The Harlem Renaissance 1920–1940

Series Editor

Cary D. Wintz
Texas Southern University

A Garland Series

Contents of the Series

The Critics and the Harlem Renaissance

Edited with introductions by

Cary D. Wintz

Texas Southern University

Garland Publishing, Inc.

New York & London

1996

Library of Congress Cataloging-in-Publication Data

The critics and the Harlem Renaissance / edited with introductions by
Cary D. Wintz.
p. cm. — (The Harlem Renaissance, 1920–1940 ; 4)
Includes bibliographical references (p.).
ISBN 0-8153-2215-1 (alk. paper)
1. American literature—Afro-American authors—History and criticism. 2. American literature—20th century—History and criticism. 3. Harlem (New York, N.Y.)—Intellectual life—20th century. 4. Afro-Americans—Intellectual life. 5. Afro-Americans in literature. 6. Afro-American aesthetics. 7. Harlem Renaissance. I. Wintz, Cary D., 1943– . II. Series.
PS153.N5C79 1996
810.9'896073—dc20 96-21608
CIP

Printed on acid-free, 250-year-life paper
Manufactured in the United States of America

Contents

The Negro in Art: How Shall He Be Portrayed?

Series Introduction

The Harlem Renaissance was the most significant event in African American literature and culture in the twentieth century. While its most obvious manifestation was as a self-conscious literary movement, it touched almost every aspect of African American culture and intellectual life in the period from World War I to the Great Depression. Its impact redefined black music, theater, and the visual arts; it reflected a new more militant political/racial consciousness and racial pride that was associated with the term "New Negro"; it embodied the struggle for civil rights that had been reinvigorated by the founding of the N.A.A.C.P. and the ideology of W.E.B. Du Bois; and it was an aspect of the urbanization of African Americans that first attracted public attention in the early twentieth century with the black migration.

Within this context it is difficult to pinpoint the chronological limits of the Harlem Renaissance. Generally the consensus among scholars is that the Harlem Renaissance was an event of the 1920s, bounded on one side by World War I and the race riots of 1919 and on the other side by the 1929 stock market crash. Some, however, have either greatly expanded or sharply restricted the time span of the movement. In 1967 Abraham Chapman wrote that he saw elements of the Renaissance in Claude McKay's poetry of 1917 and even in W.E.B. Du Bois's poem, "The Song of the Smoke," which was published in 1899.[1] Nathan Huggins argued that the Renaissance began during the years between the beginning of World War I and 1920, when the center of power in the African American community shifted from Tuskegee to Harlem, and he saw the Harlem Riots of 1935 as the end of the movement.[2] John Hope Franklin, on the other hand, wrote as late as 1980 that the Harlem Renaissance extended into the 1960s; more recently he has modified that concept, and now speaks of a first and second phase of the Harlem Renaissance, with the latter phase extending into the 1940s and beyond; he also observes that African American literary creativity was not confined to Harlem, but spread across the entire country[3] Benjamin Brawley, the preeminent African American literary historian contemporary to the Harlem Renaissance, downplayed the concept of the "so-called Negro literary renaissance," which he felt was centered around the publication of Carl Van Vechten's *Nigger Heaven* in 1926 and which he argued had no significant positive influence on African American literature.[4] Finally, Sterling Brown, one of the Harlem Renaissance poets and later a literary scholar, denied that Harlem was ever the center of a black literary movement.[5]

For the purposes of this collection the Harlem Renaissance is viewed primarily as a literary and intellectual movement. While theater, music, and the visual arts are looked at briefly, the focus is on African American literature, the assessment and criticism of this literature, and the relation of this literature to the political and social issues confronting African Americans in the early twentieth century.

The Harlem Renaissance was a self-conscious movement. That is, the writers and poets who participated in the movement were aware that they were involved in a literary movement and assumed at least partial responsibility for defining the parameters and aesthetics of the movement; black scholars and intellectuals were also aware of the Harlem Renaissance (even if they railed against it) and attempted to define the movement in terms both of literature and the political and social implications of that literature. While it was self-conscious, the Harlem Renaissance lacked a well-defined ideological or aesthetic center. It was more a community of writers, poets, critics, patrons, sponsors, and publishers than a structured and focused intellectual movement. It may be best conceptualized as an attitude or a state of mind—a feeling shared by a number of black writers and intellectuals who centered their activities in Harlem in the 1920s and early 1930s. The men and women who participated in the movement shared little but a consciousness that they were part of a common endeavor—a new awakening of African American culture and creativity; other than that what bound them together was a pride in their racial heritage, an essentially middle-class background, and the fact that all, to a greater or lesser degree, were connected to Harlem at the time that Harlem was emerging as the cultural, intellectual, and political center of black America.

Within this context, the Harlem Renaissance may best be conceptualized as a group of black writers and poets, orbiting erratically around a group of black intellectuals positioned in the N.A.A.C.P., the Urban League, and other African American political and educational institutions. These older intellectuals supported the movement, criticized it, attempted with varying success to define it, and served as liaison between the writers and the white publishers, patrons, and critics who dominated the business of literature in the United States in the 1920s. Complicating and enriching this mix was the fact that the lines between the various types of participants were not clearly drawn. James Weldon Johnson, for example, was a major promoter of the movement and a poet and novelist in his own right; Jessie Fauset, the most prolific novelist of the period, also served as literary editor of *The Crisis* and actively promoted the careers of young black writers; Countee Cullen, Sterling Brown, and Gwendolyn Bennett wrote regular literary columns, while Wallace Thurman, Langston Hughes, and several other writers attempted to publish literary magazines; and Carl Van Vechten, a white promoter of African American literature, worked closely with the Knopfs to publish black literature, authored the best-known novel of Harlem life, and almost singlehandedly created the white fascination with Harlem and African American life that characterized the 1920s.

With this definition it becomes a little easier to define the parameters of the movement. The Harlem Renaissance began in the early 1920s, when Jean Toomer published *Cane* and African American writers and intellectuals began to realize that something new was happening in black literature. The movement extended well into the 1930s and included the works of Zora Neale Hurston, Claude McKay, and Langston Hughes that were published in that decade. As long as they and other writers consciously identified with the Renaissance, the movement continued. It did not, however, encompass the younger writers like Richard Wright, Frank Yerby, or Ralph Ellison, who emerged in the 1930s and 1940s. Like so much else, these boundaries are not exact. Antecedents to the Harlem Renaissance are clear in the first two decades of the twentieth century; likewise it is easy to place some of Langston Hughes's work from the 1940s and 1950s in the Renaissance.

The goal of this series is to reprint articles and other materials that will delineate a clear picture and foster an understanding of the Harlem Renaissance. Three types of materials are included in this series. First, and most important, are the critical and interpretive materials on the Harlem Renaissance written by participants in and contemporaries of the movement. These firsthand accounts will assist readers in understanding the efforts of Harlem Renaissance writers, poets, and critics to define the movement and enable readers to glimpse the dynamics of the movement. Second, this series includes a retrospective look at the Harlem Renaissance through the eyes of participants and contemporaries, as well as by writers and critics who were involved in post-Renaissance black literature. Finally, the series presents a sample of the scholarly analysis and criticism of the movement from the 1950s through the early 1990s. The selections come from articles, essays, columns, and reviews in periodical literature; selections from memoirs, novels, histories, and books of criticism; and essays from scholarly journals. These materials are supplemented by a selection of previously unpublished materials, including letters, speeches, and essays. Not included are the literary works of the Harlem Renaissance. There are a number of anthologies of African American literature that already serve that purpose well.

This series also reflects one of the major problems confronting the study of the Harlem Renaissance in particular and African American history in general—the difficulty of accessing needed source materials. For years the study of African American history was handicapped by the fact that many of its primary sources had not been preserved or were not made available to scholars. If they had been preserved, they were housed in scattered collections and often incompletely processed and catalogued. The sharp increase in interest in African American history during the last thirty years has improved this situation enormously, but problems still persist. This series is in part an effort to make material related to one aspect of African American history more available to students and scholars. Unfortunately, it also suffers from the problem that some resources, even when located, are not readily available. For this reason a number of items by James Weldon Johnson had to be excluded; likewise, a very valuable retrospective on the Harlem Renaissance that was published initially in *Black World* is missing here. In the future, perhaps these and other barriers that impede research in African American history will be lifted.

As in any project of this nature there are scores of persons who have provided valuable support and assistance; it is impossible to name them all here. I want to especially thank Leo Balk and Carole Puccino of Garland Publishing. Leo with patience and firmness guided this series to completion; Carole worked diligently to arrange permissions for the publication of the material that appears here. In addition, I want to thank Paul Finkelman, who played a key role in helping me conceptualize the scope and nature of this project. Wolde Michael Akalou, Howard Beeth, Merline Pitre, and my other colleagues and students at Texas Southern University provided valuable feedback as the project developed. I also had wonderful assistance from the staff at the libraries

I visited while collecting the material for this series. I want to especially acknowledge the staff at the Harry Ransom Humanities Research Center at the University of Texas at Austin, the Beinecke Library at Yale University, and the Heartman Collection at the Robert J. Terry Library at Texas Southern University; in addition, librarians at the Fondren Library at Rice University, the M.D. Anderson Library at the University of Houston, the Perry Casteñeda Library at the University of Texas at Austin, and the library at the University of Houston, Clear Lake helped me track down the copies of the more elusive journals and periodicals used for this collection. I also want to thank Kathy Henderson and and Barbara Smith-Labard, who helped arrange for permission to publish previously unpublished materials from the collections at the Harry Ransom Humanities Research Center. Finally, research for this project was supported in part by a Travel to Collections grant from the National Endowment for the Humanities.

Cary D. Wintz

Notes

1. Abraham Chapman, "The Harlem Renaissance in Literary History," *CLA Journal* 11 (September 1967): 44–45.

2. Nathan Irvin Huggins, ed., *Voices from the Harlem Renaissance* (New York: Oxford University Press, 1976), 6–10.

3. John Hope Franklin, *From Slavery to Freedom: A History of Negro Americans*, 5th ed. (New York: Alfred Knopf, 1980), 383; John Hope Franklin and Alfred A. Moss, Jr., *From Slavery to Freedom: A History of African Americans*, 7th ed. (New York: McGraw–Hill, Inc., 1994), 379–80.

4. Benjamin Brawley, *The Negro Genius: A New Appraisal of the American Negro in Literature and the Fine Arts* (New York: Dodd, Mead, 1937), 231–68.

5. Sterling Brown, "The New Negro in Literature (1925–1955)." In *The New Negro Thirty Years Afterward*, ed. by Rayford W. Logan, Eugene C. Holmes, and C. Franklin Edwards (Washington, D.C.: Howard University Press, 1955).

Further Reading

Cooper, Wayne F. *Claude McKay: Rebel Sojourner in the Harlem Renaissance*. Baton Rouge: Louisiana State University Press, 1987.

Douglas, Ann. *Terrible Honesty: Mongrel Manhattan in the 1920s*. New York: Farrar, Straus, and Giroux, 1995.

Ferguson, Blanche E. *Countee Cullen and the Negro Renaissance*. New York: Dodd, Mead, 1966.

Hemenway, Robert E. *Zora Neale Hurston: A Literary Biography*. Urbana: University of Illinois Press, 1977.

Huggins, Nathan Irvin. *Harlem Renaissance*. New York: Oxford University Press, 1971.

———, ed. *Voices from the Harlem Renaissance*. New York: Oxford University Press, 1976.

Hull, Gloria T. *Color, Sex, and Poetry: Three Women Writers of the Harlem Renaissance*. Bloomington: Indiana University Press, 1987.

Kerman, Cynthia Earl, and Richard Eldridge. *The Lives of Jean Toomer: A Hunger for Wholeness*. Baton Rouge: Louisiana State University Press, 1987.

Levy, Eugene. *James Weldon Johnson: Black Leader, Black Voice*. Chicago: University of Chicago Press, 1973.

Lewis, Dadid Levering. *W.E.B. Du Bois: Biography of a Race, 1868–1919*. New York: Henry Holt, 1993.

———. *When Harlem Was in Vogue*. New York: Vintage Books, 1981.

Marable, Manning. *W.E.B. Du Bois: Black Radical Democrat*. Boston: Twayne Publishers, 1986.

Rampersad, Arnold. *The Life of Langston Hughes*. Vol 1. *I, Too, Sing America: 1902–1941*. New York: Oxford University Press, 1986.

———. *The Life of Langston Hughes*. Vol 2. *I Dream a World: 1942–1967*. New York: Oxford University Press, 1988.

Singh, Amritjit. *The Novels of the Harlem Renaissance: Twelve Black Writers*, 1923–1933. University Park: The Pennsylvania State University Press, 1976.

Sundquist, Eric J. *To Wake the Nations: Race in the Making of American Literature*. Cambridge: Harvard University Press, 1993.

Tillery, Tyrone. *Claude McKay: A Black Poet's Struggle for Identity*. Amherst: The University of Massachusetts Press, 1992.

Wintz, Cary D. *Black Culture and the Harlem Renaissance*. Houston: Rice University Press, 1988.

Volume Introduction

Both black writers and intellectuals served as critics of the Harlem Renaissance. black and white intellectuals assessed the work of individual writers and black literature in general in black and white periodicals, and in letters, speeches, and interviews. In addition, virtually every book of fiction and poetry published during the Harlem Renaissance was reviewed in both black and white periodicals. Several critics attempted either annual or periodic assessment of black literary output. For example, Alain Locke published an annual survey of black literature in *Opportunity* magazine for the years 1930 through 1938, while W.E.B. Du Bois sponsored a symposium in *The Crisis* that spanned eight months in 1926.

The role of the critics was essential. While the writers produced the literature, the critics helped define the movement and give it direction, and frequently served as a buffer between the creative artist and his or her publishers, patrons, and audience. These critics came from three groups: the black intelligentsia primarily, but not exclusively, centered in Harlem; writers who doubled as critics; and those white writers and critics who focused their attention on the Harlem Renaissance. Finally, the critics were not unanimous in their support of the movement—some argued that the literature of the Harlem Renaissance did a disservice both to African American literature and to the social and political status of the African American in the United States; some encouraged the freedom of expression and experimentation that characterized much of the writing of the Renaissance; others sought to channel African American literature into areas that served specific political, social, or literary agendas.

In the 1920s, the African American intelligentsia consisted of a diverse group of men and women scattered throughout the country who were associated with the principal African American institutions: colleges and universities, newspapers, periodicals, churches, and political and civil rights organizations like the N.A.A.C.P. and the Urban League. The most prominent of this group included James Weldon Johnson, a novelist and poet in his own right, who spent the Harlem Renaissance years first as field secretary of the N.A.A.C.P., and then on the faculty of Fisk University; Charles S. Johnson, first director of research and information at the Urban League and editor of *Opportunity* and *Ebony and Topaz,* then professor at Fisk University (and later the first African American president of that institution); Alain Locke, former Rhodes Scholar, professor of philosophy at Howard University, and editor of the Harlem issue of *Survey*

Graphic and *The New Negro*; W.E.B. Du Bois, by most measures the preeminent African American intellectual of the 1920s, who spent most of the Harlem Renaissance as an officer of the N.A.A.C.P. and editor of *The Crisis*, and who authored a number of poems and two novels during his lengthy career; William Stanley Braithwaite, a poet in his own right who was the literary critic of the Boston *Evening Transcript*, editor of the annual *Anthology of Magazine Verse* between 1913 and 1929, and after 1934, professor of creative writing at Atlanta University; and Benjamin Brawley, the most prominent African American literary historian in the early twentieth century, who spent the Renaissance years as a professor of English at Howard University, Morehouse College, and Shaw University. The most significant Harlem Renaissance writer who doubled as a critic was the novelist Jessie Fauset, who served as literary critic of *The Crisis* during the crucial early years of the Harlem Renaissance. Others who made significant contributions to the analysis and interpretation of the Renaissance included Langston Hughes, Wallace Thurman, Gwendolyn Brooks, and Claude McKay. While a number of white critics and literary scholars reviewed and commented on the literature of the Harlem Renaissance, none contributed more to the movement than Carl Van Vechten, author of the controversial Harlem novel, *Nigger Heaven*, associate of the Knopfs and their publishing house, and close friend to James Weldon Johnson, Langston Hughes, and other writers of the movement. In addition to these major players, scores of others, black and white, participated in the effort to critically evaluate the unfolding Harlem Renaissance.

This material in this volume is divided into several discrete sections. First is a selection of editorial essays, speeches, and similar materials that attempt to define and evaluate black literature as a whole, as well as individual writers and their specific works. This is followed by a selection of reviews of the published works of the Harlem Renaissance. The materials in these two sections were written by blacks and whites, and by novelists and poets as well as critics. Most were published in black periodicals like *The Crisis*, *Opportunity*, and *Southern Workman*, while others were printed in white newspapers and magazines. The third section consists of formal surveys of African American literature, the most significant of which were Alain Locke's annual review of black literature published in *Opportunity* from 1931 to 1938. Then there is a selection of interviews and correspondence in which Renaissance participants outline their views on their own work and on the literary movement. This volume concludes with the symposium, "The Negro in Art: How Shall He Be Portrayed," which W.E.B. Du Bois hosted in the pages of *The Crisis* between February and November, 1926.

The Critics and the Harlem Renaissance

A Note on the New Literary Movement

IT IS to be expected that the present resurgence of literary expression among Negroes should develop some grotesqueries, and, in certain ones a distorted sense of values. Some of these dangers it is worth pointing out as a necessary precaution against ultimate disillusionment among the Negroes themselves. For if this awakening is to be a sound, wholesome expression of growth rather than a fad to be discarded in a few seasons, it must somehow be preserved from the short-sighted exploiters of sentiment; from the immoderate and prematurely triumphant ones who think that Negro writers have fully arrived; from those superficial ones, inebriate with praise and admission to the company of writers, who are establishing by acceptance, a double standard of competence as a substitute for the normal rewards of study and practice, and in many instances, lack of talent.

The assumption back of this whole movement is that these Negro writers, long silenced by an overwhelming environment, are *beginning* to find their voices. The encouragement that they are receiving from established writers is a gracious and valuable aid to this expression. But this does not mean that simply because they are Negroes they can sing spirituals or write stories and verse or even dance *instinctively;* it does not mean that this surprise and generous commendation from the great are recognition of full admission to the status of foremost American artists and writers; nor does it mean that the standard of work is to be qualified by the fact that they are Negroes, and, being a disadvantaged race, are entitled to larger rewards. Dr. Johnson's comparison of women as minsisters to the dog that walked on its hind legs gives point to the double standard of expectation to be avoided here at all hazards. What made the dog remarkable, he thought, was not so much that it could walk on its hind legs well but that it could walk on its hind legs at all.

One very good example of the acceptance of this double standard is the belief of certain of our recent writers that the fact of being a Negro condones mediocrity of accomplishment, and that there is a sufficient virtue in being the best Negro writer. They boast of the notable contracts possible when white men of similar talents would be lost in the competition of the white world.

The notion, while it has its pleasant possibilities, has an element of grave danger in it.

Now the fields of art and letters are, fortunately, ones which hold no racial limitations for Negroes and theoretically there is no reason why talent, if developed, should not make itself felt. Roland Hayes was the best Negro singer before he began the long and dogged training of his voice. He is the greater artist by virtue of it, one of America's foremost singers, and does not rely upon racial sentiment and cultural philanthropy alone for acceptance. A Negro who is merely the best Negro doctor, or metallurgist or chemist, is in the same position of Hickville's greatest actor who goes to New York. It is a species of self-cheating which eventually injures. The danger is similar to that practiced from the other side by certain pseudo-philanthropic teachers in mixed schools who have been known to mark ordinary Negro students according to effort rather than performance, on the belief that it would be unjust to their smaller capacities to grade them with the same rigor applied to white students. This both injures and deludes the Negroes. If a book or poem is bad or mediocre it is bad and should not beckon for the shroud of race to redeem it.

The next step must be adjustment to the normal standards of American writers. Until the product of Negro writers can be measured by the same yardstick that is applied to all other writers, the Negro writer will suffer from the lack of full respect, and all that this implies.

Welcoming the New Negro

THE appearance of the *New Negro* edited by Alain Locke has drawn out many attitudes from critics who, in their variety, reflect much of the new sentiment of the American public on the Negro, who is changing his skin before their very eyes. There is, generally, the recognition of a new spirit of confidence among Negroes; of the shunting off of the usual weird fabrications of ancestry as aids to prestige; and recognition of the concern of the Negroes with their own problems and materials. The book, indeed, reveals a firm grasp of these questions—a certain notable facility of expression and a distinct overtone of agreement on racial objectives. It has commanded the best reviewers, who have not failed to sense its epochal significance in Negro life.

Oswald Garrison Villard in the *Saturday Review of Literature* regards the book as "a milestone marking the exact distance the race has travelled since Booker T. Washington's *Up From Slavery,"* and feels that these new writers contribute color, more warmth and music to our national life; create their own mold, "bow down to no Gessler hat of alleged race supremacy and ask favors of nobody." But Ernest Boyd, in the *Independent* was "as far removed as ever from enthusiasm" after reading the book, explaining that "If I had supposed that all Negroes were illiterate brutes, I might be astonished to discover that they can write good third rate poetry, readable and unreadable magazine fiction, and that their real estate in Harlem is anything but dilapidated slum property." Howard W. Odum in the *Modern Quarterly* finds a "new self discovery on the part of the Negro"—which means change in the Negro, in the relations he is to assume, in the attitude of other races, and in governmental relationships. Jim Tully in the *International Book Review* regards the book as a "direct challenge to the young white writers of the nation." V. F. Calverton offers what amounts to a sociological interpretation and envisages three stages of progress: the passionate imitation of the culture of the white race as the first, revolution in attitude marked by protest and melodramatic sentimentality as the second, and objectivity and analysis as the third. Carl Van Vechten in *Books* commends the fiction and poetry to those who are cognizant only in a vague way of what Negro youth are doing. He gives a critical appraisal of nearly all contributions, agreeing, and dissenting with a fine taste and with considerable familiarity with recent Negro literature. Herbert J. Seligman in the *New York Sun* thinks the claims of the Negroes are immoderate and Mary White Ovington in *The Bookman* concludes that "the new Negro bears little likeness to the colored man who is portrayed today on the stage and in the white man's fiction, the verbose, good natured Cohen-Cobb variety", but is "very much like his white neighbor" with a touch which is "just different enough to give us deep pleasure." H. L. Mencken in the *American Mercury* sees Negroes shedding their servile complex, notes a hearty growth, a quality of writing that could not be equalled in a similar group south of the Mason and Dixon Line, and suggests that they rid themselves of the clumsy baggage of their sentimental white patrons. Edith J. R. Isaacs in the *World Tomorrow,* quoting Mr. Locke's assertion that "something has happened beyond the watch and guard of statistics," reflects that something has happened, temporarily at least, beyond even the finer measuring rod of understanding. For nobody, not even the Negro himself, knows exactly how great and how fundamental a thing it was that happened when, in their efforts to find a solution for their race problem, the Negroes began a sudden inturning and found their spiritual freedom within themselves."

The movement as expressed in the volume prompts Carl Van Doren in the *Century* to one of the most illuminating appraisals of the entire series. He views Negroes as a tenth part of the population, handicapped but neverthless "touched by the gospel of progress which the other nine-tenths swore by"; whose work does not suffer by comparison with that of white Americans at a period when the population was about the same as Negroes, and conditions were similar. The fiction does not equal the best of Irving and Copper, the verse is higher in workmanship and poetic quality, and the prose discussions "put to shame the vexed and feverish provincialism with which Americans argued their case against Europe."

* * *

Some of the surprise and praise of the book is excessive just as some of bored insouciance to it is affected. But throughout runs a current of firm, unpatronizing evaluation which can distinguish between an evolved stage and a fad; between, let us say, *Go Down Moses* and *The Memphis Blues.*

For Negro Novelists

IT was at an informal OPPORTUNITY dinner celebrating the appearance of *The New Negro,* that the probability of stimulating Negro writers to the more sustained prose effort of a novel by a substantial prize offer, was first seriously discussed. The idea grew and the publishing house of A. & C. Boni has announced its offer of $1,000 for a novel of Negro life written by a person of Negro descent. It is an opportunity not to be lightly ignored, and a literary business man's blunt request that Negro writers who have complained of the absence of incentive, give evidence of what they can do. Formal announcement of this offer was carried in this journal last month. More particulars concerning it may be secured by writing to the publishers at 68 Fifth Avenue, New York City.

Palms

October 1926

Vol. IV
No. 1

The Negro Renaissance

by Walter White

A little over three hundred years ago, a handful of Negroes was landed on American soil at Jamestown, Virginia. For two and a half centuries other Africans were brought to America and they and their descendants held in bondage. In Africa, Negro artists, some of them of the same tribes and nations as those who were the ancestors of present-day American Negroes, had carved in ivory or wood gods and symbolic vessels and bowls used in their tribal worship. Many years later a few of these plastic creations were destined to be carried to Paris, and there and elsewhere profoundly influence what we call modern art. In Africa, too, there were given birth songs which are the ancestors, in a different genre, of our present-day Negro spirituals. Of folklore there was an abundance—expressed in language which was of the very essence of poetry.

It was not until very recent years, however, that the talent from which sprang these creations met with any considerable encouragement in the United States. It is true that there were individual Negroes who achieved eminence as artists or, more often, achieved patronizing attention. Harry Burleigh as a musician; Bert Williams on the stage; Charles W. Chesnutt as novelist and writer of excellent short stories of Negro life; Dr. W. E. B. DuBois as scholar and master of an extraordinarily beautiful and powerful prose style; Paul Lawrence Dunbar as poet; and Booker T. Washington as educator, are a few of the more familiar names of those who attained eminence.

But with the new economic security which the Negro has attained, with the greater willingness of America to receive the gifts the Negro could make and with post-war eagerness for new forms and new sensations came the wave which has hurtled the Negro into a position as artist where, at least in and near New York, he comes dangerously near becoming a fad. In music there is the extraordinary success of Roland Hayes, Paul Robeson, Lawrence Brown, Rosamond Johnson, Taylor Gordon, Julius Bledsoe, and Marian Anderson. In the field of the short story, there are Rudolph Fisher, Jean Toomer, and a number of lesser lights. In the field of novel writing there are not so many, but there are a dozen or so to my knowledge who are attempting the longer flight. On the stage are Paul Robeson again, Charles Gilpin, Evelyn Preer, Miller and Lyles and many of lesser stature. In every field of the arts Negroes are emerging, adding a richness and colorfulness which America so sorely needs. Book after book on Negro spirituals tumbles from the press. the best of them, THE BOOK OF AMERICAN NEGRO SPIRITUALS, a best-seller. Soon, too, there will doubtless appear books on the less well-known but equally vital blues, work songs, and other secular music of the Aframerican.

In no one field, however, has so much been done as in poetry. Perhaps this is the most natural mode of expression next to song that the Negro possesses. To prove this, one needs but to run over the titles of many of the spirituals — for example — "Deep River", "Go Down, Death", "Singing with a Sword in My Han' ", "Ride On, King Jesus", "Swing Low, Sweet Chariot".

Nor is this form of expression a new thing. Beginning in 1761 when a Negro girl, eight years old, Phyllis Wheatley, was landed at Boston, sold as a slave, and later wrote creditable verse, on down through Countée Cullen and Langston Hughes, the stream has been unbroken though it has changed its course many times. I have been asked in this brief introduction to discuss trends in Negro poetry—always a difficult and dangerous thing to attempt.

There was little distinctive form to poetry written by American Negroes until Paul Lawrence Dunbar came upon the scene. Well over one hundred American Negroes have published volumes of verse but until Dunbar, most of them followed the conventional schools which were then current. As has been said many times, Dunbar was the first Negro to view his people objectively. He did his best work in his dialect poems. Through them he was perhaps the first Negro to draw widespread attention to the Negro and to his possibilities as a subject for artistic treatment.

But Dunbar, on the other hand, did a certain amount of harm. Following the attention he received and the fame he gained prior and subsequent to his premature death in 1906, most Negroes who attempted to write verse, and most editors, wanted nothing from Negroes except dialect poems. So far as it goes, dialect has its advantages but, as has been pointed out by James Weldon

Johnson, there are only two stops possible with thi form—pathos and humor. The mould into which Negro poetry was set by Dunbar was broken only within the last twenty years. James Weldon Johnson, W. E. B DuBois, William Stanley Braithwaite and Claude McKay broke from the dialect school and in doing so caught up and gave form to the writing of poetry by Negroes Perhaps no other factor was so potent in broadening the fields in which the Negro poet could wander as the publication in 1922 of THE BOOK OF AMERICAN NEGRO POETRY with its introductory essay on *The Creative Genius of the Negro* by the editor of the volume, James Weldon Johnson.

The results of this renaissance just now are being seen through the publication of volumes like COLOR by Countée Cullen and THE WEARY BLUES by Langston Hughes, these two writers being by far the best known of the younger school. With many other fields in which he is expending his energy, Mr. Johnson has written little poetry during the last few years. Claude McKay has, too, been silent for a long while. Jessie Fauset has turned her attention to the writing of novels, while Mr. Braithwaite has devoted most of his time to the editing of his Anthology and to his publishing business.

To take the places of these, others have come—Mr. Cullen, Mr. Hughes and a number yet to be heard from. In this newer school are not only those who are writing first-rate Negro verse but those who are forming excellent verse which takes no cognizance of race. Though on this point I do not expect agreement, yet I am glad that both Mr. Cullen and Mr. Hughes (and the others) are not going to the other extreme— of casting overboard the gifts of their experiences as Negroes in American life From this springs a passion, a colorfulness, a strength which gives them most decided advantages over many of their white brothers who are writing verse.

The flower of the bush which has been so long sinking its roots into this rich and abundant soil of Negro life is just beginning to unfold. Mr. Cullen, Mr. Hughes, Anne Spencer, Georgia Douglas Johnson and others will doubtless produce even more beautiful poetry than they have in the past. And back of them surges up a vast number of others whose voices as yet are faint but who with experience and training will yet be heard from to the enrichment of American poetry.

WILLIAM STANLEY BRAITHWAITE

The Negro in American Literature

TRUE TO his origin on this continent, the Negro was projected into literature by an over-mastering and exploiting hand. In the generations that he has been so voluminously written and talked about he has been accorded as little artistic justice as social justice. Antebellum literature imposed the distortions of moralistic controversy and made the Negro a wax-figure of the market place: post-bellum literature retaliated with the condescending reactions of sentiment and caricature, and made the Negro a *genre* stereotype. Sustained, serious or deep study of Negro life and character has thus been entirely below the horizons of our national art. Only gradually through the dull purgatory of the Age of Discussion, has Negro life eventually issued forth to an Age of Expression.

Perhaps I ought to qualify this last statement that the Negro was *in* American literature generations before he was part of it as a creator. From his very beginning in this country the Negro has been, without the formal recognition of literature and art, creative. During more than two centuries of an enslaved peasantry, the race has been giving evidence, in song and story lore, of an artistic temperament and psychology precious for itself as well as for its potential use and promise in the sophisticated forms of cultural expression. Expressing itself with poignancy and a symbolic imagery unsurpassed, indeed, often unmatched, by any folk-group, the race in servitude was at the same time the finest national expression of emotion and imagination and the most precious mass of raw material for literature America was producing. Quoting these stanzas of James Weldon Johnson's *O Black and Unknown Bards,* I want you to catch the real point of its assertion of the Negro's way into the domain of art:

O black and unknown bards of long ago,
How came your lips to touch the sacred fire?
How, in your darkness, did you come to know
The power and beauty of the minstrel's lyre?
Who first from midst his bonds lifted his eyes?
Who first from out the still watch, lone and long,
Feeling the ancient faith of prophets rise
Within his dark-kept soul, burst into song?

There is a wide, wide wonder in it all,
That from degraded rest and servile toil
The fiery spirit of the seer should call
These simple children of the sun and soil.
O black slave singers, gone, forgot, unfamed,
You—you, alone, of all the long, long line
Of those who've sung untaught, unknown, unnamed,
Have stretched out upward, seeking the divine.

How misdirected was the American imagination, how blinded by the dust of controversy and the pall of social hatred and oppression, not to have found it irresistibly urgent to make literary use of the imagination and emotion it possessed in such abundance.

Controversy and moral appeal gave us *Uncle Tom's Cabin,*—the first conspicuous example of the Negro as a subject for literary treatment. Published in 1852, it dominated in mood and attitude the American literature of a whole generation; until the body of Reconstruction literature with its quite different attitude came into vogue. Here was sentimentalized sympathy for a down-trodden race, but one in which was projected a character, in Uncle Tom himself, which has been unequalled in its hold upon the popular imagination to this day. But the moral gain and historical effect of Uncle Tom have been an artistic loss and setback. The treatment of Negro life and character, overlaid with these forceful stereotypes, could not develop into artistically satisfactory portraiture.

Just as in the anti-slavery period, it had been impaled upon the dilemmas of controversy, Negro life with the Reconstruction, became involved in the paradoxes of social prejudice. Between the Civil War and the end of the century the subject of the Negro in literature is one that will some day inspire the literary historian with a magnificent theme. It will be magnificent not because there is any sharp emergence of character or incidents, but because of the immense paradox of racial life which came up thunderingly against the principles and doctrines of democracy, and put them to the severest test that they had known. It was a period when, in literature, Negro life was a shuttlecock between the two extremes of humor and pathos. The Negro was free, and was not free. The writers who dealt with him for the most part refused to see more than skin-deep,—the grin, the grimaces and the picturesque externalities. Occasionally there was some penetration into the heart and flesh of Negro characters, but to see more than the humble happy peasant would have been to flout the fixed ideas and conventions of an entire generation. For more than artistic reasons, indeed against them, these writers refused to see the tragedy of the Negro and capitalized his comedy. The social conscience had as much need for this comic mask as the Negro. However, if any of the writers of the period had possessed gifts of genius of the first caliber, they would have penetrated this deceptive exterior of Negro life, sounded the depths of tragedy in it, and produced a masterpiece.

American literature still feels the hold of this tradition and its indulgent sentimentalities. Irwin Russell was the first to discover the happy, care-free, humorous Negro. He became a fad. It must be sharply called to attention that the tradition of the ante-bellum Negro is a post-bellum product, stranger in truth than in fiction. Contemporary realism in American fiction has not only recorded his passing, but has thrown serious doubts upon his ever having been a very genuine and representative view of Negro life and character. At best this school of Reconstruction fiction represents the romanticized high-lights of a régime that as a whole was a dark, tragic canvas. At most, it presents a Negro true to type for less than two generations. Thomas Nelson Page, kindly perhaps, but with a distant view and a purely local imagination, did little more than paint the conditions and attitudes of the period contemporary with his own manhood, the restitution of the over-lordship of the defeated slave owners in the Eighties. George W. Cable did little more than idealize the aristocratic tradition of the Old South with the Negro as a literary foil. The effects, though not the motives of their work, have been sinister. The "Uncle" and the "Mammy" traditions, unobjectionable as they are in the setting of their day and generation, and in the atmosphere of sentimental humor, can never stand as the great fiction of their theme and subject: the great period novel of the South has yet to be written. Moreover, these type pictures have degenerated into reactionary social fetishes, and from that descended into libelous artistic caricature of the Negro, which has hampered art quite as much as it has embarrassed the Negro.

Of all of the American writers of this period, Joel Chandler Harris has made the most permanent contribution in dealing with the Negro. There is in his work both a deepening of interest and technique. Here at least we have something approaching true portraiture. But much as we admire this lovable personality, we are forced to say that in the Uncle Remus stories the race was its own artist, lacking only in its illiteracy the power to record its speech. In the perspective of time and fair judgment the credit will be divided, and Joel Chandler Harris regarded as a sort of providentially provided amanuensis for preserving the folk tales and legends of a race. The three writers I have mentioned do not by any means exhaust the list of writers who put the Negro into literature during the last half of the nineteenth century. Mr. Howells added a shadowy note to his social record of American life with *An Imperative Duty* and prophesied the Fiction of the Color Line. But his moral scruples—the persistent artistic vice in all his novels—prevented him from consummating a just union between his heroine with a touch of Negro blood and his hero. It is useless to consider any others, because there were none who succeeded in creating either a great story or a great character out of Negro life. Two writers of importance I am reserving for discussion in the group of Negro writers I shall consider presently. One ought perhaps to say in justice to the writers I have mentioned that their nonsuccess was more largely due to the limitations of their social view than of their technical resources. As white Americans of their day, it was incompatible with their conception of the inequalities between the races to glorify the Negro into the serious and leading position of hero or heroine in fiction. Only one man, that I recall, had the moral and artistic courage to do this, and he was Stephen Crane in a short story called *The Monster*. But Stephen Crane was a genius, and therefore could not besmirch the integrity of an artist.

With Thomas Dixon, of *The Leopard's Spots*, we reach a distinct stage in the treatment of the Negro in fiction. The portraiture here descends from caricature to libel. A little later with the vogue of the "darkey-story," and its devotees from Kemble and McAllister to Octavus Roy Cohen, sentimental comedy in the portrayal of the Negro similarly degenerated to blatant but diverting farce. Before the rise of a new attitude, these represented the bottom reaction, both in artistic and social attitude. Reconstruction fiction was passing out in a flood of propagandist melodrama and ridicule. One hesitates to lift this material up to the plane of literature even for the purposes of comparison. But the gradual climb of the new literature of the Negro must be traced and measured from these two nadir points. Following *The Leopard's Spots,* it was only occasionally during the next twenty years that the Negro was sincerely treated in fiction by white authors. There were two or three tentative efforts to dramatize him. Sheldon's *The Nigger* was the one notable early effort. And in fiction Paul Kester's *His Own Country* is, from a purely literary point of view, an outstanding performance. This type of novel failed, however, to awaken any general interest. This failure was due to the illogical treatment of the human situations presented. However indifferent and negative it may seem, there is the latent desire in most readers to have honesty of purpose and a full vision in the artist: and especially in fiction, a situation handled with gloves can never be effectively handled.

The first hint that the American artist was looking at this subject with full vision was in Torrence's *Granny Maumee.* It was drama, conceived and executed for performance on the stage, and therefore had a restricted appeal. But even here the artist was concerned with the primitive instincts of the Race, and, though faithful and honest in his portrayal, the note was still low in the scale of racial life. It was only a short time, however, before a distinctly new development took place in the treatment of Negro life by white authors. This new class of work honestly strove to endow the Negro life with purely aesthetic vision and values, but with one or two exceptions, still stuck to the peasant level of race experience, and gave, unwittingly, greater currency to the popular notion of the Negro as an inferior, superstitious, half-ignorant and servile class of folk. Where they did in a few isolated instances recognize an ambitious impulse, it was generally defeated in the course of the story.

Perhaps this is inevitable with an alien approach, however well-intentioned. The folk lore attitude discovers only the lowly and the naïve: the sociological attitude finds the problem first and the human beings after, if at all. But American art in a reawakened seriousness, and using the technique of the new realism, is gradually penetrating Negro life to the core. George Madden Martin, with her pretentious foreword to a group of short stories, *The Children in the Mist,*—and this is an extraordinary volume in many ways—quite seriously tried, as a Southern woman, to elevate the Negro to a higher plane of fictional treatment and interest. In succession, followed Mary White Ovington's *The Shadow,* in which Miss Ovington daringly created the kinship of brother and sister between a black boy and white girl, had it brought to disaster by prejudice, out of which the white girl rose to a sacrifice no white girl in a novel had hitherto accepted and endured; then Shands' *White and Black,* as honest a piece of fiction with the Negro as a subject as was ever produced by a Southern pen—and in this story, also, the hero, Robinson, making an equally glorious sacrifice for truth and justice, as Miss Ovington's heroine; Clement Wood's *Nigger,* with defects of treatment, but admirable in purpose, wasted though, I think, in the effort to prove its thesis on wholly illogical material; and lastly, T. S. Stribling's *Birthright,* more significant than any of these other books, in fact, the most significant novel on the Negro written by a white American, and this in spite of its totally false conception of the character of Peter Siner.

Mr. Stribling's book broke ground for a white author in giving us a Negro hero and heroine. There is an obvious attempt to see objectively. But the formula of the Nineties—atavistic race-heredity—still survives and protrudes through the flesh and blood of the characters. Using Peter as a symbol of the man tragically linked by blood to one world and by training and thought to another, Stribling portrays a tragic struggle against the pull of lowly origins and sordid environment. We do not deny this element of tragedy in Negro life—and Mr. Stribling, it must also be remembered, presents, too, a severe indictment in his painting of the Southern conditions which brought about the disintegration of his hero's dreams and ideals. But the preoccupation, almost obsession of otherwise strong and artistic work like O'Neill's *Emperor Jones, All God's Chillun Got Wings,* and Culbertson's *Goat Alley* with this same theme and doubtful formula of hereditary cultural reversion suggests that, in spite of all good intentions, the true presental of the real tragedy of Negro life is a task still left for Negro writers to perform. This is especially true for those phases of culturally representative race life that as yet have scarcely at all found treatment by white American authors. In corroborating this, let me quote a passage from a recent number of the *Independent,* on the Negro novelist which reads:

> During the past few years stories about Negroes have been extremely popular. A magazine without a Negro story is hardly living up to its opportunities. But almost every one of these stories is written in a tone of condescension. The artists have caught the contagion from the writers, and the illustrations are

ninety-nine times out of a hundred purely slapstick stuff. Stories and pictures make a Roman holiday for the millions who are convinced that the most important fact about the Negro is that his skin is black. Many of these writers live in the South or are from the South. Presumably they are well acquainted with the Negro, but it is a remarkable fact that they almost never tell us anything vital about him, about the real human being in the black man's skin. Their most frequent method is to laugh at the colored man and woman, to catalogue their idiosyncrasies, their departure from the norm, that is, from the ways of the whites. There seems to be no suspicion in the minds of the writers that there may be a fascinating thought life in the minds of the Negroes, whether of the cultivated or of the most ignorant type. Always the Negro is interpreted in the terms of the white man. White-man psychology is applied and it is no wonder that the result often shows the Negro in a ludicrous light.

I shall have to run back over the years to where I began to survey the achievement of Negro authorship. The Negro as a creator in American literature is of comparatively recent importance. All that was accomplished between Phillis Wheatley and Paul Laurence Dunbar, considered by critical standards, is negligible, and of historical interest only. Historically it is a great tribute to the race to have produced in Phillis Wheatley not only the slave poetess in eighteenth century Colonial America, but to know she was as good, if not a better, poetess than Ann Bradstreet whom literary historians give the honor of being the first person of her sex to win fame as a poet in America.

Negro authorship may, for clearer statement, be classified into three main activities: Poetry, Fiction, and the Essay, with an occasional excursion into other branches. In the drama, until very recently, practically nothing worth while has been achieved, with the exception of Angelina Grimke's *Rachel,* notable for its sombre craftsmanship. Biography has given us a notable life story, told by himself, of Booker T. Washington. Frederick Douglass's story of his life is eloquent as a human document, but not in the graces of narration and psychologic portraiture, which has definitely put this form of literature in the domain of the fine arts. Indeed, we may well believe that the efforts of controversy, of the huge amount of discursive and polemical articles dealing chiefly with the race problem, that have been necessary in breaking and clearing the impeded pathway of racial progress, have absorbed and in a way dissipated the literary energy of many able Negro writers.

Let us survey briefly the advance of the Negro in poetry. Behind Dunbar, there is nothing that can stand the critical test. We shall always have a sentimental and historical interest in those forlorn and pathetic figures who cried in the wilderness of their ignorance and oppression. With Dunbar we have our first authentic lyric utterance, an utterance more authentic, I should say, for its faithful rendition of Negro life and character than for any rare or subtle artistry of expression. When Mr. Howells, in his famous introduction to the *Lyrics of Lowly Life*, remarked that Dunbar was the first black man to express the life of his people lyrically, he summed up Dunbar's achievement and transported him to a place beside the peasant poet of Scotland, not for his art, but precisely because he made a people articulate in verse.

The two chief qualities in Dunbar's work are, however, pathos and humor, and in these he expresses that dilemma of soul that characterized the race between the Civil War and the end of the nineteenth century. The poetry of Dunbar is true to the life of the Negro and expresses characteristically what he felt and knew to be the temper and condition of his people. But its moods reflect chiefly those of the era of Reconstruction and just a little beyond,—the limited experience of a transitional period, the rather helpless and subservient era of testing freedom and reaching out through the difficulties of life to the emotional compensations of laughter and tears. It is the poetry of the happy peasant and the plaintive minstrel. Occasionally, as in the sonnet to *Robert Gould Shaw* and the *Ode to Ethiopia* there broke through Dunbar, as through the crevices of his spirit, a burning and brooding aspiration, an awakening and virile consciousness of race. But for the most part, his dreams were anchored to the minor whimsies; his deepest poetic inspiration was sentiment. He expressed a folk temperament, but not a race soul. Dunbar was the end of a régime, and not the beginning of a tradition, as so many careless critics, both white and colored, seem to think.

After Dunbar many versifiers appeared,—all largely dominated by his successful dialect work. I cannot parade them here for tag or comment, except to say that few have equalled Dunbar in this vein of expression, and none have deepened it as an expression of Negro life. Dunbar himself had clear notions of its limitations;—to a friend in a letter from London, March 15, 1897, he says: "I see now very clearly that Mr. Howells has done me irrevocable harm in the dictum he laid down regarding my dialect verse." Not until James W. Johnson published his *Fiftieth Anniversary Ode* on the emancipation in 1913, did a poet of the race disengage himself from the background of mediocrity into which the imitation of Dunbar snared Negro poetry. Mr. Johnson's work is based upon a broader contemplation of life, life that is not wholly confined within any racial experience, but through the racial he made articulate that universality of the emotions felt by all mankind. His verse possesses a vigor which definitely breaks away from the brooding minor undercurrents of feeling which have previously characterized the verse of Negro poets. Mr. Johnson brought, indeed, the first intellectual substance to the content of our poetry, and a craftsmanship which, less spontaneous than that of Dunbar's, was more balanced and precise.

Here a new literary generation begins: poetry that is racial in substance, but with the universal note, and consciously the background of the full heritage of English poetry. With each new figure somehow the gamut broadens and the technical control improves. The brilliant succession and maturing powers of Fenton Johnson, Leslie Pinckney Hill, Everett Hawkins, Lucien Watkins, Charles Bertram Johnson, Joseph Cotter, Georgia Douglas Johnson, Roscoe Jameson and Anne Spencer bring us at last to Claude McKay and the poets of the younger generation and a poetry of the masterful accent and high distinction. Too significantly for mere coincidence, it was the stirring year of 1917 that heard the first real masterful accent in Negro poetry. In the September *Crisis* of that year, Roscoe Jameson's *Negro Soldiers* appeared:

These truly are the Brave,
These men who cast aside
Old memories to walk the blood-stained pave
Of Sacrifice, joining the solemn tide
That moves away, to suffer and to die
For Freedom—when their own is yet denied!
O Pride! A Prejudice! When they pass by
Hail them, the Brave, for you now crucified.

The very next month, under the pen name of Eli Edwards, Claude McKay printed in *The Seven Arts*,

THE HARLEM DANCER

Applauding youths laughed with young prostitutes
And watched her perfect, half-clothed body sway;
Her voice was like the sound of blended flutes
Blown by black players upon a picnic day.
She sang and danced on gracefully and calm,

The light gauze hanging loose about her form;
To me she seemed a proudly-swaying palm
Grown lovelier for passing through a storm.

Upon her swarthy neck black, shiny curls
Profusely fell; and, tossing coins in praise
The wine-flushed, bold-eyed boys, and even the girls
Devoured her with their eager, passionate gaze;
But, looking at her falsely-smiling face
I knew her self was not in that strange place.

With Georgia Johnson, Anne Spencer and Angelina Grimke, the Negro woman poet significantly appears. Mrs. Johnson especially has voiced in true poetic spirit the lyric cry of Negro womanhood. In spite of lapses into the sentimental and the platitudinous, she has an authentic gift. Anne Spencer, more sophisticated, more cryptic but also more universal, reveals quite another aspect of poetic genius. Indeed, it is interesting to notice how to-day Negro poets waver between the racial and the universal notes.

Claude McKay, the poet who leads his generation, is a genius meshed in this dilemma. His work is caught between the currents of the poetry of protest and the poetry of expression; he is in turn the violent and strident propagandist, using his poetic gifts to clothe arrogant and defiant thoughts, and then the pure lyric dreamer, contemplating life and nature with a wistful sympathetic passion. When the mood of *Spring in New Hampshire* or the sonnet *The Harlem Dancer* possesses him, he is full of that spirit and power of beauty that flowers above any and all men's harming. How different in spite of the admirable spirit of courage and defiance, are his poems of which the sonnet *If We Must Die* is a typical example. Negro poetic expression hovers for the moment, pardonably perhaps, over the race problem, but its highest allegiance is to Poetry—it must soar.

Let me refer briefly to a type of literature in which there have been many pens, but a single mind. Dr. Du Bois is the most variously gifted writer which the race has produced. Poet, novelist, sociologist, historian and essayist, he has produced books in all these fields with the exception, I believe, of a formal book of poems, and has given to each the distinction of his clear and exact thinking, and of his sensitive imagination and passionate vision. *The Souls of Black Folk* was the book of an era; it was a painful book, a book of tortured dreams woven into the fabric of the sociologist's document. This book has more profoundly influenced the spiritual temper of the race than any other written in its generation. It is only through the intense, passionate idealism of such substance as makes *The Souls of Black Folk* such a quivering rhapsody of wrongs endured and hopes to be fulfilled that the poets of the race with compelling artistry can lift the Negro into the only full and complete nationalism he knows—that of the American democracy. No other book has more clearly revealed to the nation at large the true idealism and high aspiration of the American Negro.

In this book, as well as in many of Dr. Du Bois's essays, it is often my personal feeling that I am witnessing the birth of a poet, phoenix-like, out of a scholar. Between *The Souls of Black Folk* and *Darkwater*, published four years ago, Dr. Du Bois has written a number of books, none more notable, in my opinion, than his novel *The Quest of the Silver Fleece*, in which he made Cotton the great protagonist of fate in the lives of the Southern people, both white and black. I only know of one other such attempt and accomplishment in American fiction—that of Frank Norris—and I am somehow of the opinion that when the great epic novel of the South is written this book will prove to have been its forerunner. Indeed, the Negro novel is one of the great potentialities of American literature. Must it be written by a Negro? To recur to the article from which I have already quoted:

> The white writer seems to stand baffled before the enigma and so he expends all his energies on dialect and in general on the Negro's minstrel characteristics. . . . We shall have to look to the Negro himself to go all the way. It is quite likely that no white man can do it. It is reasonable to suppose that his white psychology will always be in his way. I am not thinking at all about a Negro novelist who shall arouse the world to the horror of the deliberate killings by white mobs, to the wrongs that condemn a free people to political serfdom. I am not thinking at all of the propaganda novel, although there is enough horror and enough drama in the bald statistics of each one of the annual Moton letters to keep the whole army of writers busy. But the Negro novelist, if he ever comes, must reveal to us much more than what a Negro thinks about when he is being tied to a stake and the torch is being applied to his living flesh; much more than what he feels when he is being crowded off the sidewalk by a drunken rowdy who may be his intellectual inferior by a thousand leagues. Such a writer, to succeed in a big sense, would have to forget that there are

white readers; he would have to lose self-consciousness and forget that his work would be placed before a white jury. He would have to be careless as to what the white critic might think of it; he would need the self-assurance to be his own critic. He would have to forget for the time being, at least, that any white man ever attempted to dissect the soul of a Negro.

What I here quote is both an inquiry and a challenge! Well informed as the writer is, he does not seem to detect the forces which are surely gathering to produce what he longs for.

The development of fiction among Negro authors has been, I might almost say, one of the repressed activities of our literary life. A fair start was made the last decade of the nineteenth century when Chesnutt and Dunbar were turning out both short stories and novels. In Dunbar's case, had he lived, I think his literary growth would have been in the evolution of the Race novel as indicated in *The Uncalled* and the *Sport of the Gods.* The former was, I think, the most ambitious literary effort of Dunbar; the latter was his most significant; significant because, thrown against the background of New York City, it displayed the life of the race as a unit, swayed by currents of existence, of which it was and was not a part. The story was touched with that shadow of destiny which gave to it a purpose more important than the mere racial machinery of its plot. But Dunbar in his fiction dealt only successfully with the same world that gave him the inspiration for his dialect poems, though his ambition was to "write a novel that will deal with the educated class of my own people." Later he writes of *The Fanatics:* "You do not know how my hopes were planted in that book, but it has utterly disappointed me." His contemporary, Charles W. Chesnutt, was concerned more primarily with the fiction of the Color Line and the contacts and conflicts of its two worlds. He was in a way more successful. In the five volumes to his credit, he has revealed himself as a fiction writer of a very high order. But after all Mr. Chesnutt is a story-teller of genius transformed by racial earnestness into the novelist of talent. His natural gift would have found freer vent in a flow of short stories like Bret Harte's, to judge from the facility and power of his two volumes of short stories, *The Wife of His Youth and Other Stories* and *The Conjure Woman.* But Mr. Chesnutt's serious effort was in the field of the novel, where he made a brave and partially successful effort to correct the distortions of Reconstruction fiction and offset the school of Page and Cable. Two of these novels, *The Marrow of Tradition* and *The House Behind the*

Cedars, must be reckoned among the representative period novels of their time. But the situation was not ripe for the great Negro novelist. The American public preferred spurious values to the genuine; the coinage of the Confederacy was at literary par. Where Dunbar, the sentimentalist, was welcome, Chesnutt, the realist, was barred. In 1905 Mr. Chesnutt wrote *The Colonel's Dream,* and thereafter silence fell upon him.

From this date until the past year, with the exception of *The Quest of the Silver Fleece,* which was published in 1911, there has been no fiction of importance by Negro authors. But then suddenly there comes a series of books, which seems to promise at least a new phase of race fiction, and possibly the era of the major novelists. Mr. Walter White's novel *The Fire in the Flint* is a swift moving straightforward story of the contemporary conflicts of black manhood in the South. Coming from the experienced observation of the author, himself an investigator of many lynchings and riots, it is a social document story of first-hand significance and importance, too vital to be labelled and dismissed as propaganda, yet for the same reason too unvarnished and realistic a story to be great art. Nearer to the requirements of art comes Miss Jessie Fauset's novel *There Is Confusion.* Its distinction is to have created an entirely new milieu in the treatment of the race in fiction. She has taken a class within the race of established social standing, tradition and culture, and given in the rather complex family story of *The Marshalls* a social document of unique and refreshing value. In such a story, race fiction, detaching itself from the limitations of propaganda on the one hand and genre fiction on the other, emerges from the color line and is incorporated into the body of general and universal art.

Finally in Jean Toomer, the author of *Cane,* we come upon the very first artist of the race, who with all an artist's passion and sympathy for life, its hurts, its sympathies, its desires, its joy, its defeats and strange yearnings, can write about the Negro without the surrender or compromise of the artist's vision. So objective is it, that we feel that it is a mere accident that birth or association has thrown him into contact with the life he has written about. He would write just as well, just as poignantly, just as transmutingly, about the peasants of Russia, or the peasants of Ireland, had experience brought him in touch with their existence. *Cane* is a book of gold and bronze, of dusk and flame, of ecstasy and pain, and Jean Toomer is a bright morning star of a new day of the race in literature.

BENJAMIN GRIFFIN BRAWLEY
The Negro in American Fiction

EVER SINCE Sydney Smith sneered at American books a hundred years ago, honest critics have asked themselves if the literature of the United States was not really open to the charge of provincialism. Within the last year or two the argument has been very much revived; and an English critic, Mr. Edward Garnett, writing in *The Atlantic Monthly*, has pointed out that with our predigested ideas and made-to-order fiction we not only discourage individual genius, but make it possible for the multitude to think only such thoughts as have passed through a sieve. Our most popular novelists, and sometimes our most respectable writers, see only the sensation that is uppermost for the moment in the mind of the crowd—divorce, graft, tainted meat or money—and they proceed to cut the cloth of their fiction accordingly. Mr. Owen Wister, a "regular practitioner" of the novelist's art, in substance admitting the weight of these charges, lays the blame on our crass democracy which utterly refuses to do its own thinking and which is satisfied only with the tinsel and gewgaws and hobbyhorses of literature. And no theme has suffered so much from the coarseness of the mob-spirit in literature as that of the Negro.

As a matter of fact, the Negro in his problems and strivings offers to American writers the greatest opportunity that could possibly be given to them to-day. It is commonly agreed that only one other large question, that of the relations of capital and labor, is of as much interest to the American public; and even this great issue fails to possess quite the appeal offered by the Negro from the social standpoint. One can only imagine what a Victor Hugo, detached and philosophical, would have done with such a theme in a novel. When we see what actually has been done—how often in the guise of fiction a writer has preached a sermon or shouted a political creed, or vented his spleen—we are not exactly proud of the art of novel-writing as it has been developed in the United States of America. Here was opportunity for tragedy, for comedy, for the subtle portrayal of all the relations of man with his fellow man, for faith and hope and love and sorrow. And yet, with the Civil War fifty years in the distance, not one novel or one short story of the first rank has found its inspiration in this great theme. Instead of such work we have consistently had traditional tales, political tracts, and lurid melodramas.

Let us see who have approached the theme, and just what they have done with it, for the present leaving out of account all efforts put forth by Negro writers themselves.

The names of four exponents of Southern life come at once to mind—George W. Cable, Joel Chandler Harris, Thomas Nelson Page, and Thomas Dixon; and at once, in their outlook and method of work, the first two become separate from the last two. Cable and Harris have looked toward the past, and have embalmed vanished or vanishing types. Mr. Page and Mr. Dixon, with their thought on the present (though for the most part they portray the recent past), have used the novel as a vehicle for political propaganda.

It was in 1879 that "Old Creole Days" evidenced the advent of a new force in American literature; and on the basis of this work, and of "The Grandissimes" which followed, Mr. Cable at once took his place as the foremost portrayer of life in old New Orleans. By birth, by temperament, and by training he was thoroughly fitted for the task to which he set himself. His mother was from New England, his father of the stock of colonial Virginia; and the stern Puritanism of the North was mellowed by the gentler influences of the South. Moreover, from his long apprenticeship in newspaper work in New Orleans he had received abundantly the knowledge and training necessary for his work. Setting himself to a study of the Negro of the old régime, he made a specialty of the famous—and infamous—quadroon society of Louisiana of the third and fourth decades of the last century. And excellent as was his work, turning his face to the past in manner as well as in matter, from the very first he raised the question propounded by this paper. In his earliest volume there was a story entitled " 'Tite Poulette," the heroine of which was a girl amazingly fair, the supposed daughter of one Madame John. A young Dutchman fell in love with 'Tite Poulette, championed her cause at all times, suffered a beating and stabbing for her, and was by her nursed back to life and love. In the midst of his perplexity about joining himself to a member of another race, came the word from Madame John that the girl was not her daughter, but the child of yellow fever patients whom she had nursed until they died, leaving their infant in her care. Immediately upon the publication of this story, the author received a letter from a young woman who had actually lived in very much the same situation as that portrayed in " 'Tite Poulette," telling him that his story was not true to life and that he knew it was not, for Madame John really *was* the mother of the heroine. Accepting the criticism, Mr. Cable set about the composition of "Madame Delphine," in which the situation is somewhat similar, but in which at the end the mother tamely makes a confession to a priest. What is the trouble? The artist is so bound by circumstances and hemmed in by tradition that he simply has not the courage to launch out into the deep and work out his human problems for himself. Take a representative portrait from "The Grandissimes":

> Clemence had come through ages of African savagery, through fires that do not refine, but that blunt and blast and blacken and char; starvation, gluttony, drunkenness, thirst, drowning, nakedness, dirt, fetichism, debauchery, slaughter, pestilence, and the rest—she was their heiress; they left her the cinders of human feelings. . . . She had had children of assorted colors—had one with her now, the black boy that brought the basil to Joseph; the others were here and there, some in the Grandissime households or field-gangs, some elsewhere within occasional sight, some dead, some not accounted for. Husbands—like the Samaritan woman's. We know she was a constant singer and laugher.

Very brilliant of course; and yet Clemence is a relic, not a prophecy.

Still more of a relic is Uncle Remus. For decades now, this charming old Negro has been held up to the children of the South as the perfect expression of the beauty of life in the glorious times "befo' de wah," when every Southern gentleman was suckled at the bosom of a "black mammy." Why should we not occasionally attempt to paint the Negro of the new day—intelligent, ambitious, thrifty, manly? Perhaps he is not so poetic; but certainly the human element is greater.

To the school of Cable and Harris belong also of course Miss Grace King and Mrs. Ruth McEnery Stuart, a thoroughly representative piece of work being Mrs. Stuart's "Uncle 'Riah's Christmas Eve." Other more popular writers of the day, Miss Mary Johnston and Miss Ellen Glasgow for instance, attempt no special analysis of the Negro. They simply take him for granted as an institution that always has existed and always will exist, as a hewer of wood and drawer of water, from the first flush of creation to the sounding of the trump of doom.

But more serious is the tone when we come to Thomas Nelson Page and Thomas Dixon. We might tarry for a few minutes with Mr. Page to listen to more such tales as those of Uncle Remus; but we must turn to living issues. Times have changed. The grandson of Uncle Remus does not feel that he must stand with his hat in his hand when he is in our presence, and he even presumes to help us in the running of our government. This will never do; so in "Red Rock" and "The Leopard's Spots" it must be shown that he should never have been allowed to vote anyway, and those honorable gentlemen in the Congress of the United States in the year 1865 did not know at all what they were about. Though we are given the characters and setting of a novel, the real business is to show that the Negro has been the "sentimental pet" of the nation all too long. By all means let us have an innocent white girl, a burly Negro, and a burning at the stake, or the story would be incomplete.

We have the same thing in "The Clansman," a "drama of fierce revenge." But here we are concerned very largely with the blackening of a man's character. Stoneman (Thaddeus Stevens very thinly disguised) is himself the whole Congress of the United States. He is a gambler, and "spends a part of almost every night at Hall & Pemberton's Faro Place on Pennsylvania Avenue." He is hysterical, "drunk with the joy of a triumphant vengeance." "The South is conquered soil," he says to the President (a mere figure-head, by the way), "I mean to blot it from the map." Further: "It is but the justice and wisdom of heaven that the Negro shall rule the land of his bondage. It is the only solution of the race problem. Wait until I put a ballot in the hand of every Negro, and a bayonet at the breast of every white man from the James to the Rio Grande." Stoneman, moreover, has a mistress, a mulatto woman, a "yello vampire" who dominates him completely. "Senators, representatives, politicians of low and high degree, artists, correspondents, foreign ministers, and cabinet officers hurried to acknowledge their fealty to the uncrowned king, and hail the strange brown woman who held the keys of his house as the first lady of the land." This, let us remember, was for some months the best-selling book in the United States. A slightly altered version of it has very recently commanded such prices as were never before paid for seats at a moving-picture entertainment; and with "The Traitor" and "The Southerner" it represents our most popular treatment of the gravest social question in American life! "The Clansman" is to American literature exactly what a Louisiana mob is to American democracy. Only too frequently, of course, the mob represents us all too well.

Turning from the longer works of fiction to the short story, I have been interested to see how the matter has been dealt with here. For purposes of comparison I have selected from ten representative periodicals as many distinct stories, no one of which was published more than ten years ago; and as these are in almost every case those stories that first strike the eye in a periodical index, we may assume that they are thoroughly typical. The ten are: "Shadow," by Harry Stillwell Edwards, in the *Century* (December, 1906); "Callum's Co'tin': A Plantation Idyl," by Frank H. Sweet, in the *Craftsman* (March, 1907); "His Excellency the Governor," by L. M. Cooke, in *Putnam's* (February, 1908); "The Black Drop," by Margaret Deland in *Collier's Weekly* (May 2 and 9, 1908); "Jungle Blood," by Elmore Elliott Peake, in *McClure's* (September, 1908); "The Race-Rioter," by Harris Merton Lyon, in the *American* (February, 1910); "Shadow," by Grace MacGowan Cooke and Alice MacGowan, in *Everybody's* (March, 1910); "Abram's Freedom," by Edna Turpin, in the *Atlantic* (September, 1912); "A Hypothetical Case," by Norman Duncan, in *Harper's* (June, 1915); and "The Chalk Game," by L. B. Yates, in the *Saturday Evening Post* (June 5, 1915). For high standards of fiction I think we may safely say that, all in all, the periodicals here mentioned are representative of the best that America has to offer. In some cases the story cited is the only one on the Negro question that a magazine has published within the decade.

"Shadow" (in the *Century*) is the story of a Negro convict who for a robbery committed at the age of fourteen was sentenced to twenty years of hard labor in the mines of Alabama. An accident disabled him, however, and prevented his doing the regular work for the full period of his imprisonment. At twenty he was a hostler, looking forward in despair to the fourteen years of confinement still waiting for him. But the three little girls of the prison commissioner visit the prison. Shadow performs many little acts of kindness for them, and their hearts go out to him. They storm the governor and the judge for his pardon, and present the Negro with his freedom as a Christmas gift. The story is not long, but it strikes a note of genuine pathos.

"Callum's Co'tin' " is concerned with a hard-working Negro, a blacksmith, nearly forty, who goes courting the girl who called at his shop to get a trinket mended for her mistress. At first he makes himself ridiculous by his finery; later he makes the mistake of coming to a crowd of merrymakers in his working clothes. More and more, however, he storms the heart of the girl, who eventually capitulates. From the standpoint simply of craftsmanship, the story is an excellent piece of work.

"His Excellency the Governor" deals with the custom on Southern plantations of having, in imitation of the white people, a Negro "governor" whose duty it was to settle minor disputes. At the death of old Uncle Caleb, who for years had held this position of responsibility, his son Jubal should have been the next in order. He was likely to be superseded, however, by loud-mouthed Sambo, though urged to assert himself by Maria, his wife, an old house-servant who had no desire whatever to be defeated for the place of honor among the women by Sue, a former field-hand. At the meeting where all was to be decided, however, Jubal with the aid of his fiddle completely confounded his rival and won. There are some excellent touches in the story; but, on the whole, the composition is hardly more than fair in literary quality.

"The Black Drop," throughout which we see the hand of an experienced writer, analyzes the heart of a white boy who is in love with a girl who is almost white, and who when the test confronts him suffers the tradition that binds him to get the better of his heart. "But you will still believe that I love you?" he asks, ill at ease as they separate. "No, of course I can not believe that," replies the girl.

"Jungle Blood" is the story of a simple-minded, simple-hearted Negro of gigantic size who in a moment of fury kills his pretty wife and the white man who has seduced her. The tone of the whole may be gleaned from the description of Moss Harper's father: "An old darky sat drowsing on the stoop. There was something ape-like about his long arms, his flat, wide-nostriled nose, and the mat of gray wool which crept down his forehead to within two inches of his eyebrows."

"The Race-Rioter" sets forth the stand of a brave young sheriff to protect his prisoner, a Negro boy, accused of the assault and murder of a little white girl. Hank Egge tries by every possible subterfuge to defeat the plans of a lynching party, and finally dies riddled with bullets as he is defending his prisoner. The story is especially remarkable for the strong and sympathetic characterization of such contrasting figures as young Egge and old Dikeson, the father of the dead girl.

"Shadow" (in *Everybody's*) is a story that depends for its force very largely upon incident. It studies the friendship of a white boy, Ranny, and a black boy, Shadow, a relationship that is opposed by both the Northern white mother and the ambitious and independent Negro mother. In a fight, Shad breaks a collar-bone for Ranny; later he saves him from drowning. In the face of Ranny's white friends, all the harsher side of the problem is seen; and yet the human element is strong beneath it all. The story, not without considerable merit as it is, would have been infinitely stronger if the friendship of the two boys had been pitched on a higher plane. As it is, Shad is very much like a dog following his master.

"Abram's Freedom" is at the same time one of the most clever and one of the most provoking stories with which we have to deal. It is a perfect example of how one may walk directly up to the light and then deliberately turn his back upon it. The story is set just before the Civil War. It deals with the love of the slave Abram for a free young woman, Emmeline. "All his life he had heard and used the phrase 'free nigger' as a term of contempt. What, then, was this vague feeling, not definite enough yet to be a wish or even a longing?" So far, so good. Emmeline inspires within her lover the highest ideals of manhood, and he becomes a hostler in a livery-stable, paying to his master so much a year for his freedom. Then comes the astounding and forced conclusion. At the very moment when, after years of effort, Emmeline has helped her husband to gain his freedom (and when all the slaves are free as a matter of fact by virtue of the Emancipation Proclamation), Emmeline, whose husband has special reason to be grateful to his former master, says to the lady of the house: "Me an' Abram ain't got nothin' to do in dis worl' but to wait on you an' master."

In "A Hypothetical Case" we again see the hand of a master-craftsman. Is a white boy justified in shooting a Negro who has offended him? The white father is not quite at ease, quibbles a good deal, but finally says Yes. The story, however, makes it clear that the Negro did not strike the boy. He was a hermit living on the Florida coast and perfectly abased when he met Mercer and his two companions. When the three boys pursued him and finally overtook him, the Negro simply held the hands of Mercer until the boy had recovered his temper. Mercer in his rage really struck himself.

"The Chalk Game" is the story of a little Negro jockey who wins a race in Louisville only to be drugged and robbed by some "flashlight" Negroes who send him to Chicago. There he recovers his fortunes by giving to a group of gamblers the correct "tip" on another race, and he makes his way back to Louisville much richer by his visit. Throughout the story emphasis is placed upon the superstitious element in the Negro race, an element readily considered by men who believe in luck.

Of these ten stories, only five strike out with even the slightest degree of independence. "Shadow" (in the *Century*) is not a powerful piece of work, but it is written in tender and beautiful spirit. "The Black Drop" is a bold handling of a strong situation. "The Race-Rioter" also rings true, and in spite of the tragedy there is optimism in this story of a man who is not afraid to do his duty. "Shadow" (in *Everybody's*) awakens all sorts of discussion, but at least attempts to deal honestly with a situation that might arise in any neighborhood at any time. "A Hypothetical Case" is the most tense and independent story in the list.

On the other hand, "Callum's Co'tin' " and "His Excellency the Governor," bright comedy though they are, belong, after all, to the school of Uncle Remus. "Jungle Blood" and "The Chalk Game" belong to the class that always regards the Negro as an animal, a minor, a plaything—but never as a man. "Abram's Freedom," exceedingly well written for two-thirds of the way, falls down hopelessly at the end. Many old Negroes after the Civil War preferred to remain with their former masters; but certainly no young woman of the type of Emmeline would sell her birthright for a mess of pottage.

Just there is the point. That the Negro is ever to be taken seriously is incomprehensible to some people. It is the story of "The Man That Laughs" over again. The more Gwynplaine protests, the more outlandish he becomes to the House of Lords.

We are simply asking that those writers of fiction who deal with the Negro shall be thoroughly honest with themselves, and not remain forever content to embalm old types and work over outworn ideas. Rather should they sift the present and forecast the future. But of course the editors must be considered. The editors must give their readers what the readers want; and when we consider the populace, of course we have to reckon with the mob. And the mob does not find anything very attractive about a Negro who is intelligent, cultured, manly, and who does not smile. It will be observed that in no one of the ten stories above mentioned, not even in one of the five remarked most favorably, is there a Negro of this type. Yet he is obliged to come. America has yet to reckon with him. The day of Uncle Remus as well as of Uncle Tom is over.

Even now, however, there are signs of better things. Such an artist as Mr. Howells, for instance, has once or twice dealt with the problem in excellent spirit. Then there is the work of the Negro writers themselves. The numerous attempts in fiction made by them have most frequently been open to the charge of crassness already considered; but Paul Laurence Dunbar, Charles W. Chesnutt, and W. E. Burghardt DuBois have risen above the crowd. Mr. Dunbar, of course, was better in poetry than in prose. Such a short story as "Jimsella," however, exhibited considerable technique. "The Uncalled" used a living topic treated with only partial success. But for the most part, Mr. Dunbar's work looked toward the past. Somewhat stronger in prose is Mr. Chesnutt. "The Marrow of Tradition" is not much more than a political tract, and "The Colonel's Dream" contains a good deal of preaching; but "The House Behind the Cedars" is a real novel. Among his short stories, "The Bouquet" may be remarked for technical excellence, and "The Wife of His Youth" for a situation of unusual power. Dr. DuBois's "The Quest of the Silver Fleece" contains at least one strong dramatic situation, that in which Bles probes the heart of Zora; but the author is a sociologist and essayist rather than a novelist. The grand epic of the race is yet to be produced.

Some day we shall work out the problems of our great country. Some day we shall not have a state government set at defiance, and the massacre of Ludlow. Some day our little children will not slave in mines and mills, but will have some chance at the glory of God's creation; and some day the Negro will cease to be a problem and become a human being. Then, in truth, we shall have the Promised Land. But until that day comes let those who mold our ideals and set the standards of our art in fiction at least be honest with themselves and independent. Ignorance we may for a time forgive; but a man has only himself to blame if he insists on not seeing the sunrise in the new day.

WALLACE THURMAN
Negro Poets and Their Poetry

JUPITER HAMMON, the first Negro in this country to write and publish poetry, was a slave owned by a Mr. Joseph Lloyd of Queens Village, Long Island. Hammon had been converted to the religion of Jesus Christ and all of his poems are religious exhortations, incoherent in thought and crudely excepted. His first poem was published in 1761, his second, entitled "An Address to Miss Phillis

Wheatley, Ethiopian Poetess in Boston, who came from Africa at eight years of age and soon became acquainted with the Gospel of Jesus Christ", in 1768.

This Miss Phillis Wheatley, who had been bought from a slave-ship by a family named Wheatley in Boston Harbor and educated by them, wrote better doggerel than her older contemporary Hammon. She knew Alexander Pope and she knew Ovid—Hammon only knew the Bible—and she knew Pope so well that she could write like a third-rate imitator of him. Phillis in her day was a museum figure who would have caused more of a sensation if some contemporary Barnum had exploited her. As it was, she attracted so much attention that many soft hearted (and, in some cases, soft headed) whites and blacks have been led to believe that her poetry deserves to be considered as something more than a mere historical relic. This is an excerpt from her best poem:

Imagination! who can sing thy force?
Or who describe the swiftness of thy course?
Soaring through the air to find the bright abode,
The empyreal palace of the thundering God,
We on thy pinions can surpass the wind,
And leave the rolling universe behind,
From star to star the mental optics rove,
Measure the skies, and range the realms above,
There is one view we grasp the mighty whole,
Or with new worlds amaze the unbounded soul.

She never again equalled the above, far less surpassed it. And most of the time she wrote as in the following excerpt from "On Major General Lee". (This poem would warm the heart of "Big Bill" Thompson of Chicago; he really should know about it.) A captured colonial soldier is addressing a British general:

O Arrogance of tongue!
And wild ambition, ever prone to wrong!
Believ'st thou, chief, that armies such as thine
Can stretch in dust that heaven defended line?
In vain allies may swarm from distant lands,
And demons aid in formidable bands,
Great as thou art, thou shun'st the field of fame,
Disgrace to Britain and the British name.

She continues in this vein, damning the British and enshrining the Americans until she reaches a climax in the following priceless lines:

Find in your train of boasted heroes, one
To match the praise of Godlike Washington.
Thrice happy chief in whom the virtues join,
And heaven taught prudence speaks the man divine.

Thomas Jefferson is quoted as saying that "Religion has produced a Phillis Wheatley, but it could not produce a poet. Her poems are beneath contempt". Nevertheless, Phillis had an interesting and exciting career. The Wheatleys carried her to London, where her first volume was published in 1773. She was exhibited at the Court of George III, and in the homes of the nobility much as the Negro poets of today are exhibited in New York drawing rooms. She wrote little about slavery, which is not surprising considering that save for her epic trip across the Atlantic in a slave-ship, she had never known slavery in any form. She often mentioned her homeland and once spoke of herself as "Afric's muse", but she was more interested in the religion of Jesus Christ and in the spreading of piety than in any more worldly items, save perhaps in her patriotic interest for the cause of the American colonists.

Heretofore every commentator, whether white or black, when speaking of Phillis Wheatley, has sought to make excuses for her bad poetry. They have all pointed out that Phillis lived and wrote during the eighteenth century, when, to quote from the introduction to White and Jackson's "Poetry of American Negro Poets", "the great body of contemporary poetry was turgid in the style of debased Pope". It would be too much, they continue, to expect "a poet of Phillis Wheatley's rather conventional personality to rise above this influence". In his preface to "The Book of American Negro Poetry", James Weldon Johnson contends that "had she come under the influence of Wordsworth, Byron, Keats or Shelley, she would have done greater work". Does it smack too much of lese majesty to suggest that perhaps Phillis wrote the best poetry she could have written under any influence, and that a mediocre imitation of Shelly would have been none the less mediocre than a mediocre imitation of Pope? Phillis was also influenced by the Bible, but her paraphrases of the scripture are just as poor as her paraphrases of "debased Pope".

Phillis died in 1784 and until Paul Lawrence Dunbar published his "Oak and Ivy", in 1892, American Negro poetry stayed at the level at which she had left it, although there must have been over one hundred Negroes who wrote and published poetry during this period. Most of them came into prominence during and after the

Civil War, and were encouraged by abolitionists to write of their race and their race's trials. Frances Ellen Harper is probably the best of this period. One volume, "On Miscellaneous Subjects", was published with an introduction by William Lloyd Garrison. Over ten thousand copies were circulated. Mrs. Harper also wrote and published "Moses, a Story of the Nile", in verse covering fifty-two closely printed pages. Many of her contemporaries were equally ambitious. Length was a major poetic virtue to them.

It seems highly probable that these people wrote in verse because neither their minds nor their literary tools and backgrounds were adequate for the task of writing readable and intelligent prose. They could be verbose and emotional in verse, and yet attain a degree of coherence not attainable when they wrote in prose. George M. Horton is a good illustration. He was born a slave in Chatham County, North Carolina, in 1797. It is said that he "was not a good farm worker on account of devoting too much time to fishing, hunting and attending religious meetings". He taught himself to read with the aid of a Methodist hymn-book and a red-backed speller. In 1830 he secured work as a janitor at Chapel Hill, the seat of the University of South Carolina. Here he made extra money writing love poems for amorous students. Desiring to obtain his freedom and migrate to Liberia, Horton, aided by some of his white friends, published a volume of verse entitled "The Hope of Liberty", but the returns from the sale of this volume were not sufficient for his purpose. But he remained more or less a free agent, and was allowed to hire himself out instead of having to remain on his master's plantation. In 1865, a troop of Federal soldiers, who had been quartered in Chapel Hill, were ordered north. Horton left with them and went to Philadelphia where he eventually died.

Here is a sample of his prose: "By close application to my book and at night my visage became considerably emaciated by extreme perspiration, having no lucubratory apparatus, no candle, no lamp, not even lightweed, being chiefly raised in oaky woods". And here is a sample of his verse:

Come liberty. Thou cheerful sound
Roll through my ravished ears;
Come, let my griefs in joy be drowned
And drive away my fears.

Further comment would be superfluous.

After the Civil War, the Negro found himself in a dilemma. He was supposed to be free, yet his condition was little changed. He was worse off in some respects than he had been before. It can be understood, then, that the more articulate Negroes of the day spent most of their time speculating upon this thing called freedom, both as it had been imagined and as it was in actuality.

However, none of the poetry written at this time is worthy of serious critical consideration. It was not even a poetry of protest. Although Negro poets objected to the mistreatment of their people, they did not formulate these objections in strong, biting language, but rather sought sympathy and pled for pity. They wept copiously but seldom manifested a fighting spirit. The truth is, only one American Negro poet has been a fighting poet, only one has really written revolutionary protest poetry, and that is Claude McKay, who will be considered later.

Paul Lawrence Dunbar was the first American Negro poet whose work really merited critical attention. Dunbar was the son of two ex-slaves, but supposedly full-blooded Negroes, a fact flagrantly paraded by race purists, to controvert the prevalent Nordic theory that only Negroes with Caucausian blood in their veins ever accomplish anything. He was born in Dayton, Ohio, June 27th, 1872. His father had escaped from his master and fled to Canada, but later returned to the States and enlisted for military service during the Civil War in a Massachusetts regiment. Dunbar may have inherited his love for letters and writing from his mother, whose master had often read aloud in her presence.

Dunbar attended the public school in his home town, and was graduated from the local high-school, where he had edited the school paper. Then he found employment as an elevator operator. In 1892 he delivered an address in verse to the Western Association of Writers, and shortly afterwards he published his first volume, "Oak and Ivy". In 1896, through the subscription method, he was able to publish another volume entitled, "Majors and Minors". William Dean Howells wrote a most favorable review of this volume and later paved the way for Dodd, Mead and Company to publish "Lyrics of Lowly Life", for which he wrote an introduction. Meanwhile Dunbar had visited England, and had become a great friend with Coleridge Taylor, the Negro composer, with whom he collaborated on many songs. On his return to the United States, another friend, Robert G. Ingersoll, helped him to get a position in the Library of Congress. He was only able to keep this job two years, for meanwhile he had developed pulmonary tuberculosis, and despite pilgrimages to such lung-soothing climates as the Adirondacks, the Rockies, and Florida, he finally succumbed to the disease and died in Dayton, Ohio, on February 9, 1908.

From 1892 until the time of his death, Dunbar published five volumes of verse, four volumes of collected short stories, and four novels. Not only was he the first Negro to write poetry which had real merit and could be considered as having more than merely sentimental or historical value, but he was also the first Negro poet to be emancipated from Methodism, the first American Negro poet who did not depend on a Wesleyan hymn-book for inspiration and vocabulary. Most of the poets preceding him were paragons of piety. They had all been seized upon by assiduous missionaries and put through the paces of Christianity, and their verses were full of puerile apostrophizing of the Almighty, and leaden allusions to Scriptural passages.

Yet Dunbar was far from being a great poet. First of all, he was a rank sentimentalist, and was content to let surface values hold his interest. He attempted to interpret the soul of his people, but as William Stanley Braithwaite has said, he succeeded "only in interpreting a folk temperament". And although he was, as William Dean Howells affirmed, the first "man of pure African blood of American civilization to feel Negro life aesthetically and express it lyrically", neither his aesthetic feeling nor his expression ever attained enough depth to be of permanent value.

Dunbar is famous chiefly for his dialect poetry. Yet he often regretted that the world turned to praise "a jingle in a broken tongue". He was ambitious to experiment in more classical forms, and to deal with something less concrete than the "smile through your tears" plantation larky of reconstruction times. Here perhaps was his greatest limitation. Being anxious to explore the skies, he merely skimmed over the surface of the earth.

After Dunbar, there was a whole horde of Negro poets who, like him, wrote in dialect. The sum total of their achievement is zero, but happily, in addition to these parasitic tyros there were also two new poets who had more originality and more talent than their contemporaries. And though neither of these men produced anything out of the ordinary, they did go beyond the minstrel humor and peasant pathos of Dunbar, and beyond the religious cant and doggerel jeremiads of Dunbar's predecessors. One of these men, William Stanley Braithwaite, is best known as a student and friend of poets and poetry rather than as a poet. He has yearly, since 1913, issued an anthology of American magazine verse, and has also published some academic studies of English literature.

The second, James Weldon Johnson, achieved little as a poet until recently, when he published "God's Trombones", a volume of Negro sermons done in verse. His first volume, "Fifty Years And

Other Poems", contains little of merit. The title poem, which recounts in verse the progress of the race from 1863 to 1913, has, because of its propagandist content, been acclaimed as a great poem. No comment or criticism is necessary of this opinion when part of the poem itself can be quoted:

Far, far, the way that we have trod
From heathen trails and jungle dens
To freedmen, freedmen, sons of God,
Americans and citizens.

Mr. Johnson, it seems, has also been fairly intimate with Methodist hymnbooks.

His sermon poems, while at times awkward and faulty in technique, have an ecstatic eloquence and an individual rhythm which immediately place them among the best things any Negro has ever done in poetry. Although this may not be saying much, and although, as a poet Mr. Johnson may not be adequate to the task of fully realizing the promise of these sermon poems, he has at least laid a foundation upon which a new generation of Negro poets can build. He will have to be remembered as something more than just a historical or sentimental figure. He, like Dunbar, is an important, if a minor bard; and if the Negro poet of the future is to make any individual contribution to American literature he must derive almost as much from the former's "God's Trombones" as from the latter's "Lyrics of Lowly Life".

To consider all the Negro poets who since 1913 have lifted up their voices in song would necessitate using an entire issue of any journal. It is not only an impossible task but one not worth the time and space it would require. For our present study we will touch only the high spots, passing over such people as Fenton Johnson, whose early promise has never been fulfilled; Joseph Cotter, Jr., who, it is alleged by most critics in this field, would have been a great poet had he lived but whose extant work belies this judgment; Georgia Douglas Johnson, whose highly sentimental and feminine lyrics have found favor; Arna Bontemps, who specializes in monotonous and wordy mystic evocations which lack fire and conviction, and Helene Johnson, who alone of all the younger group seems to have the "makings" of a poet.

But taking up the contemporary triumvirate—McKay, Cullen, and Hughes—all of whom have had volumes published by reputable houses and are fairly well known to the poetry-reading public, we have poets of another type. Each one of them represents a different trend in Negro literature and life.

Claude McKay was born in Jamaica, British West Indies, where he received his elementary education, served a while in the constabulary, and wrote his first poems. A friend financed his journey to America to finish his scholastic work, but McKay found himself at odds with the second-rate schools he attended here and finally fled to New York City where he became a member of the old *Masses, Seven Arts, Liberator* group of radicals and artists. During this period he received a legacy which, he tells us, was spent in riotous living. Broke, he attempted to make a living by washing dishes, operating elevators, doing porter work—the usual occupations engaged in by Negro artists and intellectuals.

McKay's first volume was published while he was still in Jamaica, a compilation of folk verse done in the native dialect. The Institute of Arts and Sciences of Jamaica gave him a medal in recognition of this first book. It is in many ways remarkable, and in it the poet gives us a more substantial portrait and delves far deeper into the soul of the Jamaican than Dunbar was ever able to in the soul of the southern Negro in America.

McKay's latter poetry is often marred by bombast. He is such an intense person that one can often hear the furnace-like fire within him roaring in his poems. He seems to have more emotional depth and spiritual fire than any of his forerunners or contemporaries. It might be added that he also seems to have considerably more mental depth too. His love poems are not as musical or as haunting as Mr. Cullen's, but neither are they as stereotyped. His sonnet to a Harlem dancer may not be as deft or as free from sentiment as "Midnight Man" by Langston Hughes, but it is far more mature and moving. All of which leads us to say that a study of Claude McKay's and of the other better Negro poetry convinces us that he, more than the rest, has really had something to say. It is his tragedy that his message was too alive and too big for the form he chose. His poems are for the most part either stilted, choked, or over-zealous. He could never shape the flames from the fire that blazed within him. But he is the only Negro poet who ever wrote revolutionary or protest poetry. Hence:

If we must die, let it be not like hogs
Hunted and penned in an inglorious spot,

. . .

Oh, Kinsman! We must meet the common foe;
Though far outnumbered let us still be brave,
And for their thousand blows, deal one death blow!
What though before us lies the open grave?

Like men we'll face the murderous pack,
Pressed to the wall, dying—but fighting back.

There is no impotent whining here, no mercy-seeking prayer to the white man's God, no mournful jeremiad, no "ain't it hard to be a nigger", no lamenting of or apologizing for the fact that he is a member of a dark-skinned minority group. Rather he boasts:

Be not deceived, for every deed you do,
I could match—out match; Am I not Africa's son,
Black of that black land where black deeds are done?

This is propaganda poetry of the highest order although it is crude and inexpert. Contrast it with these lines from Countee Cullen's sonnet "From The Dark Tower":

We shall not always plant while others reap
The golden increment of bursting fruit,
Nor always countenance abject and mute
That lesser men should hold their brothers cheap.

Countee Cullen is the symbol of a fast disappearing generation of Negro writers. In him it reaches its literary apogee. On the other hand Langston Hughes announces the entrance of a new generation, while Claude McKay, glorious revolutionary that he is, remains uncatalogued. For two generations Negro poets have been trying to do what Mr. Cullen has succeeded in doing. First, trying to translate into lyric form the highly poetic urge to escape from the blatant realities of life in America into a vivid past, and, second, fleeing from the stigma of being called a *Negro* poet, by, as Dunbar so desired to do, ignoring folk-material and writing of such abstractions as love and death.

There is hardly anyone writing poetry in America today who can make the banal sound as beautiful as does Mr. Cullen. He has an extraordinary ear for music, a most extensive and dexterous knowledge of words and their values, and an enviable understanding of conventional poetic forms. Technically, he is almost precocious, and never, it may be added, far from the academic; but he is also too steeped in tradition, too influenced mentally by certain conventions and taboos. When he does forget these things as in his greatest poem, "Heritage":

What is Africa to me:
Copper sun or scarlet sea,
Jungle star or jungle track,

Strong bronzed men, or regal black
Women from whose loins I sprang
When the birds of Eden sang?
One three centuries removed
From the scenes his fathers loved,
Spicy grove, cinnamon tree,
What is Africa to me?

and the unforgettable:

All day long and all night through,
One thing only must I do:
Quench my pride and cool my blood,
Lest I perish in the flood,
Lest a hidden ember set
Timber that I thought was wet
Burning like the dryest flax,
Melting like the merest wax,
Lest the grave restore its dead,
Not yet has my heart and head
In the least way realized
They and I are civilized

or his (to illustrate another tendency):

I climb, but time's
Abreast with me;
I sing, but he climbs
With my highest C.

and in other far too few instances, he reaches heights no other Negro poet has ever reached, placing himself high among his contemporaries, both black or white. But he has not gone far enough. His second volume is not as lush with promise or as spontaneously moving as his first. There has been a marking time or side-stepping rather than a marching forward. If it seems we expect too much from this poet, we can only defend ourselves by saying that we expect no more than the poet's earlier work promises.

Mr. Cullen's love poems are too much made to order. His race poems, when he attempts to paint a moral, are inclined to be sentimental and stereotyped. It is when he gives vent to the pagan spirit and lets it inspire and dominate a poem's form and context that he does his most impressive work. His cleverly turned rebellious poems are also above the ordinary. But there are not enough of these in comparison to those poems which are banal, though beautiful.

Langston Hughes has often been compared to Dunbar. At first this comparison seems far-fetched and foolish, but on closer examination one finds that the two have much in common, only that where Dunbar failed, Langston Hughes succeeds. Both set out to interpret "the soul of his race"; one failed, the other, just at the beginning of his career, has in some measure already succeeded.

The younger man has not been content to assemble a supply of stock types who give expression to stock emotions which may be either slightly amusing or slightly tragic, but which are never either movingly tragic or convincingly comic. When Langston Hughes writes of specific Negro types he manages to make them more than just ordinary Negro types. They are actually dark-skinned symbols of universal characters. One never feels this way about the people in Dunbar's poetry. For he never heightens them above their own particular sphere. There is never anything of the universal element in his poems that motivates Mr. Hughes.

Moreover, Langston Hughes has gone much farther in another direction than any other Negro poet, much farther even than James Weldon Johnson went along the same road in "God's Trombones". He has appropriated certain dialects and rhythms characteristically Negroid as his poetic properties. He has borrowed the lingo and locutions of migratory workers, chamber-maids, porters, bootblacks, and others, and woven them into rhythmic schemes borrowed from the blues songs, spirituals and jazz and with them created a poetic diction and a poetic form all his own. There is danger in this, of course, for the poet may and often does consider these things as an end in themselves rather than as a means to an end. A blues poem such as:

I'm a bad, bad man
'Cause everybody tells me so.
I'm a bad, bad man,
Everybody tells me so.
I takes ma meanness and ma licker
Everywhere I go.

or:

Ma sweet good man has
Packed his trunk and left.
Ma sweet good man has
Packed his trunk and left.
Nobody to love me:
I'm gonna kill ma self.

may be poignant and colorful but the form is too strait-laced to allow much variety of emotion or context. The poems produced are apt to prove modish and ephemeral. But when this blues form is expanded, as in:

Drowning a drowsy syncopated tune,
Racking back and forth to a mellow croon,
I heard a Negro play.
Down on Lenox Avenue the other night
By the pale dull pallor of an old gas light
He did a lazy sway
He did a lazy sway
To the tune o' those Weary Blues.
With his ebony hands on each ivory key
He made that poor piano mean with melody.
O Blues!
Swaying to and fro on his rickety stool
He played that sad raggy tune like a musical fool.
Sweet Blues!
Coming from a black man's soul.

the poet justifies his experiment, and ends at the same time the most felicitous and fruitful outlet for his talent.

Mr. Hughes, where his race is concerned, is perfectly objective. He is one of them so completely that he, more than any other Negro poet, realizes that after all they are human beings; usually the articulate Negro either regards them as sociological problems or as debased monstrosities. To Mr. Hughes, certain types of Negroes and their experiences are of permanent value. He is not afraid of, nor does he ignore, them. He can calmly say:

Put on yo' red silk stockings
Black gal.
Go an' let de white boys
Look at yo' legs.

. . .

An' tomorrow's chile'll
Be a high yaller.

or:

My old man's a white old man
And my old mother's black

. . .

My old man died in fine big house.
My ma died in a shack.
I wonder where I'm gonna die,
Being neither white nor black?

and reach the heights of his achievement in "Mulatto", one of the finest and most vivid poems written in the past few years. But Mr. Hughes has also written some of the most banal poetry of the age, which has not, as in the case of Mr. Cullen, even sounded beautiful.

The future of Negro poetry is an unknown quantity, principally because those on whom its future depends are also unknown quantities. There is nothing in the past to crow about, and we are too close to the present to judge it more than tentatively. McKay is called in France, an alien and a communist, barred from returning to this country. Once in a while a poem of his appears, but the period of his best work in this field seems to be at an end. Langston Hughes and Countee Cullen are both quite young, as poets and as individuals. Neither can be placed yet, nor can their contributions be any more than just intelligently commented upon. Whether they are going or will continue to go in the right direction is no more than a matter of individual opinion. All of us do know that as yet the American Negro has not produced a great poet. Whether he will or not is really not at all important. What does matter is that those who are now trying to be great should get intelligent guidance and appreciation. They seem to have everything else except perhaps the necessary genius.

From the Darker Side

IZETTA WINTER ROBB

"Yet do I marvel at this curious thing:
To make a poet black and bid him sing."
—COUNTEE CULLEN.

THE strangeness of his excellence we are not accustomed to consider, for the Negro—we always believed and even now hesitate to acknowledge his rightful place—had been to us anathema except for such times as we deigned to approve. There seemed no reason to accept him except as the servant in the house, magnanimously offering him the places we ourselves would scorn to hold. For years he was a servant, a slave to command; and then, after civil strife, the Negro found his freedom, which was only a less miserable kind of slavery, a little more tolerable than what he had known. Deeply hurting him was the hard, relentless attack which white superiority deemed righteous to inflict. With this background of a darkly-burdened race, and from a home in Harlem, and from the intellectual background of a modern collegiate institution, steps the new poet, Countee Cullen. He is the author of *Color,* a member of Phi Beta Kappa, and the acknowledged leader of American collegiate poets. He amazes us; for we, also in college, have not, many of us, a sonnet to our account in glory. Quite swiftly comes to mind as I write of this poet the memory of a girl, dark and tense, standing on the hillside before a group of students, singing spirituals. She had said, "These are the songs of my race, a race reared in pain yet seeking to comprehend God." She was exceedingly bitter, insistently defiant, and her voice, with its richness granted by heritage, pleaded for tolerance. The clear, deep resonance of her voice gave to the songs of her race a beautiful significance which is rooted in the darker side of our American culture. And then, not long ago, I heard the great Negro tenor, Roland Hayes, singing deeply his songs touched by the emotion which comes only from those who have understood harsh things in existence. He, too, sang proudly the songs of his race. But I return to Countee Cullen, the new and young poet.

There is sensuality in his verse. What precisely distinguishes his physical expressions from those of other authors of either prose or poetry is very difficult to express, but it is not completely indefinable. One cannot know at just what point crudeness enters into the expression of physical sensation, but in the poems of Countee Cullen, there is a certain physical clearness and poignancy which fairly expresses athletic litheness and agility, physical vigor as if the body had been whipped by strong winds into flaming cleanliness. Countee Cullen insists upon a sensuality which might almost be called bodily sensuousness, but which fails that because of the great, passionate intensity of his verse. His insistence on sensuality seems not a conscious thing, perhaps this very disregard of self preserves us from righteous disgust. One would say that his spontaneity is the consequence of three blended influences: the physical enthusiasm which is the mutual possession of youth, the deep emotions which ofttimes govern a poet who does not restrain himself completely to refined conventionalities, and the hereditary intensity of his race. Countee Cullen has beautifully expressed the hereditary influences which cause conflict.

All day long and all night through
One thing only must I do:
Quench my pride and cool my blood,
Lest I perish in the flood.
Lest a hidden ember set
Timber that I thought was wet
Burning like the dryest flax,
Melting like the merest wax,
Lest the grave restore its dead.
Not yet has my heart or head
In the least way realized
They and I are civilized.

Beautifully sophisticated is his *Advice to Youth* when one remembers that he, too, is very young. All youth is now possessed of the desire to test to the uttermost what has been conventionally forbidden in the glorious conventional age of the past. He likewise insists on these delights.

Since blood soon cools before that Fear
  That makes our prowess clay,
If lips to kiss are freely met,
  Lad, be not proud nor shy;
There are no lips where men forget,
  And undesiring lie.

It is the insistence of his word that astounds one. In *Bread and Wine,* voluptuous expression of life, the complaint against the awful toil in the shop is made by a soul who is tortured by relentlessness and futility in a chained existence, and then is followed by ecstatic passion.

Then tenuous with dreams the night,
  The feel of soft brown hands in mine,
Strength from your lips for one more fight,
  Bread's not so dry when dipped in wine.

But the rich, keenly cutting vitality of the writer makes for beauty cut from crudeness, at times hardly free of it, yet boldly cold and frank, not insinuating but finding the loveliness therein.

Biting deeply into the racial personality of the dark race is the cynicism which has been created by the social prejudice which has cut it with awful, red welts, and the intolerable process has been continuous. I remember once beginning an argument with the worn phrase, "People say," and the young colored woman to whom I was speaking spoke immediately with a touch of anger and despair, "People say? People say? I tell you *people say* almost anything!" Neither race has been free from prejudice. Mr. Cullen has expressed clearly the combined prejudice of both races on the question of the inter-racial friendship of two young men.

From the lowered blinds the dark folk stare,
And here the fair folk talk,
Indignant that these two should dare
In unison to walk.

Quite interesting is the poem *To My Fairer Brethren.* One girl of the negro race said a few weeks ago, "In any skilled occupation, the negro must be better than the best of the white men, or he will not be able to hold his place." They feel intensely the inequality which is inflicted by prejudiced attitudes.

Though I score you with my best,
Treble circumstance
Must confirm the verdict, lest
It be laid to chance.

And this is very true.

The rude remarks or actions which the fairer race inflicts upon the Negro are felt, and it is not given to him to find comfort in forgetfulness. When the sensitive nerves have been drawn taut and crudely touched, it is long remembered. The laughter of his race is not always there. I have seen the look of stoicism and cynical submission which is armor against renewed attack. I have seen it underneath a laugh, a kind of sardonic bravado. Told very neatly is *Incident* in which a small Baltimorean stared at eight-year-old Countee and called him "Nigger." The last verse is this:

I saw the whole of Baltimore
From May until December;
Of all the things that happened there
That's all that I remember.

From the source of like memories must have come the lovely touch of scorn, and then at times there is a word of irony against all that count themselves on the side of righteousness. Here is his word in *Black Magdalens:*

They fare full ill since Christ forsook
The cross to mount a throne,
And virtue still is stooping down
To cast the first hard stone.

But in contrast to this is delightful humor with a touch of whimsicality that lights his attitude toward those who feel that the sons of Ham shall serve eternally. The epitaph is *For a Lady I Know.*

She even thinks that up in heaven
Her class lies late and snores,
While poor black cherubs rise at seven
To do celestial chores.

Countee Cullen gives to his work gracefulness, litheness, swiftness, beauty. There is heat with the cold wind brushing across the surface, burnished gold against dull silver, swift flash of movement against a constant wall of gray. The cleverness of his thought is enhanced greatly by the subtle twist and meaning of the words. The living gracefulness of his words, even though touched at times by a crudeness which he cannot escape, or which he may not desire to avoid since conventional perfection breaks with reality, is very good whether he describes the native agility of a colored waiter at Atlantic City, the loveliness of his love's dark throat, or the crash of nature under bold skies. "But he was dying for a dream"—is it not beautiful to have said it of Christ? The great emotional freedom of his verse with the glow of intense sincerity is a part of his gift. Youth is in his work, and we would wish it that way. Blowing against our face the gay, cutting, ecstatic wind of the East, burning us with the sun, or washing us clean in cold water with luxurious tingling aftermath—all is the physical impetuosity of youth. Merging himself with nature is a part of the song:

. . . The din
A hollow log bound with a python's skin
Can make wrought every nerve to ecstasy,
And I was wind and sky again, and sea,
And all sweet things that flourish, being free.

But the note of defiance, the insistence upon freedom, is the high proud note. It is struck many times, sometimes only as the accompaniment to the motif, and then again as the central note of the theme. A whistle in the dark! He is very brave. His keen alliance with nature is a part of his extraodinary freedom; his own will in the matter is equally a part.

Across the earth's warm, palpitating crust
I flung my body in embrace; I thrust
My mouth into the grass and sucked the dew,
Then gave it back in tears my anguish drew;
So hard I pressed against the ground, I felt
The smallest sandgrain like a knife, and smelt
The next year's flowering; all this to speed
My body's dissolution, fain to feed
The worms. And so I groaned, and spent my strength
Until, all passion spent, I lay full length
And quivered like a flayed and bleeding thing.

The gradual merging of body to earth is a beautiful thing because it leads ultimately to the high cry of victory.

Right glad I was to stoop to what I once had spurned,
Glad even unto tears; I laughed aloud; I turned
Upon my back, and though the tears for joy would run,
My sight was clear; I looked and saw the rising sun.

But I cannot express adequately the intense defiance of him. It is a swift, beautiful, haughty declaration.

You cannot keep me captive, World,
Entrammeled, chained, spit on, and spurned
More free than all your flags unfurled,
I give my body to be burned.
I mount my cross because I will,
I drink the hemlock which you give
For wine which you withhold—and still,
Because I will not die, I live.

And finally, one is definitely held by the lyrical beauty of this very new young poet. One covets much the art of him who sings from the darker side of American culture. The intensity of youth, of poetic feeling, of race, beautifully blended, is the cause of admiration, and now has come the knowledge that beauty may come from Harlem.

THE Drama Section of the last two OPPQR-TUNITY Contests, while contributing new material, and a few good one act plays for the Negro Theatre, seems yet farthest behind the possibilities of its field of all the literary divisions.

On the Need of Better Plays

Excursions into the field in the past have been limited for the most part to low comedy which has succeeded commercially, and to a few propagandistic efforts of a defensive character. The attitude of the public has had something to do with this. It has accepted the stereotypes of buffoons, and Uncle Tom of Mrs. Stowe's play, and rejected by its indifference, and sometimes hostility, the efforts to revise these to more faithful pictures of reality. The recent plays of Negro life, which include Ridgeley Torrence's *Three Plays for a Negro Theatre, The Emperor*

Jones, All God's Chillun, The No 'Count Boy, The Chip Woman's Fortune, have all with the exception of the last been written by white playwrights. Negro writers have not, until very recently, sensed the possibilities of Negro drama. They have, excusably, used the drama as a field for the development of histrionic talent within the race and have lead themselves off into palpably unreal portrayal of the general plays of the stock company repertoire. They have been too ashamed of the material of their own lives to give it artistic portrayal. The new writers are beginning to see these situations and are clothing them in a new beauty. Herein lies the great future of the Negro in drama. It can provide a medium for the forceful interpretation of Negro life itself, a service which the stage undoubtedly can perform with as great, if not greater, directness and power than either fiction or poetry.

Recently there have come to us requests from inter-racial groups, for plays suitable for mixed casts, or plays that will offer aid toward softening the harsh points of racial contact. Noteworthy are the requests from the International Student Forum in England, and the Negro-Caucasian Club at the University of Michigan. Few plays that have come to our attention have been suitable for such use. This suggests still a further possibility for our developing playwrights. Taboos are weakening here and opening a new future for the creative energies of the playwrights and actors.

There has not been sufficient study of technique by the Negro playwrights. It is evident that the greatest lack at present is in the technique of play construction. Such newcomers to the field as Eloise Bibb Thompson, Willis Richardson, Frank Wilson and Eulalie Spence at least appreciate this necessity and are grounding themselves soundly in the formal procedure of presenting their materials.

There is not only opportunity for Negroes in drama but, at this stage, abundant hope; and we look to the materials of the present contest to point a way to definite accomplishment.

LS Arthur Davison Ficke to Carl Van Vechten, nd [1927].
[Harry Ransom Humanities Research Center, University of Texas at Austin.]

Dear Van Vechten:

You have asked me what I think of FINE CLOTHES TO THE JEW. I will tell you.

Langston Hughes , whose earlier poems had such great promise, here fulfills every vestige of that promise. He is a great artist; he never yields to the obvious temptation to comment on his themes, but produces the theme, stark and stripped, for the reader to feel and vibrate to. With a devastatingly ironic sense of the possibly comic quality of some of his material, he accepts that limitation and writes poetry that is usually as beautiful as it is tragic . . . [ellipses in the manuscript] Probably he is too unconscious an artist even to understand what I mean by saying that.

I was telling Witter Bynner only yesterday that it was a great pity that Bynner himself and others were encouraging, by means of prizes and little poetry magazines, the printing of so much facile verse by nice girls and boys all over the country. I told him that it misled everyone concerned–that it degraded the greatest of the arts to the level of a parlor pastime–and that it obscurred the fact that really fine poetry is usually the result of sole and passionate devotion of a lifetime. Today I am almost ready to eat my words–for I understand that Mr. Hughes' first recognition came through these mediums–and it is worth while to endure all the other rot for the sake of one authentic poet.

Hughes stands at the other pole from the clever verse writer. His technical cleverness is enormous; yet he does not exploit it. He knows, only too well, that poetry is the result of some catastrophic agony of the spirit, and he seems rarely to write from any more trivial level of experience.

The New Negro as Revealed in His Poetry

By Charlotte E. Taussig

Elemental discussions of the new Negro poets, in relation to their changed psychology, outside of the Anthologies, are rare, despite the aroused public interest on this question. Miss Taussig has succeeded admirably in providing a picture of this change, and of a group of writers, who stood at the crest of definite periods of their race's cultural growth. Here we have a DE NOVO *presentation, which is not only usefully informative, but stimulating in its appraisals. It is the substance of an address delivered before the Poetry Section of the Wednesday Club of St. Louis, the oldest and largest woman's club in the city*—Editor's Note.

IN approaching the subject of the new Negro, whether it be in his social or community life, his relations to his own or the white race, or in his artistic endeavors, it is necessary to readjust our minds and bring to its consideration a new point of view.

It is quite useless to try to understand these men and women who are making a place for themselves in art, literature and music if we continue to conjure visions of "Aunties" and "Uncles" and "Mammies." A new generation has arisen that is no longer only something to be argued about, condemned or defended, to be kept down, helped up or in its place—a generation that is fast learning that if it can give of the best, it has a chance to be judged on a universal basis. As "J. Poindexter, Colored" says in the book of that name, by Irvin Cobb, "I ain't no problem, I'se a person. I crave to be so regarded." And that many of them are becoming persons who must be reckoned with in any survey of contemporary achievement soon becomes clear to anyone who makes himself familiar with the prose and the poetry that the Negro is producing today.

Some of this has great limitations. It is often self-conscious and is propaganda rather than straight writing. But much of it, and this is particularly true of the poetry, is of such merit that it bears comparison with the best of the moderns. And this from a race who sixty years ago were slaves, of whom one in ten could read and write.

Professor Kittredge, of Harvard, once said that culture is a by-product. A by-product of what? Surely not of slavery, or oppression or discrimination. And yet in considering Negro art, this race, with a background so little fitted to make for that illusive quality, has, in this short time prepared a field too broad to cover. I have had to weed out and eliminate. I find myself not only sympathetic to, but overwhelmed by the mass of material obtainable. Because of this, I have had more and more to confine my subject matter. I cannot give even a brief survey of the Spirituals and the Blues and the Folk Legends of which these people have such a store. And so I am confining myself to one form of their expression and in line with the general subject of this section, except for a slight historical background, to the more modern phase.

I was asked the other day whether these poems were really good, whether they were being accepted by publishers and editors of magazines and awarded prizes on their worth; or because there was a rather sensational interest in the entire Negro question that was being catered to. I think the answer lies in the poems themselves.

II.

It is true that we speak of the new Negro. He is new in many ways, but that deep-lying feeling, which is inherent in the race, has found expression in poetic form for a long time. There were recognized Negro poets even when slavery existed. In 1761, Phyllis Wheatly was brought to Boston and sold on the public block. She fell into the hands of a kindly woman who taught her to read and write. She was not a great poet, but after the publication of her small volume of verse, the Lord Mayor of London sent her an inscribed copy of *Paradise Lost*, which is still preserved in the Harvard Library.

In 1829, George Moses Horton published, with the help of some white friends, a book of poems, entitled *The Hope of Liberty*. He hoped to sell enough copies to buy his freedom. But his master refused to sell him to himself; and bitterly disappointed, he stopped writing.

In 1854, a volume appeared by Frances Ellen Watkins, which showed an advance in literary merit.

WITH Paul Lawrence Dunbar, we come to the first Negro poet who can be judged by the standards generally applied. He was born in 1872, nine years after his parents had gained their freedom. With the publication of his poems, there comes the first step towards the greater power and broader vision that the Negro is enjoying. Up to and during his time, there were individuals who overcame the almost insuperable obstacles placed in their path and achieved a certain, and, in some instances, a marked success in their undertakings. Booker Washington immediately comes to mind and William Stanley Braithwaite, whose anthologies of American verse are among the most discriminating of their kind. There are others, but in each case they stood alone—an educator here—an aspiring poet there. Today we speak of Negro educators, Negro novelists, Negro musicians and Negro poets.

This has been made possible because, in the last decade, something has happened to the race that even the sociologist and the philanthropist cannot account for. It has come about partially through the shifting of the Negro population, which has made the Negro problem no longer exclusively or predominantly Southern. The trend of migration has been not only North but to the city and the great centers of industry. This migration is not to be entirely explained by the demands of war, industry or increased terrorism in the South. Neither labor demands nor the Ku Klux Klan is altogether responsible, although both have been important factors. It can be partially explained by the promise of a place where there can be found greater opportunity, more social and economic freedom and a chance to improve conditions.

Harlem is, of course, the outstanding example of a Northern Negro community. It is a city within a city, the largest Negro city in the world. The statement has often been made that if Negroes were transplanted to the North in large numbers, the race problem, with all its acuteness, and with new aspects, would be transferred with them.. 175,000 Negroes live closely together in Harlem, 100,000 more than live in any Southern city, and there is no record of race friction, nor any unusual record of crime. In a recent article in the *Survey*, a captain of police of the Harlem district is quoted as saying that, on the whole, it is the most law-abiding precinct in the city.

The Negro, and this applies especially to the educated Negro, is happier in Harlem than he can be in any other place in this country. There, group expression and self-determination have, for the first time, become possible. Each group has come with its own special motives and its own special ends. But the greatest experience of coming has been the finding of each other and the joining in common pursuits. In New York, Negroes publish their own newspapers, two magazines, *The Crisis* and OPPORTUNITY; maintain their news and circulation on a cosmopolitan scale, and any Negro with literary or artistic aspirations can find there the stimulus through association, that the white artist finds in his larger centers.

It is possible that these men and women, who are making a place for themselves in American literature, might have achieved success under less advantageous conditions. It is not necessary for all of them to live in Harlem; as a matter of fact, they don't. But it is open to them and sooner or later they drift there.

Fortunately, too, many of them have been able to go to college; some of them have studied or lived abroad, where for a time they were freed of a sense of race inferiority and with very few exceptions, all have founded their homes in the North, where segregation is less marked. Were this not the case, they might still have written good poetry. But as happened with the earlier, more isolated Negro poets, their writings would have continued to express only the emotions of their race. Today, while much of it deals with their own problems and is written in characteristic folk speech, a larger part is of universal appeal. One of the dangers which we are facing is that as the Negro writer increases his powers and becomes more generally recognized, he will cease giving us the typical products of his race. Fortunately, however, just as Roland Hayes is maintaining the best racial traditions in his conceptions of the spirituals, so some of the Negro writers feel this same need when it comes to expressing the instincts and emotions of their own people.

III.

Speaking of the place of dialect in Negro literature, James Weldon Johnson, whom we shall consider as the poet succeeding Dunbar, says: "It may be surprising to many to see how little of the poetry written by Negro poets today is in Negro dialect. Much of the subject matter which went into the making of traditional dialectic poetry they have discarded altogether, at least as poetic material. This tendency will, no doubt, be regretted by the majority of white readers, and it would be a distinct loss if the American Negro poets threw away this quaint and musical folk speech as a medium of expression; and yet these poets are working through a problem. They are trying to break away from, not the Negro dialect itself, but the limitations imposed by the fixing effects of long convention. What the colored poet in the United States needs is to find a form that will express the racial spirit by symbols from within, rather than by symbols from without, such as the mere mutilation of English spelling and pronunciation. He needs a form expressing the imagery, the idioms, the peculiar turn of thought and the distinctive humor and pathos of the Negro, but which will also be capable of voicing the deepest and highest emotions and aspirations and allow of the widest range of subject and the widest scope of treatment."

JAMES WELDON JOHNSON has been a great asset to his race. He has published two volumes, *The Book of American Negro Poetry* and *The Book of American Negro Spirituals*, which make it possible to gain a definite impression of the Negro's strivings and achievements. For the first time, in his *Fiftieth Anniversary Ode*, written in 1913, did a Negro poet break away from the brooding undercurrents which had characterized all their efforts.

After him, a new literary generation begins, giving us poetry that is racial in substance and context, but with the universal note and using consciously the full heritage of English poetry. Because he marks so definite a step in Negro poetry, I am using this poem as an example:

O BLACK AND UNKNOWN BARDS

O black and unknown bards of long ago,
How came your lips to touch the sacred fire?
How, in your darkness did you come to know
The power and beauty of the minstrel's lyre?

Who first from midst his bonds lifted his eyes?
Who first from out the still watch, lone and long
Feeling the ancient faith of prophets rise
Within his dark kept soul, burst into song?

There is a wide, wide wonder in it all,
That from degraded rest and servile toil
The fiery spirit of the seer should call
These simple children of the sun and soil.
O black slave singers, gone, forgot, unfamed,
You—you, alone, of all the long, long line
Of those who've sung untaught, unknown, unnamed,
Have stretched out upward, seeking the divine.

Johnson seems to be almost a generic name for Negro poets. There is Charles Bertram Johnson, the minister of the Second Baptist Church of Moberly, Mo., a native-born and reared Missourian, whose poetry has the virtue of sincerity and a definite melodious quality; Fenton Johnson, who takes the ideas embodied in the spirituals and transposes them into modern verse; and Georgia Douglas Johnson, who is generally considered the outstanding Negro woman poet of the day. She was born in Atlanta and received her academic education there. Later she specialized in music at Oberlin. Her first book of lyrics was entitled *The Heart of a Woman*. Mrs. Johnson is a poet who is neither afraid nor ashamed of her emotions. Through all her poems one can sense the longing for a fuller chance at life. Without one word or hint of race in all the book, there lies between its covers the full tragedy of her people.

I give a short poem of Mrs. Johnson's and one by Angelina Grimké, in order that we may hear from more than one woman:

MEMORY

Georgia Douglas Johnson

What need have I for memory
When not a single flower
Has bloomed within life's desert
For me one little hour?

What need have I for memory
Whose burning hours have met
The course of unborn happiness
Winding the trail regret?

THE BLACK FINGER

Angelina Grimké

I have just seen a beautiful thing
Slim and still,
Against a gold, gold sky,
A straight cypress,
Sensitive
Exquisite,
A black finger
Pointing upwards.
Why, beautiful, still finger are you black?
And why are you pointing upwards?

IV.

From now on the process of elimination must be drastic. One would like to dwell at length on Jean Toomer, Anne Spencer, Lewis Alexander, Lucien Watkins, Joseph Cotter, and many others. But it seems wiser to concentrate on the three Negro poets who represent the high-water mark of the new Negro poetry—Claude McKay, Langston Hughes and Countee Cullen. I shall consider them according to their age and not their merit. Each can well bear to be judged on his own.

Claude McKay was born in Jamaica in 1889 and received his early education there. He came to the United States in 1912 and for the two succeeding years was a student at the Kansas State University. Since then he has devoted himself to journalism and writing. In 1921 he visited Russia and he has spent much time in France and Germany. He was formerly associate editor of *The Liberator* and *The Masses*.

Let me quote from Max Eastman's introduction to McKay's volume of verse, *Harlem Shadows*, and briefly from an article by another critic Mr. Eastman says: "These poems have a special interest for all the races of man because they are sung by a pure blooded Negro They are characteristic of that race as we most admire it, they are gentle simple, candid, brave and friendly, quick of laughter and of tears, yet they are still more characteristic of what is deep and universal in mankind. There is no special or exotic kind of merit in them, no quality that demands a transmutation of our own natures to perceive. These poems move with a sovereignty that is never new to the lovers of the high music of human utterance. They have in them the pure, clear arrow-like quality that reminds us of Burns, Villon and Catallus and all the poets that we call lyric." And Robert Littell writing in the New Republic says: "If Mr. McKay and the other Negro poets do not always stir us unusually when they travel over poetic roads so many have traveled before they do make us sit up and take notice when they write about their race and ours. Claude McKay strikes hard and pierces deep." The following poem is indicative of his powers:

Like A Strong Tree.

Like a strong tree that in the virgin earth
Sends far its roots through rock and loam and clay
And proudly thrives in rain or time of dearth,
When the dry waves scare rainy sprites away;
Like a strong tree that reaches down, deep, deep,
For sunken water, fluid underground,
Where the great ringed unsightly blind worms creep,
And queer things of the nether world abound;
So would I live in rich imperial growth,
Touching the surface and the depth of things,
Instinctively responsive unto both,
Tasting the sweets of being and the stings,
Sensing the subtle spell of changing forms,
Like a strong tree against a thousand storms.

In his introduction to Langston Hughes' volume, *The Weary Blues* which has gone through four editions, Carl Von Vechten says: "At the moment I cannot recall the name of any other person who at the age of twenty-three has enjoyed so picturesque and rambling an existence as Langston Hughes."

Hughes was born in Joplin, Mo., in 1902. He was educated in the public schools of Lawrence, Kansas, went to high school in Cleveland, and spent one year at Columbia University. During his youth he lived for a time in Mexico City. When he left college he worked for a truck farmer on Staten Island; as a delivery boy for a New York florist, and then signed up as a sailor for a cruise of the Canary Islands, the Azores and the west coast of Africa. Returning to New York with plenty of money and a monkey he shipped again, this time for Holland. Again he came and went west, landing finally in Paris where he was employed as doorman of a night club; and later as second cook, and then waiter at one of the larger restaurants. Since 1924 he has divided his time between Harlem and Washington and has devoted himself to writing.

LANGTON HUGHES more than any of the other Negro poets breaks away from the traditional form. His poems have often almost an air of informality. They reveal the shifting scenes and places which have made up his life. They portray a ceaseless hunger for warmth and color and beauty, and almost invariably they are personal in tone, although they are not confined to an exclusive mood, and in his language form he uses a Biblical simplicity. Most of his poems are short. I have chosen to quote:

Dream Variation

To fling my arms wide
In some place of the sun,
To whirl and to dance
Till the white day is done.
Then rest at cool evening
Beneath a tall tree
While night comes gently
Dark like me—
That is my dream.

To fling my arms wide
In the face of the sun,
Dance, whirl, whirl!
Till the quick day is done.
Rest at pale evening—
A tall slim tree—
Night coming tenderly
Black like me.

The John Reed Memorial Prize awarded through the magazine *Poetry* was given to Countee Cullen for this *Threnody for a Brown Girl*, in 1925. He has also won the Witter Bynner prize. Cullen is the most prolific of these younger Negro poets. In his volume entitled *Color* of which over 6000 copies have been sold to date, he makes acknowledgement to these magazines for permission to reprint (I give this as an indication of the place he is taking): *The American Mercury, The Bookman, The Century, The Crisis, The Conning Tower of the New York World, Folio, Harpers, Les Continents, The Messenger, The Nation, Opportunity, Palms, Poetry, The Southwestern Christian Monitor Advocate, The Survey Graphic, The World Tomorrow,* and *Vanity Fair*. He is the youngest of these poets having been born in New York City in 1903. He went to the public schools and New York University where he was graduated a Phi Beta Kappa man in 1925. Young as he is, he has taken the new movement a step beyond even the strength displayed by Claude McKay. The bitterness revealed by those who have preceded him is with him converted into a question. It almost seems as if he were treasuring a dream that it may be given to his generation to solve the unsolvable problems of his race. His poems are beautiful in form, they cover a wide range of subject, reveal originality and in his longer poems he shows the ability to sustain, perhaps the most difficult achievement in artistic creation. *Judas Iscariot*, an entirely new conception, is particularly interesting as coming from a race which so naturally has the fullest sympathy for the outcast, but it is unfortunately, too long for quotation. The following sonnet is exemplary of his general style:

Yet Do I Marvel.

I doubt not God is good, well-meaning, kind,
And did He stoop to quibble could tell why
The little buried mole continues blind,
Why flesh that mirrors Him must some day die.
Make plain the reason tortured Tantalus
Is baited by the fickle fruit, declare
If merely brute caprice dooms Sisyphus
To struggle up a never-ending stair.
Inscrutable His ways are, and immune
To catechism by a mind too strewn
With petty cares to slightly understand
What awful brain compels His awful hand.
Yet do I marvel at this curious thing:
To make a poet black, and bid him sing!

I hope in presenting this subject, I have not seemed to let my sympathy get the better of my judgment. I have tried to approach it without any sense of race conflict. I have found that I could read these poems with the same disregard of the fact that they were written by a Negro as I can *The Three Musketeers*. That is, I *can* dissociate myself from the struggle and the pathos and the pity of their situation. It is this which makes me stand in awe of what these men and women are doing, in spite of what we have done to them. And I ask myself whether we who are so responsible, dare scorn any who so truly seek the light. After all, haven't they earned the right to say this—

I, too sing America,
I am the darker brother.

THE NEGRO LITERARY RENAISSANCE

BY BENJAMIN BRAWLEY

THE recent literary striving on the part of young Negro people throughout the country really began in the throes of the World War. After all discount is made, after all the tinsel is brushed away, the fact remains that the grandiose schemes of Marcus Garvey gave to the race a consciousness such as it had never possessed before. The dream of a united Africa, not less than a trip to France, challenged the imagination; and the soul of the Negro experienced a new sense of freedom. To be black ceased to be matter for explanation or apology; instead it became something to be advertised and exploited: thus the changed point of view made for increased racial self-respect. Here at least was a very solid gain.

With the new sense of freedom latent impulses not unnaturally came to the surface. "Suppressed desires" were given rein; and the revised order of things brought into prominence that quality in the Negro—romanticism—which we have all had to note is his greatest gift and also his greatest pitfall. Accordingly, with his innate love of song and the dance, he gave himself to the most intense living. Now romanticism, as one critic has said, is a disease in that it throws emphasis on sensational effects and abnormal states of mind. All America, however, was for the moment abnormal; old modes of thought and conduct were in the crucible; and the popular demand for the exotic and the exciting was best met by a perverted form of music originating in Negro slums and known as jazz. If it was a matter of getting strong effects, no other racial element in the country could possibly compete with the Negro.

Very especially did this romantic temper cultivate a mood that was of the very essence of hedonism and paganism. All of the more serious values in life were left out of account in a reckless abandon to the enjoyment of the moment. Introspection and self-pity ran riot, and there was such psychoanalysis as Freud himself hardly ever dreamed of. The result was a new form of so-called art known as the "blues," the spirit of which may be seen from the following:—

Everybody in Hoboken town—everybody an' me
Hopped upon a warehouse that was swinging around
An' went to sea;
Oh, all day long I's lookin' for trees—
Lookin' for sand, lookin' for land,
'Cause I've got dose awful, weepin', sleepin',
Got dose awful sailin', wailin',
Got dose awful deep sea blues.

Of the temper represented by jazz and the "blues" there were three results in literature and art. The first was a lack of regard for any accepted standards whatsoever. Old forms of composition were thrown overboard; young poets were led to believe that they did not need any training in technique; and a popular form of poetizing known as "free verse" was most acceptable because most unrestrained. In prose the desired outlet became a sharp staccato form of writing that Fanny Hurst and one or two others had used as a vehicle but that attacked the very foundations of grammar. The second result of the dominant mood was a preference for sordid, unpleasant, or forbidden themes. As the hectic, the reckless, or the vulgar became attractive, so did young authors tend to seek their themes in dives or cabarets or with ladies of easy virtue. A third result, a very practical result, was the turning away from anything that looked like good honest work in order to loaf and to call oneself an artist. If one could betake himself to writing and engage in the task of enlightening a benighted world, all the more could he imagine that he was doing something constructive, and he would be the greater "artist" accordingly, even if he did not know the difference between a dactyl and a spondee. The pity of it all was that the young author frequently fancied that he was creative when, as a matter of fact, he was simply imitative and coarse.

The first two of the results just mentioned we shall illustrate as we proceed; for the moment let us note especially the last. In the new periodical, *Fire,* in the midst of seven double-column pages entitled "Smoke, Lilies and Jade," there is the following (and I certainly hope the compositor will set it up exactly as we give it to him):

he wondered why he couldn't find work . . .
a job . . . when he had first come to New York
he had . . . and he had only been fourteen
then was it because he was nineteen now that he felt
so idle . . . and contented . . . or because he was an artist . . . was one an artist
until one became known . . . of course he was
an artist . . . and strangely enough so were all
his friends . . he should be ashamed that he

didn't work . . . but . . . was it five years in New York . . . or the fact that he was an artist . . .

This is the "very latest thing" in English prose as cultivated by Negro "artists." On the main point, however, that about unwillingness to work, we may note in the same periodical and also in the latest volume by the author, Mr. Langston Hughes, some lines entitled "Elevator Boy," which will hardly do for quoting in this magazine but which end thus:

I been runnin' this
Elevator too long.
Guess I'll quit now.

As to all of which we submit simply that the running of an elevator is perfectly honorable employment and that no one with such a job should leave it until he is reasonably sure of getting something better.

Such is the background and such are some of the more obvious results of the temper that just now characterizes the young Negro writers of the country. These writers, let us note in passing, have been encouraged as perhaps no group of literary young people was ever before encouraged in the history of American letters. Patronage has extended its hand; prizes offered by *Opportunity* and *The Crisis* have called forth hundreds of manuscripts; and metropolitan critics have sometimes been almost maudlin in their praise of mediocre achievement. Again and again the new striving has been termed a "renaissance," and one was given to understand that the movement had brought forth several writers of unquestioned genius and ability. It is not unfitting then, for us to look into the situation and see just what has actually been accomplished. Naturally the points that have been made will not apply in equal measure to every representative of the school; all in all, however, they will hold, and while we shall find some work of genuine promise, we shall also find a good deal that might with perfect propriety have been left undone.

The first to demand attention is Eric Walrond, whose "Tropic Death" has but recently come from the press. Mr. Walrond was born in British Guiana and in his youth gained wide acquaintance with life in the West Indies. For several years now he has been in the United States, and recently he was business manager for *Opportunity*. As to his book it is hardly too much to say that in a purely literary way, it is the most important contribution made by a Negro to American letters since the appearance of Dunbar's "Lyrics of Lowly Life." Mr. Walrond differs from other writers in the freshness of his material, in the strength of his style, in his skillful use of words, in his compression—in short, in his understanding of what makes literature and what does not. "Tropic Death" is a collection of ten stories or sketches that deal with the tragedy in the lives of the poorer people in the West Indies. Sometimes death comes to the Negro peasant through drought or starvation, sometimes through lingering and loathsome disease; or it may be that a drunken marine pulls a trigger to uphold the established order. The book is not always a pleasant one; nor is it a perfect one. Frequently the suggestion is so veiled that even the diligent reader is puzzled; and certainly a writer of Mr. Walrond's ability can now dispense altogether with hectic writing in gaining his effects. Moreover we cannot help thinking that those stories that move steadily toward a strong conclusion, such as "Drought" and "Subjection," are much more convincing than those that are more episodic, such as "The White Snake" and "Tropic Death." All told, however, the man who wrote this book knows something about writing; his style is becoming more and more chaste; and, in view of his firm grasp of his material and his clear perception of what is worth while, we feel that there is nothing in fiction that is beyond his capabilities.

Very different, but still demanding serious consideration, is the work of Walter White. Here the scene and setting are much more conventional, and the propaganda is deliberate. In "The Fire in the Flint" there is an abundance of philosophizing; the workmanship, especially near the beginning is often amateurish; and the hero at times seems incorrigibly stupid; but let us be just: before this book gets through it thrusts before the reader a situation that grips with the power of sheer tragedy and that sweeps all before it to a harrowing but inevitable close. "Flight" has been regarded as on the whole not so successful; the first part of the book is not firmly organized and the last part was evidently hastily done. Yet this novel is not without merit. It attempts something a little finer if not stronger than "The Fire in the Flint"; and the middle portion, that detailing the flight of the heroine and her fight back to respectability, holds the interest firmly. In general Mr. White's work preaches perhaps more than it expresses; accordingly, regarded purely from the standpoint of the artistic, it belongs to a different order of writing from that of Mr. Walrond. Preaching, however, has its place; and we recall that "Uncle Tom's Cabin," produced seventy-five years ago, still has power to engage the reader. So we shall have no quarrel with the author of "The Fire in the Flint" on account of his propaganda. The book has vitality, and there is still place in the world for literature with a message.

Perhaps near Mr. Walrond many people would today

place Jean Toomer, the author of "Cane," who has written both prose and verse. With this judgment we cannot quite agree, though this is not to say that Mr. Toomer's work is without merit. Again and again it is strong; but the themes are frequently unpleasant, the impressionism is often gross, and the effect is sometimes that of a shock rather than that of genuine power. Over the whole accordingly broods an air that borders on the artificial or theatrical. The fact that Mr. Toomer seems most interested in prose while his poetry shows him to the better advantage is in itself significant; it may be that the prose could stand a little more discipline.

Among the poets Claude McKay is outstanding, and it was the little volume, "Harlem Shadows," that by its appearance in 1922 did much to give impetus to the recent literary movement. Of the work of this author we have spoken at other times and places. His poetry is successful because it not only has something vital to say but because it also shows due regard for the technique of versification. The favorite form is the sonnet, and within the narrow confines of this medium the poet manages to express the most intense emotion. His work has not been perfect, but it has often been strong, and altogether one felt justified in placing a high estimate on the author's possibilities.

Through the long night until the silver break
Of day the little gray feet know no rest;
Through the long night until the silver break
Has dropped from heaven upon the earth's white breast,
The dusky, half-clad girls of tired feet
Are trudging, thinly shod, from street to street.

As for saying anything about Countee Cullen, one would seem to need to be just a little brave in view of the prizes that have been showered on this young poet and of his success with the magazines. The fact remains, however, that he has simply not yet mastered the mechanics of his art. His volume, "Color," as we understand it, brought together the best of his work up to 1925. We have read through that book twice with a fair degree of care, and we regret that we can find in it not one quotable passage. By a quotable passage we mean one that expresses a truth or a mood in such felicitous language that a reader can hardly help remembering it. Such lines or stanzas abound in well-known classics like Gray's "Elegy" and Lowell's "The Vision of Sir Launfal"; and they are even to be found in Paul Laurence Dunbar—in the first and last stanzas of "The Poet and his Song," for instance, or in the lines entitled "Life." "Color" contains no such things as these; on the contrary, on page after page there is lack of attention to the nature of dental, labial, and guttural sounds. The author does not mind writing such harsh and crowded lines as

By truths of wrongs the childish vision fails
To see; too great a cost this birth entails.

Throughout the volume the insufficiency of the poet's mastery of form is shown by a rather excessive fondness for the old ballad measure. This is very good in its way, but if used in poem after poem tends to become monotonous. And in view of Robert Buchanan's poem on the subject, Mr. Cullen was daring indeed to write on Judas Iscariot. Here, however, are four of the lines:

And when Christ felt the death hour creep
With sullen, drunken lurch,
He said to Peter, "Feed my sheep,
And build my holy church."

These lines raise not only questions of taste but questions of fact. It was not at the time of the "lurching" of his death hour that Christ said to Peter the things quoted. The text about the church came some time before the crucifixion, and that about the sheep after the resurrection. Lest we seem, however, to be unjust to this poet's work, we quote the whole of a poem of six lines, that on Joseph Conrad:

Not of the dust, but of the wave
His final couch should be;
They lie not easy in a grave
Who once have known the sea.
How shall earth's meagre bed enthrall
The hardiest seaman of them all?

One does not have to read this more than once to observe that the fourth line is easily the best. When he asks the reason why this should be so, he finds in it the dominance of liquid sounds in the line. What, however, is to be said about the juxtaposition of dental and labial in the middle of the first line, or of the harsh consonants in the second, or, worst of all, of the amazing medley of dentals and gutturals in the fifth line? Of course it may be contended that the harshness of the words is to suggest the rugged character of Conrad; but, in view of the fact that this sort of thing runs all through the book, we are not quite convinced.

About Langston Hughes the only thing to observe is that here we have the sad case of a young man of ability who has gone off on the wrong track altogether. We are sure that he can get on the right track, but it will take a strong wrench to put him there, also a little time. When Mr. Hughes came under the influence of Mr. Carl Van Vechten and "The Weary Blues" was given to the world, the public was given to understand that a new and genuine poet had appeared on the horizon. It mattered not that the thing contributed had been done years before by Vachel Lindsay; the book was full of jazz, and that was enough for the public. After all, however, it is not an author's first book that determines his quality, but the second, for the first may be an accident. "Fine Clothes to the Jew" hardly stands the test. In fact, one would have to go a long way to find more of sheer coarseness and vulgarity than are to be found between the covers of this little book. We forbear quotation. We are sorry that Mr. Hughes wrote it, and we hope that he will never write another like it.

And now *Fire*.

About this unique periodical the only thing to say is that if Uncle Sam ever finds out about it, it will be debarred from the mails. We have already given a sample of the prose cultivated by this new venture; but this "Quarterly Devoted to the Younger Negro Artists" has still other claims to consideration. The very first article ought not to have been written, to say nothing of being published; one of the poems seems to rest mainly on the strength of its swearing; and other contributions are in line with these. The temper and the grammar may both be seen from the following (the italics are ours):

> It really makes no difference to the race's welfare what such ignoramuses think, and it would seem that any author preparing to write about Negroes in Harlem or anywhere else should take *whatever phases of their life that seem the most interesting to him,* and develop them as he pleases.

Just one hundred years ago this year a young poet of England not yet quite eighteen years of age, brought out with his brother a little book called "Poems by Two Brothers." Three years later he brought out another volume, and three years later still another. By this time the critics of England had found him out, and they at last convinced him that he did not as yet have full mastery of his medium. He did not become discouraged, and he did not lose faith in himself; instead he went off for a season of study. He studied ten years before he published again; he studied Greek, Latin, and Italian poetry, and all the forms that that poetry assumed; he read history and philosophy and theology; and he criticised himself unmercifully. When he returned to the scene in 1842 he was the foremost poet of his country, and he held his place without challenge for fifty years.

The name of that poet was Alfred Tennyson, and we commend his example to the young writers of the Negro race.

The so-called renaissance has given us such a book as that by Mr. Walrond, and such work of promise as that by Mr. White and Mr. McKay; and these men would probably have written even if there had been no "renaissance" at all. In general, however, the younger group of writers has been indifferent to the need of taking pains; one after another has refused to master technique; and it is all the more to be lamented that they have been overpraised and that their vulgarity has been mistaken for art. Already, however, the day of jazz is over; charlatanry has defeated itself. He who would be a poet in the new day must not only have a vision; he must labor unceasingly to give that vision beautiful and enduring form. Only thus can there be an abiding contribution to literature; only thus can all the hopes and prizes be justified.

CONQUEST BY POETRY

BY ROBERT T. KERLIN

"*We are the music-makers,*
And we are the dreamers of dreams;
. . . .
Yet we are the movers and shakers
Of the world forever, it seems.

With wonderful deathless ditties
We build up the world's great cities,
And out of a fabulous story
We fashion an empire's glory:
One man with a dream, at pleasure,
Shall go forth and conquer a crown;
And three with a new song's measure
Can trample an empire down."

IN OUR own day and in our own country this prophesy is being fulfilled. Such is the power of song, such the might of the spirit. Peace indeed hath her victories, and the only conquests worth seeking for or worth recording are the conquests of the spirit; not of the arm of the flesh, or the weapon of war. A half-dozen or so young Negro poets have achieved more for their people in the last half-dozen years simply by the beauty of their poems than have all the belligerent editors in a half-century by their denunciations. Not that the editors were not justified—a thousand times justified. I am only comparing methods. Pragmatism is on the side of the poets.

The Negro is today singing himself into the respect of the world; not with the precious old slave spirituals, exciting compassion, but with new songs that win admiration and disarm prejudice. Verily, the music-makers are shaking an empire down and building the City of God.

The best American magazines and the best book publishers—no small number of them—are today accepting the poems and stories of young Negro writers solely upon their merit. Explain the fact on either of two hypotheses; that the publishers have grown more open-minded, or that the Negro has attained to a new excellence of artistic articulation; both explanations are sound. It requires both to explain the fact.

More and more difficult is the task of evaluating or describing the literary output of the young Negro writers of the day. It is too various for easy generalizations. There are too many strongly differentiated artists. The term "school" would be misleading and do an injustice. Connections between author and author are only incidental, as between Shelley and Keats, Coleridge and Wordsworth. Hughes and Cullen are only contemporaries and friends—and Negroes; there ends the connection. Neither belongs to a school; nor, in prose, does Fisher, Toomer, or Walrond. They are all just moderns, each with his individual art and individual materials. The time has therefore come for critical essays upon individual creators. This is to say a great deal, by implication, on the subject of recent Negro achievement in literature.

I have just finished reading the poems submitted to *Opportunity* in the "Pushkin" and the "Holstein" contests. If the eighty competitive poems were published as an anthology of contemporary Negro poetry the volume would evoke general praise and expressions of astonishment at so much talent. I do not doubt this. Acquainted as I am with Negro literature I was not prepared for this abundance of excellence. It will be interesting to compare the anthologies which are sure to appear in the next year or so—for they will be needed—with Johnson's (1922), Kerlin's (1923), and White and Jackson's (1924).

Even at the time these books were coming from the press the Negro Renaissance, now so convincing, was well on its way, yet discerned only by the few. Its present vigor may be indicated by a few items of current history. Braithwaite's "Anthology of Magazine Verse," an event of major importance in the literary annals of each year, an authoritative and unrivaled volume, contains in the 1926 issue twenty-three poems by eleven Negro poets. In a group of fifteen essays on sectional or racial contributions to American poetry during the last fifty years there is one by a Negro on Negro poetry. In view of such recognition who can doubt that the Negro has arrived. Former volumes of this series have contained poems by Negroes, but never to anything like this extent. Here, unsegregated, the Negro poet appears on his merit by the side of the white poet, competitor with him for the same honors. The fact is immensely significant. It is hostile to lynching, and to jimcrowing.

This arrival was not unheralded. Clement Wood in his "American Poets" gives several pages to Negro poets and presents a dozen or so writers with just commendation. Louis Untermeyer's "Modern American Poets," an anthology used more extensively as a textbook in colleges than any similar volume, includes Dunbar, J. W. Johnson, Alex Rogers, and Countee Cullen.

The American Negro poet is plainly in the vestibule of the Hall of Fame. At least there. He, or she, is young. Note these names in Braithwaite's "Anthology": Gwendolen B. Bennett, Anna Bontemps, Countee Cullen, Waring Cuney, Frank S. Horne, Langston Hughes, Helen Johnson, Thurman Wallace, and Lucy Ariel Williams: they are all in their twenties. Two out of the entire eleven I omitted from this list of youthfuls. They are Joseph Cotter and Georgia Douglass Johnson. They will pardon me. If I were thinking only of their poetic vigor I should class them still as young.

But the evidence of the Negro Renaissence has not even yet been fully adduced. Here is the fine little poetry magazine called *Palms*. The October, 1926, number was a "Negro Poets" number, edited by Countee Cullen. It contained poems by fifteen verse-writers, at least ten of whom are new or recent names in print. Some of them are not out of their teens and more not out of college. Thus the vestibule before mentioned is being thronged. Or shall we say the slopes of Parnassus?

The best American magazines appear to be open to talent in whatever guise it comes. But the Young Negro—with capitals, observe—will have his own. Nor are *The Crisis,* and *Opportunity,* and *The Messenger* adequate to his purpose. He will have something born of the New Day and expressing it. Hence appears *Fire;* A Quarterly Devoted to Younger Negro Artists. It is fire new, as the saying goes, and is worthy to continue flaming. Original in all its aspects, imitative of nothing but genuine African art, its decorations by Richard Bruce and Aaron Douglas emphasize the purport of its literary content: plays, poems, short stories, sketches.

Not alone by farm holdings and bank accounts nor by banks and insurance companies—though good; not alone by fulminating editorials and protesting memorials—though necessary; not alone by speeches and sermons, but by poems may freedom be achieved—freedom, and that respect for self and race which every living soul accounts the chief boon of life.

Our Negro "Intellectuals"

By ALLISON DAVIS

FOR nearly ten years, our Negro writers have been "confessing" the distinctive sordidness and triviality of Negro life, and making an exhibition of their own unhealthy imagination, in the name of frankness and sincerity. Frankness is no virtue in itself, however, as any father will tell his son, nor is sincerity. A dog or savage is "sincere" about his bestialities, but he is not therefore raised above them. The modern novel has been frankly and sincerely preoccupied with sex, but has not escaped an insane naturalism. It is a question, then, of the purpose for which one is being sincere. It is quite evident that the sincerity of Milton, of Fielding, and of Dr. Johnson is different in kind from the sincerity of Mr. D. H. Lawrence and Mr. James Joyce. If sincerity is to justify one in exploiting the lowest traits of human nature, and in ignoring that sense in man which Cicero says differentiates him from other animals,—his sense for what is decent—then sincerity is a pander to a torpid animalism.

The plea of sincerity, of war against hypocrisy and sham, therefore, is no defence for the exhibitionism of Mr. George S. Schuyler and Mr. Eugene Gordon, nor for the sensationalism of such works as Dr. Rudolph Fisher's HIGH YALLER or Mr. Langston Hughes' FINE CLOTHES TO THE JEW. The first two writers by their coarse frivolousness and scandalmongering falsely represent that the Negro has no self-respect. A bawling confession from the house-tops is a poor substitute for honest and discriminating self-examination, in race criticism as in religion. Mr. Schuyler and Mr. Gordon may be clever intellectual gymnasts; as such they belong with the vaudeville, and not with the men who set new currents of thought moving in Negro life. Of our Menckenites, however, more later; let us first include in our view those who ought to be termed our Van Vechtenites. Mr. Van Vechten is not responsible for the beginning of our literary effort to appear primitive, but he brought the movement to its complete fruition, and gave it the distinction of his patronage.

OUR writers started almost ten years ago to capitalize the sensational and sordid in Negro life, notably in Harlem, by making it appear that Negro life is distinctive for its flaming "color", its crude and primitive emotion. This facile acceptance of the old, romantic delusion of "racial literatures", which goes back beyond Taine all the way to Mme. de Stael, was a convenient mould for the energies of writers who had no tradition to guide them in treating Negro themes. What was more to the point, it interested the sophisticated reading public, at the height of the "jazz age" following the war, because it seemed to bring fresh and primitive forces to a jaded age.

These young writers hit upon two means of injecting primitivistic color in their work; one, the use of the Harlem cabaret and night life, and the other, a return to the African jungles. Since Mr. MacKay's HARLEM DANCER, the cabaret has been an unhealthy obsession with these youths, who in their relative naïveté imagine that there is something profoundly stirring about the degradation of its habitués. Even the best writers, Mr. McKay, Mr. Cullen, Mr. Hughes, and Dr. Fisher, as well as many of their less gifted imitators, have exploited the cabaret. The jazz band became the model which the Negro poet sought to imitate. It is particularly unfortunate that Mr. James Weldon Johnson should yield to this jazzy primitivism in choosing the title GOD'S TROMBONES for a work purporting to represent the Negro's religious fervor. Of course here, as always, the Negro movement must be seen in relation to the broader current of American literature. Mr. Waldo Frank, Mr. Scott Fitzgerald, and a host of other white authors were at the same time popularizing the jazz complex. In illustration, moreover, Mr. Miguel Covarrubias and Mr. Winold Reiss did more than Mr. Aaron Douglas and Mr. Richard Bruce to represent the Negro as essentially bestialized by jazz and the cabaret.

IN this mad rush to make the Negro exhibit his sensational and primitivistic qualities, our young writers did not lack white support. Mr. Carl Van Doren encouraged them in this fashion: "But if the reality of Negro life is itself dramatic, there are of course still other elements, particularly the emotional power with which Negroes live —or at least to me seem to live. What American literature decidedly needs at the moment is color, music, gusto, the free expression of gay or desperate moods. If the Negroes are not in a position to contribute these items, I do not know what Americans are." Mr. Max Rheinhardt spoke of the necessity for the Negro dramatist's remaining true to the original spontaneity of his race by portraying "pure emotion, almost independent of words or setting". This myth of the spiritual and artistic virtue of spontaneous emo-

F. Marcellus Staley *M.S.* *Cornell*	*Prince Williams* *Valedictorian* *West Virginia*	*W. H. Jones* *M.A.* *Straight*	*Croxton Williams* *Salutatorian* *A. and T., N. C.*	*William J. Sinkford* *Phi Beta Kappa* *Michigan*

tion in the Negro was enthusiastically supported by Mr. Carl Van Vechten. I think that the severest charge one can make against Mr. Van Vechten is that he misdirected a genuine poet, who gave promise of a power and technique exceptional in any poetry, — Mr. Hughes. Mr. Van Vechten disclaims any influence upon Mr. Hughes' first book, THE WEARY BLUES, for which he wrote a preface expressing undiluted primitivism. The evident reply is that the drop from the best poems of this first book to any of those in FINE CLOTHES TO THE JEW, which Mr. Van Vechten undoubtedly *did* influence, is the real proof of his having finally misdirected Mr. Hughes.

NOW came the devastating result of the primitivism which our Negro writers had concocted and made a holy cause. NIGGER HEAVEN was the *telos*, the perfect flowering of the "cabaret school". By means of the same sensational primitivism and the creation of half a dozen cabarets which Harlem could never boast, Mr. Van Vechten warped Negro life into a fantastic barbarism. What was most pernicious in NIGGER HEAVEN was the representation that the Negro upper class is identical with the pleasure-seekers and cabaret-rounders. NIGGER HEAVEN was the logical outcome of the forces our "intellectuals" had championed for five years, and in a very real sense these "intellectuals" were responsible for its writing and its success. With its appearance there arose in the minds of many Negro writers and readers some doubt concerning the whole movement toward "color" and exhibitionism. The most prominent writers, however, could not evade the natural result of their own practice, and defended Mr. Van Vechten on the ground of artistic sincerity, for which they found proof chiefly in his mixing socially with Negroes. Here again the pretense of sincerity justified the most unalleviated sensationalism. In fact, the total effect of the whole movement was that Negroes are sincerely bestial.

An atavistic yearning for the African jungles, which was entirely simulated, was the second device of these poets for adding "color" to the Negro. The desire of young poets to "dance naked under palm trees", and to express themselves in jungle loves has been the favorite device for making poetry authentically Negroid. Tom-toms, love-dances, strange passions and savage urges have been the paraphernalia of almost every budding poetaster. Even Mr. Cullen made especial use of the jungle urge in his early and best known poems, HERITAGE and THE SHROUD OF COLOR. This whole primitivistic interpretation of the Negro is the white man's facile point of view, and our Negro "intellectuals" wanted to appear as the white man would have them. The most important assertion of the related primitivism of cabaret and jungle is the work of a white poet, Mr. Lindsay's CONGO. There is nothing more foreign to the Negro's imagination than this yearning for savage Africa, and it is a false note every time it is struck by a Negro poet. The African tradition which we want to uncover and make fruitful is certainly not that of savagery, but of self-containment, fortitude, and culture.

At times the poets achieved something beautiful and significant in spite of their material and creed. Mr. McKay's poem, HARLEM SHADOWS touches on nobility and a higher imaginative view than most American realistic poetry ever reaches. The title poem of Mr. Hughes' THE WEARY BLUES created a representative symbol for the frustration and inertia into which Negro life is penned. There were poems in McKay, Cullen, and Hughes which gave evidence of a higher understanding of Negro life, but this quality of their imagination was not developed. Mr. Hughes especially chose to exploit the meretricious themes of jazz, instead of developing the powers shown in such poems as AUNT SUE'S STORIES and WHEN SUE WEARS RED. The indubitable gift of Mr. Hughes and of one or two other poets was sacrificed to a dogma, which necessitated their being atavistic and "colorful" at the expense of a full and experimental development of their imagination. The untrammeled self-expression which the supporters of the movement claimed for it was actually freedom only to be as *primitivistic* as one liked. There was no freedom from the creed that a Negro poet ought to be barbaric.

II

OUR primitivistic poets and story-tellers have been ousted from the stage lately by a rising group of young critics, writing for magazines and Negro newspapers. They are Menckenites, largely inspired by their master's attack upon Negro preachers and "misleaders", and his heralding of the self-critical Negro. Now the genuine critic is the individual who can fix upon the excellent and significant in the welter of all that is obvious and passing, and who can reveal how this seed may be made fruitful. Even though he must expose what is trivial or pernicious, he moves from a perception of what is true. Such a critic will illustrate his higher standards by the point from which he attacks false standards. His criticism, then, is vital, even in the act of denying. We do not look to him for reform and solutions, but we do expect him to give currency to real and high principles. In applying these standards with an *esprit de finesse* to the ever shifting flux of the energies which make for chaos, he will give perspective to the so-called "men of action".

A vital grasp upon standards, then, and the ability to apply them flexibly to the "gushing forth of novelties"

(*Will you please turn to page* 284)

Miss Julia Skinner / *M.A.* / *Columbia* — *Miss Leonia Lanier* / *Valedictorian* / *Atlanta* — *Miss Evelyn Lawlah* / *Ranking Student* / *Talladega* — *Joseph Jackson* / *Salutatorian* / *Livingston* — *Cyprian Cunningham* / *Phi Kappa Epsilon* / *Illinois*

Our Negro "Intellectuals"

(*Continued from page* 269)

which is the other side of life are the qualifications of the critic. Our Negro "intellectuals" have tried to substitute a display of their own and the race's eccentricities for these virtues. Mr. Schuyler and Mr. Gordon are likely to become the forerunners of a line of young critics, who will pose as the thoughtful and emancipated Negro. They will pretend to represent a positivistic and experimental attitude toward the Negro's situation, to replace the religious fatalism and inferiority complex of our older leaders. It is precisely this specious liberalism in our little Menchenites, which makes them dangerous. The Negro to-day is at a critical and strategic point of transition, where the cry of intellectual emancipation will lead him after false lights, unless he is willing to be thoroughly critical. We must avoid the recurrent, human tendency to exchange one extreme for another. Complete trust of all that parades as intelligence, and an effort to be hypercritical are not the proper cure for an inferiority complex. Smartness and a superficial cynicism are not substitutes for reflection and vision.

MR. SCHUYLER and Mr. Gordon are interested only in expressing themselves, their cleverness without taste, their radicalism without intelligence, their contempt for Negro leaders and our upper class, uninformed by serious principles. The most obvious fact concerning Mr. Schuyler's articles is their coarse flippancy which he no doubt means to be a protective hardening for the sensitiveness and race-consciousness of Negroes. But to become hardened to such terms as "smoke", "Ziggaboo", "crow", "dinge", "shine", or to take refuge in thumbing one's nose by hurling back "cracker", "peckerwood", and "hill-billy", is not to gain stoical strength, but to lose self-respect. The qualities which have kept the Negro's spirit unbroken are a gift for irony of a broader kind, and an everlasting fortitude.

Reflection and contemplation, alone, can insure the critic's virtues of perspective and balance. Reflection is made evident by one's discrimination, one's power of making vital distinctions. What Mr. Schuyler, Mr. Gordon, and their school, as well as Mr. Mencken, lack, is just this faculty of discriminating judgment. Mr. Schuyler especially reveals his lack of all standards in his frivolous and universal cynicism. In his indiscriminate jeering at all efforts to ameliorate white animosity and injustice, and at the efforts of such men as "Dr. Lampblack of the Federal Society for the Exploitation of Lynching, who will eloquently hold forth for the better part of an hour on the blackamoor's gifts to the Great Republic, and why, therefore, he should not be kept down", Mr. Schuyler betrays his own intellectual muddle.

MR. GORDON'S innocence of any standards and his intellectual confusion are illustrated by his naive theory that the tradition which the Negro wants to preserve is that of the black-face minstrel and the Stephen Foster folk. THE NEGRO'S INHIBITIONS, so far as it is at all honest and serious, is an unconscious *reductio ad absurdum* of the primitivistic creed. The Negro is to treasure his eccentricities simply because they are spontaneous and differentiate him from the white man! If Mr. Gordon had any real perception he would have found ideals based upon the character of the Negro which distinguish him from the white man in a more fundamental sense. The qualities which have moulded the Negro are not emotional crudeness and colorful spontaneity; they are fortitude, an oriental spirituality and unworldliness, and a faculty of laughing at any tendency towards self-pity, which more than anything human approaches the laughter of Mr. O'Neil's Lazarus!

WITHOUT intelligent standards, then, our Menckenites still insist upon expressing themselves. What they really set up for our improvement, in the place of standards, is their own personality. The virtue of their writing they believe to lie in the brilliance and iconoclastic smartness with which they demolish what is obviously ignorant and mean. Every man or movement treated is warped and caricatured by the necessity for displaying their own temperament. Mr. Schuyler expresses his fantastic misconception of the affluence recently acquired by Negro writers, in this fashion: "the black scribblers, along with the race orators, are now wallowing in the luxury of four-room apartments, expensive radios, Chickering pianos, Bond Street habiliments, canvas-back duck, pre-war Scotch, and high yallow mistresses". And Mr. Schuyler is "wallowing" in his own temperament! Similarly Mr. Gordon's representation that most Negroes are blind apes of everything in the white world is only a reflection of his individual desire to pose before the white public. So long as we have had romantic confessionalists, we have been acquainted with those who desire "to publish themselves", in Emerson's phrase; but when they set themselves up as serious critics, they become public dangers.

III

OUR "intellectuals", then, both those in literature and those in race criticism, have capitalized the sensational aspects of Negro life, at the expense of general truth and sound judgment. Primitivism has carried the imagination of our poets and story-tellers into the unhealthy and abnormal. A sterile cynicism has driven our Menckenized critics into smart coarseness. With regard to the primitivists, the first thing to be settled is whether our lives are to be interpreted with relation to the Negro race or the human race. Are there any traits peculiar to Negro character, and if so, are those traits especially crude emotions? It will appear, I think, that the qualities of fortitude, irony, and a relative absence of self-pity are the most important influences in the lives of Negroes, and that these qualities are the secret strength of that part of us which is one with a universal human nature. Our poets and writers of fiction have failed to interpret this broader human nature in Negroes, and found it relatively easy to disguise their lack of a higher imagination by concentrating upon immediate and crude emotions.

OUR critic "intellectuals" also lack this quality of elevation. Mr. Schuyler, Mr. Gordon, and their imitators, (at two removes from Mr. Mencken!) are preoccupied with the sordid and trivial aspects of Negro life. On the whole, the facts of Negro life are sordid; they have been so for three hundred years, as a result of slavery, and will very likely remain so for sometime to come. *We are going on our grit*, and it is these higher secret powers which I have indicated, (call them spiritual or chemical, as you like) which we must preserve and apply intelligently to our future development. Self-respect is vital if we are to retain our courage, and self-respect is precisely the quality which these critics lack. "Such conceits as clownage keeps in pay" are their qualifications, and the Negro has had enough clowning,—from his leaders down. I have already defined the true critic as the individual who holds fast to his perception of what is excellent and real, in the midst of appearances, and who applies his standards with discrimination to the flux of actual life. The genuinely qualified crtics of Negro life will fix upon the inner strength of Negro character as illustrated in the last three hundred years, and, discounting the trivial and irrelevant, will reinterpret these persistent characteristics for the new Negro to whom he will be as an eye.

Langston Hughes to the Editor of The Crisis. *July 28, 1928. Letter in response to Davis essay.*
[JWJ/Hughes/MSS 382. James Weldon Johnson Collection, Beinecke Rare Book Library, Yale University]

Lincoln University, Pa.,
July 28, 1928.

To the Editor of THE CRISIS:

Mr. Allison Davis, in his recent article, OUR NEGRO "INTELLECTUALS", makes the following assertion: "I think that the severest charge one can make against Mr. Van Vechten is that he misdirected a genuine poet, who gave promise of a power and technique exceptional in any poetry,—Mr. Hughes"....... in FINE CLOTHES TO THE JEW, which Mr. Van Vechten undoubtedly *did* influence, is the real proof of his having finally misdirected Mr. Hughes," This, to all my available knowledge on the subject, is quite untrue. I do not know what facts Mr. Davis himself may possess as to how, where, or when I have been misdirected by Mr. Van Vechten, but since I happen to be the person who wrote the material comprising FINE CLOTHES TO THE JEW, I would like herewith to state and declare that many of the poems in said book were written before I made the acquaintance of Mr. Van Vechten, as the files of the CRISIS will prove; before the appearance of THE WEARY BLUES containing his preface; and before ever he had commented in any way on my work. (See THE CRISIS for June, 1922, August, 1923, several issues in 1925; also the BUCCANEAR for May, 1925.) These poems which were written after my acquaintance with Mr. Van Vechten were certainly not about him, not requested by him, not misdirected by him, some of them not liked by him nor, so far as I know, do they in any way bear his poetic influence.

My second book is what I personally desired it to be and if the poems which it contains are low-down, jazzy, cabaret-ism, and utterly uncouth in the eyes of Mr. Davis the fault is mine,—not Mr. Van Vechten's. I do not resent Mr. Davis' criticism of my work and I know very well that a great many persons agree with him,— nay, go even farther in believing that all of my verses are tainted with the evils of utter blackness. To such people my poems are as the proverbial red rag to the bull. To say the least they seem quite distasteful to them and evidently not the kind of reading diet on which they should feed, but I am not hurt about it. I have never pretended to be keeping a literary grazing pasture with food to suit all breeds of cattle. However, for the sake of truth, I cannot allow mr. Davis' rather extravagant misstatement of fact to go unanswered, therefore this letter offering a correction.

Very truly yours,

Langston Hughes

1

Harlem Goes To Work

HARLEM may laugh loudly and without restraint; Harlem may sing joyously and with spiritual ecstacy; Harlem may dance madly and with abandon; but Harlem also goes to work!

In the early hours of the morning as the night clubs empty their hilarious crowds into the almost deserted streets, the workers of Harlem begin their day. At first only a scattered few hurry from the recesses of dimly lit hallways, and then gradually as the morning grows older the number increases. Fifth Avenue, Lenox Avenue, 7th Avenue and 8th Avenue become the parade ground of a hundred, a thousand and ten thousand silent ones who move swiftly to elevated stairways and subway entrances, or stand and wait impatiently for street cars and busses.

On the faces of these people there is no hint of that perpetual happiness which is often ascribed to the Negro. Rather their countenances bear a certain hopelessness—a sort of sullen indifference. Conversation is confined to the more or less formal greetings, and when more extended is carried on in low, subdued tones.

Harlem is the vogue in some of the current literature. If not the actual *misc en scene* it is somewhere included or referred to in order to enliven what otherwise might be dull and commonplace. The Harlem of the cabarets; of bizarre and exotic dancing; the Harlem of jazz and gin is widely known. But there is another Harlem as rich in the materials of creative literature as these which have been so much exploited. Rudolph Fisher in his recent novel, "The Walls of Jericho," touched lightly on this phase of Harlem life. In the trio whose sparkling reparteé supplies the story with the give and take of comedy and drama, Fisher presents the black workers. They, after all, are the most important, even tho the least known of all the various groups in Harlem. Their struggles and ambitions, their unremitting, tho futile, efforts to span the incessant demands of living with a meager wage, their reactions to the civic and social forces about them ultimately must determine the future of the Negro in Harlem.

Some Reflections on the Negro in American Drama

By Randolph Edmonds

THERE is drama in Negro life. The truth of this statement is seldom contested, for everyone who knows intimately the complex existence of colored America, and is in any degree capable of analyzing the subtle soil upon which the art of the theatre grows, recognizes that fact, and is usually not hesitant about saying so. It is very evident that suffering, struggle, comedy, atmosphere, and great emotional crises—the very essence of the dramatic—are found abundantly in Negro life. Since this is true, the average observer has been puzzled at the slow progress made by the Negro in the dramatic art. He becomes still more mystified when he compares the advancement made in this field with that evidenced in poetry, music, the novel and the essay. The conclusion is almost inescapable that the so-called "Negro Renaissance" has been almost a total failure in so far as the development of the drama is concerned.

If one is seeking for excuses, he does not have to search long for an explanation for this retarded progress. The verdict of history decrees a long and arduous apprenticeship both in tradition and accomplishment for marked success in the art of the theatre. Then, too, its offerings are designed to appeal to a heterogeneous crowd which brings to the playhouse all kinds of opinions and prejudices which a playwright opposes at a great risk. The world wide opposition to some of the ideas in Ibsen's plays, and the violent demonstrations at the premieres of some of the Irish plays give an indication as to what happens when the playwright presents something that is a little out of the ordinary routine thinking of the average theatre audience. Until comparatively recent times, the narrow opinion of this "compact majority" decreed that serious drama was no fit vehicle for the Negro actor. The buffoon, farce comedians, and the clown who could sing blues, spirituals, and clog dance were the roles assigned to him with the minstrel show as the vehicle. Ernest Hogan, Black Patti, Williams and Walker, Whitney and Tutt and the other early pioneers deserve great credit for taking this kind of farce and caricature from burnt cork to the height they achieved in some of their musical shows.

Although Paul Lawrence Dunbar, Angelina Grimke, E. C. Williams, and others wrote plays before the tremendous interest in Negro material began, the Nordic writers, for the most part, have furnished the vehicles for the Negro actors. Although Edward Sheldon's "Nigger" was produced earlier, Ridgley Torrence is generally looked upon as the great pioneer who started the movement which has ended in the change of attitude towards the colored thespians. The Hapgood Players presented his three one-act plays: "Granny Maumee," "The Rider of Dreams," and "Simon the Cyrenian" in 1917. This was the first time that Broadway witnessed serious Negro plays performed by Negro actors. Following closely behind Torrence came Eugene O'Neill with "Emperor Jones" which established the Irish author as the most significant playwright in America, and Chas. Gilpin as the greatest Negro actor of the period. O'Neill wrote two other plays for the Negro theatre: "Dreamy Kid" and "All God's Chillun Got Wings."

Four other noteworthy plays of Negro life bring us down to the present. I refer to the starkly realistic play "In Abraham's Bosom," by Paul Green, which won the Pulitzer prize for 1926; the sensational "Lulu Belle" which showed the potentialities of the mass scene; "Porgy," by Dubose and Dorothy Heyward, a nearer approach to the folk play than the others; and lastly "The Green Pastures," the great Negro miracle play which won the Pulitzer prize for 1930. It is unanimously agreed that the latter is the best play dealing with Negro life that has ever been written, and is one of the most significant plays ever to be produced on Broadway.

These were the most important productions in the popularization of Negro dramatic material by the white playwrights. Historical accuracy would require a discussion of many others. Prominently among these would be "Earth," by Em Jo Basse, "Goat Alley," by Ernest Culbertson, "Goin' Home," by Ransom Rideout, and the work of the Carolina Playmakers. The three big movie specials "Uncle Tom's Cabin," "Hearts of Dixie," and "Hallelujah" would come in for their share of evaluation. The net results of these and others, however, were to make the Negro a serious character in serious drama struggling for serious things.

From the standpoint of the Negro, as intimated before, the great tragedy is that playwrights of color have had so little influence in shaping these plays. Only three Negro playwrights have had plays on Broadway for any length of time. Garland Anderson's "Appearances" does not deal with Negro material. The play contains far more white characters than Negro. "Meek Mose," by Frank Wilson, the star of "Porgy," had as its theme: "The meek shall inherit the earth." The bowing and scraping of the meek old man failed to excite a large number of Harlemites, and did not contain enough farce or melodrama to satisfy the satiated Broadway theatre-goers. "Harlem," by Wallace Thurman, who wrote in collaboration with William Jordan Rapp, aroused more interest and attention. It set out to do for Harlem what "Porgy" did for Catfish Row. It did not sparkle quite as brilliantly as the so-called folk play from the lower Carolina, but it did carry on quite effectively the dramatic effect of the mass scene introduced in "Lulu Belle" and carried to its height in "The Green Pastures." One of the most important things it did was to lift Negro characterization from a spineless creature of frustration to one having a backbone.

Turning from the plays themselves to the subject matter, we get a very dismal picture, indeed. Modern naturalistic drama has been often characterized as a "bloody slice of life," and nowhere is this term more befitting than in describing these plays of Negro life. In them we see dark portrayals of human misery silhouetted against a black sky-line of woes. They reveal earthly suffering at its blackest—men and women with skins of night struggling in the anguish and agony of situations that doom them to failure and despair from the very opening of the curtain.

Superstition and voodooism are especially rampant in this part of the theatric world. In one form or another they creep into nearly all of the plays. The intelligent and the city bred react to them in the same manner as the rustics. The entire theme of "Emperor Jones" is woven around the superstitions of Brutus, the usurper. Paul Green's "In Aunt Mahaley's Kitchen" and Ridgley Torrence's "Granny Maumee" have similar themes. Lulu Belle and Abraham have their share, and in one of the dark moments Cordelia, the highly sophisticated vampire in the play "Harlem" buys a love philter from a voodoo doctor. No wonder the average Negro is sceptical about plays that purport to reveal an authentic picture of his life.

I do not contend that the tragic side of life should not be depicted. My point is that it should be grounded in the natural laws of life, and tragedy should come as a result of the fitness or unfitness of a character to perform a task. This piling up of insurmountable obstacles with their overtones of inferiority is very unsatisfactory to those who see something deeper and finer and more dramatic in Negro life, and envisage in it a real contribution to the American theatre.

The noble exception to all of this, of course, is "The Green Pastures." Negroes who have never seen the play criticize it sharply. They cannot see how a fish fry could represent the Negro's idea of heaven when they have been told all their lives about pearly gates and golden stairs. God being black is something they have never heard, except as a humorous part of the Garvey movement. The Lord accepting a ten cent cigar seems to them the height of absurdity, and the spirituals are just those old slave songs sung for the benefit of white people. In short, they conclude that it is just another show making fun of the race. Very rarely are these comments heard after they have seen the spectacle, however. Somehow the spiritual message forces its way through the comedy, music, setting and the violent contrasts of its episodes. There comes a feeling, even among the harshest critics, that here is something beautiful and powerful acted by Negroes and told in Negro dialect, and of which they need not be ashamed. The whole seems a tremendous refutation of James Weldon Johnson's statement that dialect is an instrument with only two stops, comedy and pathos.

One would naturally expect Negro plays by Negro authors to reveal the soul of the black man, to give us something of the beauty and grandeur contained in "The Green Pastures": but unfortunately this is not so. These plays are very hard to get, most of them existing largely in manuscript form; and since they have had no great influence in the popularization of Negro drama, they have not entered largely in the foregoing conclusions. Willis Richardson, Eulalie Spence, Georgia Douglass Johnson, John Matheus, Mae Miller, and Frank Wilson all won prizes in the *Crisis* and *Opportunity* contests, and with Wallace Thurman and Garland Anderson have established themselves as the leading playwrights of color. Most of them are known for their one-act plays, some of which have appeared in important collections and productions.

"The Plays of Negro Life," edited by Alaine Locke and Montgomery Gregory; "Plays and Pageants of Negro Life," edited by Willis

Richardson; the Negro play number of the *Carolina Magazine*, and the prize plays of the various contests give some indication of the kind and quality of Negro plays by Negro authors. As a whole they deal with the same subject matter, with the same type of characters as those of their Nordic contemporaries. Very little originality is manifested, and certainly there is no more piercing insight into the depth of Negro life indicated. Still further there is no catching the joyful and poetic side of life beyond the color line, no subtle suggestion of tragedy that rises in ominous overtones from black philosophy. Negro drama, as written by Negroes, is too stilted, too restrained, directly imitative of white authors, and as a rule inferior in craftsmanship with long literary speeches and almost no theatric values. There has been no riddle of the world given a solution in black terms; and after all this is the only thing that we can expect. For strictly speaking there is no such thing as Negro drama, Irish drama, French drama, and the like. Drama is a representation of universal life built around the feelings, thoughts, and clash of wills of particular people. When we speak of the drama of a nationality, we mean these universal truths colored by the temperament of a group. And certainly the reaction of Negroes to life should give us something that is distinctively different.

Now what is the best way of helping young colored authors to write the drama of their race? After all that is the most important question to consider, for it is comparatively easy to make a cursory summary of what has been accomplished so far, and point out the shortcomings with a learned affectation, and pronounce with oracular authority what should be done. To point out a simple, but effective way to remedy the situation is the thing most needed. What I have to propose is far from being original. It is based upon the obvious fact to the student of dramatic history that most of the great playwrights have been closely connected with the stage. The truth of this can be easily seen if we look for a moment at Aeschylus and the Greeks, Shakespeare and the Elizabethans, and Ibsen and the Moderns. Most of them learned the playwright's craft by actually working in the theatre.

The colored schools of this country have seemingly not awakened to the educational and aesthetic values in the development of real university theatres, and have consequently done little to facilitate the writing of Negro plays. The Howard Players, under the direction of Professor Montgomery Gregory, made a very brilliant start in 1921, but the interest soon died out when he left. Other schools have given spasmodic productions of Negro plays but none have consistently tried to develop them. The exchange productions between Morgan College and Hampton Institute last year led to the formation of an intercollegiate dramatic circuit with the development of plays of Negro life as one of its aims. It is sincerely hoped that all of the schools will unite for the same purpose.

One of the greatest contributions to Negro education could be made by a donor who would specify that his gift be used for the erection of a small theatre and the teaching of educational dramatics. The net results can be readily foreseen. It would mean the teaching of the ethical and aesthetic values of the drama to larger and larger numbers of students which would in the course of years build up a larger audience among the masses for the better forms of recreational entertainment. The popular misconception that Negro plays are designed to hold the race up to ridicule would give way to the true aim of all of the best plays; the mirroring of all that is good and true and beautiful in a people for the enjoyment and edification of humanity. It would result in more authors writing on Negro life, and writing with such sincerity and truth that universal sorrows, sufferings, and joys might be revealed through the medium of black folk.

Post-Bellum—Pre-Harlem

By CHARLES W. CHESNUTT

> *This article appeared first in* THE COLOPHON, *the beautifully printed Book Collectors' Quarterly. The Editors of* THE COLOPHON *have given us permission to reprint the article on condition that we protect their copyright and give them credit.*
>
> *Mr. Chesnutt writes: "I am very glad to learn that you like the article and have no objection whatever to you reproducing it."*
>
> *We regard this as one of the most significant literary statements of the season.*

MY first book, *The Conjure Woman*, was published by the Houghton Mifflin Company in 1899. It was not, strictly speaking, a novel, though it has been so called, but a collection of short stories in Negro dialect, put in the mouth of an old Negro gardener, and related by him in each instance to the same audience, which consisted of the Northern lady and gentleman who employed him. They are naive and simple stories, dealing with alleged incidents of chattel slavery, as the old man had known it and as I had heard of it, and centering around the professional activities of old Aunt Peggy, the plantation conjure woman, and others of that ilk.

In every instance Julius had an axe to grind, for himself or his church, or some member of his family, or a white friend. The introductions to the stories, which were written in the best English I could command, developed the characters of Julius' employers and his own, and the wind-up of each story reveals the old man's ulterior purpose, which, as a general thing, is accomplished.

Most of the stories in *The Conjure Woman* had appeared in the *Atlantic Monthly* from time to time, the first story, *The Goophered Grapevine*, in the issue of August, 1887, and one of them, *The Conjurer's Revenge*, in the *Overland Monthly*. Two of them were first printed in the bound volume.

After the book had been accepted for publication, a friend of mine, the late Judge Madison W. Beacom, of Cleveland, a charter member of the Rowfant Club, suggested to the publishers a limited edition, which appeared in advance of the trade edition in an issue of one hundred and fifty numbered copies and was subscribed for almost entirely by members of the Rowfant Club and of the Cleveland bar. It was printed by the Riverside Press on large hand-made linen paper, bound in yellow buckram, with the name on the back in black letters on a white label, a very handsome and dignified volume. The trade edition was bound in brown cloth and on the front was a picture of a white-haired old Negro, flanked on either side by a long-eared rabbit. The dust-jacket bore the same illustration.

The name of the story teller, "Uncle" Julius, and the locale of the stories, as well as the cover design, were suggestive of Mr. Harris's *Uncle Remus*, but the tales are entirely different. They are sometimes referred to as folk tales, but while they employ much of the universal machinery of wonder stories, especially the metamorphosis, with one exception, that of the first story, *The Goophered Grapevine*, of which the norm was a folk tale, the stories are the fruit of my own imagination, in which respect they differ from the *Uncle Remus* stories which are avowedly folk tales.

Several subsequent editions of *The Conjure Woman* were brought out: just how many copies were sold altogether I have never informed myself, but not enough for the royalties to make me unduly rich, and in 1929, just thirty years after the first appearance of the book, a new edition was issued by Houghton Mifflin Company. It was printed from the original plates, with the very handsome title page of the limited edition, an attractive new cover in black and red, and a very flattering foreword by Colonel Joel Spingarn.

Most of my books are out of print, but I have been told that it is quite unusual for a volume of short stories which is not one of the accepted modern classics to remain on sale for so long a time.

At the time when I first broke into print seriously, no American colored writer had ever secured critical recognition except Paul Laurence Dunbar, who had won his laurels as a poet. Phillis Wheatley, a Colonial poet, had gained recognition largely because she was a slave and born in Africa, but the short story, or the novel of life and manners, had not been attempted by any one of that group.

There had been many novels dealing with slavery and the Negro. Harriet Beecher Stowe, especially in *Uncle Tom's Cabin*, had covered practically the whole subject of slavery and race admixture. George W. Cable had dwelt upon the romantic and some of the tragic features of racial contacts in Louisiana, and Judge Albion W. Tourgée, in what was one of the best sellers of his day, *A Fool's Errand*, and in his *Bricks Without Straw*, had dealt with the problems of reconstruction.

Thomas Dixon was writing the Negro down industriously and with marked popular success. Thomas Nelson Page was disguising the harshness of slavery under the mask of sentiment. The trend of public sentiment at the moment was distinctly away from the Negro. He had not developed any real political or business standing; socially he was outcast. His musical and stage successes were still for the most part unmade, and on the whole he was a small frog in a large pond, and there was a feeling of pessimism in regard to his future.

Publishers are human, and of course influenced by the opinions of their public. The firm of Houghton, Mifflin, however, was unique in some respects. One of the active members of the firm was Francis J. Garrison, son of William Lloyd Garrison, from whom he had inherited his father's hatred of slavery and friendliness to the Negro. His partner, George H. Mifflin, was a liberal and generous gentleman trained in the best New England tradition. They were both friendly to my literary aspirations and became my personal friends.

But the member of their staff who was of most assistance to me in publishing my first book was Walter Hines Page, later ambassador to England under President Wilson, and at that time editor of the *Atlantic Monthly*, as well as literary adviser for the publishing house, himself a liberalized Southerner, who derived from the same part of the South where the stories in *The Conjure Woman* are located, and where I passed my adolescent years. He was a graduate of Macon College, a fellow of Johns Hopkins University, had been attached to the staff of the *Forum* and the *New York Evening Post*, and was as broad-minded a Southerner as it was ever my good fortune to meet.

Three of the *Atlantic* editors wrote novels dealing with race problems—William Dean Howells in *An Imperative Duty*, Bliss Perry in *The Plated City*, and Mr. Page in *The Autobiography of Nicholas Worth*.

The first of my conjure stories had been accepted for the *Atlantic* by Thomas Bailey Aldrich, the genial auburn-haired poet who at that time presided over the editorial desk. My relations with him, for the short time they lasted, were most cordial and friendly.

Later on I submitted to Mr. Page several stories of post-war life among the colored people which the *Atlantic* published, and still later the manuscript of a novel. The novel was rejected, and was subsequently rewritten and published by Houghton, Mifflin under the title of *The House Behind the Cedars*. Mr. Page, who had read the manuscript, softened its rejection by the suggestion that perhaps a collection of the conjure stories might be undertaken by the firm with a better prospect of success. I was in the hands of my friends, and submitted the collection. After some omissions and additions, all at the advice of Mr. Page, the book was accepted and announced as *The Conjure Woman*, in 1899, and I enjoyed all the delights of proof-reading and the other pleasant emotions attending the publication of a first book. Mr. Page, Mr. Garrison and Mr. Mifflin vied with each other in helping to make our joint venture a literary and financial success.

The book was favorably reviewed by literary critics. If I may be pardoned one quotation, William Dean Howells, always the friend of the aspiring author, in an article published in the *Atlantic Monthly* for May, 1900, wrote:

"The stories of *The Conjure Woman* have a wild, indigenous poetry, the creation of sincere and original imagination, which is imparted with a tender humorousness and a very artistic reticence. As far as his race is concerned, or his sixteenth part of a race, it does not greatly matter whether Mr. Chesnutt invented their motives, or found them, as he feigns, among his distant cousins of the Southern cabins. In either case the wonder of their beauty is the same, and whatever is primitive and sylvan or campestral in the reader's heart is touched by the spells thrown on the simple black lives in these enchanting tales. Character, the most precious thing in fiction, is faithfully portrayed."

Imagine the thrill with which a new author would read such an encomium from such a source!

From the publisher's standpoint, the book proved a modest success. This was by no means a foregone conclusion, even assuming its literary merit and the publisher's imprint, for reasons which I shall try to make clear.

I have been referred to as the "first Negro novelist," meaning, of course, in the United States; Pushkin in Russia and the two Dumas in France had produced a large body of popular fiction. At that time a literary work by an American of acknowledged color was a doubtful experiment, both for the writer and for the publisher, entirely apart from its intrinsic merit. Indeed, my race was never mentioned by the publishers in announcing or advertising the book. From my own viewpoint it was a personal matter. It never occurred to me to claim any merit because of it, and I have always resented the denial of anything on account of it. My colored friends, however, with a very natural and laudable zeal for the race, with which I found no fault, saw to it that the fact was not overlooked, and I have before me a copy of a letter written by one of them to the editor of the *Atlanta Constitution*, which had published a favorable review of the book, accompanied by my portrait, chiding him because the reviewer had not referred to my color.

A woman critic of Jackson, Mississippi, questioning what she called the rumor as to my race, added, "Some people claim that Alexander Dumas, author of *The Count of Monte Cristo* and *The Three Musketeers*, was a colored man. This is obviously untrue, because no Negro could possibly have written these books"—a pontifical announcement which would seem to settle the question definitely, despite the historical evidence to the contrary.

While *The Conjure Woman* was in the press, the *Atlantic* published a short story of mine called *The Wife of His Youth* which attracted wide attention. James McArthur, at that time connected with the *Critic*, later with *Harper's*, in talking one day with Mr. Page, learned of my race and requested leave to mention it as a matter of interest to the literary public. Mr. Page demurred at first on the ground that such an announcement might be harmful to the success of my forthcoming book, but finally consented, and Mr. McArthur mentioned the fact in the *Critic*, referring to me as a "mulatto."

As a matter of fact, substantially all of my writings, with the exception of *The Conjure Woman*, have dealt with the problems of people of mixed blood, which, while in the main the same as those of the true Negro, are in some instances and in some respects much more complex and difficult of treatment, in fiction as in life.

I have lived to see, after twenty years or more, a marked change in the attitude of publishers and the reading public in regard to the Negro in fiction. The development of Harlem, with its large colored population in all shades, from ivory to ebony, of all degrees of culture, from doctors of philosophy to the lowest grade of illiteracy; its various origins, North American, South American, West Indian and African; its morals ranging from the highest to the most debased; with the vivid life of its cabarets, dance halls, and theatres; with its ambitious business and professional men, its actors, singers, novelists and poets, its aspirations and demands for equality — without which any people would merit only contempt—presented a new field for literary exploration which of recent years has been cultivated assiduously.

One of the first of the New York writers to appreciate the possibilities of Harlem for literary purposes was Carl Van Vechten, whose novel *Nigger Heaven* was rather severely criticized by some of the colored intellectuals as a libel on the race, while others of them praised it highly. I was prejudiced in its favor for reasons which those who have read the book will understand. I found it a vivid and interesting story which presented some new and better types of Negroes and treated them sympathetically.

The Negro novel, whether written by white or colored authors, has gone so much farther now in the respects in which it was criticized that *Nigger Heaven*, in comparison with some of these later productions, would be almost as mild as a Sunday School tract compared to *The Adventures of Fanny Hill*. Several of these novels, by white and colored authors alike, reveal such an intimate and meticulous familiarity with the baser aspects of Negro life, North and South, that one is inclined to wonder how and from what social sub-sewers they gathered their information. With the exception of one or two of the earlier ones, the heroine of the novel is never chaste, though for the matter of that few post-Victorian heroines are, and most of the male characters are likewise weaklings or worse.

I have in mind a recent novel, brilliantly written by a gifted black author, in which, to my memory, there is not a single decent character, male or female. These books are written primarily for white readers, as it is extremely doubtful whether a novel, however good, could succeed financially on its sales to colored readers alone. But it seems to me that a body of twelve million people, struggling upward slowly but surely from a lowly estate, must present all along the line of its advancement many situations full of dramatic interest, ranging from farce to tragedy, with many admirable types worthy of delineation.

Caste, a principal motive of fiction from Richardson down through the Victorian epoch, has pretty well vanished among white Americans. Between the whites and the Negroes it is acute, and is bound to develop an increasingly difficult complexity, while among the colored people themselves it is just beginning to appear.

Negro writers no longer have any difficulty in finding publishers. Their race is no longer a detriment but a good selling point, and publishers are seeking their books, sometimes, I am inclined to think, with less regard for quality than in the case of white writers. To date, colored writers have felt restricted for subjects to their own particular group, but there is every reason to hope that in the future, with proper encouragement, they will make an increasingly valuable contribution to literature, and perhaps produce chronicles of life comparable to those of Dostoievsky, Dumas, Dickens or Balzac.

Introduction to a Speech by Langston Hughes Given at Fisk University, January 29, 1932
[JWJ 76 James Weldon Johnson Collection, Beinecke Library, Yale University.]

In any inquiry regarding the important developments in American literature within the past decade we would at once cite the degree ... the Negro artist, especially the Negro writer, as one of the most significant and vital.

The record of the American Negro's efforts in literature goes back a long way, covering a period of more than a century and a half. But it is only within the past ten years that America as a whole has been made consciously aware of the Negro as a literary artist. It is only within that brief time that Negro writers have ceased to be regarded as isolate cases of exceptional, perhaps accidental ability and have gained group recognition. It is only within these few years that the arbiters of American letters have begun to assay the work of these writers by the general literary standards and accord it such appraisal as it might merit.

This more sensitive awareness on the part of America as a whole to the existence and efforts of Negro writers; this wider recognition and appreciation of their work began with the rise of what is termed "The Younger Group." Out of the whole group a dozen have gained more or less of national recognition.

Among the writers of poetry in this group three names stand out: Countee Cullen, Langston Hughes, and Sterling Brown. (I am giving them in the order of their emergence.) This younger group of poets are not only younger in years, they are new in their response to what still remains the principal motive of poetry written by Negroes—"Race." These younger poets in their approach to "race" are less direct, less obvious than their predecessors—and they are less sensitive to the approval or depreciation of their white environment.

Langston Hughes is one of the preeminent figures in this Younger Group, and therefore has been one of the main forces in bringing about the more propitious era in which the Negro artist now finds himself. And not only does he stand preeminent among the young group of Negro poets, he has made a place for himself well up in the list of young American poets.

Mr. Hughes's work is not only fine, it is unique. After the Negro poets discarded conventionalized dialect—with its minstrel traditions of Negro life—(traditions that had but slight relation—often no relationat all—to actual Negro life), with its exaggerated, artificial and false sentimentality, its over genial optimis, he was the first to see the possibilities of the common, racy, living speech of the Negro in certain phases of real life. He took that medium, experimented with it, perfected his mastery over it, and through it has given us authentic and vital poetry—a good deal of which has come out of the rich and extremely varied experiences of his not very long life.

This uniqueness, this originality on Mr. Hughes's part has—as he will admit with a smile—brought down on his head the disapprobation of a considerable section of his own race who feel that his poetry is not sufficiently elevating; he has not written enough about nice colored people. What Mr. Hughes has done with these things taken from the so-called lower strata is, I am sure, complete justification of his work.

Langston Hughes is a cosmopolite and a rebel and both of these attributes are reflected in his poetry. He is in the main an objective poet and is apt to portray life as he sees it rather than as he feels it. And his objectivity often brings from him a sardonic laugher [sic] instead of tears. We cannot but be struck by the sudden, cynical twist he is able to give to such poems as "Mulatto", "Cross" and to a number of others. This same quality enables him often to lift a poem clear above the level of its origin—as is illustrated so well in the last wonderful ten lines of "Brass Spitoons."

A good part of Mr. Hughes's poetry is written in the Negro fold and jazz rhythms. But there are many of his poems—poems like "Fantasy in Purple" and "The Negro Speaks of Rivers" in which he shows how superb a lyrist he can be.

Ladies and gentlemen, I have the pleasure of introducing to you one of the outstanding younger poets of America and one of the vital forces in the world of Negro youth, Mr. Langston Hughes.

THE NEGRO RENAISSANCE

INFANTS OF THE SPRING. *By Wallace Thurman. Macaulay. New York.* 1932. $2.00.
ONE WAY TO HEAVEN. *By Countee Cullen. Harper & Brothers. New York.* 1932. $2.00.
THE CHINABERRY TREE. *By Jessie Fauset. Stokes. New York.* 1932. $2.00.
HOME TO HARLEM. *By Claude Mackay. Harper's. New York.* 1928. $2.50.
BANJO. *By Claude Mackay. Harper's. New York.* 1929. $2.50.
NOT WITHOUT LAUGHTER. *By Langston Hughes. A. A. Knopf. New York.* 1930. $2.50.

"BEING a Negro writer in these days is a racket and I'm going to make the most of it while it lasts. I find queer places for whites to go to in Harlem . . . out-of-the-way primitive churches, side-street speakeasies and they fall for it. About twice a year I manage to sell a story. It is acclaimed. I am a genius in the making. Thank God for this Negro Literary Renaissance! Long may it flourish!"

In these words a minor character in Wallace Thurman's "Infants of the Spring" expresses in terms of cynical self-interest what has for some time been only too apparent to some of those interested in the artistic expression of the Negro. Elsewhere in the book its hero is shown in the midst of a black and white gin party. "'This," he kept repeating to himself, 'is the Negro Renaissance and this is about all the whole damn thing is going to amount to. . . . It is going to be necessary, he thought, to have another emancipation to deliver the emancipated Negro from a new kind of slavery.'"

Yet it is only seven years ago that some of us who today find an echo of these savage words in our hearts hailed with high hopes the beautiful and colorful volume "The New Negro," edited by Alain Locke, and accepted its premise of a younger Negro generation on the threshold of a new era of accomplishment. They were no longer bound together, Locke wrote confidently, "by a common problem, but by a common consciousness" and "shedding the chrysalis of the Negro problem they were achieving something of a spiritual emancipation."

It was inevitable that this prophecy could only be partially fulfilled. From that consciousness of which Locke wrote, and probably far more from individual impulse, unregimented by any such herd instinct, has come in the intervening years some real achievement. And much more might have come if the so-called Negro Renaissance had not been ballyhooed and exploited commercially and socially, until it has been, to a large extent, degraded into a racket. It was always too much to hope that 12,000,000 Americans of any race or color could, in our chaotic civilization, achieve a solidarity of thought and experience which would result in genuine expression. The finest products of the Renaissance have been distinctly individual as, for instance, the extraordinary work of Jean Toomer. But Toomer has published little, if anything, since "Cane" appeared in 1923. Meanwhile the mystical and probably mythical concept of a common Negro consciousness has for some time been superseded by a very definite consciousness, common alike to white and black writers of a very definite and marketable fashion in literature and art for all things Negroid. Among Negroes this has resulted, among other things, in the kinds of writing which are the objects of Wallace Thurman's attack.

"Infants of the Spring," like Thurman's earlier "The Blacker the Berry," is in a sense a pioneering book. It is the first serious and aggressive attempt that I know of by a Negro writer to debunk the Negro Renaissance in a thoroughgoing manner. It is bitter, disillusioned and probably unfair in its wholesale rejection of nearly everything being done by Negro artists and writers. But in spite of this and in spite of its somewhat crude and journalistic writing, there is an exhiliration to be gained from its angry honesty. It will no doubt be glibly denounced as "unconstructive," and indeed, it makes no pretense of being anything else. For it is simply the hearty individual expression of an individual disgust with life in general and with the Negro Renaissance in particular by a writer too keenly sincere and individualistic to find an easy escape from its sterility by such frequently suggested and ready-made panaceas as flight into communism, back to a problematical "African Inheritance" or into the ranks of the bourgeois Negro writers who "have nothing to say, and who write only because they are literate and feel they should apprise white humanity of the better classes among Negro humanity."

It is especially by their type of novel and by the uncritical acclamation with which examples of it have been received, I think, that the Negro Renaissance has been debased. One can almost establish a standard novel that will combine the worst features of all of them. Almost inevitably it will have a foreword by some professional foreworder like Carl Van Vechten or maybe Zona Gale, stating among other things how novel and unique it is. If it is in the Carl Van Vechten tradition it will probably have a glossary of Harlemese and certainly it will include a scene in which a Harlem ball or soirée is invaded by uplifting or merely curious palefaces, who are promptly knocked out by the ease, beauty and sophistication of the rainbow-tinted members of the gathering. It is also practically obligatory for at least one member of the white group to make the very natural faux pas of mistaking some Negro light enough to "pass" for a Nordic, and to behave with a complete and pitiable lack of savoir faire when he discovers his mistake. To find this wearisome is not for a moment to deny that such incidents occur frequently in real life; a very great number of light Colored People must have experienced white uncouthness of this kind, but writing suffers as much from a stencil based on such incidents as it does from stencils of the Uncle Tom and Mammy variety to which these same writers very properly object. The real argument of these Negro novels could be summed up in almost every case as follows:

"I am writing this book because most white people still believe that all Colored People are cooks called Mandy or Pullman porters called George — but they aren't. They think we all live in cottonfield cabins or in city slums, but actually some of us live on Edgecombe Avenue or Chestnut Street. We don't all shout at Camp Meetings or even all belong to the Baptist or Methodist Church. *Some of us are Episcopalians.* If you were privileged to visit our homes (which you aren't, for we are just as exclusive as you are) you would find bathtubs, sets of the best authors and *etchings* on the walls! That's how refined we are. We have class distinctions, too. Our physicians' wives snub our hairdressers and our hairdressers our cooks, and so on down the line. The daughters of our upper classes are beautiful and virtuous and look like illustrations in *Vogue.* They are also far more attractive than white girls of the same class, for they come in assorted shades of bronze, tan, fawn, beige, hazel, chestnut, amber, cream, gold, lemon, orange, honey, ivory and persimmon. You would, of course, be attracted to the heroine of this book, but as you are white, you are, in nine cases out of ten, a cad with dishonorable intentions. We'll allow the tenth case out of pure magnanimity. But in any case the heroine would scorn you because in the last chapter she will marry the dark hero and be happy ever after. She might, being human, have been tempted perhaps for a moment by the wealth and power you represent and by the immunity from insult and discrimination which 'passing' would mean for her, but even if she weren't too noble and loyal to yield to such temptation in the end the call of race would be too strong for her. Joy isn't on your side of the line, nor song, nor laughter, etc., etc." We have heard all this many times before, and we are likely to hear it many times again.

Nearly all these novels have been wholly devoid of literary merit, but they have a certain documentary value in revealing what is on the minds of a large portion of the Negro Intelligentsia, as well as of many Negroes who do not technically belong to it. Among recently published novels Jessie Fauset's "The Chinaberry Tree" is an outstanding example of this type. This, her third novel, like its predecessors is dedicated to the proposition that there are Colored ladies and gentlemen and that these constitute Colored Society. As propaganda this is no sillier than the stale counter-propaganda to which it is a retort, but the fact remains that a rather serious waste of Negro intelligence and sensitiveness is still going into the writing of such books. What is obvious from them is that the long frustrated, ambitious, struggling Negroes of the upper and middle classes still accept and jealously cherish the values of capitalistic civilization. They accept these values very much as they move into white neighborhoods as white people abandon them. And in this acceptance there has been much more than the snobbery and silliness which books like Miss Fauset's make pathetically and ludicrously evident. It represents two generations of struggle and achievement away from slavery toward a promised land, a goal which as they near it has all the unsubstantiality of a mirage. One may even concede that the struggle was noble and the achievement praiseworthy, and still feel that new day of the Negro Renaissance, if it comes, will not be made by those unable to detach their emotions from this mirage. Morever, everything that can be said in favor of this goal was said once and for all, far better and more movingly than it has ever been said since in Du Bois's eloquent "Souls of Black Folk." And even the "Souls of Black Folk," somehow, dates a little today. It is, for all its beauty, a little Victorian, moralistic, and slightly rhetorical; but it is moving as its successors are not because it is passionate and militant, where they are merely complacent, because its author was in those days the leader of a forlorn hope, rather than a Negro Babbitt.

Negro Babbitry exists and there is no reason why it should not be depicted; so do Intellectual Negro groups and Negro Smart Sets, but the Negro novels written about them have very generally been novels of neurosis. Instead of novels of Negro life they have been *prospectuses*, designed to sell to white readers the idea of Negro Upper Classes. But if there have been few if any good novels written about the Negro Bourgeoisie there have been at least three first rate novels about Negro Proletarian life. All three were written by Negro poets. Negro poets have very generally been spare-time poets — and proletarians. They have been cooks, dishwashers, floor-scrubbers, shoe-shiners, waiters, stevedores, Pullman porters, stokers, or have worked at any of the various forms of rough and casual menial labor open to American Negroes.

Langston Hughes is one of these poets, who having spent much of his life in the world of labor has inevitably been close to the life of the masses of his race. It was out of this experience that he wrote "Not Without Laughter," which is not only uniquely moving and lovely among Negro novels but among books written about America. It is affirmative in a sense in which no other book by an American Negro is, for it is the story of a Negro happily identified with his own group, who because of this identification tells what is essentially, despite the handicaps of poverty and prejudice, the story of a happy childhood. The poverty was never sordid; for one thing it was country poverty in a growing small town of the Middle West, and the child had a backyard to play in, in which there was an apple tree, and flowers as well as clothes lines.

"Here the air was warm with sunlight and hundreds of purple and white morning glories laughed on the back fence. Earth and sky were fresh and clean after the heavy night rain and . . . there was the mingled scent of wet earth and golden pollen on the breeze that blew carelessly through the clear air." It was poverty, but never sodden or defeated though the child's grandmother toiled all day at her washtub washing the white folk's clothes and his mother sweated all day in the white woman's kitchen, while his handsome, vagabond father went fishing and played the guitar; even though eventually there was no place in Stanton for his pretty, fun-loving Aunt Harriet but the sinful house in the "bottoms" where on "summer evenings little yellow and brown and black girls in pink and blue bungalow aprons laughed invitingly in doorways and dice rattled with the staccato gaiety of jazz music on long tables in rear rooms; pimps played pool; bootleggers lounged in big, red cars; children ran in the streets until midnight with no voice of parental authority forcing them to an early sleep; young blacks fought like cocks and enjoyed it; white boys walked through the streets winking at Colored girls; men came in autos; old women ate pigs' feet and watermelon and drank beer; whiskey flowed; gin was like water; soft indolent laughter didn't care about anything, and deep nigger-throated voices that had long ago stopped rebelling against the ways of this world rose in song." It was poverty enlivened by singing and laughter, by strong, if casual, family affection and occasional family quarrels; by carnivals and camp meetings, by lodge meetings and regalia after the day's work was done, for: "Evening's the only time we niggers have to ourselves — Thank God for night — 'cause all day you give to the white folks." Simple and touching, yet by some miracle always avoiding sentimentality, the story is told with a happy tenderness which recalls Katherine Mansfield's dictum that in fiction the beginning of art is *remembering.* It has the courage of its tenderness for Negro things, a serene and robust acceptance of the common things, the sights and smells and sounds, the folkways and idiosyncrasies of the people who made up one little Colored boy's background; and through this acceptance and evocation of them it communicates the very feeling and texture of life.

The only other American novel I know which seems to me comparable with "Not Without Laughter" is Willa Cather's "My Antonia." Both books have, in common, somewhat the same quality of radiant sanity. Both communicate, in spite of relatively small canvases, a feeling of earth and sun and air, of a strong life with deep folk roots. In both a poetic quality is due in part to the fact that the story is told reminiscently through the eyes of a child reflecting a child's curiosity and sensibility and wonder, and that the child in each case was a potential poet. In both there is ugliness and hardship and pain, but in both these incidents are dominated by a triumphant vitality, an open-eyed resilience in the face of life. And this, too, is a quality that is characteristic of Langston Hughes and which sings through his poems whether he is writing of Beale Street Love or Railroad Blues or of

> The steam in hotel kitchens
> And the smoke in hotel lobbies

And the slime in hotel spittoons
Part of my life

and is implicit in his high-hearted chant, "I, Too":

I, too, sing America
I am the darker brother
They send me
To eat in the kitchen
When company comes
But I laugh
And eat well
And grow strong.

Tomorrow
I'll sit at the table
When company comes
Nobody'll dare
Say to me
"Eat in the kitchen"
Then.

Besides
They'll see how beautiful I am
And be ashamed.

I, too, am America.

Claude Mackay is another vagabond poet who has brought a somewhat similar experience to rich fruition in his novels "Home to Harlem" and "Banjo." Mackay, too, has worked in the white man's kitchens, and on wharves and trains and the stokeholes of steamers. He has known the life of a down-and-out beachcomber on the waterfront of Marseilles, and that of a poor farm boy in Jamaica. Older and more mature than Hughes, more complex and possibly deeper he seems to have reached by a more difficult path an adjustment which in Hughes is instinctive. While his early associations seem to have had somewhat the same happy quality as Hughes' childhood and a far more beautiful setting — what hardships there were were due to poverty rather than to color — if one may judge by his writings he seems to have experienced the full cruelties of race and class struggle after his arrival in America in 1912. He was the first of the Negro intellectuals to be a radical in the political and economic sense as well as a militant rebel on behalf of his race. His novels "Home to Harlem" and "Banjo" are full of a deep and bitter wisdom, but also full of humor and zest for life. "Home to Harlem" specializes in those aspects of Harlem life that are not mentioned in polite Harlem society, at least if white people are present: Promiscuous and happy love making, drinking, jazzing, shooting and razor flashing; the life of the high yellow "sweet-back" and of the black women who work for him; instinctive, rhythmic life — frequently joyous, but with undertones of cruelty and savagery.

These aspects are presented convincingly through the consciousness of two very different types of Negro — Jake, a simple, uneducated, American working man who delights in most of them, and Ray, the exiled sensitive Haitian student. Ray finds in Harlem the extremes of joy and despair and finally flees from it because he was entangled with a girl and feared that some day "the urge of the flesh and the mind's hankering after the pattern of respectable comfort might chase his high dreams out of him and deflate him to the contented animal that was a Harlem Nigger strutting his stuff. 'No happy-nigger strut for me' he would mutter when the feeling for Agatha worked like a fever in his flesh. . . . And he hated Agatha and, for escape, wrapped himself darkly in self-love."

Jake returning to Harlem from overseas could find joy on Seventh Avenue where "the lovely trees were a vivid green flame and . . . the smooth bare throats of brown girls were tokens as charming as the first pussy willows." He could find it at the Congo, the amusement place, entirely for the unwashed of the black belt. You could go to the Congo and turn rioting loose in all the tenacious odors of service and the warm indigenous smells of Harlem, fooping or jig jagging the night away. You would if you were a black kid hunting for joy in New York. But "Ray felt more and his range was wider and he could not be satisfied with the easy simple things that sufficed for Jake. Sometimes he felt like a tree with roots in the soil and sap flowing out and the whispering leaves drinking in the air. But he drank in more of life than he could distill into active animal living. Maybe that was why he felt he had to write.

"He was a reservoir of that intense emotional energy so peculiar to his race. Life touched him emotionally in a thousand vivid ways. Maybe his own being was something of a touchstone of the general emotions of his race. Any upset — a terror-breathing, Negro-baiting headline in a metropolitan newspaper or the news of a human bonfire in Dixie could make him miserable and despairingly despondent like an injured child. While any flash of beauty or wonder might lift him happier than a god. It was the simple, lovely touch of life that stirred him most. . . . The warm, rich brown face of a Harlem girl seeking romance . . . a late, wet night on Lenox Avenue when all forms are soft shadowy and the street gleams softly like a still, dim stream under the misted yellow lights. He remembered once the melancholy-comic notes of a 'Blues' rising out of a Harlem basement before dawn. He was going to catch an early train and all that trip he was sweetly, deliciously happy, humming the refrain and imagining what the interior of the little dark den he heard it in was like. 'Blues' . . . melancholy-comic. That was the key to himself and his race. That strange, child-like capacity for wistfulness and laughter. . . .

"Going away from Harlem . . . Harlem! How terribly Ray could hate it sometimes. Its brutality, gang rowdyism, promiscuous thickness. Its hot desires. But, oh, the rich blood-red color of it! The warm accent of its composite voice, the fruitiness of its laughter, the trailing rhythm of its blues and the improvised surprise of its jazz. He had known happiness, too, in Harlem, joy that glowed gloriously upon him like the high noon sunlight of his tropic island home."

"Banjo" is a bitter and devastating picture of the white man's civilization as it looks to the black man at the bottom of it, and of the free and instinctive life which the irresponsible and uneducated black man can still manage to live in an ever tightening, mechanical white civilization. "For civilization had gone out among these native, earthy people, had despoiled them of their primitive soil, had uprooted, enchained, transported and transformed them to labor under its laws, and yet lacked the spirit to tolerate them within its walls."

That this primitive child, this kinky-headed, big-laughing black boy of the world did not go down and disappear under the serried rush of the trampling white feet; that he managed to remain on the scene, not worldly wise, not "getting there," yet not machine-made, nor poor-in-spirit like the regimented creatures of civilization was baffling to civilized understanding. Before the grim, pale rider-down of souls he went his careless way with a primitive hoofing and a grin. From these black boys he could learn to live. . . . how to exist as a black boy in a white world and rid his conscience of the used up hussy of white morality. He could not scrap his intellectual life and be entirely like them. He did not want or feel any urge to "go back" that way. . . . Ray wanted to hold on to his intellectual acquirements without losing his instinctive gifts. "But also he knew that though it was easy enough for Banjo who in all things acted instinctively it was not easy for a Negro with an intellect standing watch over his instincts to take his way through the white man's world . . . but of one thing he was resolved: civilization should not take the love of color, joy, beauty, vitality and nobility out of *his* life and make him like the mass of its poor pale creatures. . . . Could he not see what Anglo-Saxon standards were doing to some of the world's most interesting people? Some Jews ashamed of being Jews. Changing their names and their religion . . . for the Jesus of the Christians! Educated Negroes ashamed of their race's intuitive love of color, wrapping themselves up in respectable gray, ashamed of Congo sounding laughter, ashamed of their complexions . . . ashamed of their strong appetites. No being ashamed for Ray! Rather than lose his soul, let intellect go to Hell and live instinct."

Writing of this kind is, of course, very exasperating to the Negro Intelligentsia. Some of them may protest with justice that they are being *themselves* in conforming to the standards of the white civilization in which they live, since it seems to them good except in so far as it discriminates against them; that they are not merely Negroes but Americans as well, dark Americans, to be sure, but still fulfilling themselves legitimately through the usual American channels. This clash of views is not limited to Colored Americans. Every racial minority in America, with the possible exception of the Irish, is divided between those of its members who wish to sink themselves, their blood and their differences in the majority, and the proudly or defensively race conscious who wish to take their stand on this blood and this difference. Among Colored People, particularly, the logic of facts may actually be with the first group. Owing to the extravagance of anti-Negro prejudice any person, however white, is classed as Colored if he is known to possess a single drop of Colored blood. A "Negro" thus arbitrarily created is not necessarily being himself any more when he sings spirituals or jazzes, than when he follows what are usually accepted as white behavior patterns. If Negro art has struck deeper roots, as I think it has, in the soil of the race conscious attitude it is because it has been the more affirmative and liberating. Conformity to white standards, on the other hand, has very generally meant conformity to the most standardized elements in our civilization — its negations, its drabness, its gentility. But this is not, I think, inherently or eternally true and even today the best writing is by Negroes in whom this consciousness is transcended. Thus "Not Without Laughter" is not merely a chronicle of Negro family life. The story of hard working, stay-at-home Annjee's helpless love for her vagabond husband, of Harriet's rebellion against her mother's puritanism, the true and sensitive picture of Sandy's boyhood and adolescence are rich and warm and full-flavored because of certain Negro qualities that Langston Hughes knows and loves, but the book's hold on our emotions is independent of these. They merely enhance the truth of what the perceptive artist in Hughes has felt about love between a man and a woman, about the clash of the generations, and the awakening consciousness of a boy. "Home to Harlem" has given us the most poignant and unforgettable picture of the substratum on which our commercial civilization is built in the half-dozen pages which describe Ray, the Negro student waiter, tossing in a half-waking nightmare in the vermin-infested bunkhouse of the Pennsylvania Railroad. Here Color is an added element of torture and humiliation in the life of the underdog. It makes escape from this life difficult if not impossible, but it is only part of the picture into which Mackay has distilled the very essence of the horror and despair the cruelty at the roots of our civilization must awaken sometimes in any sensitive mind. Color again is an element, but only one element in the entrancingly comic feud between the Negro cook and the Negro waiters on the dining car which ended with the cook's discomfiture and demotion. Color again plays an important part in the sweeping epic of "Banjo," but "Banjo" is an immensely rich book because it is far more than a story of Color. It is a story of beachcombing and vagabondage, of the clash not only between black and white, of civilization and primitive races, but of civilization at grips with itself, and of the detached and frequently humorous clarity, with which the beachcomber, black or white, who keeps clear of it except for the occasional necessity of working or panhandling sees it for the thing it is.

"A good story," Ray says at one point, "in spite of those who tell it and those who hear it is like good ore that you might find in any soil — Europe, Asia, Africa, America. The world wants the ore and gets it by a thousand men, scrambling and fighting, dying and digging for it. The world gets its story in the same way."

MARTHA GRUENING

Jean Toomer — Apostle of Beauty

By Eugene Holmes

> *The development of a body of critical opinion within the Negro group must accompany his advance in literature. A younger Negro student of literature essays a critical estimate of one of the Negro poets.*
>
> The Editor.

IN writing about Toomer, one is discussing a man who has been poetically quiet for the past eight years. His importance lies in this fact, gainsaid only by J. W. Johnson, since he neglects to include him in his "Second Book of American Negro Verse"—that whether or not he has written anything recently, he remains one of the more important Negro poets. There are no major Negro poets in America. And Toomer's position is justifiable in that he has exerted a very strong influence in American literature of today.

To those who offer objections to the inclusion of Toomer in a study of modern Negro poets, I reply that because of his influence and because of the unknowableness of the future of Negro poetry no study would be complete without Toomer. We can know nothing about the future of Negro poetry simply because we can form no idea about the importance of those who are writing today. We are too close to their work and since most of the younger poets have little or no repute, all we can do is judge any work tentatively. For these reasons, it can be seen that the work of Toomer must be examined for what is in it, whether he is poetically dead or not. And the mere fact that his influence has given to many poets intelligent guidance and poetic appreciation should suffice that his work be included. Lest I appear to be Toomer's apologist, let it be said that there is ample enough poetry as poetry in his one book for him to be included in any select niche of poetical art.

Not many people in America and Europe knew the name of Jean Toomer ten years ago. The few who did know him and his verse were acquainted only if they read the Double Dealer of New Orleans, The Little Review, Broom, The Liberator, S. N. 4, Prairie, Nomad and "little" magazines. It was in 1923, with the publication of "Cane" that he became known to a sizeable majority of readers in this country. In "Cane" raving critics and poetasters recognized a naturalism of such a distinctive kind that the applause was deafening.

This novel element in his poetry was distinctive because first of all, here was a Negro who composed not as a Negro, but as an artist, and secondly because there was not in his poetry any obsession of race. At first, the critics could not understand that a Negro could write poetry that did not reek with rebellion and propaganda. Toomer wrote as a poet, never as an apologist. Reading the turbulent and rebellious poetry of the McKay of that time, this poetry of Toomer's came upon the poetic horizon as a breath of sweet, cool air.

Toomer possessed what Max Eastman termed "the poetic temper." His poetry mirrored a full life of experience. It contained in the fullest sense what Prof. Whipple called "social experience," the complete cognizance of other people and of all their characteristics and inner souls. In his poetry he had probed deep down into the life-experience of his characters. He saw them as they were in all their real significance and he entered into these experiences with them, translating them into the moving poetical rhythms of "Cane."

Some critic, I forget who, years ago wrote that with Toomer, "the fashioning of beauty is ever foremost in his inspiration." And that is essentially true in almost every poem he has written. Beauty is always his medium, always his goal and always for him the summum bonum of existence. He finds in life challenge and beauty, only beauty is uppermost. It is this preoccupation with beauty that has stamped him as an important poet. It has also given the necessary influence and impetus to those younger Negro poets who did not know about what to write.

Toomer's influence, I repeat, has been great and inspirational and has found its way down the line into the work of many of these younger Negro poets. They have been impelled to see, through Toomer's eyes, the objectives in the fashioning of beauty. They have perforce seen that in order to be a poet, it is not at all necessary to try and solve the race problem. They have been led to believe also that the interests of the true poet-artist as exemplified in Toomer must be writ large in the experiences of life, as they are separated from the materialities of existence.

Those who have followed him have seen that

his poetry is always concerned with the very depths of human experience:

A feast of moon and men and barking hounds
An orgy for some genius of the South
With blood-hot eyes and cane-lipped scented mouth,
Surprised in making folk-songs from soul sounds.

In its ascendancy to universality this poetry in its tragic flight soars to greatness. He transcends the temporal and scarce worthwhile things and sings of Man:

An everlasting song, a singing tree,
Caroling softly souls of slavery.

The experiences incorporated in his poems are vividly real and are calculated to arouse the most lethargic of emotions. They stir and surge through you, effecting the katharsis that only poetry of this kind can compel. That this wealth of experience is enriched by his imagination, almost any line of his poetry will show:

"Their voices rise...the pine trees are guitars,"

Jean Toomer was born in Washington, D. C., in 1896. His parents were proud, cultured Negroes of old Creole stock. They had come from Louisiana to Washington in order to educate their children. In Louisiana they had been people of some consequence, in social position and wealth. But there were no opportunities for even a public school education in Louisiana. Mrs. Toomer's father was Lieutenant Governor Pinchback of Louisiana and played a great part in the Reconstruction Days of that state. Toomer received his public school education in the Washington public schools. After graduation from high school, he stayed in Washington for a while and then went West to study law. After two years at a law school, he gave it up and came to New York City. Here, he began to dabble in free-lance writing and contributing verse to "little magazines." His writings brought him into contact with such famous artists and critics as Alfred Stieglitz, Paul Rosenfeld, Waldo Frank, Gorham Munson and Max Eastman. He became a member of this select circle and took a great part in the wholesome critical attitude of the times.

In 1921, he decided, for some reason still unknown to him, to teach in Georgia. He went down there expectant, eyes and ears open, waiting to drink in whatever experiences teaching in Georgia would hold for him. In "Cane," and in his poetry he tells us just what those experiences were. Georgia, the Southland, the home of his fathers awakened in him something he had not known existed. He found down there a hereditary link with forgotten and unknown ancestors. Slavery once a shame and a stigma became for him a spiritual process of growth and transfiguration and the tortuous underground groping of one generation, the maturing and high blossoming of the next. He found in the life of those Georgians and their forebears a sense of mystical recognition. Of this dark fruit of experiences he had this to say:

One plum was saved for me, one seed becomes
An everlasting song, a singing tree
Caroling softly souls of slavery.

He found out that there must have existed a preordained motive in his going to Georgia. He had been able to identify himself with the "souls of slavery" that had gone before him. He saw in those simple, lovely folk a garden beautiful and lovely to behold. The supreme beauty which he found there was the vast blackness into which his heart ventured—like a man who plunges into deep water. This love of simple things, as well as of humble souls, is indeed a dominant note in his song:

O land and soil, red soil and sweet-gum tree
So scant of grass, so profligate of pines.
Now just before an epoch's sun declines,
Thy son, in time I have returned to thee,
Thy son, I have, in time, returned to thee.

As Gorham Munson wrote,* "It seems here that at last a wandering child had returned to his home, to the home of his fathers . . . so that he can immerse himself in the deep folk riches of the Georgia soil and so look for his soul in the earth."

His experiences in Georgia had prompted him to publish in 1923, "Cane," a book which most critics were anxious to style poetic prose. Back in New York, in the circle composed of Frank, Munson, Stieglitz, and Rosenfeld, he admits that he saw life much differently after his Georgia sojourn. He began to express dissatisfaction for American life. It seemed to be so chaotic and purposeless. Knowing inwardly that an artist's first obligation to himself is "personal unification," he decided to cure himself. He began looking around him to find some means whereby he might seek a different self-expression. He began to psychoanalyze himself. Then he underwent the rigorous training

* "Destinations," 1928, in which a chapter is devoted to Toomer.

prescribed by F. Matthias Alexander for "conscious control of the body." Then a summer at the Gurdjieff Institute at Fontainebleau. Here, he wrote that he had found just what he had been searching for; "I am. What I am and what I may become I am trying to find out." If that explains his poetical reticence and his Gurdjieff activities, there is nothing to say.

When Orage, Gurdjieff's representative, came to America, he took Toomer with him to Chicago where they set up an American institute. He wrote a remarkable short story, "Easter" that appeared in the 1925 Little Review. His "Values and Fictions: A Psychological Record," still unpublished, is due to appear shortly. Only a few months ago, under Gurdjieff's auspices, (privately printed) there appeared "Essentials," a book of epigrams and distiches. He says that he has not stopped writing poetry and that he will publish a volume of verse in the next few years. It will be interesting to notice what many years will have done to his poetic outlook.

Toomer had thought of becoming a composer before he turned to poetry and the novel. It is very easy to see this affinity with music. His is essentially the poet-musician's soul. Rather, he is the creative artist whose work is based on the truth of music and poetry. There is so much of musical unity in his work that the sheer artistry in it stands out vividly. Anyone who can combine vowels and liquids to form a cadence like "she was as innocently lovely as a November cotton-flower" has a subtle command of word-music. His verse is always cadenced to accord with the unusually sensitive ear.

His word-painting is based on a strict fidelity to nature, his art is founded on truth, hence its vitality. His descriptions are made on direct notations, and as he composes with the precision and vividness of an artist working with his ear close to the subject, the freshness of the first impression clings to the poem. The exactness of his notations may be seen in an epithet of color as in "Face":

Hair—
silver gray
like streams of stars,
Brows—
recurved canoes
quivered by the ripples blown by pain,
Her eyes—
mist of tears
condensing on the flesh below:
And her channeled muscles
are cluster grapes of sorrow
purple in the evening sun
nearly ripe for worms.

You cannot help seeing the face. It is evoked with a faithful precision with only a few particulars, selected with keen and original insight and painted with broad deliberate touch. I doubt if there has been such a skilful delineation done so well recently.

Toomer accepts life, yet there is in his heart a yearning for completeness and unity. There is in him a good deal of the mystic—not of the type who wants to commune with God and Nature more intimately on a mountain top—but the type who has in himself the deep aspiration for the "peace that passeth understanding."

Every poet carries his message. Toomer's is beauty and the mystery of life. He recognizes in life just so much 'sweetness and light,' color and song, pathos and tragedy, and he accepts all this because it is beautiful and mysterious. He has been wounded in life and so too have his simple, beloved people he writes about. He cares not so much for himself. For those simple, singing people, he has the deep sense of pity. He is keenly alive to their sorrows, he feels acutely the anguish and misery of man's existence, the dumb pain of nature; suffering creatures are by him passionately loved:

O singers, resinous and soft your songs,
Above the sacred whisper of the pines,
Gives virgin lips to cornfield concubines,
Bring dreams of Christ to dusky cane-lipped throngs.

His feeling of pity extends to animals and things, to the field rat who:

. . . startled, squealing bleeds,
His belly close to ground. I see the blade
Blood-stained, continue cutting weeds and shades.

He is deeply moved by the sight of dying cotton. There is intense pathos and understanding here:

And cotton, scarce as any southern snow,
Was vanishing, the branch so pinched and slow,
Failed in its junction as the autumn rake:

He is usually placed, owing to the exactness of his notations from nature and life, among the "realists" and "naturalists." Yet "realism" or "naturalism" should have no proper

(Continued on page 260)

JEAN TOOMER—APOSTLE OF BEAUTY

(Continued from page 254)

meaning in art and poetry. A poet or painter or a musician always is a visionary soul, that is, they descry the "true reality" beyond appearances. Toomer can, if he wants, deny membership in this clique, for instead, he exalts the magic of reality, not of dreams. He woke up to spiritual realities, and to the ethical side of our existence. The mystic feeling added to the poetical intensity of his lives, spreading a new glow over familiar objects and surroundings. In his descriptions even the commonplace and the obvious are clothed with a new light.

I believe that Toomer's poetry will live because it is of the stuff of pure poetry. It is the great depth of emotion implicit in his poems, and the sincerity and simplicity of style that have given him a notable place among contemporary poets. We must agree with Paul Rosenfeld* when he wrote of Toomer that he "comes to unlimber a soul and give of its dance and music."

* Paul Rosenfield, "Twenty-Four Men" (a chapter on Toomer).

JESSIE FAUSET

BY MARION L. STARKEY

THERE is something established and substantial about the appearance of a book. It is popularly supposed that authors who have published them must be substantial and established also, quite beyond care. Such, however, is by no means necessarily the case. Take for example Jessie Fauset, who has published three novels, all substantial volumes and established items in Negro literature. Yet Miss Fauset supports herself, not by her novels, but by her position as French instructor in the De Witt Clinton High School in New York City.

Nothing would please Miss Fauset more than to be able to live by her writing. She looks wistfully to the day when she can accumulate the surplus thousand or two that will enable her to devote a year or so to novels that she has in mind. "Just to see what I really could do if I had my full time and energy to devote to my work."

She confesses to studying whole issues of the *Saturday Evening Post* in a candid effort to analyze and isolate the germ of popular writing. In the meantime her own novels, though widely read, have never been best sellers. French classes, which pay better, must consume the better part of her energy.

Novels have to be written in free afternoons and during summer vacations.

She wrote all but the first eighty pages of her latest, "The Chinaberry Tree," last summer in the hours left free after she had completed an eight o'clock morning class in French at Columbia. Frequently she went from her classroom to the park along Riverside Drive and worked out the tragic complications in the life of Laurentine Strange right there and then by the Hudson.

"And never would I have got my novel done in such good season if it hadn't been for taking that French course and being thereby forced to get up early every day," she reports.

It was as a poet that Miss Fauset started her career in childhood. She came from a large and somewhat literary family, one of those old Philadelphia families she has described in both "Plum Bun" and "There Is Confusion." She had a sister who used to write romances all over the laundry paper, and a brother from whom she confidently expects important achievements in a literary way. He is Arthur Fauset, now principal of a Philadelphia school.

Her own gift for versifying did not leave her as she matured. No anthology of Negro poetry is complete without some of her delightful and often poignant lyrics. Nevertheless she has taken no serious interest in her poems, has made no effort to publish a collection of her own.

She studied in the Philadelphia schools, took her B. A. at Cornell and her M. A at the University of Pennsylvania, taught awhile in Washington, D. C., and then accepted a position on on the editorial staff of *The Crisis*, to which she had been contributing poems and sketches since her undergraduate days.

Dr. William E. B. DuBois, her chief on *The Crisis*, appears briefly but quite glamorously in "Plum Bun" under the not very heavy disguise of Van Meier. It was while working under his precept and example that Miss Fauset learned the important truth that a writer becomes a writer by dint of doing a little every day rather than by waiting for the correct mood, or for uninterrupted leisure.

What started Miss Fauset on a literary career in earnest was a novel of Negro life by the white writer, T. S. Stribling. It was not, as she saw it, a successful study of Negro life, sympathetic though it aspired to be. Negroes of the type the author depicted just did not act and react in the way he described; yet the novel was being accepted seriously by white readers.

"A number of us started writing at that time," said Miss

Fauset. "Nella Larson and Walter White, for instance, were affected just as I was. We reasoned, 'Here is an audience waiting to hear the truth about us. Let us who are better qualified to present that truth than any white writer, try to do so.'"

"There Is Confusion," in the main a study of a Negro singer and dancer whose rise to recognition is cruelly hampered by her race, was Miss Fauset's first contribution. Like all of her books, it is a story of hard-working, self-respecting Negroes, who forge steadily forward in their chosen work. It contains no descriptions of Harlem dives, no race riots, no picturesquely abject poverty. For that reason it found a publisher with some difficulty.

"White readers just don't expect Negroes to be like this," explained the first publisher to see the manuscript as he rejected it. And that fact has been Miss Fauset's difficulty ever since. White readers in their tragic ignorance persist in being surprised that life among educated Negroes goes on quite as it goes on among educated white people, but for the artificial limitations that the latter place upon the former.

Even in considering "The Chinaberry Tree" whose plot is almost wholly divorced from racial issue, the publishers repeated that cry,"But white readers don't expect this of Negroes." Miss Fauset's good friend Zona Gale had to come to the rescue with a preface before the book was published.

Her first novel, published in 1924, was followed in 1929 by "Plum Bun." The latter concerns the problem of "passing." It is the story of a fair-skinned colored girl who "passes" for some years in New York, and then returns out of preference to her own people.

"I never consider myself as working out problems in my novels; the problem story simply isn't my *genre*," explains Miss Fauset. It is not my concern to solve a problem, but to tell what strikes me as a good story.

"All of my novels have been taken from real life. Yes, as stories they are literally true. The story of Laurentine and Melissa in 'The Chinaberry Tree,' for instance, is a story that I heard when I was a girl of fifteen. It was the first tragic story I had ever heard as coming from real life, and I was profoundly impressed, intended always that some day I would write it.

"Like my other plots it had remained in my mind for years. Again and again I had worked it out so that when I came to the mechanical process of writing, I could do so in a straightforward manner, almost without revision. Of course there were certain interpolations that I put into the original story. For instance, the incident that happened to Dr. Denleigh and Laurentine at the restaurant in Pelham happened, almost exactly as it is described, to my husband and me last summer while I was writing my novel. Dr. Denleigh himself is a combination of my husband and my brother."

In private life Miss Fauset is Mrs. Herbert Harris. She married in 1929, just in time for her publishers to present her "Plum Bun" in a beautifully tooled leather binding for a wedding gift.

She and her husband make their home at present with Miss Fauset's sister, Helen Fauset Lanning, in Harlem on Seventh Avenue. It is a cooperative apartment which has been in possession of Mrs. Lanning for some years, and the fact that the neighbors there are real down-home neighbors is a matter of delight to Miss Fauset.

"You wouldn't believe you could possess such good neighbors in New York," say she. "But you should have seen them coming in and out with fruits and jellies a few months back when my sister fell seriously ill."

Miss Fauset has travelled, has been twice to Europe, is planning a trip to Los Angeles this summer to take in the Olympic games. Her favorite recreation is theatre-going; the boast of her life is that once she appeared on the Broadway stage with the French actress, Cecile Sorel.

You may have noticed me; I was part of the mob in the guillotine scene in Du Barry," she said.

Her most immediate literary plans concern a biography, whose subject she is not yet ready to make public, and then another novel whose story has been haunting her for years. But the biography comes first.

"No part of Negro literature needs more building up than biography," she stated. "It is urgent that ambitious Negro youth be able to read of the achievements of their race. When I was a child I used to puzzle my head ruefully over the fact that in school we studied the lives of only great white people. I took it that there simply have been no great Negroes, and I was amazed when, as I grew older, I found that there were. It is a pity that Negro children should be permitted to suffer from that delusion at all. There should be a sort of 'Plutarch's Lives' of the Negro race. Some day, perhaps, I shall get around to writing it."

Claude McKay to Nancy Cunard 9/18/32, from Tangier, Morocco.
[MS Cunard/recip/McKay,Claude. Harry Ransom Humanities Research Center, University of Texas at Austin.]
[The original is handwritten. Ellipses appear in the original manuscript.]

Dear Miss Cunard,

Hope I don't bore you to death asking favors but this stupid cheque drawn on N.Y. will take 25-30 days before I can cash it there (the first time sent like this) and I need the money now. My bank will not cash it spot because I have no funds left–will collect only which will take an even longer time. So will you put it through yours for me and send the equivalent in francs–preferably *mandat* which is the safest? Since both my friends who could do this are out of France you're about the quickest person I know who can fix me up.

I have finished the chapter! Now typing all I hand-wrote when the machine was in pawn–100 pages nearly. After that revision and ought to have all done by the middle of next month.

And please *don't* worry about my contribution. It will be a real relief and joy to turn to something else after a year's hard work on my peasant saga. Since you won't have fiction I am going to do an authentic bit of personal history–a travelogue and perhaps a poem and you can choose the most fitting.

I am very buoyant about my three months more lease of life–I am sending you Santori's letter–also Reides's so that when you go to Paris you will have all the necessary details in approaching him. I don't expect a whole lot from them–the French pay so little for writing–last year I got 200 francs for a short story–but whatever they give will help even out Harper's.

No, I dislike Eric Walrond. And he does me too. Think he is very pretentious light-weight. Knew him when I was on the Liberator with Max Eastman & he on the Negro World with Garvey. 1922. Garvey had given me hell and more in his paper (he had a grudge about me for showing up the preposterous side of his movement in the Liberator) because the police had broken up a Liberator affair and beaten some guests on account of my dancing with a white woman–Crystal Eastman & the N.Y. papers had made quite a scandal of it. Eric came to see me and give some inside dope on Garvey's character for me to make a comeback attack –the crassest moral stuff & besides he was working for the man. . . . Next time I heard from him was 1925 in France *he wrote* asking me to read stories for a competition in the Negro magazine "Opportunity" for which he was assistant editor & offered to place some stuff for me. I was glad to do it for I was quite broke. The stories and poems I sent in did not take the prize, but because I was known a little the magazine proceeded to print them without paying me. And so I had my agent on them to collect. The Negro magazines and papers are almost all pirates paying no attention to the ordinary journalistic procedure such as recognizing the source of reprinted stuff and *payment*. I find most of them have a way of making people pay for "write-ups" and their mug on the page.

But my ultimate success with "Home to Harlem" after years of struggling brought all the black venom out against me. I was told that Walrond said "I knew how to exploit people." And my friends of the "enemy race" whom I have shamefully exploited have never to my knowledge complained. I was called every damned thing. (Schomburg especially amazed me. Because he was always a young old dog. Full of naughty tales. Couldn't imagine him sitting well with Du Bois. But I suppose he slated me to curry favor with the Aframericans, being West Indian. Moreover when I was broke in Marseilles, he wrote me asking that I should copy my book of verse by hand for which he would pay 50 dollars. I put my novel aside & started the job just to have the ready cash & after I had begun it he said he didn't want it–had changed his mind). Schomburg who I always counted a close friend called me (in a review) a buzzard a hog and what not? Walrond (in a widely reprinted article) said I had been invited to Russia by the Soviet government and the impression was that I had become a bolshevik agent. A lie. I had to peddle autographed copies of poems, burn my friends, & work as a fireman from New York to Liverpool to get to Russia. And although the bolsheviks tried to *make* me represent the Negro race, I let them know I was a free spirit, a poet although politically my sympathies were communist.

What maddened the American [indecipherable word] was my making money out of my novel, because the whole intelligentsia crowd have a wards-of-charity mentality–a helpless looking to the powerful philanthropist for awards and scholarships. I told Walrond he ought to have use[d] his scholarship to try and achieve liberty of mind and freedom of expression. I have gone carefully through his stories and stripped of their journalistic verbiage they reveal nothing but the average white man's point of view towards Negroes. The "Palm Booth," the best one is just a "White Cargo" written by a black man.

Of the Negro writers today I think Langston Hughes is the real thing, also Wallace Thurman once he finds his stride. Rudolph Fisher, a nice humorist, Locke a kindly Professor.

The Novels of Jessie Fauset

By William Stanley Braithwaite

William Stanley Braithwaite, distinguished literary critic, herein appraises the place of Miss Jessie Fauset in American letters.

—The Editor.

I DON'T at all mind looking back—a statement I am bold to make, in face of the implied challenge of some of my readers—over thirty-five years, and publicly embrace an era, the *first* era, of creative literature by Negro writers. We have crossed a turbulent, roaring, treacherous, aesthetic Stream of Time between 1898 and 1933: between Chesnutt's "The Marrow of Tradition" say, and Jessie Fauset's "Comedy: American Style," in the growth and development of the Negro novelist.

Our creative literature, chiefly poetry and fiction, has carried the Race across this stream—a bridge, girder and gable and solid granite piers and towers, suspended fairylike in the mist of misunderstanding and calumny, dazzlingly unsubstantial in the sunlight of sympathy and encouragement—from the shores of a "backward," "inferior" people of the eighteen-nineties, to, well, to the shores of cultural and spiritual equality with our fellow-citizens of today. A magic structure and an alluring journey! Yes, by all the precepts and paradoxes of an elusive and deceptive opportunity: no, by all the confluent, Promethean flames of biological urgencies and gifts which the bloods of Europe have poured into the original stream-source from Africa. The "gay nineties" was a tragic era, the "mauve decade," of the critical fancy, was a jaundiced vision, where the Negro was concerned; and in them, the Negro was a passionate root, that sent its first fragile stems above the aesthetic soil along the borderlands of the old and the new century.

There was a girlhood at this time whose wistful dreams must have sent her bright, brown eyes staring in the direction of far horizons, where lay hidden the secrets of a peoples' pride of spirit, secrets that were miraculously endowed with *beauty;* a girlhood that was to grow into womanhood; a searcher after the lure whose priceless possession made her a bright, enchanting blossom on the literary plant that has grown so magically in the last decade.

Within a few months, a decade will have been reached since the publication of Jessie Fauset's first novel "There is Confusion." In 1928, appeared "Plum Bun," in 1931, "The Chinaberry Tree," and in November of this year, "Comedy: American Style." Four novels in not quite ten years. Only one Negro novelist has equalled this output, Dunbar. Our other novelists, Chesnutt, Du Bois, McKay, Nella Larsen, Walter White, Rudolph Fisher, Wallace Thurman, G. S. Schuyler, Langston Hughes, Countee Cullen, and Arna Bontemps, have produced three, two, and one novel, respectively. These eleven writers have described and interpreted Negro life and experience with an art built, with two or three exceptions, to the same pattern. There has not been much variation to the theme nor to the *milieu.*

Miss Fauset has done otherwise, and done it with superb courage. She stands at the head of the procession; and I deliberately invite the objection of critical opinion when I add, that she stands in the front rank of American women novelists in general. Glance at the procession of American women novelists, and their names will register the quality and character of their art, both as an expression, the rendering of human experience, the delineation of human character and nature, and environmental influences. Sara Orne Jewett, Mary E. Wilkins Freeman, Margaret Deland, Edith Wharton, Dorothy Canfield Fisher, Willa Sibert Cather, Ellen Glasgow, Kathleen Norris, Gertrude Atherton, Julia Peterkin, Zona Gale, to name a few, the most conspicuous and successful of the last two generations. If my claim is extravagant, that Miss Fauset assumes a natural and spontaneous association in this company, I am quite willing to take an immediate chastisement, and leave to posterity the relish of honoring with reiterated quotation this morsel of critical extravagance.

Can one by any extension of the critical yardstick credit any of these women novelists with the extraordinary imaginative perception of discovering a new world of racial experience and character, hitherto without psychological and spiritual map and compass, and with poignant surprise find it buffeted, baffled, scorned and rejected, by the pressure

Jessie Fauset

of an encircling political, economic, social and spiritual society, as with an intangible wall of adamant, through which it had to break for the means of survival, and more than mere survival, *progress,* and return from the discovery with both a tragedy and comedy of manners? No, Miss Jewett's Maine folk in her 'country of the pointed firs,' are fundamentally of the same dramatic substance in motive and experience as Miss Cather's Nebraska pioneers; Miss Wharton's Knickerbocker aristocrats are essentially one with the same pride and mellow grace of mind and habit as Miss Glasgow's Virginia 'first families,' the only difference that, with the former the *nouveau riche* gave a surface glitter to the jewel raping its purity, while with the latter a 'lost cause' took the sheen from the once proud texture of a feudal regime. Also these white novelists could afford to toy with some solid virtues and traditions of their craft, which often, and in several cases amongst them, mitigated their value and sincerity as literary artists. Strange as it may seem to all except those of cultivated taste and a broad knowledge of the history and traditions of aesthetic values, many of these novelists, in spite of their reputations and the authoritative praise given them, are scarcely more than deft craftsmen, manipulating the profoundest emotions of humanity for the sake of capturing their readers' attention and interest.

When Miss Fauset tremulously stepped across the threshold of American literature with "There is Confusion," in 1924, she did more than tell the story of a segment of a neglected group of American citizens of color, whose family, social and economic life, on the plane on which she placed it, was new material for the novelist; she unrecognizably made her entrance upon the American scene of letters as the potential Jane Austen of Negro literature. How is one to make clear the subtle distinction between Negro and American literature? Is Negro literature determined by the material or by the color and race of the author who creates it? If by the former, then there are a countless number of white Americans who are *Negro writers;* and yet obviously they cannot be, because by every evidence of proof these authors are known to be white men and women; if by the latter, here we have a paradox as confusing as the other circumstances, because the author of obvious Negro blood is dealing with individuals who, though they are likewise Negroes, are now, after several centuries of transportation and transformation from the native soil of the race—just as the English, the Italian, the French, the Spanish, or German, whose lives went into the colonization of these western lands, and also into the foundations of the American Republic—speaking the common language, and in the custom of living, dressing, eating, working, depend upon the same means and methods as all other Americans; thus it is not merely a question of rationality, but of truth, that the shaper of their individual and collective destinies upon the patterns of creative literature, though racially of Negro extraction or decent, is first and foremost an American author and the creator of American literature.

Thus, if it is convenient to speak of Negro literature as a classification of American literature, it is essential to insist that the standards are one and the same. And if comparisons are made, it is the character and not the quality of the material that is the chief object of appraisal and analysis. With some modification then, I repeat, that Miss Fauset, when she started her novelistic career with "There is Confusion," as the potential Jane Austen of Negro literature, after many decades of authorship by white women novelists, became the first American woman novelist to wrap her shoulders in the scarf of rare and delicate embroidery that Jane Austen's genius bequeathed to the American woman who could wear it most gracefully.

I daresay, as a novelist Miss Fauset would be credited with many a virtue by certain eminent criticis, if she were but obliging enough to ignore the *conventional* ideals and triumphs of the emerged group of the Race. She has been infinitely more honest with her characters than her critics have cared to acknowledge, indeed, to have even suspected. After all, her purpose, whether conscious or unconscious, has been to create in the pages of fiction a society which outside the Race simply did not and preferably, in accordance with granted assumption, could not be allowed to exist. The spirit, the consciousness of pride, dignity, a new quality of moral idealism, was breathed into this darker body of human nature by her passionate sympathy and understanding of its ironic position in the flimsy web of American civilization. Only recently a review of Miss Fauset's latest novel, "Comedy: American Style," in one of the leading Negro papers, resented what the reviewer charged was a lack of climax and philosophy in the recital of Olivia Cary's color obsession and the pain it brought her family. The philosophy in this latest novel, as in the three earlier ones, is not, and never was intended to be, an imposed thesis upon the surface of the story. Miss Fauset is too good an artist to argue the point; to engrave a doctrine upon so intangible an element as Truth, or to array with a misfitting apparel of rhetoric the logic which like a pagan grace or a Christian virtue should run naked as the wind through the implications that color and shape the lives of her characters and their destinies. I am afraid that Negro critical eyes as well as white critical eyes have quite often failed to discern these implications in which are contained the philosophy of a tremendous conflict; the magnificent Shakesperean conflict of *will* and *passion* in the great tragedies from "Titus Andronicus" to "Coriolanus"; for in this Negro society which Miss Fauset has created imaginatively from the realities, there is the *will*, the confused but burning *will*, to master the *passion* of the organized body of lusty American prejudice.

Philosophy, indeed! If we trace the range of American fiction—so spotty in its genuine qualities—we do not find since Hawthorne a similar, and singular, devotion of the philosophy of *rebuke* to an inhuman principle, elevated to an institution and safeguarded by both law and public opinion, as we find in these novels of Jessie Fauset's. Hawthorne's novels were the vehicle, for and presented types of human lives as, a brooding, passionate rebuke to the hard, callous Puritan spirit, which denied earthly happiness and fulfillment, the sense of joy and beauty, to the people. So in the novels of Miss Fauset, we find underlying the narrative, this same philosophy of rebuke, brooding and passionate also, against the contemporary spirit of the American people, who have elevated prejudice into an institution, safeguarded also by law and public sentiment, denying the freedom of development, of the inherent right to well-being, and the pursuit of happiness. It comes as a strange, mysterious echo out of the pages of the great romancer, to hear Miss Fauset's women, Joanna Marshall, Angela Murray and Olivia Cary (is it singular that her men are less given to this articulate yearning?) cry, in Angela's words: "Doesn't anyone think that we have a right to be happy, simply, naturally?" And Joanna, in the first of the novels, at the very end of her story in which she is drawn as a somewhat selfish, ambitious, and unintentionally hard girl, while building her career, after being twitted by Peter her lover, about her desire for greatness, replied, "No, . . . my creed calls for nothing but happiness."

Happiness and—*beauty!* these are the overtones, vibrating from the ordinary drama of men and women, young and old, acting out their tense and colorful destinies in the pages of these four novels, aloof at the core of their interests and intentions from the broad currents of American life. These people want, most of all, to be themselves. To satisfy the same yearnings and instincts, which God has given them in the same measure bestowed upon other people. When some of their members "cross over" into the white world, to enjoy the advantages and privileges for which they are fitted and worthy, as Angela Murray, and her mother Mattie, in temporary spells of adventure, Anthony Cross, and Olivia Cary did, it was not because they desired to be "white," but because a cruel, blind, and despising tradition had taught them it was wiser and more profitable "not to be colored." So far Miss Fauset has nicely balanced her survey of this extraordinary scene and the people who compose it. "There is Confusion," the first of her novels, deals with the clear-cut background and its atmosphere of a rising racial social group in New York, the action taking place largely in the pre-war years. It is mainly the story of Joanna Marshall's artistic ambition to fulfill her talents in the larger world of universal recognition and appreciation. The Marshall family is typical of many Negro families of the period, rising by hard work and moral principles to a position of respectability and influence among their own. Peter Bye, Joanna's lover, though he was careless of the distinction, brings into the story the pride of ancestry from an old Philadelphia family. That Joanna, in the end, was defeated in her purpose to achieve greatness—it is interesting to reflect upon the parallel story of Maggie Ellersley, poor and unfavored by opportunity, who strove so earnestly and honestly to be respectable in the sense that the Marshalls were, and who built her own sturdy ambitions upon the materials and services designed entirely along racial lines—she remains a more significant figure in the late realization of her love for Peter.

"Plum Bun," Miss Fauset's second novel is, perhaps, her most perfect artistic achievement, and the most balanced force of interracial experience. Its heroine, Angela Murray, not so profoundly and vividly drawn as Laurentine Strange or Melissa Paul, in "The Chinaberry Tree," nor as that superbly ironic figure Olivia Cary, in "Comedy: American Style," is nevertheless, the most successful protagonist of the white-colored girl, who tragically sought happiness in the white world. "Plum Bun," is the apogee of this mode among Miss Fauset's novels, for in Anthony Cross again, she has taken a character "over"; and he is the most unique of her male characters, one who went "white" not by choice, but because of the hatred, which the murder of his father by a southern mob, had engendered in him for white people. If the story hides a moral, it is, that if one masquerades as white because it is expedient in the search for happiness and security and not because one is ashamed, or would rather not possess the dark blood in them, then a defection which the gods ironically punish with spiritual, and often, physical tragedy. Both Angela Murray and Anthony Cross, who were lovers, following Angela's affair with Roger Fielding, the rich white youth, tasted this fortuitous draught at the hands of fate.

With her third novel Miss Fauset returns to the same general theme of racial solidarity on the higher social plane, as in her first story. In this respect it is by far the meatiest of her books. Laurentine Strange drums upon one's consciousness with the insistent and haunting lure for sympathy and understanding that one has for Hardy's Tess, and more recently for Irene Forsythe in Galworthy's "Saga." Her experience, of course, is not like that of Tess; and she is not quite that "impinging beauty" of symbolic intentions, rebelling against the acquisitive Victorian propensity of a Soames, of Galsworthy's creation. She is, nevertheless, an impinging symbol within the bound of her social *milieu,* the confluent expression in our modern era, of that free, non-obligatory mating of a white father and colored mother. Proud, unconsciously disdainful, Laurentine emerges from the older racial backgrounds by the way of a critical arbiter, who stirs the tempest in the broadening world of which she and her relatives and, the people who would be, her friends, had she allowed them to be, pass through a process of crystallization. Melissa, her cousin, accompanies her through the narrative as a foil, spontaneous, warm-heated, impulsive, but a little designing, with the potential stuff in her of a romantic disaster. The duel between these two girls is a comedy whose spirit is dipped in a vinegar of affection. And disaster, indeed, is what overtakes these girls; a disaster whose effect is somewhat artificial when revealed, and seems a bit forced and unreal. In many ways her strongest book on the theme of racial solidarity in its advanced stage, "The Chinaberry Tree" alone strikes what seems to me the one false note in Miss Fauset's artistic equipment. For the sake of the story we forgive it, however, as we forgive Thomas Hardy that equally false and absurd climax in which Tess murders her betrayer. It is a story that will take a long time for both colored and white Americans to appreciate its supreme power.

The fourth of Miss Fauset's novels, "Comedy: American Style,"—with its ironic title, for the story is a tragedy throughout—is both the most irritating and at the same time, the most powerful of her books. The story of Olivia Cary's obsession not to display the dark blood in either herself, nor in those members of her family—with the one tragic exception of Oliver, her youngest son—is one of the most devastating characterizations in contemporary American fiction. As in the case of Angela Murray, Olivia would not have cared a fig about being taken for colored anywhere, if the fact did not rob her of the things which the white world possessed, and which, she contended, were necessary for her own happiness and peace, and the happiness and peace of her children. She built this desire upon an illusion, which was not of her own creation; but finding it as she did, she began early as a child and pursued the purpose through the rest of her life until we leave her at the end of the story, that purpose to cheat the creator of the illusion. She did just the opposite, and it is the irony and paradox of her story, that those she cheated were herself, her husband and her children. Though all of them saw through her, and took the stand that honest and self-respecting colored people take, even when it is often possible for one to deceive, they could not prevail against Olivia's heartless and untiring persecution. Her husband she ruined; drove her daughter into a loveless marriage with an insiped, selfish Frenchman with an Oedipus complex; stung her youngest son into suicide; and in the end the victim of her own unrelenting fanaticism.

Olivia Cary is a tragic figure—one cannot call her a heroine, though that is the role designed for her by Miss Fauset. There is nothing glamorous about her, and yet she fascinates one with that hard, glittering frostiness of purpose, with which she wrecks and ruins. What makes her so disturbingly alive is the paradox of her morality; for she is, according to a misconception of virtue, an impeccably moral woman in the flesh. Like Becky Sharpe, after all, she touches one's sympathy, when at the end of the novel we leave her pathetically stranded in the ashes of her own once consuming desires and hopes. She is the symbol of a force that must ultimately be acknowledged and discussed frankly by both races in America, and when that discussion takes place there will be concessions and revisions on the part of white Americans which will make it possible to draw her like again as a warning.

The Growth of Negro Literature

by V. F. CALVERTON

NEGRO art and literature are, in many ways, as rich in ancient tradition as in modern challenge. The discoveries of archæologists, dating from the explorations of over a century ago, have disclosed the remnants of an African culture that hitherto was almost completely unknown. Tennyson's youthful apostrophe to Timbuctoo has a deeper meaning and import today. Timbuctoo stands now as but a single reminder of an ancient civilisation that was, perhaps, as rare in diversity and as advanced in ways of life as any civilisation, however adjacent or remote, of its time. The products of this civilisation, or if we wish to include the civilisations of Ethiopia, Ghana, Melle, and the Songhay in separate categories, then of these civilisations, are an eloquent testimony of their progress.

In the Songhay empire, for example, education was advanced to such a point that people came from all over the Islamic world to teach in its schools; and the savants of the Songhay were active also in Mohammedan countries to the north and east. In fact, throughout the Sudan, university life was fairly extensive. Ahmed Baba, one of the strongly arresting figures of his period, stands out as a brilliant example of the sweep of Sudanese erudition. An author of more than forty books upon such diverse themes as theology, astronomy, ethnography and biography, Baba was a scholar of great depth and inspiration. With his expatriation from Timbuctoo—he was in the city at the time that it was invaded by the Moroccans in 1592 and protested against their occupation of it—he lost, in his collection of 1,600 books, one of the richest libraries of his day. Ahmed Baba, of course, although the most conspicuous, was only one scholar amongst many. All through West Africa the Negroes had established many centres of learning. In their schools and universities courses were given in rhetoric, logic, eloquence, diction, the principles of arithmetic, hygiene, medicine, prosody, philosophy, ethnography, music and astronomy.[1] The Negro scholars in many instances surpassed the Arabian. In Ethiopia their contributions to culture streamed far beyond the borders of their own nation in influence and power. Every exploration and excavation of African materials adds to this historical revelation. We see rising before us, in the form of obscure manuscript, relics of apparel and architectural remains, the lives of peoples and the movements of civilisations once buried in the sands of a dead world. In this Negro ancestry there were discovered rulers who expanded their kingdoms into empires, generals who advanced the technique of military science, and scholars who brought with their wisdom an advancing vision of life.

When we realise, then, that the Negro is not without a cultural past, we can readily understand his

[1] *Negro Culture in West Africa*, by G. W. Ellis.

achievements in American art and literature in terms of environmental evolution. Most Americans, unacquainted with this past, and unappreciative of the potentialities of the black peoples, interpret the developments in Negro literature in ways that are immediately stultifying and absurd. One way is tragically familiar. Negro advance, according to this way of interpretation, is the result of the white blood infused in the black personality. The advocates of this interpretation have gone to great pains in their endeavour to prove that every Negro genius is a product of white miscegenation. Their argument that it is only through the presence of white blood that black genius can derive, is no more logical than the contention that it was only through the presence of black blood that Pushkin could develop into a white genius. Nevertheless this method of interpretation still prevails, even in circles that often pretend to be scientific. But there are other ways of interpretation that are scarcely less unfortunate in their logic—or lack of it. Another is the one that tries to treat the growth of the new Negro literature as a fad, which, in its sudden flare, reflects nothing more than an interest in the curious. The Negro, in the eyes of the critics, is an oddity, and as an artist and an intellectual is stranger far than fiction. Their explanation of his recent success is based mainly upon what they consider an aspect of patronage on the part of the reading public and the publisher. His work is greeted from the point of view of race and not of art. He is pampered as a Negro, and his work is praised often when it ought to be attacked. As a consequence, they are convinced that in a few years, as this illusion in reference to his work has begun to vanish, the interest in Negro literature will cease, and the urge in favour of its creation will correspondingly disappear.

Upon close analysis, these interpretations are seen to be at once irrelevant and futile. In the first place the Negro did advance and achieve in Africa before white blood could make its intrusion, and many Negro geniuses in America show very little trace of white blood at all; and, in the second place, his contributions to American art and literature are far more free of white influence than American culture is of English. Indeed, we may say that the contributions of the Negro to American culture are as indigenous to our soil as the legendary cowboy or gold-seeking frontiersman. And, in addition, it is no exaggeration whatsoever to contend that they are more striking and singular in substance and structure than any contributions that have been made by the white man to American culture. In fact, they constitute America's chief claim to originality in its cultural history. In song, the Negro spirituals and to a less extent the Blues; in tradition, Negro folklore; and in music, Negro jazz—these three constitute the Negro contribution to American culture. In fact, it can be said that they constitute all that is unique in our cultural life. Since Indian remains have been very largely exterminated, Indian culture, with its native originality, has been mainly lost. At least, enough does not remain to challenge the contributions of the Negro. When Dvořák sought to find an inspiration in American environment for his New World Symphony, he inevitably turned to the Negro. After all, the Negro, in his simple, unsophisticated way, has developed out of the American *milieu* a form of expression, a mood, a literary *genre*, a folk-tradition, that are distinctly and undeniably American. This is more than the white man has done. The white man in America has continued, and in an inferior manner, a culture of European origin. He has not developed a culture that is definitely and unequivocally American. In respect of originality, then, the Negro is more important in the growth of an American culture than the white man. His art is richer, more spontaneous, and more captivating and convincing in its appeal.

The social background of Negro life in itself was sufficient to inspire an art of no ordinary character. Indeed, the very fact that the Negro, by the nature of his environment, was deprived of education, prevented his art from ever becoming purely imitative. Even where he adopted the white man's substance, as in the case of religion, he never adopted his forms. He gave to whatever he took a new style and a new interpretation. In truth, he made it practically into a new thing. There were no ancient conventions that he, in his untutored zeal, felt duty-bound to respect, and no age-old traditions that instructed him, perforce, as to what was art and what was not. He could express his soul, as it were, without concern for grammar or the eye of the carping critic. As a result, his art is, as is all art that springs from the people, an artless art, and in that sense is the most genuine art of the world. While the white man has gone to Europe for his models, and is seeking still an European approval of his artistic endeavours, the Negro in his art forms has never gone beyond America for his background and has never sought the acclaim of any culture other than his own. This is particularly true of those forms of Negro art that come directly from the people. It is, of course, not so true of a poet such as Phyllis Wheatley or of the numerous Negro poets and artists of today, who in more ways than one have followed the traditions of their white contemporaries rather than extended and perfected the original art forms of their race. Of course, in the eighteenth century when Phyllis Wheatley wrote, these Negro art forms were scarcely more than embryonic. Today, on the other hand, their existence has become a commonplace to the white writer as well as the black.

In a subtle way, Negro art and literature in America have had an economic origin. All that is original in Negro folklore, or singular in Negro spirituals and Blues, can be traced to the economic institution of slavery and its influence upon the Negro soul. The Negro lived in America as a slave for over two hundred and forty years. He was forced by the system of slavery into habits of life and forms of behaviour that inevitably drove him in the direction of emotional escape and religious delirium. Existence offered him nothing to hope for but endless labour and pain. Life was a continuous crucifixion. The earth became a place of evil. As a downtrodden and suppressed race he had nothing to discover within himself that insured emancipation or escape. His revolts had all proved ineffectual. Inevitably he turned toward the white man for the materials of his " under-dog " logic. He accepted and absorbed the ideas of the ruling class, as do most subordinate groups and classes, until they became a part of his reaction. The white man's paradise suddenly became a consuming aspiration. He became enamoured of it as a holy vision. His belief in it became a ferocious faith. Its other-worldly aspect only lent it a richer enchantment. There were no realistic categories to thwart or limit its undimensioned beauty and magnificence. The scarcities of this world had no meaning in the infinite plenitude of the next. Gold could be had for the asking, and everything was as dream would have it if in a land beyond the sun.

It was as an expression of this consecrated other-worldly ardour that the Negro spirituals came into being and grew into form. There is more, far more, than the ordinary Christian zeal embodied in them. These spirituals are not mere religious hymns written or recited to sweeten the service or improve the ritual. They are the aching, poignant cry of an entire people. Jesus to the Negro is no simple religious saviour, worshipped on Sundays and forgotten during the week. He is the incarnation of the suffering soul of a race. In such a spiritual as *Crucifixion* one finds this spirit manifest. Or in such a spiritual as *Swing Low Sweet Chariot* we discover the other-worldly motif in fine, moving form.

When we turn to the Blues and Labor Songs, the economic connection is more obvious. Here we have folklore in poetic form, springing spontaneously from the simple everyday life of an oppressed people. The Blues have a primitive kinship with the old ballads that is strikingly curious upon close comparison. While the rhyme-scheme employed in the Blues is often less clever and arresting than that found in the ballads, the incremental repetitions are not less effective, and the simple, quick descriptions are often as fine in this form as the other. The labor songs, growing up as part of the workaday rhythms of daily toil, have a swing about them that is irresistibly infectious. The musical swing of the hammer, its sweeping rise and fall, is communicated, for instance, with rhythmic power in the song entitled *John Henry*. And in the familiar levée song we meet with another but not less enticing rhythm :

Where wuz your sweet mamma
When de boat went down?
On de deck, Babe,
Hollerin' Alabama Bound.

The Negro has retained unquestionably in his art a certain primitivism that is wonderfully refreshing in contrast to the stilted affectations of the more cultured styles and conceptions. We come closer to life with these primitivisms, feel beauty in its more genuine and intimate and less artificial and cerebral forms.

These primitivisms of the Negro are a singular evolution of our American environment. In describing them as primitive, we do not mean that they are savage in origin, or that the instincts of savagery linger in them, but that they are untutored in form and unsophisticated in content, and in these aspects are more primitive than civilised in character. The art of primitive peoples is often the very opposite in spirit to that of the African Negro. African art is rigid, economical of energy, and almost classic in its discipline. The exuberance of sentiment, the spirited denial of discipline, and the contempt for the conventional, that are so conspicuous in art of the American Negro, are direct outgrowths of the nature of his life in this country.

In jazz this vital and overwhelming exuberance of the American Negro reaches its apex in physical dynamics. If the origin of jazz is not entirely Negroid—that its fundamental form is derivative of Negro rhythms no longer can be disputed—its development of attitude and expression in America has certainly been chiefly advanced by the Negro. While the spirituals represent the religious escape of the Negro, the jazz rhythms vivify his mundane abandon. Today this mundane abandon has become a universal craving on the part of youth in Europe as well as in America. Since the war, the dance has become a mania. It is the mad, delirious dance of men and women who have had to seize upon something as a vicarious outlet for their crazed emotions. They have not wanted old opiates that induced sleep and the delusion of a sweet stillness of things and silence. They have not sought the escape which an artificial lassitude brings to minds tormented with worry and pain. They have demanded an escape that is active, dynamic, electrical, an escape that exhilarates, and brings restfulness only from exhaustion. Jazz has provided that escape in increasing measure as its jubilant antics and rhythms have become madder and madder in their tumult of release. To the Negro the riotous rhythms that constitute jazz are but an active translation of the impulsive extravagance of his life. Whether a difference in the calcium factor in bone structure or conjunction, accounting for an exceptional muscular resiliency, or a difference in terms of an entirely environmental disparity, be used to explain the Negro's superior response to jazz, his supremacy in this departure in music remains uncontested. Jazz, Stokowski contends, " has effected a profound change in musical outlook." In this change, Stokowski adds:

> The Negro musicians of America are playing a great part. . . . They have an open mind, and unbiased outlook. They are causing new blood to flow in the veins of music. The jazz players make their instruments do entirely new things, things finished musicians are taught to avoid. They are path-finders into new realms.

Jazz reflects something of the essential irresponsibility, or rather the irresponsible enthusiasms and ecstasies that underlie Negro life here in America, and which give to Negro art such singular distinction in verse and spontaneity. While jazz in its inferior forms is a vulgar removal from the idea of the exquisite which prevailed in music before our day, it nevertheless has the virtue of great originality and the vigour of deep challenge. In a very significant sense, indeed, it remains as the only original contribution to music that has been made by America.

If the spirit of jazz is captured almost to a point of precision in these lines from *Runnin' Wild*:

> Runnin' wild, lost control,
> Runnin' wild, mighty bold,
> Feelin' gay and reckless too,
> Carefree all the time, never blue,
> Always goin' I don't know where,
> Always showin' that I don't care,
> Don' love nobody, it ain't worth while,
> All alone, runnin' wild.

it would be a serious and most reprehensible exaggeration to maintain that it is this mood which permeates all Negro art in America. In fact, much of contemporary Negro poetry is as far removed in spirit from the jazz motif as the poetry of John Milton is from that of T. S. Eliot. There is indeed an over-seriousness, even an affected dignity in the work of many Negro poets. This tendency to an artificial loftiness of utterance, verging often upon the pompous, is more marked in the work of the Negro writers of the 19th century than of the 20th. In many cases education removed the Negro writer further from his people, and inclined his work in the direction of imitating the artificial standards of other groups rather than of advancing and perfecting those of his own. As a result, a certain naturalness and fine vigour of style were lost. While this tendency has not disappeared, a reaction has already set in against it, and today Negro writers have begun to develop a more candid approach.

In the poetry of Langston Hughes, for instance, there is a freshness even in artifice that was absent in the poetry of the 19th-century Negro. Even Dunbar, who was the leading Negro poet prior to our own day, avoided the affectations and conceits of his contemporaries only in his poems of dialect. In the verse of such writers as Albert A. Whitman, Mrs. Harper, George Moses Horton, James Madison Bell, Joseph Seamon Cotter and James David Corrothers, this literary fallacy is unpleasantly conspicuous. They aspired at the stately, when they should have aimed at the simple. Their poetry, as a consequence, was hopelessly inept and sentimental. It is only with the present day, and the emergence of the contemporary school of Negro poets, led by such figures as Langston Hughes, Countee Cullen, Jean Toomer and Claude McKay, that this type of verse has been condemned with scorn.

If the recent developments in Negro literature cannot be characterised as a renaissance, they certainly must be noted as marking off a new stage in the literary history of a people. Without question the work of Jean Toomer, Rudolph Fisher, Burghardt DuBois and Walter White in fiction; Langston Hughes, Countee Cullen and Claude McKay in verse; and Alain Locke, Franklin Frazier, James Weldon Johnson, Charles S. Johnson, Abram L. Harris and George Schuyler in the essay, has been distinguished by fine intelligence and advancing artistic vision. Surely at no other period, and certainly never in so short a time, have so many Negro writers of genuine talent appeared. If among these writers no great artist or great thinker has so far evolved, there is no reason for despair. The great achievement of Roland Hayes on the concert stage, and of Paul Robeson in the theatre, gives promise at least of similar success in the literary art in the future. The appearance of these numerous artists and the growth of this newer spirit on the part of the Negro, is really not so much a re-birth in the sense of a renaissance, as it is the hastening of an old birth which had formerly been retarded in its growth and evolution.

Steadily this trend in the New Negro literature has developed in favour of the vigorous instead of the exquisite. Challenge has become more significant than charm. The submissive acquiescences of the Booker T. Washington attitude and era have now become contemptuously anachronistic. The sentimental cry of a 19th-century poet such as Corrothers:

> To be a Negro in a day like this—
> Alas! Lord God, what ill have we done

has been superseded by the charging defiance of a 20th-century poet such as McKay:

> What though before us lies the open grave?
> Like men we'll face the murderous, cowardly pack,
> Pressed to the wall, dying, but—fighting back!

The admission of inferiority which was implicit in so much of the earlier verse, the supplicatory note which ran like a lugubrious echo through so many of its stanzas, has been supplanted by an attitude of superiority and independence on the part of such poets as Countee Cullen, Langston Hughes and Gwendolyn Bennett.

George Schuyler in prose has given this same attitude a sharp, ironic turn. His clean-cut, biting style, inevitably in keeping with his theme and purpose, is at times superb. He meets his materials with a directness that compels by its vigour. His writing is never sentimental; rather it has a hard, metallic brilliance that convinces without endeavouring to caress. In *Our Greatest Gift to America*, which deals in satiric form with the Negro's position in this country, Schuyler's criticism is acute and devastating.

As the racialism of the Negro has become more assertive and radical, a new attitude has begun to reveal itself in his fiction. There has been a marked tendency in the past, except in stories of dialect, for Negro writers to centre their attention upon the more enlightened and prosperous members of the race. In *The Fire in the Flint*, for instance, Walter White has chosen a doctor for his protagonist; in *There is Confusion* Jessie Fausset has featured a dancer as her star; in *Quicksand* Nella Larsen has selected a school teacher for her main character; and in *The Dark Princess* DuBois has made an aristocratic woman into his heroine. Today in the novels of Rudolph Fisher and Claude McKay the class of characters has shifted. In *The Walls of Jericho* and *Home to Harlem* the main characters are proletarian types, piano movers and stevedores, who are endowed with little education and less culture. The lives of these lower types are seen to be as fascinating and as dramatic as those of the upper. In fact, a certain native drama is revealed in the lives of these colored folk that is absent in the lives of most white people in the same class of society. This added drama flows from the freer and more irresponsibly spontaneous way in which these black men live. In time, no doubt, these proletarian types, since the Negro, dating from his vast migrations from southern to northern latitudes during and immediately following the war, is becoming rapidly proletarianised, will occupy an increasingly large part in the entire literary scene.

If this new literature of the Negro in America does not constitute a renaissance, it does signify rapid growth in racial art and culture. It is a growth that is as yet unfinished. Indeed, we may say it illustrates a growth that in a dynamic sense has just begun. It indicates more than the rise of a literature. It marks the rise of an entire people.

Sterling Brown: The New Negro Folk-Poet

by ALAIN LOCKE

Alain Locke

Many critics, writing in praise of Sterling Brown's first volume of verse, have seen fit to hail him as a significant new Negro poet. The discriminating few go further; they hail a new era in Negro poetry, for such is the deeper significance of this volume (*The Southern Road*, Sterling A. Brown, Harcourt Brace, New York, 1932). Gauging the main objective of Negro poetry as the poetic portrayal of Negro folk-life true in both letter and spirit to the idiom of the folk's own way of feeling and thinking, we may say that here for the first time is that much-desired and long-awaited acme attained or brought within actual reach.

Almost since the advent of the Negro poet public opinion has expected and demanded folk-poetry of him. And Negro poets have tried hard and voluminously to cater to this popular demand. But on the whole, for very understandable reasons, folk-poetry by Negroes, with notable flash exceptions, has been very unsatisfactory and weak, and despite the intimacy of the race poet's attachments, has been representative in only a limited, superficial sense. First of all, the demand has been too insistent. "They required of us a song in a strange land." "How could we sing of thee, O Zion?" There was the canker of theatricality and exhibitionism planted at the very heart of Negro poetry, unwittingly no doubt, but just as fatally. Other captive nations have suffered the same ordeal. But with the Negro another spiritual handicap was imposed. Robbed of his own tradition, there was no internal compensation to counter the external pressure. Consequently the Negro spirit had a triple plague on its heart and mind—morbid self-consciousness, self-pity and forced exhibitionism. Small wonder that so much poetry by Negroes exhibits in one degree or another the blights of bombast, bathos and artificiality. Much genuine poetic talent has thus been blighted either by these spiritual faults or their equally vicious over-compensations. And so it is epoch-making to have developed a poet whose work, to quote a recent criticism, " has no taint of music-hall convention, is neither arrogant nor servile "—and plays up to neither side of the racial dilemma. For it is as fatal to true poetry to cater to the self-pity or racial vanity of a persecuted group as to pander to the amusement complex of the overlords and masters.

I do not mean to imply that Sterling Brown's art is perfect, or even completely mature. It is all the more promising that this volume represents the work of a young man just in his early thirties. But a Negro poet with almost complete detachment, yet with a tone of persuasive sincerity, whose muse neither clowns nor shouts, is indeed a promising and a grateful phenomenon.

By some deft touch, independent of dialect, Mr. Brown is able to compose with the freshness and naturalness of folk balladry—*Maumee Ruth*, *Dark O' the Moon*, *Sam Smiley*, *Slim Green*, *Johnny Thomas*, and *Memphis Blues* will convince the most sceptical that modern Negro life can yield real balladry and a Negro poet achieve an authentic folk-touch.[1]

Or this from *Sam Smiley*:

> The mob was in fine fettle, yet
> The dogs were stupid-nosed, and day
> Was far spent when the men drew round
> The scrawny wood where Smiley lay.
>
> The oaken leaves drowsed prettily,
> The moon shone benignly there;
> And big Sam Smiley, King Buckdancer,
> Buckdanced on the midnight air.

This is even more dramatic and graphic than that fine but more melodramatic lyric of Langston Hughes:

> Way down South in Dixie
> (Break the heart of me!)
> They hung my black young lover
> To a cross-road's tree.

With Mr. Brown the racial touch is quite independent of dialect; it is because in his ballads and lyrics he has caught the deeper idiom of feeling or the peculiar paradox of the racial situation. That gives the genuine earthy folk-touch, and justifies a statement I ventured some years back: " the soul of the Negro will be discovered in a characteristic way of thinking and in a homely philosophy rather than in a jingling and juggling of broken English." As a matter of fact, Negro dialect is extremely local—it changes from place to place, as do white dialects. And what is more, the dialect of Dunbar and the other early Negro poets never was on land or sea as a living peasant speech; but it has had such wide currency, especially on the stage, as to have successfully deceived half the world, including the many Negroes who for one reason or another imitate it.

Sterling Brown's dialect is also local, and frankly an adaptation, but he has localised it carefully, after close observation and study, and varies it according to the brogue of the locality or the characteristic jargon of the *milieu* of which he is writing. But his racial effects, as I have said, are not dependent on dialect. Consider *Maumee Ruth*:

> Might as well bury her
> And bury her deep,
> Might as well put her
> Where she can sleep. . . .
>
> Boy that she suckled
> How should he know,
> Hiding in city holes
> Sniffing the " snow "?[2]

[1] This exquisite poem is in the Poetry section. [2] Cocaine.

And how should the news
Pierce Harlem's din,
To reach her baby gal
Sodden with gin?

Might as well drop her
Deep in the ground,
Might as well pray for her,
That she sleep sound.

That is as uniquely racial as the straight dialect of *Southern Road*:

White man tells me—hunh—
Damn yo' soul;
White man tells me—hunh—
Damn yo' soul;
Got no need, bebby,
To be tole.

If we stop to inquire—as unfortunately the critic must—into the magic of these effects, we find the secret, I think, in this fact more than in any other: Sterling Brown has listened long and carefully to the folk in their intimate hours, when they were talking to themselves, not, so to speak, as in Dunbar, but actually as they do when the masks of protective mimicry fall. Not only has he dared to give quiet but bold expression to this private thought and speech, but he has dared to give the Negro peasant credit for thinking. In this way he has recaptured the shrewd Aesopian quality of the Negro folk-thought, which is more profoundly characteristic than their types of metaphors or their mannerisms of speech. They are, as he himself says,

Illiterate, and somehow very wise,

and it is this wisdom, bitter fruit of their suffering, combined with their characteristic fatalism and irony, which in this book gives a truer soul picture of the Negro than has ever yet been given poetically. The traditional Negro is a clown, a buffoon, an easy laugher, a shallow sobber and a credulous christian; the real Negro underneath is more often an all but cynical fatalist, a shrewd pretender, and a boldly whimsical pagan; or when not, a lusty, realistic religionist who tastes its nectars here and now.

Mammy
With deep religion defeating the grief
Life piled so closely about her

is the key picture to the Negro as christian; Mr. Brown's *When the Saints Come Marching Home* is worth half a dozen essays on the Negro's religion. But to return to the question of bold exposure of the intimacies of Negro thinking—read that priceless apologia of kitchen stealing in the *Ruminations of Luke Johnson*, reflective husband of Mandy Jane, tromping early to work with a great big basket, and tromping wearily back with it at night laden with the petty spoils of the day's picking:

Well, taint my business noway,
An' I ain' near fo'gotten
De lady what she wuks fo',
An' how she got her jack;
De money dat she live on
Come from niggers pickin' cotton,
Ebbery dollar dat she squander
Nearly bust a nigger's back.

So I'm glad dat in de evenins
Mandy Jane seems extra happy,
An' de lady at de big house
Got no kick at all I say—
Cause what huh " dear grandfawthaw "
Took from Mandy Jane's grandpappy—
Ain' no basket in de worl'
What kin tote all dat away. . . .

Or again in that delicious epic of *Sporting Beasley* entering heaven:

Lord help us, give a look at him,
Don't make him dress up in no nightgown, Lord.
Don't put no fuss and feathers on his shoulders, Lord.
    Let him know it's heaven,
Let him keep his hat, his vest, his elkstooth, and everything.
Let him have his spats and cane.

It is not enough to sprinkle " dis's and dat's " to be a Negro folk-poet, or to jingle rhymes and juggle popularised clichés traditional to sentimental minor poetry for generations. One must study the intimate thought of the people who can only state it in an ejaculation, or a metaphor, or at best a proverb, and translate that into an articulate attitude, or a folk philosophy or a daring fable, with Aesopian clarity and simplicity—and above all, with Aesopian candor.

The last is most important; other Negro poets in many ways have been too tender with their own, even though they have learned with the increasing boldness of new Negro thought not to be too gingerly and conciliatory to and about the white man. The Negro muse weaned itself of that in McKay, Fenton Johnson, Toomer, Countee Cullen and Langston Hughes. But in Sterling Brown it has learned to laugh at itself and to chide itself with the same broomstick. I have space for only two examples: *Children's Children*:

When they hear
These songs, born of the travail of their sires,
Diamonds of song, deep buried beneath the weight
Of dark and heavy years;
They laugh.

They have forgotten, they have never known
Long days beneath the torrid Dixie sun,
In miasma'd rice swamps;
The chopping of dried grass, on the third go round
In strangling cotton;
Wintry nights in mud-daubed makeshift huts,
With these songs, sole comfort.

They have forgotten
What had to be endured—
That they, babbling young ones,
With their paled faces, coppered lips,
And sleek hair cajoled to Caucasian straightness,
Might drown the quiet voice of beauty
With sensuous stridency;

And might, on hearing these memories of their sires,
Giggle,
And nudge each other's satin-clad
Sleek sides.

Anent the same broomstick, it is refreshing to read *Mr. Samuel and Sam*, from which we can only quote in part:

Mister Samuel, he belong to Rotary,
Sam, to de Sons of Rest;
Both wear red hats like monkey men,
An' you cain't say which is de best. . . .

Mister Samuel die, an' de folks all know,
Sam die widout no noise;
De worl' go by in de same ol' way,
And dey's both of 'em po' los' boys.

There is a world of psychological distance between this and the rhetorical defiance and the plaintive, furtive sarcasms of even some of our other contemporary poets—even as theirs, it must be said in all justice, was miles better and more representative than the sycophancies and platitudes of the older writers.

In closing it might be well to trace briefly the steps by which Negro poetry has scrambled up the sides of Parnassus from the ditches of minstrelsy and the trenches of race propaganda. In complaining against the narrow compass of dialect poetry (dialect is an organ with only two stops—pathos and humor), Weldon Johnson tried to break the Dunbar mould and shake free of the traditional stereotypes. But significant as it was, this was more a threat than an accomplishment; his own dialect poetry has all of the clichés of Dunbar without Dunbar's lilting lyric charm. Later in the *Negro Sermons* Weldon Johnson discovered a way out—in a rhapsodic form free from the verse shackles of classical minor poetry, and in the attempt to substitute an idiom of racial thought and imagery for a mere dialect of peasant speech. Claude McKay then broke with all the moods conventional in his day in Negro poetry, and presented a Negro who could challenge and hate, who knew resentment, brooded intellectual sarcasm, and felt contemplative irony. In this, so to speak, he pulled the psychological cloak off the Negro and revealed, even to the Negro himself, those facts disguised till then by his shrewd protective mimicry or pressed down under the dramatic mask of living up to what was expected of him. But though McKay sensed a truer Negro, he was at times too indignant at the older sham, and, too, lacked the requisite native touch—as of West Indian birth and training—with the local color of the American Negro. Jean Toomer went deeper still—I should say higher—and saw for the first time the glaring paradoxes and the deeper ironies of the situation, as they affected not only the Negro but the white man. He realised, too, that Negro idiom was anything but trite and derivative, and also that it was in emotional substance pagan—all of which he convincingly demonstrated, alas, all too fugitively, in *Cane*. But Toomer was not enough of a realist, or patient enough as an observer, to reproduce extensively a folk idiom.

Then Langston Hughes came with his revelation of the emotional color of Negro life, and his brilliant discovery of the flow and rhythm of the modern and especially the city Negro, substituting this jazz figure and personality for the older plantation stereotype. But it was essentially a jazz version of Negro life, and that is to say as much American, or more, as Negro; and though fascinating and true to an epoch this version was surface quality after all.

Sterling Brown, more reflective, a closer student of the folk-life, and above all a bolder and more detached observer, has gone deeper still, and has found certain basic, more sober and more persistent qualities of Negro thought and feeling; and so has reached a sort of common denominator between the old and the new Negro. Underneath the particularities of one generation are hidden universalities which only deeply penetrating genius can fathom and bring to the surface. Too many of the articulate intellects of the Negro group—including sadly enough the younger poets—themselves children of opportunity, have been unaware of these deep resources of the past. But here, if anywhere, in the ancient common wisdom of the folk, is the real treasure trove of the Negro poet; and Sterling Brown's poetic divining-rod has dipped significantly over this position. It is in this sense that I believe *Southern Road* ushers in a new era in Negro folk-expression and brings a new dimension in Negro folk-portraiture.

The Negro Theatre—A Dodo Bird

by RALPH MATTHEWS

Theatrical Editor of the *Afro-American*

Ralph Matthews

A FAMOUS explorer returning from Africa once had much to tell about the Dodo Bird, an extinct fowl which, it was later revealed, did not exist at all. When one sets out to write about the Negro Theatre, he feels almost as guilty as the hapless explorer after the exposé. The Negro Theatre, as such, is a Dodo Bird.

By this I do not intimate that there are not certain cardinal Negroid elements, certain contributions of an unmistakable Afric origin, certain psychological situations that could be born only in the mind of a transplanted race, that distinguish the productions in which black folk appear from those of any other group; but my main premise stands.

Because the American theatre is a commercialised industry instead of a medium merely for the expression of art for art's sake, the Negroes who have entered this field since emancipation have not been so much concerned with developing a vital, moving force depicting the soul of an oppressed people as they were with merely eking out an existence. Their paramount concern was, what side of the Negro can we sell?

No less an individual than the eminent psycho-analyst, Dr. A. A. Brill, answered this unconscious question most effectively when he said, " Everybody likes to laugh at a black man." Thus for the edification of the dominant race there grew up in the Negro theatre a type of entertainment from which they cannot break away. The black performer was looked upon only as a buffoon and a clown.

The early minstrels were predominantly " Rufus and Rastus " ignominiousness; and the later musical comedies which appeared in the gay nineties bore such titles as *Mr. Lode of Cole*, *A Trip to Coontown*, *Darktown Follies*, and other such names that must have cut deep into the very hearts of the producers and actors themselves.

After more than 30 years there seems to have taken place but slight departure from this same discriminating procedure, as the titles of *Blackbirds* and *Hot Chocolates* all carry the same contemptuous implications.

The work of the pioneer sepia showman was pretty well circumscribed. America accepted him only in the form that exploited his inherent abilities. Thus the musical comedy field, that gave him opportunity for singing and dancing, talents that are attributed to the black man as a racial heritage, flourished; while the drama, which required application, study and artificial development, could not get a foothold until after the late war. Even this, when presented in its most pretentious forms, could not conscientiously be classed as Negro theatre, because the productions for the most part are from the pens of white playwrights. Through their productions seeps an unconscious strain of Ofay psychology that presents the Negro not as he sees himself, but as he is seen through the condescending eyes of the detached observer. Thus only the extremities of Negro life have been brought on to the stage. *Porgy*, *In Abraham's Bosom*, *Emperor Jones* and *The Green Pastures*, all by white authors, fell into this category.

We find towering high above the names of our best dramatic stars the names of Dorothy and Dubose Heywood, Paul Green, Marc Connelly and Eugene O'Neil. In musical comedies this same situation pertains. White song-writers have been employed on innumerable occasions to be the tunesmiths for sepia revues. It is not my intention to give the impression that Negroes cannot create material for their own offerings, but to show that the American scheme of things does not always allow them this opportunity. In short, the two races have been so indistinguishably associated in the theatre that any attempt to find the line of demarcation would be the problem of a Diogenes.

That the Negro has made a very definite contribution to the American theatre is an irrefutable fact. His humor can be classified in three divisions. There is the droll, " po' me " type, created by Bert Williams, in which the poor black-faced comedian becomes the butt of adversity. His hard-luck situations appeal to the sympathies of his audience whose own sense of defeatism is minimised, and they find mental escape in his misfortunes.

This brand of fun-making also carries with it the Negro's supposed irresponsible and happy-go-lucky nature exemplified in the classic observation, " Hard times don't worry me because I didn't have nothing when times was good."

Contrasted with this we find the slicker type of character brought to the fore by S. H. Dudley, in which one Negro is able to take advantage of his more ignorant brethren.

The third classification finds its humor built on suggestiveness that is quite frankly termed smut. This depends for its appeal on the ease with which the spoken word can be twisted to a base and vulgar interpretation. The latter type of humor flourished most in the houses catering exclusively to a colored clientèle prior to, and for the period immediately following, the war, when colored actors in Metropolitan houses were few.

It was also upon this same type of suggestiveness that the phonograph-record era, which gave rise to an army of blues singers and coon shouters who yodeled their way along the trail blazed by Mamie Smith, was built. Therefore, we found among the best-selling titles such songs as *My Handy Man*, who, the song says, " beats my biscuits and churns my cream," and constant references to the unfortunate gentlemen who " can't climb a hill without shifting gears."

This same type of humor, which the Negro seems unusually prolific in creating, also accounts for the popularity of Harlem night clubs where Park Rowers seek a rendezvous from the politeness of their own circles. Little of the piquant witticisms of the polished Broadway commentators, that depend on their timeliness for their laugh-provoking effects, are found in Negro revues.

Since *Shuffle Along* brought about a renaissance in Negro theatricals, so far as its relation to Broadway was concerned, there came about a gradual change in the attitude toward Negro artists. The years saw them accepted, not as monstrosities or curiosities, but as people capable of giving entertainment value for money received. At that, however, the all-colored show during the decade that followed the memorable revival remained in the experimental stage with few exceptions, of which the *Blackbirds* productions of Lew Leslie were perhaps the most outstanding.

The success of *Shuffle Along* was no accident. During the years that intervened between the balmy days of Williams and Walker, Cole and Johnson and C. Aubrey Hill's productions, and the time that Miller and Lyles and Sissle and Blake brought *Shuffle Along* to Mazda Lane, there had been developing almost unnoticed a wealth of talent in the colored theatres held together by a makeshift circuit throughout the Southland and a few acts in the white houses. It was not until they were assembled under one huge banner and given sure-fire material that their capabilities became apparent.

At first the idea of sepia choruses, garbed or ungarbed in the fashions of Follies or Vanities blondes, was frowned upon, and many predicted that Broadway would not accept them. The fact that, unlike their fairer sisters, the former supplemented their ability to wear clothes with an ability to dance with a feverish abandon that the latter could not or did not acquire, made them instant hits.

During the time that colored shows had absented themselves from Broadway the race had improved in appearance, thanks to amalgamation and the good offices of such kink destroyers as the late Mme. C. J. Walker. Broadway was, therefore, pleasantly surprised at its first baptism of high yaller femininity.

The sepia torso tossers were literal bundles of energy, and their vivaciousness gave birth to the speed-show idea with its accompanying " Charlestons," " Blackbottoms " and other dances reminiscent of the levee and the plantation, all of which had a particular appeal to the group they sought to please.

Many will contend that the Negro theatre has found its own level in the past decade and that it has taken on a definite form that has buried the stigma of the past, which once left it standing like a dingy jim-crow car on the sideline as the palace coaches of the American theatre rumbled on their way. My contention is that it has merely undergone a transition and that the basic principles upon which America has always accepted the Negro still remain.

The old musical comedy scenes which showed him in overalls against a background depicting a Mississippi levee have given way to a night club panorama, and Harlem has supplanted Dixie as the name synonymous with Negro.

The plunking banjo and the cotton-field chant have been supplanted by the moaning saxophone and the rent-party wail. The melancholy spirituals have been replaced by the equally melancholy but less reverent blues, and the rhythm of the old plantation has vanished in the path of the weird and sensuous tempo of the jungle and the transplanted beat of the tom-tom.

The " Virginia " and " Chicken wheel " of the early minstrels, and the " Cakewalk " of the pioneer musical comedies have given way to the carefree abandonment of the devil dance. The brass band in its flaming red coats has been displaced by the jazz orchestra with its dancing baton-wielders and " skat " singers. The busy interlocutor is now called a master of ceremonies.

The Negro Theatre—A Dodo Bird

The big names among Negro performers are only those who have appealed to the whimsicalities of the white race and conformed to their idea of what a Negro should be.

Those who have confined their activities exclusively to what we might term the Negro theatre, have either vanished completely from the arena or are wallowing in mediocracy. The American black man honors only those whom the gods have chosen.

Let me not detract one iota from the glory that belongs to these hearty pioneers who braved the tempest in those early days when their profession was looked down upon not only by the opposite group, but by their own race as well. I have nothing but praise for these gladiators who invaded the benighted Southland, playing in stuffy theatres, travelling in discomfort, sleeping and eating in places unfit for decent habitation. Snubbed and ignored by the better citizenry, they carried on, lifting their calling by their own bootstraps until the proper recognition could be attained.

This was the hothouse of Negro theatricals, but in the path of the vitaphone, the radio and other mechanised forms of entertainment, it has almost mouldered into decay with a few outposts still remaining. Harlem is now the mecca of the Negro theatre and Broadway is its goal. This means assimilation. A merger of talents has taken and continues to take place with the increasing years. Both groups have profited by the pooling of their respective interests and contributions. The American theatre moves on to a finer, more cosmopolitan and higher pinnacle by virtue of these changes. The Negro theatre is a Dodo Bird.

Negro Creative Musicians

by EDWARD G. PERRY

Mr. Perry is a well-known young coloured musical critic on several of the Harlem papers

MOST Americans, and perhaps a majority of the people in many other parts of the world, are of the opinion that the spirituals are the Negro's only worthy contribution to the creative music of the world. Many of these people also believe that the spirituals, in their musical origin or inspiration, are based upon or derived from African rhythms or tribal songs. This, of course, is quite erroneous, since these folk-songs of the black man's early days of plantation slavery in America contain almost nothing that is African in their origin. Therefore, they are as much the creation of a group of people—now long removed from the native land of their black ancestors—as the folk-songs of the Russian peasants. And because these songs were born of the souls of men and women, who, through the hardships of slavery, fertilised a great portion of the soil of America, they are as much a part of the native music of this continent as that of any other group. They are, in the simplicity of their rhythmical beauty and fervor, not only a noble tribute to the creative genius of the black man but they are the supreme offering of America to the music of the world.

Therefore, if the modern Negro has not demonstrated any great ability as a creative musician, or has failed to contribute any outstanding and impressible compositions to the music of America and the world, it has not been because he has not thought of or attempted to do more serious work than his well-known arrangements of the spirituals and his later popular ballads, "rag-time," and jazz compositions, but only because he is living in a highly mechanised and material civilisation—a civilisation that is in every way inconsistent to the cultural and artistic advancement of its people—that he has turned, like other present-day creative artists, to work that is much more remunerative. That is, if the younger Negro musician has not developed his talent as a creator of the higher forms of music, he has certainly contributed much to the present popularity of American jazz. Therefore, considering these things, it is no discredit to the black people of America, or the world, that their musicians have not wrought any music of divine greatness, since it is almost too much of a fact that the so-called native music of other American composers has been, and apparently continues to be, somewhat muddled and sentimental carbon copies of the music of the old European masters.

Concerning the creative ability of the Negro musician, as long ago as the early part of the nineteenth century there were many well-educated colored people in New Orleans, a number of whom were talented musicians who also gained some distinction as composers; while in Philadelphia there were several colored men who not only wrote music but were publishers of it as well. In this latter group—from 1829 to 1880—were James Hemmenway, publisher of a musical journal known as *Atkinson's Casket*, and whose better-known compositions are *That Rest so Sweet like Bliss Above*, *The Philadelphia Grand Entrée March*, and *Hunter and Hope Waltzes*; Edwin Hill, the first Negro admitted to the Philadelphia Academy of Fine Arts, and A. J. Conner, whose compositions were published by reputable music houses in Boston and Philadelphia. Other composers of this period were Justin Holland, who wrote a number of compositions for the guitar, and Samuel Milady, known as *Sam Lucas*, who was the first Negro to write popular ballads; while two of the outstanding songs of the nineteenth century were written by colored men: James Bland composed *Carry me Back to Old Virginia*, and Septimus Winner, under the *nom de plume* of Alice Hawthorne, wrote and published *Listen to the Mockin' Bird*. The former song or ballad, *Carry me Back to Old Virginia*, has become almost a classic in its sentimental appeal and popularity among the American people.

But the most distinguished of all Negro composers, Samuel Coleridge-Taylor, was an Englishman of African descent. He was born in London during the first year of the last quarter of the nineteenth century. His father, a native of Sierra Leone, was a doctor of medicine in London. Having started to study music at the age of six, Coleridge-Taylor entered the Royal Academy of Music, London, when he was only sixteen. Later he was a pupil of Villera Stanford.

Although he composed many opus numbers, including a symphony, a sonata and other compositions of chamber music, Coleridge-Taylor's best-known works are his choral music, of which *Hiawatha*, a cantata in trilogy form, is outstanding, as it has been sung at various times in almost every modern country. He also composed three oratorios—*Herod*, *Nero*, and *Ulysses*; while *A Tale of Old Japan*, his last choral work, was an unprecedented success when it was first performed. Coleridge-Taylor, because he was endowed with a supreme knowledge of the pianoforte, composed music that is intelligently original in form, and even though it is sometimes astoundingly vigorous, it is written with such clarity and imagination that it is not only sensitive and beautiful but highly impressive.

Negro Creative Musicians

While Coleridge-Taylor was creating his great choral works and other compositions in London, the musicians of his race on this side of the Atlantic were by no means idle. They were working with the lighter forms of music and writing arrangements of the spirituals. This, of course, was at the turn of the century, when most of the musicians who had any creative ability were devoting their time and efforts to the popular ballads of the period. Foremost among these composers was Will Marion Cook, who not only wrote music but was, at different times, leader of two well-trained musical organisations—the Clef Club Orchestra and the New York Syncopated Orchestra—both of which attained much prominence during the early 1900's. And it was during these days that Cook wrote such popular ballads as *The Casino Girl*, *Bandanna Land*, and *Cruel Popupa*. But the two compositions of his which have been kept alive because they reveal something of his creative genius, are *Swing Along* and *Exhortation*. Although Will Marion Cook is still living, he has written very little during the past few years. But because he so greatly influenced the younger generation of Negro musicians and other artists he is still considered with much favor.

Perhaps no Negro musician has done as much for the musical advancement of his people as J. Rosamond Johnson, who was born in Jacksonville, Florida, and received his higher musical training at the New England Conservatory of Music in Boston. At the beginning of the twentieth century he was writing the music for the light operas and operettas presented by Klaw and Erlanger, two of the most famous producers of that day. He was also responsible for the musical scores of the extravaganzas produced by Klaw and Erlanger, and therefore wrote a number of songs for the stars of their shows, who were such eminent music-hall artists as Lillian Russell, Anna Held and May Irvin. Among the popular songs he composed at this time were *Under the Bamboo Tree*, *The Congo Love Song*, *My Castle on the Nile*, and *Lazy Moon*. In 1913 Johnson became the director of Hammerstein's Opera House, London, but soon resigned and returned to New York, where he became the guiding spirit of one of the first musical institutions for Negroes in this city—the Music School Settlement. Later he turned seriously to composition and wrote some distinctive arrangements of a large number of spirituals ; his later work includes a choral development of *Nobody Knows the Trouble I See* and several art songs, among them *Since You Went Away*, *The Awakening*, and *A Song of the Heart*. The latter songs are music of the finest quality, written in an original musical manner. The music for *Lift Every Voice and Sing*, a stirring song, magnificent in its emotional appeal, was written by Johnson, with lyrics by his brother, James Weldon Johnson, the eminent literary scholar, poet, author and diplomat. *Lift Every Voice and Sing* is popularly known as the Negro national anthem. So perhaps those people who call J. Rosamond Johnson " the apostle of Negro music taken seriously " are right.

The spirituals have played an important part in the recent cultural and artistic development of the Negro. That is, during the so-called *New Negro Renaissance*, hardly any Negro singer attempted a program without including a group of spirituals. Most of them felt that their programs would have been a failure without several of the folk-songs of their race included; while one or two singers even went so far as to offer entire programs of spirituals, which, it must be admitted, were highly successful financially.

Foremost among the arrangers of the spirituals is Henry Thackeray Burleigh, a native of Erie, Pennsylvania, who studied at the National Conservatory of Music and was a pupil of the great Anton Dvorák. Burleigh is a notable personage not only among Negro musicians but among the musicians of America. For many years his name has been, and continues to be, constantly before the public as an arranger of the spirituals and the composer of many " semi-classical " or art songs. He is also baritone soloist in one of the oldest and wealthiest Episcopal parishes in New York—St. George's Church, and is a member of the editorial staff of G. Ricordi and Co., one of the largest music publishing houses in America.

While Henry T. Burleigh is often considered the creator of the American art song, he has done more to bring about the high appreciation of the spirituals than any other Negro musician, unless it be Hall Johnson, whose work will be mentioned later. Those songs of his which are sung most, apart from his distinctive arrangements of the spirituals, are *Jean*, *In the Woods of Finvara*, *Were I a Star*, *The Grey Wolf*, *Three Shadows*, *The Saracen Song*, and *Passionale*.

While a large number of spirituals have been adapted in a singularly interesting manner by older Negro musicians, Hall Johnson, a native of Pennsylvania, and a young musician of rare genius, has written some arrangements that are so harmonic and rhythmic that they surpass in musical brilliance most of the efforts of his predecessors. But Johnson has not only given us some highly original adaptations of the spirituals but has turned his attention, with much success, to other Negro folk music—work songs, secular songs and native " blues." And while he has developed much of this folk music in a rather elaborate manner, he has done so without spoiling its sensitive, earthy quality.

And when this purely racial music is sung by the Hall Johnson Negro Choir—a group of singers whose training under the direction of Johnson has brought them notable success—it is given the greatest expression. This chorus alone, if nothing else, would give Johnson an outstanding place in any future musical history of America. For the genius of his fine musicianship is so skilfully displayed by the Hall Johnson Negro Choir, whose diction, harmonic wizardry and startling variation of rhythms are musical perfection. And because he has refused to compromise with those inhibited and too self-conscious members of his race, who would destroy in their arrangements the beauty and simplicity of the Negro folk-songs, by offering them without the dialect and inspirational fervor of their native creators, his contribution to our musical culture is a significant one. Of course, Hall Johnson has also composed a number of songs, all of which reveal his exceptional musical ability.

Few Negro composers have written compositions solely for the piano or other string and wind instruments. That is, most of them have been interested in music for the voice. But R. Nathaniel Dett, who is still a rather young man, has devoted much of his time to the creation of music for the pianoforte, even though he was for a number of years director of one of the finest choirs in the country—the Hampton Choir, at Hampton Institute, in Virginia. This musical organisation is now famous internationally, as a result of their excellent training under Dett. Unlike many other musicians of his race, Dett has found much that is beautiful in African rhythms, and many of his compositions for the pianoforte have sonorous, yet weird, exotic qualities, while certain portions of his *Magnolia Suite* and *Barcarolle* have the delicate brilliancy of the music of Debussy. Dett, of course, has written some fine arrangements of the spirituals, and among his other important compositions are *In the Bottoms*, *Juba Dance*, *Marche Nègre*, and a number of songs and oratorios.

Another musician whose compositions are known for their African themes is Ira Amanda Aldridge, daughter of the famous nineteenth-century Negro actor, Ira Aldridge. Miss Aldridge, who now writes under the *nom de plume* of Montague Ring, was born in London, where she still lives. She has written a number of songs, pianoforte compositions and ballet music, and conducted a performance of one of the latter compositions at Buckingham Palace.

Returning to America, one can find in the group of finer musicians here such men as Melville Charlton, distinguished organist, who once conducted grand opera performances in the famous ballroom of the old Waldorf Astoria Hotel, New York, served as organist for the largest and wealthiest Jewish congregation in New York, and is at present holding the same position at Union Theological Seminary, New York. Charlton has written an outstanding composition for the pianoforte in *Poème Erotique*. Others in this group are Carl Diton, organist, pianist and singer, whose compositions are an organ fantasie on *Swing Low Sweet Chariot*, and a choral arrangement of *Deep River*; Clarence Cameron White, concert violinist, composer of *Bandanna Sketches*, and Hugo Bornn, composer of two piano compositions of merit—*Song of the Siren* and *Moon Revel*. And there are a few younger musicians whose names should also be mentioned here for their distinctive arrangements of the spirituals: Eva Jessye, whose volume, *My Spirituals*, contains some adaptations that are rich with rhythm and melody; Lawrence Brown, Edward Boatner, Percival Parham, William Dawson and Edward Mathews.

In the field of musical drama the Negro musician's contribution has been almost negligible. Neither as a composer or a singer has he been successful. And while there are a few men and women with fine voices who are well prepared to sing on the operatic stage, there have been few if any worthy opportunities offered for them to do so; and the Negro composer has not given enough time to the building-up of a significant background to enter the field as a composer of significance.

But only recently a young woman, whose name is Shirley Graham, completed an opera in four acts called *Tom-Tom*, which was produced during the summer of 1932 by the Cleveland Summer Grand Opera with notable success. The opera has for its dramatic theme the transition of the Negro from Africa to America; and the composer in developing the music has attempted to synchronise it with the action of the story. That is, throughout the first scene of the opera only the percussion instruments are heard beating the rhythm of the tom-toms, while the spirituals are used to develop the dramatic interest during the days of slavery, and the final scenes have a musical theme of counterpoint that reaches into the field of modern jazz. Miss Graham, like most modern composers, has apparently had some difficulty in avoiding the music of some of her European predecessors, but her score contains enough exceptional music to make it more than interesting. Therefore, while *Tom-Tom* certainly has its faults, it is up to the present time the Negro musician's most significant venture in the field of grand opera.

Of course, one cannot afford to overlook Lawrence Freeman, who has devoted almost all of his musical talent to the opera, but his compositions, even though they are often interesting, lack the skilful requirements of the musical drama; while two other musicians—Clarence Cameron White and William Grant Still—show promise of better things.

Negro Creative Musicians

While the Negro has been able to keep the spirituals as his own native creation and contribution to the music of the world—even though other musicians and composers have interwoven them into the themes of their compositions—he has been fast losing ground as the original creator of jazz. This music, which is an outgrowth of Southern " rag-time," is now universal in its appeal, and was first introduced abroad by James Reese Europe, noted Negro band leader. While the " blues," like the spirituals, are still purely racial, they are in the same field as the old " rag-time " tunes, and many jazz compositions are therefore by-products of these strange and colorful songs.

Outstanding among the composers and arrangers of the " blues " is W. C. Handy, whose *St. Louis Blues* is almost a classic in its popular appeal. There is no doubt that this composition is the work of a first-rate musician; not only has it been heard over and over again in the dance casinos of America and Europe, but it has been sung in concert halls, and symphonic arrangements of it have been performed with much success. While there are other composers of the " blues," none of them have been able to achieve the success of W. C. Handy, whose compositions deserve serious consideration wherever they are heard. Three other composers who should and must be mentioned here are James Johnson for his *Yamacraw*; Duke Ellington for the exotic *Mood Indigo*, and Porter Grainger for his sincerely original Negro music. That is, if music can be called Negroid, then the music of Porter Grainger is just that. While among the better-known composers of jazz are Noble Sissle, Eubie Blake and Thomas Waller.

In conclusion, it might be mentioned here that Pitts Sanborn, eminent American music critic, writing in a recently-published volume, *America as Americans See It*, considers jazz " America's outstanding contribution, so far, to world music." Furthermore, Mr. Sanborn says that " Jazz jumped up, full fledged, of exotic origin, born of yearning for orgiastic display, supposedly among the roustabouts on the levees at New Orleans; but we hear of it very early indeed among the shrewd tone-merchants of Tin-Pan-Alley."

All of which deserves some consideration, of course, for the above-mentioned distinguished music critic not only overlooked the spirituals, as a part of the Negro's contribution to the music of America, but he failed to give them any credit for their exceptional ability as creators and musicians of jazz. Whether this was intentionally done or an oversight it is now difficult to say, but it is hardly possible that such an erudite musical personage as Mr. Sanborn could have overlooked the black man's contribution to the music of America or of the world.

Therefore, as in many other things, it is left to the Negro writer and pulpiteer to call to the attention of the world the Negro's gifts to its cultural and artistic advancement. Perhaps the Negro's contribution has not been of any supremely great and fundamental importance in recent years, but it has surely been significant enough to be recorded in any history of American music, since the impression he has made has been, and continues to be, so definite that it is impossible for any intelligent person to overlook its worth. Musically, the Negro is growing and there is no doubt that he will rise proportionately with other creative artists of the present day.

Remarks by Langston Hughes concerning Kay Boyle's Analysis of "On the Road," nd. [MS Boyle, Kay /Misc /Hughes, Langston. Harry Ransom Humanities Research Center, University of Texas at Austin.]

1. I think it would be a mistake to limit the meaning of the story to the predicament of the artist. This is not what I intended. I was writing of the little man, wherever he is and whoever he might be, but not necessarily of the creative man. I was writing, too, of Jesus as a human being whose meaning has been lost through the organization of the church and of religion. The functioning of religion in daily life, as the Reverend King has made it function, is what I was talking about in that story. It seemed important to me that Sergeant had done as much for Jesus in getting him down off the cross as Jesus had done for Sergeant in showing him that even the Savior of men had nowhere to go except to push on to Kansas City. This idea of everything that Jesus signified being kept away from the little people and nailed up on a cross out of reach for two thousand years is an idea I've written about before. I used it in a poem I'd like to read to you now.

[Hughes inserts a poem]

2. You said in your analysis that it was important to take into consideration the time at which the stories took place. This reminds me that just about the time I wrote "On the Road" the Scottsboro case was very much in the minds of all of us. That was the case of the Negro boys who hopped a freight-train in Alabama, going from one town to another looking for work. And in the box-car that night there were two white girls, dressed up like boys, looking for work too, and the boys were accused by the girls of attacking them. I'm sure this case was in my mind when I wrote about the coal car full of cops who brought their night sticks down on Sergeant's knuckles when he tried to pull himself into the car. The Scottsboro boys had been beaten up by the cops after the girls accused them, and one was even shot to death by two sheriffs as they took him. handcuffed in a car, from one jail to another. We were all aware of these things at the time the story was written.

3. I was not having a hard time making a living just at that time, for friends had lent me a house in Carmel, California, and I was living and writing there by the sea. But I happened to go to Reno for a visit, and I decided to stay and write there for a while. That was when this story and several other were written. It was during the depression, of course, and I took a room in a boarding-house because Negroes weren't allowed in the hotels. Everybody in the boarding-house was on relief, and the boarding-house keeper herself was on relief, and the food we had was what the relief agencies handed out. Negroes weren't allowed in the gambling places either, but neither were the American Indians who lived in Reno, but at least I could buy a drink and drink it, which the Indians were forbidden by law to do. Everybody in America was looking for work then, everybody moving from one place to another in search of a job. People who lived in the west were taking trains to the east because they had heard that there were jobs in the east, and people living in the east were taking trains to the west because they'd heard there were jobs out there. Sometimes they wouldn't get any farther than Reno, whichever way

1

they happened to be going, and none of them would have any money, so they'd build big fires near the railroad tracks, outside the town, and they'd collect around those fires and live like that until they could manage to go on again. I wrote in this story, you remember, about the makeshift houses made out of boxes and tin and old pieces of wood and canvas. "You couldn't see them in the dark, but you knew they were there if you'd ever been on the road, if you had ever lived with the homeless and hungry in a depression," I wrote.

4. You spoke of D.H. Lawrence, and I want to say that it was Lawrence's work that started me writing short stories. I was in Moscow on a newspaper assignment, and I hadn't written any fiction at all. And somebody gave me D.H. Lawrence's "The Rocking Horse Winner" to read, and I thought if I could say the things I wanted to say in stories like that instead of in articles, that would be the most wonderful thing in the world. So I started writing stories, and I guess I wrote twenty or more stories in three months. I sent them off to New York and every one of them was bought by magazines. That's how it began.

OUR BOOK SHELF

W. E. B. DuBois, Emmett J. Scott, Jr., Langston Hughes

The Book of American Negro Spirituals. By James Weldon Johnson, J. Rosamond Johnson and Lawrence Brown. The Viking Press, New York.

The Basis of Racial Adjustment. By Thomas Jackson Woofter, Jr. Ginn and Company, New York.

The Wooings of Jezebel Pettyfer. By Halbane MacFall. Alfred A. Knopf, New York.

The Sailor's Return. By David Garnett. Alfred A. Knopf, New York.

The Book of American Negro Spirituals

Mr. James Weldon Johnson has edited, with an introduction, a book of Negro spirituals containing musical arrangements chiefly by his brother, J. Rosamond Johnson, and with other arrangements by Lawrence Brown. The result is peculiarly satisfying.

It is one thing for a race to produce artistic material; it is quite another thing for it to produce the ability to interpret and criticize this material. This is particularly true when the artistic gift is a matter of primitive development in the rich childhood of a people. For a long time the Negro had to depend upon white critics for the presentation of his folk songs, and while Allen and White and Krehbiel did excellent work, they lacked the inner knowledge and inspiration which would make their word authoritative. The authors of this book bring these essential things.

Mr. Johnson's introduction, which runs over forty large pages, is in itself a most entertaining comment on the folk song. He characterizes "this noble music", defends the Negro as its original creator, examines the origin and "miracle" of its production. He then speaks of our late discovery of African art in various lines both in the Motherland and in other parts of the world. He has a notable explanation of the way in which the new Christian religion came to modify African music in America and make the Negro folk song possible. The process of folk song making is explained with interesting references to "Ma" White and "Singing" Johnson.

There is a study of variations in solo and chorus singing, in the use of melody and rhythm and the curiously difficult art of rendering them, and the many methods of approach. Mr. Johnson discusses the difficulty of recording these spirituals because of the "curious turns and twists and quavers and the intentional striking of certain notes just a shade off the key". The rhythm of the work songs is analyzed and that too of the "shout" songs and of the dance which has so largely disappeared now from the Negro churches. There is a special attention paid to the fact that the folk songs were harmonized by the singers and not sung in unison as some have assumed, and Mr. Rosamond Johnson and Mr. Brown have especially brought this out in their renditions, with a great deal of care and with notable success.

The poetry of the folk songs is illustrated by many quotations, such as "De blood came twinklin' down", "Sometimes I feel like a motherless child" and others. There are several pages on Negro dialect and generous acknowledgment of the credit due those who have helped preserve the Negro spiritual. "The credit for the first introduction of spirituals to the American public and the world belongs to Fisk University." The book has words and music of 61 songs. "The collection here presented is not definitive but we have striven to make it representative of this whole field of music, to give examples of every variety of spiritual."

The musical setting as done in this book one must hear to appreciate the peculiarly high and unique quality of the work. Never before have the "Spirituals" had just this sort of original and yet true musical accompaniment. It is as though something unknown and wild and yet sensed in the song of black folk had been caught and caged forever.

The book is published by the Viking Press and it is hoped that it will have wide use and vogue.

W. E. B. D.

Our Book Shelf

Second Book of Negro Spirituals—By JAMES WELDON JOHNSON. Viking Press. $3.00.

James Weldon Johnson in his preface to the Second Book of Negro Spirituals treats a multiplicity of themes the origin and sociological significance of the spirituals, the Negroes' psychology and contribution to American folk literature and art, the philosophy of the blues, the author of ragtime and jazz and the artistic potentialities of Negro music. His facts are marshaled logically; his style is lucid and his diction frequently reaches the heights of poetic prose. No wonder, he has the soul of a poet.

When I consider the large number of dedications appearing on J. Rosamond Johnson's arrangements I recall the fact that it is related of Scriabin, the Great Russian Tone-Poet, that never did he follow the custom of a super-inscribed dedication to any influential person as an inducement for the person to cultivate a composition. The wide popularity and success of Mr. Johnson's previous undedicated compositions demonstrate that he does not have to employ any artifice to win success, and the public loves the inspiring spirituals. These facts rendered dedications unnecessary for commercial reasons, consequently uncharitable remarks concerning the dedications are palpably absurd.

The musical arrangements, while manifesting the æsthetic faculty of the composer are not always Negro. The influence of modern European harmony is occasionally perceptible. This is not to be wondered at. Any student of social science knows that races having cultural contact frequently influence each other. Did not the early Italian opera influence the German, Wagner; and did not Wagner in turn affect Italian opera? Mr. Johnson's tasteful arrangements are simpler harmonically and technically than the arrangements of some other composers. Choice offsetting is a matter of individual taste; *De gustibus non est disputandum*. The principal object is to reveal in the spirituals the soul of the Negro and this has been accomplished by the arranger.

Some prejudiced critics, especially Henry T. Finck, do not wish the Negro folk songs to be used as the basis of American composition, but prefer the songs of Stephen Foster. Finck himself admits that Foster attended Negro camp meetings and studied plantation life in general. Since the Negroes sang at the camp meetings and Foster listened, any plagiarism could not have been perpetrated by the Negroes but by Foster.

Some would have us confine our efforts to folk songs and dialect English. Would Wagner have produced his music-dramas if all Germans had confined their efforts to German folk songs? Would the painters of Europe have created their diversified styles and schools if they had executed only genre pictures? Nationalism, racial elements and local color can easily be overdone in art.

Let the Negro artists develop and sublimate not only their racial elements and small art forms but let them like the Anglo-African Samuel Coleridge-Taylor create works in the larger forms. Then will they conduce to human happiness by originating productions of æsthetic variety.

MELVILLE CHARLTON.

Book Shelf

DARK LAUGHTER, By Sherwood Anderson; a novel, published by Boni & Liveright. $2.50.

During the last two or three years American literature has been wonderfully enriched by the infusion of competent material by and about the Negro. Fiction, poetry, *belles lettres* and the literature of information and opinion have all discovered a new and interesting field for exploration and speculation; and the creative abilities of a growing group of colored writers have received an opportunity and a delighted hearing which augur well for the immediate future of American culture. Unless I am badly mistaken, Messrs. Boni & Liveright were among the first to offer encouragement and a well known imprint to this significant trend.

It was with this background of knowledge and appreciation that I opened Mr. Anderson's latest novel and his first for these publishers. Further, my interest had been whetted by a friend's remark that the Negro in *Dark Laughter* played a role somewhat similar to that of the tom-toms in that extraordinary play, *The Emperor Jones.* The crescendo of those drums was in my ears as I began the book, and I was all attention for the first far-off faintness of a similar *motif.*

Mr. Anderson's method of writing *Dark Laughter* is such that one must read it carefully, or not at all. All the attention that goes ino unravelling a snarl of yarn must be freely given if one is to follow the thread of the story without danger of breaking it, with the necessity of reknotting it later. But the effort is worthwhile. It does not, however, discover any genuine racial rhythm. To be sure, Negroes flash into the story and fade out again—as aimlessly as the fireflies of a summer evening. They are "niggers" and we are *told* that they dance, that they sing, that they are lazy, that they are unmoral, that two of them work as servants in the house which becomes the main setting for Mr. Anderson's story. And we are told from time to time that they laugh. The effect is that of grabbing sundry stage Negroes and making them "walk Spanish" across the picture of the story.

We *hear* the drums in *The Emperor Jones.* We are not told about them. They beat their way into us and dominate our pulse. Mr. Anderson's Negroes are as fireflies in the radiance of a summer moon.

Having established (to my own satisfaction, at least) that *Dark Laughter* adds nothing to the literature of the Negro, or of the interplay of races in the United States, and that, therefore, a review of this book is of no more *sociological* significance to *Opportunity* than would be a review of, say, *The Constant Nymph,* may I report that Mr. Anderson has written a most interesting story which amply repays the attention demanded of the reader by the method of telling it?

The principal male character escapes from a wife and the self-conscious Bohemia of word-and-paint slingers in Chicago. He is at work as a factory hand in a southern Indiana town when the story opens, but much is said about his Chicago background. To this Indiana town comes the woman of the story as wife of the owner of the factory. Her origin is also Chicago (of a different sort), but her immediate background is a certain erotic night in Paris after the war. Her husband is a well drawn character of the Babbitt type and at the end of the story he is left pretty flat and impotent as Bruce, with two suitcases, and Aline, with the prospect of childbirth, stumble down a pitch-black path towards the river.

In the main, the story is developed in terms of the thoughts of Bruce, Aline and her husband, Fred. Bruce, standing at his bench in the factory, turns over in his mind his life in Chicago, his escape and wanderings. Aline, with an unread book in her lap, remembers Paris, thinks about her husband, speculates about Bruce. Fred, puffing up the hill from factory to home, likewise lets his mind run free.

Here are three minds busily spinning threads of memory, thought and pure speculation. The threads are short, long, bright, dull or dark, depending upon the character and his immediate state of mind. They are spun out by the page for the reader to pick up, straighten out and twist into the yarn of the story. It takes effort but it is stimulating effort and a good yarn is the result of success. Indeed, there is a sense of disappointment in the few passages where this method would have been particularly brilliant, but where the author lapses into direct narrative.

Readers of *Opportunity* will find *Dark Laughter* a book well worth the reading. But it does not qualify as a contribution to interracial literature despite the possible implication in the title, the pattern of the story and the statement on the paper jacket. Three years ago it might have been said to qualify because then we were hungry even for crumbs.

WILLIAM H. BALDWIN.

Book Shelf

PORGY, By Du Bose Heyward, published by George H. Doran Company, New York City, Price $2.00

A few weeks ago I felt that, with a few reservations permitted, I could match Carl Van Vechten's appraisal of THE WOOINGS OF JEZEBEL PETTYFER as the best novel on the Negro by a white author that I had read. Since then, however, I have read PORGY.

Mr. Heyward is a southerner and a poet, a combination one half of which qualifies him to write of Negro life in Catfish Alley in a small South Carolina town, while the other half has undoubtedly helped him to fashion so fine and pathetic a story. Here is a white author who wastes no maudlin sentiment on his characters, yet gives one the uncanny feeling that Negroes are human beings and that white and black southerners are brothers under the skin. The story is a simple one: Porgy, a cripple from birth and therefor a beggar by profession, has had little joy in life, until he meets Bess, the loose, dissolute woman of Crown, a quarrelsome black giant who is forced to flee the town when he commits a murder. Porgy and Bess join forces and work double miracles; they adopt a baby and the future looms roseate. Then Crown returns; Porgy removes this impediment to his happiness, and provides an insurmountable defense. But the authorities want someone to identify the dead man; they draft Porgy. This is too much for Porgy's simple superstitious frame. Perhaps he fears the dead man's wounds will bleed at sight of him. He fails to appear at the inquest and is given a short term of imprisonment for contempt of court. Upon his release he finds that Bess could not prevail without him; "happy dust" and the lustful workers on the levee have beaten down her resistance. Porgy snaps like a too taut string.

As far as any white man can understand a Negro's feelings, Mr. Heyward scores; and inasmuch as there are depths in a black man's mind totally inassessible to the most adroit white plumbing, Mr. Heyward should regard his as a satisfactory performance. But he understands *white* southerners better than most other white novelists do, if we take their work as prima facie evidence. We know how the southern heat is supposed to affect all Negroes, but Mr. Heyward enlightens us in a passage on white jailers when he says, "it would have meant effort to better the living conditions, and effort on the part of a white warden in August was not to be considered"—a plain case of the kinship between the Governor and Judy O'Grady's husband.

Any book, however steeped in pathos and tragedy, that attempted to treat the Negro without due respect to his humor would do its subject an irreparable injustice. Mr. Heyward strikes the golden mean in his humorous passages; he does not offend us with the buffoonery and burlesque of which we are rightfully sick and tired. He realizes that Negro humor is an intricately subtle affair even in its most naive expressions. While I can't admire the politics of Simon Frasier, the ancient Negro attorney who "had voted the democratic ticket in the dark days of reconstruction, when such action on his part took no little courage, and accordingly enjoyed the almost unlimited toleration of the aristocracy," I can enjoy his ingenious divorce mill with its succinct eradication of existing evils thus: "I, Simon Frasier, hereby divorce Rachel Smalls and Columbus Devo for the charge of one dollar; signed, Simon Frasier."

I don't know enough about dialect to quarrel strenuously with Mr. Heyward's skill or lack of it in that field, but it does seem to me that the northern gambler, Sportin' Life, should have spoken differently from the inhabitants of Catfish Alley; even if he just had to speak dialect, the brand should have been different. I also arch a skeptic brow at "Jedus" for "Jesus;" and I can't by any stretch of imagination conceive of "I gots" for "I got;" an illiterate Negro would say "I has." But these are small and almost gratuitous objections to raise to a book that is otherwise so completely likeable. Read PORGY!

COUNTEE CULLEN.

Porgy. By DuBose Heyward. George H. Doran Company. New York. 1925. 196 *pages.*

DuBose Heyward's little novel of colored Charleston life, "Porgy", is a beautiful piece of work. It is the Iliad of a small black beggar in the underworld of labor and crime surrounded by whiskey and lust and sanctified with music, a queer and quaint religion and a great yearning flood of love.

Seldom before has a white Southern writer done black folk with so much of sympathy and subtle understanding. Heyward knows Porgy and his fellows; but his very knowledge brings forward the old and ever young criticism: Charleston has 35,000 persons of Negro descent. They include not only pitiful and terrible figures —beggars, drunkards and prostitutes—but self-supporting and self-respecting laborers and servants, artisans and merchants, professional men and housewives. There is a group of educated and well-to-do folk, beautiful in character and face, who look back on generations of freedom and comfort and accomplishment. Out of Charleston for a hundred years has flowed leadership of the colored folk of America and in Charleston still rest men and women who would be a credit to any modern nation.

And yet if Charleston were swept by a cataclysm tomorrow, and the archaeologists of the 40th century searched white men's writings to learn of its inhabitants in the 20th century, "Porgy" would remain as the best, almost the only picture. It would be a fine picture of the best type of Negro which DuBose Heyward could really know. Into the black underworld he can go almost unhindered save by that subtle veil he so delicately paints. But between him and the main mass of Charleston Negroes there is an unpassable gulf. Whose ever the fault is, the loss to art is irreparable.

W. E. B. D.

Color -- A Review

By ALAIN LOCKE

LADIES and gentlemen! A genius! Posterity will laugh at us if we do not proclaim him now. COLOR transcends all the limiting qualifications that might be brought forward if it were merely a work of talent. It is a first book, but it would be treasurable if it were the last; it is a work of extreme youth and youthfulness over which the author later may care to write the apology of "juvenilia," but it has already the integration of a distinctive and matured style; it is the work of a Negro poet writing for the most part out of the intimate emotional experience of race, but the adjective is for the first time made irrelevant, so thoroughly has he poetized the substance and fused it with the universally human moods of life. Cullen's own Villonesque poetic preface to the contrary, time will not outsing these lyrics.

The authentic lyric gift is rare today for another reason than the rarity of poetic genius, and especially so in contemporary American poetry—for the substance of modern life brings a heavy sediment not easy to filter out in the poetic process. Only a few can distill a clear flowing product, Housman, de la Mare, Sara Teasdale, Edna St. Vincent Millay, one or two more perhaps. Countee Cullen's affinity with these has been instantly recognized. But he has grown in sandier soil and taken up a murkier substance; it has taken a longer tap-root to reach down to the deep tradition upon which great English poetry is nourished, and the achievement is notable. More than a personal temperament flowers, a race experience blooms; more than a reminiscent crop is gathered, a new stalk has sprouted and within the flower are, we believe, the seeds of a new stock, richly parented by two cultures. It is no disparagement to our earlier Negro poets to say this: men do not choose their time, and time is the gardener.

Why argue? Why analyze? The poet himself tells us

Drink while my blood
Colors the wine.

But it is that strange bouquet of the verses themselves that must be mulled to be rightly appreciated. Pour into the vat all the Tennyson, Swinburne, Housman, Patmore, Teasdale you want, and add a dash of Pope for this strange modern skill of sparkling couplets,—and all these I daresay have been intellectually culled and added to the brew, and still there is another evident ingredient, fruit of the Negro inheritance and experience, that has stored up the tropic sun and ripened under the storm and stress of the American transplanting. Out of this clash and final blend of the pagan with the Christian, the sensual with the Puritanically religious, the pariah with the prodigal, has come this strange new thing. The paradoxes of Negro life and feeling that have been sad and plaintive and whimsical in the age of Dunbar and that were rhetorical and troubled, vibrant and accusatory with the Johnsons and MacKay now glow and shine and sing in this poetry of the youngest generation.

COLOR, by COUNTEE CULLEN. Harper & Brothers, New York. $2.

This maturing of an ancestral heritage is a constant note in Cullen's poetry. *Fruit of the Flower* states it as a personal experience:

My father is a quiet man
 With sober, steady ways;
For simile, a folded fan;
 His nights are like his days.

My mother's life is puritan,
 No hint of cavalier,
A pool so calm you're sure it can
 Have little depth to fear.

And yet my father's eyes can boast
 How full his life has been;
There haunts them yet the languid ghost
 Of some still sacred sin.

And though my mother chants of God,
 And of the mystic river,
I've seen a bit of checkered sod
 Set all her flesh aquiver.

Why should he deem it pure mischance
 A son of his is fain
To do a naked tribal dance
 Each time he hears the rain?

Why should she think it devil's art
 That all my songs should be
Of love and lovers, broken heart,
 And wild sweet agony?

Who plants a seed begets a bud,
 Extract of that same root;
Why marvel at the hectic blood
 That flushes this wild fruit?

Better than syllogisms, *Gods* states the same thing racially:

I fast and pray and go to church,
 And put my penny in,
But God's not fooled by such slight tricks,
 And I'm not saved from sin.

I cannot hide from Him the gods
 That revel in my heart,
Nor can I find an easy word
 To tell them to depart:

God's alabaster turrets gleam
  Too high for me to win,
Unless He turns His face and lets
  Me bring my own gods in.

Here as indubitably as in Petrarch or Cellini or Stella, there is the renaissance note. What body of culture would not gladly let it in! In still more conscious conviction we have this message in the *Shroud of Color*:

Lord, not for what I saw in flesh or bone
Of fairer men; not raised on faith alone;
Lord, I will live persuaded by mine own.
I cannot play the recreant to these;
My spirit has come home, that sailed the
    doubtful seas.

The latter is from one of the two long poems in the volume; both it and *Heritage* are unusual achievements. They prove Mr. Cullen capable of an unusually sustained message. There is in them perhaps a too exuberant or at least too swiftly changing imagery, but nevertheless they have a power and promise unusual in this day of the short poem and the sketchy theme. They suggest the sources of our most classic tradition, and like so much that is most moving in English style seem bred from the Bible. Occasionally one is impressed with the fault of too great verbal facility, as though words were married on the lips rather than mated in the heart and mind, but never is there pathos or sentimentality, and the poetic idea always has taste and significance.

Classic as are the fundamentals of this verse, the overtones are most modernly enlightened:

The earth that writhes eternally with pain
Of birth, and woe of taking back her slain
Laid bare her teeming bosom to my sight,
And all was struggle, gasping breath, and fight.
A blind worm here dug tunnels to the light,
And there a seed, tacked with heroic pain,
Thrust eager tentacles to sun and rain.

Still more scientifically motivated, is:

Who shall declare
  My whereabouts;
Say if in the air
  My being shouts
Along light ways,
  Or if in the sea
Or deep earth stays
  The germ of me?

The lilt is that of youth, but the body of thought is most mature. Few lyric poets carry so sane and sober a philosophy. I would sum it up as a beautiful and not too optimistic pantheism, a rare gift to a disillusioned age. Let me quote at the end my favorite poem, one of its best expressions:

THE WISE.

Dead men are wisest, for they know
How far the roots of flowers go,
How long a seed must rot to grow.

Dead men alone bear frost and rain
On throbless heart and heatless brain,
And feel no stir of joy or pain.

Dead men alone are satiate;
They sleep and dream and have no weight,
To curb their rest, of love or hate.

Strange, men should flee their company,
Or think me strange who long to be
Wrapped in their cool immunity.

Our Book Shelf

Books Which You Must Know About Reviewed by Sympathetic Readers. All of Them Are for Sale at THE CRISIS *Book Shop*

The New Negro, edited by Alain Locke. Albert and Charles Boni, New York, 1925. 446 *pages.*

THIS extraordinary book in many ways marks an epoch. It is in many respects sprawling, illogical, with an open and unashamed lack of unity and continuity, and yet it probably expresses better than any book that has been published in the last ten years the present state of thought and culture among American Negroes and it expresses it so well and so adequately, with such ramification into all phases of thought and attitude, that it is a singularly satisfying and inspiring thing.

It has, too, more than most books, a history. The well-known magazine, *The Sur-*

vey, which represents organized social reform in America, has always been traditionally afraid of the Negro problem and has usually touched it either not at all or gingerly. Even last year one of the editors at a great meeting of social workers in Los Angeles succeeded in talking over an hour on the social problems of America, dividing and examining them exhaustively both geographically and qualitatively, and yet said no word on the race problems.

Notwithstanding this *The Survey* has grown and developed tremendously in the last few years. I remember vividly being asked by *The Survey* to furnish it for the New Year 1914 a statement of the aims of the N. A. A. C. P. I did so and said among other things:

Sixth—Finally, in 1914, the Negro must demand his social rights. His right to be treated as a gentleman when he acts like one, to marry any sane, grown person who wants to marry him, and to meet and eat with his friends without being accused of undue assumption or unworthy ambition.

No sooner had the editors of *The Survey* read this than they telephoned frantically to some of the directors of the N. A. A. C. P. and they found easily several who did not agree with this statement and one indeed who threatened to resign if it were published. *The Survey* therefore refused to publish my statement unless this particular paragraph were excised. The statement was not published.

Since then much water has flowed under the bridge and it happened last year that the editor of *The Survey* was sitting next to Mr. A. G. Dill, our business manager, at a dinner given to Miss Fauset in honor of the appearance of her novel, "There Is Confusion". The editor looked at the company with interest and Mr. Dill began to tell him who they were. It occurred to the editor of *The Survey* that here was material for a *Survey Graphic;* still he hesitated and feared the "social uplifters" of the United States with a mighty fear. But he took one step which saved the day: He got a colored man to edit that number of the *Graphic*, Alain Locke, a former Rhodes scholar and a professor at Howard University. Locke did a good job, so good a job that this Negro number of the *Survey Graphic* was one of the most successful numbers ever issued by *The Survey*.

It was a happy thought on the part of the Bonis to have the material thus collected, arranged and expanded, combined with the painting and decoration of Winold Reiss and issued as a book which states and explains the present civilization of black folk in America. Mr. Locke has done a fine piece of editing. The proof reading, the bibliographies and the general arrangement are all beyond criticism.

With one point alone do I differ with the Editor. Mr. Locke has newly been seized with the idea that Beauty rather than Propaganda should be the object of Negro literature and art. His book proves the falseness of this thesis. This is a book filled and bursting with propaganda but it is propaganda for the most part beautifully and painstakingly done; and it is a grave question if ever in this world in any renaissance there can be a search for disembodied beauty which is not really a passionate effort to do something tangible, accompanied and illumined and made holy by the vision of eternal beauty.

Of course this involves a controversy as old as the world and much too transcendental for practical purposes, and yet, if Mr. Locke's thesis is insisted on too much it is going to turn the Negro renaissance into decadence. It is the fight for Life and Liberty that is giving birth to Negro literature and art today and when, turning from this fight or ignoring it, the young Negro tries to do pretty things or things that catch the passing fancy of the really unimportant critics and publishers about him, he will find that he has killed the soul of Beauty in his Art.

W. E. B. DuBois.

Our Book Shelf

POET ON POET

The Weary Blues—LANGSTON HUGHES. Alfred Knopf & Co. $2.00

Here is a poet with whom to reckon, to experience, and here and there, with that apologetic feeling of presumption that should companion all criticism, to quarrel.

What has always struck me most forcibly in reading Mr. Hughes' poems has been their utter spontaneity and expression of a unique personality. This feeling is intensified with the appearance of his work in concert between the covers of a book. It must be acknowledged at the outset that these poems are peculiarly Mr. Hughes' and

Photo by Nicholas Murray.

LANGSTON HUGHES

no one's else. I cannot imagine his work as that of any other poet, not even of any poet of that particular group of which Mr. Hughes is a member. Of course, a microscopic assiduity might reveal derivation and influences, but these are weak undercurrents in the flow of Mr. Hughes' own talent. This poet represents a transcendently emancipated spirit among a class of young writers whose particular battle-cry is freedom. With the enthusiasm of a zealot, he pursues his way, scornful, in subject matter, in photography, and rhythmical treatment, of whatever obstructions time and tradition have placed before him. To him it is essential that he be himself. Essential and commendable surely; yet the thought persists that some of these poems would have been better had Mr. Hughes held himself a bit in check. In his admirable introduction to the book, Carl Van Vechten says the poems have a *highly deceptive air of spontaneous improvisation.* I do not feel that the air is deceptive.

If I have the least powers of prediction, the first section of this book, *The Weary Blues,* will be most admired, even if less from intrinsic poetical worth than because of its dissociation from the traditionally poetic. Never having been one to think all subjects and forms proper for poetic consideration, I regard these jazz poems as interlopers in the company of the truly beautiful poems in other sections of the book. They move along with the frenzy and electric heat of a Methodist or Baptist revival meeting, and affect me in much the same manner. The revival meeting excites me, cooling and flushing me with alternate chills and fevers of emotion; so do these poems. But when the storm is over, I wonder if the quiet way of communing is not more spiritual for the God-seeking heart; and in the light of reflection I wonder if jazz poems really belong to that dignified company, that select and austere circle of high literary expression which we call poetry. Surely, when in *Negro Dancers* Mr. Hughes says

Me an' ma baby's
Got two mo' ways,
Two mo' ways to do de buck!

he voices, in lyrical, thumb-at-nose fashion the happy careless attitude, akin to poetry, that is found in certain types. And certainly he achieves one of his loveliest lyrics in *Young Singer.* Thus I find myself straddling a fence. It needs only *The Cat and The Saxaphone,* however, to knock me over completely on the side of bewilderment, and incredulity. This creation is a *tour de force* of its kind, but is it a poem:

EVERYBODY

Half-pint,—
Gin?
No, make it

LOVES MY BABY

corn. You like
don't you, honey?
BUT MY BABY..............

In the face of accomplished fact, I cannot say *This will never do,* but I feel that it ought never to have been done.

But Mr. Hughes can be as fine and as polished as you like, etching his work in calm, quiet lyrics that linger and repeat themselves. Witness *Sea Calm*:

How still,
How strangely still
The water is today.
It is not good
For water
To be so still that way.

Or take *Suicide's Note*:

The Calm,
Cool face of the river
Asked me for a kiss.

Then crown your admiration with *Fantasy in Purple,* this imperial swan-song that sounds like the requiem of a dying people:

Beat the drums of tragedy for me,
Beat the drums of tragedy and death.
And let the choir sing a stormy song
To drown the rattle of my dying breath.

Beat the drums of tragedy for me,
And let the white violins whir thin and slow,
But blow one blaring trumpet note of sun
To go with me to the darkness where I go.

Mr. Hughes is a remarkable poet of the colorful; through all his verses the rainbow riots and dazzles, yet never wearies the eye, although at times it intrigues the brain into astonishment and exaggerated admiration when reading, say something like *Caribbean Sunset*:

God having a hemorrhage,
Blood coughed across the sky,
Staining the dark sea red:
That is sunset in the Caribbean.

Taken as a group the selections in this book seem one-sided to me. They tend to hurl this poet into the gaping pit that lies before all Negro writers, in the confines of which they become racial artists instead of artists pure and simple. There is too much emphasis here on strictly Negro themes; and this is probably an added reason for my coldness toward the jazz poems—they seem to set a too definite limit upon an already limited field.

Dull books cause no schisms, raise no dissensions, create no parties. Much will be said of *The Weary Blues* because it is a definite achievement, and because Mr. Hughes, in his own way, with a first book that cannot be dismissed as merely *promising,* has arrived.

Countee Cullen

"The New Negro—An Interpretation"—Edited by Alain Locke—Albert and Charles Boni, publishers, New York City. **(Price $5.00—466 pgs.)**

If I were a spiritualist I should say that the spirit of old Fra Albertus had controlled the craftsman who made this book. It is a thing of rare beauty, a beauty almost prodigal. This is not a book to lend, for few persons examining its beautiful pages will have the virtue to return it. Alain Locke is fundamentally an æsthete, and Winold Reiss' appreciation of the lovely is well known. These two have done a job worthy of themselves in this volume and the House of Boni can congratulate itself on turning out such a product.

The cover design is striking, the type fresh and bold, the margins wide, the decorative illustrations novel, the drawings and symbolic sketches of Aaron Douglass powerful and effective, the two studies by Miguel Covarrubias startling in their animation, and the sixteen portrait studies in color by Winold Reiss, beautiful and revealing. The physical side of the book—utterly apart from its reading matter, makes the volume a valuable possession—one to be treasured.

However, the reading matter is worthy of the physical makeup. There are twenty essays—most of them very well done, eight stories by young Negroes, thirty-seven poems from nine Negro poets, a Negro play, two Negro folk-tales, and an excellent bibliography. Most of the matter appeared before in the HARLEM NUMBER of the SURVEY GRAPHIC. Many of us at that time felt it deserved more permanent form. Here you have it with additions. The book is divided into two parts—*the Negro Renaissance* and *the New Negro in the New World.*

The first division consists of a foreword and four introductory essays on the new Negro, his art and literature. Short stories and poetry follows, revealing to us that art and literature which has been commented upon. Here we see the genius of Jean Toomer and the technique of Rudolph Fisher; here we experience the beauty of Countee Cullen, the bitterness of McKay, the sophisticated abandon of Langston Hughes and the revealing imagery of James Weldon Johnson.

Now follows a Negro play preceded by two essays that deal with Negro drama; and then we have Negro music, spiritual and dance, revealed by essays and poems. The first division of the book ends with three essays on the hereditary culture of the Negro, followed by two folk-tales and that great poem of Cullen's—*"Heritage".*

Part two of the book is a sociological chart of the action and inter-action of the New Negro and the New World upon each other. It consists of essays under the general heading—"The Negro Pioneers"; "The New Frontage on American Life"; "The New Scene"; "The Negro and American Traditions"; and "Worlds of Color". It contains remarkable contributions by DuBois, Domingo, James Weldon Johnson, and Charles Johnson.

The collection which comprises the book has been carefully chosen and for the most part is excellent. Contributions, of course are uneven—an inevitable thing in a work of this sort. There are a few extravagant claims in some of the essays; an uncertain touch now and then, but these faults are few in number. One misses certain names and may question whether some of the subject matter might not have been handled more expertly by other writers than those chosen. But this questioning is further proof of the truth of thesis of the book—the richness of the new flowering of Negro culture.

There is however, one glaring fault in the book which we cannot overlook. It is the frequency with which the editor Mr. Locke, obtrudes himself upon the scene. Five times he appears before its footlights, reminding one of those chairmen who must make a new speech everytime he introduces a new speaker. It would have been in much better taste, we feel, if the last three essays that bear Mr. Locke's name, had been written by someone else. In fact, he assays to cover practically the same field Stanley Braithwaite has already covered in one of these essays and in another—that of the Negro Spiritual—he is open to serious criticism both as to omission and interpretation. However, his foreword and essay on the New Negro are masterly.

The book essays "to document the New Negro culturally and socially", and it does just that. It convinces its readers that the New Negro is and that he possesses gifts which the world must recognize. This book must prove a revelation to that world which has known the Negro only in terms of controversial literature and has seen only in the familiar stereotypes featured by the Cobbs and the Cohens. It will prove a revelation also to many Negroes themselves—that group which has accepted the white world's evaluation of its race. These will find new stirrings as they come to see this new Negro whose outlook is bounded only by world horizons, and who expresses his culture in terms of wonderful beauty and power.

Seldom do we find in the book-stalls, so rich and beautiful an offering, or one so revealing of the soul of a people. The book portrays indeed the resurgence of a race to a rich and high culture.

ROBERT W. BAGNALL.

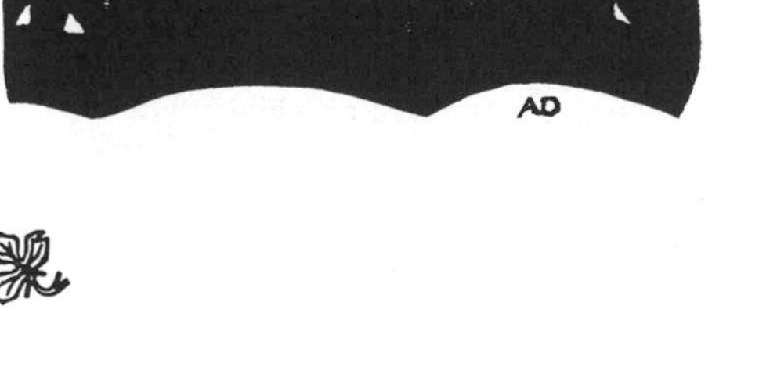

Our Book Shelf

Books Which You Must Know About Reviewed by Sympathetic Readers. All of Them Are for Sale at The CRISIS Book Shop

Color. A Book of Verse. By Countee Cullen. Harper & Brothers, New York. 1925. 108 *pages.*

COLOR is the name of Mr. Cullen's book and color is, rightly, in every sense its prevailing characteristic. For not only does every bright glancing line abound in color but it is also in another sense the yard-stick by which all the work in this volume is to be measured. Thus his poems fall into three categories: Those, and these are very few, in which no mention is made of color; those in which the adjectives "black" or "brown" or "ebony" are deliberately introduced to show that the type which the author had in mind was not white; and thirdly the poems which arise out of the consciousness of being a "Negro in a day like this" in America.

These last are not only the most beautifully done but they are by far the most significant group in the book. I refer especially to poems of the type of "Yet do I Marvel", "The Shroud of Color", "Heritage" and "Pagan Prayer". It is in such work as this that the peculiar and valuable contribution of the American colored man is to be made to American literature. For any genuine poet black or white might have written "Oh for a Little While be Kind" or the lines to "John Keats"; the idea contained in a "Song of Praise" was used long ago by an old English poet and has since been set to music by Roger Quilter. But to pour forth poignantly and sincerely the feelings which make plain to the world the innerness of the life which black men live calls for special understanding. Cullen has packed into four illuminating lines the psychology of colored Americans, that strange extra dimension which totally artificial conditions have forced into a sharp reality. He writes:

All day long and all night through,
One thing only must I do:
Quench my pride and cool my blood,
Lest I perish in the flood.

That is the new expression of a struggle now centuries old. Here I am convinced is Mr. Cullen's forte; he has the feeling and the gift to express colored-ness in a world of whiteness. I hope he will not be deflected from continuing to do that of which he has made such a brave and beautiful beginning. I hope that no one crying down "special treatment" will turn him from his native and valuable genre. There is no "universal treatment"; it is all specialized. When Kipling spoke of having the artist to

"paint the thing as he sees it
For the God of things as they are",

he set the one infallible rule by which all workmanship should be conceived, achieved and judged. In a time when it is the vogue to make much of the Negro's aptitude for clownishness or to depict him objectively as a serio-comic figure, it is a fine and praiseworthy act for Mr. Cullen to show through the interpretation of his own subjectivity the inner workings of the Negro soul and mind.

The Jazz Band's Sob

THE WEARY BLUES.
By Langston Hughes.
New York: Alfred A. Knopf. $2.

Reviewed by
DU BOSE HEYWARD

A LITTLE over a year ago the brilliant Negro journal "Opportunity" awarded a prize for a poem, "The Weary Blues," by Langston Hughes. Shortly thereafter "The Forum" reprinted the poem. Previous to the appearance of this poem very few were aware of the existence of the author, although he had been writing for seven years; an apprenticeship the results of which are evident in the pages of this volume, to which his prize poem gives its name.

"The Weary Blues" challenges more serious consideration than that generally accorded a "first book." Langston Hughes, although only twenty-four years old, is already conspicuous in the group of Negro intellectuals who are dignifying Harlem with a genuine art life. And, too, his use of syncopation in his prize poem suggested the possibility of a conflict in the rhythms of poetry paralleling that which is taking place between the spiritual and jazz exponents of Negro music.

Let it be said at once then that this author has done nothing particularly revolutionary in the field of rhythm. He is endowed with too subtle a musical sense to employ the banjo music of Vachel Lindsay, but he is close kin to Carl Sandburg in his use of freer, subtler syncopation. In fact, he has wisely refused to be fettered by a theory and has allowed his mood to select its own music. Several of the short free verse poems might have been written by Amy Lowell.

But if he derives little that is new in rhythm from his "Blues" he has managed to capture the *mood* of that type of Negro song, and thereby has caught its very essence. When he is able to create a minor, devil-may-care music, and through it to release a throb of pain, he is doing what the Negroes have done for generations, whether in the "Blues" of the Mississippi region or a song like "I Can't Help from Cryin' Sometimes," as sung by the black folk of the Carolina low country.

As he says in his "Cabaret":

"Does a jazz band ever sob?
They say a jazz band's gay.
Yet as the vulgar dancers whirled
And the wan night wore away,
One said she heard the jazz band sob
When the little dawn was gray."

That Langston Hughes has not altogether escaped an inevitable pitfall of the Negro intellectual is to be regretted. In one or two places in the book the artist is obscured by the propagandist. Pegasus has been made a pack horse. It is natural that the Negro writer should feel keenly the lack of sympathy in the South. That the South is a great loser thereby brings him small comfort. In the soul of a poet, a revolt so born may be transmuted through the alchemy of art into poetry that, while it stings the eyes with tears, causes the reader to wonder

But far more often in the volume the artist is victor:

"We have to-morrow
Bright before us
Like a flame.

Yesterday
A night-gone thing,
A sun-down name.

And dawn to-day.
Broad arch above the road we came."

And in "Dream Variation" youth triumphs:

"To fling my arms wide
In some place of the sun,
To whirl and to dance
Till the white day is done.
Then rest at cool evening
Beneath a tall tree
While the night comes on gently,
Dark like me—
That is my dream!"

It is, however, as an individual poet, not as a member of a new and interesting literary group, or as spokesman for a race, that Langston Hughes must stand or fall, and in the numerous poems in "The Weary Blues" that give poignant moods and vivid glimpses of seas and lands caught by the young poet in his wanderings I find an exceptional endowment. Always intensely subjective, passionate, keenly sensitive to beauty and possessed of an unfaltering musical sense, Langston Hughes has given us a "first book" that marks the opening of a career well worth watching.

The Weary Blues. A Book of Verse. By Langston Hughes. Alfred A. Knopf. New York. 1926. 109 *pages.*

Very perfect is the memory of my first literary acquaintance with Langston Hughes. In the unforgettable days when we were publishing THE BROWNIES' BOOK we had already appreciated a charming fragile conceit which read:

Out of the dust of dreams,
Fairies weave their garments;
Out of the purple and rose of old memories,
They make purple wings.
No wonder we find them such marvelous
things.

Then one day came "The Negro Speaks of Rivers". I took the beautiful dignified creation to Dr. Du Bois and said: "What colored person is there, do you suppose, in the United States who writes like that and yet is unknown to us?" And I wrote and found him to be a Cleveland high school graduate who had just gone to live in Mexico. Already he had begun to assume that remote, so elusive quality which permeates most of his work. Before long we had the pleasure of seeing the work of the boy, whom we had sponsored, copied and recopied in journals far and wide. "The Negro Speaks of Rivers" even appeared in translation in a paper printed in Germany.

Not very long after Hughes came to New York and not long after that he began to travel and to set down the impressions, the pictures, which his sensitive mind had registered of new forms of life and living in Holland, in France, in Spain, in Italy and in Africa.

His poems are warm, exotic and shot through with color. Never is he preoccupied with form. But this fault, if it is one, has its corresponding virtue, for it gives his verse, which almost always is imbued with the essence of poetry, the perfection of spontaneity. And one characteristic which makes for this bubbling-like charm is the remarkable objectivity which he occasionally achieves, remarkable for one so young, and a first step toward philosophy. Hughes has seen a great deal of the world, and this has taught him that nothing matters much but life. Its forms and aspects may vary, but living is the essential thing. Therefore make no bones about it,—"make the most of what you too may spend".

Some consciousness of this must have been in him even before he began to wander for he sent us as far back as 1921:

"Shake your brown feet, honey,
Shake your brown feet, chile,
Shake your brown feet, honey,
Shake 'em swift and wil'— . . .
Sun's going down this evening—
Might never rise no mo'.
The sun's going down this very night—
Might never rise no mo'—
So dance with swift feet, honey,
(The banjo's sobbing low) . . .
The sun's going down this very night—
Might never rise no mo'."

Now this is very significant, combining as it does the doctrine of the old Biblical exhortation, "eat, drink and be merry for tomorrow ye die", Horace's "Carpe diem", the German "Freut euch des Lebens" and Herrick's "Gather ye rosebuds while ye may". This is indeed a universal subject served Negro-style and though I am no great lover of any dialect I hope heartily that Mr. Hughes will give us many more such combinations.

Mr. Hughes is not always the calm philosopher; he has feeling a-plenty and is not ashamed to show it. He "loved his friend" who left him and so taken up is he with the sorrow of it all that he has no room for anger or resentment. While I do not think of him as a protagonist of color,—he is too much the citizen of the world for that—, I doubt if any one will ever write more tenderly, more understandingly, more humorously of the life of Harlem shot through as it is with mirth, abandon and pain. Hughes comprehends this life, has studied it and loved it. In one poem he has epitomized its essence:

Does a jazz-band ever sob?
They say a jazz-band's gay.
Yet as the vulgar dancers whirled
And the wan night wore away,
One said she heard the jazz-band sob
When the little dawn was grey.

Harlem is undoubtedly one of his great loves; the sea is another. Indeed all life is his love and his work a brilliant, sensitive interpretation of its numerous facets.—

JESSIE FAUSET.

THE WEARY BLUES

The Weary Blues: Langston Hughes. Alfred A. Knopf New York, 1926. $2.00

I believe there are lyrics in this volume which are such contributions to pure poetry that it makes little difference what substance of life and experience they were made of, and yet I know no other volume of verse that I should put forward as more representatively the work of a race poet than THE WEARY BLUES. Nor would I style Langston Hughes a race poet merely because he writes in many instances of Negro life and consciously as a Negro; but because all his poetry seems to be saturated with the rhythms and moods of Negro folk life. A true 'people's poet' has their balladry in his veins; and to me many of these poems seem based on rhythms as seasoned as folk-songs and on moods as deep-seated as folk-ballads. Dunbar is supposed to have expressed the peasant heart of his people. But Dunbar was the showman of the Negro masses; here is their spokesman. The acid test is the entire absence of sentimentalism; the clean simplicity of speech, the deep terseness of mood. Taking these poems too much merely as the expressions of a personality, Carl Van Vechten in his debonair introduction wonders at what he calls "their deceptive air of spontaneous improvization". The technique of folk song and dance are instinctively there, giving to the individual talent the bardic touch and power. Especially if Hughes should turn more and more to the colloquial experiences of the common folk whom he so intimately knows and so deeply loves, we may say that the Negro masses have found a voice, and promise to add to their natural domain of music and the dance the conquest of the province of poetry. Remember—I am not speaking of Negro poets, but of Negro poetry.

Poetry of a vitally characteristic racial flow and feeling then is the next step in our cultural development. Is it to be a jazz-product? The title poem and first section of THE WEARY BLUES seem superficially to suggest it. But let us see.

And far into the night he crooned that tune.
The stars went out and so did the moon.

Or this:

Sing your Blues song,
Pretty baby.
You want lovin'
And you don't mean maybe.

Jungle lover . . . .
Night-black boy . . . .
Two against the moon
And the moon was joy.

Here, — I suspect yet uncombined, are the two ingredients of the Negro poetry that will be truly and beautifully representative: the rhythm of the secular ballad but the imagery and diction of the Spiritual. Stranger opposites than these have fused to the fashioning of new beauty. Nor is this so doctrinaire a question as it seems, when considering a poet who has gone to the cabaret for some of his rhythms and to the Bible for others.

In the poems that are avowedly racial, Hughes has a distinctive note. Not only are these poems full of that passionate declaration and acceptance of race which is a general characteristic of present day Negro poets, but there is a mystic identification with the race experience which is, I think, instinctively deeper and broader than any of our poets has yet achieved.

The Negro Speaks of Rivers catches this note for us most unmistakeably:

I've known rivers;
I've known rivers ancient as this world and older than
the flow of human blood in human veins.

My soul has grown deep like the rivers.

I bathed in the Euphrates when dawns were young.
I built my hut near the Congo and it lulled me to sleep.
I looked upon the Nile and raised the pyramids above it.
I heard the singing of the Mississippi when Abe Lincoln
went down to New Orleans, and I've seen its muddy
bosom turn all golden in the sunset.

I've known rivers;
Ancient, dusky rivers.

My soul has grown deep like the rivers.

Remembering this as the basic substratum of this poetry, we may discriminatingly know to what to attribute the epic surge underneath its lyric swing, the primitive fatalism back of its nonchalance, the ancient force in its pert colloquialisms, the tropic abandon and irresistableness of its sorrow and laughter.

No matter how whimsical or gay the poet may carry his overtones after this, or how much of a bohemian or happy troubadour he may assume to be, we will always hear a deep, tragic undertone pulsing in his verse. For the Negro experience rightly sensed even in the moods of the common folk is complex and paradoxical like the Blues which Hughes has pointed out to be so characteristic, with their nonchalant humor against a background of tragedy; there is always a double mood, mercurial to the artist's touch like an easily improvised tune. As our poet himself puts it:

In one hand
I hold tragedy
And in the other
Comedy,——
Masks for the soul.

Laugh with me.
You would laugh!
Weep with me,
Would you weep!

Tears are my laughter.
Laughter is my pain.
Cry at my grinning mouth,
If you will.
Laugh at my sorrow's reign.

Alain Locke

Singers of New Songs

By ROBERT T. KERLIN

Cane—By Jean Toomer. With a Foreword by Waldo Frank. Boni and Liveright, 1923.

The Weary Blues—By Langston Hughes. With an Introduction by Carl van Vechten. Alfred A. Knopf, 1926.

Color — By Countee Cullen. Harper and Brothers, 1926.

"LIKE purple tallow flames, songs jet up. They spread a ruddy haze over the heavens. The haze swings low. Now the whole countryside is a soft chorus." So Jean Toomer, in *Cane,* describes the effect of a song spark that traveled swiftly from cabin to cabin in a Georgia night. Not all white folks, perhaps not many, will understand it. There is more primitive poetry, and more poetic mysticism, in *Cane,* than in any other book yet produced on this continent. Further on in the story comes this:

'Slave boy whom some Christian mistress taught to read the Bible. Black man who saw Jesus in the rice fields, and began preaching to his people. Moses—and Christ—words used for songs. Dead blind father of a muted folk who feel their way upward to a life that crushes or absorbs them."

Twice have I had the kinship of the African and the Indian (or Hindu) mind impressed distinctly upon me: once and again in reading Charles H. Conner's *The Enchanted Valley* (alas! so little known!) and a second time and again in reading *Cane.* It chanced that I came to this latter book direct from Mukerju's *Caste and Outcast.* Who does not know that the Negroes have an understanding of *our* Scriptures—which of course are ours only by imperfect adoption—which leaves us wondering, and ought to leave us humiliated? But I am now speaking about poetry, not religion, though the two are not far asunder. Again I quote from *Cane:*

"Ralph Kabnis, propped in his bed, tries to read. Ceiling, patterned by the fringed globe of the lamp. The walls, unpainted, are seasoned a rosin yellow. And cracks between the boards are black. These cracks are the lips the night winds use for whispering. Night winds in Georgia are vagrant poets, whispering. Kabnis, against his will, lets his book slip down, and listens to them."

When "an atom of dust in agony on a Georgia hillside" hears in the winds through the cracks of his cabin the whisperings of vagrant poets what may not be expected of that same "atom" when the agony, intensified, understood, has at command the language of Shakespeare, Shelley, Sandburg?

Cane is written partly in verse form, partly in prose: all of it has the spirit of poetry. It is, in respect to content and form, an audacious book, stamped all over with genius.

The story of Dunbar's printing and peddling his first book is well known. Something like that has been the story of all Negro books of verse hitherto. I have a shelf of such books—the cost of printing borne by the author, the burden of selling borne by the author. Is it not a notable event in the history of the American Negro, and of America, that in the first months of the year 1926 two young Negro poets had their books put forth, on their merits and trade value, just as white poets' books, by two publishing firms of first repute for orthodox business? Negro poets are in the market, no longer lost wanderers on Parnassus.

Mr. Langston Hughes has now for three or four years—he is but in his twenty-fifth year—been transposing into verse some of the rhythms of Negro life. He is the interpreter of jazz and of the life from which it springs. Harlem is his, its theatres and dance halls, its streets and tenements, its gaities and "blues." The poignant note is not long absent. This is typical:

She
Who searched for lovers
In the night
Has gone the quiet way
Into the still,
Dark land of death
Beyond the rim of day.

Now like a little lonely waif
She walks
An endless street
And gives her kiss to nothingness
Would God his lips were sweet!

It's a common story. Why weep?

The rhythm of life
Is a jazz rhythm,
Honey.
The gods are laughing at us.

The broken heart of love,
The weary, weary heart of pain—
Overtones,
Undertones,
To the rumble of street cars,
To the swish of rain.

Lenox Avenue,
Honey.
Midnight,
And the gods are laughing at us.

All this life of Harlem calls for a poet. No reporter can give it to the world. His most honest story of any event in Harlem would be a lie. Mr. Langston Hughes comes on the scene and we begin to see a new world—one that night only reveals. Here are lyrics that are akin to the deathless ones in all languages—Sappho's, Horace's, Herrick's, but most of all the Hebrew *Song of Songs.* This is an example:

Would
That I were a jewel,
A shattered jewel,
That all my shining brilliants
Might fall at thy feet,
Thou dark one.

Would
That I were a garment,
A shimmering, silken garment,
That all my folds
Might wrap about thy body,
Absorb thy body,
Hold and hide thy body,
Thou dark one.

Would
That I were a flame,
But one sharp, leaping flame
To annihilate thy body,
Thou dark one.

I would liken you
To a night without stars
Were it not for your eyes.
I would liken you
To a sleep without dreams
Were it not for your songs.

Truly those who see only with their eyes see not at all. Dancers, and jazz bands, and *chansons vulgaires,* and Charlestons, and Weary Blues hardly tell the whole story, and tell their own not at all. Hence Langston Hughes.

In 1923 a Negro student in New York University won second place among the seven hundred undergraduates of American colleges who competed for the Witter Bynner prize in poetry. The next year he was still second, and in 1925 he was first. This was Countee Cullen, aged 23. On the publication of "The Ballad of the Brown Girl" I wrote, in *The Southern Workman,* that it placed Mr. Cullen by the side of the best modern masters of the ballad —Morris, Rossetti, and any others that may be named. Of course it is imitative—all modern ballads are, and are successful just in degree as they are imitative of the old folk ballads. But there is a felicity possible in imitation, and a creativeness, which are capable of producing the thrill we expect of supreme art. I still think, "The Ballad of the Brown Girl" worthy of the praise I gave it.

But now appears Mr. Cullen's first book and this ballad is nowhere in it! My first thought is, What must be the severity of self-criticism, and the audacity, of a poet of twenty-three who will exclude from his book a poem of such merit? It was a most conceited thing to do. But I have no sooner read his ballad entitled "Judas Iscariot" than I am able to guess the reason of the exclusion. Like the author, I am willing to rest his case upon this ballad without the assistance of "The Brown Girl."

I return to his apologia, as it were, "To You Who Read My Book:"

Juice of the first
  Grapes of my vine,
I proffer your thirst
  My own heart's wine.
Here of my growing
  A red rose sways,
Seed of my sowing,
  And work of my days.

It is in an altogether manly strain, albeit with an undertone of melancholy—Mr. Cullen did well to entitle his book "Color." It is impregnated with color. Something exotic to the Caucasian, call it *color,* call it *Africanism,* call it what you will, impregnates the fabric of Cullen's verse as the murex dye impregnated the cloth of the Tyrian looms, and made the purples worn by kings. A brown girl is thus brought before you:

Her walk is like the replica
  Of some barbaric dance
Wherein the soul of Africa
  Is winged with arrogance.

An Atlantic City waiter whose subtle poise as with his tray aloft he carves dexterous avenues, as it were through a jungle, on his way to serve choice viands to ladies who pause and gaze, is thus presented:

Sheer through his acquiescent mask
  Of bland gentility,
The jungle flames like a copper cask
  Set where the sun strikes free.

In such imagery we have a poet who is going on his own. We have here a Negro poet who is as sure of himself as Keats was. Two entire poems of Cullen's I will give because, primarily, of their merits as poems, and incidentally because they exemplify, as the "Judas Iscariot" already mentioned does, the Negro's easy penetration to the meanings we of the occidental and white mind so easily miss in "our" gospel narratives.

Black Magdalens

These have no Christ to spit and stoop
  To write upon the sand,
Inviting him that has not sinned
  To raise the first rude hand.

And if he came they could not buy
  Rich ointment for his feet,
The body's sale scarce yields enough
  To let the body eat.

The chaste clean ladies pass them by
  And draw their skirts aside,

But Magdalens have a ready laugh;
  They wrap their wounds in pride.

They fare full ill since Christ forsook
  The cross to mount a throne,
And Virtue still is stooping down
  To cast the first hard stone.

SIMON THE CYRENIAN SPEAKS

He never spoke a word to me,
  And yet He called my name;
He never gave a sign to me,
  And yet I knew and came.

At first I said, "I will not bear
  His cross upon my back;
He only seeks to place it there
  Because my skin is black."

But He was dying for a dream,
  And He was very meek,
And in His eyes there shone a gleam
  Men journey far to seek.

It was Himself my pity bought;
  I did for Christ alone
What all of Rome could not have
    wrought
With bruise of lash or stone.

These two poems, which are quite typical of Mr. Cullen's quality as a poet, suggest something in the way of spiritual discernment and wisdom which is the Negro's peculiar possession. It is the same quality which appears in Mr. Roland Hayes' singing—a quality that so gets hold of your heart. It surely omens a new element in our literature, art and life. Will the Negro be duly impressed with the idea that he has this contribution to make? And, a more important question, will the Caucasian, proud of his "supreme Caucasian mind," be humbly or otherwise receptive?

It is easy enough to conceive of the American Negro outstripping every competitor in every art and in every spiritual quality or achievement. If suffering worketh patience, and patience hope, and hope maketh not ashamed, the Negroes are the privileged class, God's chosen, in America and in the world. This can hardly be construed into an argument for lynching: "woe unto him through whom the offense cometh:" but it goes far toward justifying the ways of God to men. There is a law of compensation. Sometimes it seems to be the only law in the universe worth consideration. The Negro is making deeper penetrations, or plunges, into the abysma of life and scaling painfully and gloriously loftier heights, than any other group of mortals. A wisdom is therefore coming to be his which belongs to no other. And wisdom is more precious, according to very good authority, than the choicest residential sections of cities, and Pullman privileges, and theatre seats, and equal educational opportunities. Though it is only by demanding these that those experiences come whose fruit is wisdom. And such wisdom always finds embodiment in poetry. It is now doing so.

A little more than a century ago Leigh Hunt announced in a paper of which he was the editor, three new poets. Two of them were, Shelley and Keats. It sometimes happens—once, in a century, perhaps, to or three poets of indisputable genius appear linked in some sort of union. It's in the lap of the gods whether Toomer, Hughes, and Cullen will be poets of unfilled renown or the creators of an epoch when it will no more seem a marvel

"To make a poet black, and bid him sing.'

Poets of America, by Clement Wood. E. P. Dutton and Company, 1925. $3.00

The truth seems at last in the way of being told about American literature. Macy, Calverton, Untermeyer, Mencken, Van Vechten, the Van Dorens, Clement Wood—they are making perceptible dents in the hide of that old dragon Tradition. Perhaps they will yet reach his heart. But since truth is a matter of emphasis, relation, proportion, and since the common mind is slow to get anything but easy generalizations, much yet remains to be done. The significant fact, however, is that already a tremendous amount has been done in changing the mind of college youth towards traditional estimates. For example, Page's *Chief American Poets* stands absolutely no chance with Untermeyer's *Modern American Poets*. One no longer hears any mention even of "the great New England group."

Out of the Nineteenth century only two—at the most four—American poets walk as more than ghosts in the Twentieth: the two, of course, are Poe and Whitman; the other two, in the distance, are Emerson and Lanier. The "Great Group" is not superabundantly represented. Echoes cannot go on forever. There are new voices, other themes. The Victorians, whether of Old England or New, cannot speak for the youth of the Twentieth Century. The one ultimate test of a classic is that is always modern, ageless. Our Longfellows, Lowells, Tennysons, Brownings, missed the note. They belong to a period. They do not appeal. Only poets now living, with the exception of a few who in their day upon earth were mostly neglected or scorned, read for us truly life as it is unfolding.

Professor Brander Matthews a quarter of a century ago wrote an "American Literature" in which Fitz-Greene Halleck and Joseph Rodman Drake had the honor of a chapter—one of about eight constituting the book; Sidney Lanier was awarded just half a sentence. That was the academic—and provincial—valuation. Today comes Clement Wood, a free lance in the field of letters, with "Poets of America"; Halleck and Drake are mentioned, no more; Sidney Lanier receives a chapter. Truth, I said, is a matter of proportion and emphasis. I also said that we seem to be on the road to it.

More disregardful of tradition still, Mr. Wood gives Phillis Wheatley more space than Whittier and admits James Weldon Johnson, Claude McKay, Fenton Johnson, Albery Whitman, Paul Laurence Dunbar, Countee Cullen, Georgia Douglas Johnson, William Stanley Braithwaite, Leslie Pinckney Hill, and fifteen other Aframerican poets, to a place alongside their white contemporaries as co-makers of American poetry. "Why not?" Of course. But why has it not been done all along? The Negro Spirituals, with their cry for freedom, and the Negro secular folk-rhymes, with their rollicking satire, receive as much space as all "the amiable versifiers," whilom "the Great Group," put together. Who before Mr. Wood considered them a part of "American poetry?"

A no less significant fact in the present day treatment of American literature by the text book makers is their inclusion of selections from Negro writers. Two noteworthy books of this class are Untermeyer's *Modern American Poetry,* which includes poems from four Negroes, and Heydrick's *Americans All,* which includes a story by Dunbar. These two books are widely used in high-school and college courses. Henceforth the Negro teacher in selecting the best anthologies of contemporary literature will find his own race represented. Will the writers of school texts of American history follow this example? They shall be obliged to, at no distant day.

Mr. Wood's treatment of the contribution of the Negro to American poetry is concluded with a note of prophecy:

"The music-laden soul of the Negro has not yet found an adequate poet of wide gesture; but there is every reason for anticipating that he will come; and we will be the richer for this lilting addition to the three original English strains" (Celt, Saxon, Norman).

This innovation with respect to the Negro poet is not the only rousing appeal that *Poets of America* will make to readers of OPPORTUNITY. Such chapters as those on Sandburg, Frost, Emily Dickenson, and especially the last two chapters, "Out of the Depths" and Poets to Come," are written with such a sense of the real values of poetry and of the conditions for its production, that they are bound to make a deep impression on those who see too much social injustice and too little social freedom in America. Almost the author's last words are:

"The poet asks two little favors: a fit reception for himself, a living part in your scheme of society—and that you can easily give; and justice and joy to all men—and that you may find less of a trifle." So it is: but it is the one thing worth giving your life to securing in the present day.

Though this is a good stopping place I cannot close Mr. Wood's book without putting a query to him, and to his readers not that I expect from either an answer. I have one of my own. My query is this: Why do so many poets peter out? Why does Lindsay make such a descent to drivel? Why does Masters give us so barren a book as "Starved Rock" after giving us the "Spoon River Anthology?" Where is the Carl Sandburg of "Smoke and Steel," "Chicago," and "Corn Huskers?" Why, why do so many poets peter out? I am dying to tell.

ROBERT T. KERLIN.

Our Book Shelf

Flight, by Walter White, Alfred A. Knopf. $2.50.

Just the other evening, a most charming lady asked me what I thought of this story of Mr. White's. Quite unthinkingly and most abruptly my answer came:—"It seems to me a good story gone wrong." She perceptibly disliked my remark and went on to say that she thought "Flight" a distinct advance over "The Fire in the Flint." And in the way of weak critics with charming ladies, I limited my discourse to those elements upon which we were in agreement; but here, alone at my desk I shall say what I jolly well please. It may be that I feel so strongly about this book, because I had hoped to do such a story some day myself—there are so many elements contained that are problems of my life, so many experiences that are my experiences, that I feel less than a man if I withhold the honesty of my opinion.

Let me start by saying that there is much in this book that is commendable. At least the artist has attempted something worth-while—the delineation of a soul and its harassed turbulence under the buffetings of a relentless environment. Mimi Daquin is a character worthy of a novel; she deserves treatment of a kind to place her beside Maria Chapdelaine, Mattie Frome and Salammbo. There is in her travail the lonely vicissitudes of a lost race and it irks no little to see her treated in a manner far inferior to her possibilities. It is in the failure of this central character to diffuse anything of glowing life and reality that the novel suffers its death blow. Mimi sees and acts and does but never becomes activated by the warm breath of life. This glaring fault in the development of the major character descends in proportionate measure upon the subsidiary actors. They never seem to evolve from a two dimensioned existence; these people have length and some breadth but rarely any depth. They are always either villainous or divine; either blatantly white or dastardly black, with the necromantic ability to change abruptly and unreasonably from the one extreme to the other. Witness Carl's almost inexplicable reversal of type at the arrival of his unexpected offspring. And, too, Jimmie's absolute descent into inanity and triviality after his marriage with Mimi. Such manipulation smacks of the puppet show and not of creation. And a very creaky, awkward puppet show at that; you can actually see the strings and hear the squeaking of rusty jointed marionettes.

The tale chiefly concerns Mimi Daquin, a "Creole," who after a series of misadventures among "her own people" crosses over the line and becomes the wife of a white man. Suddenly becoming conscious of the essential artistry and beauty of her own "race", as expressed in the voice of Roland Hayes, she overthrows the entire superstructure of her existence and goes flying back to "her people." One can imagine the possibility of such an happening to such a person, but Mr. White fails to convince us that his particular Mimi in her particular environment could have so acted. And so the climax meant to be intense and sweeping, strikes a hollow, blatant note. Then, too, we must conjecture that he has left this girl at the most critical stage of her career. She leaves a white world, with all its advantages of body and spirit, a position of eminence which she has developed out of the soul-sweat of her spirit, to go back to "her people." How then to be received?—how to adjust on a lower, cramped scale a life that had become so full?—how to compensate for the intense freedom of "being white?" Truly, has Mimi been left in the lurch!

Mr. White's style suffers mainly from a woeful lack of clarity. Such elementary matters as faulty sentence structure often rise to affront one. The very opening sentence of the novel is involved and cumbersome. Then, too, I was far into the second chapter before I was certain of the identity and relationships of the main characters of the story. These things should not be. "The Fire in the Flint" was at least clear-cut, simple and clearly defined. That story swept along by its very powerful simplicity; "Flight" seldom gets on the wing. The description of the Atlanta riot and part of the closing scene seem the only portions of the book that really come alive and fly. There is an interesting little psychological sidelight in the delineation of Hilda Adams' reactions to Mimi's winning of the affections of Carl. There is insight here which is no little blighted by inadequate expressions and puerile vocabulary. As further example of such inept writing, his similes are often ludicrously overdrawn and quaintly inapt.

There is throughout the story a general lack of the very contributions that Negroes are expected to make to the literature of America:—color and poetry. His Harlem is a flat, colorless assemblage of brick and black faces. Will Eric Walrond or Langston Hughes please put "our" Harlem into a novel! The people are generally colorless sketches and the attempts at the creation of atmosphere are exceedingly forced and dissatisfying. After a story like "Porgy", or even "The Black Harvest", Mr. White, has, in the inimitable Harlemese "let us down."

If I have seemed a trifle caustic, charge it to the account of my belief that Mr. White has not stood up to the conception of his story. "Flight" lacks the interest of the "Fire in the Flint," the ruggedness and power is lacking, the drama and the color. In attempting more, he has accomplished less. If he will carefully prune his next effort to eliminate the glaring faults of this novel, I expect him to really do something worth while. May his next "flight" be upon sturdier wings.

FRANK HORNE.

"FLIGHT"**

BEAUTIFUL Creole Mimi in "Flight" from home and race and self and back again at last to race—this is Walter White's heart-compelling story of a mulatto. I use the term in its broadest sense.

Mr. White pictures accurately and graphically the plight in which the mulatto so often finds himself, almost wrecked between the Scylla of ostracism on the part of the white race and the Charybdis of suspicion on the part of his black race.

To the colored reader, probably, there is nothing new in the sociological or psychological revelations of the colored people in the various communities of Atlanta, Philadelphia, in Harlem, where Mimi lived and struggled for existence. The novelty lies in the fact that Walter White is proving successfully that life is life; and if the life of the white man can be made interesting in literature so can the colored author make a place for his people in literature. Nor will it be alone the grotesque, unfortunately illiterate Negro who will occupy this place. In fact the life of the cultured mulatto provides a far richer field for artistic literary development than the Nordic. A greater variety of complexes, due to his mixed blood, creates an involved psychology often misunderstood. Economic conditions force him into a false racial misrepresentation of himself and the tragedy and pathos and sardonic humor concomitant with such a situation provide material for endless "Mimi" stories awaiting the pen of the sympathetic author.

Such a story as "Flight", told with the forceful ingenuousness of Mr. White, can never leave the reader apathetic—he will be either strongly on the offensive or on the defensive.

"Flight" to me means "Mimi". I should have preferred that title—with apologies to Mr. White. Treated less didactically Mimi would have been a stronger character. Mr. White is so very matter of fact that at times he falls back on a natural reportorial style that detracts from the artistry he has attempted to maintain in this his second novel. Mimi is too much the victim of her creator and particularly so in the finale. She seems deprived of her individuality and becomes mechanical accomplice to the plot rather than an intelligent woman striving to break through the whims of fate to a spiritual freedom. However, she is a long-awaited colored heroine. Mimi is throughout a serious, intelligent, tragic figure. She is distinctly an individualist. Behind her is an ancestry of dare-devil adventures, ardent lovers and leisured-gentry. She asserted, at an early age, her inherited independence of spirit and a precocity of thought that both alarmed and gratified her father who indulged her in both. Small wonder then that when suddenly swept by the fire of early youth she loved intensely and without limit. But later she scorned to allow the weakling who had exploited her love to legalize her prospective maternity through marriage. The subsequent ostracism accorded Mimi caused her to take flight North and begin a lone battle to make a living for two. And it is around Mimi in a succession of flights that Mr. White has woven his dramatic tale of colorful American Negro life.

NORA E. WARING.

---

* Cincinnati's Colored Citiens. By W. P. Dabney. Dabney Publishing Co., Cin'ti.

** Flight. By Walter White. Alfred A. Knopf, New York.

Correspondence

Dear Sir:

I have before me Mr. Frank Horne's amazing review—in the July issue of OPPORTUNITY—of Mr. White's latest novel, "Flight." I do not like this review. In fact so violently do I object to it that I am moved to put pen to paper to state my reasons for objecting. I read this review with mingled feelings—surprise, anger, pity. Surprise, that a reviewer apparently so erudite should have written such an unintelligent review. Anger, because such a book had been given to so ununderstanding a person for review. Pity, because the reviewer had so entirely missed the chief idea of the book. . . .

May I quote a little from the review as I go along?

"Mimi Daquin is a character worthy of a novel; she deserves a treatment of a kind to place her beside Maria Chapdelaine, Mattie Frome and Salammbo." Just why, I wonder, did your reviewer choose the passive French-Canadian girl, the trapped Mattie, and the Salammbo of ancient Carthage, with whom to disparage the sensitive, rebellious, modern Mimi? Certainly, these are for their own environment and times, excellent characters. But so is Mimi for hers. And would not Galsworthy's unsurpassable Irene Forsyte, or Jacobsen's Maria Grubbe have been more effective for purposes of comparison as well as for disparagement? They, like Mimi Daquin, threw away material things for the fulfillment of their spiritual destinies.

"There is in her travail the lonely vicissitudes of a lost race. . . ." Which "lost" race? It is here that your reviewer stumbles and falls. It is here that we detect his blindness. It is here that we become aware that he fails to realize that this is the heart of the whole tale. A lost race. Yes. But I suspect that he refers to the black race, while Mr. White obviously means that it is the white race which is lost, doomed to destruction by its own mechanical gods. How *could* your reviewer have missed this dominant note, this thing which permeates the whole book? It was this that made Mimi turn from it. Surely, the thesis of "Flight" is "what shall it profit a man if he gain the whole world and lose his own soul?" "Then, too, we must conjecture that he leaves this girl at the most critical stage of her career." We do *not* conjecture anything of the kind. We know it. And we were meant to know it. Authors do not supply imaginations, they expect their readers to have their own, and to use them. Judging by present day standards of fiction, the ending of "Flight" is the perfect one, perfect in its æsthetic coloring, perfect in its subtle simplicity. For others of this type, I refer your reviewer to Sherwood Anderson's "Dark Laughter," to Carl Van Vechten's "Firecrackers," to Joseph Hergesheimer's "Tubal Cane."

"She leaves a white world with all its advantages of body and spirit . . . to go back to 'her people.'" Here it is again, your reviewer's inability to grasp the fact that Mimi Daquin came to realize that, for her, there were no advantages of the spirit in the white world, and so, spiritual things being essential to her full existence she gave up voluntarily the material advantages. . . .

To my mind, warped as I have confessed by the Europeans and the American moderns, "Flight" is a far better piece of work than "The Fire in the Flint." Less dramatic, it is more fastidious and required more understanding, keener insight. Actions and words count less and the poetic conception of the character, the psychology of the scene more, than in the earlier novel. "Flight" shows a more mature artistry.

It may be that your reviewer read the book hastily, superficially, and so missed both its meaning and its charm.

NELLA IMES.

Correspondence

My dear Mr. Johnson:

When I first read Nella Imes' answer to my criticism of Walter White's *Flight,* it had been my intention to let the matter drop there, else we be accused of creating much ado about nothing. But the realization of this charmingly energetic partizanship in a literary matter within my own group, aroused by my own controversial review, so tickled my innate and unpardonable vanity, that words fairly bubble from my pen in reply. Perhaps when we are more critically mature and colder of blood, neither Mrs. Imes nor myself will bother to express our opinions in so open and positive a manner. But now, I welcome her into the lists of critical controversy.

Your correspondent's answer is most brilliantly illogical. She falls headlong into a similar pathetic fallacy with the novel she so zealously defends, in that she, too, mistakes the *intention* for the accomplishment, the *conception* for the expression. Hardly anyone—just really anyone—could have missed the intention. For even such as I, did not Mr. White most graciously include, first a dissertation by Professor Henry Meekins on the perils of industrialism to the soul, and almost immediately following several other pages in which Mr. Chuan, the visiting "mogul," holds forth at great length on eastern vs. western civilization? Did I not applaud Mr. White for assuming such an exacting and high-minded assignment? So that it is surely Mr. White, and not I, who must be accused of "missing the point." The conflict of spirituality and materialism was indicated but never *incorporated* into the being of Mimi. The idea was pointed out, but never woven into the warp and woof of the story. I am certain that Mr. White *meant* to, but it is *he* that missed the point.

It is perfectly evident that we agree that the *intention* was worthy, so that our disagreement must center upon the degree of accomplishment. The briefest method is to clear away the objections Mrs. Imes makes to portions of my own review. She objects most strenuously to my choice of Maria Chapdelaine, Mattie Frome and Salammbo as subjects for comparison with Mimi, saying that they were excellent for their times and environment while Mimi is for hers. There are so many illogical non sequiturs here that I really do not know where to start. First, Mrs. Imes must understand that these inestimable ladies were chosen as examples of consummate skill in character creation and analysis and, as such, constitute the company to which Mimi should have aspired. And in the idea of Mimi being "modern" and Marie and the rest relegated to "their times and environment," Mrs. Imes commits her cardinal sin against literature. Mimi "modern" to be sure! And when did Maria's "thousand aves" die? When will sacrifice in the name of love die? They will always be "trapped" Matties. Is not Hamlet "modern"? Mrs. Imes is surely aware that there is no such thing in the kingdom of art as "times" and environment. Not only is a thing of beauty a joy forever, but a character simply, powerfully and beautifully alive is forever modern. "Judging by present day standards," you say. What is my concern with "present day standards"? We are judging here a professed work of art, to somewhere take its place beside "Hamlet" and "An American Tragedy." Mr. White has presumed to rush in where Conrad and Dumas have so fearfully trod. Does Mrs. Imes mean that I am to judge it as last week's best book by a Negro—to say that it is fair for its moment and its race? My concern is neither with chronology nor pigmentation, but with the eternal verity of art, and in this intense and glaring light, *Flight* is a poor book. I am evaluating this story as literature, an artistic accomplishment. In its final appraisal, what do I care what he *meant* to do if he didn't do it; what is it my concern of the hours consumed or the mental anguish if Mimi never comes to life? He offers her up unto the altar of art, he challenges all art in his gesture and in that light have I judged him. George Jean Nathan aptly says, "Criticism is the art of appraising that which isn't in terms of what it should be, and that which should be in terms of what it isn't. The rest—is mere handshaking."

Mrs. Imes insists that "spiritual things were essential to her full existence" in speaking of Mimi, and that her final flight back to her people was prompted by these yearnings for spirituality. What made her think she would find solace there? Surely not the same people that drove her from pillar to post with her child of love? Surely not in the petty jealousies and tinsel of Mr. White's Harlem? Where was she to satisfy this "intense spirituality" among her own people? It was this fact that prompted me to observe that Mimi had been deserted at the most critical stage of her career. Mrs. Imes agrees with this statement, claiming that Mr. White *meant* to do so. She truly frightens me at times by the clarity of insight she has as to the *intentions* of Mr. White. I agree with Mrs. Imes that "authors do not supply imaginations" but they themselves must be possessed of enough imaginative power to at least indicate the *direction* in which they wish to be followed. After all, the imagination is a bridging function and the author should at least survey the ground, give me some river to cross, indicate a spot here and there that the bridge is to touch, suggest some distant horizon into which my far flung bridge is to disappear. If not that, then Mr. White's novel might just as well have been written in some such manner as this:—

"Mimi — colored—disillusioned—white — disillusioned No. 2—colored No. 2 . . . please use imagination."

Let me close, Mr. Johnson, by thanking you again for the privilege of reviewing *Flight* and answering Nella Imes. This interest she displays as well as that which has come to my ears from other quarters have been most gratifying. But I remain quite incorrigible. I firmly attest that Mr. White is a jolly fine fellow, but I as vehemently insist that he has not written a jolly fine book.

Very sincerely yours,

Frank Horne.

CORRESPONDENCE

Editor, OPPORTUNITY:

Sir: I think it is a swell idea to have Mrs. Imes and Mr. Horne disagreeing *in print* over the merits or lack of them in my novel, "Flight." Most human beings buy a particular brand of soap or garters or cheese because they constantly see advertisements of that brand and not so much because other brands are wholly inferior. The same rule applies largely to books. That is the reason why most authors (including the author of "Flight") prefer treatment of their work in this order: first, favorable reviews; second, unfavorable notices; third, and most distasteful of all, a damning silence. To help avoid the latter is partly the reason for this letter.

Mr. Horne's letter in the October number of OPPORTUNITY would be, I confess reluctantly, much more convincing even to me if there did not stick out from it like sore thumbs such phrases as "to somewhere take its place" or "to at least indicate" or "it is he *that* missed the point." Ordinarily, it would be ungracious to mention such things as needlessly split infinitives or solecisms. But when they come from the pen of so erudite and confident a critic—well, shall I say, it is a bit surprising.

Mr. Horne's chief grievance against Mrs. Imes seems to be that he cannot understand why, after reading his piece, Mrs. Imes should continue to imagine that she comprehended Mimi's plight or Mimi's reasons for the things she does in "Flight." His "'jolly fine" review of my book apparently should have convinced Mrs. Imes that she was all wrong when she found a certain pleasure in reading the story. Mrs. Imes, under Mr. Horne's expert tutelage, should have known better than to think that I had not "deserted" Mimi when the experiment of going white caused Mimi to decide that, with all the faults that Negroes undoubtedly possess, she could find greater spiritual happiness with them than with the more mechanized whites. After reading Mr. Horne's letter, I apparently was entirely wrong in assuming that any person possessing even normal intelligence could learn anything from life. For this grave error I suppose I owe Mr. Horne a profound apology. For his consolation, I want to say that when I wrote of Mimi it seemed to me reasonable that the things she experienced both as colored and as white brought her a new perspective and a new power of appraisement of the Negro and his life.

It is beginning to become apparent that hereafter I must write two versions of any book I want understood—one of them designed for readers of normal intelligence or better; the other supplied with maps, charts, graphs and pictures and written in words of not more than two syllables. I suppose I am recalcitrant but, even after Mr. Horne's erudite strictures and his profound dicta, I am afraid I am not yet convinced that I "deserted" Mimi. Of course I might have adopted the fairybook formula of ending the story with the line ". . . and she lived happily ever afterwards." If it will make him any happier, I shall be glad to inscribe that line in Mr. Horne's copy of "Flight."

Boiled down to simple language, the controversy between Mrs. Imes and Mr. Horne seems to me to be this: for Mr. Horne, "Flight" is a rotten book; for Mrs. Imes, it is not so bad. Being violently prejudiced, my inclinations are towards the point of view Mrs. Imes holds. A few years ago, when I was around Mr. Horne's age, I was as certain of the absoluteness of everything in life as he apparently now is. Perhaps age is gently touching me for the older I grow and the more I see of life in its various phases, the less sure am I that everything in life can be definitely classed as white or black. Instead, truth and life and art and all the other tags and labels which we adopt to save ourselves the pain of thinking seem to me to consist of relative shades of gray. The particular shade depends on the experiences, knowledge, understanding or prejudices of the individual who holds a given opinion whether that opinion be sound or not. Perhaps in a few years from now Mr. Horne will not speak with quite the assured air of a combination Anatole France and H. L. Mencken.

And it was so sweet of Mr. Horne to label me as "a jolly fine fellow" even if I can't for the life of me see what that has to do with "Flight."

Sincerely yours,

WALTER WHITE.

Charles S. Johnson to Carl Van Vechten, August 10, 1926 [on Opportunity letterhead]. [JWJ/Van Vechten/Corres. James Weldon Johnson Collection, Beinecke Rare Book Library, Yale University.]

Dear Mr. Van Vechten:

You were good to send me an autographed copy of your *Nigger Heaven.* I began reading it rather promptly with the taut expectancy which I dare say will not be lacking in many of that widening audience of yours who have been warned of the imminence of this book. It demands a responsible review in OPPORTUNITY. Despite a number of standing requests, I have asked James Weldon Johnson to review it. It would insure a balanced and brilliant appraisal if he consents.

When I had put down the book I found myself in quite a flurry. The reaction which is perhaps least important to a person for whom literature is a profession, forces itself up into first place so far as I am concerned. It is to me a new focusing, deft orientation to artistic treasures kicked about for years, the first achievement of a novel of Negro life with fascination springing from emotions other than patronizing sympathy,—the point of beginning for a really vital novel by a Negro about his own life. I hope I am saying this with the appropriate restraint. It has universality. It requires no particular racial philosophy to enjoy it. It is worth knowing that this sort of thing is possible. That is the interest of the book for me. Byron symbolizes to me more than you perhaps intend—he is both the nebulous fringe and the disconcerting heart of young Harlem. Mary is alive with a placid intensity, a really glowing charm. At points however, as you etch her, a Negro writer would be accused of propaganda. Lasea is immortal. In one spot you crowd together more Negroisms of speech than I have ever heard before in anything called a conversation, but I think that the cabaret scene has been described once for all. I experienced no such disconcerting factual jolts as one so often encounters in reading of familiar scenes and situations. Your observation and honesty are to be thanked for this altho you managed to get what many Negroes will regard as "family secrets." I can't say that I was convinced by the manner in which you describe Dick Sill's going white, page 182, but that is a small item.

Summing up, I don't seem to find much to object to in *Nigger Heaven,* and I am almost ashamed at the excess of enthusiasm to which I was tempted. I might make a stir about your title and be a good "race man" but fundamentally I am too anxious to have the sting of this term extracted in the fashion that such employment promises to do it. As an afterthought I might say that aside from the purely artistic qualities of the book, I take to myself the satisfaction that a valuable thing is accomplished intellectually when one may see that Negroes spend some of their time, between suffering and solutions of problems to laugh at their own foibles and at the Gargantuan foolishness of their white brother. A most ungracious thing to say but my supreme tribute to the book is that I wish a Negro had written it: and along with my hopes for the success go my hopes that one eventually will equal it.

Sincerely
Charles S. Johnson,
EDITOR

1

Color

Yet do I marvel at this curious thing:
To make a poet black, and bid him sing!

COLOR, the new book of poems by Countée Cullen, was read before our studio fireplace last night. Cullen's dedication of his book, "To my Mother and Father This First Book", translated, means this: "I love my Mother and Father. This my first achievement I lay at their feet. I am ashamed of nothing in this book: it is me as they know me, me at my best. It is a beginning. I shall write other books, better books, books which I shall dedicate to other people—— but this is Their Book— my First Book— and I want them to know how much I love them."

And the divisions of the book: Color, Epitaphs, For Love's Sake, and Varia, comprising seventy-four poems, picture his mind clearly: a mind troubled with the thought of race, sad and rebellious by turns as the fact of man's inhuman cruelty to his brother is borne in upon him. He is a frequent thinker on Death, a Living Fool who envies the Dead Wise, and wishes he were "wrapped in their cool immunity." He is a lover of John Keats and the Bible, and is desperately in love with Love. Like Dowson, his loved one is still without love for him:

Oh, for a little while be kind to me
Who stand in such imperious need of you,
And for a fitful space let my head lie
Happily on your passion's frigid breast.

There is a strong Heine-Dowson quality to these

lines; but in *Judas Iscariot*, *Heritage*, and *The Shroud of Color*, — far more important poems— he is . . . Countée Cullen.

Sympathetic? Listen to his poem *Near White*:

Ambiguous of race they stand,
By one disowned, scorned of another,
Not knowing where to stretch a hand,
And cry, "My sister" or "My brother"

But ah, the bitter, the shocking, the tragic knowledge— "My color shrouds me in." For eight months he was blind and deaf, his heart bleeding, his soul trembling, stricken:

Once riding in old Baltimore,
Heart-filled, head-filled with glee,
I saw a Baltimorean
Keep looking straight at me.

Now I was eight and very small,
And he was no whit bigger,
And so I smiled, but he poked out
His tongue, and called me, "Nigger."

I saw the whole of Baltimore
From May until December;
Of all the things that happened there
That's all that I remember.

And then, with the curious flaring hopelessness of his race, and with his poet's soul, he speaks of God:

I doubt not God is good, well-meaning, kind,
And did He stoop to quibble could tell why

The little buried mole continues blind,
Why flesh that mirrors Him must some day die,
Make plain the reason tortured Tantalus
Is baited by the fickle fruit, declare
If merely brute caprice dooms Sisyphus
To struggle up a never-ending stair.
Inscrutable His ways are, and immune
To catechism by a mind too strewn
With petty cares to slightly understand
What awful brain compels His awful hand.
Yet do I marvel at this curious thing:
To make a poet black, and bid him sing.

Countée Cullen is one of the greatest of the younger American poets. At twenty two, after one year of publication, he finds it necessary to acknowledge his indebtedness to seventeen magazines for permission to reprint a part of the poems in his book. There are enough *good* poems in this "little collection" for five ordinary books of verse.

Countée Cullen. Twenty-two. Watch him.

J. M. W.

NOTE

PALMS takes pleasure in announcing that Countée Cullen has consented to act as Editor for a Negro Poets' Number of the magazine.

*Romance and Tragedy in Harlem—A Review**

By JAMES WELDON JOHNSTON

FROM its intriguing prologue to its tragic end, here is an absorbing story. Whether you like it or dislike it you will read it through, every chapter, every page. Mr. Van Vechten is the first white novelist of note to undertake a portrayal of modern American Negro life under metropolitan conditions. Mr. Van Vechten is also the only white novelist I can now think of who has not viewed the Negro as a type, who has not treated the race as a unit, either good or bad. In *NIGGER HEAVEN* the author has chosen as his scene Harlem, where Negro life is at its highest point of urbanity and sophistication, and there the entire action of the story is played out. The economy of stage Mr. Van Vechten imposes for himself enables him to gain in dramatic intensity but it does not limit him in the scope of the action. The story comprehends nearly every phase of life in the Negro metropolis. It draws on the components of that life from the dregs to the froth.

It was inevitable that the colorful life of Harlem would sooner or later claim the pen of Carl Van Vechten. He has taken the material it offered him and achieved the most revealing, significant and powerful novel based exclusively on Negro life yet written. A Negro reviewer might pardonably express the wish that a colored novelist had been the first to take this material and write a book of equal significance and power. Mr. Van Vechten is a modernist. In literature he is the child of his age. In *NIGGER HEAVEN* he has written a modern novel in every sense. He has written about the most modern aspects of Negro life, and he has done it in the most modern manner; for he has completely discarded and scrapped the old formula and machinery for a Negro novel. He has no need of a *deus ex machina* from the white world either to involve or evolve the plot. There is, of course, the pressure of the white world, but it is external. The white characters are less than incidental. The story works itself out through the clashes and reactions of Negro character upon Negro character. Its factors are the loves, the hates, the envies, the ambitions, the pride, the shamelessness, the intelligence, the ignorance, the goodness, the wickedness of Negro characters. In this the author pays colored people the rare tribute of writing about them as people rather than as puppets. This representation of Negro characters in a novel as happy or unhappy, successful or unsuccessful, great or mean, not because of the fortuitous attitudes of white characters in the book but because of the way in which they themselves meet and master their environment—a task imposed upon every group—is new, and in close accord with the present psychology of the intelligent element of the race. The only other full length novel following this scheme that I can recall at this moment is Jessie Fauset's *THERE IS CONFUSION*. It is a scheme for the interpretation of Negro life in America that opens up a new world for colored writers.

There are those who will prejudge the book unfavorably on account of the title. This was the attitude taken by many toward Sheldon's *THE NIGGER,* perhaps, the finest and fairest play on the race question that has yet been successfully produced in New York. This attitude is natural, but it is probable that the reaction against the title of the novel will not be so strong as it was against the title of the play which was produced sixteen years ago. Indeed, one gauge of the Negro's rise and development may be found in the degrees in which a race epithet loses its power to sting and hurt him. The title of Sheldon's play was purely ironic, and the title of *NIGGER HEAVEN* is taken from the ironic use of the phrase made by the characters in the book. But whatever may be the attitudes and opinions on this point, the book and not the title is the thing. In the book Mr. Van Vechten does not stoop to burlesque or caricature. There are characters and incidents in the book that many will regard as worse than unpleasant, but always the author handles them with sincerity and fidelity. Anatoles and Rubys and Lascas and number kings and cabarets and an underworld there are as well as there are Mary Loves and Byron Kassons and Olive Hamiltons and Howard Allisons and Dr. Lancasters and Underwoods and Sumners and young intellectuals. There are, too, Dick Sills and Buda Greens, living on both sides of the line, and then passing over. It is all life. It is all reality. And Mr. Van Vechten has taken these various manifestations of life and, as a true artist, depicted them as he sees them rather than as he might wish them to be. But the author again as a true artist, deftly maintains the symmetry and proportions of his work. The scenes of gay life, of night life, the glimpses of the underworld, with all their tinsel, their licentiousness, their depravity serve actually to set off in sharper relief the decent, cultured, intellectual life of Negro Harlem. But all these phases of life, good and bad, are merely the background for the story, and the story is the love life of Byron Kasson and Mary Love.

Mary is a beautiful, golden-brown girl who works as an assistant librarian in one of the New

**Nigger Heaven*—By Carl Van Vechten. Alfred A. Knopf. $2.50.

York public libraries. She is intelligent, cultured and refined. She is sweet, pure and placid until she meets Byron; she remains sweet and pure, but her placidity is shattered, the emotions which she sometimes feared she did not possess are stirred to the depths. Byron, bronze-colored, handsome, proud, impetuous and headstrong has just been graduated from the University of Pennsylvania. At college he had made a literary reputation in the university periodicals; his professors had encouraged him; so he comes to Harlem to make writing his profession and to conquer New York. He and Mary first meet at a gay week-end house party given by a wealthy woman of the smart set at her country home on Long Island—a house party at which Mary is sadly out of place. They meet again at a dinner given by the Sumners, one of the well-to-do, cultured colored families of Harlem. Byron calls to see Mary at her home, and the beginnings of love burst into a flame. The author makes an idyl of the awakening of love in Mary's heart. Byron starts out buoyant and sanguine. He receives a small monthly allowance from his father, but he must work to supplement that sum while he makes his way as a writer. He smarts under the rebuffs he meets with in trying to find work he considers in keeping with his training. He grows bitter and cynical under failure. He finally takes a job as an elevator boy, but this job he fails to hold. In the meantime he is devoting such time as the distractions of New York leave him to irresolute efforts at his writing. But there is something wrong with his stories, he sends them out and they regularly come back. Byron begins to slip. Mary tries to give him the benefit of her intelligent opinion and her knowledge of literature but his pride will not let her. His pride also keeps him from going for assistance to the Sumners and other influential friends to whom his father had given him letters; he does not want to be "patronized" by them. Byron cannot adapt himself, he cannot bend the bars of his environment to accommodate his own needs and desires. He has already failed, but he is not yet lost. Mary's love is what he needs to keep him steady, but the very fullness of her love raises for him a wall which his rebellious nature will not permit him to get over or through. Mary's love has developed in a two-fold manner, passionately and maternally; she jealously wants her handsome young lover wholly for herself, and she wants to watch over him and guide and protect him as she would a child, which in many respects he is. Byron is irritated by her jealousy and her attitude of guardianship he resents. He realizes that he is a failure compared to the young intellectuals and professional men of Mary's acquaintance and he feels that she, too, is pitying him, is patronizing him; and he will not be patronized. He begins to think of the fascinating, exotic Lasca Sartoris, whom he had met and danced with at a big charity ball. Her wit and beauty had amazed him and the talk about her purple past had stirred his imagination. He compares the tender, solicitous Mary with this superb woman, Lasca, who tramples all conventions under her shapely feet, who recognizes no limitations, who takes what she wants. Why couldn't he know intimately such a woman? That would be life—that would be inspiration.

One day Byron receives a letter from Russett Durwood, the editor of a great magazine, asking him to call regarding a story he had sent in. It is the story that carries all of Byron's hopes, his great story. He forgets all about Lasca. He rushes as fast as his feet can carry him to Mary. It is Mary to whom he wants to break the good news. He is again the buoyant, sanguine and the lovable Byron. He is sure of success now, he has regained his self-confidence and self-respect, Mary's love and solicitude are now grateful to him. The outcome of the interview is a lecture from the great editor on the defects of the story. He has sent for Byron because he is interested in Negro literature and Negro writers. He has seen from parts of Byron's story that he has talent and ability and can write. But "why in hell" doesn't he write about something he knows about? Negro life—Harlem—West Indians, Abyssinian Jews, religious Negroes, pagan Negroes, Negro intellectuals all living together in the same community. Why continue to employ the old clichés that have been worked to death by Nordics? Why not use this fresh material before a new crop of Nordics spring up and exploit it before Negro writers get around to it? Byron is stricken dumb, he can make no answer. He drags himself out of the building and makes his way to Central Park. Through whirling emotions of disappointment and heartbreak there surges a flame of fury. He will go back to the editor and tell him what he thinks of him; he will not stand to be treated as a Nigger. But he does not; instead, he sinks upon a park bench discouraged, disheartened, beaten. He hears a woman's voice calling him, he raises his head to see Lasca beckoning him from her luxurious limousine, Lasca, who takes what she wants. She takes Byron. She showers him with all the fragrance, the beauty, the wild ecstacies, the cruel-sweets of love that her perfect body and her lawless soul know. Byron, now, has not only failed, he is lost. And yet his is a fate before which self-righteousness should take no occasion to preen itself. One must, indeed, be much of a prig not to make some allowances for youth caught in the circle of the lure of Lasca, the courtesan supreme. Lasca keeps Byron for a period, then, as she had done others before, she throws him out, banishes him wholly, and takes Randolph Petijohn, the number king. From here on Byron's journey downward is steep and fast. His moral disintegration is complete. He pleads, he raves, he broods. He becomes obsessed with the desire for revenge; and he procures a revolver and haunts the cabarets, lying in wait for the two objects of his hatred. One night in the Black Venus, drunk to the point of irresponsibility, he sees the number king enter. While Byron is trying to bring together his dissolved will for the accomplishment of his purpose a shot rings out and Petijohn falls dead. The shot

(*Continued on page* 330)

Romance and Tragedy in Harlem

(*Continued from page* 317)

had been fired by Anatole, the Scarlet Creeper, who also had a grudge against the number king. Byron, playing his futile role in the drama out to the end, springs up, stands over the prostrate form and is emptying his revolver into the dead body when the law lays its hands upon him. An absorbing, a tragic, a disquieting story.

Byron is at many points a symbol of the tragic struggle of the race thrown as it is in an unsympathetic milieu and surrounded by fateful barriers. But Byron's story is especially true as an individual story. It is a true story—and an old story. It is the story of many a gifted and ambitious young colored man who has come up to New York as the field for success, and has been sucked in and down by the gay life and underworld of the great city. It is the story of talent and brilliancy without stamina and patience. The theme has been used before. Paul Dunbar used it in a measure in *THE SPORT OF THE GODS,* and I myself skirted it in a now forgotten novel. But never before has it been so well and fully used.

The book is written with Mr. Van Vechten's innate light touch and brilliancy, but there is a difference; Van Vechten, the satirist, becomes in *NIGGER HEAVEN* Van Vechten, the realist. In every line of the book he shows that he is serious. But however serious Van Vechten may be, he cannot be heavy. He does not moralize, he does not over-emphasize, there are no mock heroics, there are no martyrdoms. And, yet—Mr. Van Vechten would doubtless count this a defect—the book is packed full of propaganda. Every phase of the race question, from Jim Crow discriminations to miscegenation, is frankly discussed. Here the author's inside knowledge and insight are at times astonishing. But it is not the author speaking, he makes his characters do the talking, and makes each one talk in keeping with his character. If the book has a thesis it is: Negroes are people; they have the same emotions, the same passions, the same shortcomings, the same aspirations, the same graduations of social strata as other people. It will be a revelation, perhaps, a shock to those familiar only with the Negro characters of Thomas Nelson Page, Thomas Dixon and Octavius Cohen. It is the best book Mr. Van Vechten has done, and that is saying a good deal when we remember *PETER WHIFFLE.*

NIGGER HEAVEN is a book which is bound to be widely read and one which is bound to arouse much diverse discussion. This reviewer would suggest reading the book before discussing it.

Books

CARL Van Vechten's "Nigger Heaven" is a blow in the face. It is an affront to the hospitality of black folk and to the intelligence of white. First, as to its title: my objection is based on no provincial dislike of the nickname. "Nigger" is an English word of wide use and definite connotation. As employed by Conrad, Sheldon, Allen and even Firbanks, its use was justifiable. But the phrase, "Nigger Heaven", as applied to Harlem is a misnomer. "Nigger Heaven" does not mean, as Van Vechten once or twice intimates, (pages 15, 199) a haven for Negroes—a city of refuge for dark and tired souls; it means in common parlance, a nasty, sordid corner into which black folk are herded, and yet a place which they in crass ignorance are fools enough to enjoy. Harlem is no such place as that, and no one knows this better than Carl Van Vechten.

But after all, a title is only a title, and a book must be judged eventually by its fidelity to truth and its artistic merit. I find this novel neither truthful nor artistic. It is not a true picture of Harlem life, even allowing for some justifiable impressionistic exaggeration. It is a caricature. It is worse than untruth because it is a mass of half-truths. Probably some time and somewhere in Harlem every incident of the book has happened; and yet the resultant picture built out of these parts is ludicrously out of focus and undeniably misleading.

The author counts among his friends numbers of Negroes of all classes. He is an authority on dives and cabarets. But he masses this knowledge without rule or reason and seeks to express all of Harlem life in its cabarets. To him the black cabaret is Harlem; around it all his characters gravitate. Here is their stage of action. Such a theory of Harlem is nonsense. The overwhelming majority of black folk there never go to cabarets. The average colored man in Harlem is an everyday laborer, attending church, lodge and movie and as conservative and as conventional as ordinary working folk everywhere.

Something they have which is racial, something distinctively Negroid can be found; but it is expressed by subtle, almost delicate nuance, and not by the wildly, barbaric drunken orgy in whose details Van Vechten revels. There is laughter, color and spontaneity at Harlem's core, but in the current cabaret, financed and supported largely by white New York, this core is so overlaid and enwrapped with cheaper stuff that no one but a fool could mistake it for the genuine exhibition of the spirit of the people.

To all this the author has a right to reply that even if the title is an unhappy catch-phrase for penny purposes and his picture of truth untruthful, that his book has a right to be judged primarily as a work of art. Does it please? Does it entertain? Is it a good and human story? In my opinion it is not; and I am one who likes stories and I do not insist that they be written solely for my point of view. "Nigger Heaven" is to me an astonishing and wearisome hodgepodge of laboriously stated facts, quotations and expressions, illuminated here and there with something that comes near to being nothing but cheap melodrama. Real human feelings are laughed at. Love is degraded. The love of Byron and Mary is stark cruelty and that of Lasca and Byron is simply nasty. Compare this slum picture with Porgy. In his degradation, Porgy is human and interesting. But in "Nigger Heaven" there is not a single loveable character. There is scarcely a generous impulse or a beautiful ideal. The characters are singularly wooden and inhuman. Van Vechten is not the great artist who with remorseless scalpel probes the awful depths of life. To him there are no depths. It is the surface mud he slops about in. His women's bodies have no souls; no children palpitate upon his hands; he has never looked upon his dead with bitter tears. Life to him is just one damned orgy after another, with hate, hurt, gin and sadism.

Both Langston Hughes and Carl Van Vechten know Harlem cabarets; but it is Hughes who whispers

"One said he heard the jazz band sob
When the little dawn was grey".

Van Vechten never heard a sob in a cabaret. All he hears is noise and brawling. Again and again with singular lack of invention he reverts to the same climax of two creatures tearing and scratching over "mah man"; lost souls who once had women's bodies; and to Van Vechten this spells comedy, not tragedy.

I seem to see that Mr. Van Vechten began a good tale with the promising figure of Anatol, but that he keeps turning aside to write in from his notebook every fact he has heard about Negroes and their problems; singularly irrelevant quotations, Haitian history, Chesnutt's novels, race-poetry, "blues" written by white folk. Into this mass he drops characters which are in most cases thin disguises; and those who know the originals have only to compare their life and this death, to realize the failure in truth and human interest. The final climax is an utterly senseless murder which appears without preparation or reason from the clouds.

I cannot for the life of me see in this work either sincerity or art, deep thought, or truthful industry. It seems to me that Mr. Van Vechten tried to do something bizarre and he certainly succeeded. I read "Nigger Heaven" and read it through because I had to. But I advise others who are impelled by a sense of duty or curiosity to drop the book gently in the grate and to try the *Police Gazette*. W. E. D. B.

In Our American Language

By WALDO FRANK

I HAVE been reading Mr. Eric Walrond's "Tropic Death"—a collection of short stories just brought out by Boni and Liveright. My ultimate impression of the book is rather paradoxical. It seems to me that what stands in the way of the book, as a work of art, is its chief feature of interest and importance: to wit, its language. Mr. Walrond is using a raw instrument—a language whose relation with literary English is not organic at all. And the very fact that his instrument is raw, unwieldy, forces his attention so hypnotically to it, that some of the life-energy is drawn from the tales he tells. The reader, too, finds himself thinking of Mr. Walrond's language: finds himself seeing (and often being moved by) Mr. Walrond's words, rather than by the pictures and the dramas they are supposed to flesh.

I do not know Mr. Walrond's age: but I think this is his first book. And I should say, that the deep æsthetic fault I find in it is the highest sort of promise. That he has stories to tell is clear enough. That he has not successfully—or at least not organically—told them here is due to his preoccupation with ground work;—with what is indeed today the American artist's basal task, as it was, when Whitman wrote his magnificent Primer on the American language.

I find that I know nothing about Mr. Walrond's background. I do not know even if that background is "American" in the restrictive sense of the word employed by citizens of the United States. I suspect he comes from the West Indies: and in this case, his background is probably English. I find myself hoping that this is so. For if it is, my own claim about the true and whole America is strengthened. I should like to think that Mr. Walrond speaks English with a London accent, and that his grandfather was a British Squire who drank small beer at breakfast. For if this is so, the Americanism of Eric Walrond is all the more convincing: his profound affinity in language and in language-sense with the rest of us—whose background may be Scandinavian or Russian or Jewish or Spanish becomes less possibly accidental, more certainly the result of an organic occurrence in our cultural world.

The superficial elements in this book "Tropic Death" strike me indeed as not American at all. Everything I do not like about it strikes me as not American. I find here taints of what I might call the *Vanity Fair* school: cleverisms, forcednesses, devotions to brash effects for their own sake, which bungling American writers have tried to naturalize from the sophisticated schools of France and England. No matter. Although I found many words and phrases which brought to my reminiscent lips such syllables as Conrad, Cocteau, Huxley, it was clear enough to me that these pages were American: that no one but an American could feel and form language like that upon these pages.

Recognition is swift and instinctive: to explain it is hard. We meet the brother of a friend. We say, assuredly enough, "You look like my friend's brother." But if we must analyze aloud our certainty, we are liable to be stumped. How can I make clear that the basis of this book—the very substance of its language—relates it to Poe, Melville, Thoreau even—and to their contemporary successors: excludes it radically, moreover, from the noble and long lineage of English literary prose?

There is, for one thing, the matter of accent. There is, for another, the matter of swift, angular approach to his subject. The American author comes up to his vision from a different angle: his approach is not curved, not gradual, but swift and abrupt. What he finally sees moreover, is not an analyzed, dimensioned object but an unanalyzed whole. English prose gives you a Cube, for instance, as a geometric figure, holding its planes and its angles. American prose gives you that Cube as a blunt hard impact. And of course, I realize that if this is American prose, Henry James—to take an illustrious example—is not American at all, but English. Mr. Walrond who, for all I know, may be a subject of the King, *is* in his language an American. And I hereby claim him!

Wherefore, having cavalierly made him my brother, I claim the right to scold him. I don't like your sophistications, brother Walrond. I wish you'd realize that you'll wield your noble youthful language better if you'll take it *easier*. Perhaps one of your ancestors was a Caribbean peasant. When he wielded the hoe or the knife, did he not grasp it loose in his brown hand? Do you likewise with your language. Let your fine instrument lie easy in a palm half-open. I prophecy that forthway a miracle will happen. Your story will open, too. It will achieve overtones, undertones, vistas, dimensions—which in this book it lacks.

Fine Clothes to the Jew

By Langston Hughes.
New York: Alfred A. Knopf. $2 net.

Reviewed by
[redacted]

WHEN Langston Hughes published his first volume less than a year ago under the title of "The Weary Blues" he sounded a new note in contemporary American poetry Like practically all first books of lyric poetry the quality was uneven. At its worst it was interesting, because it was spontaneous and unaffected. At its best the poems contained flashes of passionate lyrical beauty that will probably stand among the finest examples of the author's work. This irregularity of quality is to be expected in a volume that is in a way a spiritual biography of the poet. Writing has been an escape; it has registered the depths, and it has caught the fire of the emotional crises through which its author has passed. Because Langston Hughes had suffered with intensity and rejoiced with abandon and managed to capture his moods in his book he sounded an authentic note.

Unfortunately, writing poetry as an escape and being a poet as a career are two different things, and the latter is fraught with dangers. In "Fine Clothes for the Jew" we are given a volume more even in quality, but because it lacks the "high spots" of "The Weary Blues" by no means as unforgettable as the first book. The outstanding contribution of the collection now under review is the portraiture of the author's own people. Langston Hughes knows his underworld. He divines the aspirations and the tragic frustrations of his own race, and the volume is a processional of his people given in brief, revealing glimpses. Here is a boy cleaning spittoons, who sings of his work: "A bright bowl of brass is beautiful to the Lord." And here is the psychology of the Negro bad man in a single stanza:

> I'm a bad, bad man
> 'Cause everybody tells me so.
> I'm a bad, bad man,
> Everybody tells me so.
> I takes ma meanness and ma licker
> Everywhere I go.

In "The Death of Do Dirty," "The New Cabaret Girl," "Prize Fighter," "Ballad of Gin Mary."eral poems bear-vator Boy" and the, the Negro prosti- [redacted] sharply etched impressions that linger in the memory.

The "Glory Hallelujah" section of the book contains a number of devotional songs which have the folk quality of the spiritual. A lovely example is the "Feet o' Jesus":

> At de feet o' Jesus,
>   Sorrow like a sea.
> Lordy, let yo' mercy
>   Come driftin' down on me.
>
> At de feet o' Jesus,
>   At yo' feet I stand.
> Oh, ma little Jesus,
>   Please reach out yo' hand.

From the section "From the Georgia Roads" tragedy emerges in the poignant, "Song for a Dark Girl."

> Way down South in Dixie,
>   (Break the heart of me),
> They hung my black young lover
>   To a cross-roads tree.
>
> Way down South in Dixie,
>   (Bruised body high in air),
> I asked the white Lord Jesus
>   What was the use of prayer.
>
> Way down South in Dixie,
>   (Break the heart of me),
> Love is a naked shadow
>   On a gnarled and naked tree.

"Fine Clothes to the Jew" contains much of beauty, and in most of the poems there is the same instinctive music and rhythm that distinguished the poet's best earlier work. Against this must be set what appears to me to be an occasional conscious striving for originality, as in the title, and the employment in one or two of the poems of a free verse that invades the territory of prose. But if this second book does not lift the art of the author to a new high level it does appreciably increase the number of first-rate poems to the credit of Langston Hughes, and it renews his high promise for the future.

NEW YORK WORLD

FEB 6 1927

The Growth of a Poet

Langston Hughes Evokes Stirring Emotions From the Life of His Race

By Walter F. White

IT IS probable that most of the sophisticated and near-sophisticated have by now heard Bessie or Clara Smith sing either in the flesh or on phonograph records one or more of the infinite number of songs known as "blues." If the prospective reader of Langston Hughes's "Fine Clothes to the Jew" (just published by Alfred A. Knopf) or his earlier "The Weary Blues" has not heard at least one of these songs as sung by a Negro singer, I urgently recommend that he do so before tackling the poems. For the blues are strictly limited both as to poetic pattern and meaning. As the name implies, blues are sung as plaintive expressions of utter despondency. Almost always there is expressed some idea of suicide through drowning or "laying ma head on de railroad track." Inevitably the repetition of a single emotion in time grows monotonous and often triteness cannot be avoided because there are few changes to be rung on the blues theme. The human voice of a Bessie Smith is needed to transmute and vary the subtle overtones and in that manner give the needed variety.

So, too, is the form rigidly fixed, one line repeated and a third line to rhyme with the first two. In a paragraph Mr. Hughes explains that "sometimes the second line in repetition is slightly changed and sometimes, but very seldom, it is omitted. The mood of the Blues is almost always despondency, but when they are sung people laugh." Frequently a beautiful bit of imagery darts through one of these songs or a poignant catching up of a profound emotion in a single line. Take, for example, two stanzas of Mr. Hughes's "Homesick Blues" in which both of these gifts are seen:

De railroad bridge's
A sad song in de air.
De railroad bridge's
A sad song in de air.
Ever time de trains pass
I wants to go somewhere.

Homesick blues, Lawd,
'S a terrible thing to have,
Homesickness blues is
A terrible thing to have.
To keep from cryin'
I opens ma mouth and laughs.

IT may be questioned, however, how much further blues can be utilized as poetry because of its rigid limitations. Out of the blues form it is possible and probable that a more inclusive poetic form may develop but that form would not be blues as the term is now interpreted. It will be interesting to watch these changes as they are developed by Mr. Hughes and others who may follow him in the growth of either a more universal medium of expression or a broadening of the scope of the moods themselves. Mr. Hughes's friends and admirers may perhaps have some apprehension that too diligent working of this vein may cramp him or lessen the fine, flowing, ecstatic sense of rhythm which he so undoubtedly possesses.

For he has seen the immense store of material for poetry which is in the life of the Negro. When he leaves the more confining form of the blues Mr. Hughes evokes magnificently stirring emotions from the life of Negro porters and prostitutes and others of humble estate. For example, take the last ten lines of this poem, "Brass Spittoons":

Hey, boy!
A bright bowl of brass is beautiful to the Lord.
Bright polished brass like the cymbals
Of King David's dancers,
Like the wine cups of Solomon.
Hey, boy!
A clean spittoon on the altar of the Lord.
A clean bright spittoon all newly polished—
At least I can offer that.
Com' mere, boy!

I WOULD like to quote several other poems and give in Mr. Hughes's own words the fine flavor of his new book—poems like "Ruby Brown," "Porter," "Prayer Meeting," "Magnolia Flowers," "Song for a Dark Girl," "Laughers," or two or three others equally fine. But that would be fair neither to Mr. Hughes nor his publisher for then there would be some who would not buy the book. It is a book that should be bought and one that will grow upon its readers in its evocation of beauty and rhythm and color and warmth. And if the reader has heard Clara or Mamie Smith croon and moan the blues, the first eight and the last nine poems in "Fine Clothes to the Jew" won't seem as monotonous as they perhaps might otherwise be judged.

A VOICE OF THE COLORED PEOPLE

Langston Hughes, as drawn by Winold Reiss. Mr. Hughes's second volume, "Fine Clothes to the Jew," has just been published

A Poet for the People—A Review*

By MARGARET LARKIN

IN casting about for a precise category in which to identify the work of Langston Hughes, I find that he might be acclaimed a new prophet in several fields, and very likely he does not think of himself as belonging to any of them.

There is still a great deal of talk about "native American rhythms" in poetic circles, and the desirability of freeing poetry from the stiff conventions which Anglo Saxon prosody inflicted upon it. In turning to the rhythm pattern of the folk "blues," Langston Hughes has contributed something of great value to other poets, particularly since he uses the form with variety and grace.

"De po' house is lonely,
An' de grave is cold.
O, de po' house is lonely,
De graveyard grave is cold.
But I'd rather be dead than
To be ugly an' old."

This apparently simple stuff is full of delicate rhythmic variety through which the long ripple of the form flows boldly. The "blues" are charming folk ballads and in the hands of this real poet present great possibilities for beauty.

Ever since I first heard Langston Hughes read his verse, I am continually wanting to liken his poems to those of Bobby Burns. Burns caught three things in his poems: dialect, speech cadence, and character of the people, so that he seems more Scotch than all of bonnie Scotland. It is a poet's true business to distil this pure essence of life, more potent by far than life ever turns out to be, even for poets. I think that Hughes is doing for the Negro race what Burns did for the Scotch—squeezing out the beauty and rich warmth of a noble people into enduring poetry.

In hearing a group of young poets reading their new poems to each other recently, I was struck with their common tendency to intricacy, mysticism, and preoccupation with brilliant technique. Their poems are competent and beautiful, and the antithesis of simple. To any but other poets, skilled in the craft, they are probably as compeltely mysterious as though in a foreign tongue. The machine age and the consequent decline of the arts has driven many poets and artists into the philosophy that art is the precious possession of the few initiate. Poets now write for the appreciation of other poets, painters are scornful of all but painters, even music, most popular of all the arts, is losing the common touch. Perhaps this is an inevitable development. Yet the people perish. Beauty is not an outworn ideal, for they still search for it on Fourteenth street. While the poets and artists hoard up beauty for themselves and each other, philosophizing upon the "aristocracy of art," some few prophets are calling for art to come out of rich men's closets and become the "proletarian art" of all the people.

Perhaps Langston Hughes does not relish the title of Proletarian Poet, but he deserves it just the same. "Railroad Avenue," "Brass Spitoons," "Prize Fighter," "Elevator Boy," "Porter," "Saturday Night," and the songs from the Georgia Roads, all have their roots deep in the lives of workers. They give voice to the philosophy of men of the people, more rugged, more beautiful, better food for poetry, than the philosophy of the "middle classes."

This is a valuable example for all poets of what can be done with simple technique and "every day" subjects, but it is particularly valuable, I believe, for other Negro poets. Booker T. Washington's adjuration to "educate yourself" has sunk too deep in the Race philosophy. As in all American life, there is a strong urge to escape life's problems by reaching another station. "The life of a professional man must surely be happier than that of a factory worker," America reasons. "A teacher must surely find greater satisfaction than a farmer." Poets, influenced by this group sentiment, want to write about "nicer" emotions than those of the prize fighter who reasons

Only dumb guys fight."
If I wasn't dumb
I wouldn't be fightin'
I could make six dollars a day
On the docks,
And I'd save more than I do now.
Only dumb guys fight."

or the pondering on circumstance of the boy who cleans spitoons

"Babies and gin and church
and women and Sunday
all mixed up with dimes and
dollars and clean spitoons
and house rent to pay.
Hey, boy!
A bright bowl of brass is beautiful to the Lord.
Bright polished brass like the cymbals
Of King David's dancers,
Like the wine cups of Solomon.
Hey, boy!"

Yet this, much more than the neurotic fantasies of more sophisticated poets, is the stuff of life.

There is evidence in this book that Langston Hughes is seeking new mediums, and this is a healthy sign. If he were to remain the poet of the ubiquitous "blues" he would be much less interesting. He will find new forms for himself, and I do not believe that he will lose his hold on the simple poignancy that he put into the "blues" as he adds to his poetic stature. The strong, craftsmanlike handling of "Mulatto," one of the best poems in the book, the delicate treatment of "Prayer," the effective rhythm shifts of "Saturday Night" are promises of growing power.

Not all of the poems of *Fine Clothes to the Jew* are of equal merit. Many of them are the product of too great facility. To be able to write easily is a curse, that hangs over many a poet, tempting him

**Fine Clothes to the Jew* by Langston Hughes. Alfred A. Knopf, Publishers. $2.00.

to produce good verse from which the fine bead of true poetry is lacking. But even the most demanding critic cannot expect poets to publish perfect volumes. It ought to be enough to find one exquisite lyric like the "New Cabaret Girl" surcharged with an emotion kept in beautiful restraint,

"My God, I says,
You can't live that way!
Babe, you can't
Live that way!"

and here are many such.

Keats in Labrador*

A *Review* by E. MERRILL ROOT

MODERN American poetry has had two chief faults: a hard clear technique; a hard objective content. With brilliant exceptions, like Edna Millay (that tiger, tiger burning bright), or like the grace notes of Robert Frost (that eagle-sized lark), it has seldom been poetry that sings and that shines. If it shone — as in Amy Lowell's scissor-blades and patchwork, it did not sing; if it sang—as in the jazz records to be played on the Victrola of Vachel, it did not shine. Much of the rest of it has not been Christian enough to escape the hard intellectuality of Puritanism: like the bleak Pilgrim Fathers, it wears black: it knows little of the Lilies of the Field and the Many Mansions. It has been "just a plate of current fashion" with "not a softness anywhere about it," like the formal lady in *Patterns;* it has seldom been "Eve with her body white, supple and smooth to her slim fingertips."

Therefore I, for one, welcome poetry that sings and that shines; poetry that is no plumed hearse, but a dancing star.

"I who adore exotic things
Would shape a sound
To be your name, a word
that sings
Until the head goes
round."

So sings Countee Cullen, unashamed. And it is no boasting: it is a literal description of his sensuous rhythms, his translation of heart's blood into words, his imagery that is not the decorative cameos of the Imagists, but the suns that roar through heaven and the scarlet flowers that grow mystically from the black and humorous earth. Here is poetry that is not written with phosphorescent brains, but with the soul's blood. Here is poetry that soars on deep-damasked wings.

Countee Cullen's title is *Copper Sun.* And in the book we are transported into a fresher world, where the sun is a blazing copper drum sounding reveille over the morning hills, and the trees are heavy with the "golden increment of bursting fruit," and the delicate reeds quiver under the feet of the wind, that angel of the unknown color.

A Charles Cullen Illustration for "Copper Sun"

Technically considered, the book is a delight and a triumph. Whether we stir to the rolling echoes and the dying fall of its music, as in that haunting and perfect poem, *Threnody;* or thrill to the subtlety of emotion incarnated in the simplicity of art—the tears, idle tears of *Pity the Deep in Love;* or marvel at imagery as inevitable as the green hills haloed with the copper sun of morning, we acknowledge Countee Cullen a master of living magic.

"One to her are flame and
frost;
Silence is her singing lark;
We alone are children, lost,
Crying in the dark.
Varied feature now, and
form,
Change has bred upon her;
Crush no bug nor nauseous
worm
Lest you tread upon her.

Pluck no flower lest she
scream;
Bruise no slender reed,
Lest it prove more than it
seem,
Lest she groan and bleed.
More than ever trust your
brother,
Read him golden, pure;
It may be she finds no other
House so safe and sure.

. . . .

Lay upon her no white stone
From a foreign quarry;
Earth and sky be these alone
Her obituary."

Such lines seem the earth's own green hieroglyphs. To paraphrase the poet: Earth and sky be these alone Poetry's commentary!

And (as always) it is only out of the fullness of the blood that the mouth chants. These are no Arrows of Scorning shot by an impotent brain, no acrobatics of a honeyless wasp, no finger-exercises by the Precocious Child trying to see how different he can be from Mr. Longfellow. These are pulses

**Copper Sun*, by Countee Cullen, Harper & Bros.

translated into poetry. Here is the revolt, fierce but forgiving, of *From the Dark Tower;* the "grief wound up to a mysteriousness" of *Threnody,* where personal anguish merges into pantheistic mysticism; the ache and ecstasy of love, sung with a simple inevitability that equals A. E. Housman, and a breadth of range that surpasses Edna Millay; the fear of all flesh (as in *Protest*) for the dark halo . . . Here are magic casements opening on many seas: and Countee Cullen has himself stood at every casement and looked from each with his own eyes. His is no poetry at second brain: no tinsel of words, but a tissue of experience. He is no mirror but a face; no phonograph but a voice.

In lyricism more musical and rich, in a subtle sensuousness which shows that the years have brought him more philosophic eyes, *Copper Sun* surpasses *Color.* If I find any luck and lapse, I miss those great poems, those longer epics of philosophy, *Heritage* and *Shroud of Color.* I want to see Countee Cullen again fight a campaign and not merely a battle, with full pomp and circumstance justify man's ways to God. Yet tho he perhaps shows a relapse in scope of attack, he shows an advance in the quality of his philosophy. He is still death-shadowed; he still feels the "little room" which fifty—or fifty times fifty—Springs give to our immortal longings; but he wanders less resolutely in the Valley of the Shadow. In *Threnody,* in *Epilogue,* he shows a philosophic advance: he steps out of the dark halo that hovers over us as from an eagle's wings: he sees death as it is—an accident and not an essence—a relapse of the mortal body, but a return to the immortal energy: he may yet say, with Whitman, "To die is different from what we expect—and luckier." Also, in the *Litany of the Dark Peoples,* he has written one of the finest manifestoes of generosity that has been written in modern years: in serenity of vision and triumph it transcends even those great poems (which belong to our common race of Adam) *Heritage* and *Shroud of Color.*

> "And if we hunger now and thirst,
> Grant our witholders may,
> When heaven's constellations burst
> Upon Thy crowning day,
> Be fed by us and given to see
> Thy mercy in our eyes,
> When Bethlehem and Calvary
> Are merged in Paradise."

And Countee Cullen has developed, too, a new suggestion of fighting faith, a gav insouciance of Yea-saying, that is an advance. Thus the poet is one whose

> "Ears are tuned to all sharp cries
> Of travail and complaining,
> His vision stalks a new moon's rise
> In every old moon's waning.
> And in his heart pride's red flag flies
> Too high for sorrow's gaining."

Hegelian paradox set to gay music *(More than a Fool's Song)*, banter with the superstition called Fate *(Ultimatum)*, the Higher Scepticism of Epilogue, show that he is, more than most of our modern American poets, a singer after sunset—and before sunrise. Whether he knows it or not, the best in him is shaking itself loose of Disillusionment and Decay and Fallen-petal Pessimism and all our resolute, dreary Apostles of the Unholy Catholic Church of Death Everlasting, from Masters to Mencken.

I am presumptuous, but if a critic has any worth, he must be conscious of the artist's unconscious: he must translate into idea the urge and ultimatum of the blood which the artist translates into image. What, then, is the *elan vital* back of Countee Cullen's blood?—An emphasis on color and on copper suns, on the subjective and the lyric, on the heart as well as the head, on poetry that shines and that sings: in short, on Romance. That is his peculiar worth: that makes him rare and radiant. And, in future, what should be his further path and destiny? It seems to me that, having done all he can do to give immortal poignance to the ache and transcience of flesh, he should go beyond good and evil, above life and death, into spirit. In denial of negation and in acceptance of affirmation, in the victorious synthesis of animal and angel, in instincts made rhythmic with intellect, in spirit defeated yet superb like Spartacus . . . there, with Shelley, he will find "life, empire, and victory." My wish for him is that he leap to the forefront of the battle; that he become the first poet in modern America to accept the universe like a master-spirit. And my wish is not merely a love and a hope, but (thanks to the tocsin that already sounds in his poetry) a faith.

Countee Cullen belongs to a great race that, because of American savagery, stupidity, and jealousy, has had to walk the Valley of the Shadow. If he will rise above tragic circumstance, as we poor dwellers on Waste Lands and Main Streets are not strong enough to do, if he will (to quote Carlyle) "seek within himself for that consistency and sequence which external events will always refuse him (and us)," he can be the first American poet to become Nietzsche's child—"Innocence is the child, and forgetfulness, a new beginning, a game, a self-rolling wheel, a first movement, a Holy Yea."

Meanwhile, tho he is not yet the spiritual leader of a new day, he is one of the few poets of our generation. He sings and shines like Edna Millay, and has more wholesome life in his blood; his blood (if not always his brain) is world-accepting and life-affirming like Frost's grey elfin mysticism, and he has richer color, tho not an idiom as unique and great as Frost's tang and accent.

Countee Cullen loves Keats; therefore he will know what I mean—and how much I mean—when I say that in his sensuous richness of phrase, in his sweetness of heart, in his death-shadowed joy, he reminds me of Keats. The great tree has fallen; but from the mystic root comes up this shoot and sapling with the same rich leaves. Countee Cullen, it seems to me, is much what the young Keats would be if he wore flesh again in this minor and maddening age, this fever and fret of a fiercer Capitalism, this welter thru which war has plunged like a dinasaur trampling daffodils, this fox-fire age of cerebral realism, this Labrador of the soul which we call America.

OUR BOOK SHELF

The Autobiography of an Ex-Colored Man, by James Weldon Johnson. Alfred A. Knopf, New York. $3.00. With an Introduction by Carl Van Vechten.

IT was in 1912 that the reading public among Negroes and friends of Negroes was shaken to its inner core by the appearance of a book, surely the strangest that had ever been written by or about the Negro. *The Autobiography of an Ex-Colored Man,* published anonymously, evoked wide and varied speculation. Was the author really a Negro? Was it not perhaps some white man, who having observed the phenomenon of the fair colored man, slipped over into the ranks of the Caucasians, was perhaps venting his delicate satire on the American public? Negroes generally believed that the author was "one of ours". There were too many little subtle ear-marks of the man born, bred and nutured in the traditions of the race. No mere white man could hope to penetrate into the mysteries of racial psychology. But the wonder died down, as wonders have a fashion of doing, and the book was out of print before the secret of its authorship leaked out and became generally known.

But the memory of the remarkable work clung, and therefore it is felt that Alfred A. Knopf has performed a distinct service to present day literature by bringing out another edition of this delicate satire. For satire it is, couched in the most subtle form. The same sort of satire that Swift perpetrated in *Gulliver's Travels,* bland, lucid, arresting by its very naiveté. Or perhaps the kind of disarming narrative that Defoe writes in his apparent autobiographies, the supreme art of putting oneself into the soul of another, albeit that other has probably only existed in one's imagination.

Carl Van Vechten has written an introduction to this late edition. He acknowledges his indebtedness to the book in making his studies of the Negro, and compares it to Booker Washington's *Up From Slavery* which it rather resembles in manner and diction. Its dispassionate, impersonal air, with complete lack of verbiage, fine writing, hysterics, passion, adjectives or rhetorical involutions does suggest Mr. Washington's style. But as suggested by Mr. Van Vechten, the limitations of *Up From Slavery* are not to be found in the Autobiography.

Fifteen years ago, when the book appeared, there was no Harlem, as we know it now. Negro night life had moved from the Thirties, which are described in the Autobiography, to the Fifties. The early scenes of the book lie in the Thirities, twenty-five years ago, in the hey-dey of George Walker and Cole and Johnson and hansom ccabs and the Floradora sextette and all the rest of the hectic days of the early twentieth century. The child of mysterious parentage, such as the author describes himself in the earlier chapters, was common enough in the South of thirty or forty years ago, but fortunately no more. And for that the race may heave a sigh of relief and thankfulness. Jazz was unknown, but Lottie Collins had glorified rag-time, and the big Negro shows of the time were making it classic. Cabarets were "Clubs" and vice was gilded, not painted. Life was a bubble and froth in the cup of pleasure, but its bubbles were perhaps caused by real champagne, and not by bootleg substitutes.

All this Mr. Johnson has made live in his pages. Somehow you move with him through all his vicissitudes—in the little Connecticut town, among the Spanish soeaking cigar-makers, in the beautiful town of Jacksonville (here certainly Mr. Johnson was at home), in the noisome dens of the gambling clubs of New York; in France, in England, and back at home in his own country. He makes you feel his griefs from the very supression of his own emotions. And here is where the sheer art of the book is evident. The author expresses both objectively and subjectively emotions both complex and powerful. He is shaken to the soul by grief, tormented by indecisions, perplexed by grave problems, and you feel it all with him, albeit you are, at the same time, standing with him on the

THE
AUTOBIOGRAPHY
OF AN
EX-COLOURED MAN
JAMES WELDON JOHNSON

From the Jacket of "The Autobiography of An Ex-Coloured Man"

outside of the emotional area watching the writhings of the nameless individual who acts as protagonist.

Another great claim upon the imagination of the present day reader lies in the musical hints which Mr. Johnson gives of what he was later to elaborate. The "Ex-Coloured Man" was primarily a musician, and it was as a musician that he had hoped to create his career. Hence his interest in the folk-songs of the Negro, and his dismay when he found he must throw over his chosen career if he were to be white. Had he lived now, it would have only served as a whet to his ambition, whether white or black, to write of the music of the Negro. In the book we find precursors of the scholarly and exhaustive introductions to the two books of Negro Spirituals, edited by Mr. Johnson, and to *God's Trombones.* There are glimpses of the classic "Singing Johnson" and "John Brown, the Preacher", now well-known to Mr. Johnson's readers. "The day will come," he avers, "when this slave music will be the most treasured heritage of the American Negro." A bold prophecy, but that day has come, and more than that, for this slave music is the biggest thing in the modern musical world.

The book runs the whole gamut of the life of an American Negro not only twenty-five or thirty years ago, but of today, from the debauched slave woman with her octoroon offspring, to the very latest style in lynchings—which the author describes with so few lines that it seems almost like a dry-point etching, nauseatingly vivid and terse. It describes every variety of American Negro from the crudest field hand to the cultured professional man and their wives in the inner circles of fashionable Washington. In a small space he has epitomized the life and soul of the Negro, as surprisingly true then as now. There have been additions to the charmed circle of the culturally elect, yet the soul of the race is essentially the same. And the lynchings go on as merrily and as vividly, yea, even more so, as ever, so that the thoughtful Negro may still feel "Shame at being identified with a people that could with impunity be treated worse than animals. For certainly the law would restrain and punish the malicious burning alive of animals."

We, who must be always looking for the moral of any story, may rejoice to find it in the last sentence, "I cannot repress the thought that after all, I have chosen the lesser part, that I have sold my birthright for a mess of pottage." For so it must ever be for the man or the woman of any race or nationality whatever, who turns his back upon his own people for his own fancied gain—the canker worm of self-distrust and shame at his own cowardice will eat at his heart until he shall close his eyes upon a deceitful world.

Alice Dunbar Nelson.

OUR BOOK SHELF

Caroling Dusk: An Anthology of Verse by Negro Poets. Edited by Countee Cullen. Harpers, $2.50.

WITH an unhappy heritage of poverty, prejudice, and contempt to combat, and with the happy heritage of ambitious minds, singing hearts, and a simple faith in ultimate goodness and justice, these carolers have the conflict and impetus necessary for the production of art.

Out of satisfaction and completion no true art can emerge. Right art foundations exist in the life of the lonely human being attempting to fashion, out of his loneliness and his pride, a vision of loveliness and truth to live by. If poetry comes to him "as naturally as the leaves to the tree", if rhythm is born in his blood, he is able to make audible and permanent for his own and other ears the joy and the sorrow within his heart.

In *Caroling Dusk* one hears the voices emerging, some of them high and clear, and some of them groping for melody.

In an age that is growing altogether too self-conscious, poetry is suffering greatly from over-intellecutalization. In proportion as it grows cerebral it grows sterile and unsatisfactory. We ask our poets for the bread of life, and most of them give us the uncomforting stone of cold mentality. Poetry is losing simplicity, intuition, emotional color, and human values which, in the past, have made it a consolation and a revelation to man.

In *Caroling Dusk* we find immediate responses to the beauty seen by the singers; responses colorful and glowing with a real abundance of life. These are fashioned into simple and sincere songs. We find here a wide range of human emotion—pathos, pity, irony, pride, hate, love and humor.

Moreover, among most of these poets there is sufficient depth of thought and intellectual quality to give weight and meaning to their verse . Happily, the Negro has not yet learned to divorce heart and mind, and cleave to mind alone; he can therefore write a complete poem, born in pain out of his completeness of being.

Grass Fingers, by Angelina Weld Grimke, is pleasingly whimiscal. However, anyone who can write so delicately should know better than to mar her work, even on purpose, with such a tongue-twister as, *"A clenched claw cupping a craggy chin"*.

Claude McKay's *America* has genuine force, and his *Flame-Heart* is an adroitly done bit of tropical nature. Several stanzas in his *Desolate* are remarkably lovely, and the whole has the haunting effect of *La Belle Dame Sans Merci*.

Beneath the ebon gloom of mounting rocks
The little pools lie poisonously still.
And birds come to the edge in forlorn flocks,
And utter sudden plaintive notes and shrill,
Pecking at fatty grey-green substances;
But never do they dip their bills and drink.
They twitter sad beneath the mournful trees,
And fretfully flit to and from the brink,
In little dull brown, green-and-purple flocks,
Beneath the jet-gloom of the mounting rocks.

And green-eyed moths of curious design,
With gold-black wings and brightly silver-dotted,
On nests of flowers among those rocks decline—
Bold, burning blossoms, strangely leopard-spotted,
But breathing deadly poison at the lips.
Oh, every lovely moth that wanders by,
And on the blossoms fatal nectar sips,
Is doomed in drooping stupor there to die—
All green-eyed moths of curious design
That on the fiercely-burning rocks recline.

Sterling A. Brown, in *Salutamus* and *Challenge*, strikes a resounding note; then turning to the ballad he shows us in *Maumee Ruth*, the *Odyssey of Big Boy*, and the thoroughly enjoyable *Long Gone*, his mastery of a lighter form and of tragedy in a comic mask. Langston Hughes will have to look to his laurels.

Hughes is fairly represented here. The memorable lines from *Homesick Blues*.

"De railroad bridge's
A sad song in de air * * *"

and the poem *Mother to Son*, with its pathetic brave philosophy, are the high points of his group.

Gladys May Casely Hayford writes warm golden poems of Africa. We wish Jean Toomer would strive more to be the poet, and less the articulate Negro. We would like to have space to review adequately the work of others, including especially Arna Bontemps, Georgia Douglas Johnson, Effie Lee Newsome, and Anne Spencer.

There is no doubt that the poems by Countee Cullen constitute the finest group in the anthology; *To Lovers of Earth: Fair Warning* reaches as high a level as any short poem we have seen this year. If Countee Cullen continues writing with the maturity shown in his poems of the present year, he will be one of the great poets of America. *Idella Purnell.*

THE BROWSING READER

Cullen's "Caroling Dusk",
Lock and Montgomery's
"Plays of Negro Life"
and other books.

COUNTEE CULLEN'S "Caroling Dusk", (Harpers', $2.50), is the fourth anthology of Negro American poetry to appear in the last five years. The others were: James W. Johnson's "Book of American Negro Poetry", (1922); Robert T. Kerlin's "Negro Poets and Their Poems", (1922); and White and Jackson's "Anthology of Verse by American Negroes", (1924). It is astounding to find so little duplication. Of the poets represented in Cullen, twenty-eight are not mentioned by Johnson, chiefly because they had not begun to write, while many of the poems in Cullen are later works of the older poets. This points to a virility and new birth of Negro literature. As the author says: "This anthology, by no means offered as *the* anthology of verse by Negro poets, is but a prelude, we hope, to that fuller symphony which Negro poets will in time contribute to the national literature and we shall be sadly disappointed if the next few years do not find this collection entirely outmoded". The editing is delicately and discreetly done and the self-written biographies add much to its charm.

Alain Locke and Montgomery Gregory have edited "Plays of Negro Life", (Harpers', $5.00), which supplies a wide demand. The authors were associated in pioneer work in dramatics at Howard University some years ago. Mr. Locke says in his introduction: "This anthology garners the yield of this experimental and ground-breaking decade as far as the one-act play is concerned, and in that form, which has been the bulk of the recent development, presents the worth-while repertory of the Negro Theatre to date. Here really is a new province in our national literature. From opposite approaches, there has been a notable collaboration between the Negro play-wright attempting, on the one side, to advance Negro drama as such and to provide the talent of the Negro actor with a fit vehicle and a native medium and, on the other side, the quest of modern American realism for new material and a deeper, firmer grip upon the actualities of American life. Half the plays in this volume represent one wing of this advance, and half, the other".

Among the writers represented are the white O'Neill, Torrence and Green, while among the colored are Wilson, Matheus, Spence, Toomer, Richardson and Johnson. The editing and proof reading in this volume leave something to be desired. There are many obvious slips.

Aaron Douglas has decorated both these volumes with his usual arresting skill.

The fourth edition of Woodson's "Negro in our History", (The Associated Publishers, 1927), is a mighty volume of 616 pages; too large by far for a school text book, but excellent for college and home reference. It has become the best handy encyclopedia of the Negro in America that one could buy.

Walter Fleming's history of the "Freedmen's Savings Bank", (University of North Carolina Press, $2.00), is a story of philanthropy and fraud told by a man who is no friend of Negroes but more than willing to expose with dispassionate impartiality this disgraceful episode. No Negro should be ignorant of these facts. Steiner and Brown's study of the "North Carolina Chain Gang" from the same press, ($2.00), is an excellent detailed study of local crime and punishment. It is depressing but ought to form a basis of intelligent reform.

W. E. Walling's "The Mexican Question", (Robins Press, $2.00), defends this true thesis: "If we intervene or interfere in Mexico the world will conclude that America's foreign policies are to be made henceforth by the business interests and that the people have either been mastered or have voluntarily abdicated. From that moment every nation would be on its guard against us and ready to combine and use every means to prevent further encroachments and the further aggrandizement of American capital. Already the economic rapprochement of France and Germany is largely accounted for, as the German Foreign Minister Stresemann, pointed out in his Nobel Peace Prize speech, by the desire of these European nations 'to defend themselves from oppression and absorption' by this new extra European Power.

"That way madness lies."

W. E. B. D.

THE BROWSING READER

TWO NOVELS

Nella Larsen "Quicksand" (Knopf)
Claude McKay "Home to Harlem" (Harper and Brothers)

I HAVE just read the last two novels of Negro America. The one I liked; the other I distinctly did not. I think that Mrs. Imes, writing under the pen name of Nella Larsen, has done a fine, thoughtful and courageous piece of work in her novel. It is, on the whole, the best piece of fiction that Negro America has produced since the heyday of Chesnutt, and stands easily with Jessie Fauset's "There is Confusion", in its subtle comprehension of the curious cross currents that swirl about the black American.

Claude McKay's "Home to Harlem", on the other hand, for the most part nauseates me, and after the dirtier parts of its filth I feel distinctly like taking a bath. This does not mean that the book is wholly bad. McKay is too great a poet to make any complete failure in writing. There are bits of "Home to Harlem", beautiful and fascinating: the continued changes upon the theme of the beauty of colored skins; the portrayal of the fascination of their new yearnings for each other which Negroes are developing. The chief character, Jake, has something appealing, and the glimpses of the Haitian, Ray, have all the materials of a great piece of fiction.

But it looks as though, despite this, McKay has set out to cater for that prurient demand on the part of white folk for a portrayal in Negroes of that utter licentiousness which conventional civilization holds white folk back from enjoying—if enjoyment it can be called. That which a certain decadent section of the white American world, centered particularly in New York, longs for with fierce and unrestrained passions, it wants to see written out in black and white, and saddled on black Harlem. This demand, as voiced by a number of New York publishers, McKay has certainly satisfied, and added much for good measure. He has used every art and emphasis to paint drunkenness, fighting, lascivious sexual promiscuity and utter absence of restraint in as bold and as bright colors as he can.

If this had been done in the course of a well-conceived plot or with any artistic unity, it might have been understood if not excused. But "Home to Harlem" is padded. Whole chapters here and there are inserted with no connection to the main plot, except that they are on the same dirty subject. As a picture of Harlem life or of Negro life anywhere, it is, of course, nonsense. Untrue, not so much as on account of its facts, but on account of its emphasis and glaring colors. I am sorry that the author of "Harlem Shadows" stooped to this. I sincerely hope that he will some day rise above it and give us in fiction the strong, well-knit as well as beautiful theme, that it seems to me he might do.

Nella Larsen on the other hand has seized an interesting character and fitted her into a close yet delicately woven plot. There is no "happy ending" and yet the theme is not defeatist like the work of Peterkin and Green. Helga Crane sinks at last still master of her whimsical, unsatisfied soul. In the end she will be beaten down even to death but she never will utterly surrender to hypocricy and convention. Helga is typical of the new, honest, young fighting Negro woman—the one on whom "race" sits negligibly and Life is always first and its wandering path is but darkened, not obliterated by the shadow of the Veil. White folk will not like this book. It is not near nasty enough for New York columnists. It is too sincere for the South and middle West. Therefore, buy it and make Mrs. Imes write many more novels.

Social science in America has so long been the foot ball of "nigger"-hating propaganda that we Negroes fail to get excited when a new scientist comes into the field. We have had our fill of Bean, Smith, Brigham and McDougal, so that when a young student turns to the Negro problem, we assume he is going to come out exactly where he went in. When Melville Herskovits started anthropological measurements in Harlem, the only hope we had was that he was a pupil of Franz Boaz. But he proved to be more than this. Herskovits is a real scientist. That is: a man who is more interested in arriving at truth than proving a thesis of race superiority.

His book, "The American Negro", (Knopf) built up from a number of papers and studies is, in a real sense, epoch-making. First of all, he proves by a series of careful measurements and compilations that the American Negro is a new definite group. All of that nonsense fostered by the United States Census as to mulattos is swept away. I myself told the Census authorities of 1910 when I collaborated with them, that their figures on mulattos made a serious under-estimate and was laughed at for my pains. Now comes Herskovits and proves by a wide study that less than one-fourth of the Negroes of the United States are of unmixed Negro blood and that forty per cent of them have as much or more white blood as Negro. This in itself is neither advantage nor disadvantage; but it shows on the one hand the idiocy of talking about the Negro as an "unassimilable" and distinct race in the United States, and of arguing about American Negroes from the same premises as we argue about the Bantu.

Indeed the interesting thing about Mr. Herskovits' conclusions is that we have in the American Negro, by actual physical measurements, a group which resembles in many important respects, a pure race. That is: the intermixture has gone on for so long and the "racial" inbreeding and inter-thinking have become so strong, that a singular group stability has been attained. Moreover, one feels that this group stability has been even more largely a matter of social and rational accomplishment than of mere physical descent.

The implications of Herskovits' studies are really tremendous, not simply for the race problem in the United States, but also for the whole question of human contact, intermingling of blood and social heredity. It is a little book of 92 pages and costs a trifle. It ought to be in every Negro's library.

We may end this review with one interesting quotation.

"The American Negroes are, after all, a homogeneous population. They are also a greatly mixed group. How may one reconcile these two statements? It is not so difficult when one really considers the proposition from all angles. For is it not true that all human groups represent large amounts of mixture? This brings us back to the theory of race. Students have wondered at the number of varieties of human types, and have been unable to account for them. They have also been at a loss to account for the degree to which all the so-called 'races' of man seem to shade from one type into another; with never the sharp lines of demarcation that are found when we divide one biological species from another."

W. E. B. D.

BOOK REVIEWS

Home to Harlem. By Claude McKay. Harper & Bros., New York. 1928. Price $2.50.

THE over-civilized or supersensitive will not enjoy reading all of Claude McKay's "Home to Harlem." It carves into a raw, red bit of Harlem life on the level of the longshoreman. The none too closely related incidents of the story are bound together by the happy, fearless, virile Jake, and all his companions are pictured with a sincerity and trueness to their environment that takes away sordidness. McKay is no outsider searching for dregs in Harlem. He gives us a series of authentic pictures, interesting and fascinating to anyone interested in human life with capacity to get outside a circumscribed area of life and enter into another at least as genuine.

Jake takes a turn in the dining car and we are taken behind the scenes there, and into the hell-hole provided by the Pennsylvania Railroad for its Negro employees in Pittsburgh. Most of the time we are with him in Harlem where his incidental and unsought conquests enrich the life he knows. In contrast to Jake, who is unhampered by any but self-education in his manner of living, comes Ray, brilliant, sensitive, and saturated with the pre-war European dramatists, but a tragic figure in his inability to relate his knowledge and philosophy to the environment in which he found himself.

Passages in the book are poetry, many are rich; all are sincere. As a picture of phases of Harlem life it has a sociological interest apart from that of style and incident value. Those who like people for their human qualities, even though they be crude and unmoral, will like "Home to Harlem."

—A. B. D., Jr.

Home to Harlem, By Claude McKay. New York. Harper and Brothers, $2.50.

A matter of very nearly ten years ago I ventured the opinion in the *New York Evening Post* that the time was ripe for an awakening among writers of the Negro race, as well as of the white, to the richness of the fictional material lying ready to honest hands, not alone in the relations of the two races with all their implications; but in the fair and just presentation of the life and character of the Negro element of this country's population.

It was natural for me as a Southerner to think first of the vast amount of literary ore in my part of the country that awaited minting as soon as capable writers could be found who were able to free themselves of conventional prejudice and see their tasks in terms of art rather than in terms of propaganda for white supremacy, or propaganda of any sort—one kind, as it happens, is quite as dangerous as another to the intention of the artist.

But at the time I should not have been so insistent that Negro writers themselves would do their full share if I had not realized that along with a changing attitude on the part of the white South toward many aspects of race relations, the new colored centers of population were promising to offer sufficient detachment from the more disagreeable aspects of the situation to give one great hopes of what writers developed there might accomplish.

How well the prophesy has been fulfilled has now become literary history. Beginning with T. S. Stribling's "Birthright," H. A. Shand's "White and Black" and Clement Wood's "Nigger," every one significant of a breaking up of old prejudices and new desire to be fair to the Negro, and passing along to such fine recent novels as Du Bose Heyward's "Porgy" and Julia Peterkin's "Black April," the movement has grown without check. We have had stirring novels from Walter F. White, and Arthur Huff Fausett has written short stories good enough to win the O. Henry prize he came very near receiving a year or so ago.

If there has been much activity among Southerners and if we have witnessed something like a revolution in fiction dealing with Negroes, they have been busying themelves in Harlem and other cultural centers. How much Harlem has been discussed around New York in recent years is too well known to need commenting upon; the wealth of literary material there has up to this time, however, gone relatively neglected.

With due respect to Carl Van Vechten's aims and intentions in "Nigger Heaven" I did not like the book overmuch. But I do like Claude McKay's "Home to Harlem" which I have been a long time getting to in this article. And what I like most about it is its absolute candor, its complete freedom from an attempt to apologize or explain or gloss over.

Mr. McKay's story of the exploits, amorous and otherwise, of Jake, who abandoned the War when he saw there was little chance for real fighting, rings true, and because it does its characters are understandable and sympathetic. Jake likes his women and his liquor, neither of which he has any trouble of obtaining; he has a rousing "come-day, go-day, God-send-Sunday" attitude toward life that is refreshingly primitive; he lives simply and straightforwardly and with no restraint or concern for the morrow.

Mr. McKay's Harlem is the Harlem of pre-Prohibition days, although one is privileged to suppose that the scene has changed but little since speakeasies supplanted friendly old corner saloons. It is a Harlem where women fight for their men, and men for their women, a Harlem of casual attachments, with or without financial arrangements, of bloodsucking money-lenders, and gamblers, pimps, "sweetmen," and so on. It has vivid color as Mr. McKay describes it; it is a satire on civilization as we imagine it should be, a modern symphony scored for saxophones and snare-drums which were once tom-toms.

For contrast to the free and easy Jake, big, handsome, and reckless, there is the interesting Haytian, Raymond, whom Jake meets while serving as a dining car waiter. Raymond knows the history of his own land, the glory of Toussaint L' Ouverture and the courage of Dessalines; he knows other literature, and the exercise of his desires, which so pleases Jake and fills his life, makes no appeal to a young man upon whom the tragedy of race weighs heavily. Jake's Americanism, which makes him suspicious of such a person, is one of the most subtly delightful touches in the book. It is something the author must have met himself, since he is a Jamaican.

Loose in structure, "Home to Harlem" is held together by Jake's search for a brown-skin girl he has met his first night back in New York after his trip abroad. She and Jake delight each other, but he forgets her address, and many things happen to him before he meets her again by accident. This is a love-story, a little crude, perhaps, but not in the least without its genuine element of romance.

Mr. McKay has interpolated one chapter which is a very fine short story. It is Raymond's narrative of the suicide of a pimp, who really loved the woman he sent into the streets.

I have said that Mr. McKay's book gives me the feeling of fidelity to the phases of life which he touches. The picture is not meant to be complete, to be sure, but what is put down before us is done with an eye that looks straight nad unblinkingly at the object. There are moments when the style falters slightly, but on the whole the quality of the writing is good.

The book is rich in Harlem slang, as for example, "Ah-Ah" as a synonym for dumbbell; "dickty shines" for well-dressed, pretentious members of Jake's own race, "chocolate-to-the-bone" as the description of the color of one of the characters, and life described as "a be-be itching of a place." I haven't the remotest notion what the last means, but it is highly decriptive.

Aside from these critical matters, "Home to Harlem" is a thoroughly entertaining book, in which there are drama, tragedy, comedy, romance, pathos and most of the other elements one asks for in literature. Mr. McKay has done well, it seems to me, and I hope that more novelists of his stature will be discovered among his people.

Herschel Brickell.

Quicksand, by Nella Larsen. Alfred Knopf. $2.50.

TO tell the story of a cultivated and sensitive woman's defeat through her own sex-desire is a difficult task. When the woman is a mulatto and beset by hereditary, social and racial forces over which she has little control and into which she cannot fit, her character is so complex that any analysis of it takes a mature imagination. This, I believe, Miss Larsen is too young to have. the book, *Quicksand*, is a first novel. The attempt is to present Helga Crane not as a young colored woman, but as a young woman with problems unique to her temperament, and her background one largely of her own choice. Supposedly, save for a deep-rooted weakness, she has the vitality to manipulate the machinery of her days. But of this we are never quite convinced. As portrayed, the character is not quite of one pattern. Now it is Helga, the aesthete, the impulsively intelligent girl whom we feel; now it is Helga, the mulatto, suffering from an inferiority complex about her mixed ancestry, her lack of social status. Since she is supposedly complex, her character should be turned to us as a jewel of many facets. Instead we get it as a piece of bright red glass or as smoke-colored.

Besides the difficulty of incomplete characterization there is the fault of fine-writing in the worst sense of that word. The opening paragraph is a good example of that elaborateness of uninteresting detail into which Miss Larsen plunges in order to assure us that her Helga is cultured and modern.

"Helga Crane sat alone in her room, which at that hour, eight in the evening, was in soft gloom. Only a single reading lamp dimmed by a great black and red shade, made a pool of light on the blue Chinese carpet, on the bright covers of the books which she had taken down from their long shelves, on the white pages of the opened one selected, on the shining brass bowl crowded with many-colored nasturtiums beside her on the low table, and on the oriental silk which covered the stool at her slim feet. It was a comfortable room, furnished with rare and intensely personal taste, flooded with Southern sun in the day, but shadowy just then with the drawn curtains and single shaded light. Large, too. So large that the spot where Helga sat was a small oasis in a desert of darkness. And eerily quiet."

Born of a Danish mother and a colored father, an outcast from the American branch of her mother's family and a curiosity to the Danish branch, educated carefully by a pitying uncle, Helga has decided to devote her life to the betterment of her father's race. For this purpose she has become a teacher in Naxos, the most advanced of the Negro schools. For this reason, likewise, she has engaged herself to James Vayle, a young man of acknowledged social position in the settlement there. She wants a place in life, and social position, and work. But her mind is too keen to accept the patronizing attitude of the leaders in education, and her adjustment to the environment impossible; therefore she breaks with it.

In Chicago she suffers only a brief time from poverty and rejection and then becomes the companion of a lecturer on race problems. This older woman befriends her, finds her a congenial position in a New York insurance company for colored people and leaves her in a delightful social background and living with her own niece, Anne Grey.

In New York the problems are few. She moves among Harlem's most intellectual people. Her aesthetic sensibilities have full play in Anne's charming home. "Bonneted old highboys, tables that might be by Duncan Phyfe, rare spindle-legged chairs, and others whose ladder backs gracefully climbed the delicate wall-panels" and "Anne, herself, pretty maybe, brownly beautiful—with the face of a golden Madonna grave and calm and sweet, with shining black hair and eyes." These facts of daily life gave Helga freedom. She seems about to decide upon a suitable marriage to a properly wealthy man when restlessness again grips her and luck flies into her hands. She receives five thousand dollars from a penitent uncle and decides to leave Harlem. Reveling in the thought, she chooses a dress to announce her plan:

"What should she wear? White? No, everybody would, because it was hot. Green? She shook her head, Anne would be sure to. The blue thing. Reluctantly she decided against it; she loved it but she had worn it so often. There was that cobwebby black net touched with orange, which she had bought last spring in a fit of extravagance and never worn because on getting it home both she and Anne considered it too decollete, too outre. She was going "because there were moments when it was as if she were shut up, boxed with hundreds of her race, closed up with that something in the racial character which had always been, to her, inexplicable, alien."

In Copenhagen, Frau Dahl (her aunt treats her like an exotic doll, dresses her and parades her and puts her in the marriage market. When an excellent offer comes from a Danish artist, Helga refuses it. Another flight and she is back at Anne's wedding to Dr. Anderson. Dr. Anderson, first met as Helga's principal in Naxos, has moved shadow-like through the pages. Helga has always shown some slight interest in him. But nothing has prepared us for the sudden shift in her that comes now. There is a silly incident. Dr. Anderson, in his cups, embraces her. When he formally apologizes, she, realizing that she wants him, slaps him for his conventionality. Suddenly all the forces of passion are loose in her. Finding no outlet, she turns to revivalistic religion of a stupid sort, then, more illogically, to a flabby, dull minister who happens to take her home from the church meeting. Having given herself to him, she marries him with a certain exultation in her own power.

She is, of course, lost. As a minister's wife she can for a time be pleased with her "status" (a bit pitiful, but certain). For a time she has drugged peace in the flesh. Then come children, weariness, serious illness. She is brought back to living to discover her mistake and her hatred of her husband. She makes many resolutions for freeing herself only to discover her body laden with a fifth child. The end is, I suppose, a sordid death.

But in none of the latter Helga have we found any particular meaning. If she was at all the young woman of the first of the book, she cannot be the older woman of the latter half. There is no continuity of development, no wholeness here.

Miss Larsen writes a little too carefully of the objective evidences of culture and too carelessly of the refinement within the woman herself. We are told again and again that Helga is restless, unhappy, passionate, but we don't believe it until, arbitrarily, Miss Larsen introduces proofs of action.

Quicksand is, for all this comment, a good tale, and a good first novel. Miss Larsen's prettiness of style may, with more writing, become power. She will undoubtedly learn a more effectual working out of laws of cause and event within characters. She has already the ability to interest us in her people and their problems.

But she has not in this first book anything of the usual richness and fullness of character presentation, or the zestful interest in life in Harlem that other novelists of Negro life have given us.

Eda Lou Walton.

OUR BOOK SHELF

Dark Princess, by W. E. Burghardt Du Bois. Harcourt, Brace and Company. 311 pp. Price $2.00.

DARK PRINCESS is the mingling of an allegory on the world union of the darker races, and certain realistic pictures of the economic and political problems of the Negro in the United States. The allegory contains many glints of the moving and poetical style that has made the work of Dr. Du Bois, as visionary and prophet, so note worthy. The realism of the vivid studies of a crushed rebellion among the Pullman porters, and of the web of machine politics in Chicago, will help us to understand some of the new forces at work in Negro life. But the marriage of the symbolic and the real is not particularly happy. We feel that Dr. Du Bois has undertaken too heavy a load for even his real talents: to chant the lyric hope of a common cause among the non-white races for world equality; to present the sordid intrigues of white and black exploiters in crime, vice, and the big graft; and to mould the entire book as propaganda—this many-stringed bow does not send the arrow into the bull's-eye of our emotions or our reason. The propaganda spoils the lyric novel that Dr. Du Bois could have written; and the machinery of fiction obscures the clear-cut facts of these problems with which the author is so intimately acquainted. Nevertheless, *Dark Princess* is a gallant effort, with pages of real beauty, but probably most significant for its incidental sidelights on present social and political phenomena among the Negroes.

For example, Matthew Town, the hero, throws up his medical career because the Dean of his school will not let him study obstetrics since the women may object to one of his race. Here is a real problem: how to overcome race prejudice so that Negroes may be competently trained as physicians. Equally illuminating is the picture of Matthew's struggle to organize the porters, and his efforts to forestall the violent methods of the radicals in his race. And most interesting of all is the detailed study of the political relations between the Negro boss, Sammy Scott, in a Chicago district in which the Negroes have gained political control by their votes, and the white man's machine. The process here is one that is going to be duplicated in many other places. It must be said that Dr. Du Bois's verdict is not very encouraging: the Negro boss delivers his voters for exploitation and corruption just as does the white boss.

The symbolism of the Dark Princess, lovely head of an Indian state, is not convincing. She represents the ideal of an unselfish seeking for a common hope among all the non-white races of the world. Matthew meets her at a dinner in Berlin where Japanese, Arabs, Egyptians, and others, are making plans for common action. He finds a new color line drawn by these other races against the Negro. But he loves the Princess, who understands the aspiration and potential strength of the American Negro, and throughout the rest of the book their lives cross until in the final scene is revealed the fruit of their love—a man child who is the future Maharaiah of Bwodpur. This is a thrilling idea, but in the telling is mostly melodrama. Indeed, melodrama marks much of the tale: the Princess appears at the most unexpected and unnatural places (once on a Ku Klux Klan special train), and all because the plot requires her interventions or symbolic presence.

The tale of Matthew follows him through dabblings with leaders of violence, the disintegration of the Pullman porters' strike, prison for alleged participation in a plot to wreck the aforesaid Klan special, a time-serving political career and marriage in Chicago, and a final renunciation of Congress for the ideal (and the love) of the Princess. He is sometimes moving in his bewildered search, but generally a symbol pulled by strings for the author's purposes.

As a novel, the book is full of vivid and amusing scenes. The tragic figure of Jimmy, the porter, who is lynched for an alleged but untrue familiarity with the wife of a Klan potentate, is real. The dinner of white and Negro leaders at which Matthew is to be named as candidate for Congress is deft and full of counterpoint. Best of all is the study of Sara Andrews, the clever secretary of Sammy Scott, who marries Matthew to make a career for him. This is an excellent character study. She it is who seizes the limelight and intrigues the interest in the whole center of the story. She is not a very admirable person, and I believe not typically a Negro, but she appears as an authentic human being, unique, contradictory, physically real and psychologically veracious. Sammy Scott and the whole environment and deeds of these two are faithfully and picturesquely rendered. If all the persons in Dr. Du Bois's treatise were done in this quiet, full-bodied fashion, the novel would stand first among all Negro novels.

The theses of the author prove as interesting as the story. They seem to be:

1. The non-white races should join in a common effort to secure a place in the world comparable to their traditions and gifts.
2. Race discrimination will exist within the membership of this union.
3. International intermarriage of leaders of these races will furnish a bond of sympathy and understanding stronger than impersonal propaganda.
4. The Negroes in the United States have made extraordinary progress and are now mostly willing to consolidate their gains and trust to slow social and educational processes for the advance toward a completer independent destiny.
5. Violence will gain the Negro nothing. His labor unions are as yet ineffectual. They disintegrate under economic pressure. The political power of the Negro offers hope. But here personal self-seeking and the native corruptions of politics undermine the idealism and aims of those Negroes who desire racial integrity and progress toward power. The white economic instruments will buy and use venal Negro politicians. But the idealism of the women Negro voters may give true leaders an instrument whereby certain fine ends may be secured.

Certain of these theses require stronger proofs than allegorical romance.

Leon Whipple.

BOOK REVIEW

Dark Princess. By W. E. Burghardt Du Bois. Published by Harcourt, Brace and Company, New York City. Price $2.00

FOR many years Dr. W. E. B. Du Bois has been considered one of the foremost Negro thinkers. By many persons he has literally been worshiped; by others he has been greatly feared and even hated.

"Dark Princess" which is Dr. DuBois's most recent adventure into the field of romance, is a thrilling tale which will be eagerly read by his friends who will find in it a summary of much sober thinking on the subject of mental and spiritual conflict arising among Negroes when an attempt is made to "keep the Negro in his place" and interfere with the Negro in his uphill climb to success by way of the leading professions.

This book will doubtless be regarded by those who fear or hate Dr. Du Bois as a subtle, though powerful, argument in favor of winning Negro supremacy or domination by political chicanery and "direct (or violent) action" of organized Negroes against intrenched white interests, which, if not purely selfish in many instances, are, to say the least, far from being altruistic or Christian.

The story itself is interesting, though in spots it is so realistically told that it will probably offend the sensibilities of those people, both white and Negro, who have been brought up to believe firmly that any serious breach of the moral code is unforgivably reprehensible. Dr. Du Bois has the story-teller's art at his full command. His tale unfolds itself so naturally, so simply, and so dramatically, that the ordinary reader—the person who reads for the sake of the story chiefly—will probably not be vividly aware, as are thoughtful students of race relations, of its stirring, yes, its compelling, effect on youth, who, in all places and at all times, are eager for change, for reform, and for the quick realization of equality and social justice.

Matthew Towns, the principal character—and he can hardly be called a *hero*, because of his obvious limitations of character and achievement, although he is a man who has descended into a human hell—wishes to become a physician. When the time comes, however, for his training in obstetrics his dean makes clear the objections some white people have to a Negro attending prospective white mothers. Matthew endures a crushing spiritual revulsion of feeling. In anger and in despair he quits his work in the medical school. His whole soul is in revolt against the white world. The bottom of life, for him, falls out. He is alone with himself in a world that he feels is full of cruel prejudice and unalterable misunderstanding. His soul is seared. He must get away from the United States. He travels and he keeps on suffering in spirit more and more acutely.

In Berlin he meets a beautiful woman of Indian blood—a woman who, at the hands of the British, has had her own soul seared deeply and permanently. This dark princess and Matthew, who have been dramatically thrown together, see eye to eye on the problem facing the colored races of the world in their struggle for self-realization and for more complete freedom against those organized white interests which seem always confining and crushing.

Matthew returns to the United States and tries to bury himself in hard, physical work. He enters the Pullman service and, at every turn, endures experiences which goad him to bitterness and despair. Finally, he is brought face to face with the lynching of his dearest friend. Again the dark princess crosses his path and he rises to heroic heights. He is an unsung martyr.

Following a brief, soul-trying experience in jail he faces a new life for which he has had little training—life in the whirlpool of Chicago politics—life among whites and Negroes who prey upon their weak and sinful neighbors. He is used as a pawn in a game played almost in spite of him.

"Dark Princess" might well be called "a study in revolt." Matthew Towns revolts against white hypocrisy; the princess, against prejudice; Sara Andrews, against the drabness of everyday living; Sammy Scott, against white political domination; the white politicians of Chicago, against the rising tide of Negro power and economic independence. Everywhere there is revolt against things as they are, without adequate or constructive programs of reform.

Perhaps, after all, "Dark Princess" is truer to life itself than the modern pollyannas and sentimentalists are willing to admit. If this is true, then Dr. Du Bois has written another book which will help men and women, especially in America, to lay aside the masks of smugness and complacency and then face a world that is in confusion—a world in which, for many persons, things or possessions mean more than ideas and ideals — a world in which shrewdness and social climbing and power of exploitation are rated more highly than they should be, even by well-meaning, code-adhering guileless followers of tradition.

The problem of the "Dark Princess" is finding the plan of emancipation. It is not, however, solved; but it is discussed from many angles. Those who read this book intelligently and sympathetically must think a little more seriously and constructively about the dark-skined peoples of the world who are thinking and who are finding a way out.

Friends of Hampton Institute who read "Dark Princess"—and it is hoped that many of them will read this modern romance—should be reminded, when they study the career of Matthew Towns and try to account for his actions, that, for sixty years, Hampton has been training Negro men and women to give their best to society and that many Hampton-trained students have gone into leading professions and achieved real success. —W. A. A.

THE BROWSING READER

The Walls of Jericho." A Novel by Rudolph Fisher, Knopf. $2.50.

THIS is another story of Harlem, following the footsteps of "Nigger Heaven" and "Home to Harlem." The casual reader wading through the first third of the book might think it nothing else but a following of these pathfinders into the half-world north of 125th Street. But a little persistence and a knowledge of what Rudolph Fisher has already accomplished in his remarkable short stories, will bring reward. For the main story of a piano mover and a housemaid is a well done and sincere bit of psychology. It is finely worked out with a delicate knowledge of human reactions. If the background were as sincere as the main picture, the novel would be a masterpiece. But the background is a shade too sophisticated and unreal. Mr. Fisher likes his two characters, Jinx and Bubber, and lingers over them: but somehow, to the ordinary reader, they are only moderately funny, a little smutty and certainly not humanly convincing. Their conversation has some undoubted marks of authenticity, for this kind of keen repartee is often heard among Negro laborers. But neither of these characters seems human like Shine.

Mr. Fisher does not yet venture to write of himself and his own people; of Negroes like his mother, his sister and his wife. His real Harlem friends and his own soul nowhere yet appear in his pages, and nothing that can be mistaken for them. The glimpses of better class Negroes which he gives us are poor, ineffective make-believes. One wonders why? Why does Mr. Fisher fear to use his genius to paint his own kind, as he has painted Shine and Linda? Perhaps he doubts the taste of his white audience although he tries it severely with Miss Cramp. Perhaps he feels too close to his own to trust his artistic detachment in limning them. Perhaps he really laughs at all life and believes nothing. At any rate, here is a step upward from Van Vechten and McKay—a strong, long, interesting step. We hope for others.

OUR BOOK SHELF

THE LIGHTER TOUCH IN HARLEM

THE WALLS OF JERICHO. By Rudolph Fisher. New York. Alfred A. Knopf. $2.50.

AS a "City of Refuge" (which occupied him in his short story of that name), a battleground of "jungle and modern industrialism," a "Nigger Heaven" of cabarets and parties, a "Mecca of the New Negro," Harlem does not here interest Dr. Fisher He is concerned rather with its strictly human values, with giving it a place in universal experience. To this end he has taken for his subject the love-story of a piano-mover and a housemaid—in itself a fact of no little significance. In his earlier short fiction Dr. Fisher has been characterized by Alain Locke as adding Uncle Remus to O. Henry. Certainly in this first novel, in subject-matter, treatment, and tone, there is more of O. Henry than Uncle Remus—O. Henry the humorist and entertainer as well as the realist of metropolitan life.

Dr. Fisher is to be congratulated on having avoided what he would call the "crassly obvious" devices of local color, by which the white novelist thinks to lend a touch of the racial and exotic. He does not have to plaster his narrative with blues and spirituals, with symposia and orgies—sign-posts and posters crying, "So this is Harlem!" Vague spiritual aches and longings for expression, problems and passions—his characters have them, but they are first of all individual and only incidentally racial. Shine, the piano-mover hero, with his hard-boiled recklessness and cynical "line", fights the battle of Jericho and the walls come tumbling down. But the walls are those he has built up around himself, the bullying hardness of a "rat" who has come up from the orphan asylum and the shine-stand to wrestle daily with danger and wiles—a "steel man lined with cast-iron." Jinx and Bubber, his comic assistants and Greek chorus, are racial enough in the extravagant, aggressive contentions and distortions of their curiously perverted friendship. But the "joreein" tall talk of folk-lore has become vaudeville. Merrit, the blond "dickty" lawyer, who takes a grim, defiant joy in the discomfiture of the "fays" he hoaxes and baits, attempts an extension of the colony. But, in the words of the young rector, Bruce, "even though he claims a racial interest, he has admitted that the chief motive is personal after all." "Improvement" likewise finds a place here; but whether of the black or the white variety (the pompous J. Pennington Potter with his panacea of "social admixture" or the absurd Miss Agatha Cramp with her grossly ignorant "uplift"), intellectuals and reformers are in for a "razz". The fact that a "jig", the debonair and dangerous pool-parlor proprietor, Henry Patmore, using white prejudice as a cover, beats the "fays" to the job of wrecking Merrit's house, would seem to be sufficient evidence that Dr. Fisher's real concern is not so much with conflict between the races as with conflict among the different social strata and color casts within the race; not so much with race, in fact, as with essential humanity. The independent and detached attitude of the new Negro writer toward his material is summed up in Bruce's query! "Why is it that a shine can never do anything except as a shine?" And the sophisticated attitude toward race is wittily expressed as follows:

> Here is the hedonistic paradox if anywhere, that one best learns the facts of a race by ignoring the fact of race. If Nordic and Negro wish truly to know each other, let them discuss not Negroes and Nordics; let them discuss Greek lyric poets of the fourth century, B. C.

In the same way one best *reveals* the facts of race by ignoring the fact of race. This is the goal toward which Dr. Fisher's novel points, a position already vigorously asserted by many of his fellow-artists. Having achieved a suitable adjustment to his Nordic neighbors (call it "acculturation" or "cultural maturity", as you will), the Harlem writer is turning inward for material, digging deeper into the problems and humors of adjustment on the various levels of Harlem society. And the tone is inevitably one of satire, of irony, directed at both himself and his neighbor.

Dr. Fisher satisfies, however, by being sufficiently racial and local, for all that his aim is critical rather than documentary. His story cuts a wide swath in the welter of Harlem life. Local color and gusto it undeniably has—the color and gusto of character, atmosphere, and idiom, with all the racy vulgarity of the "rat's" lowbrow tastes. Here is the lowdown on 1928 styles of beauty, dress, lovemaking, and exploitation—for "amusement, profit, uplift" —along Harlem's Fifth and Seventh Avenues. Dr. Fisher writes with equal authority and zest of the conquest of territory in the early days, the inimitable variety of the General Improvement Association's Annual Costume Ball, a piano-mover's conception of an Episcopal service in terms of a musical show, his Harlemese version of a sermon on the battle of Jericho, the technique of piano-moving, "jiving", and pool-room brawls. All this with a certain unconventionality and novelty in that he passes up the allurements of Harlem's dens of abandoned revelry and (except for the purposes of glancing satire, as in the "Litter Rats' Club") its coteries of art and culture, as well as the temptation of capitalizing popular personalities. Add to this native juice and savor the pattern of careful vignettes (though the structure of the novel may be beyond him) and a clarity and dignity notable amidst a turbulence of hot, obscure loves and hates. A civilized novel dealing with (for all their underlying primitiveness) civilized characters—as much New York as they are Negro.

Dr. Fisher's poise is engaging to behold—the cool hard composure born of perfect familiarity with his material; the irony of a sophisticated intelligence that is capable of playing with ideas as well as recording facts; the tropic "nonchalance" of a race that "accepts things not with resignation but with amusement." One is even willing to grant Dr. Fisher his slight theatricality of tone and ostentation of style as a concession to his material, an adaptation of means to end in order to reproduce faithfuly the sensationalism of a lusty, melodramatic life. Like melodrama, caricature "here strides . . . naked, and unashamed." A flaw in tone, a lack of perspective, or only a convenient and deliberate adjustment? Who shall say? Side by side with the uncomplimentary comic valentines of Nordics like Miss Cramp are the equally ludicrous cartoons of Negroes; if on the subject of race Dr. Fisher says to the Nordics, "Touch me not," to his own people he says, "Hands off." One would like to credit him with the impartiality of the "dancing and destructive eye" of the best satire.

Within the limits he has set himself Dr. Fisher has achieved ample mastery. Those who look here for the passion that might be expected of one on the inside looking out will be as disappointed as those who demand perspective of one on the outside looking in. His is a frankly hedonistic attitude, eschewing protest, poetry, and pity alike. Here are the suave aplomb and the easy assurance of one at home in his subject, the self-possession of self-understanding, the adroit irony and clever banter of, if not exactly the light, at least the lighter touch.

B. A. Botkin.

THE BROWSING READER

OUR MONTHLY SERMON

THESE are happy days for those who are writing and reading Negro literature. For a time all of us were a little afraid that the almost sudden flare of interest in Negro writing and the desperate effort of new young dark writers, was a spasmodic thing, likely to be overdone instead of being the ground-swell of a great movement.

As time goes on, all of us are becoming more and more convinced that there is here now a movement, a great development, and not simply a fad. But this can only become assured as there is built up back of the new Negro writers a strong wide and sane body of readers. It does not mean that these readers necessarily all be black, but obviously the people who are most interested in this literature must form the bulk of its readers.

It is all a matter of habit. We do not, as colored people, systematically and regularly buy books. We do systematicallly and regularly buy dinners far beyond the needs of our bodies; we buy expensive clothes; we are going in for furniture and decoration, and we are traveling each year more and more widely. Against this, there is but one criticism; namely: this ration must be balanced by book-buying. The family that spends $500 a year for rent can surely, without strain, spend $10 a year for books. If it costs $15 to attend the Odd Fellows Ball, it is quite possible that $10 on the Ball and $5 on two recent books, would be a more profitable investment.

LATEST LITERATURE

OUR desk is filled with all sorts of things calling for attention. There is, for instance, the "Survey of Negro Colleges and Universities". It is a volume in 20 or more chapters, forming Bulletin Number 7, 1928, of the Bureau of Education in the United States Department of the Interior. It calls for long and careful study, and we shall from time to time refer to it. Meantime, however, what a contrast this Report is from the Thomas Jesse Jones Report of 1916! That Report was a clear and distinct endeavor to decry the Negro colleges, except a few guided by white men, and to endorse and advertise industrial education. Today, the whole program of industrial education as worked out in the Nineties, is a confessed failure. The Negro college has come into its own, and this Report of the United States Government is a dignified, encouraging message which recognizes that Negro education is going to follow the same lines as all education of human beings.

Among the new books that have come to us are "Mamba's Daughters", by Du Bose Heywood, (Doubleday, Doran and Company); "The Blacker the Berry", by Wallace Thurman, (Macauley); "Plum Bun", by Jessie Fauset, (Stokes); "This Side of Jordan", by Roark Bradford, (Harpers); "The Pedro Gorino", Captain Harry Deane and Sterling North, (Houghton Mifflin); "What the Negro Thinks", by Robert R. Moton, (Doubleday, Doran and Company); "Unhappy India", by Lajpat Rai; "Living India", by Savel Zimand, (Longmans), the "Magic Island" by W. S. Seabrooke, (Harcourt, Brace.)

Of most of these we shall speak again.

"The Conjure Woman", (Houghton-Mifflin Company), the earliest of Mr. Charles W. Chesnutt's books, has, to our great delight, re-appeared in a new edition. Joel Spingarn writes the foreword and says:

"Mr. Chesnutt's novels, published over a quarter of a century ago, mark an era both in the history of the Negro and in the history of American literature. They are the first novels in which an American of Negro descent has in any real sense portrayed the fortunes of his race. Paul Laurence Dunbar had more or less successfully introduced the material in brief snatches of song and in brief studies of character and incident, but he failed, like other and feebler predecessors, in his attempts at a more extended treatment in the form of a novel. Mr. Chesnutt is a true pioneer, but we should be underestimating his achievement if we thought of it merely in terms of its subject matter or material. Only the archaeologist is interested in this kind of priority: what is important is not that Mr. Chesnutt was the first to discover or deal with the material, but that he was the first to give it life."

We hope to see all of Mr. Chesnutt's novels in new edition.

I HAVE JUST READ

"MAMBA'S Daughters", by Du Bose Heywood, (Doubleday, Doran and Company), is an excellent book and worth reading, but I do not like it. Partially, this is a subjective recoil at feeling the hands of strangers at the heart of my problem. The attitude is unfair and almost silly, and yet it has a certain real justification. I assume that the white stranger cannot write about black people. In nine cases out of ten I am right. In the tenth case, and Du Bose Heywood is the tenth case, the stranger can write about the colored people whom he knows; but those very people whom he knows are sometimes so strange to me, that I cannot for the life of me make them authentic.

I have no doubt but that Catfish Alley in Charleston, New Orleans and Galveston, breeds people like Mamba and Porgy. But they are in no sense typical American Negroes today; and when their story is coupled with the trite tale of the old Charleston white aristocracy, I am full of resentment.

The story of Charleston aristocrats has been done to death; here it is written again with singular delicacy and understanding. But I am no longer interested in the way in which a small group of privileged people set themselves at the top of the world and make its people their cherry. When, in addition to this, and as a part of the same story, there comes the debauchery and exploitation of the lowest of the black low, I again renege. I want the story of real, ordinary people, black and white.

Of course, this criticism is unfair because the author was writing frankly of those two classes of people. And given his task, he did it well. He even reached tentatively up and showed how out of the mud of the alley grows a flower of song and how terribly Mamba strove for that granddaughter; but with all of the successful artistry of the book, I do not like its subject.

FOR quite similar reasons, I like Jessie Fauset's "Plum Bun": (Elkin, Mathews and Marrott in London, and the Frederick Stokes Company in the United States).

"Plum Bun" talks about the kind of American Negroes that I know. I

(*Will you please turn to page* 138)

The Browsing Reader

(*Continued from page* 125)

do not doubt the existence of the debauched tenth, but I cannot regard them as characteristic or typical, and while there is a certain tang and unusualness to their adventures, enough of their sort is as good as a feast, and God knows we have surely latterly had the feast!

"Plum Bun" is a work of sincerity and finish and of extraordinary human interest. It will not attract those looking simply for the filth in Negro life, but it will attract and hold those looking for the truth. It is a story of a little colored family in Philadelphia with two daughters, one brown, and the other able to pass for white. The novel is the story of her "passing"; of the depths and heights to which it led, and of the sanity which it finally evolves. The characters are drawn surely and clearly and the plot is easy and natural.

PERIODICALS

WE have received a file of the extraordinarily interesting *"Oedaya"*, published in Holland, edited by Noto Soeroto, and dealing most interestingly with the race problems of the Dutch, particularly the Javanese and the Guianians.

The first number of Volume Two of *Africa*, journal of the International Institute of African Languages and Cultures, comes to us. It is edited by Diedrich Westermann. The trend of the first volume is kept up. The slogan is always "Educate Africans as Africans and not as Europeans", which in its practical application means to keep the Negro from acquiring modern education. Outside of this, the Quarterly tends to follow the lines of German scientific periodicals. Monroe N. Work is the only American Negro that has appeared in its pages.

It is singular how we tend to forget the obviously good and indispensable. Here is the *Journal of Negro History* edited by Carter G. Woodson, entering its 14th year of life. It keeps up its solid worth—scientific accuracy, and careful editing. Recent numbers have contained articles on the "Mandate System in Africa", the "Mohammedan slave trade", the "Negro in the Pacific Northwest", and the Annual Report of the Director.

The January number of the *International Review of Missions*, published in London, is a special double Number, with a Report of the Jerusalem meeting of the International Missionary Council. The conclusion of the Council's "Survey on Africa" says:

"The increasing recognition in some parts of Africa of the right of Africans to participate in government, seen, for example, in the Native Council of Transkei and the elected membership of the legislative councils in parts of West Africa, is in contrast to the racial animosity seen in other parts, which inevitably effects both legislation and administration. Inadequate provision for African education, forced labour and other forms of exploitation still exist."

PHONOPHOTOGRAPHY IN FOLK MUSIC. Metfessel and Seashore. University of North Carolina Press.

THIS is an interesting attempt made possible by a grant of the Laura Spelman Rockefeller Memorial to photograph Negro songs.

"This group of songs constitutes the first sustained effort to preserve selections from a particular type of folk music by the method of phonophotography. The camera has been substituted for the conventional phonograph, and scientific notation has been substituted for the conventional musical notation.

"In this age of extraordinary spread of civilization into the remotest parts of the earth, primitive folk traits are being obliterated and lost at an amazing pace. Shall we preserve the native songs of our Indians, our Negroes, our Hawaiians, our Filipinos? Shall the scientific collection of the songs of the most primitive peoples be taken seriously, together with other anthropological collecting? Let us hope that the present trial of instruments and methods of collecting songs in the field may arouse investigators to a recognition of the great value of this type of collections and the necessity of doing it at an early date, unless we shall forever lose the opportunity of recording permanently some of the most interesting expressions of folk life which are now being wiped out by the march of civilization."

THE BROWSING READER

OUR MONTHLY SERMON

WHO determines what Negro artists shall write about? And what white authors shall say about Negroes? The publishers, of course. But who guides the publishers?

Doubtless, publishers know something of the spiritual trends of the times. Doubtless, they assume a certain kind of leadership, but after all, the person who in the long run determines what the publisher shall issue in book form, is the buyer. No, it is not the reader of books. The reader of books in the long run indirectly influences the buying. He guides the buyers, sometimes and somewhat. He talks to his friends and in this way helps the buyer to come to his decision. But the person who buys books is the one who is the real ruler in the situation. It is book buyers that make Octavius Roy Cohen and Carl Van Vechten, just as the book buyers make DuBose Heyward and Claude McKay. They can make others. They can, if they will, bring new editions of all Chesnutt's novels; they can make Jean Toomer break his long silence. They can bring new voices and new souls into the articulate world.

THE BROWSING READER

I HAVE just read three novels: Claude McKay's "Banjo", (Harper's), Nella Larsen's "Passing", (Knopf), and Wallace Thurman's "The Blacker the Berry" (Macauley).

The first two novels are second adventures in fiction; the one by a poet; the other by a new writer. The third, has been the basis of a rather successful popular musical show.

BANJO

CLAUDE McKAY'S "Banjo" is a better book than "Home to Harlem". It is full of experience, vivid, and, of course, colorful as all McKay's work must be. It is described as "a story without a plot", but it is hardly even that. It is in no sense a novel, either in the nature of its story or in the development of character. It is, on the one hand, the description of a series of episodes on the docks of Marseilles; and on the other hand a sort of international philosophy of the Negro race. It is this latter aspect which seems to me to make it of most value.

The first aspect of the book is negligible. It is really a continuation of experiences like Jake's in "Home to Harlem". Here are a lot of people whose chief business in life seems to be sexual intercourse, getting drunk, and fighting. Their comments on this kind of life are picturesque, but there is nothing intriguing and there is a great deal of repetition. The characters, while minutely described, do not stand out. Even, the Arab woman, Latnah is vague and unfinished, while Banjo himself lacks even the interest of Jake. Ray, alone, (a character taken over from the former novel), seems like flesh and blood, and probably is largely a counterpart of the author.

The race philosophy, on the other hand, is of great interest. McKay has become an international Negro. He is a direct descendant from Africa. He knows the West Indies; he knows Harlem; he knows Europe; and he philosophizes about the whole thing. He speaks of Ray's urge to write:

"He was always writing panhandling letters to his friends, and naturally he began to feel himself lacking in the free splendid spirit of his American days. More and more the urge to write was holding him with an enslaving grip and he was beginning to feel that any means of achieving self-expression was justifiable."

He defends plain talk about Negros:

"I think about my race as much as you. I hate to see it kicked around and spat on by the whites, because it is a good earth-loving race. I'll fight with it if there's a fight on, but if I am writing a story—well, it's like all of us in this place here, black and brown and white, and I telling a story for the love of it."

With the characteristic reaction of the West Indian who does not thoroughly know his America, he is bitter about "society" Negroes in America and contrasts them with the society he saw in the West Indies:

"In my home we had an upper class of Negroes, but it had big money and property and power. It wasn't just a moving-picture imitation. School-teachers and clerks didn't make any ridiculous pretenses of belonging to it. I could write about the society of Negroes you mean, if I wrote a farce . . .

"If you think it's fine for the society Negroes to fool themselves on the cheapest of imitations, I don't. I am fed up with class. The white world is stinking rotten and going to hell on it . . .

"The best Negroes are not the society Negroes. I am not writing for them, nor the pork-chop-abstaining Negroes, nor the Puritan Friends of Color, nor the Negrophobes nor the Negrophiles. I am writing for people who can stand a real story no matter where it comes from."

Turning from such bitter criticism of his own race, he slashes at the whites:

"You don't know why the white man put all his dirty jokes on to the race? It's because the white man is dirty in his heart and got to have dirt. But he covers it up in his race to show himself superior and put it on to us. The Yankees used to make jokes out of the Germans. Then when the Germans got strong enough to stop that, they got it out of the Irish and Jews. When the Irish and Jews got too rich and powerful in politics, they turn to Italians and Negroes."

And finally comes this evaluation and comparison:

"All the things you say about the Negro's progress is true. You see race prejudice over there drives the Negroes together to develop their own group life. American Negroes have their own schools, churches, newspapers, theatres, cabarets, restaurants, hotels. They work for the whites, but they have their own social group life, an intense, throbbing, vital thing in the midst of the army of whites milling around them. There is nothing like it in the West Indies nor in Africa, because there you don't have a hundred-million strong white pressure that just carries the Negro group along with it. Here in Europe you have more social liberties than Negroes have in America, but you have no warm group life. You need colored women for that. Women that can understand us as human beings and not as wild over-sexed savages."

As a book of racial philosophy, "Banjo" is most inspiring. And for this very reason perhaps "The Home to Harlem" aspect,—the dirt of the docks and the maudlin indulgence, fades away as the book evolves, and Banjo himself becomes almost a forgotten person when he returns from working in coal to take up his role as hero.

PASSING

NELLA LARSEN'S "Passing" is one of the finest novels of the year. If it did not treat a forbidden subject—the inter-marriage of a stodgy middle-class white man to a very beautiful and selfish octoroon—it would have an excellent chance to be hailed, selected and recommended. As it is, it will probably be given the "silence", with only the commendation of word of mouth. But what of that? It is a good close-knit story, moving along surely but with enough leisure to set out seven delicately limned characters. Above all, the thing is done with studied and singularly successful art. Nella Larsen is learning how to write and acquiring style, and she is doing it very simply and clearly.

Three colored novelists have lately essayed this intriguing and ticklish subject of a person's right to conceal the fact that he had a grandparent of Negro descent. It is all a petty, silly matter of no real importance which another generation will comprehend with great difficulty. But today, and in the minds of most white Americans, it is a matter of tremendous moral import. One may deceive as to killing, stealing and adultery, but you must tell your friend that you're "colored", or suffer a very material hell fire in this world, if not in the next. The reason of all this, is of course that so many white people in America either know or fear that they have Negro blood. My friend, who is in the Record Department of Massachusetts, found a lady's ancestry the other day. Her colored grandfather was a soldier in the Revo-

(*Will you please turn to page 248*)

Browsing Reader

(*Continued from page* 234)

lutionary War, and through him she might join the D. A. R. But she asked "confidentially", could that matter of "his—er—color be left out?"

Walter White in "Flight" records the facts of an excursion of a New Orleans girl from the colored race to the white race and back again. Jessie Fauset in "Plum Bun" considers the spiritual experiences and rewards of such an excursion, but the story of the excursion fades into unimportance beside that historical document of the description of a colored Philadelphia family. That characterization ought to live in literature.

Nella Larsen attempts quite a different thing. She explains just what "passing" is: the psychology of the thing; the reaction of it on friend and enemy. It is a difficult task, but she attacks the problem fearlessly and with consummate art. The great problem is under what circumstances would a person take a step like this and how would they feel about it? And how would their fellows feel?

So here is the story: Irene, who is faintly colored, is faint with shopping. She goes to a hotel roof for rest and peace and tea. That's all. Far from being ashamed of herself, she is proud of her dark husband and lovely boys. Moreover, she is deceiving no one. If they wish to recognize her as Spanish, then that is their good fortune or misfortune. She is resting and getting cool and drinking tea. Then suddenly she faces an entirely different kind of problem. She sees Clare and Clare recognizes her and pounces on her. Clare is brilliantly beautiful. She is colored in a different way. She has been rather brutally kicked into the white world, and has married a white man, almost in self-defense. She has a daughter, but she is lonesome and eyes her playmate Irene with fierce joy. Here is the plot. Its development is the reaction of the race-conscious Puritan, Irene; the lonesome hedonist, Clare; and then the formation of the rapidly developing triangle with the cynical keen rebel, Irene's husband.

If the American Negro renaissance gives us many more books like this, with its sincerity, its simplicity and charm, we can soon with equanimity drop the word "Negro". Meantime, your job is clear. Buy the book.

The Blacker the Berry

IT is a little difficult to judge fairly Wallace Thurman's "The Blacker the Berry". Its theme is one of the most moving and tragic of our day. The first chapter states it clearly:

"Emma Lou had been born in a semi-white world, totally surrounded by an all-white one, and those few dark elements that had forced their way in had either been shooed away or else greeted with derisive laughter. It was the custom always of those with whom she came into most frequent contact to ridicule or revile any black person or object."

Here is the plight of a soul who suffers not alone from the color line, as we usually conceive it, but from the additional evil prejudice, which the dominant ideals of a white world create within the Negro world itself. The author has one passage which will make every colored reader thrill:

"'Emma Lou Morgan.'

"The principal had called her name again, more sharply than before and his smile was less benevolent. The girl who sat to the left of her nudged her. There was nothing else for her to do but to get out of that anchoring chair and march forward to receive her diploma. But why did the people in the audience have to stare so? Didn't they all know that Emma Lou Morgan was Boise High School's only nigger student? Didn't they all know—but what was the use. She had to go get that diploma, so summoning her most insouciant manner, she advanced to the platform center, brought every muscle of her lithe limbs into play, haughtily extended her shiny black arm to receive the proffered diploma, bowed a chilly thanks, then holding her arms stiffly at her sides, insolently returned to her seat in that forboding white line."

This is the theme, but excellent as is the thought and statement, the author does not rise to its full development. The experience of this black girl at the University is well done, but when she gets to Harlem she fades into the background and becomes a string upon which to hang an almost trite description of black Harlem.

The story of Emma Lou calls for genius to develop it. It needs deep psychological knowledge and pulsing sympathy. And above all, the author must believe in black folk, and in the beauty of black as a color of human skin. I may be wrong, but it does not seem to me that this is true of Wallace Thurman. He seems to me himself to deride blackness; he speaks of Emma's color as a "splotch" on the "pale purity" of her white fellow students and as mocking that purity "with her dark outlandish difference". He says, "It would be painted red—Negroes always bedeck themselves and their belongings in ridiculously unbecoming clothes and ornaments."

It seems to me that this inner self-despising of the very thing that he is defending, makes the author's defense less complete and less sincere, and keeps the story from developing as it should. Indeed, there seems to be no real development in Emma's character; her sex life never becomes nasty and commercial, and yet nothing in her seems to develop beyond sex.

Despite all this, the ending is not bad, and there is a gleam of something finer and deeper than the main part of the novel has furnished. One judges such a book, as I have said, with difficulty and perhaps with some prejudice because of the unpleasant work in the past to which the author has set his hand. Yet this book may be promise and pledge of something better, for it certainly frankly faces a problem which most colored people especially have shrunk from, and almost hated to face.

W. E. B. D.

OUR BOOK SHELF

MAMBA'S DAUGHTERS

MAMBA'S DAUGHTERS. By DuBose Heywood. Doubleday Doran Co., 1929, Garden City. $2.50.

TO those among us whose gods are the gods of Babbitry this will not be a satisfactory book. As in *Porgy*, Heyward shows here his flair for the picturesque elements in lowly life. He does show our so-called upper strata. But he deals more fully with Mamba, the crafty, and Hagar, the massive, than with either Lissa, the self-centered artist, or the bourgeoisie she is circled by. One reader at least thinks that this is as it should be; that there is no outsider who can adequately deal with our so-called "society" whether his intention be to satirize smugness or to bear witness that there can be intelligence and grace.

The heart of this novel is Charleston. All the romantic coloring is here; the heavy hanging wisteria, the rose gardens, the old mansions; the famous gates with their wrought iron urns and scrolls, the historic landmarks, the St. Cecelia Society. Set in this framework there is the familiar idyl of Southern chevalier and Northern bride, of a little Spartan mother fighting to keep her family prestige. Striking athwart the old, are such strange changes as the industrializing, the Northern speeding up of the town, the strivers from the North, craving oddly enough the acolade of South Carolina approval! Most significant of differences between this and Southern novels of older vintage is that the Negro characters are no longer conceived of as a colorful background, as docile, faithful retainers. The Negroes in this portrait, and not the sentimental whites, are the ones painstakingly delineated. Because of this, Heyward gains strength and humanity.

This is a story of many threads, tied together in the simplest of knots. Saint Julien de Chatigny Wentworth is traced from an ineffectual dreamer, through commissary manager at the Phosphate Mines, where he learns something of the Negro, to a rather solid business man, successfully wedded. Mamba's line is triple. Mamba's schemes led her from waterfront dives, through attendance on the Wentworths, to Mrs. Atkinson's household with its superior advantages for her grandchild, Lissa; Hagar's herculean labors permit her daughter, Lissa, to take music lessons; Lissa's splendid voice finally brings her to the Metropolitan Opera House.

Of these many stories the most striking in both the telling and the thing told is the life of Hagar. There is heartbreak in this woman's struggle against things she cannot understand. Forbidden the city limits, because she trounced a swindler, she goes to the phosphate pits where she labored under the broiling sun, saving her meagre earnings for Lissa. When Lissa is abducted by Prince, alias Gillie Bluton, a notorious woman chaser, she kills him with her bare hands. Panic struck at thoughts of the many tentacled *Law*, she returns to the camp, signs a false confession, "sets up" the camp to a treat, and then with a superb though futile gesture, drowns herself. She had saved Lissa's body, she would save Lissa's name.

Two meetings between the three generations are unforgettable. "The sight of Lissa leaning against her grandmother filled Hagar with a new sort of loneliness that hurt her more than the past days of separation. Finally she rose to go. This time she did not take the child in her arms and kiss her, but patted the little head gently with big hands. "Well, so long," she said and turned abruptly away." Her last words are as memorable, when Lissa is about to go away forever to New York and triumph, and she, to death.

"Good bye, chile. Don't be afraid. Nuttin' going hahm yo'."

There are some unconvincing parts. Lissa's artistic triumph is hastily presented. It is by a severe twist of circumstance that Prince, who had attempted to seduce Lissa should be the very Gillie whose life Hagar had saved. That Saint should be in New York exactly at the time that Lissa is hurried there, seems too coincidental; and Mamba's ubiquity at the right moment in her early toadying days seems almost black magic. Reverend Grayson is not entirely believable. Occasionally hackneyed situations are here, the Negro preacher fulminating against liquor and exposing his own nearly emptied flask. Some generalizations, rather freely given—such as "He was a gentleman—and therefore used to appraising Negro labor"—are hardly in step with Heyward's generally steady approach to fairmindedness.

Among many valuable pictures of the South, Heyward shows us the travesty of justice. One woman is sentenced to seven years for stealing a few dollars worth of second hand clothes. Labor conditions in the phosphate mines approach peonage. Proc Braggart, with his Negro henchman, pauperizes and terrorizes the workers, feeding fat his pocketbook and his ancient grudge. Besides collecting mythical taxes, fining the owners of stray dogs!!!, running the only licensed gambling hell, and engaging in other amenities of the land noted for "understanding the Negro," he had killed six Negroes. His last victim had not scurried to the roadside to escape Proc's speeding buggy, but had stopped and shouted at him. A shotgun had taught him better manners.

Familiar Negro types are here such as Maum Netta, ante-bellum relic, Mamba, who fools the white folks, Maum Vina, withered Circe of folk ways, Davy, "quick on his figgers," Gillie Bluton, tool of the white man, Gardinia, magnificent tigress; many others from field hands to artists. The color prejudice existent within the group is satirized; the smugness of the "drawing pioneers" is called "copybook gentility." We have ostensibly the gamut of our types and interests. But in the so-called higher reaches Heyward seems less sure of himself. His material is obviously second hand and consequently second rate. Let no one therefore be misled by the variant types to call the book "representative." No single book can be; this is *one* observer's book about people, with the omissions to be expected.

It would be too easy and too uncritical, however, to dismiss this book with the statement—"But *why will* he select such scenes and such folk." Those whose deities are pocketbooks and fine cars and what they misname "Kult-choor" will of course fail to see the warm humanity about Mamba and Hagar. But Heyward, it seems to me, has shown their unselfish devotion to be as humanly noble as Mrs. Kate Wentworth's tightlipped facing of poverty, and certainly nobler than Mrs. Atkinson's distracted grabbings for social approval. If we must call any of these women children, Mrs. Wentworth with her Old South pattern of thinking, and Mrs. Atkinson with her Babbitry are the childish ones.

The poetic sense of life revealed by Heyward in *Porgy* and *Jazzbo Brown* is much in evidence in this book. Among the many authentic and beautiful bits is the one closing the book. Mamba, after the triumph of her line, sits upon the doorstep, and hears and sees the departing steamboat, northward bound: "Git along, den," she says partonizingly. "Git along. Ah ain't holdin' yo'. An' when yo' get whar yo' is goin', 'member what Ah tol' yo' an' gib my gal huddy fuh me. . . ."

STERLING A. BROWN.

unusually well protected, makes her ever fair game for exploitation.

Mr. Thurman has painted a vivid picture of Alva, the good looking male, who works spasmodically, lives by his wits and when opportunity offers, on the bounty of women. One gets to know him very well before the tale is ended. His god is pleasure. His master is gin. His credo is Alva first, last and always. Under his gaiety he is vain, petty and unscrupulous. One expects nothing of him beyond the cavalier treatment which he accords Emmy Lou from beginning to end. And though the latter from her first glimpse of him pursues him and for several years lavishes herself upon him, one never acquires any conviction that she really loves him. In the beginning he is for her an outlet, a symbol of escape from a shroud of color, from the squirrel-in-cage existence which she finds herself leading. Later he is an obsession of which she is eventually freed. And painful as the process of freeing is, it is doubtful that though it leaves Emmy Lo-sadder, it leaves her any wiser.

With the rest of his characters the author has dealt variedly. In the portrayal of some of them he shows flashes of real genius. Others he handles clumsily and with too great detail for their importance in the story. He spends a great deal of time describing scenes and persons at the University of Southern California without giving any sense of reality to the picture. While the story of Emmy Lou's life there is as necessary to a complete understanding of her as is the description of her family and early home life, yet the background of her University life is as stilted and unreal as a poorly executed stage setting. It is only when the scenes are laid in Harlem that the author seems sure of himself and glides easily through his descriptions. And yet even there there is too much that is purely descriptive, not enough that is creative, too much that is hackneyed, not enough that is new. McKay has done it better. Thurman, like McKay, has seen much, but unlike McKay, he has not yet assimilated his experiences. He is yet lost and fumbling in the morass of them. He suffers a bit from both emotional and intellectual indigestion. Van Vechten's Harlem, though a different and less pleasant Harlem, is much more real. Rudolph Fisher's short stories have a much surer touch.

Rudolph Fisher's short stories come to mind because the story of Emmy Lou Morgan as the author presents it in *Blacker the Berry* is short story material strung out into novel length by undue emphasis on the affairs of unimportant characters and a great deal of tiresome repetition, by digressions into other possible short stories, such as that of the love affairs of Braxton, Alva's roommate.

Placed beside the Muir translation of Lion Feuchtwanger's powerful and brilliant "Ugly Duchess" which was read during the same interval, the immaturity and gaucherie of the work of this young man from the west strikes one with a force that is infinitely disheartening. Disheartening and alarming because one wishes for the chronicles of the Negro that same finished workmanship, that same polished perfection that characterizes the best in Anglo-Saxon letters. The vogue today, however, for literature by Negroes and about Negroes, is so great that there is no apparent incentive or compulsion to conform to any academic standards in the matter of construction,

THE BLACKER THE BERRY. By Wallace Thurman. Macauley, New York. $2.50.

WITH a play that performs nightly to a capacity house on Broadway and a book that has run into several editions Wallace Thurman, a young Negro, who has recently come out of the West, apparently has joined the ranks of the successful. And yet one wonders whether it is a success of artistic achievement or a success consummated because Mr. Thurman has become a devotee of the most fashionable of American literary cults, that dedicated to the exploitation of the vices of the Negro of the lowest stratum of society and to the mental debauching of Negroes in general.

The Blacker the Berry is a story of a girl, possessed on her mother's side of the best sort of lineage that the American Negro knows, but with a despised black skin, a legacy from a roving black father. Merely tolerated at home in Idaho among her lighter kin, she seeks a happier and fuller life at the University of Southern California where again her ambitions for comradeship are thwarted because of her ebony hue. She abandons her college work and eventually arrives in Harlem where once more color prejudice forces her downward in the social scheme of things until the end of the book leaves her economically adjusted as a school teacher but bitter, disillusioned and alone, an emotional derelict.

In spite of Emmy Lou Morgan's easy virtue and lack of fastidiousness all that the author can do fails to make her vicious. Nor does he even succeed in making her indiscretions exciting. He simply has created an incredibly stupid character. The moral that evidently is intended to adorn this tale is to the effect that young women who are black are doomed to a rather difficult existence should they aspire to anything but life in its most humdrum and sordid forms. But somehow it seems that were she as fair as a lily, a young woman, at once so dominated by the urge of sex and so stupid, would succeed in being exploited by the gentlemen of her acquaintance in one way or another. The exploitation might not take forms so crude, but stupidity in a woman, unless that woman be expression or finish. The more quickly the novelty of the Negro theme wears off and publishers and critics begin to exact from Negro writers that same high standard which they do from others, the more quickly may we expect something better from writers like Wallace Thurman who are capable of things infinitely better than they give.

EUNICE HUNTON CARTER.

OUR BOOK SHELF

BANJO, by Claude McKay. Harper and Brothers. $2.50.

HERE is a tale of the breakwater of Marseilles and of that human flotsam and jetsam that is daily cast upon its shores. Through the pages of Mr. McKay's story move African Negroes, European Negroes, American Negroes, Irishmen, Frenchmen . . . one might even say that the people of the world pass flamboyantly through this new novel from the hand that wrote *Home to Harlem.*

Home to Harlem was the story of Negroes at work in America. Dishwashing, pullman-portering, stevadoring and then the sweet abandon that comes with well-earned rest. On the other hand, *Banjo* is a symphony of vagabondry. Here we have the loafers and other unfortunates who have been cast high on the shores of life by the tides of wandering. With the same palette he used in *Home to Harlem* the author daubs on the same rich colors, paints in the same turbulent stream of living. If there is one conclusion to be drawn from these two books of Mr. McKay's, it is that Negroes are always colorful, always interesting whether they be basking in contented leisure of work finished and coffers full or lying sodden with drink upon the beach of "lost men." It is with an unsullied curiosity that the author looks about him for the little earmarks that make Negroes outstanding in a world where all men are abandoned.

Banjo is longer, more studied than *Home to Harlem.* Yet there is little more plot to this new book than there was to the first novel. It is more the rambling mural of Banjo and his buddies, Malty, Dengel and Ginger than a composite picture. Briefly Lincoln Agrippa Daily, for that is Banjo's real name, has one passion in life and that is his banjo and the sweet, insinuating music his agile fingers make from it. Close to his heart is the dream of having a Negro band to play from cafe to cafe in the gay city of Marseilles. We follow him through the medley of his travels with a small group of musicians. He takes the love that Latnah, the East Indian girl, offers casually . . . in the code of the breakwater. And then Ray of *Home to Harlem* memories comes into the picture and becomes Banjo's fast friend. Jake, whom we knew in the earlier book comes on the scene for a brief moment. The book ends with Ray and Banjo cutting away from the rest of the "gang" to find new ports. Rather than the conventional idea of a solid plot with all events threading up, this book is a series of impressionistic scenes from the lives of several individuals in Banjo's "gang." And yet by some magic the book does not suffer because of this looseness. Perhaps it is akin to impressionism in painting where the aggregate of associated parts becomes a mental and emotional whole. One feels that after all life as a beach-comber would be just a hodge-podge string of events.

Again as in *Home to Harlem* Mr. McKay is in native waters. This book is no superficial glazing of the surface of beach-life in Marseilles. Most certainly the author knows the lingo first-hand; he must have been in and out the *bistros* he pictures hundreds of times. And who but one of Claude McKay's intellect, adrift in the by-ways of life, could reproduce so poignantly the many nuances of Negro thought and discussion. Here is where the book reaches supreme heights . . . in those heated discussions between Africans, Sengalese and American Negroes. The talk of Marcus Garvey, the blind devotion of his West Indian follower, the endless arguments on which nation is least prejudiced against Negroes—all this is typical to Negroes who at least have speaking intelligence and an abundance of time on their hands. It was the excellence of these scenes in the book that made me wish that there had been no attempt to tell a story but instead a personal treatise from the McKay viewpoint on life in the civilized world, being a Negro, and the conglomerate musings of a cosmopolite. He makes so many priceless observations. Latnah's resentment against Banjo, not because he was untrue to her but because she who was brown was left behind when he went in search of a white woman . . . that devil-may-care loyalty that Negro "hoboes" bear toward each other . . . the fine distinctions between the way African, West Indian and American Negroes acted when they were drunk.

No doubt this book will bring down upon its head the wrath of the circumspect, as did *Home to Harlem.* With this I have little patience. Granted that the book is filled with expressions that are considered risque in "the best" parlor circles. True, that it is for the most part concerned with slices of life that would in social surveys be considered sordid. In spite of these admissions I hazzard the guess that Claude McKay was little concerned with the incident he was depicting. To him this tale was life as he saw it about him in Marseilles. There is no snigger of wrong emphasis in his discussion of the most taboo subject. He seems to tell his story with the same naivete that a child has when it makes some shocking statement with no undercurrent of thought. I wondered as I read the book how the people who will criticize it from a moral standpoint would

CARNEGIE LIBRARY, KNOXVILLE, TENN.
BOOKS MOST CALLED FOR IN MAY 1929

FICTION

"Bridge of San Luis Rey"	By Wilder
"Strange Case of Miss Anne Spragg"	By Bromfield
"With Malice Toward None"	By Morrow
"Brook Evans"	By Glaspell

NON-FICTION

"Safari"	By Johnson
"Negro Poets and Authors"	By Kerlin
"New Negro"	By Locke
"Psychology of the Pre-School Child"	Baldwin and Stecher
"Table Setting and Service"	By Lutes
"Careers"	By Rogers
"Strange Interlude"	By Eugene O'Neill

have written a novel around Marseilles. But I suppose the answer to that is that one should not choose Marseilles for a subject under any circumstances.

Banjo is a full-length novel, rounding out its three hundred some pages with solid writing. It has power and courage. And by a strange twist of life where ugliness may be intriguing, it has beauty.

GWENDOLYN B. BENNETT.

PASSING, by Nella Larson. Alfred Knopf, Inc. $2.00

NELLA Larson's "Quicksand" was a novel of achievement and promise. The same may be said of her second novel.

There should be as many ways of telling a story as there are story-tellers—and there are, when it comes to the truly great among them. For the giant uses his chosen method with so subtle an artistry, with so dazzling a power, with so passionate an earnestness, that the method is not merely enriched but transformed into something more and different, thus becoming his very own.

Of the various modes of classifying story-methods, the most obvious and least painless is to set down

I. Direct
II. Indirect

and let it go at that.

In her new novel, Miss Larsen has forsaken the direct telling of "Quicksand" for an indirect telling, thereby losing the advantage of straight impact upon the sense and sensibility of her readers. Had the material been used directly as the life of Clare Kendry, had Miss Larsen christened her story, "The Girl Who Passed," it might have marched more vividly before our eyes, more nearly searched our hearts. Yet in that case, we should, perhaps, have missed some of the shades of intellectual and emotional reaction to the fact of *passing*, in the lives that touch upon and are touched by the "having" Clare.

We see Clare chiefly through the eyes of Irene Redfield, in this fashion acquiring what may be the norm of reaction to *passing*, by a cultured woman of the Negro social group, in a great metropolitan area in the United States of America, today. We are given the reactions of sundry other individuals and types—both Negro and Caucasian. Witness Gertrude the butcher's wife, Dr. Brian Redfield who needed *something* more, Hugh Wentworth literary godling, the golden Felise. And we cannot forget John Bellew, husband of the beautiful eager Clare who wanted to barter and at the same time eat her cake. He symbolizes the extreme of wooden-headed white reaction to dark blood.

The background of "Passing"? It is less diversified, less rich if you will, than the background of "Quicksand." There we had a southern college, Chicago, New York, Copenhagen and again the South—this time a small town church and parsonage. In "Passing" we have concentrated Harlem, with only a flashback to Chicago. But it is the story not the physical background that counts here. It is the story plus the psychological background and ether.

I like "Passing", for its calm clear handling of a theme which lends itself to murky melodrama. But this quality of calmness and clearness does not and has not entailed the blinking of a single element in the stupid Nordic complex and its unlovely sequelae. The tragedy is told with an economy of words, but its full import is unmistakable. A throb of *the urge to speak out* runs through it.

Also, in the novel under discussion, we have a competent piece of story-telling: both plot and people move logically to their appointed end. Yet somehow, it fails to be a great story, and with the given ingredients, it might have been great and greatly moving. I wish with all my heart that instead of bringing forth another novel next year, Mrs. Imes would, after a decade of brooding, give the world its needed epic of racial interaction between thinking members of the American social order belonging to both African and European stocks.

Novels may be transcripts or interpretations of life; and life being so mammoth an affair must be viewed in sections, large or small. These sections may be marked off horizontally like well-behaved geologic strata or cut perpendicularly into segments, like a birthday cake.

A ripe artist of gargantuan powers and stature may cut perpendicularly, study life in all its layers, set before us its tremendous light and shadow, paean and threnody, with delicate precision or a passionate "Behold!"

There is no layer or segment of humanity that is *verboten* to the maker of novels, if he be an honest workman. And the honest reader need not flinch from honest fact or honest interpretation of any phase of life. Yet certain literary somebodies and other literary nobodies would have us believe that only life in the raw or bloody-rare is life at all and worth writing up. The pity of it!—if "Walls of Jericho" and "Home to Harlem' perched upon our bookshelves with "Plum Bun" and "Passing" nowhere to be seen.

Doctors, lawyers, men of affairs, their wives and daughters are neither less valuable nor less richly human members of society than jazz boys and girls, roustabouts and drunks—though it takes a more gifted, understanding and highly experienced artist to make them breathe and move and speak so that we know them for what they really are, so that we ourselves breathing, moving and speaking with them, come to perceive more clearly what we ourselves really are—of one blood with them and all humanity.

MARY FLEMING LABAREE.

OUR BOOK SHELF

Plum-Bun, by Jessie Fauset. Frederick A. Stokes Company. $2.50.

AND now we have another book from the pen that gave us "There Is Confusion." This later book, "Plum-Bun," is of a little wider scope than Miss Fauset's earlier book. True, she has started the children who are to be the men and women of her book in the familiar background of Philadelphia; true, that the author is concerned with the same ordinary well-bred Negro of intelligence and education; but on the other hand this last book seems to come to grapple with a larger, more potent element in Negro life—passing for white. For that reason I am prepared to say that the theme of Jessie Fauset's second novel is of more importance in the scheme of Negro letters than her first book.

The story carries us with two sisters, Angela and Virginia Murray, through their childhood, spent in peace and calm in Philadelphia, to their adolescence when they both arrive in New York City—the one passing for white and the other caught in the warm, multicolored whirl of Harlem. The greater portion of the book is given over to the difficulties as well as pleasures that Angela encounters as a Negro who is passing for white. Miss Fauset has approached this problem through the interesting side-light of the opinions of the white people with whom Angela comes in contact. There is Matthew Henson, a Negro, who loves Angela in the old Philadelphia days; Roger Fielding, a Nordic, who loves her in the New York days; and Anthony Gross, who is, himself, a Negro almost forced into *passing*, through whose love Angela finally wins her way back to the race she has deserted.

Many there will be who will quibble over Miss Fauset's fortunate choice of incident by which all her characters and happenings are brought together. This will not be altogether fair since "Truth is stranger than Fiction." I'll wager that Miss Fauset could match every incident in her book with one from real life. I imagine this book will be even less convincing to members of the white race. They still conjecture over the possibility of a Negro's completely submerging himself in their group without a shadow of detection. But here again Miss Fauset can smile benignly up her writing sleece and know whereof she speaks.

Most of us will see in many of this book's characters some of the real figures that people our Negro world. It Meier and Miss Powell were fashioned. Then on the other hand most of know a hundred or so charming Virginias. The models have not suffered from Hiss Fauset's handling.

The author writes with a quaint charm about Philadelphia. One feels as one reads parts of the book that deal with Philadelphia that the author is with wistful reminiscence looking back into scenes that she, herself, has lived. There is a tenderness of touch that Miss Fauset bestows upon these scenes. I found particular pleasure in her apt, yet subdued, picture of Sunday afternoon in a middle-class Negro home. Her descriptions of New York scenes in the latter part of the book never ring with the same fervor that these earlier scenes do. I should like to see the author take some simple segment of Philadelphia life and write an entire book around that scene. I imagine that it would have all the simple serenity and mellowness that haunts the queer, little narrow streets of that city. Somehow, for all Miss Fauset's cosmopolitan wanderings, I feel that Philadelphia has left an indelible print on her heart.

The author of this story does not seem concerned to a great extent with the inner workings of her characters. In this day of over-emphasis on the mental musings of people and things this may be called a fault but I feel that the author was wise in not delving into the mental recesses of people to whom so much was happening. This is a task for a master psychologist. Who can tell how the minds of white Negroes work? Is it not a problem to stump the best of us that they who are so obviously white should feel a "something" that eventually draws them from the luxury and ease of a life as a white person back to the burden of being a Negro? Miss Fauset tells her story, packed as it is with the drama and happenings of a life of passing for white. It is better for the story that Miss Fauset avoided too much of a metaphysical turn.

When one has finished reading *Plum-Bun* one naturally wonders what Miss Fauset will write next. Most certainly she knows well the better class of Negroes who have been so long an enigma to the reading public at large. I think it fitting that she busy herself about bringing them to light. Books about cabarets, stevedores, et al, are prevalent enough. Why not this gentlewoman's pen that dips so choicely into the lives of black folk who go to school and come home to the simple niceties of living "just like all the white folks do?"

GWENDOLYN BENNETT.

BOOK REVIEWS

The Black Christ and Other Poems. By Countee Cullen. Putnam, New York. Price, $2.00.

THE author of "The Black Christ" would not ask to be discussed simply as a Negro poet; he is a poet without racial adjectives. He believes that there can be no line of separation between the poetry of the white and black races:

"Never shall the clan
Confine my singing to its ways
Beyond the ways of man."

Yet by the sheer necessity of his own experiences, and those of his people in America, this poet must deal with the sorrows of the black, and must be sensitive to their hopes and fears. He has discharged his soul in the closing poem in this his latest book, "The Black Christ". This must be considered the most significant poem which we have had so far from this poet; but fine as it is, it is not the masterpiece which we may yet have from him. It is in the metre familiar to us in "The Everlasting Mercy," a poem which has had evident influence over this poet. It is the story of a lynching, told by the brother of the man who is pursued by the angry mob. In desperation the singer tells how he hid the fugitive in a cupboard, and afterwards like hounds the pursuers broke into the room; and out of the hiding-place a figure steps. He was the same as the one who had been hidden, in "form and feature, bearing, same": yet he seemed "one I had never known". It was the Christ, though they did not know Him, who had come once more to be crucified, identifying himself with the doomed Negro. Afterwards, when the lynching is over, and the mother and brother are mourning for the one who is lost, in the night the brother reappears, wondering how the crowd had been persuaded to depart, and for the rest of their lives the mother and her sons in another land spend their days in praise to Him, the Black Christ Who had gone once more to Calvary

"Betrayed a thousand times each morn
As many times each night denied."

There is a tree in the Southland, only a tree to others, but to those who knew the secret it is the Cross on which Christ took the place of the hunted Negro. For this Christ always makes Himself one with men; He is the Other Self.

"If I am blind, He does not see:
If I am lame, He halts with me."

This is a noble theme, in which the heart of this poet finds a way of clinging to his faith even in the presence of human cruelty.

"Two brothers have I had on earth,
One of spirit, one of sod,
My mother suckled one at birth;
One was the Son of God."

There are evident marks of immaturity in this poet's work; he sometimes embroiders his theme with decorations which are purely literary; he has not set himself free from the dangerous spell of Masefield. But when all that is admitted, he is a true poet with a moving theme, and with a passionate faith, which finds refuge in the mystic union of his people, and of all suffering peoples, with the Eternal Christ, Who is crucified till the end of the world.

—Rev. Edward Shillito

OUR BOOK SHELF

THE BLACK PEGASUS

The Black Christ and Other Poems, by Countee Cullen. Harper & Brothers. $2.00.

NO phenomenon in American social life is so impressive as the emergence of the Negro into a prominent place in all aspects of American culture during the last decade. In the field of poetry, the names of James Weldon Johnson, Claude McKay, Georgia Douglas Johnson, Langston Hughes, William Stanley Braithwaite, and dozens more loom large on the horizon. Not one of these names is better known than that of Countee Cullen.

His work has appeared in the leading magazines, and in special collections already published. He has a genuine singing gift, a keen honesty, a penetrating vision. His fault has been that he has followed too closely certain outworn patterns in English verse. In spite of this he is a significant figure in our poetry.

His latest volume does not seem, to this critic, to mark an advance over his former ones. The title poem is a moving study of lynching, using an incident which should have made an immortal poem. The weakness in it can be seen from this fact: On one page, he has the principal character, Jim, say:

"We never seem to reach nowhere"

Soon the same character is talking in this sickly poetic speech:

" 'Twere best, I think we moved away."

No person ever spoke like this today: and when the same character pursued by lynchers, face bloodied, delivers a speech to his family, almost seven pages long, in this same false diction, instead of escaping from the lynchers, the end becomes grotesquely unnatural.

Much of the book is better than this. But, to be a great poet, Countee Cullen must do what other great poets do: he must write in the simple, natural speech, without artificiality. He has the singing gift; and beauty and poetic immortality will be his, when he uses his gift straightforwardly, unwarped by bookish phrases.

CLEMENT WOOD.

A Negro Miracle Play

Reviewed by HOWARD BRADSTREET

"THE GREEN PASTURES"
A PLAY BY MARC CONNELLY
Suggested by Roark Bradford's Southern Sketches
"Ol' Man Adam an' His Chillun"
At the Mansfield Theatre, New York City

CAST OF CHARACTERS

Gabriel	*Wesley Hill*
The Lord	*Richard B. Harrison*
Adam	*Daniel L. Haynes*
Eve	*Inez Richardson Wilson*
Cain	*Lou Vernon*
Cain's Girl	*Dorothy Randolph*
Zeba	*Edna M. Harris*
Cain the Sixth	*James Fuller*
Noah	*Tutt Whitney*
Noah's Wife	*Susie Sutton*
Shem	*Milton J. Williams*
Flatfoot	*Freddie Archibald*
Ham	*J. Homer Tutt*
Japheth	*Stanleigh Morrell*
First Cleaner	*Josephine Byrd*
[illegible]	*Florence Fields*
Abraham	*J. A. Shipp*
Isaac	*Charles H. Moore*
Jacob	*Edgar Burks*
Moses	*Alonzo Fenderson*
Zipporah	*Mercedes Gilbert*
Aaron	*McKinley Reeves*
Pharaoh	*George Randol*
Joshua	*Stanleigh Morrell*
King of Babylon	*Jay Mondaaye*
Prophet	*Ivan Sharp*
High Priest	*J. Homer Tutt*
Hezdrel	*Daniel L. Haynes*

TO see *The Green Pastures* once is to desire to see it again. To stand through the performance, in the absence of seats, is not a test of endurance inasmuch as one forgets he is standing. Both statements label it as a remarkable play. Yet both of these statements might be made now and again of some other performance of outstanding interest.

The Green Pastures is still more remarkable for other reasons. It is based on the mind of the Negro and is given by a Negro cast yet its content transcends the color line; it deals with religion, the Bible, and Biblical characters yet creates sympathy not sacrilege. It has entered two of the most dangerous fields — race and religion — and emerges without controversy or race accentuation. In these respects it is a truly remarkable accomplishment.

It is reliably stated that several producers declined the play in manuscript form, and it is not surprising that such was the case. A politician may sound out his public before committing himself on a delicate point. In this instance a huge cast must be assembled, and a huge expense undertaken in the face of odds that it might fall completely flat, or worse yet, arouse a storm of protest for racial or religious reasons.

GABRIEL

Biblical scenes and characters are portrayed faithfully in the manner in which they have taken form in the minds of all imaginative children throughout the ages, and as they still exist in the minds of many grown persons who still retain their childhood ideas on religious matters. It is not easy to say why the result is free from sacrilege. The average person, from the first scene, relaxes into unreasoning acceptance and appreciation, much as he might enjoy mulling over photographs of himself taken along the line of years, all of them seeming so unlike his present self, and yet affectionately and smilingly treasured.

Whatever the undercurrent of thoughts or impressions, the outstanding feature of the performance is Richard B. Harrison. It is possible that there might be somewhere throughout the realm another person who could portray the Lord as well as he, but it is difficult to imagine

NOAH AND THE LORD

anyone doing it better. He stands out in memory regardless of scene or episode. He gives sincerity to the character—a seeming impossibility—because of the sincerity within himself, which he is able to project to his audience. An actor of ordinary stage experience, no matter how talented, could not produce the same effect, and with due appreciation of others in the cast, the peculiar appeal of the play is due to Mr. Harrison in the pivotal part.

In fact it is the contrast between the richness of his portrayal of the Lord, and the professionalism of the others that the play falls short of complete perfection. If it were possible to train a group after the manner of the players at Oberammergau, or even that of the Russian players, there would be a complete atmosphere of religious sincerity which does not now exist. To a surprising degree Mr. Harrrison offsets the deficiencies of others by his carrying power in a role which demands superiority over them. He is the Lord, why should he not be superior?

Although Mr. Harrison stands out in retrospect, *The Green Pastures* is by no means a "one-man" play, nor has he created a part in the way that Frank Bacon created *Lightnin'*. It is a marvelous coincidence that Mr. Harrison was available for a role that demanded a Mr. Harrison to portray. The hearer is completely convinced that the qualities he depicts are part of his personality; that it is a rare type, and one whose possession draws from the public an affection given to but few of the outstanding artists.

The play does not depend upon thrilling scenes for its interest. There are but few of these—perhaps the most outstanding being the admirably conceived picture of the "exodus."

The country has learned in recent years that there are scattered throughout the land a large number of people who still interpret religion and Biblical figures in the realistic way shown in *The Green Pastures*. It would be difficult, however, to imagine a group of white persons performing the same play with the same effect—no matter with how deep a religious fervor. Instead of suggesting inferiority of the Negro race, the effect of the play is the reverse; instead of stimulating an attitude of superiority towards primitive beliefs, the effect is to soften and warm the heart. Unconsciously a tribute is given to the human qualities of the Lord, faith is renewed in the experience that unobtrusive goodness draws people together regardless of age or race.

THE EXODUS

This Negro

Not Without Laughter. By Langston Hughes. Alfred A. Knopf. $2.50.

HERE is the Negro in his most picturesque form—the blues-loving Negro, the spiritual-singing Negro, the exuberant, the impassioned, the irresponsible Negro, the Negro of ancient folk-lore and romantic legend. "Good-natured, guitar-playing Jim Boy"; Angee Rogers loving Jim Boy no matter where he goes or whom he lives with; Aunt Hager, the old mammy of a dead generation, "whirling around in front of the altar at revival meetings . . . her face shining with light, arms outstretched as though all the cares of the world had been cast away"; Harriet, "beautiful as a jungle princess," singing and jazzing her life away, sneering at sin as a white man's bogy, and burying beneath peals of laughter "a white man's war for democracy"; and Sandy, seeing his people as a "band of black dancers captured in a white world," and resolving to free them from themselves as well as from their white dictators—these are the Negroes of this novel, these the people who make it live with that quick and intimate reality which is seldom seen in American fiction.

"Not Without Laughter" continues the healthy note begun in Negro fiction by Claude McKay and Rudolph Fisher. Instead of picturing the Negro of the upper classes, the Negro who in too many instances has been converted to white norms, who even apes white manners and white morality and condemns the Negroes found in this novel as "niggers," McKay, Fisher, and Hughes have depicted the Negro in his more natural and more fascinating form. There can be no doubt that the Negro who has made great contributions to American culture is this type of Negro, the Negro who has brought us his blues, his labor songs, his spirituals, his folk-lore—and his jazz. And yet this very type of Negro is the one that has been the least exploited by contemporary Negro novelists and short-story writers. It has been white writers such as DuBose Heyward, Julia Peterkin, Howard W. Odum, and Paul Green who have turned to this Negro for the rich material of their novels, dramas, and stories. These writers, however, have known this Negro only as an exterior reality, as something they could see, listen to, sympathize with, even love; they could never know him as an inner reality, as something they could live with as with themselves, their brothers, their sweethearts—something as real as flesh, as tense as pain. Langston Hughes does. As a Negro he has grown up with these realities as part of himself, as part of the very air he has breathed. Few blurs are there in these pages, and no fumbling projections, and no anxious searching for what is not. Here is this Negro, or at least one vital aspect of him, as he really is, without ornament, without pretense.

All this praise, however, must not be misconstrued. "Not Without Laughter" is not without defects of style and weaknesses of structure. The first third of the novel, in fact, arrives at its points of interest with a pedestrian slowness; after that it picks up tempo and plunges ahead. Unfortunately, there are no great situations in the novel, no high points of intensity to grip and overpower the reader. Nor is there vigor of style—that kind of vigor which could have made of Sandy's ambition to emancipate his race, for example, a more stirring motif. But "Not Without Laughter" is significant despite these weaknesses. It is significant because even where it fails, it fails beautifully, and where it succeeds—namely, in its intimate characterizations and in its local color and charm—it succeeds where almost all others have failed.

V. F. CALVERTON

OUR BOOK SHELF

NOT WITHOUT LAUGHTER

Not Without Laughter. By Langston Hughes. Alfred A. Knopf. $2.50.

We have in this book, laconically, tenderly told, the story of a young boy's growing up. Let no one be deceived by the effortless ease of the telling, by the unpretentious simplicity of *Not Without Laughter.* Its simplicity is the simplicity of great art; a wide observation, a long brooding over humanity, and a feeling for beauty in unexpected, out of the way places, must have gone into its makeup. It is generously what one would expect of the author of *The Weary Blues* and *Fine Clothes to the Jew.*

Not Without Laughter tells of a poor family living in a small town in Kansas. We are shown intimately the work and play, the many sided aspects of Aunt Hager and her brood. Aunt Hager has three daughters: Tempy, Annjee and Harriett. Tempy is doing well; having joined the Episcopalian Church she has put away "niggerish" things; Annjee is married to a likeable scapegrace, Jimboy, guitar plunker and rambling man; Harriett, young, full of life and daring, is her heart's worry. She has a grandchild, Sandy, son of Anjee and Jimboy. And about him the story centers.

Sandy with his wide eyes picking up knowledge of life about the house; Sandy listening to his father's blues and ballads in the purple evenings, watching his Aunt Harriett at her dancing; Sandy at school; Sandy dreaming over his geography book; Sandy at his job in the barbershop and hotel; Sandy at his grandmother's funeral; Sandy learning respectability at Aunt Tempy's,—and learning at the same time something of the ways of women from Pansetta; Sandy in Chicago; Sandy with his books and dreams of education—so run the many neatly etched scenes

But the story is not Sandy's alone. We see Harriett, first as a firm fleshed beautiful black girl, quick at her lessons; we see her finally a blues singer on State Street. The road she has gone has been rocky enough. She has been maid at a country club where the tired business men made advances; she has been with a carnival troupe, she has been arrested for street walking. We follow Annjee in her trials, and Jimboy, and Tempy. And we get to know the wise, tolerant Aunt Hager, beloved by whites and blacks; even by Harriett who just about breaks her heart. Lesser characters are as clearly individualized and developed. We have Willie Mae, and Jimmy Lane, and Joe Willis, "white folks nigger," and Uncle Dan, and Mingo, and Buster, who could have passed for white. The white side of town, the relationships of employers with laundresses and cooks, all these are adequately done. The book, for all of its apparent slightness, is fullbodied.

One has to respect the author's almost casual filling in of background. The details are perfectly chosen; and they make the reader *see.* How representative are his pictures of the carnival, and the dance at which "Benbow's Famous Kansas City Band" plays, and the gossip over back fences! How recognizable is Sister Johnson's "All these womens dey mammy named Jane an' Mary an' Cora, soon's dey gets a little somethin', dey changes dey names to Janette or Mariana or Corina or somethin' mo' flowery than what dey had."

As the title would suggest the book is not without laughter. Jimboy's guitar-playing, Harriett's escapades, the barber shop tall tales, the philosophizing of the old sheep "who know de road," all furnish something of this. Sandy's ingenuousness occasionally is not without laughter. But the dominant note of the book is a quiet pity. It is not sentimental; it is candid, clear eyed instead—but it is still pity. Even the abandon, the fervor of the chapter called *Dance,* closely and accurately rendered (as one would expect of Langston Hughès) does not strike the note of unclouded joy. We see these things as they are: as the pitiful refugees of poor folk against the worries of hard days. It is more the laughter of the blues line—*laughin' just to keep from cryin'.*

The difference between comedy and tragedy of course lies often in the point of view from which the story is told. Mr. Hughes' sympathetic identification with these folk is so complete that even when sly comic bits creep in (such as Madame de Carter and the Dance of the Nations) the laughter is quiet—more of a smile than a Cohen-like guffaw. But even these sly bits are few and far between. More than Sandy's throwing his boot-black box at the drunken cracker, certainly a welcome case of poetic justice, one remembers the disappointments of this lad's life. Sandy went on Children's Day to the Park. "Sorry," the man said. "This party's for white kids." In a classroom where the students are seated alphabetically, Sandy and the other three colored children sit behind Albert Zwick. Sandy, in the white folks' kitchen, hears his hardworking mother reprimanded by her sharp tempered employer. And while his mother wraps several little bundles of food to carry to Jimboy, Sandy cried. These scenes are excellently done, with restraint, with irony, and with compassion.

Sandy knows the meaning of a broken family, of poverty, of seeing those he loves go down without being able to help. Most touching, and strikingly universal, is the incident of the Xmas sled. Sandy, wishful for a Golden Flyer sled with flexible rudders! is surprised on Christmas Day by the gift of his mother and grandmother. It is a sled. They had labored and schemed and sacrificed for it in a hard winter. On the cold Christmas morning they dragged it home. It was a home-made contraption—roughly carpentered, with strips of rusty tin along the wooden runners. "It's fine," Sandy lied, as he tried to lift it.

Of a piece with this are the troubles that Annjee knows—Annjee whose husband is here today and gone tomorrow; Annjee, who grows tired of the buffeting and loses ground slowly; and the troubles of Aunt Hager who lives long enough to see her hopes fade out, and not long enough to test her final hope, Sandy. . . . Tempy, prosperous, has coldshouldered her mother; Annjee is married to a man who frets Hager; Harriett has gone with Maudel to the sinister houses of the bottom. "One by one they leaves you," Hager said slowly. "One by one yo' chillen goes."

Unforgettable is the little drama of Harriett's rebellion. It is the universal conflict of youth and age. Mr. Hughes records it, without comment. It is the way life goes. Harriett, embittered by life, wanting her share of joy, is forbidden to leave the house. The grandmother is belligerent, authoritative, the girl rebellious. And then the grandmother breaks. . . . "Harriett, honey, I wants you to be good." But the pitiful words do not avail; Harriett, pitiless as only proud youth can be, flings out of doors—with a cry, "You old Christian Fool!" A group of giggling sheiks welcomes her.

Of all of his characters, Mr. Hughes obviously has least sympathy with Tempy. She is the *arriviste*, the worshipper of white folks' ways, the striver. "They don't 'sociate no mo' with none but de high toned colored folks." The type deserves contempt looked at in one way, certainly; looked at in another it might deserve pity. But the point of the reviewer is this: that Mr. Hughes does not make Tempy quite convincing. It is hard to believe that Tempy would be as blatantly crass as she is to her mother on Christmas Day, when she says of her church "Father Hill is so dignified, and the services are absolutely refined! *There's never anything niggerish about them—so you know, mother, they suit me."*

But, excepting Tempy, who to the reviewer seems slightly caricatured, all of the characters are completely convincing. There is a universality about them. They have, of course, peculiar problems as Negroes. Harriett, for instance, hates all whites, with reason. But they have even more the problems that are universally human. Our author does not exploit either local color, or race. He has selected an interesting family and has told us candidly, unembitteredly, poetically of their joy lightened and sorrow laden life.

Langston Hughes presents all of this without apology. Tolerant, humane, and wise in the ways of mortals, he has revealed beauty where too many of us, dazzled by false lights, are unable to see it. He has shown us again, in this third book of his—what he has insisted all along, with quiet courage:

Beautiful, also, is the sun.
Beautiful, also, are the souls of my people. . . .

STERLING A. BROWN.

BOOK REVIEWS

Not Without Laughter. By Langston Hughes. Published by Alfred A. Knopf. Price, $2.50

IN this his first novel, Langston Hughes has given a very human and intensely fascinating account of a struggling Negro family living in a small Kansas town. But more than contributing a story of absorbing details, this talented writer has done an unusual thing in paying a tribute to a hard-working washerwoman, one of those noble black pioneers to whom we owe an unpayable debt, and whom we should remember with gratitude and veneration.

This family consisted of Hager Williams, a widowed mother, her three daughters, and a little grandson, Sandy. From the beginning of the story it is Hager who is the pivotal center around which the others move. It is she who is the angel of mercy, administering willingly and efficiently to all in the little community who come to her for comfort, sympathy, and care. It is she who daily and incessantly toils over the washtub, praying, hoping, and longing for her three daughters to grow up to useful and respectable womanhood. But Annjee, the eldest, marries the shiftless Jimboy; Tempy, after graduating from high school, unites with the upper class of society, and feels too elevated to recognize or associate with those on the level of her hard-working mother and other members of her family; Harriett, the youngest, and the sorest trial to her mother, soon tires of poverty with its stings and insults, yearns for a gayer life which will afford time and opportunity for freedom and laughter, and runs away to join the stage. The ageing Hager, still robust and strong, undaunted and courageous, places her fond hopes in little Sandy, "the lovable edition of his worthless father, Jimboy." Cheerily, she speaks:

"But they's one mo' to go through school yet, an' that's ma little Sandy. If de Lawd lets me live, I's gwine make a edicated man out o' him. He's gwine be another Booker T. Washington. I wants him to know all they is to know, so's he can help this black race o' our'n to come up an' see de light an' take they places in de world. I wants him to be a Fred Douglass leadin' de people, that's what!"

This is the inspirational thread of the story, and although the author leads the little hero, Sandy, through many winding paths, both dangerous and difficult, he never allows him to lose sight entirely of the star pointed out to him by his devoted grandmother. The portrayals are often touching, sometimes humorous, but always human, sympathetic, and fascinating. Mr. Hughes employs his characters to discuss many of the problems which cloud the present-day atmosphere — wrongs that go unrighted, pleas that fall unheeded, and the many "whys" that somehow remain unanswered. Each chapter vibrates with power, interest, and beauty, but one is particularly impressed by the story, "Nothing But Love," which the gray-headed old woman, out of her own experiences, relates to little Sandy, as they sit together on the front porch of their little cottage in the cool of the summer evening. This is a little classic within itself.

The last chapter presents Sandy at the age of seventeen, a bright, industrious, and promising youth, determined to have an education but face to face with the perplexing situation of how to work and help his needy mother and at the same time continue in school. At this point, Harriett, now a popular stage artist, appears and renders valuable assistance toward the solution of the difficulty.

Such a novel would naturally bring in pictures of poverty, sorrow, and sometimes cruelty; yet true to the type of people depicted, these pictures are balanced by scenes of laughter — a song of blues, the strains floating from a guitar in the hands of a black artist, a dance, or perhaps a humorous tale — for the characters must laugh. And Sandy concludes, as he watches the jovial, good-natured group, that this must be the reason why so many poverty-stricken Negroes live so long: "no matter how hard life might be, it was not without laughter."

The story ends with the swelling of a chorus from the meeting house of black worshippers—"We'll understand it better by and by," and it leaves the reader wondering if this is an indication that Mr. Hughes is planning sometime soon to write the sequel to this narrative. We hope so, for we feel that Sandy is a real flesh and blood brother, and we want to follow him further.

—ALICE M. PAXTON

Walt Carmon "Away from Harlem" review of Not Without Laughter, The New Masses, *October 30*

Not Without Laughter, the first novel by Langston Hughes, is a definite contribution to both Negro and proletarian literature in America.

Coming at this moment, however, it takes on added importance: it is the first definite break with the vicious Harlem tradition of Negro literature sponsored by Van Vechten and illustrated by Covarrubias.

This literary tradition has vulgarized the burlesqued the Negro as have the stage and the movies. It has seduced talented young Negro writers with easy money and quick recognition to be found in a synthetic cabaret bawdiness which is but a libel on 12 million American Negroes, most of them wage slaves.

Even Taylor Gordon, artist and genial human, makes his autobiography *Born To Be* a series of off-color episodes moralized into: "Don't sit on the green grass nude if you don't know your botany." He can thank Van Vechten.

And our own Claude McKay in *Home To Harlem* and *Banjo*, despite all their virtues, makes them definite products of this travesty of Negro life.

It is not surprising that genuine talent should have sacrificed artistic honesty, race pride and even class consciousness. Like the Negro worker, the Negro writer has been Jim-Crowed unmercifully. Honest novels of Negro life with their tragedy and bitterness were as unwelcome as the novels of the white woker. For years, this perverted literature has been practically the only opening in the literary field for the Negro writer. He has been allowed only to porter and clown at the literary bawdyhouse.

That Langston Hughes in his first book has had the courage to break with this tradition is evidence of his artistic honesty and a proletarian experience that has served him well. Hughes has been a seaman, porter, busboy and student.

As far back as 1924, I recall how enthusiastically we discussed his first poems then appearing in the *Workers Monthly*. They appeared later in the fine little collection *Poems for Workers* edited by Manuel Gomez, who was also editor of the *Workers Monthly* at that time. The poems were spirited, bitter poems of a proletarian and the work of a sensitive, competent literary craftsman.

In later poems in the *New Masses* and the following two books of verse: *The Weary Blues* and *Old Clothes to the Jew* [sic] the same note was dominant. But here it was already laden with the scent of the vicious Van Vechten patronage which Hughes still acknowledges.

In *Not Without Laughter*, the break with the Harlem tradition is not complete. But the novel is far beyond *Home to Harlem*, for instance. While McKay consciously daubs his canvas for the well paying market, Langston Hughes, closer to proletarian reality, gives us a vivid picture of a Negro working class family in midwest America.

One is struck immediately with the remarkable similarity to Agnes Smedley's *Daughter of Earth*, published last year. The kinship is a proletarian class kinship; the life is one that both black and white workers share in common.

The Indian father in Agnes Smedley's novel is not unlike the Negro, Jimboy, of *Not Wothout Laughter*: a transient worker, restless, always moving: "Jimboy was always goin . . . what was there in Shanton anyhow for a young colored fellow except to dig sewer-ditches for a few cents an hour or maybe porter around a store for seven dollars a week."

But where the Indian drowns his unrest in drink, the Negro Jimboy plays a guitar and sings blues, shouts and jingles: the songs he had learned as a wharf hand, railroad worker and porter in Natchez, Shreveport and Dallas. Some of these are folk-songs he learned in the pine woods of Arkansas from the lumber camp workers, earthy songs "desperate and dirty like the weary roads where they were sung.

Daughter of Earth took its bias from the bitterness of a woman. *Not Without Laughter* is steeled in the hatred of an oppressed race. Both are marred as class novels in this way. Yet both are proletarian as well. Agnes Smedley's story was a bitter, gray story. *Not Without Laughter* also gray, has brillaint gay tones of laughter, dance and music. Some of its passages are unmistakenly the work of a poet.

The Negro worker feels the heel of race oppression. He is "Nigger" to his white playmates in childhood. He is discriminated against in grade and high school. Later in life he is restricted to miserly paid menial labor. The white boss exploits him and his white misguided fellow-worker often discriminates against him on the job and in the trade union. Langston Hughes lets us see how bitterly the Negro worker feels this. It is not strange that class issues are beclouded by race feeling.

Harriet, hardheaded funloving girl who turns prostitute and later becomes a successful blues singer is told by her mother that her sister must guard her health. "What for," she asks, "to spend her life in Mrs. Rice's kitchen?"

And Harriet voices all the bitterness against a white religion which helps to oppress such a great part of her race: "Your old Jesus is white" she says, "He's white and stiff and don't like niggers!"

Dsicrimination, lynching, exploitation, the proletarian Negro feels as a class. But his oppresser is almost always white and the bitterness and hatred is misdirected at the white race as a whole.

Not Without Laughter is primarily a race novel. It concludes in a misty pointless fashion. There is no clear class consciousness nor revolutionary spirit which distinguished some of Hughes' early poems. But under its black skin, there is red proletarian blood running through it. With all its faults, *Not Without Laughter* goes far beyond Harlem. It is *our* novel.

REVIEW

oetry to the Novel to G

Sincere Picture of Neg o Life in America

LANGSTON HUGHES'S novel, "Not Without Laughter" (Knopf, $2.50), will confound many soothsayers and prematurely pessimistic critics. For the poet has proven that he can write prose adequate for the story he has to tell, and he has not concerned himself either with Harlem's Midnight Nans or the southland's cottonfield sweet men. He has depicted, rather, as the blurb on the jacket so conveniently states, a "deeply human picture of a simple people, living in a typical Kansas town, meeting, as best they can, the problems of their destructive, complex environment." He has done this, that is, for 249 pages of his 308-page novel. Remember this reservation for future reference.

Aunt Hagar Williams is an aged Negro woman, a pious, homespun, ample-bosomed individual, beloved by all with whom she comes into frequent contact. She lives her simple life, immersed in the steam and suds of her washtubs, dedicated to the welfare of her children, to the grace of God, and to the service of her neighbor should he be in need of her assistance. And, as a reward for this exemplary conduct, makes such an impression upon the community in which she lives that notice of her death merits, "in small type on its back page," the following paragraph from the Daily Leader:

> Hagar Williams, aged colored laundress, of 419 Cypress Street, passed away at her home last night. She was known and respected by many white families in the community. Three daughters and a grandson survive.

One of these surviving daughters, Tempy, is a victim of that lamentable American disease for which there seems to be no antitoxin: Keeping up with the Joneses, the Joneses in Tempy's case being bourgeois whites. With a smattering of what she believes to be culture, a few parcels of income property, and a husband who works for the Government, Tempy spends her time trying to convince herself and the world at large that she is neither part nor parcel of the peasant environment in which she happened to be born. While Tempy sounds as if she might be interesting, she is actually the most poorly delineated character in the novel. The reason is obvious. Being constantly surrounded by a legion of Tempy's prototypes, Mr. Hughes has not been as objective in this portrayal as he might have been had Tempy, like most of his other characters, been more indigneous to the novel's milieu.

The youngest daughter, Harriet, is a naive hedonist, early and easily seduced by flashy clothes, torrid dancing, spontaneous song fests, stimulating beverages and amorous dalliance. Frustrating all efforts to keep her in school or to make her amenable to menial labor, she gleefully, if not always successfully, defies the wrath of Aunt Hagar's God and Charlestons down a gaudy, primrose path.

THE other daughter, Annjee, is the mother of Hagar's one grandchild, Sandy. Annjee is distressingly normal. She works hard, complains but seldom, has no desire to be either a Tempy or a Harriet, and loves her husband, the irresponsible Jimboy, intensely, constantly, albeit, he is subject to the "travelin' blues," and walks off from Annjee and her child whenever the spirit so moves him.

It is with Sandy, the son of this haphazard union, whom "Not Without Laughter" primarily concerns itself. Around him most of the action is woven, through his eyes much of the story is reflected, and it is the problem of Sandy's adjustment to his environment, a problem more or less peculiar to the maturing Negro child, which occupies many pages of the novel.

It is not Sandy, however, but Aunt Hagar, Harriet, Jimboy and Annjee who remain alive in the reader's mind once the novel is completed. And of these Aunt Hagar is by far the most indelible, a fact which explains the reference made to page 249 some paragraphs ago. For when Aunt Hagar dies and crosses over Jordan, the reader is hard put to retain his former high pitch of interest. Simultaneously with her death, Harriet, Jimboy and Annjee also fade into the background. It is too great a bereavement. Either the novel should have managed to end itself at this point or Aunt Hagar's demise should have been postponed. Certainly her heav'nly home could have done without her for a few more years. Her presence is vitally necessary to the more mundane "Not Without Laughter."

Following the death of his grandmother, Sandy is forced to sojourn with the dicty Tempy, his mother having decided to trail the truant Jimboy. Tempy keeps him in school, urges him to abjure bad company, and, being a myopic disciple of Dr. W. E. B. DuBois, attempts to invest him with ideals diametrically opposed to those disseminated and held dear by his dead grandmother, a loyal, if vague, disciple of Booker T. Washington. Sandy seems destined to pursue a middle course, and we leave him optimistically facing the future, appropriately misunderstood by Annjee, obligingly relieved of Tempy, and, surprisingly enough, encouraged and aided by Harriet, whose aversion to the straight and narrow path has brought her a measure of fame and fortune on the stage.

"NOT WITHOUT LAUGHTER" is an enviable first performance. Belonging to a more decorous school, it lacks the dramatic intensity, the lush color, and tropical gusto of Claude McKay's "Home to Harlem." It also lacks the pallid insipidity and technical gaucheries of certain other contemporary novels by Negroes which are best left unnamed and forgotten. But it does present a vivid, sincerely faithful and commendable picture of peasant Negro life in a small American town, a town which vacillates uncertainly, spiritually and physically, from one side of the Mason Dixon line to the other.

In a moment of post-college exuberance, while considering Mr. Hughes's first book of poems, "The Weary Blues," the present reviewer stridently declaimed that it's author was possessed of "an unpredictable and immeasurable potential." After five years, the language might be more simple and more choice, but the spirit of the phrase would remain unchanged. For, as in his poetry Mr. Hughes carried a beacon light for Negro poets, he now, with this volume, advances to the vanguard of those who have recourse to the novel in an earnest endeavor to depict the many faceted ramifications of Negro life in America.

WALLACE THURMAN.

GOD SENDS SUNDAY. By Arna Bontemps. Harcourt Brace & Co. $2.00.

THOSE who already know Mr. Bontemps as a poet will not be surprised at the artistry evinced in this novel, although they may be surprised at the manner of its manifestation; those to whom his work is new, will realize that Mr. Bontemps has abilities to be reckoned with. *God Sends Sunday* is a good first novel.

One might be forgiven for not suspecting from Mr. Bontemps' restrained, pensive, subjective lyrics that he could turn out such a robustly humorous, frank, and detached novel as this. The cadence and fall of the "Nocturnes" has gone over into the syncopation of folk balladry. There is still an obvious concern with finesse of expression, but the book is hardboiled and at times cruel.

The plot is simple, almost too simple. It has to do with the ups and downs of Little Augie, or more exactly, of the up and the down. Little Augie was a jockey in the era of checkered clothing and the brass rail, in one of the most gilded sections of the gilded age, the sporting life hangouts of New Orleans and St. Louis. Leaving Harlem and cotton plantations this novel goes to the racetracks. Mr. Bontemps thus introduces to the fiction of Negro life a new character, and a new milieu, both colorful, and both authentic parts needed to fill out the saga of Negro life. Little Augie is of the brotherhood of Joe Gans, and Jack Johnson, and the jockeys found in James Weldon Johnson's *Black Manhattan*: Isaac Murphy, Tiny Williams and Jimmie Lee. Now on the crest of popularity, and now gone.

Little Augie, unable because of his puniness to do the heavy work of the farm, becomes a lover and knower of horses. At his first chance he runs away down the river to capitalize his skill. About the stables he must have found many horseshoes because his luck is miraculous. From a taunted runt he becomes the idol of the day. To cover up his sense of personal inadequacy, he affects the beau brummel.

At the top of the sporting wheel, Augie meets Della Green, who in spite of her goodness to him cannot keep him from remembering Florence Dessau, a quadroon of New Orleans, who 'stood out like a sunflower among daisies.' Of Della he does think enough to shoot casually a rough 'maquereau' who had been unwise enough to beat her. Little Augie could stand anything except the beating of his women by other men. But having killed for Della and having beaten her up rather tamely, he returned to Florence, who had been living as the mistress of Little Augie's first employer. Florence plays around with him until his luck turned and then she quits him. "Yo' luck done change, Lil Augie. Its leavin' time."

Suddenly he looked tired and old. "Yes, ma luck done gone down." . . .

"Its mor'n a notion, Lil Augie. I done got used to havin' things. Y'all men done spoilt me."

The wheel comes around full circle. Lil Augie, broke and disconsolate, hoboes to California where he finds his sister Leah. This part of the book, in elegiac strain, shows the tiny outcast dreaming of vanished glory, of the cakewalk where he had triumphed, of his startling wardrobe and of the greenbacks that many times had filled his hat. The book ends with Lil Augie, running away from the effects of a brawl, headed for Tia Juana, a broken, foolish old man, living in dreams of glory he had known so many years ago that he could not remember how many.

The merits of the book are those of folk ballads. The movement is swift and direct, the telling simple and interesting. Such melodrama as there is seems part and parcel of the whole scheme. Of course some incidents such as the double murder of Tom Wright and Joe Bailey seem too much in the ballad manner and unconvincing. 'In the same instant his six gun barked. Root a toot toot . . . toot toot,' is a sentence throwing back too obviously to *Frankie and Johnnie*. The characterization of most of the people is vague; even Lil Augie is flat; one doesn't get an all around look at him. Leah and Florence and Badfoot are disappointingly sketchy. Moreover, Augie's meteoric rise and fall are both too sudden, and for a novel with such chances for local color as this one, the background is too shadowy. We don't see the life of the stables, we don't get in the paddock, we don't see Augie at the peak of his triumph in the races themselves. The big race that spelled his doom is telephoned to us. If Mr. Bontemps had only exercised his undeniable skill in words on some of these.

The prose is sensitive and balanced. The dialect almost everywhere rings true, and is at times inspired. The folk humor is good. *"Anybody'll shoot what carries a gun," Barner said. "Hell, I seen a gun pop off layin on a table."* And although Augie with Florence and Della doesn't always support credence, still at times he is made appealing and wistful—a genuine creation in our gallery of folk portraits. One will remember him, 'no bigger than a minute' daring the husky race track gamblers to 'try a barrel' with him. One will remember him singing his blues and in his other attempts to impress Della. One will remember him, as Aaron Douglass has caught him on the excellent bookjacket, dreaming of the days that were. One would like to remember him at the moment of his real triumphs, riding the winner home, and feeling as he thundered over the finishing line past the judges stand, an ecstasy of which even Della and Florence, and a flowered vest were merely prolongings and second rate substitutes.

STERLING A. BROWN.

"God Sends Sunday," by Arna Bontemps (Harcourt, Brace, $2.00).

ARNA BONTEMPS' first venture in fiction is to me a profound disappointment. It is of the school of "Nigger Heaven" and "Home to Harlem." There is a certain pathetic touch to the painting of his poor little jockey hero, but nearly all else is sordid crime, drinking, gambling, whore-mongering, and murder. There is not a decent intelligent woman; not a single man with the slightest ambition or real education, scarcely more than one human child in the whole book. Even the horses are drab. In the "Blues" alone Bontemps sees beauty. But in brown skins, frizzled hair and full contoured faces, there are to him nothing but ugly, tawdry, hateful things, which he describes with evident caricature.

One reads hurriedly on, waiting for a gleam of light, waiting for the Sunday that some poor ugly black God may send; but somehow it never comes; and if God appears at all it is in the form of a little drunken murderer riding South to Tia Juana on his back.

I suppose I am not tuned right to judge this book and am a prey to hopeless prejudices. Somehow, I cannot fail to see the open, fine, brown face of Bontemps himself. I know of his comely wife and I can imagine a mother and father for each of these, who were at least striving and ambitious. I read with ever recurring wonder Bontemps' noble "Nocturne at Bethesda;" but here in this, nothing of that other side is even hinted.

Well,—as I know I have said several times before,—if you like this sort of thing, then this will be exactly the sort of thing you will especially like, and in that case you ought to run and read it.

W. E. B. D.

The Crisis

TWO BOOK REVIEWS

BY GEORGE A. KUYPER

COMING from the finely-chiseled, epigrammatic, intense poetry of Countee Cullen into the pages of his latest work —a first novel*—the sensitive reader will undoubtedly experience a feeling of disappointment, and, in spite of another poet's fair success with a first novel published last year, will ardently wish that first rate poets be less versatile. For in this latest attempt to picture life as it is (or is supposed to be) lived in Harlem, there is a combination of some really forceful characterization together with a goodly measure of the bizarre and much that is flat, stale, although perhaps profitable—readers being what they are. If there is some truth in a periodical article which appeared recently, regretting the Negro artist's weakness in catering to the white man's *conception* of what Negro life in Harlem is, and not portraying colored men and women as they really are—then over a third of this novel seems to help in proving the truth of that thesis. The vital imagination of Cullen's poetry, which with his acute wit and his keen epigrammatic expression made his name one to be reckoned with in discussing modern American poetry, is lacking, and I feel that here is a first novel of which at least one third had better been consigned to a waste-paper basket.

The novel is a dual story. Its main theme is the story of one-armed Sam Lucas, a wanderer, who made his living with a razor and a deck of cards, largely by attending church revivals, and when the sinners held back from the converts' bench, brandishing his razor and cards, confessing his "sins," giving himself to God, and thus starting a procession of converts. But on a New Year's eve in Harlem his act is responsible for bringing the stubborn Mattie to the mourners' bench, as a result of which she finds a lasting religious fervor and falls in love with Sam. Although Sam has his worries and doubts about her, "for he felt that she was like some new and strange being, unlike the other women he had known. The

*"One Way to Heaven" by Countee Cullen. Harper and Brothers. New York. $2.00.

others had been like himself, creatures of action and not of speech. . . . .But this girl . . . was strange and mysterious. . . . He could read his doom in her face: no guest for a fitful expenditure of passion, but love that was deep and severe like a halter around his neck." (Mattie is described by her aunt as the "stickin' kind, and whenever she goes into anything she goes in for keeps.") They are married; Sam finally finds work as a ticket chopper in a Harlem moviehouse and falls in love with the pretty usher. The melodramatic ending to this triangle is not quite convincing.

The rest of the novel deals with an extremely bizarre group headed by Constancia (christened Constance) Brandon, a polysyllabic Negro pseudo-intellectual at whose home white and black poets and novelists, black duchesses, a British millionaire, a blues singer, and others gather. She "was the mirror in which most of social Harlem delighted to gaze and see itself"; the height of her success was achieved when she secured for her salon a Southern professor to lecture (for a fee) on "The Menace of the Negro to our American Civilization." The two groups are held within the covers of the same book by the coincidence of Mattie's being Constancia's maid. The wedding that Constancia arranges for her maid and Sam is a Mad-Hatter's party, with a second rate poet offering as a wedding present volumes of his poetry and a blues singer offering some of her phonograph records. The author's purpose may be a contrast between the high life of the witty and pretentious and the humble life of the simpler church folk; however, the contrast is only weakly evident. More than a third of the book is devoted to Constancia and her circle—the stronger story of Mattie and Sam accordingly suffers by what is too evidently an interlude of burlesque on the would-be intelligensia.

In Countee Cullen's poetry we have been led to expect a perfection of style—a precision of phrase. In this first novel he is clumsy and frequently heavy-humored. "Donald had drunk more than a score of cocktails which Mattie and Porter were dispensing with a prodigality shocking in a country addicted to prohibition" is not even fifth-rate humor. " 'But she's awfully nice, just the same' "; "They ate for the most part in silence, finding the business of eating too heavenly to be defiled by many words"; "Their hands were spread out across the white altar-covering like so many flags of supplication and truce"; "He wished he knew how to tackle her"; "She was not totally deficient in brains"; "Constance never moved an eyelash to corral"; "Lest it be thought that Constancia was built along strictly frivolous lines"; "the slightly nonplused son"; "Now as she led the famished-seeming lecturer"; "At the dropping of a handkerchief the duchess would willingly recite"—these are evidences rather of a precocious novel hidden away in a trunk for years and suddenly brought to light than of the work of a man gifted with language.

There is one passage which may well be a rock on which the critic is meant to stumble—"Not many people had read Herbert's novel, although it had been out for several months and had been commented upon in the Negro and white press (denounced by the former as an outrage against Negro sensibilities and lauded by the latter as being typically Negro)." It is neither; but it is a novel with several interesting characters, some hilarious scenes, and a great deal of pretty poor writing.

In last month's issue of the *Southern Workman,* kind words, tempered somewhat, were said about the Associated Publishers. The praise this time need not be tempered; for this firm has published a book worthy of unqualified commendation.*

This year of the bicentennial of Washington's birth will no doubt witness the production of many books about various aspects of his life. Here is one which is worth a careful reading, not merely by those who are interested in the Negro, but as a significant and highly interesting study of this great American. It throws considerable light on the character of George Washington in particular, and on the general conditions of the Negroes in America during his lifetime.

The introduction states that although Washington's life has been written many times, "as the master of slaves he has had but little consideration; and his true picture must ever remain unpainted while his attitude toward the Negro people . . . remains obscure." The book presents that attitude in a well-documented, carefully written, and interesting study of the gradual change of Washington's views. At first we see him educated "by tradition," holding the belief of the aristocratic planter class to which he belonged by birth, that slavery was right. In his early twenties he was a slaveowner and a slave-purchaser. He was a humane one, however, his diaries abounding with references to his sick Negroes and the steps taken to care for them. Yet he was a stern task-master, working out mathematically a scale of maximum efficiency to be held to (a plan he continued in regard to his estate even while bur-

*"George Washington and the Negro" by Walter H. Mozych. Associated Publishers. Inc., Washington, D. C. $2.15

dened with the duties of president). He saw to it that Mount Vernon was systematically and successfully operated.

During the Revolution, however, Washington gradually freed himself from these prejudices, helped along partly by the necessity of enlisting Negroes in the Continental army, a plan of which at first he heartily disapproved. In 1775 he wrote, "From the number of Boys, Deserters, and Negroes which have been inlisted in the troops of this Province, I entertain some doubts whether the number [of recruits] required can be raised here." But becoming alarmed when he considered the consequences of the Negroes' following the invitation of Lord Dunmore, the Colonial Governor of Virginia, who promised freedom to all indented servants who joined his Majesty's troops, Washington reconsidered his earlier stand, and toward the end of that year, without Congress' approval, he ordered recruiting officers to *re*enlist free Negroes who had served in the army at Cambridge. By the end of the war, partly because of the influence of Lafayette, Washington became an avowed opponent of the slave system, but not daring to speak out because of his stronger desire for the building up of a united nation, and realizing that the raising of the slave question would cause disruption. But he had proceeded far down the road from the prejudiced Virginia plantation-owner attitude, for in a letter to Lafayette he wrote: "To set the slaves afloat at once, would, I really believe, be productive of much inconvenience and mischief; but by degrees it certainly might, and assuredly ought to be effected; and that too by legislative authority."

Although he owned slaves, his "human nature constantly asserted its conviction against the slave system." In 1794 he wrote, "I have another motive which makes me earnestly wish these things—it is indeed more powerful than all the rest—namely to liberate a certain species of property—which I possess very repugnantly to my own feelings; but which imperious necessity compels, and until I can substitute some other expedient, by which expenses, not in my power to avoid (however well I may be disposed to it) can be defrayed." Three years later he wrote to his nephew, "I wish from my soul that the legislature of this State could see the policy of gradual abolition of slavery." He did not free his own slaves because of financial considerations. In 1799 he again wrote to his nephew, "I have more working Negroes by a full moiety than can be employed to any advantage. . . . To sell the oversurplus I cannot, because I am principalled against this kind of traffic in human species. To hire them out is almost as bad, because they could not be disposed of in families to any advantage, and to disperse the families I have an aversion. What then is to be done? Something must or I shall be ruined." That is, he was adhering to certain humane principles even at the risk of financial ruin. A few months later he died. By his will he accomplished his wish, for that document provided, in detailed directions, for the gradual emancipation of his slaves after the death of his wife.

The exposition of Washington's changing attitude toward the Negro is the central topic around which are gathered many incidental themes which throw much light on the period. A chapter is devoted to his relations with Phillis Wheatley.

The whole book is carefully documented. Interesting appendices treat of Kosciusko, the Polish patriot's attitude toward the Negro; of Crispus Attucks; and of the important part played in the attack on Stony Point by Pompey, a Negro slave. A detailed index is added.

The preface states correctly: "A very human story, therefore, is to be found in the evolution of his regard for human rights as unfolded by his changing attitude toward the Negro."

OUR BOOKSHELF

The Chinaberry Tree. By Jessie Fauset. Stokes. $2.

MANY Negroes, I imagine, are weary of the eagerness with which white critics praise the folk songs of their race. However truly spirituals and blues may be said to form one of the richest heritages of art for contemporary America, they can scarcely be held the product of either a contemporary or a cultivated society. The writer who now attempts to duplicate them is only a romantic balladist, singing tepid echoes of what was once sincere and passionate, while his white contemporaries are absorbed in strenuous and conscious analysis of their own complex psychology. But the Negro artist who seeks instead to live in the present has too often leaped sensationally from primitivism to sophistication. He has lost the genuine though limited culture of the folk songs. But he has sometimes failed to realize that what he has substituted for it is less genuine and equally limited. When Carl Van Vechten's *Nigger Heaven* was published, many Negroes were shocked at what they felt was a burlesque of Harlem life. Mr. Van Vechten was accused of presenting only those superficial aspects of Negro life that whites on an outing would look for when they discarded their good sense along with their prejudices. Yet to an impartial view, Mr. Van Vechten had merely stylized a little more consciously the same glamor of wine and women that has formed the substance of the usual novel by Negroes themselves. If they have seen where Mr. Van Vechten did not its tragic implications, they have chosen to strangle them in melodrama.

Now the significance of Miss Fauset's *Chinaberry Tree* is that it is one of the first novels (the first I happen to have read) that takes Negro life seriously. Miss Fauset has shown in it that the life of Negroes can be complex as well as merely passionate. Doubtless she has been aided by choosing to treat not of Harlem Negroes but of a small New Jersey community less isolated from the contagion of white example. The setting, therefore, is no back drop to a burlesque show but an all pervasive though scarcely mentioned element of its action. Yet the ideal of respectability that dominates the book is more than an adoption of its stuffy Puritanic survival in the suburban life of bourgeois whites. For any race that suffers consciously from surrounding prejudice, the attainment of respectability is the one sort of imitation that can eradicate it. What to the white artist, who was, so to speak, born respectable and has grown with education unnecessarily deeper into its toils, is the stimulus of the Negro tradition is precisely that directness and intensity of instinctive expression which for the Negro must be suspect and controlled since his immediate need is for the enrichment of the conscious and the intellectual.

Miss Fauset's Negro community has perhaps become too fervidly aware of this necessity for respectability. Her characters have acquired a veneration for chastity which was certainly not caught from white Montclair but from Queen Victoria. In Red Brook the sins of the fathers descend in fact with some addition at least into the second generation. The merit of *The Chinaberry Tree* from a sociological view point is that this attitude, however cruel and insufficient, is without hypocrisy, and that the important characters transcend it. This difference in moral values, however far from modern it would be regarded for a white community, enriches the theme of the novel. The fortunate lovers, though fairly nervous over the chastity of the two cousins, are more than gallant in ignoring the lack of it in the cousins' parents. Their attitude and a similar one in two charming families of friends relieves what would otherwise be a disagreeably petty situation, one cousin, influenced by the dominating sentiment, priding herself upon a purity of descent lacking to the other until the shocking discovery that she too is illegitimate. This action takes on further color by being thrown into a society which, barring the ideal of respectability, has multiple interesting stratifications determined by wealth, education, profession (though not strangely enough after the Harlem revelations, by degree of color), and which is much more conscious of its segments than a white community since they are all alike crowded within the pale. Motivation in such a novel is as fertile a source of interest as situation. The white reader finds *The Chinaberry Tree* interesting not only because it affords him a more authentic picture of Negro life than the Harlem novels, but because it reveals a greater consciousness of the problems of plot and characterization.

The most serious weakness of the book is to be found in certain aspects of its action. One puts aside the occasional infelicities of diction in which clothes and table linen are described in the savory cliches of department store advertisements. It is more serious that the reader is given no explanation how in so gossipy a town Malory's family could have lived for many years without people generally knowing of his unfortunate blood relationship to the girl he loves. His father's affair with Melissa's mother, though it took place in a distant city and could be known only by inference, is precisely the sort of event that in a small community becomes common knowledge to everybody except some of the persons most concerned. If the plot demands both ignorance of this and Malory's periodic retirement into the gloom of his mother's house, probability demands that the family locate itself a little further away, within the week-end radius. This improbability becomes the more conspicuous because Miss Fauset willfully, appetizingly delays the revelation. And so when it does come, there is scarcely time to justify Melissa's recochet into the patient arms of her former admirer. But the most dispensable part of these slow final pages describes a trip to New York which is not simply relief from the relevation, but an opportunity seized for sketching the sights and especially for recounting the first experience of race prejudice in the novel. The manner in which Miss Fauset treats the incident makes one wish that she sometime devote a whole rich tragic novel to the subject. But it is irrelevant to the atmospere of so completely colored and so placid a society as the Red Brook of the novel which Miss Fauset has appropriately ended beneath the familiar chinaberry tree, the symbol of true love and beauty and the security of home.

EDWIN BERRY BURGUM.

INFANTS OF THE SPRING. Wallace Thurman. The Macaulay Company, $2.00.

THE "infants of the spring" are a group of young people—Negro artists and would-be artists and a trio of white persons who have varied interests in Negroes. These gather for a stormy Bohemian interval in a lodging house in Harlem called Niggerati Manor and then go their way, not wholly unaffected by the canker of their experiences there.

Unfortunately the orgiastic nature of much that goes on in Harlem has been dwelt on so often lately that a good part of *Infants of the Spring* simply leaves one with a helpless sensation of having had to eat again something one has already digested with ease several times before. Moreover, the lengthy speeches throughout the book are monotonous and boring. Mr. Thurman evidently wants more than anything else to demonstrate a thesis concerning the peculiar difficulties that confront young Negro artists,—because they are young, because they are Negroes, and because they desire to express themselves. But it is difficult to ascertain just what particular thesis he had in mind. The subjects of his numerous declamations cover a wide range; economics, social work, art, philosophy, present-day sex morality and what-not, discussed now from the Negro, now from the Negro-white, now from the purely detached point of view. Besides the fact that this diffuseness of expressed ideas obscures good elements of characterization, satire, and dialogue, the ideas themselves are never brought to a single point of unity. They are left at loose ends, the implication being that they have not yet achieved complete harmony in the mind of the author. The endeavor to analyze and present the problems of the Negro artist is a worthy one. But the problems considered in this book do not seem as yet to have been thoroughly thought through by the writer himself, and so *Infants of the Spring* has that inevitable underdone taste which flavors the bulk of literary output today.

What should have been a creation of significance and colorful beauty is no more than a series of sensationally exotic and sordid scenes whose only excuse for being is the occasional serious thought and genuine feeling, badly arranged, however, which intersperse them. For it is not enough to face and attempt to portray stark truth and bitter reality. It is necessary to pass beyond to an affirmed whole-view of them and build upon the strength of that. Only from such inner freedom and power can anything worth-while arise.

LOIS TAYLOR.

"Infants of the Spring," Wallace Thurman, [author review].
[Contempo,/Misc/ Thurman, Wallace. Harry Ransom Humanities Research Center, University of Texas at Austin.]

Infants of the Spring is a novel which the author was impelled to write. The characters and their problems cried out for relaese. They intruded themselves into his evey alien thought. And assumed importance which blinded him to their true value.

The faults and virtues of the novel, then, are the direct result of this inescapable compulsion. And now that this book is a printed reality, the author muses: Had I waited five years before setting this material down, it might have been more refined and seemed less jejune. But it might also have lacked the earnestness and spontaneity necessary for vivid presentation. And I might never have been able to produce anything else without these present unworthy characters wilfully insinuating themselves, wreaking havoc.

All of which is an acceptable excuse for having written an unsatisfactory novel. But most certainly no excuse for having allowed it to be published.

Boheminanism [sic], in the popular sense of the term, came to the present author too late to be the youthful fourteen year old adventure it should have been, and too early to be clarified by twenty-five year old maturity. It came during that uncertain middle period of his life, (he was eighteen then), when it was alternately fascinating and repellant, more the former than the latter, but sufficiently both to unbalance him. The result is *Infants of the Spring*, a novel which undoubtedly has contributed much to the author's individual growth, but which he fears will do little to impress a critical public.

Critical public? Hardly. It would be more apt to apply the adjectives, prejudiced, myopic. For this public, with lamentingly few exceptions, is so stereotyped in its mental attitudes, and so intent on surface values, that, for the moment, no Negro novelist can expect intelligent critical guidance or encouraging appreciation.

This is not, mind you, an excuse for a bad novel, nor the empty caviling of a disgruntled author. It is rather a barbed arraignment of those who classify as bad any creative work which does not concur with their biased and pre-conceived illusions of the material presented.

Negroes, themselves, resent any novel, no matter how meritorious, which does not deal with what they call "the better class of Negroes". Meaning the semi-literate bourgeoisie to whom keeping up with the Jonese implies doing nothing of which bourgeoisie whites might disapprove. Someday a harassed Negro author is going to accept the challenge, and truthfully depict this sector of Negro society. And then! . . . . . well . . . . [ellipses in the original manuscript] I only hope none of my contemporaries deprives me of the pleasure.

Literate whites, too, have peculiar ideas concerning the material Negro authors should utilize. The more emancipated they are supposed to be from mob delusions, the more insistent they are that the Aframerican novelist limit himself to one certain type of character, the earthy, naive Negro to whom life is just a bowl of cherries, but who is ultimately strangled by the pits.

The reasons for all this, of course, is that few whites or blacks can conceive of Negroes being human beings, subject to the same variations, emotional, physical and mental, as are the rest of God's chosen anthropoids. The poor black brother has been a problem for so long, the world in general seems to forget that the business of living in our present day civilization can humanize even a transplanted and highly synthetic Ethopian.

Wallace Thurman

Along This Way*

A Review of the Autobiography of James Weldon Johnson

By William Stanley Braithwaite

FOR many of us contemplating the perusal of this Autobiography of "Jim" Johnson, there was a kind of eagerness which set up a rare and peculiar scale of anticipations. Of all the works produced by Negro authorship since the so-called literary renaissance in the early nineteen-twenties, no single work intrigued the curiosity concerning the intimacies and relationships of a conspicuously successful figure in the aesthetic and controversial life of the race and the nation, as the record of this man who has been educator, lawyer, popular song-writer, librettist, translator, poet, novelist, editor, journalist, orator, diplomatist, and as a publicist the spear-head of a militant organization, shot in all directions over the country in a crusade to pierce the armor of American race-prejudice, oppression, and injustice.

William Stanley Braithwaite interprets "Along This Way" from the standpoint of the critic and the artist.

—The Editor.

Since the "Up From Slavery" of Booker T. Washington a generation ago, there have been, in this era of bumper-crops in autobiographies, but two stories of self-recorded Negro lives, that I recall, presented to the general public: Dr. Moton's "What the Negro Thinks" and Taylor Gordon's "Born To Be," antiphonal as they are in environment and purpose; with such fleeting glimpses, in supplement, as Dr. Du Bois, Benjamin Brawley and Claude McKay, have given us of fragments of their lives in periodical contributions. In a sense this Autobiography of James Weldon Johnson is unique, quite apart from the many-gifted character of its subject, for it takes shape and expression out of the qualities which make that character to become both a challenge to, and a triumph over, the critical authorities of American life.

There is a dual emphasis that should be laid upon any consideration of this pulsing human story, a duality that will be secretly recognized by every intelligent reviewer of the book in the literary press, but seldom, I fear, to be recorded by them in print. To date I have failed to notice, in any of the reviews of the book, this distinction made, or commented upon. This duality of which I speak is the duality of every gifted Negro whose physical life, by chance or circumstance of his public activities, is forced into the pattern of the eternal *problem*, but whose spiritual life transcends that pattern and adds to the radiance of the universal vision of mankind. Therefore ,we are confronted with columns, in the white press, summarizing the many episodes related in the Autobiography, of the author's personal experiences with prejudice and attempted discriminations, which inevitably precipitate a tragic, humiliating, or humorous climax. These experiences have been common to countless numbers of humble Negroes, with little variations from the attitudes and reactions taken by the more gifted and famous; but these experiences will not be corrected nor eliminated from the social and civic consciousness of American life until that consciousness has become saturated with a recognition of the verities which this thrilling, and often, fascinating, story of James Weldon Johnson's life teaches on its spiritual and cultural side.

In the familiar shaping of an epigramatic idea, God makes James Weldon Johnson a creative artist, but he made himself a race-agitator. He had an intellectual motivation for the cause into which he threw the energies and devotions of his manhood's prime; and while the heat of debate, the tactics and strategies were pursued with ardour and often with consummate skill, there was none of the passion nor exalted moods of rationalization, which forged the spirit of Douglass or Washington or Du Bois on the anvil of a diabolical oppression. If these race champions, Douglass, Washington, and Du Bois, flame across the pages of race and American history with a greater glory for stirring the hearts of their people with higher hopes and clearer visions, and a more determined effort to realize them, than James Johnson, that same history will record in its footnotes and appendices, that with Booker T. Washington he stands forth

*Along This Way—An Autobigoraphy By James Weldon Johnson. The Viking Press. $3.50.

as one of the two best organizers of a racial program.

The fourteen years that James Johnson gave to his labors with the N. A. A. C. P. were years for which the race should be immensely grateful. They left him weary, and I believe, somewhat disillusioned. Not the Negro, I hasten to explain, was disillusioned, but the man, the artist. And one cannot fully understand this mood without reading with particular attention the last ten or fifteen pages of this Autobiography.

That all through these fourteen years of organization and agitation, James Johnson was disturbingly aware of the creative impulses which haunted his more prosaic duties, he gives testimony near the end of his Autobiography, in the statement: "I got immense satisfaction out of the work which was the main purpose of the National Association for the Advancement of Colored People; at the same time, I struggled constantly not to permit that part of me which was artist to become entirely submerged. I had little time and less energy for creative writing."

There is a bit of wistful pleading in the statement; to me like the mystic echo of the Voice that spoke gently but radiantly in the Galilean hills, "I am the true vine. . . . Now ye are clean through the word which I have spoken unto you." And the implication interposes like a thin veil through which one peers along the vista of this Autobiography to behold a dim pageantry of ideals and realities, half fantasy, half tragical, of a human soul. One hears echoing out of this dim recess of a spirit, sensitive to the harsh and intimidating taboos of American life, the symphonic movements of experience which carried that spirit in triumph upon the crest of the environment that would quell and silence it. This is the other aspect of that dual character of this Autobiography of which I spoke, the spiritual element which lifts the individual out of the prescribed pattern into which an hypocritical concept has woven him, and gives him a symbolic balance in the ultimate scheme of social unity in a free democracy.

There are four sections of Mr. Johnson's Autobiography which fascinated me. The first two are of great significance to the race as ideals of attainment to be emulated. First is the story of the author's parentage, childhood and youth, up to and through those years which carried him to the threshold of his college life; they are chronicled with a fullness and charm which make these pages a lone and singular contribution of Negro authorship to American literature. Next is Mr. Johnson's invasion, with his brother Rosamond and Bob Cole, of the musical and theatrical world and the brilliant success they achieved in contributing songs and librettos to many of the best-known light operas of the opening years of the century. I only regret that Mr. Johnson did not write with the same anecdotal detail about the personalities and associations, which he knew in the later years of his literary successes. Perhaps he thought the associates and the famous figures of the musical portion of his career, when he was still a young man, had receded sufficiently into the past to give him the freedom to sketch them and the affairs of their world more copiously and intimately, while his friendships and associations in the more recent world of American letters, as well as that other world of the more sombre hue, wherein notable and self-sacrificing men and women of both races were pledged together in a warfare of service against injustice, were too well-known and in the public view, for him to write about them with the same detachment and freedom. Rich as the Autobiography is with the crowded figures of notable men and women in the aesthetic world of yesterday and today, it would have been made richer by the intimate portraitures of the author's immediate contemporaries.

The third section of the Autobiography which stirred and entranced me was the leading part Mr. Johnson took in the fight for the Dyer Anti-Lynching Bill. His account of this fight to enact into Federal legislation a remedy for the most shameful deeds of violence and lawlessness of which America was guilty above all other nations making up the civilized society of today, is, though compressed into a comparatively few pages, an epic of fortitude, tact, patience and perseverance. And the fourth recital of Mr. Johnson's colorful career, is the description of his visit to Japan as a member of the Institute of Pacific Relations, to attend the Conference at Kyoto.

Why this latter episode of his career should so impress me I cannot explain to my satisfaction. It covers scarcely more than twelve or fifteen pages. It had been nothing unusual for American Negroes, from Frederick Douglass, Mary Church Terrell, Dr. Robert R. Moton, Dr. Du Bois, John Hope to young Richard Hill, through the struggling years when the race was winning the intellectual right to a representation in world movements for the betterment of human society, to attend foreign conferences as accredited delegates. These, however, met in Europe. Could it be that there was something racially significant that the Institute of Pacific Relations Conference which took Mr. Johnson to Japan, and to that Garden Party given for its members by the Emperor of Japan, was more than an intellectual and social gesture? Did one, as one read Mr. Johnson's simple, but impressive, description of the affair and the picture of the arrival of the Imperial family and court upon the scene, feel some magic by which the spectacle was transformed into an allegory of the Past and Future, of Time and Race? If an allegory is evoked did it fuse the spirit of the dark people who had mastered with the dark people who were rising to a mastery of their own? And the framework to hold the allegory, the fact that both dark peoples had been freed of a bondage but a few years apart!

James Weldon Johnson has lived a crowded life and he has recorded it minutely in this Autobiography, which is incontestably the first work of its kind in American literature. Unlike any other autobiography, that of Frederick Douglass, Booker T. Washington, or even Dr. Moton, it escapes from that category of racial recitals in the narrower sense, and remains the narrative of a man who for sixty years of his life has passed through an amazing series of social and intellectual adventures and events which lifted him steadily to a foremost place as an American citizen. And yet I think, the word brilliant must be used to describe the picture which Mr. Johnson has composed of the *social life, the domestic manners and habits, loyalties, and ethical foundations*, which pertain to the lives of Negroes. As Colonel Higginson told a skeptical and indifferent nation a generation or two ago, that the Negro like all other peoples was "intensely human," in his ideals and aspirations, in his habits and conduct, and nowhere in a literal record of his experiences have we had so brilliant a presentation of this truth as in this Autobiography. Except for that menacing shadow which eternally hovers along the boundary line of the Negro's contact with the objective mood and sentiment of a self-deluded Nordic superiority, page after page of this Autobiography might well be the chronicle of an upper middle-class American gentleman, his family and friends. But like all individuals of exceptional spiritual gifts, there are moments when the spirit of the author is hard pressed with problems and decisions which to solve and make, affect him purely as an individual; beyond their consequences he had to make note, because of that Man-Negro dualism upon which fate and circumstance placed its accent at critical stages of his career. How hampered his career might have been otherwise if Mr. Johnson had lacked that sense of humor and philosophic detachment which so plentifully sprinkles the pages of his Autobiography, it is not difficult to see.

On arriving in France with his brother and Bob Cole, preparatory to the theatrical engagement for which the latter two were booked in London, Mr. Johnson writes: "From the day I set foot in France, I became aware of the working of a miracle within me. I became aware of a quick readjustment to life and to environment. I recaptured for the first time since childhood the sense of being just a human being. I need not try to analyze this change for my colored readers; they will understand in a flash what took place. For my white readers . . . I am afraid that any analysis will be inadequate, perhaps futile. . . . I was suddenly free; free from a sense of impending discomfort, insecurity, danger; free from the conflict within the Man-Negro dualism and the innumerable maneuvers in thought and behavior that it compels; free from the problem of the many obvious or subtle adjustments to a multitude of bans and taboos; free from special scorn, special tolerance, special condescension; special commiseration; free to be merely a man."

I could wax either sentimental or philosophic over that paragraph. Any estimate of the confession Mr. Johnson makes, of the emotions that moved him on arriving in France, is certain to be colored by both moods. But I venture to predict that an America acquainted with this Autobiography as it should be—and as I think it will be—will be cleansed of much in its heart that is contemptible and unjust, and will make it unnecessary in the future for one of her citizens to express such a mood. A life such as Mr. Johnson has lived, a career such as he has achieved and a record such as he has made of both in the pages of this Autobiography, is one of the surest guarantees of that fulfillment in the future.

THE WAYS OF WHITE FOLKS. Stories by Langston Hughes. Alfred A. Knopf. $2.50.

LANGSTON HUGHES' development has been steady, sure and positive. His works from 1926 to 1931 are links in this evolution. Save for occasional retrogressions (*Dream Keeper, Dear Lovely Death, Popo and Fifina*) which are allowable in the development of the sincere fellow-traveller, Hughes' career has been brilliant and straightforward. His work, it is true, has not always possessed the anti-bourgeois note so evident in his work from 1931 to 1934. Nevertheless, it was reasonable to believe that Hughes would go further in the only direction in which an artist should go, than any of his colleagues of the "New Negro Renaissance."

Langston Hughes, was in 1926, an integral part of that unhealthy "New Negro" tradition. He shared the beliefs in the new theories of bourgeois estheticism as much as Cullen, Toomer and McKay. Even so, the poems in "Weary Blues" signified the arrival of a remarkable poetic genius. And in "Not Without Laughter," he had broken almost definitely with the "Harlem Tradition." Today, with the publication of "The Ways of White Folks," Hughes has travelled much further, nearer his goal of true revolutionary literature. It must be remembered that there had to be a good deal of excision, a complete denial of bourgeois traditions and parlor radicalism before he could write "Scottsboro Limited," "Columbia," "Good Morning, Revolution" and "The Ways of White Folks."

Since it is difficult to review these fourteen stories in any but a laudatory fashion, it should not be incorrect to analyze the entire content as well as the author. First, Hughes has shown that he has mastered the objective short story form. These stories are as nearly perfect as one could desire. They are not unlike the stories of Pauteileimon Romanov, and of Romanov's master, Tchekov. The resemblance extends to the superb irony, the simplicity and the splendid craftsmanship.

Every word seems to be weighed, tested, burnished and carefully inserted. There is such economy of structure, the stories are told so ably, that one experiences the feeling of having read what might have been a novel. There is in this book a sense of ease, but yet vivid writing. These stories remain indelibly on the mind. You live them. They constitute special experiences for you. These properties belong to great art.

Eight years ago, Hughes, in defending Negro Art, wrote, "If white people are pleased, we are glad. If they are not, it does not matter. We know we are beautiful. And ugly too." Now, he writes of these same white people. Now, his approach is a class approach. Now, he does not mean all white folks, but as Berry says "some white folks." Hughes, realizing the struggles in existence between two classes, conceives of those white people who in their control, circumscribe and influence the lives of the Negro masses. He writes of Negroes in relation to white people who are part of their very existence. This is so for Hughes because all men stand in relation to each other as parts of a social whole. He is interested in Negro and white class psychology, in their class differentiations. He uses working class themes, showing the intensity of the exploitation of share-croppers, bookkeeper, domestic and laborer.

When read together, these stories present a rather tightly knit pattern. Taken together, they show an indictment against the decadence of capitalistic society. When read singly, such stories as "A Good Job Gone," "Little Dog," "One Christmas Eve," etc., may evoke the remarks that they are good as stories go, but that they are not examples of bourgeois realism or of revolutionary literature. Such criticism is specious, of course, when these stories are taken together. For, one of the largest effects gained in the body of the book is in the use of irony and satire, concealed and open. Also, his ability to generalize is characteristic of his anti-bourgeois outlook. This characteristic enables him to apply his scalpel to Negroes and whites alike.

In "Father and Son," the most powerfully absorbing story in the volume, the author states his belief in the knowledge that the union of white and black workers will be the single force which will smash American Capitalism. "Crucible of the South, find the right powder and you'll never be the same again—the cotton will blaze and the cabins will burn and the chains will be broken and men, all of a sudden, will shake hands, black men and white men, like steel meeting steel!" That is why Hughes' art is social. Call it propaganda if you like. He has succeeded, nevertheless, in overcoming his former schematism and abstractness. He has succeeded in depicting social relations in a realism of the highest order.

All the stories are excellent. There are, of course, some which stand out as being more powerful, such as "Red Headed Baby," "Father and Son," "Cora Unashamed," "Home," and "Rejuvenation Through Joy."

The thing which makes this volume one of the most outstanding contributions to American literature is the fact that Hughes understands the people about whom he writes. He understands their relations—exploiting and exploited—to each other. He knows what the solution of these problems of a capitalist society will be. No longer will he attempt to solve any problems, art, racial or personal, within the framework of capitalism. He knows that if he is to write in such a society, he must portray life as he sees it. He must come to terms with the life of his time. Above all, he must point the way out. In this volume, Hughes justifies his experiment and his use of the short story form finds a most felicitous outlet for his talent.

E. C. HOLMES

NEW YORK TIMES

JUL 1 - 1934

The Impact of Races

THE WAYS OF WHITE FOLKS. By *Langston Hughes.* 248 pp. *New York: Alfred A Knopf.* $2.50.

MR. HUGHES is a talented writer; he is also a Negro; and it is difficult to decide which comes first. As an artist, it may be a limitation that he concerns himself entirely with the interrelations of the black and white peoples. It was undoubtedly his intention to include only such stories in this collection, and he is not limited in his perceptions and knowledge of either Negroes or whites.

He writes about the impact of one race upon the other with the confidence of the intelligent, self-respecting man. He is scornful of the meretricious friendliness that certain pretentious whites offer to Negroes. He deplores the slave-conditioned, scraping humility that certain Negroes possess. He can be amused as well as infuriated, malicious as well as tender. Perhaps it is because he is none of these things to excess that what he has to say is so effective.

Of the fourteen stories in this volume, "Home" is the most moving and probably represents what is nearest to the author's heart. In it a gifted young Negro violinist goes back to see his mother in a Missouri village after an absence of eight years. He is ill and a little homesick after a long period in Europe playing with a successful orchestra. In Berlin, in Vienna, in Paris, he did not have to think of the color line; but at home he is just an "uppty nigger." Racked by his cough, humiliated by his reception, the boy plays at a church benefit at which his humble, pious mother is delighted because white folks condescend to come.

A faded music teacher is the only person who understands what he plays or how well he is playing. But she is white and she stops him on the street one night and shakes his hand. The home-town whites, coming out of a picture show, start to mob him. The sick boy wonders feebly why she stopped him; he knows he'll never get back to his mother now. "And when the white folks left his brown body, stark naked, strung from a tree at the edge of the town, it hung there all night like a violin for the wind to play."

This theme recurs in a number of Mr. Hughes's stories; and it is important. No matter what progress the Negro makes, no matter what homage he receives in foreign lands or from small urban groups in this country, he is eventually blocked. The white folks will stop him with weapons that range from condescension to lynching. He is supposed to be something naïve, charming and jungle—as in Mr. Hughes's mocking tale, "A Slave on the Block"—or a lazy good-for-nothing or a monster. White folks have defined his character and they won't let him step out of it. This is what Mr. Hughes says in his strongest stories. In his weakest, such as "The Blues I'm Playing," he seems to be guilty of the orthodox practice of upholding the primitive against the sophisticated.

Two of the best stories in the book, "Passing" and "A Good Job Gone," top others, not because of their theses but because in them the author refrains from marginal comments. His philosophy is implicit in his subject-matter; it does not need the explanations in which he occasionally indulges. Only an insecure creator wants to underline his thoughts; and Mr. Hughes is definitely not one of those. As a poet and a novelist his writing position was made sturdy. As a short-story writer he here confirms his earlier performances.

LEANE ZUGSMITH.

Stormy Weather

Langston Hughes' autobiography, "The Big Sea," records the travels that brought him to the place he occupies in literature today. Negro writing of the twenties. A review by Ralph Ellison.

THE BIG SEA, *by Langston Hughes. Alfred A. Knopf. $3.*

LANGSTON HUGHES' autobiography, *The Big Sea*, is a story of the writer's life from his birth in 1902 up to 1930. It is a highly exciting account of a life which in itself has encompassed much of the wide variety of Negro experience (even within the Jim-Crow-flanked narrowness of American Negro life there is much variety). Before he was twenty-seven, Langston Hughes had lived in Kansas, Missouri, Ohio, New York, and Washington, D. C., on this side of the world; and on the other side he had lived in France and Italy and he had visited Africa. He had known the poverty of the underprivileged Negro family and the wealth of his successful businessman father. He had taught school in Mexico, gone to college at Columbia, shipped to Africa on a freighter, worked as a doorman in Paris, combed the beaches of Genoa, bussed dishes in a Washington hotel, and had received the encouragement of Vachel Lindsay for the poetry he was making of these experiences.

Hughes' family background is no less broad. It winds and spreads through the years from a revolutionary grandmother whose first husband had died with John Brown, to include a great-uncle who was a Reconstruction congressman from Virginia, US minister to Haiti, and the first dean of Howard Law School. Hughes' early life was marked by economic uncertainty, while his father, who left his wife and child to seek freedom in Mexico, was a rich man. Despite its revolutionary source there was even room on Hughes' family tree to include a few bourgeois Washington snobs. This wide variety of experience and background is enough in itself to make *The Big Sea* an interesting book and to recommend it as an important American document. It offers a valuable picture of the class divisions within the Negro group, shows their traditions and folkways and the effects of an expanding industrial capitalism upon several generations of a Negro family.

But *The Big Sea* is more than this. It is also a story told in evocative prose of the personal experiences of a sensitive Negro in the modern world.

In the wake of the last war there appeared that phenomenon of literary and artistic activity among Negroes known as the Negro Renaissance. This movement was marked by the "discovery" of the Negro by wealthy whites, who in attempting to fill the vacuum of their lives made the 1920's an era of fads. Negro music, Negro dancing, primitive Negro sculpture, and Negro writing became a vogue. The artificial prosperity brought by the war allowed these whites to indulge their bohemian fancies for things Negroid. Negro writers found publishing easier than ever before. And not strange to the Marxist is the fact that the same source which furnished the money of the period had also aroused the group energy of the Negro people and made for the emergence of these writers. But this in a different way.

The wave of riots and lynchings released by the war ushered in a new period in the struggle for Negro liberation. Under this pressure Negroes became more militant than ever before in attacking the shortcomings of American democracy. And in the sense that the American Negro group is a suppressed nation, this new spirit was nationalistic. But despite its national character, the group was not without its class divisions. It happened that those who gave artistic expression to this new spirit were of the Negro middle class, or, at least, were under the sway of its ideology. In a pathetic attempt to reconcile unreconcilables, these writers sought to wed the passive philosophy of the Negro middle class to the militant racial protest of the Negro masses. Thus, since the black masses had evolved no writers of their own, the energy of a whole people became perverted to the ends of a class which had grown conscious of itself through the economic alliances it had made when it supported the war. This expression was further perverted through the bohemian influence of the white faddists whom the war had destroyed spiritually, and who sought in the Negro something primitive and exotic; many writers were supported by their patronage.

Into this scene Langston Hughes made his first literary steps. Two older writers, Claude McKay and James Weldon Johnson, have treated the movement in their autobiographies. But neither has given a realistic account of the period or indicated that they knew just what had happened to them. Hughes himself avoids an analysis, but his candid and objective account of his personal experience in the movement is far more realistic than theirs. For the student of American letters it should offer valuable material.

There are many passages in *The Big Sea* in which Hughes castigates the Negro bourgeoisie, leaving no doubt as to what he thought of its value. Declining its ideological world, he gained his artistic soul: he is one of the few writers who survived the Negro Renaissance and still has the vitality to create. While his contemporaries expressed the limited strivings of this class, Hughes' vision carried him down into the black masses to seek his literary roots. The crystallized folk experience of the blues, spirituals, and folk tales became the stuff of his poetry. And when the flood of 1929 wrecked the artistic houses of his fellows, his was balanced firm upon its folk foundation. The correctness of his vision accounts for his development during that period of his life which follows the close of this book, and which we hope will be made the material of a forthcoming volume.

In his next book, however, we hope that besides the colorful incidents, the word pictures, the feel, taste, and smell of his experiences, Langston Hughes will tell us more of how he felt and thought about them. For while the style of *The Big Sea* is charming in its simplicity, it is a style which depends upon understatement for its more important effects. Many NEW MASSES readers will question whether this is a style suitable for the autobiography of a Negro writer of Hughes' importance; the national and class position of the writer should guide his selection of techniques and method, should influence his style. In the style of *The Big Sea* too much attention is apt to be given to the esthetic aspects of experience at the expense of its deeper meanings. Nor—this being a world in which few assumptions may be taken for granted—can the writer who depends upon understatement to convey these meanings be certain that they do not escape the reader. To be effective the Negro writer must be explicit; thus realistic; thus dramatic.

The Big Sea has all the excitement of a picaresque novel with Hughes himself as hero. This gives the incidents presented a unity provided by a sensitive and unusual personality; but when Hughes avoids analysis and comment, and, in some instances, emotion, a deeper unity is lost. This is that unity which is formed by the mind's brooding over experience and transforming it into conscious thought. Negro writing needs this unity, through which the writer clarifies the experiences of the reader and allows him to recreate himself. Perhaps its lack of this unity explains why *The Big Sea* ends where it does.

For after 1930 Hughes was more the conscious artist. His work followed the logical development of the national-folk sources of his art. Philosophically his writings constitute a rejection of those aspects of American life which history has taught the Negro masses to reject. To this is accountable the power of such poems as *Ballad of Lenin*, *Letter to the Academy*, *Elderly Race Leaders*, *Ballad of Ozzie Powell*, and *Let America Be America Again*. It is the things which he rejects in American life that make for the strength of the Negro writer. This amounts to the recognition of the new way of life postulated by the plight of the Negro and other minorities in our society. In accepting it the writer recognizes the revolutionary role he must play. Hughes' later work, his speeches before the International Congress of Writers for the Defense of Culture at Paris and his presence in Madrid during the Spanish war, shows his acceptance of that role.

Because he avoided the mistakes of most Negro writers of the twenties, Hughes' responsibility to younger writers and intellectuals is great. They should be allowed to receive the profound benefits of his experiences, and this on the plane of conscious thought. Then, besides the absorbing story of an adventurous life, we would be shown the processes by which a sensitive Negro attains a heightened consciousness of a world in which most of the odds are against his doing so—in the South the attainment of such a consciousness is in itself a revolutionary act. It will be the spread of this consciousness, added to the passion and sensitivity of the Negro people, that will help create a new way of life in the United States.

RALPH ELLISON.

NEW YORK, N. Y.
OCT 28 1940

Forerunner and Ambassador

The Big Sea: An Autobiography, by Langston Hughes. New York: Alfred A. Knopf. 335 pages. $3.

THE DOUBLE ROLE that Langston Hughes has played in the rise of a realistic literature among the Negro people resembles in one phase the role that Theodore Dreiser played in freeing American literary expression from the restrictions of Puritanism. Not that Negro literature was ever Puritanical, but it was timid and vaguely lyrical and folkish. Hughes's early poems, "The Weary Blues" and "Fine Clothes to the Jew," full of irony and urban imagery, were greeted by a large section of the Negro reading public with suspicion and shock when they first appeared in the middle twenties. Since then the realistic position assumed by Hughes has become the dominant outlook of all those Negro writers who have something to say.

The other phase of Hughes's role has been, for the lack of a better term, that of a cultural ambassador. Performing his task quietly and almost casually, he has represented the Negroes' case, in his poems, plays, short stories and novels, at the court of world opinion. On the other hand he has brought the experiences of other nations within the orbit of the Negro writer by his translations from the French, Russian and Spanish.

How Hughes became this forerunner and ambassador can best be understood in the cameo sequences of his own life that he gives us in his sixth and latest book, "The Big Sea." Out of his experiences as a seaman, cook, laundry worker, farm helper, bus boy, doorman, unemployed worker, have come his writings dealing with black gals who wore red stockings and black men who sang the blues all night and slept like rocks all day.

Unlike the sons and daughters of Negro "society," Hughes was not ashamed of those of his race who had to scuffle for their bread. The jerky transitions of his own life did not admit of his remaining in one place long enough to become a slave of prevailing Negro middle-class prejudices. So beneficial does this ceaseless movement seem to Hughes that he has made it one of his life principles: six months in one place, he says, is long enough to make one's life complicated. The result has been a range of artistic interest and expression possessed by no other Negro writer of his time.

Born in Joplin, Missouri, in 1902, Hughes lived in half a dozen Midwestern towns until he entered high school in Cleveland, Ohio, where he began to write poetry. His father, succumbing to that fit of disgust which overtakes so many self-willed Negroes in the face of American restrictions, went off to Mexico to make money and proceeded to treat the Mexicans just as the whites in America had treated him. The father yearned to educate Hughes and establish him in business. His favorite phrase was "hurry up," and it irritated Hughes so much that he fled his father's home.

Later he entered Columbia University, only to find it dull. He got a job on a merchant ship, threw his books into the sea and sailed for Africa. But for all his work, he arrived home with only a monkey and a few dollars, much to his mother's bewilderment. Again he sailed, this time for Rotterdam, where he left the ship and made his way to Paris. After an interval of hunger he found job as a doorman, then as second cook in a night club, which closed later because of bad business. He went to Italy to visit friends and had his passport stolen. Jobless in an alien land, he became a beachcomber until he found a ship on which he could work his way back to New York.

The poems he had written off and on had attracted the attention of some of his relatives in Washington and, at their invitation, he went to live with them. What Hughes has to say about Negro "society" in Washington, relatives and hunger are bitter poems in themselves. While living in Washington, he won his first poetry prize; shortly afterwards Carl Van Vechten submitted a batch of his poems to a publisher.

The rest of "The Big Sea" is literary history, most of it dealing with the Negro renaissance, that astonishing period of prolific productivity among Negro artists that coincided with America's "golden age" of prosperity. Hughes writes of it with humor, urbanity and objectivity; one has the feeling that never for a moment was his sense of solidarity with those who had known hunger shaken by it. Even when a Park Avenue patron was having him driven about the streets of New York in her town car, he "felt bad because he could not share his new-found comfort with his mother and relatives." When the bubble burst in 1929, Hughes returned to the mood that seems to fit him best. He wrote of the opening of the Waldorf-Astoria:

> Now, won't that be charming when the last flophouse
> has turned you down this winter?

Hughes is tough; he bends but he never breaks, and he has carried on a manly tradition in literary expression when many of his fellow writers have gone to sleep at their posts.

RICHARD WRIGHT

Stories and Poetry of 1926

THE past year had yielded authentic recognition for the short stories and poetry of OPPORTUNITY, which, in all but one instance are the brilliant work of our new Negro writers. The Anthology compiled by Edward J. O'Brien under the title *Best Short Stories of* 1926, includes Arthur Huff Fauset's Symphonesque, which received first prize in the Second OPPORTUNITY Contest, and lists among the distinguished stories of the year, the following: *The Typewriter* by Dorothy West; *Muttsy* and John Redding Goes to Sea by Zora Neale Hurston; *Mr. Bradford Teaches Sunday School* by John Matheus; a *Christmas Journey* by Louis L. Redding; *Two Gentlemen of Boston* by Florida Ridley; *The Boll Weevil Starts North* by Benjamin Young; and *Black and White at the Negro Fair* by Guy B. Johnson.

The *Anthology of Magazine Verse*, Sesqui-centennial edition, compiled by William Stanley Braithwaite, includes these names and poems: *Hatred* and *Lines Written at the Grave of Alexander Dumas* by Gwendolyn Bennett; *Blight, Homing* and *Golgotha Is A Mountain*, by Arna Bontemps; *Lines to Certain of One's Elders* and *Confession* by Countee Cullen; *No Images* by Waring Cuney; *The Tragedy of Pete* by Joseph S. Cotter; *On Seeing Two Brown Boys in a Catholic Church* by Frank Horne; *The Black Runner* and *Lethe* by Georgia Douglas Johnson; *The Road* and *Fulfillment* by Helene Johnson; *God's Edict* by Wallace Thurman; *Northboun'* by Lucy Ariel Williams.

The O. Henry Memorial Awards volume will also reprint Arthur Fauset's *Symphonesque*.

Represetation for Negro writers in these anthologies is the largest of any period in their history; and what they have to their credit they have commanded by the sheer force of their materials and the deftness of their workmanship. Their work now speaks for itself; and, to the glory of their skill, it speaks for Negroes.

1928: A Retrospective Review

By ALAIN LOCKE

THE year 1928 represents probably the flood-tide of the present Negrophile movement. More books have been published about Negro life by both white and Negro authors than was the normal output of more than a decade in the past. More aspects of Negro life have been treated than were ever even dreamed of. The proportions show the typical curve of a major American fad, and to a certain extent, this indeed it is. We shall not fully realize it until the inevitable reaction comes; when as the popular interest flags, the movement will lose thousands of supporters who are now under its spell, but who tomorrow would be equally hypnotized by the next craze.

A retrospective view ought to give us some clue as to what to expect and how to interpret it. Criticism should at least forewarn us of what is likely to happen. In this, as with many another boom, the water will need to be squeezed out of much inflated stock and many bubbles must burst. However, those who are interested in the real Negro movement which can be discerned behind the fad, will be glad to see the fad subside. Only then will the truest critical appraisal be possible, as the opportunity comes to discriminate between shoddy and wool, fair-weather friends and true supporters, the stock-brokers and the real productive talents. The real significance and potential power of the Negro renaissance may not reveal itself until after this reaction, and the entire top-soil of contemporary Negro expression may need to be ploughed completely under for a second hardier and richer crop.

To my mind the movement for the vital expression of Negro life can only truly begin as the fad breaks off. There is inevitable distortion under the hectic interest and forcing of the present vogue for Negro idioms. An introspective calm, a spiritually poised approach, a deeply matured understanding are finally necessary. These may not, need not come entirely from the Negro artist; but no true and lasting expression of Negro life can come except from these more firmly established points of view. To get above ground, much forcing has had to be endured; to win a hearing, much exploitation has had to be tolerated. There is as much spiritual bondage in these things as there ever was material bondage in slavery. Certainly the Negro artist must point the way when this significant moment comes, and establish the values by which Negro literature and art are to be permanently gauged after the fluctuating experimentalism of the last few years. Much more could be said on this subject,—but I was requested to write a retrospective review of the outstanding literary and artistic events of 1928 in the field of Negro life.

Nella Larsen

Photograph by James L. Allen

The year has been notable particularly in the field of fiction,—a shift from the prevailing emphasis in Negro expression upon poetry. In this field there were three really important events,—Claude McKay's *Home to Harlem*, Rudolph Fisher's *Walls of Jericho* and Julia Peterkin's *Scarlet Sister Mary*. An appraisal of the outstanding creative achievement in fiction a year ago would not have given us a majority on the Negro side. That in itself reflects a solid gain, gauged by the standard I have set, — for no movement can be a fad from the inside. Negro fiction may even temporarily lose ground in general interest, but under cover of the present vogue there has been nurtured an important new articulateness in Negro life more significant than mere creativeness in poetry. For creative fiction involves one additional factor of cultural maturity,—the art of social analysis and criticism. If *Home to Harlem* is significant, as it notably is, for descriptive art and its reflection of the vital rhythms of Negro life, *Walls of Jericho* is notable in this other important direction,—the art of social analysis. The ironic detachment of the one is almost as welcome as the emotional saturation of the other; they are in their sveral ways high-water marks in fiction for the Negro artist. Those who read *Home to Harlem* superficially will see only a more authentic "*Nigger Heaven*", posterity will see the peculiar and persistent quality of Negro peasant life transposed to the city and the modern mode, but still vibrant with a clean folkiness of the soil instead of the decadent muck of the city-gutter. Moreover *Home to Harlem* will stand as a challenging answer to a still too prevalent idea that the Negro can only be creatively spontaneous in music and poetry, just as Mr. Fisher's book must stand as the answer to the charge that the Negro artist is not yet ripe for social criticism or balanced in social perspective.

Claude McKay

The scene of Harlem is of course more typical of modern Negro life than a South Carolina plantation, but the fact that the year has produced another novel from the South almost equal to *Porgy* is one of outstanding importance. *Scarlet Sister Mary*, by a veteran protagonist of the new school of Southern fiction, represents not only an acme of Mrs. Peterkin's art, but evidence that the new attitude of the literary South toward Negro life is firmly established. To be rooted deep enough for tragedy, layers beneath the usual shallowness and sentimentalism of the older Southern fiction, is of course an achievement for the literature of the South, apart even from the fact that this artistic growth has been achieved in the field of Negro fiction.

Indeed this new attitude of the white writer and artist toward Negro life has now become an accepted attitude, it registers more than the lip service of realism, for it is equally a tribute to the deeper human qualities of black humanity. Dr. Odum's *Rainbow Round My Shoulder* is another case in point. Paul Green's more recent plays and stories reinforce the same motive. Even *Black Sadie* by T. Bowyer Campbell, of the Far South, almost achieves the same respectful approach and the even-handedness of treatment which spells the banishment of propaganda from art.

Of course, it is the problem novel which is the acid test for propaganda. *Dark Princess*, marking the reappearance in fiction of the versatile Dr. DuBois, for all its valuable and competent social portraiture, does not successfully meet this test, but falls an artistic victim to its own propagandist ambushes. This novel by the veteran must on this account cede position in this field to the quite successful thrust of the novice, — Nella Larsen's *Quicksand*. This study of the cultural conflict of mixed ancestry is truly a social document of importance, and as well, a living, moving picture of a type not often in the foreground of Negro fiction, and here treated perhaps for the first time with adequacy. Indeed this whole side of the problem which was once handled exclusively as a grim tragedy of blood and fateful heredity now shows a tendency to shift to another plane of discussion, as the problem of divided social loyalties and the issues of the conflict of cultures. As one would expect, foreign fiction is showing us the way in this, just as it previously did with the "light ironic touch and the sympathetic charm" which is now so accepted an approach to the Negro peasant figure. In the discussion of this social tragedy type, Mrs. Millin has again touched it masterfully this year in *The Coming of the Lord*, it has been too melodramatically stated, though with evident seriousness in *White Nigger*, and rather competently handled by Esther Hyman in *Study in Bronze*.

Even in the literature of the comic approach, stereotypes no longer reign supreme. E. L. C. Adams' *Nigger to Nigger* actually documents the contemporary peasant Negro with real humanity and accuracy; and Roark Bradford's *Ol' Man Adam an' His Chillun* seriously tries to emulate *Uncle Remus*. One of the strange and not too reassuring features of the present situation is the comparative silence of the Negro writers in the field of humor and comic portrayal. There can never be adequate self-portrayal until some considerable section of our own literature rings to the echo with genuine and spontaneous Negro laughter.

After the extraordinary productiveness of the past years in poetry, the subsidence in this field has been inevitable and is wholesome. The gap has been filled in part by the industrious gleanings of the anthology makers; and in another more creative direction in the development of several important literary schools or coteries outside of the central pioneer group in New York. This movement, which I have elsewhere characterized as the spread of beauty to the provinces, is one of the most potential effects of the Negro cultural revival. Notable instances have been the formation of a literary group in Boston which has sponsored the occasional publication of *The Quill,* the revival of the younger ultra-expressionist group who published *Fire* and who now are publishing *Harlem*, the continued activity of the Philadelphia group that is responsible for the publication of *Black Opals,* the revival of one of the earliest founded of all these producing artistic groups, the *Stylus* group at Howard University, Washington, and the crystalization of several writing dramatic and art groups in Chicago and Indianapolis. This movement of general response to the impulses from the metropolis, has been paralleled by a general quickening of interest in the study of Negro life by white groups over a very wide area, for which two progressive centers have been largely responsible,—Chicago, through the sponsoring of a campaign plan of introducing Negro art and cultural achievement to the general public by a "Negro Art Week" program; and the liberal group at the University of North Carolina, who have been so consistently and effectively pursuing a constructive and valuable program of research and publication with their studies of Negro life and culture, of which the total now is nearly a score of indispensible contributions. In this connection the second issue of *The Carolina Magazine,* devoted to Negro poetry, with the projected third issue on the Negro folk play, must be mentioned as showing a parallel interest and liberal tendency on the part of the younger Southern college generation.

Rudolph Fisher, M. D.

In the field of drama, the Theatre Guild's presentation of *Porgy* has eclipsed everything else, and warrantably. The demonstration of the power and unique effects of Negro ensemble made by this play is a contribution of importance, over and above its intrinsic delightfulness. Broadway is more anxious for Negro plays than ever before; a little too anxious, therefore an unusual list of artistic and commercial failures due primarily to half-baked plays hurried through to exploit the present vogue. Meanwhile the typical musical revue type goes merrily and profitably on, with just a crack or two in the banal stereotypes and several laudable attempts at Negro opera,—*Voodoo* and *Deep Harlem.* In the field of the amateur stage, where the hope of Negro drama still focuses, there has been a slight growth in the activity of Negro playing groups, with outstanding achievements centering this year in the work of the Karamu Theatre of the Gilpin Players, at Cleveland, Ohio, and the successful participation of the Dixwell Players in the Yale Theatre Tournament at New Haven. Paul Green has consolidated many of his unpublished or separately published plays in a volume *In the Valley and Other Carolina Plays,* which is almost another contribution to the Negro Theatre, by reason of the fact that a majority of these plays are of Negro subject-matter.

Sociological literature usually if not most technical is ephemeral: this year has exceptionally produced two books of profound interpretative value; Raymond L. Buell's two volume survey of the racial situations of colonial Africa, *The Native Problem in Africa,* and the volume just published on *The American Negro* as the special issue of The Annals of the American Academy of Political and Social Science. This last, for all its authoritativeness, actually succeeds in vitalizing and humanizing the large majority of its subject-matter, and therefore marks a new era in the official sociology of the race problem. A third event of prime importance in this field is the publication of the extensive classified *Bibliography of the Negro,* prepared by the Tuskegee

Bureau of Records under the editorship of Monroe Work.

There has been unusual activity in the field of art, stimulated in part by the Harmon Awards in this field and the institution of an annnal show of the work of Negro artists. Prior to this, special shows of the work of Negro artists had been inaugurated by the management of the Harlem Branch Public Library, and on a larger scale exhibits of Negro painting, sculpture and decorative art, including exhibits of African art have been held at the Chicago Art Institute, under the auspices of the Chicago Negro in Art Week Committee, at Fisk University, at Howard University, Hampton Institute, Rochester Memorial Gallery, San Diego, California, and at the exhibit rooms of the new Harlem Museum of African Art in the Harlem Public Library. The increased output of the younger Negro artists is directly attributable to the fresh stimulus of these new channels of public interest and support. An individual fact of more than individual importance was Archibald Motley's one man show at the Ainslee Galleries, New York. Among white artists generally a new interest in Negro types has matured culminating in special exhibitions such as Winold Reiss's Penn Island series of Negro type studies, Captain Perfielieff's series of Haitian sketches, Erick Berry's North African types, Covarrubias's recent African series, Mrs. Laura Knight's studies, and Annette Rosenshine's sculpture studies; to mention only in passing such notable single things as Wayman Adams' *Foster Johnson*, James Chapin's *Negro Boxer* and Epstein's *Paul Robeson*. Indeed the reflection of another interest in the field of the fine arts than that of the casual genre study is one of the most recent and hopeful devlopments in the whole range of new trends.

I have reserved for brief final treatment what is in my judgment the most significant of all recent developments; the new interest in Negro origins. If there is anything that points to a permanent revaluation of the Negro, it is the thoroughgoing change of attitude which is getting established about Africa and things African. Africa has always been a subject of acute interest; but too largely of the circus variety. A sudden shift from the level of gross curiosity to that of intelligent human comprehension and sympathy is apparent in the current literature about Africa. In their several fields, recent publications like the translation of Blaise Cendrar's anthology of African folk-lore, *The African Saga*, Captain Canot's *Adventures of an African Slaver*, Mrs. Gollock's two informative books—*Lives of Eminent Africans* and *Sons of Africa*, Donald Fraser's *The New Africa* and Milton Staffer's symposium entitled *Thinking with Africa*, the publication of the new quarterly journal of the International Institute of African Languages and Culture called "Africa", and very notably, I think, J. W. Vandercook's *Black Majesty* represent in about the space of a year's time a revolutionary change not only in interest but in point of view and approach. Really this is not to be underestimated, because a revaluation of the Negro without an equivalent restatement of the Negro background could easily sag back to the old points of view. But with so thoroughgoing a transformation of opinion and an approach which implies cultural recognition to the Negro in his own intrinsic rights, no such reaction can reasonably occur; it will encounter the resistance of facts instead of the mere fluid tide of sentiment. Even when the reaction comes that was predicted at the outset of this article, there will be a vast net gain that can be counted upon as a new artistic and cultural foundation for a superstructure which it really is the privilege and task of another generation than ours to rear.

A DECADE OF NEGRO LITERATURE

BY ROBERT T. KERLIN

IN 1920 scarcely more than four American Negro authors had attained to general circulation: Dunbar, Washington, Chesnutt, DuBois: these about complete the list. It is true that a respectable Negro library could have been assembled, but the authors would have been as unfamiliar to the white reader as the kings of Ethiopia.

Marvelously different is the situation in 1930. The four have increased five-fold. Let us try, in brief space, to get a comprehensive view and an understanding of this new literature. Its import can hardly be exaggerated. Such literary activity, bringing forth such various productions in verse and prose, of recognized merit, must have far-reaching results. Unquestionably it has had such results. Our exposition here shall be historical rather than critical, for a plain statement of facts, with a minimum of appraisal, will be the best service at this time.

One novelist had the Negroes in 1920: Charles W. Chesnutt, whose stories had appeared in the *Atlantic Monthly*, and had been republished in book form by the respectable firm of Houghton and Mifflin. This decade has brought forth six novelists whose work is in no way inferior to Chestnutt's: Walter White, with "Fire in the Flint" and "Flight"; Jessie Fauset, with "There is Confusion" and "Plum Bun"; Claude McKay, with "Home to Harlem" and "Banjo"; Nella Larsen, with "Quicksand" and "Passing"; Rudolph Fisher, with "The Walls of Jericho"; and Wallace Thurman, with "The Blacker the Berry." DuBois's "The Black Princess" belongs in this decade, but he had previously written "The Quest of the Silver Fleece"; and the republication of Johnson's "The Autobiography of an Ex-Colored Man." I defer appraisal.

As large a number of writers have attained distinction in the short-story. Several have been included, or starred, in O'Brien's annual "Best Short-Stories." A half a score exhibit a mastery of technique with excellence of style and—shall I say—that stuff out of which living literature is made? Besides the novelists mentioned above, most of whom belong here also, there are Arthur Huff Fauset, Eugene Gordon, Zora Neale Hurston, John Matheus, Dorothy West, Gertrude

Schalk, and the list is not complete. The exotics, Jean Toomer, author of "Cane," and Eric Walrond, author of "Tropic Death," must be double starred.

In the drama, a field but lately entered by the Negro, only a few writers have exhibited special aptitude and talent. The collection entitled "Plays of Negro Life," edited by Alain Locke and Montgomery Gregory, contains plays by six Negroes: Frank Wilson, John Matheus, Eulalie Spence, Jean Toomer, Georgia Douglas Johnson, and Willis Richardson. The files of the *Crisis* and *Opportunity*, however, contain other, usually one-act, plays that encourage an expectation of greater activity in this field during the next decade.

In the essay and treatise the chief writers were already conspicuous, but to a very limited public, and that almost entirely Negro, before 1920: DuBois, Brawley, Braithwaite, Miller, Pickens, Johnson, Woodson. Nevertheless, their best work comes in our decade. Scholarly books, distinguished by a general dignity of style, in some instances brilliancy, have come from these and reached a wide public. Among the newer entrants are Alain Locke, Charles S. Johnson, Walter White, George S. Schuyler, Wallace Thurman, E. Franklin Frazier, and Charles H. Wesley. Several other writers of sociological or economic treatises or racial studies should no doubt be added. Principal Moton's two books, "Finding a Way Out" and "What the Negro Thinks," prove him worthy, in the field of letters, to have inherited the mantle of his great predecessor at Tuskegee.

The soul of the Negro, in the elder day, found expression in song—the Spirituals—in oratory, particularly sermons, and in autobiography. In these times it finds expression, its most satisfying and consummate expression, in poetry. Of course, poetry is singing thought, it is distilled autobiography, it is oratory addressed to God. The young Negro, with his racial heritage of a musical soul, and his natural gift of picturesque phrasing, and his acquisition of the classic forms of verse—and with his intolerable placement in an alien and hostile society—stands a chance, the great chance, in the next generation, to transcend all his competitors in poetry. Meanwhile, we have poets of such heralded excellence as Langston Hughes, with "The Weary Blues" and "Fine Clothes to the Jew"; Countee Cullen, with "The Ballad of the Brown Girl," "Color," "Copper Sun," and "The Black Christ"; Leslie Pinckney Hill, with "The Wings of Oppression," and "Toussaint L'Ouverture"; Georgia Douglas Johnson with "Bronze"; Claude McKay, with "Spring in New Hampshire," and "Harlem Shadows"; James Weldon Johnson, with "God's Trombones." In the anthologies many other good craftsmen in verse will be found. *The Crisis* and *Opportunity* in nearly every issue bring out new names, representative of the large annual crop of college graduates. For several years now an increasing number of Negro poets, all youthful, have found a place in Braithwaite's "Anthology of Magazine Verse" by the side of their fellow-singers of the white race.

The verse anthologies bear witness to a remarkable interest in Negro poetry. In Kerlin's "The Voice of the Negro," 1920, a handful of lyrics culled from Negro magazines and newspapers of the times was presented to show how the Negro was beginning, in the new era then dawning, to express himself in impassioned verse. Then came Johnson's "The Book of American Negro Poetry," 1922; Kerlin's "Negro Poets and Their Poems," 1923; White and Jackson's "Anthology of American Negro Verse," 1924; Cullen's "Caroling Dusk," 1927; and Locke's "Four Negro Poets," 1927. Also to this extraordinary list must be added the community anthologies of verse—sometimes of verse and prose—put forth by the young literati of Boston ("The Quill"), Washington ("The Stylus"), Philadelphia ("Black Opals"), and by various colleges. They are tastefully made, usually with arresting illustrations and decorations; and the literary craftsmanship attests discipline and ambition. Immensely significant is the fact that *The Carolina Magazine* of the University of North Carolina has for the last three years issued an exclusively Negro number, edited by a Negro, and with only Negro contributors.

Talley's "Negro Folk-Rhymes," 1922, and Odum's "Rainbow Round My Shoulders," 1928, and "Wings on My Feet," 1929, are significant of a special direction of interest akin to that which has led to the collection of ballads and folk tales in other lands or among other groups.

Two general anthologies of verse and prose—Locke's compendium, "The New Negro," 1925, and Calverton's "An Anthology of American Negro Literature"—deserve to be designated as the two indispensable books to begin with for whoever would acquaint himself with the Negro literature of this period.

Closely allied to these verse anthologies are the collections of Spirituals. Most of this work, no doubt, was accomplished before our decade, but the following important books have been published only in the last two or three years: Johnson's "The Book of American Negro Spirituals" and "The Second Book of American Negro Spirituals"; Fisher's "Seventy

Negro Spirituals"; Dett's "Religious Folk Songs of the Negro"; and Eva Jessye's "My Spirituals."

A people's soul demands and finds many forms of expression. Energy, mental, moral, physical, will of necessity express itself creatively, making embodiments such as houses, stores, banks, theatres, schools, churches, lodges, poems, novels, songs, dances, machines, pictures, and lives. In all these forms the evidence of recent Negro advancement has forced itself into the general mind. Much, no doubt, remains to be accomplished in the diffusion of this knowledge, but a new day has dawned. A new attitude toward the Negro, particularly in the South, is the great result, briefly stated. More and more white people south of the Mason and Dixon line are conceding to the Negro his reasonable demand to be considered a human being, with full scope for human growth and human happiness. The Negro in these last ten years has been achieving a New Emancipation—an emancipation that like his first one involves both races, most providentially. And this conquest has been, not by might nor by power, violently displayed, but by song, by poetry, by the achievements of the spirit. May it proceed!

This Year of Grace

By ALAIN LOCKE

OUTSTANDING BOOKS OF THE YEAR IN NEGRO LITERATURE

Fiction

SWEET MAN—Gilmore Millen. The Viking Press.

GULF STREAM—Marie Stanley. Coward Mc Cann.

OL' KING DAVID AN' THE PHILISTINE BOYS—Roark Bradford. Harper & Bros.

BLACK GENESIS—Roark Bradford. Harper & Bros.

NOT WITHOUT LAUGHTER—Langston Hughes. Alfred Knopf, Inc.

Drama

THE GREEN PASTURES—Marc Connelly. Farrar & Rinehart.

SCARLET SISTER MARY—Julia Peterkin. Bobbs Merrill Co.

Poetry and Belles Lettres

SAINT PETER RELATES AN INCIDENT OF RESURRECTION DAY—James Weldon Johnson. The Viking Press.

SHADES AND SHADOWS—Randolph Edmonds. Meador Publishing Co.

BLACK MANHATTAN—James Weldon Johnson. Alfred Knopf, Inc.

Music

THE GREEN PASTURES SPIRITUALS—Hall Johnson. Farrar & Rinehart.

TIN PAN ALLEY—Isaac Golberg. John Day Co., Inc.

Biography

AGGREY OF AFRICA—Edwin Smith. Richard R. Smith, Inc.

JAMES HARDY DILLARD—Benjamin Brawley. Fleming H. Revell Co.

SCHOOL ACRES—Rossa B. Cooley. Yale University Press.

PAUL ROBESON, NEGRO — Eslanda Goode Robeson. Harper & Bros.

Folk Lore

THE NEGRO SINGS A NEW HEAVEN—Mary Grissom. University of North Carolina Press.

FOLK CULTURE ON ST. HELENA'S ISLAND—Guy B. Johnson. University of North Carolina Press.

FOLK-SAY. A Regional Miscellany, 1930. B. A. Botkin. University of Oklahoma Press.

HEBREWISMS OF WEST AFRICA—Jos J. Williams. Lincoln Mac Veagh.

Social Discussion

THE NEGRO PEASANT TURNS CITYWARD—Louise V. Kennedy. Columbia University.

THE RURAL NEGRO—Carter G. Woodson. The Associated Publishers.

THE NEGRO WAGE EARNER—Lorenzo Greene and Carter G. Woodson. Associated Publishers.

BLACK YEOMANRY—T. J. Woofter. University of North Carolina Press.

THE NEGRO IN AMERICAN CIVILIZATION — Charles S. Johnson. Henry Holt.

THE BLACK WORKER—Sterling Spero and Abram Harris. Columbia University Press.

SINCE it is 1930 that is under retrospective review, there is no need for that superstitious unction which made every year of our Lord a year of grace. The much exploited Negro renaissance was after all a product of the expansive period we are now willing to call the period of inflation and overproduction; perhaps there was much in it that was unsound, and perhaps our aesthetic gods are turning their backs only a little more gracefully than the gods of the market-place. Are we then, in a period of cultural depression, verging on spiritual bankruptcy? Has the afflatus of Negro self-expression died down? Are we outliving the Negro fad? Has the Negro creative artist wandered into the ambush of the professional exploiters? By some signs and symptoms. Yes. But to anticipate my conclusion, —'Let us rejoice and be exceedingly glad.' The second and truly sound phase of the cultural development of the Negro in American literature and art cannot begin without a collapse of the boom, a change to more responsible and devoted leadership, a revision of basic values, and along with a penitential purgation of spirit, a wholesale expulsion of the money-changers from the temple of art.

I think the main fault of the movement thus far has been the lack of any deep realization of what was truly Negro, and what was merely superficially characteristic. It has been assumed that to be a Negro automatically put one in a position to know; and that any deviation on the part of a white writer from the trite stereotypes was a deeply revealing insight. Few indeed they are who know the folk-spirit whose claims they herald and proclaim. And with all the improvement of fact and attitude, the true Negro is yet to be discovered and the purest values of the Negro spirit yet to be refined out from the alloys of our present cultural currency. It is, therefore, significant that this year has witnessed a waning of creative expression and an increasing trend toward documentation of the Negro subject and objective analysis of the facts. But even after this has been done, there will remain the more difficult problem of spiritual interpretation, so that at last we shall know what we mean when we talk of the Negro folk-spirit, the true Negro character, the typical Negro spirit. At present we do not know, and at last 'it can be told.'

One of the symptoms of progress in the field of fiction is the complete eclipse of the propaganda novel, and the absence of formula and problem even in the novels of white Southern writers. A review of Gilmore Millen's *Sweet Man* says: "The book might have been written by a Negro, so accurate it seems in its details, so eager it seems in sympathy and understanding of the black people." Marie Stanley's *Gulf Stream*, the frank study of the cross-fires of the caste in an Alabama village, may lack the maturity of the best Southern fiction of its subject, but it outdoes them all in sensitive delineation. "You ask those poor blacks," says Berzelia to the Catholic priest, "to worship a simpering white woman with a rosy child in her arms; No, Father, its against reason, and they've got the right idea! We are done with your white God, they say, give us a God of our own who will understand us, who is black like ourselves! But all the same, they hadn't the courage or the pride or what not to go the whole way. For she's a Madonna with No-Kink on her hair. That's where they failed themselves, Father. They've made her hallowed hair straight; they lacked the courage for the kink. What a pity." When a sensitive mulatto heroines's daughter, near-white herself, swings deliberately back to a black marriage in "poignant opposition" to her mother's ambition for white recognition, you may be sure that the Negro sphinx has come nearer to our literary Thebes. May some real young genius, black or white, go blithely out of the walls to question her.

That almost has happened with the first novel of Langston Hughes,—*Not Without Laughter*. If this book were a trilogy, and carried its young hero, Sandy, through a typical black boy's journey from the cradle to the grave we might perhaps have the all-too-long-prayed for Negro novel. As it is despite immaturity of narrative technique, this novel is one of the high-water marks of the Negro's self depiction in prose. *Not Without Laughter* owes its inspiration to a force far different from the flippant exhibitionism by which some of our younger writers aimed to out-Herod *Nigger Heaven*. Indeed it was born in Mr. Hughes poetry, which aims to evoke the folk temperament truly and reverently; and in its best chapters, *Storm*, *Guitar* and *Dance*, its style palpitates with the real spiritual essences of Negro life. Should its promise be fulfilled, we shall have a Negro novelist to bracket with Julia Peterkin and Du Bose Heyward.

Meanwhile, the Southern tradition flows on in a stream of fiction claiming the virtues of accurate folk-lore. Although many removes from either serious or flippant caricature, it is still fictional enough to be labelled fiction, and treated no more seriously than that implies. Roark Bradford has the gift of genuine low comedy; and low comedy is heavens above the bogs of burlesque and slapstick. *Black Genesis*, *Ol' King David*, and the current *John Henry* are good surface transcriptions of Negro humor and folk idiom. However, if *The Green Pastures* had not been lifted up several levels by the skillful dramaturgy of Marc Connelly and the intuitively reverent acting and singing of a great group of Negro actors, Bradford's *Ol' Man Adam* would never have put off the limitations of Mississippi clay and taken on the imperishable garments of immortality.

Green Pastures is a controversial subject, especially among Negroes. Is it a true version of the Negro's religion? By the warrant of the Spirituals and the characteristic Negro sermons, it is too drably realistic, and not apocalyptic enough. But it is certainly not what some have accused it of being, a white man's version of what he thinks Negro religion ought to be. In spite of a heaven of jaspar walls, golden wings and crowns and harps, the true Negro peasant spirit would stop to tilt a halo and to scratch an itch. As a recent poem of Langston Hughes puts it,

> *"Ma Lawd ain't no stuck-up man.*
> *Ma Lawd, he ain't proud.*
> *When he goes a 'walkin*
> *He gives me His hand.*
> *You ma friend, He 'lowed."*

And so *Green Pastures*, in spite of questionable detail and a generous injection of "Black Zionism," achieves spiritual representativeness of the deepest and most moving kind. Incidentally, by one of its typical ironies, the stage has provided a really great play from one of the feeblest of Negro novels; while *Scarlet Sister Mary*, one of the greatest of Negro novels, has fallen far below mediocrity in its dramatized form. Miss Barrymore's fault largely,—but it is a wholesome lesson to the yet only half-convinced American stage that there is some peculiar power in Negro acting. Blackface, let us hope, has received a final setback in its threatened advance on the legitimate stage.

Except for a slender volume by James Weldon Johnson, and some significant magazine verse of Sterling Brown and Langston Hughes, there has been a noticeable lull in the output of the Negro poets. Of course, a good deal of poetizing upon the race question, both by white and Negro sentimentalists, still persists; but that is far from making Negro poetry,—the obsessions of these dilettantes notwithstanding. Indeed, Mr. Johnson's poem, *St. Peter Narrates an Incident of Resurrection Day,* comes itself somewhat under the same criticism, as a half-ironical, half-sentimental bit of propaganda in couplet stanzas.

It is in *Black Manhattan* that James Weldon Johnson makes the literary year his happy debtor. This chronicle of the life of the Negro, knit ingeniously into the general history of New York, decade by decade, is a fine and permanently valuable bit of documentation of the Negro's social and cultural history. No one can read it without surprising enlightenment, or without a subtle appreciation of the forces which have prevented the Negro from being spiritually segregated in the life of America. One gets the same impression from those chapters of *Tin Pan Alley,* by Dr. Goldberg, that traces the ragtime and jazz elements as they have carried the Negro's contribution through the stream of popular music into the very lifeblood of the national life. The climax of the year on the musical side, however, is the publication of the *Green Pastures Spirituals,* arranged by one of the most gifted and genuine of Negro musicians, Hall Johnson. Indeed this publication but makes available a small fraction of the extensive repertory of folk music of the Hall Johnson Negro Choir, which I consider to be the greatest and most typical Negro choral organization we possess.

There have been a number of biographies in the year's list; all most acceptable in substance, but pitiably fettered, with one exception, to the missionary mode, that baneful genre whose conventions have smothered the humanity out of Negro biography since anti-slavery days. The life of Dr. Aggrey chronicles an important chapter and an outstanding pioneer in the modern educational uplift of Africa; *School Acres,* by Miss Rossa Cooley, interestingly tells the story of Penn School and the Penn Island community in its heroic struggle toward economic and spiritual freedom; and Mr. Brawley's life of Dr. Dillard, tells in terms of the life work of this liberal Southern friend and co-worker in the development of mass education for the Negro, the remarkable story of the recent advances in this field. However, from no book of essentially missionary approach can the flesh and blood sense of Negro life be reflected. And yet the life of any beyond average Negro is one of the most fascinating and complicated human documents of this age. Presented in the grand style and the modern manner, it should add a new note even in a period of admitted biographical virtuosity. Sensing this, no doubt, Eslanda Goode Robeson has written a boldly intimate but too worshipful biography of her great and versatile husband. The life of Paul Robeson makes him a symbol; and perspective will make it more and more evident. But welcome as are the facts and details of this intimate chronicle, to me, it rather seems in total effect like a great statue half spoiled by an over-elaborate pedestal. Still this biography stands for the breaking of the confining mould that too long has kept Negro life from the effects of great biography.

Perhaps Negroes as individuals will never come to their latent humanity until the traditional conceptions of the folk itself are revised. Therein lies the hope and the interest in the increasing number of painstaking and respectful studies of Negro folk life and folk-lore. The activity of the University of North Carolina group, and the prolific output of their press, has been a major factor in this new movement. In time it will have completely revised the stock notions of the Negro, and afford for both the social scientist and the artist a reliable body of folk material, and suitable criteria of what is genuine and truly representative. The article by Professor Guy B. Johnson in the 1930 edition of *Folk Say* on *Folk Values in Recent Literature of the Negro,* indeed the whole section on Negro folk material, ought to be read by any and all interested in the latest trends in the appreciation and development of this important aspect of native American material. The substantial gain of the year has seemed to be a gain in the deeper understanding of the significance of Negro material not in the narrow sense of its peculiarities and differences, but as an integral part of the American tradition and as part of the common cause of all art,—Southern, Northern, Negro, working toward the self-expression of native American culture.

A notable series of sociological studies has reenforced this effort to understand the Negro more scientifically and objectively. The Association for the Study of Negro Life and History has added to its long list of studies the work on *The Rural Negro* and another on the *Negro Wage Earner;* while from the Columbia University Press comes the quite detailed study of the urban migration of the Negro in the last decade. We must add to this Mr. Woofter's study of the rural Negro community at closer range, with some attempt at social interpretation beyond the usual superficial reportorial statistics. However, the tradition of that most inhuman of sociological instruments, statistics, dies hard in this field which, to me, seems to have suffered particularly from its inadequacies. Professor Charles Johnson's very competent *The Negro in American Civilition,* may be either the last stand of statistics on this question or, as I prefer to hope, the watershed of transition from the most arid peaks of the statistical pleateau down into fertile regions of living social interpretation. Just on the eve of this stocktaking comes the economic study of *The Black Worker*, by Sterling Spero and Abram Harris, raising two long denied hopes; that for objective interpretation and integration of the facts of Negro life with general social and economic tendencies. By partially fulfilling these, and its definite consciousness of their absolute desirability, this book may be the turning point in the sociology of the American Negro. One gains from Dr. Johnson's book the impression that the necessary preliminaries of fact-finding have about reached the point of final adequacy and that much, almost too much, awaits critical appraisal and interpretation. From the latter book, comes the definite raising of a new and important point of view. Negro life, considered in isolation, cannot be scientifically interpreted; often its phenomena are but effects of causes located far outside its boundaries, and only in terms of the common factors is any diagnostic view to be obtained.

So, to conclude, the constructive gains of the year have been in the literature of criticism and interpretation rather than in the literature of creative expression. Likewise self-expression has, on the whole, encountered what we hope is only a temporary lag. However, greater objectivity and a soberer viewpoint are good gift-horses to stable, and lest they flee overnight, let us lock the stable-doors. The sober Reformation reenforces and clinches the bouyant Renaissance; at least, so it went once upon a time. I am all for history repeating herself on this point. Certainly we shall not have to wait many years to see; meanwhile, in penance for many who have boasted, let some of us pray.

We Turn to Prose

A Retrospective Review of the Literature of the Negro for 1931

By Alain Locke

THE LITERATURE OF THE NEGRO FOR 1931

Historical and Biographic:

Slave Trading in the Old South. Frederic Bancroft. J. H. Furst Co. $4.00.

George Washington and the Negro. Walter H. Mazyck. Associated Publishers. $2.00

The Black Napoleon. Percy Waxman. Harcourt, Brace & Co. $3.50.

Negroes of Africa. Maurice Delafosse, translated by Fligel man. Associated Publishers. $3.15.

* * *

Sociological:

Brown America. Edwin R. Embree. The Viking Press. $2.50.

The Negro Wage Earner. L. J. Greene and Carter Woodson. Associated Publishers. $3.25.

The Black Worker. Sterling D. Spero and Abram Harris. Columbia University Press. $4.50.

The Mobility of the Negro. Edward E. Lewis. Columbia University Press. $2 25.

Racial Factors in American Industry. Herman Feldman. Harper & Bros. $4.00

Race Psychology. Thomas Russell Garth. McGraw Hill Co. $2.50.

The Negro in American National Politics. Wm. F. Nowlin. Stratford Co. $2.00.

The Negro Family in Chicago. E. Franklin Frazier. Chicago University Press. $3.00.

* * *

Drama and Folklore:

Brass Ankle. Du Bose Heyward. Farrar & Rinehart. $2.00.

The House of Connelly. Paul Green. Samuel French. $2.50.

Never No More. James Knox Millen. Unpublished.

Cold Blue Moon. Howard W. Odum. Bobbs-Merrill Co. $2.50.

John Henry. Roark Bradford. Harper & Bros. $2.50.

The Negro Sings a New Heaven. Mary Grissom. University of North Carolina Press. $2.50.

Po' Buckra. G. M. Shelby and S. G. Stoney. Macmillan Co. $2.50.

Folk-Say; A Regional Miscellany. Ed. E. A. Botkin. University of Oklahoma Press. $3.00.

The Carolina Low Country. Members of the Society for the Preservation of Spirituals. Macmillan Co. $5.00

Belles Lettres and Criticism:

The Book of American Negro Poetry. Second Edition. Ed. James Weldon Johnson. Harcourt Brace and Co. $2.00.

Outline for the Study of Negro Poetry. Sterling A. Brown. Ibid $.50.

Readings from Negro Authors. Eva Dykes, Otelia Cromwell and Lorenzo D. Turner. Harcourt, Brace & Co., $1.50.

The Negro Author. Vernon Loggins. Columbia University Press. $5.00.

* * *

Poetry:

The Negro Mother and other Dramatic Recitations. Langston Hughes. Golden Stair Press, N. Y. $.25.

Jasbo Brown and Selected Poems. Du Bose Heyward. Farrar & Rinehart. $2.00.

* * *

Fiction:

God Sends Sunday. Arna Bontemps. Harcourt, Brace & Co. $2.00.

Black No More. George Schuyler. The Macauley Co. $2.00.

Not Only War. Victor Daly. Christopher. $1.50.

Zeke. Mary White Ovington. Harcourt, Brace & Co., $2.00.

The Chinaberry Tree. Jessie Fauset. Frederick A. Stokes, $2.00.

* * *

Africana:

Africa View. Julian Huxley. Harper & Bros. $5.00.

Forty Stay In. J. W. Vandercook. Harper & Bros. $2.50.

Fools' Parade. J W. Vandercook. Harper & Bros. $2.50.

Four Handsome Negresses. R. Hernekin Baptist. Jonathan Cape & Harrison Smith. $2.00.

Slaves To-Day. George Schuyler. Brewer, Warren & Putnam. $2.50.

Ivory: Scourge of Africa. Ernest D. Moore. Harper & Bros. $4.00.

Caliban in Africa. Leonard Barnes. J. B. Lippincott & Co. $3.00.

As in the world at large, for that increasingly important literary province of Negro life, this has been a year of sober, serious, soul-searching scrutiny and reflection. We have turned from sentiment to thought, from myth to reality, from comedy and farce to tragedy and problem-play, from fiction to folk-lore, from argument to statistics, from dictums to doubts and questions, and even on the creative side from poetry to prose. The Negro can no longer complain about not being taken seriously. Indeed if there is any real ground for complaint, it is now on the other side,—that of being taken too seriously. For though the outlines of the Negro projected by the cold November sun of our day are realistically sharp and clear, at the figure's feet lies an ever-lengthening shadow. The problem has come back to plague both our houses, after an all too brief exile since its brave banishment by the blithe creative spirit of the Negro Renaissance. Negro and white authors alike are obsessed nowadays with the social seriousness of the racial situation, and seem convinced of an imperative need for sober inventory, analysis, and appraisal.

And so, we start our yearly review with the sociological end of the spectrum, and can only come gradually through to the upper zone of pure creative literature, of which, indeed there is little,—far too little. But there is consolation in the fact that a new foundation of fundamental truth is being laid down rather rapidly, as a basis, we hope, for a superstructure of later humane and vital interpretation of Negro life. All the minds preoccupied today with the Negro are truth-seeking, even those who do not find it, and more serious revision of the old views and notions has come from the press this year than could have been wildly dreamed of or was ever demanded by those who chafed and smarted under what they called the "conspiracy of misrepresentation." Northern and Southern, Negro and white alike, have come to closer realistic grips with present fact and historic situation and record, and if truth can lead us to higher beauty, the prospect is hopeful.

In the field of historical research, four outstanding revaluations face us with disillusioning force and authority. There is that closely documented, but critically penetrating picture of the slave regime by Bancroft, *Slave Trading in the Old South,*—which finally disposes of the old romantic legend, and sends that subtly seductive tradition to a stony grave. There is great significance in this; not merely from the angle of historic justice. The Negro past holds for both the white and the Negro artist the materials of the greatest American tragedy and the most epical of American themes; but only in the death of the old hypocrisies and sentimental evasions can this material come to artistic life. It is more than a mere historical service, then, which this brave book has done. From a Negro author, we get a supplementary picture,—clear, proportioned and scrupulously just, of the early dilemmas of the race question in colonial times, as they plagued and puzzled the Father of his Country. Caught between his patriarchal tradition as slave-holder and plantation proprietor and the humanitarianism of the period and the abolitionist convictions of Lafayette and Kosciusko, George Washington makes an excellent subject for the new historical realism, and Mr. Mazyck has given an illuminating, carefully documented picture. And in *Black Napoleon,* Mr. Waxman has more nearly approached a full-length historical portrait of a Negro than any other commentator on Toussaint L'Ouverture, or for that matter any other Negro biography. There are a few other Negro figures worthy of the best and most serious historical interpretation; after this pioneer work, they will most certainly have their proper attention in due course. And of great significance also, is the publication by the Association for the Study of Negro Life and History of the competent primer of Negro African history, written by the scholarly Delafosse, who knew much of the territory of West Africa by first-hand experience and was a competent Arabic scholar to digest the best authorities, the Arabic chronicles and travel sketches that are our only historical sources for these facts.

Then comes a series of sociological treatments, of which it can be said almost without exception that they are objective, scholarly and authoritative. The most popular, Mr. Embree's *Brown America,* leans heavily on the newer findings in anthropology and social research, and though consciously a book for the layman, has the scientific temper and an objective approach. It is challenging in the freshness and fairness of its liberalism, and has the virtue of seeing the Negro as an integral part of democracy and its problems rather than as a special and separate problem. This integration of the Negro problem with the context of American life, economic, industrial, educational, political is the pronounced trend of all the other volumes listed, with the single exception of the study of the Negro in Politics, which has at least the constructive significance of being a ground-breaker in this important field. Especially Spero and Harris' study of the Negro and labor is a work with an important integrating tendency; and may be said to mark the beginning of the end of that hitherto endless succession of studies of the Negro *in vacuo,* which have given all of us the impression that the Negro question is something to be solved by itself, almost without reference to the other more fundamental social, political and economic problems of our day. After the enlightenment, one wonders how we could have fallen victim to such uncommon-sense delusions; however,—such is the actual fact. Feldman's book, *Racial Factors in American Industry,* has the same salutary lesson; and special comment should be given to the careful, critical examination with which Professor Garth breaks down all the pseudo and near-scientific theories of racial superiorities and inferiorities; substituting an individual and environmental explanation of human divergencies and difference. On the whole, no such formidable batch of sociological material has appeared in any five year period as this sober, fact-finding twelvemonth has yielded.

Shall we lighten our picture, if we turn to

the drama? Scarcely even there. A reasonably successful Broadway review had a framework of grim melodrama; and three outstanding plays of Negro life, all by white Southern playwrights, have failed or been short-lived because they have been too grim and sobering. *Brass Ankle*,—a study of miscegenation, *The House of Connelly*,—a post-mortem of the decline of the Old Regime in Charleston, and *Never No More*,—a realistic dramatic transcript of a sample lynching, all testifying to the suddenly acquired passion for truth, the bare truth and whole truth, no matter whose ox is gored or whose feelings are harrowed. Well,—the sackcloth has been too harsh and the ashes too gray and choking, but tinsel, paint and whitewash have practically been chased off the legitimate stage as far as serious drama of Negro life or situation is concerned. This, too, is a great service and achievement; may the problem-play, which seems now to be the dominant trend, quicken into real tragic and dramatic life and release its deeply significant possibilities. Du Bose Heyward, Paul Green, and James Millen are steadily moving us toward a tragic Negro drama with light and power and universality.

In my judgment, the pivot of the revaluation of Negro life is and for a long time yet must be the new Negro folk-lore. It was in this field that the white Southern mind made its first significant recanting, after discovering that there was a Negro whom even they didn't know. A good deal of this extensive chronicling of the unwritten Negro saga is still tinctured with the old tradition. Roark Bradford, particularly, still romanticizes overmuch and lays on his local color with too broad and flat a brush; but *John Henry* is closer to real folk-lore than anything he has previously done. Professor Odum continues his careful documentation of the Negro roustabout, whom he often seems to mistake for a true peasant,—perhaps reluctantly, as solace for the almost complete disappearance of the pure soil peasant, whom the Southern fathers had under their very eyes but could not deeply appreciate. So this priceless figure is left either to the sentimental lament of a point of view represented by the elaborate volume, *The Carolina Low Country*, published by members of the Charleston Society for the Preservation of Spirituals or to the synthetic reconstruction of the regional folklorists who collaborate in *Folk-Say*. The real Negro peasant and his world lie somewhere between these two; and somewhat elude the direct grasp of either. However, it may just be that one view superimposed on the other can in time painstakingly recreate him. This is not said in disparagement; rather in prophecy and to encourage both the scientific and the sentimental reconstruction of the half-lost Negro folk-lore. In the first volume, there is an essay by Robert W. Gordon on the *Negro Spiritual*, which is a substantial contribution to this much-discussed but little understood folk phenomenon; and a hundred pages of the book is given over to recording a number of fine originals and variants, with locale definitely mentioned, — a feature that would be priceless did we have it for the familiar classics among the spirituals.

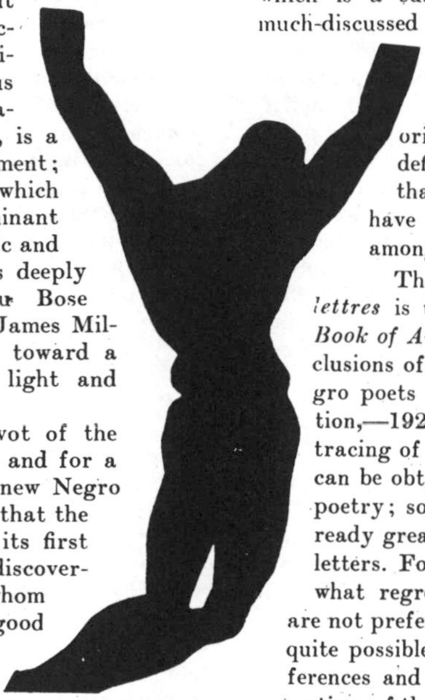

From the Book Jacket of "Slaves Today"

The significant item in *belles lettres* is undoubtedly the reissue of the *Book of American Negro Poetry*, with inclusions of the younger generation of Negro poets since the date of the first edition,—1922. The most representative tracing of the Negro creative temper that can be obtained comes from his output in poetry; so this anthology extends its already great service to the cause of Negro letters. For this very reason, it is somewhat regrettable that the racial themes are not preferentially stressed, although it is quite possible to make too much of the differences and too little of the common lyric motives of the Negro poets. Sterling Brown's companion, *Outline for the Study of Negro Poetry*, is a syllabus of more than pedagogic importance; it is critically interpretative in a way most helpful even to the mature, general reader. In its critical maturity, slender though it is, it contrasts sharply with the strictly pedagogic approach of the much larger *Readings From Negro Authors*, by Dykes, Cromwell and Turner. This book is, of course, excellent for school use, but has the limitations of that emphasis to what seems to me an unnecessary degree. For after all, the justification of Negro expression, considered separately, lies in the content significance and its representativeness of group thought and feeling,—

and the book is not especially sensitive or discriminating with respect to these values. In *The Negro Author*, Vernon Loggins, carefully exploring the unique resources of the Schomburg Library, has given a very competent and exhaustive historical and critical analysis of Negro authorship from the beginnings up to 1900. So again, in this field, more available material has been brought forward, and the stage set for the commencement of more intensive interpretation and criticism.

The poetry output this year is unusually scant. There is a fine volume of verse in the offing,—Mr. Sterling Brown's *Southern Road*, which will appear in the spring. A small volume by Langston Hughes by no means comes up to the standard of his earlier volumes; and deserts his poetic platform of folk-poetry for the dubious plane of entertainment and propaganda. So the single palm in the field of poetry this year goes to the versatile and genuine Du Bose Heyward, whose *Jasbo Brown* really adds to the sublimated folk-poetry on the Negro theme. But for this really lyric echo, one of the finest strains of the Negro tradition would this year have remained completely silent, unless we count several magazine publications of Sterling Brown's. These verses have authentic flavor, in spite of their metrical competence, and lead us to eager expectancy of fresh creative achievement to the credit of the younger Negro poet.

The year's fiction list holds five novels,—four of them by Negroes. Certainly a year of prose. All the more so, when we consider the style and content of these volumes. *God Sends Sunday* is the only one with anything of the folk flavor or, by any stretch of the imagination, a poetic style. It is probably the last, and one of the best of the low-life novels; this quite moving story of "Little Augie," the gay and hectic jockey of the palmy nineties; for the swing has gone as definitely to the problem novel as it has toward the problem play. Miss Ovington's *Zeke* is frankly a human interest story, attempting to evoke sympathy for the "other side of the picture." Despite high purpose and true details, in ensemble effect, it scarcely succeeds. *Not Only War*,—Mr. Daly's complicated novelette of the World War similarly fails to move with the conviction necessary to good fiction. However, it does break ground on a field that eventually will yield a great novel. It is certainly to be marvelled that with all the fiction of the war, the paradoxical story of the American Negro fighting a spiritual battle within a physical battle has just now been attempted. Mr. Schuyler's *Black No More* is significant. It has a theme worthy of a great satirist. That it sinks in places to the level of farce and burlesque, and yet succeeds on the whole, is evidence of the novelty and the potential power of the satirical attack on the race problem in fiction. I believe that one of the great new veins of Negro fiction has been opened by this book:— may its tribe increase!

A really mature novel has come from the pen of Miss Jessie Fauset. Her apprenticeship is now definitely over; both in style and theme. *The Chinaberry Tree*, is one of the accomplishments of Negro fiction. The tragedy of mixed blood and the bar sinister leads a half brother and sister to the near tragedy of marriage and the actual tragedy of unmerited expiation of the sins of their father. Like its analogue in classic literature this is one of the great themes of all times; and its Negro peculiarities only tend to give it deeper tragedy and universality. Miss Fauset handles it very competently, with conviction, force and reserve, and at the same time adds materially to the picture of her favorite milieu, — the upper strata of Negro life where responsibility, culture and breeding are the norms. She only requires one or two colleagues to establish what we might call a "Philadelphia" as distinguished from the "Harlem" school of fiction. For this too, there is a place and a time; and after the exploitation of the low-life level that we have had, it would really seem to be the appropriate hour,—provided, of course, we no longer are in danger of returning to the pitfalls of propaganda or the mirages of psychological compensation.

Comment on African literature should

From the Book Jacket of "God Sends Sunday"

constitute an article by itself; for the material is extensive and significant. It must suffice us to show that here, likewise, the truth will out. Even Baptist's extravaganza, *Four Handsome Negresses*, has the effect of showing the relativity of the Nordic and the African norms of life, and leaves us quite puzzled as to which has greater vitality. And all the other books listed dig in to one side or other of the African situation and bring up not a one-sided missionary view, or a partisan certainty and superiority, but tragic conflict, uncertainty and dilemma. Most ironical of all are Mr. Moore's quite frank story of the plunder-motive in "*Ivory: Scourge of Africa*" and Mr. Schuyler's sarcastic account of the slave-trading tyranny of the Americo-Liberian overlords in the little black Republic. These are sad books, that offer little hope, but they do show the factual approach, which is perhaps in itself distantly hopeful. Mr. Vandercook's two books, different as they are in tone, have underneath the primitivism of his well-known formula a frank and realistic approach to the African scene, which at least in its local color aspect leaves nothing to be experienced but the actual physical fatigue and danger of the journey. On the side of human characterization, however, there is much to be desired, if we are not satisfied by bare type portrayal. And certainly the French and German colonial literature has led us far beyond this simple technique, even for African portraiture. The remaining books are new high-water marks in colonial problem literature, because they each recognize the tragic character of the conflict between the European and the African, and by inference suggest the impossibility of resolving it. *Africa View* is especially profound and humane; I should say no finer view was to be gotten on the realistic plane than this which the fine scientific temper of Mr. Huxley has made available for us. Especially as an Englishman's book, it heralds a new spiritual sensitiveness to racial values alien to the English and European standards and conventions,—and such a new orientation might conceivably mark the beginning of a new colonial mind. If one had only time for one recent book about Africa, this is the book he should read. But one doesn't read one book nowadays, either about Africa or about the Negro; there is an interest deeper than superficial curiosity and more universal than mere ethnologic or sociological interest. Science has at least shown us the serious human interest and problem involved. May art in time give us a philosophy of creative interpretation and understanding.

Black Truth and Black Beauty

A Retrospective Review of the Literature of the Negro for 1932

By ALAIN LOCKE

FICTION:

Glory, by Nan Bagby Stephens. John Day: New York. $2.50.
Bright Skin, by Julia Peterkin. Bobbs-Merrill Co. $2.50.
Amber Satyr, by Roy Flannagan. Doubleday, Doran. $2.00.
Georgia Nigger, by John L. Spivak. Brewer, Warren & Putnam. $2.50.

* * *

By Negro Authors:

One Way to Heaven, by Countee Cullen. Harper & Bros. $2.00.
Gingertown, by Claude McKay. Harper & Bros. $2.50.
Infants of the Spring, by Wallace Thurman. Macaulay Co. $2.00.
The Conjure Man Dies, by Rudolph Fisher. Covici-Friede. $2.00.

* * *

SOCIOLOGICAL:

The Negro Family in Chicago, by E. F. Frazier. University of Chicago Press. $3.00.
The Free Negro Family, by E. Franklin Frazier. Fisk University Press. $1.00.
Race, Class and Party, by Paul Lewinson. Oxford University Press. $3.75.
The Negro in the Slaughtering and Meat-Packing Industry in Chicago, by Alma Herbst. Houghton, Mifflin Co. $3.00.
The Southern Negro as a Consumer, by Paul K. Edwards. Prentice Hall Co. $3.00.
American Minority Peoples, by Donald Young. Harper & Bros. $3.50.

* * *

DRAMA AND BELLES LETTRES:

Black Souls, by Annie Nathan Meyer. Reynolds Press: New Bedford. $1.50.

POETRY:

The Southern Road, by Sterling Brown. Harcourt, Brace & Co. $2.00.
The Dream Keeper and Other Poems, by Langston Hughes. Alfred Knopf, Inc. $2.00.
Scottsboro, Ltd., by Langston Hughes. The Golden Stair Press. $.50.

* * *

CHILDREN'S BOOKS:

Popo and Fifina, by Arna Bontemps and Langston Hughes. Macmillan & Company. $1.50.
The Railroad to Freedom, by Hildegarde Hoyte Swift. Harcourt, Brace & Co. $2.50.

* * *

ANTHROPOLOGY:

Sea Island to City, by Clyde V. Kiser. Columbia University Press. $3.50.
Folk Culture on St. Helena Island, by Guy B. Johnson. University of North Carolina Press. $3.00.
A Study of Some Negro-White Families in the U. S., by Caroline Bond Day. Peabody Museum Publication. Harvard University-Cambridge. $2.50.
Voodoos and Obeahs, by Jos. J. Williams, S. J. The Dial Press. $3.00.

* * *

BIOGRAPHY:

Daughters of Africa, by G. A. Gollock. Longmans, Green & Co. $1.25.
Selected Speeches of Booker T. Washington, by E. Davidson Washington. Doubleday, Doran & Co. $2.00.
Woman Builders, by Sadie Daniels. Associated Publishers, Washington, D. C. $2.50.
The English Hymn, by Benjamin G. Brawley. Abingdon Press. $2.00.

IT becomes more obvious as the years go on that in this matter of the portrayal of Negro life in American literature we must pay artistic penance for our social sins, and so must seek the sober, painful truth before we can find the beauty we set out to capture. Except in the rarest instances, in the current literature of the Negro, we continue to find more of the bitter tang and tonic of the Reformation than the sweetness and light of a Renaissance; and rarely, it seems can truth and beauty be found dwelling, as they should, together. Yet rare instances, gleams here and there, do convince us that in the end we shall achieve the promise that was so inspiring in the first flush of the Negro awakening,—a black beauty that is truth,—a Negro truth that is purely art; even though it may not be all that we need to know. This year one volume gives us special hope, being just that single stroke revelation of both truth and beauty. It is *The Southern Road,* a volume of verse by Sterling Brown; and for that reason I count it the outstanding literary event of the year.

But again, the output of the year is predominantly prose; and not only as last year sober, fact-seeking prose, careful human document study, but this year, in many instances, sharp-edged, surgical prose, drastically probing, boldly cutting down to the quick of the Negro problem. It is as if at last in the process of problem analysis, the scalpels of the scientific and the realistic attitude had suddenly been pushed through the skin and tissues of the problem to the vital viscera in a desperate effort to "kill or cure." Fiction is as bold and revealing as sociology; and at no time have writers, black and white, seemed more willing or more successful in breaking through the polite taboos and the traditional hypocrisies to the bare and naked, and often, tender truth about this or that vital situation of the American race problem. It is a good sign and promiseful omen, even if our nerves do twitch under the shock or wince at the sudden pain. Indeed the scientific approach is revealing the condition of the Negro more and more as just a special phase or segment of the common life, and even as a problem, as but a special symptom of general social ills and maladjustment. The most significant new trend I am able to discover in this year's literature is this growing tendency not to treat the Negro entirely as a separate or special subject, but rather as part of a general situation, be it social, economic, artistic or cultural. A score of books that cannot by any stretch be listed as "literature of the Negro," have important analyses of one aspect or another of Negro life. In "America as Seen by Americans," three of the chapters touch vitally on the Negro, and wise editing has frankly realized it. Again, a book like Ehrlich's masterly study of John Brown,—"God's Angry Man," treats the Negro all the more epically by putting him properly into sane but dramatic perspective. So although books like Donald Young's *American Minority Peoples* or Paul Lewinson's *Race, Class and Party* have enough special relevance to be listed, many of the most important commentaries do not. A recent review of T. S. Stribling's novel of Reconstruction, *The Store*—makes this appropriate statement:—"In this novel, Mr. Stribling shows the consequences to both Negroes and whites by a skilful series of interactions. Any system inevitably enmeshes all its members equally though diversely." When such a basic fact is fully realized and carried out in literary and sociological practice, we shall be on the last stage of our constantly improving technique in handling the fascinating but difficult theme of Negro life. Except for folk literature and occasional "genre" studies, then, we must expect a return by both white and Negro authors to the common canvas and the large perspective.

In fiction this year, four realists, three of them white southerners, turn to the delineation of the southern scene; each with a certain measure of pioneering success. Miss Stephens, author of the well-known drama *Roseanne,* pictures the same figures, Roseanne and the erring parson, Cicero Brown in full length portraiture in *Glory.* Her novel is most successful in its depiction of a rural Georgia village, with its dual life; and a real advance is scored in the handling of local color material. For Miss Stephen's picture is movingly human and true; it is only with her characterization that she has difficulties, and here only because her motivation is more melodramatic than tragic. Miss Peterkin, more seasoned, ventures forth from her beloved plantation milieu to carry the heroine of *Bright Skin* to Harlem. Here she is less at home, and naturally enough is not completely successful in her portrayal of the mulatto heroine,—Cricket. Yet withal each of

Illustration by E. Simms Campbell, from Popo and Fifina, by Arna Bontemps and Langston Hughes. Macmillan and Co., Publishers.

these stories is a considerable step toward the triumph of the new southern realism in handling the Negro character and setting sincerely, sympathetically, and truthfully; and both writers have the right idea that Negro life must be treated with a certain amount of poetry, at the same time that sentiment is rigorously excluded. And so, step by step, southern fiction about the Negro approaches great art.

A third novel, *Amber Satyr,* introduces a bold new theme. Roy Flannagan, as a Virginian, breaks the traditional taboos and portrays the love story of Sarah ,a white farmer's wife, and Luther ,the mulatto hired man. It is not just a formula situation or a formula solution; even though the outraged southern gods decree a lynching. *Amber Satyr* is real, moving tragedy; and is a harbinger of what southern fiction will be when it is courageously and truthfully written. No fiction can be great on mere courage and truthfulness, however, and the possibilities of Mr. Flannagan's or Miss Stephens' subjects cannot be judged from these two first novels, any more than their own mature possibilities as writers. But these are particularly significant beginnings. *Georgia Nigger* is the fourth novel in this group. Here is the pure propaganda novel, but with that strange power that propaganda takes on when it flames with righteous indignation. This story of peonage and the southern chain gang and prison labor system is vital fiction for all its biting polemic; it may well be the Uncle Tom's Cabin of this last vestige of the slave-system, even though David Jackson, its black hero, will never become the household idol that Uncle Tom became. Still John Spivak has seized on one of the legitimate uses of fiction, and within the limits of journalistic virtues, has written a powerful and humanly moving novel. It surely is a symptom of a new realism in the air, especially when we place beside it its counterpart, Harrison Kroll's more balanced, but equally revealing story of "poor white" peonage and plantation feudalism, *Cabin in the Cotton.* It is evident that the reform novel is taking on a new lease of life.

Meanwhile, the Negro writer of fiction, as might be expected, leans backward, away from propaganda and problem fiction. But the flight from propaganda does not always bring us safely to art. In fact, when the great Negro writer of fiction comes forward, he will probably steer head-on into what for a lesser talent would be the most obvious and shoddy propaganda and transform it into a triumphant victory for art. For the present, there is only one talent with a masterful touch, and he, less successful with the novel than the short story. But undoubtedly Claude McKay's collection of stories, *Gingertown*, has maturity, skill and the universal touch. His stories run from the tropical Jamaican village to "high Harlem," and then to the river-front of Marseilles, but in all there is real flesh and blood characterization and really human motivation, whether the accent be tragic, comic, or as is favorite with McKay, ironic. Nothing in the whole decade of the "Negro awakening" is to be more regretted than the exile of this great talent from contact with his most promising field of material; for even from memory and at a distance, he draws more powerfully and poignantly than many who study the Harlem scene "from life."

From right within Harlem two novels have come, neither as successful artistically as McKay's fiction. These are Countee Cullen's first novel *One Way to Heaven*, and Wallace Thurman's second novel, *Infants of the Spring*.

Illustration by E. Simms Campbell, from Popo and Fifina, by Arna Bontemps and Langston Hughes. Macmillan and Co., Publishers.

Both are path-breaking, however, as to theme. *One Way to Heaven*, the story of Sam Lucas, card gambler but professional penitent at revival meetings, is a story that just barely misses distinction. The duel in Sam's life is unfortunately external; had it been cast as a psychological conflict, there would have been high tragedy and real achievement. Mr. Cullen also ambitiously attempts to weld a low-life and a high society theme into the same story. Desirable as this is, it is a task for the seasoned writer; but as it is, Sam and Mattie's romance and tragedy do not mesh in naturally or effectively with the activities of Constantia Brown, whose maid Mattie is, and Constantia's intellectual set. Mr. Thurman's novel also misses fire, with a capital theme to make the regret all the keener. *Infants of the Spring* is the first picture of the younger Negro intelligentsia, and was conceived in the satiric vein as a criticism of the Negro Renaissance. Here is a wonderful chance for that most needed of all styles and most needed of all attitudes: self-criticism and perspective-restoring humor are indispensable in the long run in the artistic and spiritual development of the Negro. But they are not forthcoming from Mr. Thurman's sophomoric farce and melodrama or the problem-talk that his characters indulge in. The trouble with the set whom he delineates, and with the author's own literary philosophy and outlook, is that the attitudes and foibles of Nordic decadence have been carried into the buds of racial expression, and the healthy elemental simplicity of the Negro folk spirit and its native tradition forgotten or ignored by many who nevertheless have traded on the popularity for Negro art. As the novel of this spiritual failure and perversion, Mr. Thurman's book will have real documentary value, even though it represents only the lost wing of the younger generation movement.

Finally, Rudolph Fisher turns completely away from the serious and the stereotyped to write a Harlem "mystery story," *The Conjure Man Dies*. It is a refreshing *tour de force*, all the more so because one of the flaws of Negro fiction is the failing of taking itself too seriously. But the leaven of humor, and the light touch, will be even more welcome when they come in the context of the serious, literary novel of Negro life by the artist who should know it deepest and best, the young, intellectually emancipated Negro.

This difficult combination of intimacy and detachment is just what distinguishes *The Southern Road* by Sterling Brown. It is no exaggeration to say that this young newcomer among the poets has introduced a new dimension into Negro folk portraiture. A close student of the folk-life, he has caught along with the intimate particularities of Negro thought and feeling, more of the hidden universalities which our other folk-poets have overlooked or been incapable of sounding. The dominant angle of sweet or humane irony has enabled this poet to see a Negro peasant humble but epic, care-free but cynical, sensual but stoical, and as he himself says, "illiterate, but somehow very wise." It is a real discovery, this new figure who escapes both the cliches of the rhetorical propagandist poets and equally those of the "simple peasant" school. Undoubtedly, it is a step in portrayal that would have been impossible without the peasant portraits of Jean Toomer and Langston Hughes, but it is no invidious comparison to point out how much further it goes in the direction of balanced spiritual portraiture.

Meanwhile, as the folk-school tradition deepens, Langston Hughes, formerly its chief exponent, turns more and more in the direction of social protest and propaganda; since *Scottsboro Ltd.* represents his latest moods, although *The Dream Keeper* and *Popo and Fifina* are also recent publications. The latter is a quite flimsy sketch, a local-color story of Haitian child life, done in collaboration with Arna Bontemps, while *The Dream Keeper* is really a collection of the more lyrical of the poems in his first two volumes of verse, supplemented by a few unprinted poems,—all designed to be of special appeal to child readers. The book is a delightful lyrical echo of the older Hughes, who sang of his people as "walkers with the dawn and morning," "loud-mouthed laughers in the hands of fate." But the poet of *Scottsboro, Ltd.* is a militant and indignant proletarian reformer, proclaiming:

"*The voice of the red world*
Is our voice, too.
The voice of the red world is you!
With all of the workers,
Black or white,
We'll go forward
Out of the night."

And as we turn to the sociological scene, it does seem that the conflicts of Negro life can no longer be kept apart from the general political and economic crises of the contemporary world. Even historical studies like *Race, Class and Party* or Professor Frazier's two competent studies of Negro family life, one the free Negro family and the other, modern family adjustments, as they are taking place in a typical urban center like Chicago, point unmistakeably to the Negro situations as just the symptoms and effects of general conditions and forces. Similarly a labor study like Miss Herbst's narrative of the struggle of Negro labor to organize in Chicago, or an economic study of economic power like Professor Edward's, both force home the same lesson that the Negro position is a reflex of the dominant forces in the local situation. I have already referred to this trend in several independent lines of investigation. It suggests at least a new attitude of looking beyond the narrow field of Negro life itself for our most significant explanations and more basic causes; and even suggests expecting basic remedies to come from general social movements rather than just the narrow movements of race progress, however helpful or indicative they themselves may be. Possibly the most constructive of all points of view will turn out to be that reflected in Professor Young's *American Minority Peoples.* Here we have the case of the various minorities compared against the common reactions of the dominant majority, and a tracing of common lines through their differences. Two advantages are obvious; one the broader chance of discovering basic reasons, and then also, the possibility of foreseeing the possibilities not only of minority advance, but as Professor Young far-sightedly suggests, minority coalition under the stress of common persecution and suffering. To the conservative thinker or the good-will humanitarian, such alternatives may seem to be unwelcome and unwarranted bogeys, but one of the real services of social science

Illustration by E. Simms Campbell, from Popo and Fifina, by Arna Bontemps and Langston Hughes. Macmillan and Co., Publishers.

should be a level-headed exploration of all the possibilities in a situation under analysis. And certainly, no one with a scientific-minded or realistic approach could overlook the possibility of such developments. This will be even more apparent as the special research of the Negro question integrates itself more and more with the competent analysis of the common general problems of which the Negro problem is a traditional, but loose and unscientific conglomerate.

In the other fields, the literary output is interesting, but not of outstanding significance. For all their common focus in the rather uniquely primitive life of the St. Helena Island group, Professor Johnson's book, *Folk Culture on St. Helena Island* and Dr. Kiser's study of the break-up and change of pattern between that and migration from there to Harlem, these two studies have only descriptive virtue. Only occasionally do they reveal the mechanisms of the interesting changes or survivals which they chronicle. That deep secret still eludes the anthropologist, and one comes away from these studies only with an impression of the infinite variability and adaptability of the human animal. Decidedly more venturesome is Father Williams' provocative study of *Voodoos and Obeahs* in Haiti. He rightly distinguishes Voodoo as originally a pagan survival, coming from the traditional Ashanti and West Coast cults, driven underground and fusing with black magic or Obeah, which "was originally antagonistic to Myalism or white magic, until the ban of missionarism brought them together in common outlawry." This is a really important suggestion, illustrating more than a mere "description of facts." Controversial as such interpretations must be, eventually our only scientific explanations must come from the analysis of historical roots and causes. Another promising start in true anthropological interpretation is in the volume of family genealogies and anthropometric comparison of direct descendants brought together by Mrs. Day under the auspices of Professor Hooten of Harvard University, who writes the sponsoring foreword. Here we have the very antithesis of bold and highly conjectural tracing of clues, in painstaking and detailed comparisons within limited but exhaustively controlled areas. This is a pioneer and promising approach, put forward undoubtedly more to prove and vindicate a method than to establish as final the very tentative conclusions or suggestions about mulatto trends.

Passing mention must be made of a delightful child's biography of Harriet Tubman in Mrs. Swift's *The Railroad to Freedom*, a continuation of Mrs. Gollock's school biographies of prominent African characters, this time *Daughters of Africa*, companion volume to *Sons of Africa*, and *Women Builders*, a series of life sketches of prominent Negro women, compiled by Miss Sadie Daniels, and published by the press of the Society for the study of Negro Life and History. Professor Brawley has also added to his long list of publications another volume, *The History of the English Hymn*. But generally speaking, the field of biography and *belles lettres* has not been as much to the fore as usual; nor has the field of drama; in which several stage presentations have been at best only partial successes, and the only published play,—*Black Souls* by Mrs. Annie Nathan Meyer, decidedly a propaganda piece, of good intentions and laudable sympathy, but decidedly weak in dramatic conception and execution.

It would seem, then, that the year on the whole had been more notable for path-breaking than accomplishment, with exceptions already noted. It is to the promise of their fulfillment, however, that we look forward to another year and another crop of what still has to be called "Negro Literature."

The Saving Grace of Realism

RETROSPECTIVE REVIEW OF THE NEGRO LITERATURE OF 1933

By ALAIN LOCKE

FICTION AND BIOGRAPHY

Banana Bottom, by Claude McKay. Harper & Bros., N. Y. $2.50.

Comedy, American Style, by Jessie Fauset. Frederick Stokes, N. Y. $2.00.

Kingdom Coming, by Roark Bradford. Harper & Bros., N. Y. $2.50.

Roll, Jordan, Roll, by Julia Peterwin and Doris Ulmann. R. O. Ballou, N. Y. $3.50.

Along This Way—Autobiography of James Weldon Johnson. The Viking Press, N. Y. $3.50.

* * *

HISTORY AND SOCIOLOGY

The Last Slaver, by George S. King. G. P. Putnam, N. Y. $2.00.

A Century of Emancipation, by Sir John Harris. J. M. Dent, London. 5 s.

Slavery in Mississippi, by C. S. Sydnor. Appleton-Century Co., N. Y. $3.50.

Plantation Slavery in Georgia, by R. G. Flanders, University of North Carolina Press. $3.50.

Races and Ethnic Groups in American Life, by T. J. Woofter. McGraw-Hill Co., $2.50.

The Anti-Slavery Impulse, by G. H. Barnes. Appleton-Century Co., N. Y. $3.50.

Liberalism in the South, by Virginius Dabney. University of North Carolina. Chapel Hill. $3.50.

Lynching and the Law, by J. H. Chadbourn. University of North Carolina Press. $2.00.

The Tragedy of Lynching, by A. F. Raper. University of North Carolina Press. $2.50.

The Negro in America, by Alain Locke. American Library Association, Chicago. 25c.

The Mis-Education of the Negro, by Carter G. Woodson. Associated Publishers, Washington, D.C. $2.15.

The Negro's Church, by B. E. Mays and J. W. Nicholson. Institute for Social and Religious Research, New York. $2.00.

* * *

AFRICANA AND EXOTICA

Mandoa, Mandoa, by Winifred Holtby. Macmillan Co. $2.00.

The Adventures of The Black Girl in Her Search for God, by Bernard Shaw. Dodd, Mead and Co., New York. $1.50.

Congo Solo, by Emily Hahn. Bobbs-Merrill, Indianapolis. $2.75.

Chaka—An African Romance, by Thomas Mofolo. trans. by F. H. Dutton. Oxford University Press. $3.00.

At Home with the Savage, by J. H. Driberg. William Morrow & Co., New York. $3.50.

AS year by year the literature by and about the Negro not only maintains its volume, but deepens and clarifies in quality, there can be no doubt that the Negro theme has become a prominent and permanent strain in contemporary American literature. No mere fad or fashion could have sustained itself for ten or more years with increasing momentum and undiminished appeal and effect. In fact, as the fad subsides, a sounder, more artistic expression of Negro life and character takes its place. What was once prevalent enough almost to be the rule has now become quite the exception; the typical Negro author is no longer propagandist on the one hand or exhibitionist on the other; the average white author is now neither a hectic faddist nor a superficial or commercialized exploiter in his attitude toward Negro subject matter;—and as a result the unexpected has happened, sobriety, poise and dignity are becoming the dominant keynotes of the developing Negro theme.

But fortunately the dignity and sobriety are not the stiff pose and starched trappings of the moralist,—although the Negro artist is still considerably beset by moralizing Puritans, just as the white author is plagued by a babbitized host of Philistines—but instead the simple, unaffected dignity of sympathetic and often poetic realism and the sobriety of the artist who loves and respects his subject-matter. It was one thing to inveigh against the Negro stereotypes in fiction, drama, art and sociology, it was quite another to painfully reconstruct from actual life truer, livelier, more representative substitutes. But just this our contemporary realism has carefully sought and almost completely achieved,—and only realism could have done so, all the contentions of the puritanical idealists to the contrary. Social justice may be the handiwork of the sentimentalists and the idealists, but the only safe and sane poetic justice must spring from sound and understanding realism.

We can trust and encourage a literary philosophy that can sustain the devoted art of a Julia Peterkin, that can evoke from the liberal white South a book like *The Tragedy of Lynching,* that can transform gradually the superficial, caricaturish interest of the early Roark Bradford into the penetrating, carefully studied realism of his latest novel, *Kingdom Coming.* And to the extent that James Weldon Johnson's autobiography represents a new and effective step in Negro biography, it can be attributed to the sober, realistic restraint that dominates it in striking contrast to the flamboyant egotism and sentimentality of much of our previous biographical writing. So we must look to enlightened realism as the present hope of Negro art and literature, not merely because it is desirable for our art to be in step with the prevailing mode and trend of the art and literature of its time,—important though that may be—but because both practical and aesthetic interests dictate truth as the basic desideratum in the portrayal of the Negro,—and truth is the saving grace of realism. As it matures, we may expect this new realism to become more and more humane, and as it mellows to take on cosmopolitan perspective,—perhaps the one new dimension that can carry it beyond the boundaries of national literature to the classic universality of world literature. Readers of *Opportunity* have had a rare foretaste of this humane cosmopolitanism in the observations and attitudes of the well-tempered realism of the accomplished author of *The Good Earth*,—Mrs. Pearl Buck.

Comment on the fiction of the year is comparatively easy when referred to this general trend; in theme or problem no book of the year is out of step with realism, and in style only one,—Miss Fauset's, dissents. In *Banana Bottom*, Claude McKay turns to his native Jamaica, with complete success so far as local color and setting are concerned, and with moderate success in the story of Bita whose life dramatizes a provincial duel between peasant paganism and middle class Puritanism. Real and tragic as the struggle is, one has the feeling that McKay cannot yet handle the problem type story as skillfully as the story of local color, although he has added another important province to Negro fiction. Bita's renunciation of middle-class respectability and her English missionary training in marrying the peasant Jubban might have been made more inevitable, and thus the more moving. McKay's treatment, however, is always stylistically mature and nowhere borders on the amateurish, and his very real characters are far removed from mere types. The same cannot be said for Miss Fauset's latest novel,—*Comedy, American Style*, which though it makes a distinct contribution in its theme, fails to capitalize it fully by forceful style and handling. The one dark child in a family of striving, middle class, prejudice-conditioned Negroes, dominated by an ambitious, lily-white mother, is the setting for one of the really great and original Negro classics, whether it be treated as tragedy or social comedy. This situation Miss Fauset has admirably documented, so that an important segment of Negro life is opened up; but the characterization is too close to type for the deepest conviction, the style is too mid-Victorian for moving power today, and the point of view falls into the sentimental hazard, missing the deep potential tragedy of the situation on the one hand, and its biting satire on the other. Yet Negro fiction would be infinitely poorer without the persevering and slowly maturing art of Miss Fauset, and her almost single-handed championship of upper and middle class Negro life as an important subject for fiction.

Artistically then, the honors still go afield to the more mature fiction of peasant life and the Southern milieu,—for how much longer we dare not predict, but certainly to date. The steady maturing of Roark Bradford's art has already been mentioned. *Kingdom Coming* is masterful fiction, all the more acceptable because the Negro characterization is true and deeply sympathetic. But for a forced and melodramatic ending the novel would have been a masterpiece. As it is, some of the best chapters in all Southern fiction on plantation life have been written, and an important contender has been added to the lists of the liberal Southern realists.

Roll, Jordan, Roll masquerades as non-fiction; but it really is a folk novelist's note book; a workmanlike palette by which one can gauge the technique of Miss Peterkin's intensely studied portraiture of the Southern Negro. It is illuminating to see the actual types from which she has been making up her characters all these years. That they are real Negroes, no one could possibly deny, but the author has the happy but unfortunate illusion that they are the generic Negro,—and that they scarcely are. For one thing, they are too bucolic, too tinted with Miss Peterkin's own Theocritan fancy; and for the other, they are a bit too local and sectional to be generic. This by no means signifies that this careful and sympathetic recording is unwelcome; on the contrary, I would bracket the book with James Weldon Johnson's autobiography as the year's outstanding literary achievement in the Negro field. With Doris Ulmann's superb photographic studies, Negro folk portraiture has been raised to a plane so purely and perfectly artistic that one marvels how realism could have accomplished it. When will the scientific folk-lorists wake up to the possibilities of art as the medium of the truest portrayal of human types?

Along This Way takes its place, too, in this borderland between fact and fiction, where the values of both are happily blended. For although it is the sober narrative of an outstanding individual's experience, the Johnson autobiography is also the history of a class and of a generation. It is the story of the first generation of Negro culture, with all of the struggles, dilemmas and triumphs of the advance guard of the Negro intelligentsia. It could just as well have been the type story of Black Bohemia,—a story that must some day be written, if Weldon Johnson had not been so versatile in adding to his achievements as a musical comedy librettist, song-writer and poet those of the journalist, the diplomat and the race publicist. With the panoramic sweep before him, our author doubtless could not stop for the intimate and careful picture of the Bohemia of Will Marion Cook, Williams and Walker, Cole and Johnson; but what the story lacks in dramatic intensity, it gains in composite variety and representativeness. *Along This Way* is indispensable for the understanding of the upper levels of Negro life. At the same time it is one of the best cross-section pictures of that little known zone of inter-racial cultural collaboration between black and white intellectuals and artists which starting with the vogue of Negro art in New York is spreading gradualy throughout all liberal culture centers of the nation. Mr. Johnson is a little too close to his scene for daring or thorough appraisal; and he is too much the diplomat to attempt to anticipate posterity's verdict on things he has seen and experienced, with the single and praiseworthy exception of Negro rights,—a subject on which he has always been consistently outspoken and uncompromising. Yet, with it all, one or two more biographies are needed, lest the reading public jump to hasty generalizations about the Negro intellectual and artist in the same unfortunate way in which they have insisted upon generalizing about the peasant Negro.

* * *

Turning now to straight history and sociology, we find a formidable list, which valuable although it is, suggests that Negro life will not be immune from that modern plague called "research." *Slavery in Mississippi* and *Slavery in Georgia* suggest a possible monograph on slavery in every one of the slave states and territories; and there have been three or four contenders for the dubious honor of "*The Last Slaver*." Personally I would trade one synthetic and interpretative study like Gaines' *The Southern Plantation* for a dozen such detailed historical studies. This is not anti-historical bias, or even lack of recognition that we are just beginning to approach that objective frame of mind from which the real history of slavery can be written. It is rather the contention that what modern social science needs most is an analysis of social forces, attitudes and traditions rather than a rehearsal of facts; even though the record stands badly in need of rewriting. For that very reason, we single out as notable such interpretative studies as Professor Barnes book on *The Anti-Slavery Impulse*, Virginius Dabney's study of the inner conflict of the South in his *Liberalism in the South*, and most of all, Mr. Raper's brilliant and fearless study of lynching. Why in these days of medals and official rewards, have we no way of acknowledging and encouraging such constructive liberalism and scholarship as has centered in Chapel Hill, and sent out through the University of North Carolina Press such a steady and illuminating stream of studies of Negro life and the race question?

It is encouraging to notice that Negro historical scholarship and social analysis keeps pace, more or less, with the increasing general academic interest in the study of the Negro. The list of Negro authorship in this field would be well balanced indeed if it could include Dr. Du Bois's promised publication on *The Negro in the Reconstruction*,—now delayed until spring. But even without this much awaited study, there is no dearth of sound interpretative comment on race history and sociology. The year has seen the first comprehensive study of the Negro church by two competent, young Negro investigators, and with the studies announced and under way, it requires no prophet to predict for next year an unprecedented leap forward of Negro historical and sociological scholarship. This will particularly reveal, if I am not much mistaken, along with such veterans as Dr. Woodson and Dr. Du Bois, an entire younger generation of scholars whose general point of view may be differentiated as a conviction that Negro life needs now to be studied in its inter-relationships with the general life of which it is an integral part. That shift of the modern sociological point of view, from faint beginnings several years back, is now registering almost to the point of becoming the dominant and conceded attitude among all modern-minded students of the race question, whether they be Negro or white. Dr. Woodson alone holds to the counter-thesis of racialist history, and states the case more radically than he has ever stated it in his *Mis-Education of the Negro*. Here, at least, is a challenging defense of propagandist history and an educational emphasis upon race tradition and racial morale. We must ponder this "Black Zionism" carefully, *pro* and *con*—for when the dilemmas of the Negro's position in America are fundamentally intellectualized, this issue that Dr. Woodson so provocatively raises will be found to be the basic and critical question involved. Personally I think the sooner the question is faced the better,—especially since as yet our policies and programs have not quite come to the fork of the road at which a policy of assimilation must part company with a policy of racial self-determination.

Lastly, but not least, comes Africa. This year the travelogues are by no means as numerous,—and we can afford to ignore them in noticing the new genres that are growing into prominence. Inaugurated by such books as Julian Huxley's *Africa View*, the Anglo-Saxon mind is at last achieving a spiritual appreciation of native values. The continental mind, especially the French, but also, it must be said, the German, has long since made this discovery and reflected it in its colonial literature. What they admit directly, the Anglo-Saxon mentality seems to need to admit by indirection, except in an occasional brief and brave passage in men like Llewellyn Powys, E. A. Rattray, Julian Huxley. But in a satiric allegory, no less a personage than Bernard Shaw suggests to white civilization that it should not be so cock-sure of itself, or so confident that its God sanctions its brutal and egotistical missionarism. Small wonder that he has to conjure up the shade of Voltaire to ward off the racial recoil! But if Mr. Shaw's caution to 'Let Africa alone' is suggestive, how much more so, Miss Holtby's concrete satire,—"*Mandoa, Mandoa*." Here is the real antidote for the virus of missionarism and self-deceptive imperialism. It is an achievement when there is enough of the spirit of self-criticism and relative evaluation to make such a book possible. May its tribe increase!

Of the same new outlook, thought not satirical, is Emily Hahn's *Congo Solo*. Here is a frank, sensitive and uncondescending narrative of equatorial Africa as it is, with no partisanship either for or against the colonial system. Yet as a frank statement of its intimate workings in terms of the life of the governed villages, there can be little doubt that the colonial system would rather have an indignant moralistic diatribe than the subtle indictment of this simple story. Little by little the new respect for native custom and institutions in their own setting is establishing itself, and with the corollary that it is necessary to understand the institutions and traditions of primitive peoples before interfering with their lives. This thesis is more academically carried through in one of the best popular treatises on the life of primitive peoples, Professor Driberg's *At Home with the Savage*. This book is especially competent in its discussion of the legal and political institutions of the Baganda and other East African peoples, and has the virtue of describing their social values in addition to their mere externalities of form and ceremonial.

Then there is that unexpected new thing out of Africa,—a native non-missionary biography, —the narrative of the great Zulu war-lord,—Chaka, by a native scholar who knows and respects the tribal tradition, and yet can evaluate it against its European equivalents. There is much talk in some quarters of a revival of native lore and art as part of the new program of native education. However, if this is to be a missionarized product, it will never rehabilitate native values or soundly integrate the tribal tradition and its sanctions with the necessary admixture of European learning and technique that any modern system of education must also give. The emergence of real native letters is, therefore, something to be heralded with great joy. A sounder and more intelligent interest on the part of the American Negro in the cultural development of Africa could certainly help forward this revival of the suppressed native traditions, and in my opinion, we have more to gain thereby than we have to give.

* * *

To conclude,—a year of material stress and depression has not adversely affected the literature of the Negro, although many a manuscript may have gone unprinted. Indeed it may be that the deepening sobriety and poise of the books that have appeared is in part due to the absence of printing press pressure before and high-pressure salesmanship after the literary event. The natural urge and urgency of the creative impulse, we hope, will suffice for the future, and to aid it the critical and measured appreciation of a public that by now is accustomed to this vein of literary expression. It is to be hoped that Negro authorship will quicken its somewhat lagging pace, and especially reassert its peculiarly intimate medium of poetry. The next field of award for the Du Bois literary prize is poetry, and the wise policy of withholding the award when material of high quality is lacking suggests that the poets, veteran and fledgling, groom themselves. The award for non-fiction prose goes this year to James Weldon Johnson most de-

(Continued on Page 30)

THE SAVING GRACE OF REALISM

(Continued from Page 11)

servedly; although *Black Manhattan* is crowned rather than *Along This Way* because of calendar limits. Together these two books do certainly represent the most distinguished contribution in non-prose fiction from any Negro author recently. And then, it is sad, but fitting to chronicle against the year's gains a really tragic loss in the early death of Walter H. Mazyck, the most promising of our younger historical writers, whose singular combination of accurate scholarship, clear analytical judgment of men and of issues, and limpid clarity and ease of expository style made him a figure of the greatest promise. His *George Washington and the Negro* was one of the finest bits of historical analysis and writing we have produced; his unfinished biography of Colonel Young will appear, but it grieves me greatly to contemplate the complete loss of his premeditated study of Lincoln for which he was deliberately maturing his talents.

The Eleventh Hour of Nordicism*

Retrospective Review of the Literature of the Negro for 1934.

By ALAIN LOCKE

BIBLIOGRAPHY OF LITERATURE OF THE NEGRO: 1934

FICTION

So Red the Rose—Stark Young, Charles Scribners Sons, N. Y.—$2.50.
Unfinished Cathedral—T. Stribling, Doubleday, Doran, N. Y.—$2.50.
Transient Lady—Octavus R. Cohen, Appleton-Century, N. Y.—$2.00.
Let the Band Play Dixie—Roark Bradford, Harper Bros, N. Y.—$2.00.
Come in At The Door—William March, Harrison Smith & Haas, N. Y.—$2.50.
Candy—L. M. Alexander, Dodd, Mead & Co., N. Y.—$2.50.
Portrait of Eden—Margaret Sperry, Liveright & Co., N. Y.—$2.50.
Deep River—Clement Wood, William Godwin, Inc., N. Y.—$2.00.
Stars Fell on Alabama—Carl Carmer, Farrar & Rinehart, N. Y.—$3.00.
The Ways of White Folks—Langston Hughes, Alfred Knopf, Inc., N. Y.—$2.50.
Jonah's Gourd Vine—Zora Hurston, J. B. Lippincott, Philadelphia—$2.00.
With Naked Foot—Emily Hahn, Bobbs-Merrill, Indianapolis—$2.00.
Black God—D. Manners—Sutton, Longmans Green, N. Y.—$2.50.

BELLES-LETTRES

Negro, An Anthology—Nancy Cunard, Wishart & Co., London, England—£2 /$11 plus duty.
Le Noir, A School Anthology—Mercer Cook, American Book Co., N. Y.—$1.00.
John Brown, Terrible Saint—David Karsner, Dodd, Mead & Co., N. Y.—$3.00.
American Ballads and Folk Songs—John A. and Alan Lomax—Macmillan Co., N. Y.—$5.00.
Beale Street, Where the Blues Began—G. W. Lee, Robert Ballou, N. Y.—$2.50.

DRAMA

John Brown—Ronald Gow, Mss.
Dance With Your Gods—Perkins, Mss.
Africana—Donald Heywood, Mss.
Roll On, Sweet Chariot—Paul Green, Published as "Potters Field"—McBride.
Kykunkor or The Witch Doctor—Asadata Dafora, Mss.
Six Plays for a Negro Theatre—Randolph Edmonds, Walter Baker Co., Boston—$.75.
Stevedore—Paul Peters and George Sklar, Covici-Friede, N. Y.—$1.50.

HISTORICAL AND SOCIOLOGICAL

Negro White Adjustment—Paul E. Baker, Association Press, N. Y.—$2.00.
Life on the Negro Frontier—George R. Arthur, Association (Y. M. C. A.) Press, N. Y.—$2.00.
The Negro Professional Man and the Community—Carter G. Woodson, Associated Publishers, Washington, D. C.—$3.25.
The Shadow of the Plantation—Charles S. Johnson, University of Chicago Press—$2.50.
Race Relations—W. D. Weatherford and Charles S. Johnson—D. C. Heath & Co., N. Y.—$3.20.
A Guide to Studies in African History—Willis Huggins and John G. Jackson—Wyllie Press, N. Y.—$1.25.
Race Consciousness and the American Negro—Rebecca C. Barton, Aronld Busck, Copenhagen. $2.00.
Negro Americans, What Now?—James Weldon Johnson, The Viking Press, N. Y.—$1.25.

EDUCATION

The Physical and Mental Abilities of the American Negro—Yearbook No. 3—Journal of Negro Education, Howard University, July issue, 1934—$1.50.
The Evolution of The Negro College—Dwight O. W. Holmes, Columbia University Press—$2.25.
The Education of the Negro in the American Social Order—Horace Mann Bond, Prentice-Hall, N. Y., $2.75.

AFRICANA

Liberia Rediscovered—James C. Young, Doubleday, Doran, N. Y.—$1.50.
Native Policy in South Africa—Ifor L. Evans, The Macmillan Co., N. Y.—$2.00.
Rebel Destiny—Melville and Frances Herskovits, McGraw Hill, N. Y.—$3.00.
The Education of Primitive Peoples—Albert D. Helser, Fleming Revell Co., N. Y.—$3.00.
The African To-day—D. Westermann, Oxford University Press, N. Y.—7s. 6d.

A RETROSPECTIVE review must needs ask the question: what have been the dominant trends in the literature of the year? I make no apology for presenting my conclusions first, although I vouch for their being conclusions and not preconceptions. Only toward the end of a long list of reading was there any semblance of dominant notes and outstanding trends. But in retrospect they were unmistakably clear; each writer somewhere along the road, no matter what his mission, creed or race, had met the Zeitgeist, had been confronted with the same hard riddle, and had not been allowed to pass on without some answer. Even in the variety of answers, the identity of the question is unmistakable. Of course, for almost no one has it been an overt or self-conscious question: the artist is concerned with his own specific theme and knows first-hand only the problems of his own personality. But the Zeitgeist is as inescapable as that goblin of chatter-box days that

*This is the sixth article in the series of Retrospective Reviews by Dr. Alain Locke, which save for the year 1930 have appeared in *Opportunity* each year since 1929.

wormed himself as tape through the key-hole of a bolted door to become a real ogre again as soon as he had twisted through: if the artist bars the front-gate, it slips round to the back-door, and when he bolts that, up through the trap-door of the sub-conscious or down the chimney of his hearth or in between the windows of his observation of life, the dominant question of the day relentlessly comes in sooner or later. It is the small-souled artist who runs and cringes; the great artist goes out to meet the Zeitgeist.

What is the riddle for 1934? Time was when it was some paradox of art, some secret of Parnassus. To-day, it is a conundrum of the market-place, a puzzle of the cross-roads,—for the literary Sphinx sits there at the crossroads of civilization ceaselessly asking, "Whither, Mankind?" and "Artist, Whither goest thou?" The social question will not down, no matter what the artist's other problems. For the Negro writer, this has been:— Shall I go left or right or take the middle course; for the white writer:—Shall I stick with the Nordics or shall I desert their beleaguered citadel?" It is the eleventh hour of capitalism and the eleventh hour of Nordicism, and all our literature and art are reflecting that. Naturally it is the latter which for the literature of the Negro theme is the matter of chief concern.

One wonders by what strange premonition artists are so suddenly and keenly aware of such crises, until one realizes that they are after all the spiritually sensitive, the barometers of the spirit and the sentinels of change. And now, with striking unanimity they are all agog over Nordicism. Many are for it, passionately, vehemently, but they are just as symptomatic of a present crisis and an impending change as those who are boldly and deliberately recanting it. Dominant ideas behave that way at their critical moments, and before their last relapses always have these hectic fevers and deliriums of violent assertion. Rampant fascism and hectic racialism are in themselves omens of the eleventh hour, as much and more than the rising liberal tide of repudiation and repentance. There is no millenium around the corner, art has little or no solutions, but it is reflecting the decline of a whole ideology and the rise of a new conception of humanity,—as humanity.

Until some evidence is before him, the reader may think this an unwarrantable conclusion from such a provincial segment of contemporary literature as the fiction of Negro life traditionally is. But after glancing at the list of novels on this theme, let him consider that the fiction of Negro life for the year 1934 contains five or six of the best sellers of the year's fiction crop, one prize novel, two choices of the Book-of-the-Month and two of the Literary Guild. The unquestioned prominence and popularity of the theme itself is significant. To that we must add the advance in the treatment that the year has registered. Of course, the old pattern gets itself repeated; Stark Young makes a virtue of a romantic throw-back adequately exposed and criticized for *Opportunity* readers in Sterling Brown's recent review. But in the light of many another novel of the South on this same list, who would begrudge the old plantation tradition this beautiful but quavering swan-song? Personally I am not as concerned as some over the persistence of the old tradition, for alongside *So Red the Rose,* and *Transient Lady,* and *Let the Band Play Dixie* there comes also from the same South the corrective antidotes, *Stars Fell on Alabama,* and lest that be cited in spite of its evident close study as a Yankee's novel, then the work of native Southerners like Stribling's *Unfinished Cathedral,* Margaret Sperry's *Portrait of Eden,* William March's *Come in at the Door* and Clement Wood's *Deep River.* It is true no deep vindication comes from the unusual frank realism of these novels of the new school, but for all their present defeatist denouements, they show a South in the throes of a dilemma tragic for both sides and insoluble because of the local traditions. What more can we ask of art; it is only the logic of history that can go further,—and of that such art is a prophet and forerunner.

In *Unfinished Cathedral,* Miltiades Vaiden does take a stand, even though futile, against the lynching mob, and yet fate after forcing him to taste the bitter dilemma of the lynching of his own son, confronts him once again, after the tragedy of his own daughter, with the same situation in the black side of the family escutcheon, and the curtain catches him repudiating even the sacred aristocratic tradition of patronage as he drives off his quadroon half-sister. And in *Stars Fell on Alabama,* Mr. Carmer gets down to the real folk-lore that Joel Chandler Harris coated over, exposes realistically its sordid rootage in the bogs of illiteracy and primitive reversions and boldly suggests that such conditions know no racial boundary. Carl Carmer anatomizes Alabama, and for all his poetic love of the primitive shows the other devastating side of the deep South.

In *Come in at the Door,* William March tells a most unusual story, that of the close psychological relationship between an impressionable white lad, Chester Hurry, and Simon Baptiste, his educated mulatto tutor, whom he unwittingly dooms and from whose spirit, in self-imposed expiation, he can never successfully disentangle his own inner life. Remembering that psychological intimacy is the last taboo, more sacrosant than the admission of sex intimacies, we ought to see the tradition cracking to the core in a book like this, in spite of its poetic diffidence. Then in *Portrait of Eden,* we come under the bold pen of a woman writer to the most unromantic and frank portrayal of the seamy side of the South that I have yet encountered. The hero, Doctor McIntyre, working to reconstruct the almost unreconstructable, has an educated Negro colleague, who is lynched; he himself is murdered by "a cracker imbecile," and in the words of another reviewer, his enemies are "virulent Babbitry, political corruption, barbarous Fundamentalism, primitive superstition and personal feuds." Here is another South, and it is as much the South as that other one of colonels and colonel's ladies, wide porches, rambler roses, juleps and magnolias. For one, I would not deny the South its romanticism; if realism reminds us that it is not the whole story. Even Octavus Roy Cohen in *Transient Lady* has left the banter of black servant's dialogue for the bitter feuds of the townsfolk; and only Mr. Bradford remains in the groove of the old tradition, if we except the apologetic *So Red the Rose.* Bradford's stories cannot be dismissed because of their social philosophy: they are powerful sketches based on acute though narrow vision. If he ever broadens the angle, the South will have another Uncle Remus.

Everyone realizes that *Candy,* Mrs. Alexander's much read novel, is in the Peterkin tradition, and I suppose will complain that another stereotype is forming. I suppose this is so, but why should the Negro theme be exempt from this general phenomenon of imitation for which we have yet discovered no antidote but the shifting effect of time? The day is fast approaching when no few fixed types can be generalized as portraying the sum-total substance of Negro life and character. Then and then only the invidiousness of certain types will disappear (I admit and deplore their present invidiousness). But the only remedy is the portrayal of the neglected types. And then, too, in the formula of Scarlet Sister Mary and Cricket and Candy, there is one significant strand of the recantation of Nordicism,—the genuine admiration and envy of the primitive and the reaction from Puritanism. No student of the current trend of morals and convention ought to grieve too deeply over the implied slight of the amoralist mores of these South Carolina plantations; the novels of Greenwich Village and Hollywood, except for the setting, reveal the same attitudes and reactions. My complaint is that Mrs. Alexander, for all her studious effort, is no Julia Peterkin, as yet.

Finally, if it is Nordic bear-baiting that the fans call for, no partisan propagandist could have framed a more poetic-justice type of plot than Clement Wood's story of the marriage, quarrel and reunion of a daughter of the South and Elden, the Negro concert singer, even though their private Eden has to be in exile. But *Deep River* is a provocative and not a sincerely artistic or competent novel. One regrets that a theme of such ultimate implications has been reached before the proper maturity of those tendencies we have been discussing; for the present, only irony can make them real or effective with any considerable number of readers.

And just this mechanism has been used in the more successful of the stories of the first Negro writer whose fiction we discuss, Langston Hughes in his much discussed *The Ways of White Folks.* Here is the militant assault on the citadel of Nordicism in full fury, if not in full force. Avowedly propagandist, and motivated by radical social philosophy, we have here the beginnings of the revolutionary school of Negro fiction. But though anti-bourgeois and anti-Nordic, it is not genuinely proletarian. But it is nevertheless a significant beginning, and several stories in the volume, notably *Father and Son* rise far above the general level of rhetorical protest and propagandist reversal, achieving rare irony and real tragedy. But for pure folk quality, even the sort that a proletarian school of Negro fiction must think of achieving, Zora Hurston's first novel has the genuine strain and the most promising technique. This is not surprising to those who know the careful apprenticeship she has served in the careful study of the South from the inside. John Buddy's folk talk, and later his sermons as "Rev. Pearson" are rare revelations of true Negro idiom of thought and speech, and if the plot and characterization of this novel were up to the level of its dialogue and description, it would be one of the high-water marks of Negro fiction. It is for this reason that I look forward to Miss Hurston's later work with more curiosity and anticipation than to that of any of our younger prose writers. For years we have been saying we wanted to achieve "objectivity":— here it is. John's first and last encounters with a train are little classics. "You ain't never seed nothin' dangerous lookin' lak dat befo', is yuh?" "Naw suh and hit sho look frightenin'. But hits uh pretty thing do. Whar it gwine?" "Oh eve'y which and whar." The train kicked up its heels and rattled off. John watched it until it had lost itself down its shiny road and the noise of its going was dead. And then the last encounter: "He drove on but half-seeing the railroad from looking inward. The engine struck the car squarely and hurled it about like a toy. John was thrown out and lay perfectly still. Only his foot twitched a little. . . . 'Damned, if I kin see how it happened,' the engineer declared. 'God knows I blowed for him.' . . . And the preacher preached a barbaric requiem poem. So at last the preacher wiped his mouth in the final way and said. 'He wuz uh man, and nobody knowed 'im but God,'—and it was ended in rhythm."

However it is when we turn from the Southern to the African scene that we sense the full force of the anti-Nordic tide that seems to have set in. For here we have the almost unqualified worship and glorification of the primitive, combined with a deep ironic repudiation of the justifying illusions of the "white man's burden." The native now not only dominates the scene, but it is his philosophy that triumphs or at least has the last word. Fatalism and futility brood over the scene like the heat and the fever, and if anything wins, it is nature. Indeed in *Black God,* Miss Manners-Sutton suggests that it is black magic that casts the die: M'Kato waiting for years for vengeance for his maimed hands and the rape of his sister sees a pilgrimage of death overtake trader, missionary, free-booter, government officer, outcast adventurer, and eventually his long awaited enemy. The jungle everywhere exacts its expiating toll for the intrusions of white civilization; a different story from the romantic conquests in the fiction of a decade back. And only the weapon of magic, bribed from the native witch doctor, stops the avenging path of the "Black Master," native agitator and foe of the white man's power, who has undermined the Governor's self-confidence and authority and even become the paramour of his wife. It is a pity to sketch this lurid outline of melodrama, when the real charm and value of the book lies in the ironic etchings of character and description which make the substance of the book so superior to its theme and plot that one quite wishes there were no plot. Nevertheless, the justifications of our main conclusion must be pointed out.

Finally comes Emily Hahn's *With Naked Foot,* a masterpiece of observation, style and conception. Miss Hahn has served a fine apprenticeship in *Congo Solo,*—she knows her terrain and her human subject-matter perfectly. Now she has chosen a daring and a great theme and lifts the last shroud of silence from the tragedy of sex and love as it entangles the white man and the black woman, alien to each other in folkways, but not in basic emotions and common human needs. Mawa has a child by her first master-husband,—Joachim, who throughout the succession of four liasons remains the light and hope of her life. One by one they died or went, and Mawa holds her precarious superiority over her tribesmen as the mistress of the powerful. The Portuguese shop-keeper, the fat trader, the lean, meticulous government officer, and finally the romantic American school teacher with a conscience; they all succumbed to Mawa's charms and the African loneliness. At last it is Adam Kent's conscience that proves her undoing, he hurt her with a kind of love of which she knew nothing and wounded her life to the quick in trying to save her child from the primitive environment to which he only partly belonged. And as he passes out of her life, Mawa or the hull of Mawa sinks back into the chattel marriage she has defied so long to become the headsman's ageing concubine. Here is the compound tragedy of individuals and of the civilizations they represent, told with the swift deft touch and with ironically tempered understanding. This book will be cited years from now as one of the significant atonements for Nordicism: may it and its like provide the catharsis we have awaited so long!

One can afford to linger over the fiction of the year because of the almost complete cessation of poetry. Somehow the poetic strain has dwindled in quantity and quality; the occasional poems of Cullen and Hughes are below the level of their earler work, and only the muse of Sterling Brown seems to mature, and then only with a satirical and somewhat sardonic twist. Evidently it is not the hour for poetry; nor should it be, —this near-noon of a prosaic, trying day. Poets, like birds, sing at dawn and dusk, they are hushed by the heat of propaganda and the din of work and battle, and become vocal only before and after as the heralds or the carolling serenaders. The poetry section of the Cunard *Anthology* for example has for the most part an iron, metallic ring; interesting as it is, it is nevertheless hot rhetoric, clanging emotion. That is indeed the dominant note of this whole remarkable volume; making it one of the really significant signs of these times. There is much of unique informational and critical value in these eight hundred pages which document both the wrongs and the achievements of the black man and capitalize for the first time adequately the race problem as a world problem. But the capital "P" is for propaganda, not poetry, and the book hurls shell, bomb and shrapnel at the citadel of Nordicism. And again we must pause to notice that the daring initiative in so many instances comes from the white woman artist and author: strange, we say until we remember Lucretia Mott and Harriet Beecher Stowe. In passing, we must mention a noteworthy revival of John Brown by David Karsner, to goad the militancy of our day with the tonic of the militancy of our grandfathers' generation.

Still the pealing of the tocsin bell, however timely, cannot completely crowd out the old carefree romanticism and drown out entirely the strum of the guitar and the plunk of the banjo. The Lomax collection of *American Ballads* is with us to recall the immense contribution of the Negro to the balladry of the country, and George Lee's *Beale Street* comes to remind us vividly of the picturesque, swaggering and racy origin of the "Blues." Mr. Lee knows his Beale Street from its respectable end to the river bottoms where "River George" blustered and ruled. Incidentally the story of River George is one of the gems of the book; to my mind he is a better ballad subject than John Henry. In fact I confess to liking the picaresque side of this book; the respectabilities are pitiably pompous by contrast, and one regrets often that the author has chosen to mix his narrative. Yet to leave out the strange incongruities that the ghetto policy creates on Beale Street and elsewhere in Negro life would perhaps be false to the realities of Negro life; Mr. Lee has his justification in fact, if not in the congruities of art.

Turning now to the Negro drama of the year, we find a curious mixture of primitivism and modernism. Perkins' *Dance with Your Gods* and Heywood's *Africana* obviously each tried to exploit the vogue which *Kykunkor* started. To the credit of Broadway be it said that their tawdry tinsel and melodramatic shoddy failed; where the authentic and moving vitality of *Kykunkor* succeeded. Mr. Horton, (Asadata Dafora by original name) has really made a contribution to the drama of the African theme and setting; only its difficult intricacies of dance, pantomime, chant and drum-orchestra technique will prevent its sweeping the Negro stage with cleansing and illuminating fire. The production should by all means have a photo-sound recording; it is a classic of a new genre and will be eventually a turning point in Negro native drama.

The Broadway that is to be commended for thumbing down several specious fakes is to be chided for dooming Paul Green's *Roll On, Sweet Chariot*. Of course it was a cumbersome chariot, too overworked and overlaid with trappings (Mr. Green frequently overloads his plays with ideas and clogs his dramatic machinery), but the theme idea was good and significant. But for the present sound development of Negro drama, anyway, we need the tributary rather than the commercial theatre. It is for such a theatre obviously that Mr. Randolph Edmonds has written his *Six Plays for a Negro Theatre*. Professor Koch is right in his preface when saying: "This, so far as I know, is the first volume of its kind. (He means by a Negro playwright). It suggests new horizons." And Mr. Edmonds is theoretically right when he calls for a few Negro plays that are not defeatist and that are pivoted on the emotions and interests of Negro audiences. But, though they may be considerably redeemed by good acting, these historical and situational melodramas are hardly the stuff of great or highly original Negro drama. But their author has the temperament and the enthusiasm necessary for hardy pioneering, and he has bravely crossed some dramatic Rubicon,—even if the Alps are still ahead.

Finally here is a play that, though it has not scaled the dramatic heights, has burrowed under. Coming into the thick of the race problem by the unusual route of the class struggle and its radical formulae, this vehicle of the Theatre Union has not only made a box-office success but has harnessed the theatre to propaganda more successfully than has been done in this generation. Its clock, so to speak, strikes eleven for capitalism and Nordicism by the same pounding realistic strokes. No matter where one stands on the issues, there is no denying the force and effect of "Stevedore." Only a driving, pertinent theme could carry such amateurish dialogue and technique; but then, *Uncle Tom's Cabin* was one of the worst plays dramatically in the long history of the American stage, but look at its record and its results, in and out of the theatre! Certainly two of the most powerful issues of the contemporary scene have met in *"Stevedore,"* and a synthesis of race and class as a new type of problem drama may just as well be taken for granted. The applause which has greeted this play may well have national and international repercussions, and I do not envy the consternation of Nordic ears.

The second section of Retrospective Review will be published in the February issue.

The Eleventh Hour of Nordicism

By ALAIN LOCKE

(Part II.)

WHERE it is a question of Nordicism, sociology might reasonably be expected to be in the vanguard; however it is not so. Sociology,—at least the American brand, is a timid science on general principles and conclusions; fact-finding is its fetich. It particularly side-steps conclusions on the race question, and Negro sociologists, fearing to break with the genteel academic tradition in this respect, have usually been more innocuous than their white confreres,—making a great virtue and parade of inconsequential fact-finding and bland assertions of inter-racialism. That this situation is finally changing after nearly two decades dominated by such attitudes is due to the influence of just a few strong dissenting influences,—the most important of which has come from the militant but unquestionably scientific school of anthropologists captained by Professor Boas. They have dared, in season and out, to challenge false doctrine and conventional myths, and were the first to bring the citadel of Nordicism into range of scientific encirclement and bombardment. An essay in itself could be written on the slow but effective pressure that now has ringed the Nordic doctrines and their advocates round with an ever-tightening scientific blockade. The gradual liberalizing of the American historians and sociologists on the race question has been largely due to the infiltration of the conclusions of cultural anthropology, with its broader perspective and its invalidation of the basic contentions of historical racialism. Yet in the face of this, Negro educators have just made a belated beginning with the study of anthropology and the application of its findings to racial history and the social analysis of contemporary racial situations. At last, however, some beginning has been made.

Dr. Locke brings to a close his critical appraisal of the literature of the Negro for 1934. All the books mentioned in this article may be secured through OPPORTUNITY.

—The Editor.

An item,[1] omitted from our first list, *"Race and Culture Contacts,"* edited from the proceedings of the Twenty-eighth Meeting of the American Sociological Society, aside from interesting papers on *Traditions and Patterns of Negro Family Life* by Professor E. F. Frazier and on *Negro Personality Changes in a Southern Community* by Professor Charles S. Johnson, has important theoretical papers by Professor Robert E. Park on *Race Relations and Certain Frontiers* and Professor W. O. Brown on *Culture Contact and Race Conflict.* In fact for years, Professor Park has been insisting on the application of some general principles of culture contacts to the analysis of the American race problem (our most insidious and unscientific assumption has been and still is that this question is completely *sui generis*). Here in this paper he discusses general phenomena of racial intermixture and through an analysis of mixed blood status tries to get at the basic phenomena of ethnic conflict and change. Professor Brown undertakes more boldly (thank God for a bit of theoretical boldness occasionally) to trace "the process or natural history of race conflict," and tentatively develops a "race conflict sequence through six steps to the ultimate liquidation of conflict in the cultural assimilation and racial fusion of the peoples in contact." I suggest that even with the dangers of hasty generalization, a major interpretative contribution to the fruitful analysis of the race problem has either been made or will grow out of this approach and its comparative technique. Such work lifts the discussion immediately from that futilely academic plane of mere fact-finding upon which our best trained minds, black and white, have been considering the race question for nearly a generation. Though not devoted exclusively to our special subject, I would star this book as the most significant sociological item of the year, in this field of course, because of the promise and significance of this new approach to the scientific discussion of the race question.

From such thought-provoking viewpoints, one naturally turns with impatience to the traditional grooves of fact-finding and inter-racial reporting. Under the title of *Negro-White Adjustment*, Paul E. Baker makes a very exhaustive and painstaking summary of inter-racial work and organization, which is redeemed partially from the category of a catalogue by the attempt to analyze the platforms and classify

[1]Race and Culture Contacts, by E. B. Reuter—McGraw Hill Co., New York City.

the techniques of inter-racial work in America. Similarly, Mr. George R. Arthur, of the Y. M. C. A. and the Rosenwald Fund, gives an interpretive analysis and history of the welfare work of the twenty-five separate Y. M. C. A.'s in *The Negro Frontier,* with a deserved chronicle of Mr. Julius Rosenwald's contributions and his philosophy of their mission as "frontiers of adjustment in the urbanization of the Negro." It may seem ungrateful to label books of this type as manuals of professional inter-racial work, but they are in the sense that they are committed, unconsciously for the most part, to a definite philosophy of the race question and see the facts of the situation in terms of these commitments. No new light on the nature of the question or of possible new attacks and approaches need be expected under these circumstances, no matter how careful or exhaustive the analysis of the situation. Gradualism and good-will are the dogmatic commitments of this school of social thought,—and that's that.

The Shadow of the Plantation by Professor Charles S. Johnson is a triumph of recording sociology, the general limitations of which we have already discussed. Such detailed description cannot issue, as Dr. Park in his preface seems to think, in interpretative sociology, because the comparative basis and approach are lacking. For example, the conditions described in backward rural Alabama are not merely a relic of slavery and the "belated shadow of the old plantation," but a decidedly different modern deterioration, which though an aftermath of slavery, is actually the product of contemporary exploitation and the demoralization of the rural community life of the South. It is not primarily racial; but a question of a set of conditions as vividly shown by Carl Carmer's *Stars Fell on Alabama;* in this sense a better version of the situation, even in the scientific sense, though a reputed work of fiction. A more interpretative purpose and accomplishment can be credited to Weatherford and Johnson's *Race Relations,*—an elaborate and much belated text-book covering the whole range of the main historical and sociological aspects of the American race problem. The freshest contributions seem to be the discussion of *"Programs Looking Toward Solution or Amelioration of Race Relations"* and the chapter discussing *"Can There be a Separate Negro Culture?"* Rarely has either topic been put into the frame of full or objective discussion, and it is a distinct service to have done so.

Another wing of Negro scholars have definitely taken the less objective approach and philosophy; and of these Dr. Carter G. Woodson is the pioneer and leader. More and more, this erstwhile factual historian deliberately abandons that point of view and strikes boldly out for corrective criticism and the partisan encouragement of group morale. Dr. Woodson's stocktaking of the *Negro Professional Man and the Community* is weighted as much with trenchant criticism, soundly constructive for the most part, as it is with a factual report of the rise and service of the Negro professional classes. The thesis of the peculiar importance of these groups in Negro life is well sustained and explained, and the diagnosis that today we are seriously suffering from a faulty distribution of our professional group is worth immediate and serious consideration. On the whole, this is a book every Negro professional man or prospective professional should be required to read. Dr. Willis N. Huggins has compiled a useful syllabus outline of references and source materials in *African History* and the wider aspects of the color prob lem, conceived very much in the same school of semi-propagandist thought that Dr. Woodson is responsible for. An inevitable product of the reaction to Nordic bias, such corrective history and sociology has its definite place and value, even though such a position is difficult to universalize. Until the pseudo-science of the Nordics is completely routed, there will be a grave need for such militant history and for a critical, opinionated sociology.

In *Negro Americans, What Now?,* James Weldon Johnson tries and rather succeeds in striking a happy medium. It is an attempt at pithy, common-sense analysis of the racial situation, its alternatives and of the major objectives of the struggle. It is neither surprising nor discrediting that in the final weighing, the N. A. A. C. P. platform of political and civil rights action should receive very favorable, perhaps preferential emphasis. The value of the analysis lies in the succinct way in which issues usually clouded with partisan bias and emotion are clarified and touched with the wand of common sense; oddly enough an infrequent salt in the problem loaf. One quotation I should like to risk, because it is important: "What we require is a sense of strategy as well as a spirit of determination. . . . I have implied the fact that our policies should include an intelligent opportunism; by which I mean the alertness and ability to seize the advantage from every turn of circumstance whenever it can be done without sacrifice of principle." This is one of my reasons for characterizing this book as 'glorified common-sense on the race question.' It has anticipated its radical critics by saying: "Conservatism and radicalism are relative terms. It is as radical for a black American in Mississippi to claim his full rights under the Constitution as it is for a white American in any state to advocate the overthrow of the existing national government. The black American in many instances puts his life in jeopardy, and anything more radical than that cannot reasonably be required."

Finally, attention must be called to a contribution from the distant perspective of the International Peoples College in Denmark, Rebecca Barton's *Race Consciousness and the American Negro,*—essentially a philosophical study of the psychological complications and complexes of racial consciousness as reflected in Negro literature. This is a painstaking study from a pioneer angle, and only the lack of intimate knowledge of the suppressions that do not get into the literature has prevented its being an interpretation of major and final importance. This book must be taken into consideration in the new social criticism which is just below the horizon.

The field of Negro education is at last in scholastic bloom. To chronicle this is a mild reflection on the profession, but now it can be told. Of course, the obvious handicaps of the profession and the lowered tone of a segregated fraternity have accounted for the lack of productiveness in this field. *The Journal of Negro Education* climaxes a very creditable but young career with a Yearbook on *The Physical and Mental Abilities of the Negro,* a symposium that reflects not only valuable collaboration between white and Negro scholars but the interpretative focussing that only Negro auspices can give to issues that too long have had controversial discussion on uneven terms. The further historical contribution of Professor Dwight O. W. Holmes in his study, *The Evolution of the Negro College* and the analytic study of Professor Horace Mann Bond on *The Education of the Negro in the American Social Order* balance the educational field's contribution in a way that suggests providence since it is not the result of collusion. If the competent discussion of the educational problems and situations of the Negro pick up from this new start, we may anticipate a new phase of development in this numerous but somewhat stagnated and stultified profession. In Dean Holmes' book the dramatic historical role of the Negro college as the pivot of advance during Reconstruction is importantly documented, and in Dean Bond's book, the present inadequacies and injustices of public provision for Negro education are pointedly briefed and analyzed; to mention only one phase of the constructive contributions of these welcome contributions. In all, there is fortunately reflected a growing tendency not to regard the educational problems of the Negro as different in kind, but only in degree; with a definite trend toward rejoining the mainstream of educational thought after a period of regrettable but inevitable isolation, which has been the heaviest cost of the policy of educational segregation.

In the field of Africana, the contributions this year are not voluminous, but they are significant. In *Liberia Rediscovered* we have little more than a veiled justification of the Firestone policy in that sad tangle of democracy and imperialism, and in Ivor Evans' *Native Policy in South Africa,* we have a faint beginning at objectivity in the discussion of the worst racial situation in the world,—that of the Union of South Africa and adjacent protectorates and mandates. The significant books are those by Helser, Herskovits and Westermann. Dr. Herskovits, this time in collaboration with his wife, resurveys the Suriname cultures of the South American Guinea Negroes after a sojourn in the original home of these cultures, West Africa. He, or rather they, find more evidence than previously for their contention that there are important transplanted survivals of African cultures in the Western hemisphere. Eventually as the outlines of these are retraced, we may be able to reconstruct in rough outline the cultural derivations of various groups of Negroes or various stages in the fading out of these original traits and traditions. In addition to its serious anthropological bearings, *Rebel Destiny* is fascinating reading and proves that sound folk-lore can be as entertaining as pseudo folk-lore.

Helser's book on *"Education of Primitive People"* is primarily an attempt to find a practical technique of missionary education based upon some sensible recognition of the place and worth of the native tradition in such a program. Carried out a little more thoroughly, the study would have constituted a contribution on the part of the practise of social training in primitive society to our own changing system of educational aims and technique. Such a contribution must in time be made, and when it arrives the final reversal on the missionary psychosis of "Greenland's icy mountains and India's coral strand" will have been put into the record. That book will then justify what an over-enthusiastic admirer has said of this one: "A revelation not only of what education among a primitive people may be but of what real education essentially is."

Professor Westermann is co-director of the *International Institute of African Languages and Cultures,* and writes almost pontifically on *"The African of To-Day."* The point of view is that of modified imperialism, naturally,—the benevolent trusteeship conception, the advocacy of the new compromise of indirect rule and the encouragement of integral African traditions with economic but not serious cultural penetration.

(Continued on Page 59)

THE ELEVENTH HOUR OF NORDICISM

(Continued from Page 48)

Of course, it remains to be proved that this reconstructed imperialism is possible; and sound and just, even if possible. However, the brief for it is carefully and humanely advanced by Dr. Westermann, with as much detailed anthropological information as to what is really going on in Africa by reason of the contact and conflict of cultures as is gathered between any two book covers. The study is, therefore, a gift horse that cannot be looked too harshly in the mouth by serious students of the African scene, even though the inspiration is too extra-racial to be a final or a truly representative picture of the African to-day. That picture must, of course, come eventually from the African himself. But in the process that we have been discussing all along, namely the recanting of Nordicism, this book and its dominant point of view represent one long delayed and welcome admission,—namely, that there are elements of permanent value in African cultures and their tradition, and that the complete displacement of these cultures would be an irreparable loss. The idea that they yet have their complementary contribution to make to the cultures of the white man is, of course, below the horizon as yet, but not so far below as not to give some hints of its impending rise.

Deep River: Deeper Sea » » »

Retrospective Review of the Literature of the Negro for 1935.

• By ALAIN LOCKE

BIBLIOGRAPHY OF LITERATURE OF THE NEGRO: 1935.

FICTION

Kneel to the Rising Sun—Erskine Caldwell, Viking Press, N. Y.—$2.50.
God Shakes Creation—David Cohn, Harper & Bros., N. Y.—$2.50.
Stephen Kent—Hallie F. Dickerman, The Hartney Press, N. Y.—$2.00.
Siesta—Berry Fleming, Harcourt, Brace & Co., N. Y.—$2.50.
Ollie Miss—George Wylie Henderson, Frederick Stokes Co., N. Y.—$2.50.
Mules and Men—Zora Hurston, J. B. Lippincott, Phila.—$3.00.
A Sign for Cain—Grace Lumpkin, Lee Furman, N. Y.—$2.50.
Deep Dark River—Robert Rylee, Farrar & Rinehart, N. Y.—$2.50.
South—Frederick Wight, Farrar & Rinehart, N. Y.—$3.00.

DRAMA

Roll, Sweet Chariot—Paul Green, Samuel French, N. Y.—$1.50.
Porgy & Bess—A Folk Opera, George & Ira Gershwin & Du Bose Heyward, The Theatre Guild, N. Y.
White Man—Samson Raphaelson, Samuel French, N. Y.—$2.00.
Mulatto—Mss.—Langston Hughes, Vanderbilt Theatre, N. Y.
The Two Gifts—Arthur C. Lamb, in Grinnell Plays, Dramatic Publishing Co., Chicago. (one act).

BIOGRAPHY AND BELLES LETTRES

Early Negro American Writers—Benjamin Brawley, University of North Carolina Press—$2.50.
A Saint in the Slave Trade: Peter Claver—Arnold Lunn, Sheed & Ward, Inc., N. Y.—$2.50.
Richard Allen: Apostle of Freedom—Chas. H. Wesley, Associated Publishers, Washington, D. C.—$2.15.

POETRY

The Medea and Some Poems—Countee Cullen, Harper & Bros., N. Y.—$2.00.
Black Man's Verse—Frank Marshall Davis, Black Cat Press, Chicago—$3.00.
Saint Peter Relates an Incident—James Weldon Johnson, Viking Press, N. Y.—$2.00.
The Brown Thrush—An Anthology of Negro Student Verse— Malcolm Roberts Pub. Co., Memphis, Tenn., $1.25.

EDUCATION AND SOCIOLOGY

Negroes in the United States—U. S. Census Publication, Washington—$2.25.
Fundamentals in the Education of Negroes— Bulletin No. 6—Office of Education. Dept. of the Interior—Washington, D. C.—$.10.
The Courts and the Negro Separate School— Journal of Negro Education: July, 1935. Yearbook No. 4—Howard University, Washington, D. C.—$2.00.
Negro Politicians—Harold Gosnell, University of Chicago Press—$3.50.
The Collapse of Cotton Tenancy—Chas. S. Johnson, Edwin R. Embree, and W. A. Alexander, University of North Carolina Press, N. C.—$1.00.
90° in the Shade—Clarence Cason, University of North Carolina Press—$2.50.
Black Reconstruction—W. E. B. DuBois, Harcourt, Brace & Co., N. Y.—$4.50.

AFRICANA

In a Province—Laurens van der Post, Coward-McCann, N. Y.—$2.50.
Voodoo Fire in Haiti—Richard Loederer, Doubleday, Doran & Co., N. Y.—$2.75.
A la Belle Flore—Eugene Duliscouet, Editions Delmas—Bordeaux—12 fr.
The Leopard Princess—R. S. Rattray, Appleton-Century Co., N. Y.—$2.00.
The Story of An African Chief—A. K. Nyabongo, Chas. Scribners, N. Y.—$3.00.
Africa Dances—Geoffrey Gorer, Alfred A. Knopf, Inc., N. Y.—$3.50.
Black and White in East Africa—R. C. Thurnwald, Keegan, Paul Co., London—21 s.
Africa: A Social, Economic and Political Geography— Walter Fitzgerald—E. P. Dutton & Co., N. Y.— $5.00.
The Arts of West Africa—Sir Michael Sadler, Oxford University Press—$2.00.
African Negro Art—James J. Sweeney, Museum of Modern Art, N. Y.—$2.50.

DEEP river; deeper sea!-even a landlubber knows that! How much water, then, is under our literary keel? Out with the critical plummet! But there's the hitch; in 1934 we felt and announced the shock of the break-water, we know we are further downstream,—the view has suddenly widened, the sense and tang of the sea are anticipating the actual sight of it, and yet,—the waters are shallower than they were upstream and the current has slackened. Where, then, are we?

If the reader has patience, let us try a simile. A generation back, Negro literature and art were shallow trickles and stagnant puddles in the foothills; in some instance, perhaps, choked sluggish creeks behind rural millponds. Meanwhile, the poets cried out: "Yonder's Parnassus," and the critics blubbered: "We want the sea, nothing will do but the sea." But art had no such magic; water cannot run uphill and doesn't forthright leap dams and ditches. So 'poetic justive,' 'universal values,' 'high life and vindication' were yearned for in vain. Consequently, racial expression had to run inevitably the traditional course; in turns, to trickle in babbling brooks of rhetoric, dally in sentimental shallows and romantic meadows, run headlong and raucously over the sticks and stones of controversy, slow down as it gathered soil and complexion from its native banks and clay bars, chafe impatiently against barriers of prejudice, give over much of its substance to alien exploitation before gaining depth and strength enough to overleap the dam of provincialism, spurt forward, dangerously, in a waterfall of deceptive freedom, spin and eddy in self-confusion, labor toward a junction with the mainstream, press along jointly in an ever-deepening channel, though at the cost of the muddy murk of realism and the smelly muck of commercialism, at last, under the accumulated impetus of all this, to meet and challenge,—and lose, to the sea.

The reader has a right to query: "And are we really there?" Even by the simile,—not yet. Just on the threshold of the sea, nature gives us the paradox of the shallow delta with its unproductive mixture of sea sand and river soil and its unpalatable blend of salt and fresh water. And so, in this matter of the literary course of the deep, dark river of Negro literature, here we are at the end of 1935, I think, on the wide brackish waters of the delta, waiting not too comfortably or patiently in the uninviting vestibule of the ocean of great, universalized art. The scenery is monotonous, the air unsavory, the course weed-grown and tricky; half of the literature of the year isn't literature but a strange bitter bracken of commingled propaganda and art. Yet one optimistic factor stands out, in spite of all this, the horizons are wider,—wider than they have ever been: and thus the promise of the sea is assuredly there. Before too very long, the tang, taste, color and rhythm of our art will have changed irreparably from the purely racial to the universal, and those who have cried for the sea will doubtless cry for the loss of their river.

Meanwhile, our art is again turning prosaic, partisan and propagandist, but this time not in behalf of striving, strident racialism, but rather in a protestant and belligerent universalism of social analysis and protest. In a word, our art is going proletarian; if the signs mean anything. Yesterday it was Beauty at all costs and local color with a vengeance; today, it is Truth by all means and social justice at any price. Except for the occasional detached example, those who hope for the eventual golden mean of truth with beauty must wait patiently,—and perhaps, long. Just now, all the slime and hidden secrets of the river are shouldered up on the hard, gritty sand bars and relentlessly exposed to view. Almost overnight, in the fiction and drama of Negro life, generation-old taboos have been completely broken down; in a dozen steely mirrors, miscegenation shows not its intriguing profile but its tragic full face and economic exploitation and social injustice their central tragedy of common guilt and imminent retribution, not just the stock side-show of Negro melodrama. Hollywood still plays with a picture-book version of the old romantic South, but in serious contemporary letters, the work of Erskine Caldwell, though extreme, is typical. Here, the South is on the grill of a merciless realism, administered for the most part by disillusioned and disillusioning white southerners to whom the poor white and the Negro peasant are common victims of a decadent, top-heavy and inhuman system, for which they see no glory and no excuse. This increasing trend has caught the southern defensive completely off-guard because it has made no concessions to its argumentative set; it has just confronted the orators and propagandists with overwhelming and almost photographic reporting. After all, none of us can get away from bare facts in the glare of sun or spotlight; no one can read through Caldwell's *Kneel to the Rising Sun* or Berry Fleming's *Siesta,* or out of the field of fiction, Clarence Cason's *90° in the Shade* and ever be quite the same. Especially important are they for the Negro reader, who suffers acutely from the blindness of familiarity as well as from the blinkered distortion of his own case and problem. As incurable a southern as Edward Larocque Tinker calls *Siesta* "a truthful picture of how the present generation in deep Dixie lives, loves and thinks,"—"an adult novel drawn from true American sources."

I suppose that in this matter of the new radical literature of the American South, there will always be two schools, both for the creators and the consumers, the artists and the critics. Caldwell, of course, represents the social protest approach and Miss Lumpkin's *Sign for Cain* is the most daring and logical expression of that point of view to date, barring, of course, Mr. Caldwell's own brilliant pioneering; Clarence Cason will, I think, more and more come to fame as the brave pioneer of the 'psychographic' analysts, for whom the mind-sets of the South are the keys to the situation rather than the class economics of the Marxian Caldwellites. In which case, it seems to me, Cason, though no novelist, has founded or grounded a school of southern fiction, of which Berry Fleming is, to date, the most brilliant and promising exponent. My own sympathies, temperamentally determined no doubt, are with the psycho-analysts; but I grant the power, integrity and increasing vogue of the Marxians. What is of greater importance than this issue of approach and technique is the overwhelming agreement of both schools on the evidence of fact. They corroborate each other on the facts of the case startlingly; and together they raise up a new plateau both for the artistic and the social understanding of the South and the Negro. Both, incidentally, insist that each must be understood in basic common terms, and that the tragedy of the one is the tragedy of the other. Such developments, coming at this critical time of social reconstruction, have a meaning all too obvious. What is more amazing is the acceptance of these truths in substantial quarters in the South, due somewhat to the irrefutability of the facts, but also in large part to the happy circumstance that most of this writing is "indigenous criticism." Human nature is pretty much like that, everywhere,—and here's a toast to,—and a prayer for, the most desired of all desirables,—indigenous criticism on the part of the creative and articulate Negro himself. Until this shall come, the Negro can really produce no truly universal or even fully representative art. Let the white artist study Negro life objectively and wholly in terms both of itself and its context, as he is showing rapid and wholesome signs of doing; let the Negro artist do so likewise! There is the sea, of which I have spoken.

Some of the younger Negro writers and artists see this situation in terms of what is crystallizing in America and throughout the world as "proletarian literature." What is inevitable is, to that extent at least, right. There will be a quick broadening of the base of Negro art in terms of the literature of class protest and proletarian realism. My disagreement is merely in terms of a long-term view and ultimate values. To my thinking, the approaching proletarian phase is not the hoped-for sea but the inescapable delta. I even grant its practical role as a suddenly looming middle passage, but still these difficult and trying shoals of propagandist realism are not, never can be, the oceanic depths of universal art; even granting that no art is ever groundless or timeless.

But to return briefly to our 1935 crop of Negro fiction. Readers keen on comparative values may wonder why I have not yet mentioned *Deep, Dark River,* Robert Rylee's moving tragedy of Mississippi injustice and persecution. It is more of a novel structurally and more a specific study of Negro character than *Siesta.* But the last few years of fiction have just about illuminated us on the question "What is the South"; the forward turn now is to tackle that more courageous and hopeful analysis; "What makes it like that," in other words the *why* rather than just the *how* of the South. In these terms then, even Frederick Wight's half aesthetic travelogue *South* is more significant, though less powerful, for it tries to explain and is ever conscious of the great dilemmas in southern life by which it is set over against itself. It is important and brave for Mr. Rylee, himself a southerner, to admit, through the mouth of his white Portia, Mary Winston, in talking to Mose, in jail for murder: "You see, Mose, the story you have told me is not a story that can be told in a court room. You are a Negro and Mr. Birney is a white man. A Negro can't tell that a white man was living with his wife or that a white man sent a Negro to kill him. No jury would free you if you made that defense," but it is still more important and profound to say of the eastern Cotton Belt, as Berry Fleming does, "This is the heart of the South; you can't get any farther into the South than this. This is Anglo-Saxon and African, this is the original cotton country . . . and these three states have one-third of all the fertilizer factories in the United States. The fertilizer factory isn't on any of their state seals, but it ought to be . . . the unfertility of the soil makes a hard living. You have to put almost as much money into the ground as you get out." For when Mr. Fleming goes on to say that beauty doesn't grow out of soil like that, he might also have included justice. Diagnosis is better than description; although the day is yet young since frank description came on the horizon, this sort of analysis is still younger.

Mrs. Hallie Dickerman has written an interesting first novel *Stephen Kent,* frank in theme, true enough to fact, but handled with timid sentimentality. Several years ago it would have been an advanced novel because of its frank treatment of miscegenation and the peculiar Southern dilemmas of the "blot on the escutcheon." However, it does not break with the old conventional formula of blood atavism and calmly accepts the rules of caste as framing irrevocable tragedy even for the thoughts of the characters themselves. Thus Stephen Kent's magnanimity in not claiming his white mother actualizes few of the deep potentialities of the plot, and despite a courageous theme, makes a milk and water contrast to the blood, iron and steel of the prevailing trend.

Negro writers of fiction come forward with but two offerings out of the rapidly increasing field. However, both are real contributions to local color and characterization, though unfortunately not in theme or social philosophy. George Wylie Henderson's first novel *Ollie Miss* is a mature and competent study of Negro farm life and its elementals so far as that can take us without any suggestion of its place in the general scheme of things. Just such detached but intimate recording is also done in Miss Hurston's folk-lore collection, *Mules and Men,* which has the effect of novel vignettes because of her great power of evoking atmosphere and character. It has been many years since the younger Negro writers have had as firm a grip on their material as here indicated; which is so positive a gain that it is probably ungracious to complain of the lack of social perspective and philosophy. While not particularly incumbent on Miss Hurston by reason of the folk-lore objective of her work, there is yet something too Arcadian about hers and Mr. Henderson's work, considering the framework of contemporary American life and fiction. The depression has broken this peasant Arcady even in the few places where it still persisted, and while it is humanly interesting and refreshing enough, it is a critical duty to point out that it is so extinct that our only possible approach to it is the idyllic and retrospective. On the other hand, this same rare native material and local color in the flesh and bone of either the proletarian or the sociological strains of fiction would carry into them the one lacking dimension of great art.

On the dramatic front, however, folk-lore is in the ascendancy with the undoubted and deserved success of *Porgy and Bess*; since in the field of the problem play no real succession to last season's strong play *Stevedore* has come forward in spite of the obvious candidacy of Langston Hughes' current Broadway offering of *Mulatto*. Granting the difficulty of any unpleasant theme on the American stage, it is strange to account for the general lack of success of the serious Negro problem play. Playwrights, black and white, must meet this challenge, for the audience cannot be entirely blamed when one after the other, with the most sympathetic reading, plays in this category smoulder rather than flame. I think it is a problem of craftsmanship primarily, recalling how long the southern realistic novel smouldered before it broke clear and bright. *Porgy* deserves its success, both as a play and as opera, it surges irresistibly with life and is totally convincing. The other themes can do the same, when master craftsmanship appears. Even without master craft a certain flare for the dramatically vital gave real life to *Stevedore*. But *Roll, Sweet Chariot,* though well studied, over-studied perhaps, is cryptic; Raphaelson's *White Man,* with an incandescent theme, sputters and goes feebly defeatist at the end—(though even at that, it is a considerable advance in the treatment of the psychology of inter-marriage over "All God's Chillun Got Wings),—and *Mulatto* merely noses through on the magnificent potentialities of its theme, which for the most part are amateurishly smothered in talk and naive melodrama. Of course, Broadway merely takes a pot chance as yet on serious Negro plays; they are usually hastily rehearsed, poorly staged, and superficially seasoned. But the playwrights themselves must force the issue and above all else let their characters grow up to the full stature of the heroic. Well studied genre or pastiche characters carrying through great themes in only two dimensions will never put over the serious drama of Negro life.

The Negro actor has demonstrated his capacity under great handicaps of inadequate materials; it is tragic, especially in view of her enforced and we hope temporary retirement, to think of the puny roles Rose McClendon has had for the expression of her truly great dramatic genius. Of course, any role in which she would not have been positively mis-cast ought to have been open to her. But she has had to battle not only a limited chance, but even there, half-baked characterization, type roles that ill-befit great dramatic powers. Imagine, for example, to take the case of *Mulatto,* a Cora who really became the Colonel's mistress as the door closed and then shifted suddenly back to the mode of the domestic servant as it opened again to company; it is for such reasons that I place primary blame, not on the audience, the producers and Broadway traditions, but upon the faulty dramaturgy of two-thirds of the plays of Negro life, irrespective of the authorship being professional or amateur, black or white. Negro drama needs full gamut and an open throttle; and not what it has so often had, either skill without courage, or courage without skill.

Turning to *belles lettres,* we witness an obvious revival of biography, and this with the rumors of a projected biographical series of Negro leaders and the promised revival of the plans for an Encyclopedia of the Negro, indicates a decided awakening of the historical impulse. All three of the books in this field extend to the general reading public little known historical material that should be theirs. In the context of a vindication of saintliness and mystical apprehension of the supernatural, Arnold Lunn gives us a vivid biography of *St. Peter Claver,* who labored thirty-eight years during the eighteenth century for the alleviation of the victims of the slave trade. Professor Brawley brings within reach of the general reader biographical and critical material on the least known of our literary fields—the Negro writers of the colonial and early anti-slavery periods, with well-culled selections from their works. Professor Wesley has written the first complete biography of *Richard Allen,* founder of African Methodism and pioneer racialist. All this is more than welcome, even though none of the work is in the contemporary vein of biography. Paucity of material and the Puritan repressions of those who did make the contemporary records of these worthies has undoubtedly crippled their biographers for drawing psychological portraits of their subjects. They will possibly thus remain in the daguerrotype and wood-cut outlines in which they are already familiar to researchers; the gain is that this material is now at the ready disposal of the general reader, competently presented and attractively readable.

Two veteran poets have come to the fore with their medals on, so to speak. In spite of the new material, there are no new notes and no new poetic highs. In general, these two volumes of Countee Cullen and James Weldon Johnson do not advance their poetic reputations. The choruses of Cullen's translated *Medea* are finely turned, with virtuosity in fact, and it is good to have available again the cream of Weldon Johnson's *Fifty Years and other Poems,* now out of print. However, Negro poetry cannot expect in this day of changing styles and viewpoints to live successfully on its past. That is why I turned most feverishly to the pages of *The Brown Thrush: Anthology of Verse by Negro Students.* Perhaps my present impatience with the elder generation is that I found so many weak and tiring echoes of Dunbar, Johnson, Hughes and Cullen there. Natural enough, no doubt, but if so, why not Whitman, Swinburne, Frost, Millay or Jeffers? In fact, Negro poetry has no excuse today for being imitative at all, and little excuse for being tenuous and trite in substance. For the new notes and the strong virile accents in our poetry today, we must shift from Harlem to Chicago; for there are Willard Wright whose verse sees the light in the *New Masses* and other radical periodicals and Frank Marshall Davis, who really brings fresh talent and creative imagination to this waning field. Both of these younger poets owe more to the Langston Hughes inspiration than to the academicians, but each in his own individual way has gone deeper into the substance of the folk life, though neither of them so deeply as that other more mature poet, Sterling Brown, who regrettably publishes so little of what he writes. I insist that we shall not know the full flavor and potentialities either of tragic or comic irony as applied to Negro experience until this sturdy, incisive verse of Brown's is fully published. For years we have waited for the sealed vials of irony and satire to open and for their purging and illuminating fire to come down in poetic flashes and chastizing thunderbolts. And for some reason, the gods withhold the boon. The puny thrust that passes for irony, the burlesque smirk that masquerades as satire try one's critical soul, until one remembers illuminatingly that outside antiquity, only the Irish and the French have the gift of it. But it might have been in the gift-box of the Negro, seeing he had such need of it.

(*To Be Continued in the Next Issue*)

Deep River: Deeper Sea » » »

Retrospective Review of the Literature of the Negro for 1935.

• By ALAIN LOCKE

Dr. Locke, distinguished commentator on the art and culture of the Negro, concludes his Retrospective Review for 1935.

ADDENDA: LITERATURE OF THE NEGRO,—1935
PART II.

NEGRO HISTORY IN THIRTEEN PLAYS: ed. Willis Richardson and May Miller, Associated Publishers, Washington, D. C. $3.25.

THE STORY OF THE NEGRO RETOLD: Carter G. Woodson, Associated Publishers, Washington, D. C. $2.15.

DANIEL A. PAYNE: Josephus Coan. A. M. E. Book Concern, Philadelphia, Pa. $1.50.

EVEN in the cold ashes of sociology, some new fires are burning; like a refiner's furnace in books like Cason's *90° in the Shade,* like a flaming torch in a book like Dr. DuBois's *Black Reconstruction.* The subject needs both heat and light; more light, but in the impending crisis, heat, too, is salutary. In the small but searching volume, *The Collapse of Cotton Tenancy,* even that arch-advocate of objective sociology, Professor Charles S. Johnson, in the company of Edward R. Embree and Will A. Alexander, points an accusing finger and calls for present-day social reconstruction. This is a healthy symptom of progress in the artificially isolated and conservative field of Negro history and sociology. I take it that there will not be many more books written in this field that will ignore the general social and economic crisis and the necessary and vital linkage of the Negro situation with the general issues. Although not fully repudiated, this handicap and blight of several generations standing is now definitely on the wane.

Of course, separate discussion of racial issues and interests is necessary and inevitable, but a separate and special ideology, especially one based on outmoded social concepts, never has been desirable, although until recently it has been all too frequent. Yet one can scarcely approve in full of Dr. DuBois's passionate leap to close the gap and throw the discussion of the Negro problem to the forefront battle-line of Marxian economics, even though *Black Reconstruction* is one of the most challenging worthwhile books of the year. This merely because it is more difficult to apply the Marxian formula to the past decades of Negro history, and that inaccurately done, really detracts considerably from the main purpose and accomplishment of the work,—viz. a crashing counter-interpretation of the Reconstruction period and a justifiable impeachment of its American historians. Ultimately,—soon perhaps, we shall have the other problem realized in a scientifically economic interpretation of the Negro's status in American life and history; meanwhile we gratefully salute Dr. DuBois's spirited and successful historical challenge.

A useful publication, purely factual and statistical, comes from the government press, compiling the figures of the 1930 U. S. Census as they relate to the *Negroes in the United States.* For the first time, this appears under the acknowledged editorial supervision of Charles E. Hall, veteran Negro statistician of the Census department. Under the editorial supervision of Dr. Ambrose Caliver, and the imprint of the U. S. Department of Education, comes a small but pithy publication,—*Fundamentals in Negro Education,* collating the findings of last year's conference on Negro education. The pamphlet gives the best statement available of the state of Negro education in terms of the present crisis.

The Year Book issue of the *Journal of Negro Education* brings forward, similarly, a most opportune subject, in fact the crucial one of the separate Negro school. Although the pattern of previous volumes is followed, and thus the symposium issues are well balanced, *pro* and *con,* the trend of the argument is decidedly against the principle and practise of educational segregation, and forecasts a militant reaction against it. Most of the disputants advocate challenging its legality before the courts, such as has been recently done in the University of Maryland case, so successfully prosecuted under N.A.A.C.P. auspices by the young Washington attorney, Charles H. Houston. The symposium and its conclusions anticipated the case, it should be noted, in estimating its significance as a gauge of educational opinion among Negroes.

As has been hinted, *The Collapse of Cotton Tenancy,* although not completely militant, turns its back definitely upon palliative measures in the problems of the rural South. It pictures vividly the present plight of the cotton tenant farmer, and though interested in the Negro particularly, uses the more scientific concept of the share-cropper, be he black or white. The authors conclude that the present crisis in southern agriculture is the final stage of the generation-old breakdown of the plantation system, that this system must be radically changed, and that there is no solution short of converting the share-tenant into an owner tenant with whatever legal and governmental aids are necessary. So, whichever way we turn, from the economic, historical or psychological angle, a more radical and challenging point of view confronts us. One warns, another challenges, still another, as with Cason, almost vivisects; but none condone, placate or play hopeful Pollyana. We ought, at least know where we are and not be victims of time-old illusions.

As one might expect, the field of Africana is a baffling mixture of tinsel and gold; this year's yield has some of the profoundest and some of the most superficial interpretations yet made of primitive life and custom. Surely one of the worst is Loederer's *Voodoo Fire in Haiti,* where again the unhappy isle is distorted by the flippant sensation monger, looking for cheap, glamorous exotic primitivism. The verdict of competent scholarship is that the Haiti of Seabrook, Craige and Loederer simply does not exist except in the hectic imagination of these journalist-adventurers. They see largely what they preconceive, superficially document it, and are off with their wares to the eager but misguided devotees of the cult of the jungle. Those who know the jungle life more expertly come out with sober and radically different interpretations.

An instance, and an encouraging contrast is Captain Rattray's novel of a primitive African cult, *The Leopard Priestess.* It is a novel, and should perhaps have been listed with our fiction, but for the fact that its folk-lore and background are too important. The author knows his Africa from years of study and intensive experience. Authentic mystery, accurate primitive magic and ceremonial, appropriate tropic situations follow the fate of the guilty lovers; they are enmeshed in an even more typical African guilt than the lovers of Batouala, and the stark simplicity of their fate convinces us that a real African romance has been written. Had it the stylistic excellence of Batouala, it would be the undisputed classic that the latter still is.

Another competent and illuminating record of African custom and thought is the story of a native African chieftain's son, told by Akiki Nyabongo, himself an educated native of Uganda. Mr. Nyabongo has little need of a dubious veil of fiction to decorate his narrative, unless it be to save some embarrassment in this nearly autobiographical story of the conflict between native and European mores in the youth and adolescence of little Prince Ati. In some respects, this is the first book to bring out from the inside the dilemmas of the intelligent African involved in education at the hands of missionaries and tutelage from the self-appointed trustees of their civilization. Time and again the ignorant disdain of native custom is clearly and cleverly illustrated, and more than once, the native tradition comes off best. One cannot refrain from repeating the refreshing incident of the young prince reading to his father and his assembled wives, after the year-long diatribes of the Reverend Mr. Hubert on polygamy, of the passages from the Holy Bible detailing the story of King Solomon with his seven hundred wives and three hundred concubines. A gale of laughter is sometimes more effective than a blast of polemics.

In a Province, a problem novel of South Africa, reports for the first time effectively the main outlines of the class struggle and the industrial dilemmas of that quarter of the globe. Laurens van der Post is a painstaking artist as well as a competent reporter,—and the book betokens a new breath of artistic liberalism from the stagnant conservatism of its traditional background.

Professor Fitzgerald's social and economic geography of Africa is a path-breaking analysis that ought to be the base of whatever prescribed studies of Africa are given in our colleges. The arts and antiquities of Africa are important for the true understanding of African life, and nothing is less known and more misunderstood by the average American Negro) but without a scientific, objective basis such as this study of the great continent affords, they are a deceptive veneer. That is why, with an interest of long standing in such subjects as Professor Sadler's book on *The Arts of West Africa,* Mr. James Sweeney's admirable essay and catalogue on African art prepared for the Museum of Modern Art's remarkable spring show, or even Monsiuer Carré's fine preface on the Benin civilization and its art prepared for the recent Knoedler Gallery show, I still insist that a fundamental knowledge of African geography and the economics of the colonial situation are indispensable in any sound and comprehending knowledge of the land of our forefathers.

Those who need the short-cut of an interpretation combining several of these factors into a single book will, therefore, welcome and praise Geoffrey Gorer's *Africa Dances,* to my thinking, the book of the year. Starting out as an aesthetic caravan, studying the African dance, the magic key of taking Feral Benga, the talented Sengalese dancer, as devoted and respected travel companion, opened for Mr. Gorer, though a novice

(Continued on Page 61)

DEEP RIVER: DEEPER SEA

(Continued from Page 43)

in Africa, doors closed to missionaries, traders, government agents and even canny anthropologists. And so, natives, chiefs, fetish priests, colonial society, high, low and middle-rank, townsmen, coastmen, hinterlanders all flit graphically across Mr. Gorer's diary pages with a life-like vividness and candid reality. Of course, all praise to Mr. Gorer's own temperamental equipment, sensitiveness, amazing candor, freedom from prejudice of civilization and color (many who have immunity from one of these are chronic victims of the other), and a contagious power of description; but with all these, he could have forgotten the magic open sesame of an African friend and sponsor. He magnanimously admits this, so there is little virtue in calling attention to it, except to praise the book, which I do in everything but its pessimistic conclusions,—and this only because Africa has survived so much that it seems likely that she will survive even the modern plagues of imperialistic exploitation.

God Save Reality! « « « « «

PART I. Retrospective Review of the Literature of the Negro: 1936

• By ALAIN LOCKE

BIBLIOGRAPHY OF LITERATURE OF THE NEGRO: 1936

FICTION:

Death Is a Little Man—Minnie H. Moody, Julian Messner, N. Y.—$2.50.
Big Blow—Theodore Pratt, Little Brown & Co., Boston, —$2.50.
Courthouse Square—Hamilton Basso, Scribner & Sons, N. Y.—$2.50.
A White Man and A Black Man In the Deep South—James Saxon Childers—Farrar & Rinehart, N. Y.—$2.50.
The sub-plots of
Gone With the Wind—Margaret Mitchell, Macmillan, N. Y.—$3.00.
Absolom, Absolom—Wm. Faulkner, Random House Press, N. Y.—$2.50.

* * *

Under the Sun—Grace Flandrau, Chas. Scribner's, N. Y. —$2.50.
African Witch—Joyce Cary—Wm. Morrow, N. Y.—$2.50.

* * *

POETRY and BELLES LETTRES:

April Grasses—Marion Cuthbert, The Woman's Press, N. Y.—75 cents.
No Alabaster Box and Other Poems, "Eve Lynn"—Alpress, Phila.—$1.50.
We Lift Our Voices and Other Poems—Mae V. Cowdery Alpress, Phila.—$1.50.
Poems in *The American Caravan*: *1936*—Willard Wright —Wm. Morrow & Co., N. Y.—$3.95.
We Sing America: *An Anthology*—Marion Cuthbert—Friendship Press, N. Y.—$1.00.

* * *

Belles Images—Rene Maran, Editions Delmas, Paris—8 fr.
Poems, Prose and Plays by Alexander Pushkin—trans. by Yarmolinsky and Deutsch—Random Press, N. Y.—$3.00.

* * *

DRAMA:

White Man—Samson Raphaelson, National Theatre, N. Y.
One Way to Heaven—Mss. Countee Cullen and Arna Bontemps—Hedgerow Theatre, Moylan, Pa.
When the Jack Hollers—Mss. Langston Hughes and Arna Bontemps—Gilpin Players, Cleveland.
New Theatre League Plays: N. Y.—25 cents each:
1. *Trouble with the Angels*—Bernard Schoenfeld.
2. *Mighty Wind a Blowin'*—Alice H. Ware.
3. *Angelo Herndon Jones*—Langston Hughes.

Federal Theatre Project—Negro Unit—Lafayette Theatre, N. Y.
Walk Together Chillun—Frank Wilson.
The Conjure Man Dies—Rudolph Fisher.
Turpentine—J. A. Smith and Peter Morell.
Obey's *Noah*—dramatized by Carlton Moss.
Shakespeare: *Macbeth*—dramatized in Negro style by Orson Welles.
Bassa Moona—African Dance Drama by Momodu Johnson and Norman Coker.

* * *

NEGRO MUSIC AND ART:

Negro Musicians and Their Music—Maud Cuney Hare—Associated Publishers, Washington, D. C.—$3.15.
The Negro and His Music—Alain Locke, Associates in Negro Folk Education, Washington, D. C.—25 cents.
Hot Jazz—Hughes Panassié—N. Witmark & Co., N. Y.—$5.00.
Swing That Music—Louis Armstrong—Longmans, Green & Co., N. Y.—$2.50.
Negro Folk Songs—John and Allan Lomax—Macmillan Co., N. Y.—$3.00.
Folk Songs of Mississippi—Arthur Hudson, University of North Carolina Press—$5.00.
Rolling Along in Song—ed. by Rosamond Johnson—Viking Press, N. Y.—$3.50.
Negro Art: *Past and Present*—Alain Locke, Associates in Negro Folk Education, Washington, D. C.—25 cents.

* * *

SOCIOLOGY, BIOGRAPHY & RACE RELATIONS:

Alien Americans—B. Schrieke—Viking Press, N. Y.—$2.50.
A Preface to Racial Understanding—Charles S. Johnson —Friendship Press, $1.00.
Preface to Peasantry—Arthur Raper—University of North Carolina Press—$3.50.
The Story of the American Negro—Corinne Brown—Friendship Press—$1.00.
Twelve Negro Americans—Mary Jenness — Friendship Press—$1.00—paper—60 cents.
Paul Laurence Dunbar—Benjamin G. Brawley—University of North Carolina Press—$1.00.
From Harlem to the Rhine: *Story of New York's Colored Volunteers*—Arthur W. Little—Covici-Friede, N. Y.—$3.00.
The French Quarter—Herbert Asbury—Alfred Knopf, Inc., N. Y.—$3.50.
My Great Wide Beautiful World—Juanita Harrison—Macmillan Co., N. Y.—$2.50.
God in a Rolls Royce—John Horsher—Hilman-Curl, N. Y.—$2.50.

* * *

ECONOMICS, POLITICS and COLONIAL PROBLEMS:

The Negro As Capitalist—Abram Harris, American Academy of Political and Social Science, Phila.—$3.00.
The Negro Labor Unionist of New York—Charles Franklin—University of Columbia Press, N. Y.—$3.75.
The Negro Question in the United States—J. S. Allen—International Publishers, N. Y.—$2.00.
A World View of Race—Ralph J. Bunche—Associates in Negro Folk Education, Washington, D. C.—25 cents.
Out of Africa—Emory Ross—Friendship Press, N. Y.—$1.00.
How Britain Rules Africa—George Padmore, Lathrop-Lee & Shepard, N. Y.—$3.50.
Haiti and Her Problems—Dantes Bellegarde—University of Porto Rico Press.
Negroes and the Law—Fitzhugh Styles — Christopher Press, Boston—$3.50.
Pro-Slavery Thought of the Old South—William Sumner Jenkins—University of North Carolina Press—$2.50.
The Negro School Curriculum: *A Symposium* — July issue—Journal of Negro Education, Washington, D. C.
Adult Education Among Negroes—Ira DeA. Reid—Associates in Negro Folk Education—25 cents.

* * *

AFRICANA:

The Gentle Savage—Richard Wyndham—Wm. Morrow & Co., N. Y.—$2.75.
Journey Without Maps—Graham Greene.
Civilizations of the Negro: Part III, of Murchison's *Handbook of Social Psychology* — Clark University Press, $6.00.

Of Negro literature and art Dr. Locke speaks with authority. This is the eighth article on Contemporary Literature of the Negro written for "Opportunity" by the urbane professor of philosophy at Howard University. These articles have appeared each year since 1929 except the year 1930.

TRUTH may be stranger than fiction, but fiction is certainly more confusing than reality. And especially so, the modern fiction of the South, which means, in large part, the fiction of Negro life; since the Negro is almost the pet obsession of the Southern novelist. Once, however, it was a solid South, fictionally speaking, and a stereotyped Negro. Now the pendulum has swung to another bad extreme: one is bewildered by the contradictions of the divergent interpretations and must agonize over the problem "Which South" and "What Negro"! Every author almost has his "private South," and in desperation, one is forced to say: "God save Reality!", since the writers can't.

The publishers' blurb for Minnie Hite Moody's *Death Is a Little Man* says: "you will not find here the depraved South of *God's Little Acre* or *Tobacco Road;* not the soft, aristocratic South of *So Red the Rose,* nor the labor-troubled South of *A Sign for Cain.* Neither the mumbo-jumbo of *Stars Fell on Alabama* nor the sinister mob-rule of *Deep Dark River* have been set down here for your entertainment. This is just a tender, heartfelt story of simple people!" All of which is more than half true. But it is not true, as they continue to assure, that its reading "will do no more than make you glad you've read it"; and not from any defect of the book, which is a carefully observed, convincingly told story, but from the fact that again the South is a burning issue, and there are only two ways of reacting to it. There are the novels that condone and those that condemn; emotional neutrality is almost impossible.

There are, of course, degrees of attitude on both sides. *Death Is a Little Man* condones subtly, perhaps regretfully,—but condones just the same. But it should be read; it is far from being a mere white man's picture of the Negro. Ernie's life in the typical Shantytown "Bottoms" is vividly pictured; her trials, marital and otherwise, are well portrayed, we aver, her husband's temptations and persecutions are carefully documented; the moods are correct; considering the level of life the book reports, it is a true document of the outward action of Negro life and of its articulate speech, all that an outsider can hear. But of the private thought, and even Mrs. Moody's Negroes have it,—half of it subconscious and the rest slyly suppressed beneath their conventional servility,—of that, not a word. But where is the blame? With not a single sustained serious piece of fiction by a Negro author in this year's list, I think it is too easy a way out to blame white authorship for not reporting what it does not, cannot hear. Mrs. Moody guesses at some of it intuitively, but she catches only swaggering fatalism for the men, Christian resignation for the women;—which again is the half truth or a fraction over. But the rest! That part of the question is up to the Negro novelist in a day when the Negro cannot complain that he is a victim of literary neglect. We strain our ears and wait.

Moreover, although the trend in contemporary Southern fiction is to admit the inextricable tangle of white and black lives in the Southern scheme, it is not to be expected, either on moral or literary grounds, that the Negro character should always receive specialized attention. For this reason I have not listed as fiction of the Negro the year's two most sensational Southern novels: Margaret Mitchell's *Gone With the Wind* or William Faulkner's *Absolom, Absolom,* for all their importance, sectional as well as racial. Mammy is far from a stock or minor character in this best seller of Secession apologetics; and the half-wit mulatto son of Faulkner's Quixotic hero, Colonel Sutpen, is after all the living symbol of Faulkner's morbid and satirical obituary of the "Old Regime." The one manages her mistress by the age-old Negro subtlety of flattering servility; the other stands as the futile indictment of miscegenation. But after all, the tragedy is on both sides and for the general reading public, it is the South, not the Negro that matters. However, how is that public divided: hundreds of thousands of copies for the sentimental, nostalgic resurrection of historical ghosts; and only thousands for the revealing, but tedious surgery of Faulkner's post-mortem. However no amount of romancing will conceal the fact that the old South is dead; and whoever must know why it died, must have read *Sanctuary, Light in August* and now *Absolom, Absolom.*

The popular verdict may be with the condoning apologists (and this classification does not impugn motives, in fact admits that much which affects the public this way originates less harmfully as escapist day-dreaming), but the literary verdict, and this year's weight of numbers, is for those who criticize and by implication condemn.

We can take them in order of degree. Theodore Pratt's *Big Blow* is a melodrama of love and social antagonisms in Florida. Its real achievement is the fearless realism of its portrayal of white "cracker" low-life, showing its common denominators with the black peasant life surrounding it, Holy Roller revivals, barbecues and all. But Wade Barrett's love of Celie brings him into the snares of the community's prejudice, and the symbolic "Big Blow" is a hurricane that pens Wade, Celie and the fear-stricken Negro they have saved from a lynching party in a shack with a social as well as an atmospheric storm over their heads. This story is good melodrama, good sociology, and entertaining prose.

Better still, in literary and social values is Hamilton Basso's *Courthouse Square*. It too is a drama of the chronic feud of race in Southern life; with a white victim (as is frequent now in contemporary Southern fiction). The third generation of Southern liberals, David Barondess seeks a haven after a disillusioning life in the North in his ancestral and typical Southern town. He and his father espouse the cause of an enterprising Negro physician struggling to found a hospital sanitorium for his people. The antagonisms of property owners, politicians and a newspaper editor kindle the "poor whites" to mob action, the Negro section is attacked, the hospital burned and, in saving the Negro physician from their fury, David is felled, seriously beaten and wounded, in Macedon's Courthouse Square. This is really a contribution to Southern fiction, not because it pleads the Negro cause, but because it turns an accurately focussed wide-angle lens on the contemporary Southern scene. Incidentally, it is beautifully written.

Duplicating another native Alabamian's feat (Clement Wood's precedent-breaking novel of fifteen years ago), James Saxon Childers writes *"A Novel about a White Man and a Black Man in the Deep South."* It is a breathtaking title, and a breathtaking story: if just a little less tense and didactic, it would be a classic. But that is pardonable, if one considers what Southern Medes and Persians this story defies. Gordon Nicholson of a prominent Birmingham family becomes the college friend of Dave Gordon, Negro fellow student, at a Northern college. After interludes typical of their generation, the World War in France for one, Harlem professional life for the other, they meet again in Birmingham, and continue their friendship on the plane of what the orthodox South calls "social equality," but what is to them and a few understanding liberals, common interests. One is avocationally an author, the other a composer; after workaday journalism and college teaching they exchange confidences and aspirations in stimulating companionship. Whisperings, mutterings, threats, then violence spell out the rising crescendo of reactionary Birmingham's indignation, but they fight out their hazardous friendship, to the costly tune of Gordon's social connections, Anne, his sister's broken engagement, Dave's narrow escape through Gordon and a liberal lawyer friend's loyalty from a framed up charge of arson. Finally, at the point of moral victory, fate steps in with the suicide of Anne, too weak to stand the community pressure. They stick out this tragic Southern Ophelia's funeral, write each other consoling letters, but at the end the shadow of it all accumulatively falls between them and they stoically realize the cost and drift apart. This sounds defeatist, but the reactions of the main characters, especially Gordon's frequent rhetorical challenges and protests, puts the moral defeat elsewhere, and where, most readers will agree, it belongs. Falling just short of being a classic of style, Mr. Childers' novel is a classic of human insight and courageous social analysis. It is unmistakeable evidence of the new leaven in the old Southern lump.

Turning from the fiction of the "Black Belt" to that of the "Dark Continent," we find two significant indictments. Grace Flandrau goes back to her familiar Congo for nine psychological studies of white men's lives in Central Africa; and the upshot of all the tragic complications registers a moral verdict: defeat for political and economic and human exploitation, success for scientific research and truly humanitarian effort. Miss Flandrau never set out to defend such a thesis, which makes her reporting all the more convincing; but the colonial administrators, adventurers and other parasites of the colonial system do come to naught (truth telling observers have said so since the days of Joesph Conrad), and in that sense the jungle conquers and has the last laugh. Her explorers and medical research characters, however, finally "come through" to the mutual gain of black and white. It is indeed strange the way in which, even in fiction, the truth will out. Finally, Joyce Cary, veteran of the British Nigerian civil service, but Irish by birth, tells an amazing true story of witchcraft in *"The African Witch."* For seeing beneath the surface of African life, Mr. Cary has at last understood witchcraft as Africa's system of mass control, and chronicles the shrewd, vindictive victory of the juju priestess, Elizabeth Aladai over the white colony, her Caucasian loving brother, who had been to Oxford, the intriguing courtiers of the Emir who would not have her brother for the chieftain's successor, and the people themselves whose force she ruthlessly used. I stressed Mr. Cary's ancestry; nothing short of Irish intuition could have discovered what has escaped so many British eyes and ears, and only Irish irony could tolerate Africa's last laugh at all, for Aladai comes in between Colonel Rackham and Jude, his fiancee, between Louis Aladai and his ambition to mix white and black civilization, and even between Elizabeth and her own ambition to make her brother rule. Not that futility is the last word about Africa; but that the beginning in important African fiction must be honesty and penetration; and that Mr. Cary eminently has.

Turning to poetry, once the Negro literary stronghold, we find most of our poets versifying; and that in these days means the condoning school of thought or its near neighbor, the escapist mode of compensation. Miss Marion Cuthbert, who atones somewhat later by a well edited and readable racial anthology for young people, *We Sing America,* in her volume of original poems, *April Grasses* is as typically in the vein of minor lyricism as the title suggests. A just critic, without being too arbitrary, would have to insist on one of two turns for these versifiers, either that they should put more of the honest-to-goodness substance of life into their work or write and rewrite until their lyrics become technically mature. The same applies to another fragile, anaemic volume of verse *No Alabaster Box and Other Poems* by "Eve Lynn." Her sponsor boasts "that not once does she refer to the peculiar problems of her own group" (she does in one or two places, just the same)—but adds that "hers is a heart that transcends the narrow bonds of race and seeks to encompass that mysterious realm of "love ye one another," by which I infer, he means "the universal." Downright fine, if the poet in question does succeed in reaching the universal. But to escape the narrow bonds of race and shoal on the flats of minor poetry, that is the thrice repeated tragedy of this school of Negro literary escapism. One wonders when some tide of actuality will rise high enough to sweep some of these poets across their Tennysonian sand-bars.

Stanley Braithwaite is a happier sponsor of Mae Cowdery's *"Lift Our Voices,"* although some of her poetry, too, is tangled in not too congruous or vital imagery and merely precipitates personal love lyricism when the poetic fish come to market. Garden pools, spring clouds, and summer clover are all too frequent. But Miss Cowdery, who has always had real poetic possibilities, gathers her talents to a real focus in places, especially her title poem with its:

"Beat out the brazen brass of the sun
Give us sharp pointed stars
To cleanse our hands of your cowardly clay,
Shut out the brazen music of patriot bands,
Give us the soft humming of rain
To soothe our weary ears. . . .
O Liberty, you have been a vow too long! . . . .

* * *

We cannot build our dreams
Into strong towers of reality
On your faltering foundations—
We cannot let our thoughts run free
In a sluggish pool of prejudice!

* * *

We must clear this humid air
Of vows and promises never kept,
Of fear and false confidence,
That we may fill the lungs
Of our young with the cold wind,
The clear pure wind of courage!

* * *

O audience
So unaware of our music,
We are a symphony reaching the final movement,—
Fortissimo!"

The fortissimo Miss Cowdery heralds, comes thundering in, gusty, lusty and not too clear throated in the poetry of a so-called proletarian poet like Willard Wright, whose poems in *The American Caravan* are doubly significant:—of a new strain in Negro poetry and a slow maturing of one of our really vital poetic talents. Willard Wright faces crude reality and dares to try to render it poetically, which is the contemporary poet's real job; in time it will ring more clearly and artistically.

Across the water, and a literary generation removed, Rene Maran, still faithful to his poetic master, Henri de Regnier, brings out his fourth,—a slender volume of poems, *Belles Images.* Not exactly happy images, but crystal clear in their observation of life and sharpened by a skillful style to a poetic focus. For one who has come to grips with reality in a masterful way as in *Batouala* and *The Book of the Jungle,* these diversions are warrantable, and our ambitious stylists should be sentenced to read them. In fact —(to continue this year's curtain-lecture mood), what seems to me primarily wrong with our younger poets is that they haven't read enough of the great poetry that has preceded them. It would silence some, and reform others. One book that they—and all others should read, now that it is cheaply available in English, is the collected work of Alexander Pushkin. In spite of the fault finding with the translation by those more competent than I to judge, it is a great satisfaction, human and racial, to have this master's work handily available. There is no other way, at second hand, to realize what this literary colossus meant to Russian literature and what, today, at his centenary, he means to world literature. No one expects another Pushkin to rise soon, here or elsewhere, but he has a message for today's writers; one of penetrating insight into life, realistic courage, love and understanding of folk materials, ability to criticize without hate, power to reduce a mood to potent symbols.

Drama we must treat impressionistically, mainly because less than half of the increasing activity in the drama of Negro life is available to the reader in printed form. But without its consideration, a picture of contemporary culture as it relates to racial interests would be impossible. Outstanding above all else is the great momentum that the Federal Art and Drama projects have given to Negro talent, both in the field of interpretation and creative writing. Freedom from box-office risks and anticipated indifference, the development for the first time of sound group organization promise a chance for Negro art and artists such as they have never before enjoyed. Next outstanding is the anxious and for the moment not too productive attempt of the radical or revolutionary Theatre to follow up its strike hit of *Stevedore* with Negro plays of social analysis and criticism. They have made a good beginning under the auspices of the New Theatre League, but even they would scarcely claim it to be more than a beginning. Intimate technical acquaintance with the theatre has been the Negro playwright's chief handicap and the Federal projects in New York and many other centers promise to remedy that.

The Gilpin players have presented *When the Jack Hollers*, a pioneering attempt at satire and farce by Langston Hughes and Arna Bontemps, and the Hedgerow Theatre has made another beginning in middle class drama of Negro life in presenting *One Way to Heaven* dramatized from Countee Cullen's novel by the author and Mr. Bontemps as collaborator. The New Theatre League prize plays are nest eggs of the radical theatre. No one doubts their ultimate purpose or the desirability of turning the Negro problem play to vital account. But they hardly more than lay a foundation for this vital dramatic future. Mrs. Ware's ground breaking of the share-cropper situation is welcome though not smashingly dramatic; *Trouble With the Angels*, the revolt of the Green Pastures' cast, is too anecdotal to fully develop its implications, and *Angelo Jones* is too obviously dramatized propaganda. Yet, these are good beginnings. Far beyond that stage, though yet short of maturity, has been the considerable repertory of the *Lafayette Theatre Federal Drama Unit*. Next to their phenomenal *Macbeth*, which was a revelation of what fresh and daring adaptation can do, when supported by such acting as Eric Burroughs in Hecate and the general ensemble gave, must be rated *Turpentine*, a labor drama of the Carolina log camps. More than any play of the New Theatre group, this drama brought the thesis of labor and class struggle dramatically to life. *Walk Together Chillun*, in spite of one or two vital characters, was not sufficiently convincing of its theme; the feud of religious and secular leadership in the Negro community; and the W.P.A. version of *Noah* was little more than an experiment in staging and mechanical stage effects; a good apprenticeship experience, however. On Broadway, Sam Byrd's stage presentation of *White Man*, (reviewed last year), proved this reviewer's contention as to the unconvincing character of its denouement. Finally, with tremendous significance, *Bassa Moona*, first project of the *African Dance Unit*, follows the promising trail of *Kykunkor*—with an African plot, setting, chants, dances and special drum orchestra music. *Macbeth* and *Bassa Moona* point the lesson of success by the pathway of originality and raciness as over against the dead hand of imitation, propaganda and the set formula.

The literary phenomenon of the year is the sudden simultaneous appearance of seven publications on Negro music. Negro music has been rising to spectacular dominance in American and world music;—that we have known for a long time. But suddenly we seem to have become aware of the need for a critical stock-taking. Fortunately most of these critical and historical appraisals are the careful work of experts. Maud Cuney Hare, who devoted a lifetime to the defense of serious Negro music by lecture recitals with Theodore Richardson, gathered industriously a remarkable volume of information, critical and historical, about Negro music and musicians. She lived to see the manuscript on its way to publication, and it was completed, with an appendix on African music, by Dr. Woodson, her publisher. The book is indispensable to the serious student of Negro music. It is written, however, with a pronounced bias against jazz and popular music in general, and with what the writer believes a false conception of an antithesis between folk forms and art forms in music. From the opposite point of view, I have written, in the new series of *Bronze Booklets*, sponsored by the *Associates in Negro Folk Education*, of Washington, D. C., a critical analysis of Negro music, about which it is only appropriate to say that it was independently written. The two schools of thought on this question thus come forward simultaneously to the benefit—or confusion, of the interested reader.

The folkists and folk-lorists in this field seem to have conspired; four studies of Negro popular music surge at the reader. Hughes Panassie's monumental analysis of jazz, known for several years to specialists who have followed the serious European literature of the subject, has at last been adequately translated—a hard task: since like other European critics, Panassie takes his jazz as seriously and critically as one traditionally takes Bach. For the layman, there is the infinitely easier but authoritatively competent narrative of Louis Armstrong; who justifies his admirers by a remarkable demonstration of modest simplicity and sanity in his story of "how he grew up with jazz" and how jazz "went wrong" on Tin Pan Alley before the vogue of "Swing" and pure Negro idiom brought it back to its original folk spontaneity. His geuss is that "swing is America's second big bid to bring forth a worthwhile music of its own." Let us hope Louis is as good a prophet as he is a musician!

On the trail of American folk songs, the Lomax brothers have been the most indefatigable and successful hunters. This time they have found a folk bard, by the not too encouraging name of "Lead Belly" and have documented the living reality, music, words, commentary and all. Such research should have been made before the older generation died off; but since it wasn't, we must be grateful to the Lomaxes. Professor Hudson, not to be outdone found a certain "Two-time Tommy" in a Mississippi penitentiary, and got another bonanza; as far as folk ballads go, unfortunately without the most vital part,—the music. Recently a Marxian critic has taken the professional folk-lorists to task, saying "the professional collector of Negro folklore simply capitalizes upon the artificial peculiarities of a group kept in systematic impoverishment and ignorance. Minstrelsy was originally a definite expression of the Southern land-owners, who defended slavery by adorning it with the mellifluous phrases of Stephen Foster and Daniel Emmett." I presume that he would not altogether approve either of "Lead Belly" or "Two-Time Tommy," and many readers will agree, most of the latter without reading these three and five dollar volumes. However with Soviet Russia spending millions of roubles on folk-song and folk-lore collection for its many minorities, one anxiousy awaits the opening of the Marxian counter-offensive in folklore: Mr. Gellert made a good start a year or so ago. Only one thing is certain: folk-life is basic and precious, and no good Marxian can deny that. A comprehensive anthology of Negro songs of all types has been announced by the Viking Press, edited by the quite experienced hand of Rosamond Johnson. A companion volume to *The Negro and His Music, Negro Art: Past and Present* has been written for the Bronze Booklet series by the writer.

We began with the cry: God Save Reality! In the confusion of the critics and the partisanships of the artistic creeds and camps, perhaps we should have said, in the 18th Century phrase: "God save the Gentle Reader."

God Save Reality! « « « « «

Part II. Retrospective Review of the Literature of the Negro: 1936

• By ALAIN LOCKE

ADDENDA TO BIBLIOGRAPHY OF LITERATURE OF THE NEGRO: 1936

Minty Alley—A Novel—C. L. R. James, Martin, Secker & Warburg, London, 7/6.

Toussaint Louverture—A Play—in Life and Letters Today, London.

The Black Laws of Virginia—June P. Guild, Whittet & & Shepperson, Richmond, Va.

The Negro in the Philadelphia Press—George E. Simpson, University of Pennsylvania Press, $2.00.

Opportunities for Medical Education of Negroes—E. H. L. Corwin & G. E. Strugees. Charles Scribners, N. Y., $1.50.

The Moveable School Comes to The Negro Farmer—T. M. Campbell, Tuskegee Press, Ala.

THE layman will doubtless not have expected reality from the novelist, poet and dramatist, but will expect it of the economist and sociologist. But I, for my part, would rather take my chance with the fraternity of re-creative insight and imagination than with the professedly objective analysts and reporters. For they, like philosophers, idolize their "isms" while pretending to worship "fact"—(only,— philosophers don't always pretend), and at their worst, are like downright social theologians, peddling their pet panaceas for society's final and everlasting salvation. A critic's job, as I see it, with this increasingly controversial and competitive situation, is to tag and label as properly and fairly as he can and let the public buy and eat, each to his own pocketbook and taste. And so, by their schools, we shall know them.

Speaking of schools of economics and sociology, however, it is pathetically interesting to note how many otherwise intelligent people approach the Negro question with hopelessly antiquated categories. They only half realize that Booker T. Washington is long since dead, and would undoubtedly have changed tactics in the shifting issues of our times, as his professed followers have not, and do not seem to comprehend that Dr. Du Bois has left a deftly moulted skin occupying his traditional position and is nesting in quite another. And to me, it seems their primary motivation is their own mental comfort,—for the changes are too obvious for open eyes to overlook. Fortunately—(or unfortunately for the "comfortables-at-all-costs"), we have today not only an amazing gamut of positions, a rich variety of schools of interpretation but, most important of all, ever lessening of the old fallacy of trying to have a special yardstick for the Negro problem and a separate formulae for its solution apart from the basic general problems of our contemporary society. Even for those who reject it—(or them, since the Marxist positions are so sub-divided), the class theory must be credited at least with this fundamental gain,—that it carries through a 'sauce for the goose, sauce for the gander' analysis and links the Negro question into the general scheme and condition of society. But this year's literature of the social aspects of Negro life ranges through almost the whole spectrum of possible views; strict Communist interpretations, the Communist opposition, a revised Marxist interpretation, several non-Marxist but modernistic economic and anthropological analyses, two schools of economics,—the traditional and the institutionalist, studies of the race question from the labor unionist angle, Y.W.C.A. and Methodist church humanitarian liberalism, orthodox and liberal imperialism, and the now professionalized gradualism of the missionaristic-philanthropic approach, which is the contemporary survival of the Hampton-Tuskegee school of thought. Hardly a notch is missing, unless it be the C.I.O. craft-union labor philosophy, which has its important conception of the industrial and economic problems of the black laborer. Here, then, they string themselves out for the wisely critical reader to window-shop through the whole display or for the impatiently practical to get the right-size sociological hat or an economic shoe to fit, with perhaps an aesthetic tie and kerchief to match.

Alien Americans, by an eminent and experienced Dutch colonial administrator who studied the American race question under the auspices of the Rosenwald Fund, has the advantage of perspective and urbane detachment. It is a good precedent to set,—to discuss American minority problems and attitudes over a common denominator, and Dr. Shrieke discusses the Chinese and the Japanese in the West, the Mexicans in the South and Mid-West, the American Indians, the Filipino and then the bulk of the Negro problem. His conclusion, however, that, even though the product of a traditional and common American policy, there is a progressive slackening of prejudice with education and enlightenment toward the other groups, but a "petrification" of the attitudes toward the Negro, really contradicts, if true, his original assumption that they are the same social phenomenon, only different in degree. Likewise, his essentially economic solution, claiming that "a systematic effort must be made to free the South from its colonial economy" and proposing the "development of a free peasant economy in the rural South" is not in exact alignment with the author's differential diagnosis; nor the statement:—"For anyone who studies southern problems objectively, it is evident that there is an identity of black and white interests. Up till now the plantation legend has impeded the realization of this fact. Will it be otherwise in the future?" In spite of such inconsistencies and its frankly pessimistic turn, Dr. Schrieke's book should be widely read; his graphic and incisive description of the American patterns of racial discrimination has seldom, if ever, been equalled. His account of what he calls the "Great Southern Legend," of the concrete inconsistencies of southern ways and morals, his pointed suggestion that "the black spectre rules the South" all register a high score for the descriptive and analytical side of a most stimulating study. It is perhaps too much to expect, especially from a foreign visitor, equal excellence of diagnosis and proposed remedy.

Under the auspices of the Friendship Press, in a well-intentioned and valuable project of the study of the race question by Methodist church groups, Professor Charles S. Johnson contributes *A Preface to Racial Understanding*. That this book is obviously a primer for the great unenlightened does not excuse Dr. Johnson's equally obvious lapse from the advanced position of last year's book,—*The Collapse of Cotton Tenancy,* to the "coaxing school" of moralistic gradualism and sentimental missionary appeal, especially since these concessions are almost entirely absent from another book in the same series;—Corinne Brown's *Story of the American Negro,* which states the Negro's case with its moral challenges unblunted and its sociological warnings clear. The constructive effect of much painstaking and competent exposition is thus regrettably off-set by such evasive and wheedling gradualism; as reflected in statements like:—"In the field of race relations, it is not so important that there should be envisaged exact solutions, for there will inevitably be differences of opinion . . . it is important that there should be principles guiding these relationships, and that these principles should be high. . . . A sound principle of action, thus could well be: "Respect thy neighbor as thyself, even if thou canst not love him, and do not permit that he or thyself be treated with disrespect." A primer may warrantably be elementary, but it need not slur fundamentals.

Arthur Raper, Field and Research Secretary for the Commission on Interracial Cooperation, gives us a convincing statement of fundamentals in his *Preface to Peasantry,* and with it perhaps a hint as to what Dr. Schrieke specifically meant by his "creation of a free peasant economy in the South." For Mr. Raper, after an intensive survey of typical plantation farm areas, concludes: "With no reasonable hope that an adequate civilization for the majority of the rural dwellers will come either with the rejuvenation or with the collapse of the cotton plantation system, the reclamation of Greene and Macon counties and of much of the cotton South awaits a constructive land policy" . . . a policy enabling "the poorest farmers to build up the soil, to own livestock, to raise vegetables and fruits for their own tables, to cooperate with their fellows in making their purchases and in producing and marketing crops—in short, if it enables landless farmers to attain ownership and self-direction on an adequate plane. Comfortable homes, more doctors, better schools, and wholesome human relations can be maintained only through such basic economic advances. These are not simple matters, and their accomplishment will require the investment of large sums of public money and an administrative personnel with scientific training and a bold faith in the common man." With such thoroughgoing and almost revolutionary specifications, "a free peasant economy" does have a constructive connotation and an attractive challenge as a proposed solution. Mr. Raper's trenchant report of the ways in which the New Deal's agricultural relief measures were thwarted by the traditions and practises of the old regime calls for timely consideration of stringent safeguards for the next steps in the government's agricultural program for the South. Here is a vital book with a modern message; giving added evidence of the way in which the basic and realistic approach to race questions is gaining ground.

Turning aside, however, for a while from the mass aspects of things, we encounter a considerable batch of biography in the literature of the year, with an interesting human sample array of personalities. *Twelve Negro Americans,* by Mary Jenness, is also a Friendship Press book, taking a cross-section view of the Negro social pyramid at an unusual level,—that of social work and uplift projects, calculated to appeal particularly to the missionary aim of the series. These life stories of a leading liberal pastor, a pioneer organizer of cooperatives, a Jeannes school supervisor, the organizer of the Tuskegee farm extension service, several social workers and student and young peoples leaders show both the trends and the typical personalities of an important segment of race leadership. On this level of human interest and appeal, the humanitarian and moralistic notes are not out of place; indeed, have their proper usefulness provided the palliatives of social work and uplift movements are not posed as "ways of solving the race problem," which they are not and cannot be. It is only this implication that detracts from this readable collection of human interest and "success" stories.

Professor Brawley gives us this year a much needed biography of *Paul Laurence Dunbar;* so needed that it may seem ungrateful to mention its limitations. However, it is far more successful as an extended essay of literary criticism than as biography. For a Victorian biography of an only semi-Victorian poet and an entirely un-Victorian personality misses the most vital of all biographical objectives, — the re-creation of a personality. A sugar-coated Dunbar, like a sugar-coated Bobby Burns, may even go further than taking the flavor out of biography, since the dilemmas of the personality had connection with the leading motives in the poetry, it may also take a vital dimension out of the critical analysis and literary interpretation. And for this reason the first biography of Dunbar, welcome though it is, can never take rank as the definitive one.

In *From Harlem to the Rhine,* Colonel Arthur Little elaborately documents the epic story of the New York 15th Regiment in the World War. It is written with candor and obvious devotion, and only misses being a great tribute by the narrow margin of bad dialect reporting and little realization of the irony of the whole venture. As it is, with its concrete vindication of the black soldier and its remarkable tribute to Jim Europe, an important gap in Negro history has been filled in, from an undisputable eye-witness. It is good reading for Negroes, but should be prescribed reading for whites, for it is as ironic comment on American democracy as ever has been or could be written. Another missing chapter of American social history comes clear in Herbert Asbury's history of the New Orleans underworld,—*The French Quarter.* It is racially important in many respects, not merely for the reports of the "Quadroon balls," the voodoo cults of Marie Laveau et al, and the levities of Basin Street: for the whole social history of the South is laid bare in epitome, even though in perhaps its extremest example. And now for two other not too edifying but significant exposures: John Horsher's journalistic expose of George Baker, "Father Divine, styled *"God in a Rolls Royce"* and the naive, self-expose of Juanita Harrison, in her autobiographic travelogue of a trip round the world, called *My Great Wide Beautiful World,* which should be sub-titled The World Through a Mental Chink. Here certainly is biography with the important modern dimension of human psychology, baffling though it is. Page 80 of the biography of Harlem's self-styled "God" quotes a Negro high school graduate with two years' training at Boston University declaring on the court witness stand that "he believes Father Divine is God" and a white stenographer employed by the Board of Child Welfare testifying to the same effect; two instances, we should say, of seriously deluded thousands. But follow the phenomenon to its root in human suffering and social maladjustment, and the secret of these crowd hypnotists is an open one. Follow even the other line of causation to the social trauma that created the powerful over-compensations of these megalomaniacs, and realize that it was a bad day for society when Garvey was snubbed in his Jamaica boyhood for his dark complexion, and likewise, when, as Horsher reports, in his boyhood town of Savannah, George Baker confronted a socially false Christianity in the guise of a Jim Crow church and Sunday School, which he refused to attend, and later when he "was sent to jail for sixty days for riding in that part of a trolley car reserved exclusively for whites."

From such psychological acorns, with strong personalities, powerful movements grow, dangerously irrational in their creed, but dynamically righteous in their spirit and conviction. So what Mr. Horsher reports as a farce conceals a deep human and social tragedy. As to *My Great Wide Beautiful World,* the significance fortunately is only individual: an illiterate carried round the world is at the end of the trip, and in the volume that reports it, an illiterate still. And is so, whether a moronic millionaire or a moronic menial. The latter is more unusual, however: Barnum after all may have been the best American sociologist.

Now to more important subjects:—economics, politics and colonial questions. Professor Abram Harris has added an incisive study, *The Negro as Capitalist,* to his important project of a survey of the economic history of the Negro. Begun in *The Black Worker* as a partial study of the role of Negro labor in the development of modern industrialism, and specifically as "the role of the Negro industrial worker from the end of the Civil War to 1929," Dr. Harris now covers the history of the Negro as capitalist and investor from pre-Civil War days to the early years of the present depression. Taking advantage, however, of his well-known thesis about the plight and prospects of a "black bourgeoisie," which he has always viewed as a helplessly handicapped "effort to gain economic status and social respectability by erecting within the larger framework of capitalism a small world of Negro business enterprise, hoping thereby to develop his own capitalist-employer class and to create employment opportunities for an increasing number of Negroes in the white collar occupations," our author extends his economic study into definite sociological implications. From the comparative failure of Negro banking, which beside Negro insurance, has been the largest scale capitalistic effort of Negroes, he argues the improbability of any successful economic petty capitalism as a secure foundation for a Negro middle class; not so much on grounds of inexperience or incompetency (although plenty of that is revealed by the detailed history of Negro business enterprise and particularly Negro banking), but on the grounds that the large-scale capitalistic organization of American business today makes the success of any small-scale capitalist enterprise difficult and highly improbable. So, though its primary significance is as a very thoroughgoing technical economic study, there are practical and sociological corollaries to Dr. Harris's work that must be given serious consideration. His concluding chapter on the "Plight of the Negro Middle Class" would probably be borne out by an equally competent analysis of Negro insurance and retail store enterprise, but caution requires the statement that these conclusions are based mainly on an analysis of Negro banking, taken, however, as a sample.

Charles L. Franklin has written on the crucial subject of the labor front a clear factual analysis and history of the Negro worker of New York City in relation to labor union membership and organization. In spite of substantial improvement in the total numbers of Negroes in labor union affiliation, Dr. Franklin's figures show that Negro membership in unions of the highly skilled workers is negligible and that Negroes constitute a higher proportion in the membership of independent unions than in affiliates of the American Federation of Labor. He finds also that in Manhattan a pre- and post-N.R.A. survey reveals sudden increase in the disposition of Negro labor to organize, as between 3.8 per cent before 1928 and 9.3 per cent with a total unionization quota of 39,574 at present estimate; showing some creditable and significant gains for this period. Such a study needs either to be duplicated for other important industrial centers or made on a national scale, in which case the industrial profile of the Negro can be determined on this all important question of differential occupations labor union affiliation, with opportunity then to compare the policies of the craft and the industrial unions, and labor trends.

In *The Negro Question* by J. S. Allen, we have the most rigid but at the same time most rigorous Marxian analysis of the American Negro's situation yet written. It redefines the Black Belt in close but commendably lucid statistics and proves the persistence of the plantation system in a large area of the United States which includes millions of blacks and whites in what it justly calls "semi-feudal conditions of semi-slavery," since under the prevailing conditions of farm tenancy and share cropping not only is there a sub-American standard of living but the system of wage labor has never there become the basis of the economic structure of the region. A South thus X-rayed to its economic bones is a startling and challenging revelation: no polemic dust in the air can long obscure such facts. Mr. Allen then applies the Communist formula to this situation with results equally startling and challenging; with his greatest dilemma, of course, the issue between the economic common denominator theory of the proletariat and the politico-cultural formula of self-determination and cultural autonomy for oppressed minorities or in this case, the "oppressed majority"—(50.3 being the latest census figure of the ratio of the Negro population of this Black Belt area and it being 40 per cent of the total Negro population or roughly five millions). He decides for the latter, not without careful consideration of the arguments for and against; especially the Norman Thomas criticism that self-determination is impossible under capitalism and unnecessary under socialism. Anti-Communists should read *The Negro Question,* not so much to agree or be converted, as to realize what alternatives social medicine must experimentally face and try before conceding the desperate measures of social surgery. That the plantation system is economic cancer is something that all can afford to learn and agree upon.

In the international perspectives of the race question, there is also increasing realism of analysis and here and there, increasing radicalism of suggested remedy. Emory Ross paints a sober picture in *Out of Africa,* which never could have come out of the missionary movement a decade ago; it is tantamount to an admission of an unholy alliance of the church with imperialism and a warning of the complete incompatability of the two programs. Similarly, but much more radically, George Padmore presents a detailed indictment and expose of the procedures and techniques of contemporary imperialistic exploitation in *"How Britain Rules Africa,"* ending with the realistic conclusion that "the British and the French empires are colored empires, since Africans, Arabs, Egyptians, Indo-Chinese, Hindus, etc., form the overwhelming majority of their populations . . . and neither England nor France can face another European crisis without the military and economic support of the colonial peoples." In a more dispassionate and urbane vein, Dantes Bellegarde, the esteemed former Haitian Minister to this country, discusses in four lectures delivered at the University of Porto Rico, *Haiti and Her Problems,* indeed in the concluding lecture, the whole frame-work of Latin American relations. His formula, as might be expected, is international liberalism, trade agreements and honest diplomacy. Finally, Professor Bunche has written for the Negro Folk Education series a very readable digest of the latest scientific and political theories of race, relating them to the issues of modern imperialism and the racial aspects of colonial policy. It is Dr. Bunche's contention, however, that the primary objectives of imperialism are economic consequences of capitalistic expansion, and that race policies and attitudes are their *ex post facto* rationalizations. For the same series, Professor Ira Reid has written a manual of adult education principles and techniques for the use of adult education group executives and teachers, stating the specific objectives and experience to date of the adult education movement among Negroes.

Especially because there is a considerable list of *Addenda,* space scarcely permits further detailed mention, except of the thought provoking issue of the *Journal of Negro Education* on the *Negro School Curriculum* and the most competent and enlightening section on *West African Civilization of the Negro* by Professor Melville Herskovits. The additions reveal a West Indian novelist and playwright of considerable power and much promise, C.L.R. James, author of *Minty Alley,* a realistic novel of Jamaica city life and a full length *Toussaint Louverture,* scheduled for performance by the London Stage Society. In Part I, Richard Wright was inadvertently referred to as Willard Wright and John and Allan Lomax, father and son, as the "Lomax brothers."

Jingo, Counter-Jingo and Us » » »

PART I. Retrospective Review of the Literature of the Negro: 1937

● By ALAIN LOCKE

Biography of Literature of the Negro: 1937

FICTION:

Us Three Women—Roger Wiley & Helen Wood, Penn Publishing Co., $2.00

Jordanstown—Josephine Johnson, Simon & Schuster, N. Y., $2.00

Night at Hogwallow—Theodore Strauss, Little, Brown & Co., Boston, $1.25

Children of Strangers—Lyle Saxon, Houghton Mifflin Co., Boston, $2.50

River George—George W. Lee, Macaulay Co., N. Y., $2.00

Sad Faced Boy—Arna Bontemps, Houghton Mifflin Co., Boston, $2.00

Their Eyes Were Watching God—Zora Neale Hurston, J. B. Lippincott, Philadelphia, $2.00

These Low Grounds—Waters Edward Turpin, Harper & Bros., N. Y., $2.50

Big Boy Leaves Home—Richard Wright, in 1936 New Caravan: W. W. Norton, N. Y. $3.95

The Ethics of Living Jim Crow—Richard Wright in *American Stuff*, Viking Press, N. Y., $2.00

* * *

POETRY AND BELLES LETTRES:

I Am the American Negro—Frank Marshall Davis, Black Cat Publishing Co., Chicago, $1.50

Sterling Brown, Claude McKay and others in *American Stuff*—edited by Henry Alsberg.

Anthology of Negro Poetry—B. Wormley & C. Carter, New Jersey WPA Project.

From the Deep South—edited by Marcus B. Christian, Privately printed, New Orleans.

The Negro Genius—Benjamin Brawley, Dodd, Mead & Co., N. Y., $2.50

Negro Poetry and Drama—Sterling Brown, Bronze Booklet No. 7—Associates in Negro Folk Education, Washington, D. C., 25c.

The Negro in American Fiction—Sterling Brown, Bronze Booklet No. 6, 25c.

Rolling Along in Song—J. Rosamond Johnson, Viking Press, N. Y., $3.50

* * *

BIOGRAPHY:

A Long Way From Home—Claude McKay, Lee Furman, Inc., N. Y., $3.00

Let Me Live — Angelo Herndon, Random House, N. Y., $2.50

Pushkin—Ernest J. Simmons, Harvard University Press, $4.00

Negro Builders and Heroes — Benjamin Brawley, University of North Carolina Press, $2.50

The Incredible Messiah—Robert Allerton Parker, Little, Brown & Co., Boston, $2.50

DRAMA:

How Come Lawd—Donald Heywood, The Negro Theatre Guild, N. Y.

The Case of Philip Lawrence—adapted by Gus Smith Federal Theatre Project, New York

The Trial of Dr. Beck—Hughes Allison, Federal Theatre Project, Newark, New Jersey

Jute—Kathleen Critherspoon, Morgan College Players.

* * *

SOCIOLOGY AND RACE RELATIONS:

Half-Caste—Cedric Dover, Martin Secker & Warburg, London—10s 6d.

Our Racial and National Minorities—Brown & Roucek, Prentice-Hall, Inc., N. Y., $5.00

Caste and Class in a Southern Town, John Dollard, Yale University Press, $3.50

The Etiquette of Race Relations in the South—Bertram Wilbur Doyle, University of Chicago Press, $2.50

The Negro's Struggle for Survival—S. J. Holmes, University of California Press, $3.00

Interracial Justice—John LaFarge, America Press, N. Y., $2.00

The Negroes in a Soviet America—J. W. Ford & J. S. Allen, Workers' Library, N. Y.

Reconstruction—James S. Allen, International Publishers, N. Y., $2.00

The Negro in Washington in "Washington: American Guide Series." Federal Writers Project. $3.00

The Negro and Economic Reconstruction—T. Arnold Hill. Bronze Booklet No. 5. 25c.

Negro History in Outline—Arthur A. Schomburg, Bronze Booklet No. 8. Associates in Negro Folk Education, Washington, D. C. 25c.

Negro Year Book—edited by Monroe N. Work. Tuskegee Institute Press. $2.00

* * *

ANTHROPOLOGY AND AFRICANA:

Life in a Haitian Valley—Melville J. Herskovits, Alfred A. Knopf, Inc., N. Y., $4.00

Suriname Folk Lore—Melville J. and Frances Herskovits, Columbia University Press. $5.00

Introduction to African Civilizations—Willis N. Huggins and John G. Jackson, Avon House, N. Y., $2.50

The Savage Hits Back—Julius Lips, Yale University Press, $5.00

Africa Answers Back—Akiki Nyabongo, Routledge & Sons, London—7s 6d

Stone Age Africa—L. S. B. Leakey, Oxford University Press, London, $2.75

Prehistoric Rock Pictures in Europe and Africa—Leo Frobenius and Douglas Fox, Museum of Modern Art, N. Y., $2.00

Reaction to Conquest—Monica Hunter, Oxford University Press, $10.00

Race Attitudes in South Africa—I. D. MacCrone, Oxford University Press, $4.25

Out of Africa—F. G. Carnochan and H. C. Adams, Dodge Publishing Co., $2.75

This is the ninth article on Contemporary Literature of the Negro written for "Opportunity" by the professor of philosophy at Howard University, who speaks of Negro literature and art with authority. These articles have appeared each year since 1929 except the year 1930.

THE literature of the year, both by Negro and white authors, still continues to be racially tinged, some of it pro, some of it anti, little or none of it objective enough to be called "neutral." And yet some of it, for all that, is healthy and sane and true enough to be called art rather than propaganda and science rather than polemic or partisan jingo. Jingo is a touchy word since the caustic but stimulating article of Mr. Benjamin Stolberg on "Minority Jingo" in the *Nation,* (October 23). Neverthe--less let's consider, by way of an aperitif, jingo, counter-jingo and "us" ; us meaning Negro.

Like Mr. Stolberg, I also say: "Good Lord, deliver us from jingo!"—But unlike him, yet like a philosopher, I must begin with the beginning. And 'minority jingo' isn't the beginning, and so, not the root of the evil, evil though it may be. Minority-jingo is counter-jingo; the real jingo is majority jingo and there lies the original sin. Minority jingo is the defensive reaction, sadly inevitable as an antidote, and even science has had to learn to fight poison with poison. However, for cure or compensation, it must be the right poison and in the right amount. And just as sure as revolution is successful treason and treason is unsuccessful revolution, minority jingo is good when it succeeds in offsetting either the effects or the habits of majority jingo and bad when it re-infects the minority with the majority disease. Similarly, while we are on fundamentals, good art is sound and honest propaganda, while obvious and dishonest propaganda are bad art. Thus, I think, we must not load all the onus (and ridicule) upon the pathetic compensations of the harrassed minority, though I grant it is a real disservice not to chastise both unsound and ineffective counter-argument. The Negro has a right to state his side of the case (or even to have it stated for him), as for example in Professor Lips' *The Savage Hits Back* and Melville Hershkovits' *Life in a Haitian Valley,* antidotal to reams of falsification like Seabrook's *Magic Island,* or Erskine Caldwell's *You Have Seen Their Faces* poking out its realistic tongue at *Gone With the Wind* and *So Red the Rose.* But some of these counter-arguments have the racial angle and are interested in the group particularities, (notice I didn't say peculiarities) while another has the class angle and significantly includes the Negro material relevant to that. We must not praise or condemn either because of its point of view but rather because of its accomplishment in terms of its point of view. It happens that in each of these cases there is sound science and good art on the side of the opposition, and much majority jingo is debunked accordingly. The minority is entitled to its racial point of view provided it is soundly and successfully carried through. However, we shall have to take account of volumes a little later,—and some of them by Negro authors, that deserve every inch of Mr. Stolberg's birch.

As I see it, then, there is the chaff and there is the wheat. A Negro, or anyone, who writes African history inaccurately or in distorted perspective should be scorned as a "black chauvinist," but he can also be scotched as a tyro. A minority apologist who overcompensates or turns to quackish demagogery should be exposed, but the front trench of controversy which he allowed to become a dangerous salient must be re-manned with sturdier stuff and saner strategy. Or the racialist to whom group egotism is more precious than truth or who parades in the tawdry trappings of adolescent exhibitionism is, likewise to be silenced and laughed off stage; but that does not invalidate all racialism. There are, in short, sound degrees and varieties of these things, which their extremisms discount and discredit but cannot completely invalidate. I am not defending fanaticism, Nordic or Negro or condoning chauvinism, black or white; nor even calling "stalemate" because the same rot can be discovered in both the majority and the minority baskets.

I merely want to point out that minority expression has its healthy as well as its unhealthy growths, and that the same garden of which jingo and counter-jingo are the vexatious and even dangerous weeds has its wholesome grains and vegetables, its precious fruits and flowers. Selective cultivation, then, rather than wholesale plowing-under or burning over should be the sane order of the day. Transposing back to our main theme, which is literary, this would mean corrective criticism rather than general excommunication, intelligent refereeing instead of ex-cathedra outlawing. For there can be proletarian jingo as well as bourgeois and capitalist jingo and class jingoism as well as the credal and racial varieties.

As for the Negro cause in literature there is a double concern,—we are threatened both by the plague of bad art and the blight of false jingo. And jingo is more deceptive with the gloss of art and more subtly effective with the assumed innocence and disinterest of art. By all means let us be on our guard against both. Mr. Stolberg was performing a much needed critical service, then, in giving a forceful warning against any double standard in criticism, against any soft tolerance of the fallacies and opiates of internal minority chauvinism at the very time when we were making a point of the exposure and discrediting of majority jingoism. It is a matter of keen regret that much of the cultural racialism of the "New Negro" movement was choked in shallow cultural soil by the cheap weeds of group flattery, vainglory and escapist emotionalism. To that extent it was neither sound racialism nor effective and lasting counter-assertion. The first generation of these artists, (1917-1934), were primarily handicapped by having no internal racial support for their art, and as the movement became a fad the taint of exhibitionism and demagogery inevitably crept in. They are not to be excused entirely for having prostituted their wares and their artistic integrity. But a sounder cultural racialism would have avoided these pitfalls, would have aimed at folk realism and the discovery of basic human and social denominators to be thrown under the numerators of racial particularities for a balanced and factorable view of our group life, and in my judgment a second generation of Negro writers and artists, along with their white collaborators, are well on the way toward such a development. Some of them are writers like Langston Hughes, Zora Hurston, Arna Bontemps, Sterling Brown, whose life bridges both generations, while others, like Richard Wright, Waters Turpin, Hughes Allison, Frank Davis belong entirely to the younger generation. Their more penetrating, even-handed and less-illusioned portrayal of Negro life is realizing more deeply the original aims of what was too poetically and glibly styled "The Negro Renaissance." Although in self-extenuation, may I say that as early as 1927 I said:—(Ebony and Topaz: "Our Little Renaissance") —'Remember, the Renaissance was followed by the Reformation.' Another quotation,—if I may:—"The Negro Renaissance must be an integral phase of contemporary American art and literature; more and more we must divorce it in our minds from propaganda and politics . . . the self-expression of the New Negro, if conditions in the South were more conducive to the development of Negro culture without transplanting, would spring up as just one branch of the new literature of the South, and as one additional phase of its cultural reawakening."

This is just what has happened or is happening. Josephine Johnson's *Jordanstown* is in the strict sense not a novel of Negro life, but a novel of the tragedy of labor organization in the sharecropper South; but it is notable for its rare and penetrating perception of the basis of the race problem and the Negro's position in the small town rural areas and for its daring analysis of the integration of Negro and white lives. Similarly Theodore Strauss's *Night at Hogwallow,* which details not only the lynching of an innocent Negro by a labor gang of mixed southerners and northerners but gives a more detailed account of the crowd psychology of the mob than I recall having ever read. It is both good art and good sociology; all the more notable and promising because it is Mr. Strauss's first publication. Mrs. Johnson is a Pulitzer Prize veteran which gives weight and occasionally edge to her laurels. Her sociology, too, is indisputable; she goes as far as balanced realism can go, and gives a vital sense of tragedy over and above the documentation. Incidentally, it is to be noted that most socialistic novels refuse to consider themselves defeatist in the tragic death of their main characters, as in this case of the martyrdom of Adam, the militant labor leader. Why should they? Yet why should tragedy in other contexts invariably raise the hue and cry of "defeatism"?

Defeatism in art is where the issues are unfairly joined, and where the implications, social or psychological, are vicious or mis-representative. Both bad art and poor sociology alike can lead to that. In sinister conjunction they lead to falsity in a novel like *Us Three Women,* for all its profession of detailed documentation of the lives of three Negro women and their southern friends. The book is a deceptive survival of the old Plantation Tradition, which still thrives perniciously and unabashed in Hollywood plots, children's stories and popular romance fiction very generally. However, one is meeting it less and less on the level of serious realistic writing: *Us Three Women* being one of these exceptions.

Two novels, one by a white and the other by a Negro author, although unevenly matched in artistry, go a long way toward proving that the return to the plantation need not be trite or reactionary. Lyle Saxon's *Children of Strangers,* has some sentimental tourists looking on at the crucial scene in Famie's tragic life, taking snap-shots in the assurance that she looks "so typical" and that they are the "happiest people —not a care in the world." This after a lifetime of struggle after her early seduction, her ostracism by her proud Creole relatives, her vain and pathetic sacrifices for her illegitimate son, and the final breach of the law of her land-owning clan that spells her final sacrifice. Even with the romantic touch and the charm of the old tradition, Saxon sacrifices neither truth nor social perspective; and this novel will only seem defeatist to local color tourists on the one hand and fanatical proletarians on the other. With far less artistic power, George Lee's *River George* is yet noteworthy. The flaw probably lies in the too concocted expansion of the legend of River George, so dramatically told in the author's *Beale Street,* who was just a John Henry "bad man" of the slums, into a race-defiant protagonist of the oppressed sharecroppers. So, as other critics have noted, the first half or more of the story runs convincingly and the second not at all. Arty dialogue and sophomoric interlardings contribute to this; but the attempt to over-modernize material out of its tradition is risky. But the Negro novelist, though he needs criticism, needs to be read. He is definitely on his way somewhere. And the average Negro should know what is being written about him; he needs that analytical dimension in his life. Otherwise, his life is the cultural equivalent of living in a house without a mirror.

Part of the Negro novelist's dilemma is his obviously divided public. Few have the courage to write straight across the stereotypes of the whites and the hyper-sensitive susceptibilities of the blacks. And yet in no other way can great writing or a great master emerge. As good an author as Arna Bontemps, for example, writing belligerent and heroic *Black Thunder* (Macmillan—1936),—which by the way was inadvertently and regrettably omitted from our 1936 list, this year writes a children's story which barely escapes from the melon-patch stereotypes. Wistful here and there, in a revamped setting of three little black southern adventurers in Harlem, there is still an unfortunate reversion to type even after all allowances are made for the unrealistic tradition of the child story. Whereas *Black Thunder* was historical fiction of considerable power and decided promise. Even though a highly fictionalized version of an historic slave insurrection, it documented Negro character and motivation in unconventional and all but convention-breaking ways.

And now, Zora Hurston and her magical title: *Their Eyes Were Watching God.* Janie's story should not be re-told; it must be read. But as always thus far with this talented writer, setting and surprising flashes of contemporary folk lore are the main point. Her gift for poetic phrase, for rare dialect and folk humor keep her flashing on the surface of her community and her characters and from diving down deep either to the inner psychology of characterization or to sharp analysis of the social background. It is folklore fiction at its best, which we gratefully accept as an overdue replacement for so much faulty local color fiction about Negroes. But when will the Negro novelist of maturity who knows how to tell a story convincingly,—which is Miss Hurston's cradle-gift, come to grips with motive fiction and social document fiction? Progressive southern fiction has already banished the legend of these entertaining psuedo-primitives whom the reading public still loves to laugh with, weep over and envy. Having gotten rid of condescension, let us now get over over-simplification!

Just this Waters Turpin attempts in *These Low Grounds,*—and for a first novel more than half succeeds in accomplishing. A saga sweep of four generations of a family is daring for a fledgling writer, but the attempt is significant, not merely in breadth of canvas but in the conception that the Negro social tragedy is accumulative and the fight with the environment, dramatic or melodramatic for the individual is heroic and epical for the race. So from pre-Civil War Virginia to Baltimore, Philadelphia, New York and the contemporary Eastern Shore Maryland of the Salisbury lynching (Shrewsbury is the fictional name of the town), Turpin doggedly carries his story and the succession of parents, children and grandchildren. The modern scene, especially rural Maryland, is well painted, and the futility of the odds of prejudice dramatically shown. It is in the dating of the generations—a task for a scholarly writer of historical fiction, and the characterization of his central figures that one finds it necessary to speak of the high promise rather than the finished attainment of this book. As it should be, it is a moving tale of courageous matriarchy, closer to Heywood's *Mamba's Daughters* than anything else in the fiction of Negro life unless still further back we recall, as we oftener should, Clement Wood's *Nigger.*

In *American Stuff,* under the editorship of Henry Alsberg, the Federal Writers Project presents its cross-section miscellany, with a reasonably representative participation of Negro writers and poets. Of the prose, Richard Wright's thumb-nail sketches of prejudice,—*The Ethics of Living Jim Crow,* is by far the most powerful and thought-provoking. However, one is left wondering whether cold steel rather than hot steel would not have been better as an etching tool; but it is encouraging to see Negro writers turning to irony on their way to the maturer mastery of satire. Incidentally, gleams of the latter are in Sterling Brown's poetic contribution to this volume,—*All Are Gay.* To me the growing significance of Richard Wright still pivots on his last year's performance of 1936 in "The New Caravan,"—*Big Boy Leaves Home,* the second serious omission of my last year's chronicle. It must be mentioned even after this delay because it is the strongest note yet struck by one of our own writers in the staccato protest realism of the rising school of 'proletarian fiction'. There is a legend that the spring really begins in some surprising after-midnight March clash of lightning and thunder. To my ears and with reference to the new generation note, *Big Boy Leaves Home* sounds like an opener similarly significant to Jean Toomer's startling and prophetic *Cane*. Lusty crude realism though it is, it has its salty peasant tang and poetic glint, two things that one likes to think necessary for Negro folk portraiture rather than drab, reportorial realism, no matter how often tried.

Poetry proper still lags, as indeed for the last four years. A creditable anthology of Negro poets for popular use has come from the Newark, New Jersey, WPA project and a slender volume of original verse has been printed in New Orleans under the guidance of Marcus B. Christian, himself a rising poet of some distinction. His *Southern Sharecropper* in July OPPORTUNITY excels anything in this small volume, however. Frank Davis's *I Am The American Negro* becomes thus the outstanding verse effort of the year. Yet the book has too many echoes of the author's first volume and overworks its mechanism of rhapsodic apostrophes flung out in flamboyant Whitmanesque prose poetry. The mannerism dulls the edge of his social protest and again suggests hot untempered steel. Alone it would be notable, but it is not a crescendo in the light of the achievement and promise of the author's initial volume. In occasional publication there is also another Chicagoan poet, Robert Davis, with much the same ideology, but a more restrained style. Indeed until the recent publication of the *New Challenge* under the sponsorship of a New York group, it began to look as though the center of the literary scene was shifting from Harlem out to the Mid-West, and even with that promising recovery, Harlem must still look to its literary laurels.

In the Bronze Booklet series, Sterling Brown has outlined in carefully documented sequence and penetrating interpretation the course of the Negro theme in American poetry and drama in *Negro Poetry and Drama* and of the Negro theme in American fiction in *The Negro in American Fiction*. It is not too much to say that this is a greatly needed critical service, especially since the dimension of social interpretation has been brilliantly stressed. On the contrary, in *The Negro Genius,* Professor Brawley, enlarging and bringing up to date his *The Negro in Literature and Art,* has stuck to his previous method of mere chronicle narrative with trite praise and blame evaluations. Apart from the lack of social interpretation, this is not analytical criticism of the kind it models itself after,—Arnold, Lowell and Gates. But more of that later. Concluding our *belles-lettres,* Rosamond Johnson has a creditable anthology of Negro folk-song, in which he has achieved considerable perspective and corrected in a simpler style of arrangement the over-ornate style of arrangement that somewhat marred his volumes on the Spirituals.

Proportionately, it seems, as poetry has withered away, biography has waxed strong, following a dominant trend in contemporary letters. Negro biography is a province of potential importance; if ever the anomalies of the race problem are caught between the cross-fire of close grained fiction and well-defined biography, we shall at last know something about its intriguing dilemmas and paradoxes. But Negro biography has yet to grow up either to the grand manner or the expertness of contemporary biography and autobiography. The single figure in the grand manner is a figure of purely historical interest and only sentimentally connected,—Pushkin. The extent to which his mixed ancestry influenced either his career or his personality are highly debatable; he was Russian among the Russians, and stands clearly only as a striking example of cultural assimilation and the timeless and spaceless universality of first-water genius, over and above cultural and national traits. But while I would not loud pedal Pushkin's ancestry, I also see no point in ignoring it, and some point in giving it a sustained pedal for a bar or so for the color-deaf ears of the prejudiced.

Coming nearer to our time and locality, the other biographies stack up interestingly, but to no Alpine heights. Curiously in contrast, McKay's autobiography exploits a personality while Angelo Herndon's exploits a cause. Balanced biography can come from neither overemphasis. Yet an important chapter of the younger generation Negro life has been documented and oddly enough both trails lead to Moscow, one in terms of cosmopolitan vagabondage and the pursuit of experience for experience's sake, the other in the hard rut of labor struggle and the proletarian movement in the deep South. The clash of individualism and collectivism, of aestheticism versus reform, of the contemporary dilemmas of race and class could not be better illustrated if these books had been pre-arranged and their respective authors' lives accordingly. Because of its live issues and heroic attitude *Let Me Live* has no apologies to offer even in juxtaposition with the clever style and picaresque charm of *A Long Way From Home*.

(Continued on Page 27)

JINGO, COUNTER-JINGO AND US

(Continued from Page 11)

It was Professor Brawley's *Negro Builders and Heroes* that precipitated the Stolberg article and that had to sustain the full force of that blast against compensatory racialism. Exhibit A sociology, as I have said before, has bred a vicious double standard; the American success story (a majority pathology, by the way) has added its shabby psychology of Pollyanna optimism and sentimentalism, and the combination, I agree, although still the meat and bread of many professional inter-racialists and well-intentioned inter-racial movements, is stale cake on the contemporary table. Not so indigestible, once you acquire a taste for it, its chronic use induces, if I may keep up the metaphor, two serious symptoms of acute indigestion, cultural vertigo and split or dislocated social vision. Inevitable a generation ago, tolerable a half generation back, it is today not only outmoded but for the younger generation, dangerously misleading. Irrespective of personalities, then, it is time to call a halt on it.

The Incredible Messiah, from the other side of the racial fence points the same moral: its

Jingo, Counter-Jingo and Us » » »

PART II. Retrospective Review of the Literature of the Negro: 1937

• By ALAIN LOCKE

Great interest has been evinced by Dr. Locke's critical comment in the January issue. Here is the second and final instalment of Retrospective Review of the Literature of the Negro for the year 1937. All the books listed by Dr. Locke may be secured through OPPORTUNITY.

DRAMA, as far as propaganda is concerned, is the broncho of the arts; most playwrights who venture dramatic jingo finish in the dust while a riderless horse makes a hasty and disorderly exit. It takes genius to balance a problem in the dramatic saddle; yet if ever a problem gets itself effectively dramatized, nothing in the whole run of art can be as spectacular or compelling. But the many-phased Negro problem still awaits its Ibsen or even its Bernard Shaw. *Stevedore, Turpentine, Run, Little Chillun,* and *Mulatto* are still the best we have to show, and with each the dramatist finishes out of control and nearly unhorsed. As for the 1937 drama field, only in combination do they register any noteworthy placing; as single performances they scarcely rate as successes. Donald Heywood's *How Come, Lawd,* on which the promising Negro Theatre Guild unwisely gambled away its future, was a flat failure. It attempted to raise the previously successful formulae of *Stevedore* and *Turpentine* to a melodramatic folk-play, but instead of generating the conviction of persecution or the premonition of class war, *How Come Lawd* hatched a Deadwood Dick welter of corpses. Leaning on an already successful play for support, Gus Smith of the Lafayette Federal Theatre project, more than half successfully dramatized *The Case of Philip Lawrence.* Here was the set-up for a great Negro play,—the ghetto drag-down of a successful college athlete whose family and friends had no boot straps to lift themselves by, and little helpful conception of the success he yearned for. But a gangster racket and infatuation bring him down with a melodramatically contrived "framing" for murder, from which he escapes at the end only by a hair's breadth capture of the racket boss. Had social fate rather than a jealous, revengeful gangster been Philip Lawrence's downfall, real tragedy might have ensued instead of a Hollywood finish. Dramatically the strongest of the crop, *The Trial of Dr. Beck* revealed a promising newcomer to the thin ranks of Negro playwrights, Hughes Allison. His play, a success of the Newark Federal Theatre project, enjoyed a brief but effective Broadway showing at the Maxine Elliott. But here again a vital racial theme was overlaid with the trappings of an Oppenheimer crime story and two acts of well-documented but melodramatic court scenes. Though there is much talk of color complexes and considerable arraignment of the paradoxes of prejudice,—all to the good as among the first effective dramatization of these issues, both Dr. Beck's lily-whitism and his sister's-in-law counter color hate are far from being what they should be, the real protagonists of the play. Instead, Pinkertonian detective tactics and an over-idealized lawyer are the short-circuiting artifices by which Mr. Allison gets justice done and his moral put over. Still the talent of Hughes Allison, more mature in dramatic technique and depth of characterization than any Negro playwright to date, warrants hopeful watching and encouragement. The Morgan College Players are responsible for presenting the one creditable work of the white dramatist in Negro drama for 1937. Various professional concoctions of Broadway producers, two of them by George Abbott, have fortunately been as short-lived as they were mercenary and misrepresentative. At least this negative gain seems to have come about,—that except in the movies and on the vaudeville stage, the Broadway stage formula for a successful Negro play has obviously worn itself out. *Jute,* on the other hand, is the very antithesis of the Broadway play, but probably for that very reason a portent of what Broadway must come around to. Its strong bitter social realism, smacking of *Tobacco Road* on the one hand and *Stevedore* and *Waiting for Lefty* on the other, is the much needed antidote to too much *Black Boy, Sweet River* and *Brown Sugar.* In social content, Phillistine Negro protests notwithstanding, *Jute* is significant and promising for the social content of vital Negro drama.

In the ever important field of social analysis and criticism, one general change is increasingly obvious; "race sociology" is growing up. It is less frequently nowadays a puny missionary foundling or the awkward patronized protege of the interracial sentimentalists. Here and there it is sociology of full strength and maturity. And even where it is not, the pretension to scientific accuracy and objectivity is a significant omen.

Certainly one of the best and most illuminating of this year's race studies is Cedric Dover's *Half Caste*. With a panoramic swoop of world perspective on the race question, the book achieves a unique coordination of the phenomena of race. With eagle-like penetration of vision, international imperialism and fascist nationalism are seen to have common denominators of repressive, self-righteous racialism. Relentlessly the biological and cultural stalking horses of race prejudice are unmasked and the politico-economic objectives of race policies exposed. This is deftly done because the problem is tackled in terms of its crucial dilemma, the half caste, who as Mr. Dover senses, is the Dalmatian sword over the heads of all racialists: For the factualities of the human hybrids contradict either the theories or the practises of racialism; which then stands biologically contradicted or morally condemned. No other survey to date has given so wide a perspective on human hybridization or such a realization of its common factors, the similarity of situations and policies, the uniformity of its social dilemmas, and perhaps most important of all, the preponderant numbers of the mixed bloods. In the chapter on the American Negro, *God's Own Chillun,* the author achieves an illuminating analysis of the general situation, with pardonable lapses of proportion in the detailed statements of Negro achievement in which he has followed several uncritical and provincial sources. But the general soundness of his main thesis saves serious distortion, and it will be salutary for all who lack objective perspective on the American race question, Negro chauvinists included, to review the situation in this unusual and broad scientific frame of reference.

In *Our Racial and National Minorities,* under the editorship of Professors Brown and Roucek, the polyglot character of America is documented by some thirty spokesmen for national and racial sub-groups of our population. James Weldon Johnson has a double inning on Negro American achievement history and *The Negro and Racial Conflicts.* The approach of the whole study is too superficial for any sound interpretation of the interaction of minorities or the cultural problems involved in dual loyalties. Cultural pluralism and its educational objectives are, however, rather convincingly presented. The special degrees of isolation and differential treatment involved in the cases of the Negro, Indian, Mexican and Oriental minorities are dangerously minimized in the interest of the general thesis that we are all cultural hyphenates and that cultural reciprocity is our soundest, most progressive type of Americanism. Professor Johnson in keying his chapters in with this platform has not glossed over the particular injustices and inconsistencies of the Negro's position, but he has not sufficiently stressed the unusual cultural assimilation of the American Negro as compared with other minorities or the special inconsistencies of majority behaviour toward the Negro.

With *Caste and Class in a Southern Town* and *The Etiquette of Race Relations in the South,* we pass to sociological anatomy of the most scientific and painstaking sort. And yet what we get eventually in both cases is not any enlightenment as to social causes but only elaborations of the mechanisms of caste control and majority dominance. Can it be that this descriptive analytic point of view is hopelessly undiagnostic and therefore just so much academic "busy work?" Both works agree that caste rather than class describes the racial cleavage, and that its outlines are only correctly traced by examining in detail custom patterns in the social mores. But neither gives any very clear understanding of what economic interests and political policies all these elaborate mechanisms serve. In short, the vital question, it seems to me, is not the *how* but the *why* of these social differences and differentials.

In *The Negro's Struggle for Survival,* subtitled "a study in human ecology," Professor Holmes of the University of California assembles the Negro's biological statistics elaborately and tries to trace trends and prospects. In most of these balancings, our author finds Negro survival outdistancing or off-setting its handicaps, whether directly biological like the birthrate or socio-economic like the influence of poverty, migration and hybridization. However, toward the conclusion the banished bugaboo of race ascendancy comes back to threaten serious issues should the Negro rate of population increase decidedly to disturb the present balance. The author then predicts "population control" as the probable outcome. Even with the psuedo-scientific coating of "eugenics," this is the abandonment of the plane of science for that of politics and is a disappointing conclusion for an otherwise factual and objective book.

On the sound platform that "the essential human rights of Negroes do not appertain to them as Negroes, but simply as members of the human family" and that "modern Catholic sociologists see in the tendency to subordinate all considerations of the dignity of the human person to the unbridled quest of material gain the primary source of interracial, as well as of economic, industrial and international injustice," Father La Farge works out a program of really radical equalitarianism differing only in its sanctions and reform machinery from the economic radicals. In spite of this wide difference of proposed remedy, it is interesting to note this startling agreement in diagnosis. "Cheap labor," says Reverend La Farge, "brings cheap lives. And from cheap lives follow customs and maxims sanctioning the cheapening of lives."

In *The Negro in a Soviet America,* J. W. Ford and J. S. Allen expound the now familiar Communist formula for revolutionary socialism and minority self-determination. It has become too much of a formula perhaps, but that does not remove its realistic thrust as a contending alternative to the yet unsuccessful reformism of moral appeal and legislative guarantees. *Reconstruction* by J. S. Allen gives a much less doctrinnaire analysis of the relation of the Negro to the political and economic interests of the nation and the South. Particularly revealing are documentary evidences of Negro statesmanship in realistic political and labor programs from 1865 to 1879 that were frustrated by the tacit alliance of Northern industrialists and Southern Bourbons not to insist on thoroughgoing reconstruction or political power for the Negro in the South. This picture of American history after 1878 as a counter-revolution to the Civil War is an important and plausible interpretation; it culminated not merely in the setback to Negro advance but in the stultification of the labor movement for several decades and of the full functioning of democratic machinery even up to the present. A few close students of history have known this all along, but it is important that the layman should know it as well.

T. Arnold Hill's *The Negro and Economic Reconstruction* in the Bronze Booklet series also presents an indispensable layman's manual on the connection of the Negro question with past and present labor issues and programs. Volume No. 8 of the same series presents a readable and well-proportioned outline of *Negro History,* by the well-known bibliographer and source collector, Arthur A. Schomburg. But also in social history, which has been so neglected in Negro historical effort, most promising beginnings have now been made in various guide books of the Federal Writers Project. With Virginia, Louisiana and New York documentary chronicles in preparation, the project leads off very auspiciously with a revealing account, edited by Sterling Brown, of *The Negro in Washington* in the Washington: American Guide Series.

In *Life in a Haitian Valley,* Professor Herskovits vindicates even more brilliantly than in his previous books his thesis of acculturation. Studying the Haitian peasant rituals, he discovers not only substantial traces of African religions, especially the Dahomean Vodun cults, but clearly demonstrates the prevailing Haitian popular religion to be an amalgam of this, Catholicism and local superstition. This points to a completely general human pattern of acculturation, with none of the specious doctrines of innate racial primitivism or mysterious blood survivals, the favorite formulae of the culture-mongers who thrive on fashionable exoticism and bad anthropology. Cut free from such false implications, the search for African survivals is merely an excursion into social history. There is cold comfort for Nordicism or any other racial condescension in any such results, and for this service the Haitian cause in particular and the Negro cause in general have much to be grateful for in such studies as this and the previous volume of *Suriname Folk Lore,* documenting even more extensively striking survivals and parallels in the folk lore of the Negroes of Dutch Guiana. Nigerian and Dahomean patterns, both of behavior and thought, are found strikingly perpetuated.

But while we are shutting doors to Nordic jingoists, we should not be opening them to Negro jingoism. And such we must frankly label *Introduction to African Civilizations* by Huggins and Jackson. On a brittle thread of sentimental interest in Negro blood admixture, pre-historic Cromagnons, semi-Semetic Mediterraneans, Egyptians, Ethiopians, ancient and modern, South and West African peoples of diverse stocks are all hodge-podged into an amateurish hash of the black man's vindication. Such facts and conjectures are warrantable offsets to rampant and hysterical Nordicism provided they escape the same fallacies they challenge. But when they commit the same errors of over-generalization, assumption of fixed racial character and instinctive heredities, and worse than all, the ignoring of distinct culture groupings, the results must be repudiated as just as pseudo-scientific as the conclusions and prejudices they try to counteract. A much more intelligent and effective statement of the counter-case comes from an African author, Akiki Nyabongo, whose *Africa Answers Back* continues the pointed critique he began with his *Story of an African Prince.*

With a most laudatory preface by Malinowski, and a thrilling and trenchant account of his own liberal stand against German Nazi oppression and censorship, Professor Lips launches out in his *The Savage Hits Back* into an extensive documentation of the manner in which primitive peoples have represented the white man,—ruler, trader, missionary and colonial administrator. It is sufficient indictment of fascism that so indirect a criticism of colonial exploitation should seem dangerous enough to persecute and exile a scholar for daring to compile it. But this is neither the first nor the most impressive vindication of the primitive or even the African as artist. In fact most of the representations treated betray the native art in a bastard genre both with respect to style and subject matter, and necessarily we must discount its artistic and allow principally its sociological or cultural importance. Most of this work is therefore in the minor category of genre and even caricature; though of course it is interesting documentary proof that the native both sees and sees through the white overlords and takes due recourse to shrewd and half-concealed ridicule. Only rarely, however, do the European forms and accoutrements blend harmoniously with the native styles of expression, so that there is much more that must be labelled curiosa than can be called art proper. Nevertheless Professor Lips has documented very unmistakably the colored world's reaction to cultural jingoism and the loss of prestige which is taking place under the surface of professed respect. For exposing this significant symptom he merits our gratitude, even though we may not entirely grant his prophesy of a "future collision of the white and colored worlds" and his contention that "it is not class cohesion that will be the decisive factor in such a collision but the sense of race unity."

A joy to the scientific type of mind is the way in which both anthropology and the analysis of culture contacts are slowly disengaging themselves from the fog of prejudice and preconceived racialisms. Whether one grants the thesis of Frobenius that the similarities of prehistoric art indicate wide diffusion into Europe of African peoples or whether one holds with Leakey that parallel or roughly similar culture sequences worked themselves out both in Europe and different areas of the African continent, it is only too obvious in either case that the net conclusion is one of the basic similarity and parity of the human species. No sounder antidote for false racial pride or propagandist history could be found than in the cultural anthropology which is giving us increasing evidence along these new lines of the antiquity and the versatility of primitive man.

To the same collaborated authorship, as *Prehistoric Rock Pictures,* we owe the illuminating collection of African fables and creation myths in *African Genesis* (Stackpole Sons, N. Y.—$3.00). Berber, Fulbe, Soudanese, Rhodesian, —these tales are of wide range and diverse cultural quality, but they are all indicative of a more seasoned folk-lore and a higher level of literary form than other collections reveal, even the celebrated Cendrars *Anthologie Negré.* Interestingly enough, in some of them Frobenius believes he has discovered common symbols and rituals to early Egyptian mythology.

The really authoritative studies of African colonial contacts as they effect changes and breakdowns and fusions of cultures bear out the same liberal relativism of values. Notable among such are Monica Hunter's *Reaction to Conquest* and MacCrone's *Race Attitudes in South Africa,* each of which in a very different way illustrates the principle that one civilization more often demoralizes a different culture than it civilizes or improves it. In brief, according to the more recent scientific accounts, the white man makes his own burden and then has to carry it, not to mention the disproportionate profit he makes on the other side of the imperialistic ledger.

Although unnecessarily fictional for so detailed and painstaking a narrative of native folk ways, Carnochan and Adams' *Out of Africa* is a remarkably sympathetic biography of Kalola, chief of the Nyamwesi serpent cult. Nowhere has a better analysis of such ritual fetishism been drawn, with the balance carefully kept between black and white magic, conjure and tribal medicine, superstition and sound institutional tradition. In such books as we have reviewed, the African counter-statement is just beginning to gather momentum, but it certainly will have its day of assertion. However, let us hope that it will be a scientific, sanely directed counter-statement, and not another deluge of bigotry, hysteria and counter-prejudice. Not for moral reasons, but for effectiveness, let us be saner than our opponents. And let us welcome as champions only those who are scientifically convinced and convincing.

An Illustration from "Shuttered Windows"

The Negro: "New" or Newer

A Retrospective Review of the Literature of the Negro for 1938.

• By ALAIN LOCKE

PART I.

IT is now fifteen years, nearly a half a generation, since the literary advent of the "New Negro." In such an interval a new generation of creative talent should have come to the fore and presumably those talents who in 1924-25 were young and new should today be approaching maturity or have arrived at it. Normally too, at the rate of contemporary cultural advance, a new ideology with a changed world outlook and social orientation should have evolved. And the question back of all this needs to be raised, has it so developed or hasn't it, and do we confront today on the cultural front another Negro, either a newer Negro or a maturer "New Negro?"

A critic's business is not solely with the single file reviewing-stand view of endless squads of books in momentary dress parade but with the route and leadership of cultural advance, in short, with the march of ideas. There is no doubt in the panoramic retrospect of the years 1924 to 1938 about certain positive achievements:—a wider range of Negro self-expression in more of the arts, an increasing maturity and objectivity of approach on the part of the Neg artist to his subject-matter, a greater diversity styles and artistic creeds, a healthier and firm trend toward self-criticism, and perhaps mc important of all, a deepening channel towa the mainstream of American literature and a as white and Negro artists share in ever-increa ing collaboration the growing interest in Neg life and subject-matter. These are encouragi and praiseworthy gains, all of which were co fidently predicted under the convenient b dangerous caption of "The New Negro."

But a caption's convenience is part of its da ger; so is its brevity. In addition, in the case question, there was inevitable indefiniteness to what was meant by the "New Negro." Ju that question must be answered, however, befo we can judge whether today's Negro represen a matured phase of the movement of the 2(or is, as many of the youngest Negroes thi and contend, a counter-movement, for whi incidentally they have a feeling but no nam These "bright young people" to the contrar it is my conviction that the former is true ar that the "New Negro" movement is just comir

•

Fiction

The Dead Go Overside—Arthur D. Howden Smi Greystone Press, N. Y., $2.50.

Tommy Lee Feathers—Ed Bell, Farrar & Rineha N. Y., $2.50.

How Sleeps the Beast—Don Tracy, M. S. Mill C N. Y., $2.00.

The Back Door—Julian R. Meade, Longmans, Gre & Co., N. Y., $2.50.

Point Noir—Clelie Benton Huggins, Houghton M flin Co., Boston, $2.50.

Aunt Sara's Wooden God—Mercedes Gilbert, Chr topher Publishing House, Boston, $2.00.

Uncle Tom's Children—Richard Wright, Harper Bros., N. Y., $2.50.

Love at the Mission—R. Hernekin Baptist, Lit Brown & Co., Boston, $2.50.

What Hath a Man—Sarah Gertrude Millin, Harp & Bros., N. Y., $2.50.

into its own after a frothy adolescence and a first-generation course which was more like a careen than a career. Using the nautical figure to drive home the metaphor, we may say that there was at first too little ballast in the boat for the heavy head of sail that was set. Moreover, the talents of that period (and some of them still) were far from skillful mariners; artistically and sociologically they sailed many a crooked course, mistaking their directions for the lack of steadying common-sense and true group loyalty as a compass. But all that was inevitable in part; and was, as we shall later see, anticipated and predicted.

But the primary source of confusion perhaps was due to a deliberate decision not to define the "New Negro" dogmatically, but only to characterize his general traits and attitudes. And so, partly because of this indefiniteness, the phrase became a slogan for cheap race demagogues who wouldn't know a "cultural movement" if they could see one, a handy megaphone for petty exhibitionists who were only posing as "racialists" when in fact they were the rankest kind of egotists, and a gilded fetish for race idolaters who at heart were still sentimentalists seeking consolation for inferiority. But even as it was, certain greater evils were avoidod—a growing race consciousness was not cramped down to a formula, and a movement with a popular ground swell and a folk significance was not tied to a partisan art creed or any one phase of culture politics.

THE most deliberate aspect of the New Negro formulation—and it is to be hoped, its crowning wisdom—was just this repudiation of any and all one-formula solutions of the race question, (its own immediate emphases included), and the proposed substitution of a solidarity of group feeling for unity within a variety of artistic creeds and social programs. To quote: "The Negro today wishes to be known for what he is, even in his faults and shortcomings, and scorns a craven and precarious survival at the price of seeming to be what he is not. He thus resents being spoken of as a social ward or minor, even by his own, and to being regarded a chronic patient for the sociological clinic, the sick man of American Democracy. For the same reasons, *he himself is through with those social nostrums and panaceas, the so-called 'solutions' of his 'problem', with which he and the country have been so liberally dosed in the past. Religion, freedom, education, money—in turn he has ardently hoped for and peculiarly trusted these things; he still believes in them, but not in blind trust that they alone will solve his life-problem."*

How then even the *enfants terribles* of today's youth movement could see "cultural expression" as a substitute formula proposed by the "New Negro" credo I cannot understand, except on the ground that they did not read carefully what had been carefully written. Nor would a careful reading have been auspicious for their own one-formula diagnosis of "economic exploitation" and solution by "class action." Not only was there no foolish illusion that "racial prejudice would soon disappear before the altars of truth, art and intellectual achievement," as has been asserted, but a philosophy of cultural isolation from the folk ("masses") and of cultural separatism were expressly repudiated. It was the bright young talents of the 20's who themselves

5

went cosmopolite when they were advised to go racial, who went exhibitionist instead of going documentarian, who got jazz-mad and cabaret-crazy instead of getting folk-wise and sociologically sober. Lest this, too, seem sheer rationalizing hind-sight, let a few direct quotations from *The New Negro* testify to the contrary. Even more, the same excerpts will show that a social Reformation was called for as the sequel and proper goal of a cultural Renaissance, and that the present trends of second generation "New Negro" literature which we are now passing in review were predicted and reasonably anticipated. For reasons of space, quotations must be broken and for reasons of emphasis, some are italicized:

"A transformed and transforming psychology permeates the masses. . . . In a real sense it is the rank and file who are leading, and the leaders who are following. . . . It does not follow that if the Negro were better known, he would be better liked or better treated. (p. 10) . . . Not all the new art is in the field of pure art values. There is poetry of sturdy social protest and fiction of calm dispassionate social analysis. But reason and realism have cured us of sentimentality: instead of the wail and appeal, there is challenge and indictment. Satire is just beneath the surface of our latest prose and tonic irony has come into our poetic wells. These are good medicines for the common mind, for us they are the necessary antidotes against social poison. Their influence means that *at least for us* the worst symptoms of the social distemper are passing. And so the social promise of our recent art is as great as the artistic. (p. 52) . . . Each generation, however, will have its creed, and *that of the present* is the belief in the efficacy of collective effort, in race cooperation. This deep feeling of race is *at present* the mainspring of Negro life. . . . It is radical in tone, but not in purpose and only the most stupid forms of opposition, misunderstanding or persecution could make it otherwise. Of course, the thinking Negro has shifted a little toward the left with the world trend, and there is an increasing group who affiliate with radical and liberal movements. But fundamentally *for the present* the Negro is radical on race matters, conservative on others, in other words a "forced radical," a social protestant rather than a genuine radical. Yet under further pressure and injustice iconoclastic thought and motives will inevitably increase. Harlem's quixotic radicalisms call for their ounce of democracy today lest tomorrow they be beyond cure. (p. 11).

IT is important, finally, to sum up the social aspect of the New Negro front with clarity because today's literature and art, an art of searching social documentation and criticism, thus becomes a consistent development and matured expression of the trends that were seen and analyzed in 1925.

"The Negro mind reaches out as yet to nothing but American wants, American ideas. But this forced attempt to build his Americanism on race values *is a unique social experiment,* and its ultimate success *is impossible except through the fullest sharing of American culture and institutions. There should be no delusion about this.* American nerves in sections unstrung with race hysteria are often fed the opiate that the trend of Negro advance is wholly separatist, and that the effect of its operation will be to encyst the Negro as a benign foreign body in the body politic. This cannot be—even if it were desirable. The racialism of the Negro is no limitation or reservation with respect to American life; it is only a constructive effort to build the obstructions in the stream of his progress into an efficient dam of social energy and power. Democracy itself is obstructed and stagnated to the extent that any of its channels are closed. Indeed they cannot be selectively closed. So the choice is not between one way for the Negro and another for the rest, but between American institutions frustrated on the one hand and American ideals progressively fulfilled and realized on the other." (p. 12).

The generation of the late 30's is nearer such a cultural course and closer to such social insight than the tangential generation of the late 20's. Artistic exploitation is just as possible from the inside as from the outside, and if our writers and artists are becoming sounder in their conception of the social role of themselves and their art, as indeed they are, it is all the more welcome after considerable delay and error. If, also, they no longer see cultural racialism as cultural separatism, which it never was or was meant to be, then, too, an illusory dilemma has lost its paralyzing spell. And so, we have only to march forward instead of to counter-march; only to broaden the phalanx and flatten out the opposition salients that threaten divided ranks. Today we pivot on a sociological front with our novelists, dramatists and social analysts in deployed formation. But for vision and morale we have to thank the spiritual surge and aesthetic inspiration of the first generation artists of the renaissance decade.

And now, to the literature of this year of reformation, stir, and strife.

In fiction, two novels by white authors remind us of the background use of Negro materials that used to be so universal. Many such have been ignored as not basically "Negro literature" at all. However these two, Clelie Benton Huggins' *Point Noir* and Arthur Smith's *The Dead Go Overside,* do exhibit significant if limited use of Negro historical and local color materials. The latter particularly, documenting intensively New England's part in the slave traffic, weaves a melodramatic love story and sea rescue over the sombre details of a New Bedford fishing schooner's conversion into a slave raider and a sturdy personality deteriorating as it passes from codfishing to the more prosperous job of manhunting. Also picaresque is Ed Bell's *Tommy Lee Feathers,* a local color novel of Marrowtown, a Tennessee Negro community. Reasonably well studied local color and characterization are seldom met with in the rustic humor school of Negro fiction, so *Tommy Lee Feathers* registers progress even in its broad stroke characterizations of the exploits of the town's "Black Angels," Tommy's football team, and the more conscious angels of Sister Feather's "Sanctified

Church." One does not, of course, expect serious social commentary under this idiom. But too much "safe" entertainment of this sort has laid the groundwork for bad sociology.

However, it is noteworthy how much serious social commentary there really is in this year's crop of fiction, from both the white and the Negro authors. Already we are used to the semi-doctrinal criticism of the Erskine Caldwell school, which by the way he continues with usual unsparing and unrelieved realism in his latest volume of stories, *Southways,* but there are other and as I think more effective brands of realism. Certainly one of the most convincing and moving bits of documentary fiction on the racial situation is Don Tracy's reportorial but beautifully restrained *How Sleeps the Beast.* More even than the famous movie *Fury,* this novel gives the physiology of American lynching; not just its horror and bestialities, but its moods and its social mechanisms. Vince, who starts out by saying to his girl, "I ain't goin', I got no truck with lynchin's" eventually goes under her taunts; Al Purvis, whose life poor Jim had saved, starts out to rescue him but succumbs to social cowardice and mob hysteria; the Sheriff is jostled from official indifference to sectional hate at the sign of a "Yankee meddler," and a newspaper reporter hunted by the mob for fear of exposure barely escapes the same fate by sleeping the night through in the "malodorous room marked *'Ladies',*" after having been ordered out the back-door of the local Eastern Maryland Shore hotel while the mob pickets the entrance. In realism charged with terror, but tempered with pity and understanding, Don Tracy has written in the Steinbeckian vein the best version yet of this great American tragedy and of the social obsessions that make it happen.

More notable still, because about a more normal social subject, is Julian Meade's saga of Mary Lou Payton, the most fully characterized domestic Negro servant in all the tedious range of Negro servitors in American fiction. *The Back Door* is a book of truthful, artistically-balanced human documentation. Mary Lou's always precarious hold on the good things in life, on both domestic job and self-respect, on her amiable tobacco-worker lover beset by the wiles of looser women on the one hand and unemployment and occupational disease on the other, on her cherished but socially unrewarded respectability that every other week or so confronts the dreaded advances of Frank Anderson, the philandering white rent-collector, on even the job itself, are all portrayed with pity and sympathetic irony. *The Back Door* is as much a step above *Porgy* as *Porgy* was above its predecessors. Its deftly true touches—the wedding ring bought on installments and eventually confiscated, the lay-off that enables Jim to half conquer his consumptive cough, the juvenile blackmail of "Mr. Willie's" retort, "I know durn well *you* hook a plenty on the sly" as reply to Mary's frantic, "Mr. Willie, please don't bother them sandwiches," even the unwitting irony of the waiting ladies' missionary hymn,

"Can we whose souls are lighted
With wisdom from on high,
Can we to men benighted
The lamp of life deny?"

are all triumphs of the school of delicate realism well contrasted with the bludgeoning effects of the school of rough-shod realism. To the small sum of Southern classics must be added this tender saga of Stoke Alley and Chinch Row.

TO the fine achievements just mentioned, two Negro writers make this year a sizeable contribution. In the first, Mercedes Gilbert's *Aunt Sara's Wooden God,* the theme of the story is more important than its literary execution. Despite a too lenient introduction by Langston Hughes, this first novel is no masterpiece, not even a companion for *Ollie Miss* or *Jonah's Gourd Vine* with which it is bracketed; but it is promising and in subject matter significant. William Gordon, the illegitimate son, is the favored but profligate brother, Aunt Sara's "Wooden God."

An Illustration from "Araminta's Goat"

7

From the beginning a martyr to his mother's blind partiality, Jim, the darker brother, takes from start to finish the brunt of the situation—the childhood taunts, the lesser chance, the lion's share of the farm work while William is in school or frittering away time in Macon, then the loss of his sweetheart, Ruth, through the machinations of William, and finally imprisonment for William's crime. Amateurish overloading, as well as the anecdotal style of developing the episodes of the story, robs the book of its full tragic possibilities. William's eventual return to a death-bed reconciliation and Aunt Sara's pious blessings is only relieved by his attempted confession and Jim's heroic resolve not to disillusion Aunt Sara. Our novelists must learn to master the medium before attacking the heavier themes; a smaller canvas dimensionally done is better than a thin epic or a melodramatic saga. Here is a great and typical theme only half developed, which someone—perhaps the author herself—must some day do with narrative power and character insight.

IN contrast, Richard Wright in *Uncle Tom's Children* uses the novella with the sweep and power of epic tragedy. Last year the first of these four gripping tales, *Big Boy Leaves Home,* was hailed as the most significant Negro prose since Toomer's *Cane.* Since then it has won the *Story Magazine* award for the national WPA's Writers' Project contest, and a second story, *Fire and Cloud,* has won second prize in the O. Henry awards. This is a well-merited literary launching for what must be watched as a major literary career. Mr. Wright's full-length novel is eagerly awaited; perhaps in the longer form the nemesis of race injustice which stalks the fate of every chief character in the four stories will stalk with a more natural stride. One often feels in the shorter form that the nemesis makes forced marches. This is not a nerve-wrecked reader's cry for mercy; for we grant the author the terrible truth of his situations, but merely a plea for posterity that judges finally on the note of universality and artistry. By this criterion *Big Boy* and *Long Black Song* will last longer for their poignant beauty than *Down By the Riverside,* certainly, and perhaps also, *Fire and Cloud.* Yet as social indictments, the one of white oppression and ingratitude and the other of black cowardice and gullibility, these very two have the most documentary significance. The force of Wright's versions of Negro tragedy in the South lies in the correct reading of the trivialities that in that hate-charged atmosphere precipitate these frightful climaxes of death and persecution; an innocent boy's swimming prank in *Big Boy,* a man's desperate need for a boat to rescue his pregnant wife during a Mississippi flood, a white salesman's casual infatuation while trying to sell a prosperous black farmer's wife a gramophone, a relatively tame-hearted demonstration for food relief in the other three stories. And so, by this simple but profound discovery, Richard Wright has found a key to mass interpretation through symbolic individual instances which many have been fumbling for this long while. With this, our Negro fiction of social interpretation comes of age.

Love at the Mission is Mr. R. Hernekin Baptist's sternly tense story of the frustrations of three daughters of Pastor Oguey, a South African missionary. Hedged about by the double barriers of race and Puritanism, Hortense, the eldest, becomes involved in morbid jealousy of her younger sister's love affair, plots to poison her father, the symbol of this isolation, blames it after the fashion of the country on the African serving boy. But finally she has to stand for her intended crime and wither jealously in prison. Fani, the African nurse and housekeeper, is the counter-symbol of black paganism tolerant of this intruding Puritanism but never quite corrupted by it. Indeed the novel is really a pictorialized analysis of the futility of missionarism, and is of considerable significance because of its frank and carefully-studied approach to the clash of native and Nordic *mores.* In key so far as conclusions go, Sarah Gertrude Millin, with greater maturity, has analyzed the South African paradox from the point of view of an English civil servant with a tender conscience. Henry Ormandy, the hero of *What Hath a Man,* is outwardly successful as an individual but is haunted to the end of his career by his realization of the futility of the white man's self-im-

Juvenile

Shuttered Windows—Florence C. Means, Houghton Mifflin Co., Boston, $2.00.

Araminta's Goat—Eva Knox Evans, G. P. Putnam's Sons, N. Y., $2.00.

Country Life Stories—Elizabeth Perry Cannon and Helen Adele Whiting, E. P. Dutton & Co., Inc., N. Y., 65c.

Bantu Tales Retold—Pattee Price, E. P. Dutton & Co., Inc., N. Y., $1.50.

Negro Folk Tales—Helen Adele Whiting, Associated Publishers, Washington, D. C., $1.10.

Negro Art, Music and Rhyme—Helen Adele Whiting, Associated Publishers, Washington, D. C., $1.10.

The Child's Story of the Negro—Jane D. Shackelford, Associated Publishers, Washington, D. C., $1.40.

posed mission of imperialism. Mrs. Millin has woven into the earlier part of the story, when Ormandy encounters Cecil Rhodes just after the raid of Matabeleland, remarkable documentary evidence that Rhodes himself had a troubled conscience and paused once in his ruthlessness. But the very brevity of such a gesture in a cold-blooded game keynotes Mrs. Millin's indirect but quite effective indictment of imperialism as does also Henry's lonely, terrorful death. This too, although on the surface a novel of character study, is a novel of social protest; another David's pebble against our modern Goliath. The cause of social justice has been well served this year by the novelists.

A PROMISING symptom is the rapid growth of serious and sympathetic juvenile books on the Negro theme. Mrs. Florence Means in *Shuttered Windows* has written a story of an educated girl from the North, Harriet Freeman, and her struggle for the enlightenment of the illiterate South Carolina Island folk. Eva Knox Evans adds to her already well-known Jerome Anthony series of Negro child stories a sympathetic and quizzical tale of *Araminta's Goat.* Two gifted Negro teachers have collaborated to bring out a laudable public school reader series, beginning with *Country Life Stories,* a book that deserves wide circulation. Mrs. Helen Adele Whiting, Miss Cannon's collaborator in the foregoing, has independently brought out through the Associated Publishers two attractively bound and illustrated child's books, *Negro Folk Tales* and *Negro Art, Music and Rhyme*; the first much more successful in diction than the latter, but both only laudable pathbreakers in the important direction of introducing African legends and simplified race history to children. Dutton has also brought out Pattee Price's rhymed versions of *Bantu Tales,* genuinely true to folk idiom, which is all to their credit, but not too successfully adapted to the average child mind. All this is symptomatic of an important trend, of as much significance for general social education as for mere child entertainment. The crowning achievement in this field, however, is *The Child's Story of the Negro,* written by Miss Jane Shackelford. Here in fascinating style the riches of race history are minted down in sound coin for juvenile consumption and inspiration. More attractive format would make this real contribution a child's classic, and it is to be hoped that a second edition will make this advantageous addition.

Returning to the adult plane, the situation of poetry must claim our attention briefly. Time was when poetry was one of the main considerations of the Negro renaissance. But obviously our verse output has shrunk, if not in quantity, certainly in quality, and for obvious reasons. Poetry of social analysis requires maturity and group contacts, while the poetry of personal lyricism finds it hard to thrive anywhere in our day. Especially so with the Negro poet whose cultural isolation is marked; to me it seems that this strain of expression is dying a natural death of spiritual suffocation, Beatrice Murphy's anthology of fledgling poets, *Negro Voices,* to the contrary. Here and there in this volume one hears a promising note; almost invariably, however, it is a poem of social analysis and reaction rather than one of personal lyricism. To the one or two veterans, like Hughes, Frank Davis, Louis Alexander, a small bevy can be added as discoveries of this meritorious but not too successful volume: Katherine Beverly, Iola Brister, Conrad Chittick, Marcus Christian, Randolph Edmonds, Leona Lyons and Helen Johnson. However it is clear that the imitation of successful poets will never give us anything but feeble echoes, whether these models be the classical masters or the outstanding poets of the Negro renaissance, Cullen, McKay and Hughes. If our poets are to serve well this generation they must go deeper and more courageously into the heart of real Negro experience. The postponement of Sterling Brown's expected volume *No Hidin' Place* thus leaves a lean poetic year of which the best garnerings, uneven at that, are Frank Marshall Davis's *Through Sepia Eyes* and Langston Hughes's *A New Song.* Both of these writers are vehemently poets of social protest now; so much so indeed that they have twangy lyres, except for moments of clear vibrancy such as Hughes's *Ballad of Ozzie Powell* and *Song of Spain* and Davis's *Chicago Skyscrapers,* the latter seemingly the master poem of the year in a not too golden or plentiful poetic harvest. On the foreign horizon the appearance of the young Martiniquian poet, L. G. Damas, is significant;

9

Poetry

Exile—Leslie M. Collins, Privately printed, Fort Valley, Ga.

Pigments—L. G. Damas, La Pleiade Press, Paris.

Poems in All Moods—Alfred Cruickshank, Port of Spain, Trinidad, $1.00.

Negro Voices—Edited by Beatrice M. Murphy, Henry Harrison, N. Y., $1.50.

Through Sepia Eyes—Frank Marshall Davis, Black Cat Press, Chicago, 50c.

A New Song—Langston Hughes, International Workers Order, N. Y., 15c.

Drama

Big White Fog—Mss., Theodore Ward, Chicago Federal Theater.

Haiti—Mss., William Du Bois, New York Federal Theater.

The Divine Comedy—Mss., Owen Dodson, Yale University Experimental Theater.

Don't You Want to be Free?—Langston Hughes, One Act Play Magazine, Nov., 1938.

●

otherwise the foreign output, like the domestic, is plaintive and derivative.

Whereas poetry languishes, drama seems to flourish. The honors are about evenly divided between the experimental theatres and the Federal Theatre Project. The latter, with several successful revivals, *Run Little Chillun* among them, had as new hits Theodore Ward's *Big White Fog* and William Du Bois's moving though melodramatic *Haiti* to its credit. On the other hand, the experimental theatre has given two Negro playwrights a chance for experimentation both in form and substance that may eventually lead somewhere. Dodson's *The Divine Comedy,* the Yale Theatre's contribution, is a somewhat over-ambitious expressionistic rendition of Negro cult religion that shows promise of a new writing talent, while the Harlem Suitcase Theatre's *Don't You Want to Be Free?* has vindicated the possibilities of a new dramatic approach. Both are to be watched hopefully, but especially the latter, because a people's theatre with an intimate reaction of the audience to materials familiar to it is one of the sound new items of a cultural program that in some of the arts, drama particularly, has stalled unnecessarily. This theatre and the Richmond Peoples' Theatre, under the auspices of the Southern Youth Congress and the direction of Thomas Richardson, supply even better laboratory facilities than the drama groups of the Negro colleges, laudable as their Intercollegiate Dramatic Association is. It is to be hoped that real folk portraiture in drama may soon issue from these experiments. In the dramatized "Blues Episodes" of *Don't You Want to Be Free?,* and in the promising satirical sketches that the same theatre has recently begun, I see potentialities such as I have previously discussed at length. I am not only anxious to see them develop but anxious for some further confirmation of the predicted role of the drama in the Negro movement of self-expression in the arts. Not that an individual critic needs to be sustained, but since the course was plotted by close comparative study of other cultural movements, some national and some racial, rather that the history of this phase of our cultural development should demonstrate the wholesome principle that the Negro is no exception to the human rule. For after all, it is the lesson of history that a cultural revival has been both the symptom and initiating cause of most people's awakenings.

Dr. Locke will conclude his discussion of the literature of the Negro for 1938 in next month's OPPORTUNITY.

The Negro: "New" or Newer

A Retrospective Review of the Literature of the Negro for 1938.

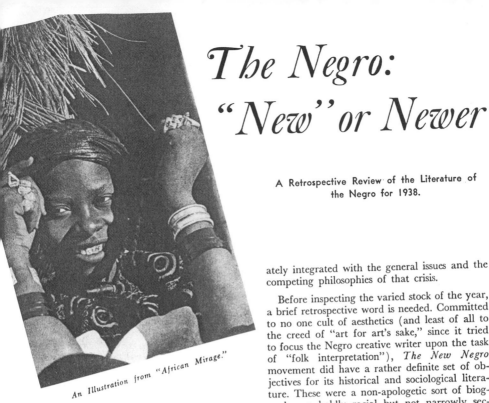

An Illustration from "African Mirage."

• By ALAIN LOCKE

PART II.

AS we turn now to the biographic, historical and sociological literature of the year, we find the treatment of the Negro, almost without exception, maturing significantly. There is, on the whole, less shoddy in the material, less warping in the weaving, and even what is propaganda has at least the virtue of frank, honest labeling. The historical cloth particularly is of more expert manufacture and only here and there exhibits the frousy irregularities of amateur homespun. General social criticism reaches a record yardage; and so far as I can see, only the patient needle-point of self-criticism has lagged in a year of unusual, perhaps forced production. Forced, because undoubtedly and obviously the pressure behind much of this prose of social interpretation is that of the serious contemporary economic and political crisis. But fortunately also, a considerable part of this literature is for that very reason, deliberately integrated with the general issues and the competing philosophies of that crisis.

Before inspecting the varied stock of the year, a brief retrospective word is needed. Committed to no one cult of aesthetics (and least of all to the creed of "art for art's sake," since it tried to focus the Negro creative writer upon the task of "folk interpretation"), *The New Negro* movement did have a rather definite set of objectives for its historical and sociological literature. These were a non-apologetic sort of biography; a boldly racial but not narrowly sectarian history; an objective, unsentimental sociology; an independent cultural anthropology that did not accept Nordic values as necessarily final; and a social critique that used the same yardstick for both external and internal criticism. A long order—which it is no marvel to see take shape gradually and by difficult stages. Again to satisfy the skeptical, let quotations from *The Negro Digs Up His Past* attest:

> "The American Negro must remake his past in order to make his future. Though it is orthodox to think of America as the one country where it is unnecessary to have a past, what is a luxury for the nation as a whole becomes a prime social necessity for the Negro. For him, a group tradition must supply compensation for persecution and pride of race the antidote for prejudice. History must restore what slavery took away, for it is the social damage of slavery that the present generation must repair and offset."

But this call for a reconstructed group tradition was not necessarily pitched to the key of chauvinism, though there is some inevitable chauvinism in its train. Chauvinism is, however, the mark and brand of the tyro, the unskilled and unscientific amateur in this line, and we have had, still have and maybe always will have our brash amateurs who rush on where scientists pause and hesitate. However, this was recognized, and warned against, and was spoken of as the mark of the old, not of the newer generation. It was said:

"This sort of thing (chauvinistic biography and history) was on the whole pathetically over-corrective, ridiculously over-laudatory; it was apologetics turned into biography. But today, *even if for the ultimate purpose of group justification,* history has become less a matter of argument and more a matter of record. There is the definite desire and determination to have a history, well documented, widely known at least within race circles, and administered as a stimulating and inspiring tradition for the coming generations. But gradually as the study of the Negro's past has come out of the vagaries of rhetoric and propaganda and become systematic and scientific, three outstanding conclusions have been established:

"First, that the Negro has been throughout the centuries of controversy an active collaborator, and often a pioneer, in the struggle for his own freedom and advancement. This is true to a degree which makes it the more surprising that it has not been recognized earlier.

"Second, that by virtue of their being regarded as something 'exceptional,' even by friends and well-wishers, Negroes of attainment and genius have been unfairly disassociated from the group, and group credit lost accordingly.

"Third, that the remote racial origins of the Negro, far from being what the race and the world have been given to understand, offer a record of creditable group achievement when scientifically viewed, and more important still, that they are of vital *general* interest because of their bearing upon the beginnings and early development of culture.

"With such crucial truths to document and establish, an ounce of fact is worth a pound of controversy. So the Negro historian today digs under the spot where his predecessor stood and argued."

THE mere re-statement of this historical credo of the New Negro (1925) shows clearly that not only has it not been superseded, but that it has yet to be fully realized. Indeed it was maintained at that time that the proper use of such materials as were available or could be unearthed by research was "not only for the first true writing of Negro history, but for *the rewriting of many important paragraphs of our common American history.*" One only needs an obvious ditto for sociology, anthropology, economics, and social criticism to get the lineaments of a point of view as progressive, as valid, and as incontestable in 1939 as fifteen years ago.

Indeed we may well and warrantably take this as a yardstick for the literature which we now have to review. Professor Brawley has excellently edited the *Best Prose of Paul Laurence Dunbar;* a service as much to social as to literary criticism. For by including with the short stories excerpts from his novels, Dunbar's pioneer attempts at the social documentation of Negro life are brought clearly to attention. Less artistic than his verse, Dunbar's prose becomes nevertheless more significant with the years; here for the most part he redeems the superficial and too stereotyped social portraiture of his poetry and shakes off the minstrel's motley for truer even if less attractive garb. Robinson's volume of stories, *Out of Bondage,* is, on the other hand, such thinly fictionalized history as to have little literary value and only to be of antiquarian interest. It is hard, no doubt, to galvanize history either in fiction or biography, but Arthur Huff Fauset's crisp and vivid *Sojourner Truth* proves that it can be done. This—beyond doubt the prize biography of the year and one of the best Negro biographies ever done—takes the fragile legend of Sojourner and reconstructs an historical portrait of illuminating value and charm. It lacks only a larger canvas giving the social background of the anti-slavery movement to be of as much historical as biographic value; and even this is from time to time hinted back of the vigorous etching of this black peasant crusader.

Just this galvanic touch is missed in the scholarly and painstaking biography, historical critique, and translation of the poems of *Juan Latino,* by Professor Valaurez Spratlin. Thus this detailed documentation of the ex-slave Humanist, the best Latinist of Spain in the reign of Philip V and incumbent of the chair of Poetry at the University of Granada, rises only momentarily above the level of purely historical and antiquarian interest. In the verses of Latino there was more poetics than poetry, but the *Austriad* faithfully reflected the florid Neo-classicism of Spain of the 1570's; the biography could and should have shed a portraitistic light, if not on the man, then at least on his times, for concerning them there is plenty of material.

The Life of George Washington Carver, under the slushy caption of *From Captivity to Fame,* is a good example of what race biography once was, and today should not be. Purely anecdotal, with an incongruous mixture of petty detail and sententious moralisms, it not only does not do the subject justice, but makes Dr. Carver a "race exhibit" rather than a real human interest life and character. One is indeed impressed with the antithesis between the sentimental, philanthropic, moralistic approach and the historico-social and psychological approaches of modern-day biography. They are perhaps ir-

Biography and Belles Lettres:

The Best Short Stories of Paul Laurence Dunbar—Edited by Benjamin Brawley, Dodd, Mead & Co., N. Y., $2.75.

Out of Bondage and Other Stories—Rowland E. Robinson, Charles E. Tuttle Co., Rutland, Vermont, $2.50.

From Captivity to Fame, The Life of George Washington Carver—Raleigh H. Merritt, Meador Publishing Co., Boston, $2.00.

Black Dynamite—Nat Fleischer, Ring Publishing Co., Madison Square Garden, N. Y., $1.50.

Sojourner Truth—Arthur Huff Fauset, University of N. C. Press, $1.00.

William Alpheus Hunton—Addie W. Hunton, Association Press, N. Y., $2.00.

Against the Tide—A. Clayton Powell, Sr., Richard R. Smith & Co., N. Y., $2.00.

The Black Jacobins—C. L. R. James, The Dial Press N. Y., $3.75.

Tell My Horse—Zora Neale Hurston, J. B. Lippincott Co., Philadelphia, $2.00.

Linea de Color—I. Pereda Valdez, Editions Ercilla, Santiago y Chile.

El Negro Rio-Platense y otros Ensayos—I. Pereda Valdez, Editions Garcia, Montevideo, Uraguay.

Juan Latino: Slave and Humanist—Edited by V. B. Spratlin, Spinner Press, Inc., N. Y., $2.00.

Negro and African Proverbs in *Racial Proverbs*—S. G. Champion, Geo. Routledge & Sons, London, $10.00.

reconcilable. Mrs. Addie Hunton's biography of her well-known husband, William Alpheus Hunton, pioneer leader of the Y.M.C.A. work among Negroes, is an example and case in point. A point of view that spots a career only by its idealistic highlights, that is committed to making a life symbolic, whether of an ideal or a movement, that necessarily omits social criticism and psychological realism, scarcely can yield us what the modern age calls biography. It is more apt to be the apologia of a "cause." In spite of such limitations, the Hunton biography is a record worth reading just as the life behind it was thoroughly worth living, but neither a moralistic allegory nor a thrilling success story like Pastor Clayton Powell's creditable autobiography will give us the objective social or human portraiture which the present generation needs and for the most part, desires.

The Black Jacobins by the talented C. L. R. James is, on the other hand, individual and social analysis of high order and deep penetration. Had it been written in a tone in harmony with its careful historical research into the background of French Jacobinism, this story of the great Haitian rebel, Toussaint Louverture, and his compatriots Christophe and Dessalines, would be the definitive study in this field. However, the issues of today are pushed too passionately back to their historic parallels—which is not to discount by any means the economic interpretation of colonial slavery in the Caribbean, but only a caution to read the ideology of each age more accurately and to have historical heroes motivated by their own contemporary idiom of thought and ideas. There is more correctness in the historical materials, therefore, than in the psychological interpretation of these truly great and fascinating figures of Negro history.

UNLESS it be characterized as the breezy biography of a cult, Zora Neale Hurston's story of voodoo life in Haiti and Jamaica is more folklore and *belles lettres* than true human or social documentation. Scientific folk-lore, it surely is not, being too shot through with personal reactions and the piquant thrills of a travelogue. Recently another study has given Voodooism a more scientifically functional interpretation and defense, and Voodooism certainly merits an analysis going deeper than a playful description of it as "a harmless pagan cult that sacrifices domestic animals at its worst." Too much of *Tell My Horse* is anthropological gossip in spite of many unforgettable word pictures; and by the way, the fine photographic illustrations are in themselves worth the price of the book. The social and political criticism, especially of the upper-class Haitians, is thought-provoking; and caustic as it is, seems no doubt deserved in part at least. One priceless epigram just must be quoted: "Gods always behave like the people who make them."

Contrasting in thoroughness and sobriety with these excursions into *Caribbeana* are the two works of the Uraguayan race scholar, Ildefonso Pereda Valdes. Through the studies of Fernando Ortiz, the learned scholar of Afro-Cubana, and the work in Afro-Braziliana by Dr. Arthur Ramos, shortly to be published in abridged translation by the Association for the Study of Negro Life and History, the field of the Negro elements in Latin American culture is at last being opened up to the scientific world generally, and to the North American reader in particular. Not yet translated, Senor Valdes's studies are an important extension of this most important field. In *Linea de Color,* he largely interprets the contemporary culture of the American and Cuban Negro while in *El Negro Rio Platense,* he documents the Negro and African elements in the history, folklore and culture of Brazil, the Argentine and Uraguay, and traces Negro influences from Brazil right down into furthermost South America. Important studies of Negro idioms in the popular music of Brazil, of African festivals and superstitions in Uraguay and the valley of the Rio de la Plata open up a fresh vein of research in the history and influence of the Negro in the Americas. In *Linea de Color* are to be found pithy urbane essays on Nicholas Guillen, the Afro-Cuban poet, the mulatto Brazilian poet, Cruz E Souza, and on African dances in Brazil. In the other volume, more academic essays on the Negro as seen by the great Spanish writers of the Golden Age in Spain and several other cosmopolitan themes attest to the wide scholarship of Senor Valdes. It is refreshing and significant to discover in far South America an independently motivated analogue of the New Negro cultural movement. *Linea de Color* reciprocates gracefully by giving a rather detailed account of the North American Negro renaissance in terms of its chief contemporary exponents, cultural and political. It has been an unusual year for Negro biography and folk-lore, the latter capped academically by the exhaustive collation of African and Negro American proverbs in Champion's monumental *Racial Proverbs*.

AS is to be expected, the documentation of Negro life in the Federal Writers' Project, *The American Guide Series,* is varied, uneven and ranges through history to folklore and from mere opinion to sociology. But on the whole the yield is sound and representative, due in considerable measure to the careful direction of these projects from the Federal editorial office. *New York Panorama,* however, in its sections on the Negro, misses its chances in spite of the collation of much new and striking material. Moderately successful in treating early New York, it fails to interpret contemporary Harlem soundly or deeply. Indeed it vacillates between superficial flippancy and hectic propagandist expose, seldom touching the golden mean of sober interpretation. In *The New Orleans City Guide* the Negro items are progressively integrated into the several topics of art, music, architecture, folk lore and civic history in a positively refreshing way. This exceeds the usual play-up of the Creole tradition at the expense of the Negro, and for once in the Creole account the Negro element is given reasonable mention. The *Mississippi Guide* is casual, notable for its omissions in its treatment of the Negro; and savors as much of the reactionary tradition of the Old South as the New Orleans Guide does of the liberal New South that we all prefer to hold with and believe in. The Old South is an undeniable part of the historical past; but as a mirror for the present it is out of place and pernicious.

Thus liberal studies like *A Southerner Discovers the South* by Jonathan Daniels and Frank Shay's *Judge Lynch: His First Hundred Years* become the really important guides to social understanding and action. They, with most of the solid literature of the New South—which someone has said is the necessary complement of the New Negro—keep accumulatively verifying these basic truths: that the history of the South itself is the history of the slave regime, that the sociology of the South is its aftermath and retribution, and that the reconstruction of the entire South is its dilemma and only possible solution. Whatever common denominator solution can be found is the problem of the present generation. Thus for Mr. Shay, lynching is rightly not just the plight of the Negro but the disease of law and public opinion; while for Mr. Daniels the Negro is not so much a problem as a symptom. This realistic third dimension now being projected into the consideration of the race problem is the best hope of the whole situation, and should never be lost sight of by any observer, black or white, who wishes today to get credence or give enlightenment.

For this reason, Professor Stephenson's study of *Isaac Franklin: Slave Trader and Planter of the Old South* is as social history of the newer, realistic type as much a document of Negro history as it is of the socio-economic story of the plantation regime. Factual almost to a fault, it is a model of careful objective statement; no one can accuse this author of seeing history through colored spectacles of opinions. Only slightly less objective, and even more revealing is Professor Bell Wiley's study of *Southern Negroes*: 1861-1865. But a decade ago so frank and fair an account of the Negroes during the crisis of the Civil War would have been very unlikely from the pen of a Southern professor of history and certainly unthinkable as a prize award of the United Daughters of the Confederacy. Southern abolitionism, Negro unrest and military service to both sides, the dilemmas of Southern policy and strategy, are not at all glossed over in a work of most creditable historical honesty. Almost a companion volume, by chance has come Professor Wesley's penetrating study entitled *The Collapse of the Confederacy.* Here surely is a fascinating division of labor—an analysis of the policy of the Confederacy by a Negro historian and of the status and behavior of the Negro population during the same period

Historical and Sociological:

Chapters on the Negro in *The American Guide Series*—Federal Writers Project—*The Mississippi Guide,* Viking Press, Inc., N. Y., $2.50; *The New Orleans City Guide,* Houghton Mifflin Co., Boston, $2.50; *New York Panorama,* Random House, Inc., N. Y., $2.50.

Isaac Franklin, Slave Trader and Planter of the Old South—Wendell Holmes Stephenson, Louisiana State University Press, $2.00.

The Negro in Louisiana—Charles B. Roussève, Xavier University Press, New Orleans, $2.00.

The Collapse of the Confederacy—Charles H. Wesley, Associated Publishers, Inc., Washington, D. C., $2.15.

Southern Negroes: 1861-1865—Bell Irvin Wiley, Yale University Press, New Haven, $3.00.

Judge Lynch: His First 100 Years—Frank Shay, Ives Washburn, Inc., N. Y., $2.50.

A Southerner Discovers the South—Jonathan Daniels, The MacMillan Co., N. Y., $3.00.

The Black Man in White America—John G. Van Deusen, Associated Publishers, Washington, D. C., $3.25.

The Negro and the Democratic Front—James W. Ford, International Publishers, N. Y., $2.00.

Howard University Studies in Social Science, Vol. I.—Edited by Abram L. Harris.

The 1938 Year Book: Journal of Negro Education: Relation of the Federal Government to Negro Education, $2.00.

The Negro College Graduate—Charles S. Johnson, University of N. C. Press, $3.00.

American Caste and the Negro College—Buell G. Gallagher, Columbia University Press, $2.50.

●

by a white historian. Dr. Wesley carefully and incisively documents the economic breakdown of the Confederate economy, showing its military defeat as merely its sequel. He is also insistent on the too often forgotten facts of the Confederacy's last frantic dilemma about military emancipation and the proposed use of Negro soldiers to bolster its shattered man-power. Thus both the historical and the contemporary Southern scene have this year had significant, almost definitive interpretations.

The fascinating subject of *The Negro in Louisiana* has unfortunately not had anything approaching definitive treatment at the hands of Professor Rousseve; for his volume, a creditable ground-breaker, has too much sketchiness and far too little social interpretation to match worthily the rapidly rising level of Southern historical studies.

Turning from the regional to the national front, we find the discussion of the race problem gains by the wider angle of vision and attack. We find also one great virtue in the economic approach, apart from its specific hypotheses—an insistence on basic and common factors in the social equation. The economic interpretation of the race question is definitely gaining ground and favor among students of the situation. Both studies in the long anticipated Volume I of the *Howard University Studies in Social Science* have this emphasis, the one explicitly, the other by implication. Wilson E. Williams' dissertation on *Africa and the Rise of Capitalism* breaks pioneer ground on the importance of the slave trade in the development of European commerce and industry in the 16th, 17th and 18th centuries and establishes the thesis that it was a "very important factor in the development of the capitalist economy in England"—one might warrantably add, of Western capitalism. The second essay, by Robert E. Martin, skillfully analyzes *Negro Disfranchisement in Virginia,* not in the traditional historical way, but by documenting the shifts of political policy and the mechanisms of majority-minority interaction, thus bringing to the surface conflicts of interest and motives too often unnoticed or ignored. Apart from such clarifying information these studies, reflecting the trend of the graduate instruction of which they are products, seem to predict a new approach in this field with broad implications and deep potentialities.

IN contrast to this critical economic attack, J. W. Ford's *The Negro and the Democratic Front* hews rather dogmatically to the official Marxist line, but with frank and zealous insistence. Its frankness is a virtue to be praised; as is also the value of having a clear, simply-put statement of the Communist interpretation of major national and world issues from the angle of the Negro's position. Though largely a compendium of Mr. Ford's addresses, it does focus for the layman a unified picture of radical thought and programs of action. Quite to the opposite, John G. Van Deusen in *The Black Man in White America* has taken up the cudgels for gradualism, gratuitously and with feeble effect. To a book seven-eighths full of patiently assembled and well-organized facts about every important phase of Negro life, Professor Van Deusen adds the banalities of philanthropic platitudes and dubious advice. He counsels "patience," expects "education and understanding" and in another paragraph "that universal solvent: Time" to solve the Negro problem, yet admits that "the greatest part of the work of conciliation remains to be accomplished." If there were some automatic strainer to separate fact from advice and opinion, this book would be a boon to the average reader, for there are regrettably few up-to-date compendiums of the facts about Negro life.

In education, there are three books of note this year. The Yearbook of the *Journal of Negro Education,* in keeping with the high standard of all its five annual year-book issues, documents exhaustively and in many regards critically *The Relation of the Federal Government to Negro Education.* Similarly exhaustive, with elaborate deduction of trends but little or no overt social criticism, Professor Charles Johnson's study of *The Negro College Graduate* offers for the first time since DuBois's *Atlanta Studies* an objective and composite picture of the college-bred Negro. Significant conclusions are the relatively low economic standard of the Negro in professional service and the serious displacement of trained Negro leadership from the areas of greatest mass need. It may be plead that an objective survey study should only diagnose and must not judge or blame. But just such vital correlation with social policy and criticism of majority attitudes is boldly attempted in President Buell Gallagher's book, *American Caste and the Negro College.* Instead of just describing the Negro college, Dr. Gallagher spends seven of his fourteen chapters analyzing the social setting and frame of reference of the Negro college, namely the American system of color caste with its taboos and techniques of majority domination and minority repression. Then he illuminatingly decides that in addition to its regular function as a college, a Negro college has imposed upon it the function of transforming and transcending caste, or to quote: "the segregated college has a special set of responsibilities connected first, with the problem of transforming the caste system" and second, "with the success of the individual member of the minority group in maintaining his own personal integrity in the face of defeat, or of partial achievement." If for no other reason, such keen analysis of the social function of Negro education would make this an outstanding contribution; but in addition, the diagnosis is sound, the prescriptions liberal and suggestive, and the style charming. Indeed a noteworthy contribution!

AFRICAN life has a disproportionately voluminous literature, since any European who has been there over six weeks may write a book about it. It is safe to say that over half of this literature is false both as to fact and values, that more than half of what is true to fact is false in interpretation, and that more than half of that minimal residue is falsely generalized—for Africa is a continent of hundreds of different cultures. So, the best of all possible interpreters is the intelligent native who also knows, without having become de-racialized, the civilization of the West. Next best is the scientific interpreter who uses the native informer as the open sesame to African social values. The virtue of Rene Maran's *Livingstone* is that he himself knows by long acquaintance that same equatorial Africa which was Livingstone's country. Jose Saco speaking of slavery in Brazil, Dantes Bellegarde speaking for Haiti and, with some reservation for amateurishness, J. A. Jarvis speaking for the Virgin Islands make their respective books welcome and trustworthy as native opinion upon native materials. The same should have been true for Nnamdi Azikiwe's *Renascent Africa* but for the almost adolescent indignation distorting the outlines of a statement of native West African conditions, grievances and programs. Even so, an expression of native opinion is valuable at any price. Just as radical, in fact more so in spite of its cool reasoning, is George Padmore's *Africa and World Peace.* In addition to being one of the sharpest critiques of imperialism in a decade of increasing anti-imperialist attack, this book vividly expounds the close connection between fascism and imperialism, on the one hand, and fascism and African interests and issues on the other.

Turning to the less controversial, we have from Professor Herskovits a monumental and definitive two-volume study of the Dahomean

Africana:

Livingstone et L'Exploration de L'Afrique—Rene Maran, Nouvelle Revue Francaise, Paris, 25 fr.

Renascent Africa—Nnamdi Azikiwe, Zik Press, Lagos, 12s. 6d.

Africa and World Peace—George Padmore, Secker & Warburg, London, 7s. 6d.

Historia de la Esclavitur de la Raza Africana en el Nuevo Mundo—Jose A. Saco, La Habana Press.

Le Nation Haitienne—Dantes Bellegarde, J. de Gigourd, Paris, 25 fr.

Brief History of the Virgin Islands—J. Antonio Jarvis, The Art Shop, St. Thomas, V. I., $3.00.

Dahomey, An Ancient West African Kingdom, 2 Vols. —Melville J. Herskovits, J. J. Augustin, N. Y., $12.00.

Black and Beautiful—Marius Fortie, Bobbs-Merrill Co., Indianapolis, $3.50.

Out of Africa—Isak Dinesen, Random House, Inc., N. Y., $2.75.

African Mirage—Hoyningen Huene, Charles Scribner's Sons, N. Y., $3.75.

Kings and Knaves in the Cameroons—Andre Mikhelson, G. P. Putnam's Sons, N. Y., $3.00.

culture. A careful historical and functional approach yields a sympathetic view of a much misunderstood people, and both illustrates and fortifies a growing trend toward the independent interpretation of African life not in terms of Nordic *mores* and standards but of its own.

So conceded is this point of view becoming that even the best travel literature is now being keyed to it. *Black and Beautiful* is one such, not just by wishful thinking in its title but by virtue of twenty-five years of "going native" by the author, Marius Fortie. His natives are individuals, not types; several of them were his "wives" and sons, and he speaks passionately for and in behalf of his "adopted people," a far cry indeed from the supercilious traveler, missionary or civil servant. Even Andre Mikhelson's *Kings and Knaves in the Cameroons,* mock-heroic and ironic, is a cynical fable castigating "so-called European civilization"; while Isak Dinesen's *Out of Africa* gives a delicately sensitive and respectful account of Kenya native life and the Kikuyu, the Somali and the Masai. The approach is human rather than anthropological and we have that to thank for a general impression that these peoples have a future and not merely a tragic present and an irretrievable primitive past. An impassioned defense of pagan primitivism is the subtle theme uniting the impressionistic diary pictures of *African Mirage,* by Hoyningen-Huene, by considerable odds one of the most understandingly observed and beautifully written volumes in the whole range of this literature. Even with all of our scientific revaluation, all our "New Negro" compensations, all our anti-Nordic polemics, a certain disrespect for Africa still persists widely. There is only one sure remedy—an annointing of the eyes. *African Mirage* seems to me almost a miraculous cure for cultural color-blindness. Such normality of social vision is surely one of the prerequisites also for effective history, sociology and econmics; no scientific lens is better except mechanically than the eye that looks through it. Let us above all else pray for clear-minded interpreters.

Another of the excellent photographs from "African Mirage."

The Poet and the Race Problem

By Edward Shillito

IT WAS in a room overlooking the noisy traffic of the Edgware road in London, that I talked on May-day with Countee Cullen, the author of "Color" and "Copper Sun." The noise did not trouble him; he loved great cities and was at home in them, whether it be New York, where his home was, or Paris, whence he had come to London. I remembered how Rabindranath Tagore had told me that he could not write poetry in the noise of the city, but Mr. Cullen, the young Negro poet, does not find that the roar of the street silences him. In that very street, I told him, another poet had spent many hours, some of them sad hours: Edgware road will always be sacred to those who love Francis Thompson. He too knew and loved "The Hound of Heaven." So we talked of the things which unite all who love poetry, for in that heavenly kingdom there is no black nor white.

From his own poems I knew that Mr. Cullen had dealt much with the life of the Negro. What an amazingly beautiful thing is his "Litany of the Dark People"! All the glory of the dark race is there. But I wondered whether it was his wish to be a Negro poet, and whether there was any school of poets deliberately claiming this province of experience, and even uniting themselves within it.

Appeal to the Universal

On the contrary, the poet told me he always wanted to write on themes which would appeal to all men everywhere, upon those experiences of life and death which are universal. He had sought to do this, but he had not been permitted. ("Poems and hums are not things that you get," said Winnie the Pooh, in Mr. Milne's famous book; "they are things that get you.") Mr. Cullen, like all true poets, had been under constraint: he did not want to be a Negro poet; he is not a Negro poet in any rigid sense of the word, but he is a poet constrained by the lot of his people, by their joys and more by their sorrows, to sing of these things. "Somehow or other, however," he has said, "I find my poetry of itself treating of the Negro, of his joys and his sorrows—mostly of the latter—and of the heights and depths of emotion which I feel as a Negro."

There is no school of Negro poetry, I gathered from him, if by that is meant a distinctive technique or language. Some writers, he told me, are experimenting in the old-time language of the Negro preachers; he mentioned, in particular, "God's Trombones," a book in which this can be seen. But for the most part the poets of his race did not seek to separate themselves from other poets who share with them the same tongue and the same great traditions. Nor did he think there was a distinctive Negro school of painting, though he told me of at least one artist of genius who has gone back to the early African traditions and memories for material to serve his art. But the Negro in America, whether as poet or artist, for the most part thinks of himself as an American, not as an African.

It is to the music and singing we have to look if we are seeking for the characteristic and distinctive gift of the Negro race to the world. (On the Sunday before Paul Robeson had filled the largest hall in London with a program chiefly of "spirituals.") In the art of painting and in literature the Negro would work alongside others; in music he had something to offer of his own to the wealth of nations.

The Negro's Gift

Would any more spirituals be written? Spirituals, he answered, were never written as works of art: they were the spontaneous cries which rose from the soul of a people; no one man wrote them, but a people. And still to hear them in their true setting, it would be necessary to go to an old-time meeting in some place untouched by modern analytic methods. Old spirituals may still be recovered, but there will be no spirituals written by modern poets. We spoke of the way in which the note of those sorrow-songs are prolonged in other forms, and he agreed that in his own poems that note is still heard, as in his "From the Dark Tower," or in the exquisite "Threnody for a Brown Girl."

But is there a better day dawning? I found Mr. Cullen confident and full of hope that in the new time there will be a cooperation, unknown before, between the white and the black races. Every day the relations between them become better. Youth is not content to accept ancient shibboleths. Those who share common intellectual and artistic interests will find, and are finding, new ways of cooperation. It was more to the imaginative writers and artists than even to the preachers that Mr. Cullen looked for his hope of reconciliation. If there were indeed racial discriminations which still met the Negro, it was gladly admitted by the poet that the relationships between the two great races were steadily improving.

It has often been said that the supreme glory of Africa will be the glory of a people which can forgive and turn the other cheek. Would that be so? It has always been so, I was told; the Negro will sorrow, but he cannot long bear resentment. He has always been ready to turn the other cheek:

> And if we hunger now and thirst
> Grant our withholders may,
> When heaven's constellations burst
> Upon Thy crowning day,
> Be fed by us and given to see
> Thy mercy in our eyes
> When Bethlehem and Calvary
> Are merged in Paradise.

915

There the Africa speaks, which shall bring this honor and glory into the kingdom of God.

It was not to a fusion between races that the poet looked as the true reconciliation, but to a fellowship, side by side, each race giving its treasures to the other.

"The Black Christ"

The title of the book at which Mr. Cullen is at work is "The Black Christ." This will be a miracle poem in which Christ re-experiences crucifixion in the lynching of a Negro. Mr. Cullen is the son of a Methodist minister; he has found it necessary, if he was to keep his hold upon the Christian faith, to express it in such a way. It will be published in the autumn at the sign of Harpers. It will be eagerly awaited by many who have read the earlier poems of this man who is but twenty-five years of age, and has started with noble promise up the slopes of Parnassus.

Of the poets who have influenced him, as I knew he would, he named Keats first of all. He had sung of him:

> Endymion, your star is steadfast now,
> Beyond aspersion's power to glitter down;
> There is no redder blossom on the bough
> Of song, no richer jewel in her crown.

I was a little surprised to find that, among living poets, he greatly admired A. E. Housman, that somber and yet deeply compassionate poet, who many years ago wrote "A Shropshire Lad"; yet it was not surprising that the Negro scholar should see and admire the perfect finish with a narrow range of those songs, written by a Cambridge classical scholar concerning the common lot of man.

For the reconciliation of man with man, of race with race, all the powers available should be welcome. All will be needed, and not least the artists and the poets who will lead us into this land of beauty in which, as in the blessed kingdom of God, there can be no Jew nor Greek, no white nor black.

New York Amsterdam News, nd [just after Quicksand published–Apr 1928?]. "New Author Unearthed Right Here in Harlem," by Thelma E. Berlack. [Knopf/uncatalogued/permanent title folders/Larsen, Nella. Harry Ransom Humanities Research Center, University of Texas at Austin.]

In the heart of Harlem–on West 135th Street, to be exact–lives a new writer. But this person, 5 feet 2 inches in height and weighing 122 pounds, is not a native New Yorker. She was born in Chicago 35 years ago.

A high school education in Chicago, one year at Fisk University in Nashville, Tenn., and three years at the University of Copenhagen, Denmark, make up her general educational career.

"I have lived East only twelve years," she said as she seated herself comfortably on the long sofa in her spacious living room. (This room, by the way, has the air of a Greenwich Village studio with its vari-colored pillows, paintings, books and more books, flowers, large and small vases, and other furnishings.

Twelve busy years these have been, for in this period she has done much specialized work. She was assistant superintendent of nurses at Lincoln Hospital for a year, did social service work for the Board of Health, worked as an assistant children's librarian in the Seward Park branch of the Public Library and later as the children's librarian in the West 135th street branch.

For three years, however, this little woman has had trouble with her health. She no longer goes out to business.

Who discovered this writer? Carl Van Vechten–and in her living room is an autographed photograph of him. Five months in her head and six weeks on the typewriter is the time is[it] took her to write her book. The publishers, Alfred A. Knopf, Inc., 730 Fifth avenue, have made her promise to do two more for them–neither is to be of the propaganda type.

"Madame X," or whatever you want to call her, is a modern woman, for she smokes, wears her dresses short, does not believe in religion, churches and the like, and feels that people of the artistic type have a definite chance to help solve the race problem.

Her hobbies are doing her own housework, and there is much to do to keep a five-room apartment so clean (and from the smell from the kitchen door she must be an excellent cook), sewing and playing bridge.

For nine years she has been married to a man who holds a Ph.D. degree in physics from the University of Michigan. He is employed downtown by an engineering company.

The only relatives she has in this country are her mother, who is white, and a half-sister. Her father, a Danish West Indian, died before she was old enough to know much about him. All of his people live in Denmark.

By now you must know "the lady in question" is Nella Larsen, author of "Quicksand," a review of which appeared last week in the Amsterdam News.

New York Telegram, 4/13/29.
[Knopf/uncatalogued/permanent title folders/Larsen, Nella. Harry Ransom Humanities Research Center, University of Texas at Austin.]
[The word Negro was not capitalized in the original text. Ellipses and brackets appear in the original manuscript.]

Nella Larsen ("Passing") has skin the color of maple syrup. Her costume of shading greys makes it seem lighter than it really is. When she was two her father, a West Indian negro, died. Her mother soon married one of her own race, a Dane. "I don't see my family much now," she says. "It might make it awkward for them, particularly my half-sister."

Nella Larsen has the uplift of the negro buried near her roots. "Propaganda isn't the way to accomplish it," she says.

Her years as a children's librarian in New York (she is in the Ghetto now) may be escape from her desire for the luxury of ten children. You would have to read the flap on her new book to know she had won the prize in literature and a bronze medal by the Harmon Foundation in its annual award for "distinguished achievement among the negroes." Also that she was head nurse of the hospital at Tuskeegee Institute.

Her voice is like a muted violin. You have to listen for it. She is proud of her poise. She laughingly admits it is acquired. Underneath her satin surface Nordic and West Indian are struggling. It hurts one way and helps another. She doesn't mind being shooed up the employees' entrance in hotels, because her Nordic side waits for such a situation; her negro side understands it.

Nella Larsen's philosophy toward life is answered:–"I don't have any way of approaching life . . . [in the article] it does things to me instead." She admits she is a fatalist if you point it out to her.

The "unforgivable sin" is being bored. She selects only amusing and natural people, not too intellectual. She would never pass because "with my economic status it is better to be a negro. So many things are excused them. The chained and downtrodden negro is a picture that came out of the civil war."

Nella Larsen's husband is a research physicist . . . colors (green especially) and words have an emotional effect on her . . . she loves bridge . . . bad food annoys her . . . her favorite authors are Galsworthy and Carl Van Vechten, the latter "to some of us is a savior, to others a devil" . . . Roland Hayes and Robeson are the artistic leaders of her race . . . Countee Cullen is another Edna St. Vincent Millay "with something left out" . . . and she is not quite sure what she wants to be spiritually . . . books, money and travel would satisfy her materially . . . her greatest weakness is dissatisfaction . . . she is convinced recognition and liberation will come to the negro only through individual effort . . . she would like to be twenty-five years younger [15 years old??]. She collects things–beautiful and [rare?].

"Negro Writers Come into their Own," Marion L. Starkey, 41 St. Nicholas Terrace, Apartment 65, New York City, sent to the Boston Herald, nd [April 1929], interview with Nell Walter White.
[Knopf/uncatalogued /permanent title folders/Larsen, Nella. Harry Ransom Humanities Research Center, University of Texas at Austin.]

NEGRO WRITERS COME INTO THEIR OWN

So says vivacious Nella Larson [sic–typescript consistently misspells Larsen], one of them, who foresees a far reaching and sunny effect upon American Literature.

"Why I really shouldn't wonder," said Nella Larson, tamping the cigarette Walter White had just given her with her slim brown fingers, "If right now the unknown Negro author of genuine ability hasn't an easier road to recognition than the unknown white writer.

"Of course it wouldn't do to make a dogmatic statement to that effect. I don't know that anyone, least of all myself, has ever taken a census to demonstrate that Negro writers have no difficulty with editors. Naturally, they must have.

"But for myself, I have had almost no trouble ever in getting placed, and that seems to be the experience of all my own immediate circle of writing friends. Editors not only welcome us, they actually seem to be on the lookout for us.

"They seem eager to give us the opportunity to show ourselves to the world as we appear to each other, and not as we formerly appeared in magazine literature, as a strange race of blackface comedians engaged in putting on a perpetual minstrel show. It may be just a fad on their part, but I think it's an awfully good fad."

They were deep in an overstuffed lounge in the library at Knopf's, these two young writers out of that most fascinating "racial capital" in all the world–modern Harlem–Nella Larson and Walter White. Each had just brought out a new book, each was chaffing the other (and a consultant reader strayed from the editorial rooms) concerning their literary produce.

Miss Larson's latest and second novel in "Passing". "To pass", in modern Harlem and Dixie parlance means to take advantage of a light skin to avail onself [sic] freely of the privileges of the paleface sector.

Miss Larson herself does not "pass", for though one half her blood is Danish, her skin has the coloring of brown honey. She is petite and chic and duskily lovely and has lustrous eyes. Her Scandinavian strain shows chiefly in the strong and beautiful modeling of her heart-shaped face.

But Mr. White's speciality has been "passing" through the South to obtain evidence on lynchings. His new book, following two novels, is "Rope and Faggot, Biography of Judge Lynch." He is not only white but actually fair, with a light moustache and blue eyes.

There was little talk of lynching with them, however. Wearied of two years' work on that memorable volume of his, Mr. White was much disposed to change the subject. And so was Miss Larson who never, if she can help it, reads about lynchings or Jersey torch murders or subway suicides, who fears that she has no great aptitude for the sociological and economic problems involved in the race question.

She went on talking about "the rising tide of color" as it concerns literary matters in America.

"Even if their interest in our writing is a fad," she went on, "It's a fad that is bound to have a very good and much needed educational effect. Until quite recently it was almost impossible for a Negro to sell a veracious story of Negro life. The only Negro stories that were considered were the burlesques like–let's see–"

"Like Uncle Remus?"

"Uncle Remus?" Her lovely eyes widened. "Oh dear, no! I love Uncle Remus. Not one word against B'rer Rabbit and B'rer Fox and Tar Baby sez 'ee. No, I was thinking rather of the Octavus Roy Cohen sort of thing.

"It's good natured enough I admit, and quite harmless as far as intentions go, but in that it has given people who take such stories seriously a biased, distorted impression of us, I think it's really harmful.

"But now the tide is turning. White writers themselves are painting much truer pictures of us. Do you know Julia Peterkin in 'Black April' and 'Scarlet Sister Mary'? I love 'Black April'–all but that awful part about April's feet. And there's Du Bose Heyward and T.S. Strioling–oh we owe a great deal to white authors.

"But more important is this being encouraged to express ourselves. We have Claude McKay the West Indian–'Home to Harlem' and poems, our Dr. W.E.B. Du Bois, Jean Toomer, Countee Cullen the poet–yes, he's a man, peculiar name, isn't it?–and Jessie Roadman Fauset– 'There is Confusion,' oh yes, and Walter White here with 'Fire in the Flint' and 'Flight,' the novels that preceded this lynching book.

"It is so interesting to conjecture what our realest contributions will be. Of course, there's our folk music which we have given already. Walter here has said that our spirituals constitute the only original folk music that America can boast.

"I think, however, that is putting it too strongly. For one thing there are marvelously imaginative Indian songs, and besides that there really are such things as white folk songs–for instance that really lovely thing 'Foggy, Foggy Dew.' But no one questions the beauty of our songs like 'Stan' Still Jordan' and 'I Walk in the Moonlight.'

"You know, what I think will be our contribution to American literature once we have done writing so much about our problems and sorrows, is our vitality, our native sunniness of temperament.

"This aspect of the Negro is very vivid to me, because, as you know, I am half Danish, and for a considerable part of my life, first when I was a very small child, then when I was 17 to 21, I was brought up in Copenhagen where I got well acquainted with the Scandinavian half of myself.

"They are wonderful people, the Scandinavians, intelligent, broadminded and prosperous, and yet in spite of all that are on the whole a strangely unhappy lot. It's hard to understand it."

"Perhaps," suggested Mr. White, "They read Ibsen too much."

"Oh, I shouldn't wonder, Walter!" laughed Miss Larson in her husky contralto. "Too much Ibsen. Of course, that accounts for everything. But no, I mean it. They really

2

seemed to me an unhappy people. And so many suicides as there are in those Northern countries!

"I can't see why. They have had peace and prosperity for so long. But perhaps that is exactly it. Perhaps that have had too much. Possibly the best of their future is all behind them, as the saying goes, and they have little that is dramatic and interesting to look forward to.

"And perhaps that partly explains why we are so happy–because everything lies still ahead of us. For all their troubles do you often hear of a Negro committing suicide? So seldom! Our folk do have good times in spite of everything. Work all day, hard grinding labor, and still ready to laugh half the night through. I don't think there's a race in the world with more capacity for sheer enjoyment.

"Who can tell what achievements we have ahead of us, what we shall make of ourselves in America? Oh, I think it's a wonderful thing to belong to the Negro race! No matter what adjustments, what sufferings are yet to come, the very worst surely, the blackest part of the shadow lies behind us. We are going forward into the light.

"Do you know, speaking of my gloomy Scandinavian half-brothers, I shouldn't wonder if, once we have done with all these problems that Walter spends his time investigating, we won't be the influence that keeps American literature prevailingly sunny-tempered in the end.

"We may supply just that tendency needed to counteract the gloom of those frightfully intellectual Scandinavians who are busy raising crops of problem novels out in the mid-Western prairies. The black influence in American literature will be in the end the influence of the sun."

Miss Larson was perhaps afraid that she was giving herself away as a Pollyanna. Anyway, she suddenly announced that for herself she is a very morbid, easily depressed sort of person, and that the heroine of "Passing" dies at the end. "Though does that make my book a tragedy? Don't most people do that–in the end?"

The talk turned to race and racial intercourse and racial barriers.

"I have no enthusiasm for barriers," said Miss Larson, "But I do know that colored people are happier as a whole in their own society. It's not so much that there is prejudice, but that race is race wherever you go and whichever race you belong to, and you're happier among your own kind. Negroes who mingle freely in white society are, in my experience, looked on rather askance in Harlem.

"For myself I have never in my life suffered any real unpleasantness because of race, and my husband, whose experience is simply amazing, has been so pleasantly received everywhere that he claims and I think believes that there is no such thing as the color line. Here in the North of course.

"My husband is Elmer Imes, graduate of Oberlin–his father was the first Negro ever admitted–and he has his Ph.D. from the University of Michigan. He is now a research physicist with an Engineers Development concern here in New York.

"In his work he is thrown exclusively with whites, belongs to their technical societies, attends their dinners. Why he's even been to conventions in Atlantic City where we are expressly not welcomed–and has never met with anything but hospitality and good fellowship.

"It isn't that he 'passes.' Not in that sense. He is fully as dark as I–wouldn't you judge so, Walter? It is merely that he has never had anything but kindness from whites in his life, expects nothing else, gets nothing else.

"–no more cigarettes, Walter. I must get back."

She stood up and pulled her smart little black hat over her blue-black hair. For the past four years Miss Larson has been a lady of leisure and letters, but just now she is busy as a librarian at the Rivington Street Branch Library, down on the Lower East Side, in anticipation of organizing a library in Harlem.

"Good luck on 'Passing'!' said Walter White. "I hope it's a best seller. I hope it's banned in Boston."

"It won't be," said Miss Larson. "I'm much to innocuous to get banned anywhere. And don't go insinuating things against Boston. I love Boston.

"I don't think there's any place in the world where a colored person can come and go with more complete absence of embarrassment. People are delightful there. I have so many friends who feel just the same way, who have a very special feeling for Boston.

"And what about all those tables of yours in the back of that lynching book? Ever since lynchings have been recorded there's not been one in Massachusetts, and only two in New England. You must talk to me about Boston!

"I must run. Remember me to Gladys, Walter, and to Jane and Pidge." It seems that Walter White's family includes a 22 months son named Darrow for Clarence and called Pidge for short.

"Thank you. I will. And I know it's going to be a best seller this time," said Mr. White.

"Oh no. The best seller is always next time. Goodby both, and my love to Boston." And Nella Larson had gone into the gray and silver April afternoon.

"Langston Hughes, Novelist," by Louise Thompson, 435 Convent Ave., New York City, nd [at the time of the publication of Not Without Laughter–typescript in]. [Knopf/ uncatalogued/permanent title folders/Hughes, Langston/Bio. Harry Ransom Humanities Research Center, University of Texas at Austin.]

With the appearance of *Not Without Laughter* (Alfred A. Knopf, Inc.) July 25, Langston Hughes will take his place in the literary world for the first time as a novelist. As the author of *The Weary Blues* and *Fine Clothes to the Jew*, Mr Hughes is already very well known the country over, and there has been a great deal of interest evidenced in the announcement of his forthcoming novel.

"Many people will be looking for a novel quite different from *Not Without Laughter*," he said to me the other day.

"Why?" I asked.

"Well, you see, they will be expecting a sensational Harlem novel of night club life and 'bad' people. The people in the book are simple, lowly people but they are not really 'bad' people. Many colored people did not like my poems, but I am hoping that they are going to like the novel."

Thinking about this conservation sometime later, the idea came to me that perhaps it was their not knowing Langston Hughes that had caused many people to misinterpret his poetry as immoral or "in the gutter." And I wondered if it might not be of interest to my friends in California, as it has been to me, to understand how Langston Hughes could write a novel of simple, working class people living unsensationally and more or less calmly in an insignificant midwestern town.

Langston Hughes is a true bard of Negro life. He has a keen eye for the colorful and a sensitive ear for the rhythmical in the life of the Negro, and a sympathetic understanding of his struggles to exist in a world too often unfriendly and cold. As a writer of the people he naturally turns for his material to the lowly classes where life is lived in less pretense and is actuated more by emotion and instinct. He has sought to give voice to the suffering, the joy and the desires of his own people wherever he found them–in a Harlem night club, Beale Street, and now in a little town in Kansas. He has interested their song and dance, work and play, in verse and prose pulsating in like tempo. To him there are no bad and good people. Life is colorful, intense and pathetic wherever he finds it–a woman crying her heart out in blues for her lover, the "little yellow bastard boy" sobbing against his white father, the frenzied jazzers in a cabaret playing their jazz-band sob. Always he bores deep into the heart of his people and writes of their happiness or despair, but always one finds in his work that pathetic note of one who not only understands but suffers with his people.

It is not strange then that in this novel Langston Hughes should write of working class people out in Kansas, where he himself spent part of his boyhood. The story winds itself around a colored family of three generations–Aunt Hager, her daughters and her grandson. The attitude toward the life about them would of course be different from each generation, and in his portrayal of the slave-like devotion to [sic–of] the old woman to white folks and the bitter hatred of her young daughter for those same people, Mr. Hughes shows equal sympathy. In the young grandson he focuses the hope of the Negro–that his children may learn and escape from the life he has had to endure. Working out his

1

story in this vein Mr. Hughes has escaped from the note of futility most often sounded in Negro novels by white authors, and from the despair and hopelessness of many novels by Negro authors, without, however, becoming either unreal or over-optimistic. Only in the portrayal of the oldest daughter of Hager does he reveal himself as unsympathetic, and it is not hard to understand this difference of treatment, since imitation of white people and disparagement of everything black are, to him, capital sins.

Mr. Hughes is vitally interested in how Negroes are going to accept his novel. He says of himself: "I want to write novels about colored people for colored people. I should like to have a novel published by a Negro publisher some day." Before his novel was handed into the publisher he had it read by a Negro working man to see if it would have an appeal for him.

Often the accusation is made that many of our Negro writers are catering to the white public–are writing what they think white people will want to read about Negroes. On the other hand the publishers say that Negroes are not reading books written by their own writers, and that any extensive advertising or large issuance of review copies of forthcoming novels to the Negro press is not warranted. Publishers are in business for profits, and writers cannot publish very many books that do not sell, so it is obvious that if there is not a Negro book reading public one must be built up before we can expect more of our writers to be able to write sincerely and with great appreciation of their own people. It is to be hoped that the numbers of Negroes who read *Not Without Laughter* will be great enough to encourage other Negro writers to follow Langston Hughes into the rich field of real Negro material as yet barely touched, and to convince publishers that there is a Negro public to be considered.

Langston Hughes is one of the most unassuming persons one could meet. Wherever he may be, among any group, he carries the same air of charming boyishness and friendly interest in life about him. He has been living quietly over in New Jersey since his graduation from Langston University last year, and aside from his own work, he has found time to encourage and sponsor the work of others. In the spring of this year he made a brief trip to Cuba and found among Cuban Negroes a lively interest in the activities of the American Negro. Sines his return he has set about, unpretentiously but effectively, awakening an interest here in America for the work of Cuban Negro artists. He has translated the poems of leading Cuban Negro poets which have been accepted by various American magazines. The common saying is to know Langston Hughes is to like him, and it is to be hoped that the issuance of his new novel will widen the interest in and support of one who has already proved his right to the place of spokesman for his people.

Wallace Thurman to Langston Hughes, Tuesday, nd [1928] from 267 W 136, New York. [JWJ/Hughes/Corres/Wallace Thurman. James Weldon Johnson Collection, Beinecke Rare Book Library, Yale University.

[Excerpts from letter, Wallace Thurman to Langston Hughes]

Hello there! –

Just finished Claude's book–Tis the best novel any Negro has published. Just like that. And I too await the holocaust. Good thing he's in Marseilles! ! ! ! Decadent is the name of our Renaissance. Cane another word.

You know I am not good enough to be in Countee's ball. I mean marriage. What I had in mind to tell you was that Otto cut some fellow up at the Hamilton Lodge Ball! Eli! Eli! -- Whee —. Unfortunately I forgot the date and missed it–the ball I mean.

. . . .

More scandal–

I'm in love!

Didn't ask?

You're a dear about –what's his name–Kellin. Soon as royalties come in I'll clear up the rest. Cary, Jean, James Weldon.

But Claude's novel–oh how I want to review it. And nobody asked me to.

Working on another play and on an auto-biography *not to be published*. Then *267* is my next opus.

1

Wallace Thurman to Langston Hughes, nd [1928?], from Mamaronec. [JWJ/Hughes/Corres/Wallace Thurman. James Weldon Johnson Collection, Beinecke Rare Book Library, Yale University.]

For an experiment I submitted my novel to Doubleday. The reader's report was priceless. "This is a very articulate novel for a Negro." And on "It has none of the decor or sensationalism of Nigger Heaven and Home to Harlem," and "It is a good novel but would advise against publishing. Would not be a commercial success. However, we may consider it."

Screw 'em.

Meanwhile I am making it longer for Boni-Liveright. And it is *not* a good novel but will be before published.

Have you read Dark Princess?

Wallace Thurman to Langston Hughes, Friday, nd [1929] from Santa Monica. [JWJ/ Hughes/Corres/Wallace Thurman. James Weldon Johnson Collection, Beinecke Rare Book Library, Yale University.]

[Excerpts from letter, Wallace Thurman to Langston Hughes]

[Wallace Thurman complaines that he is broke–devastated by the cost of his divorce]

"While friend wife takes a trip to Reno and has a nice little pile of hubbies royalties. The show flopped terribly in Chicago. Thanks to Negro propaganda. Don't ever marry. Had I remained single I would be financially secure for the next year. As it is I am broke, attorneys are over a thousand richer, and Louise has a couple of thousand, with two more in sight should I ever make more money. In fact I am almost glad to be broke again. Every person I know, save you, Jeanette, and Harold Jackman have borrowed money from me. And all are pouting because I cannot lend additional sums. I lent out almost eight hundred dollars. Paid $2200 worth of debts. I return to New York (maybe) to starve again next winter unless I get another break. Such is life. . . .

[Thurman describes the fun he is having, travels to Mexico, Catalina]

Am working on my novel, have finished book of essays, and am also working on a novelized version of Harlem, a new play, and a story for James Cruze to do in the movies. . . .

Found Banjo turgid and tiresome. Passing possessed of the same faults as Quicksand. Rope and Faggot good for library reference. Nella Larsen can write, but oh my god she knows so little how to invest her characters with any life like possibilities. They always outrage the reader, not naturally as people have a way of doing in real life, but artificially like ill-managed puppets. Claude I believe has shot his bolt. Jessie Fauset should be taken to Philadelphia and cremated. You should write a book. Countee should be castrated and taken to Persia as the Shah's eunuch. Jean Toomer should be beshrined as a genius and immortal and he should also publish his new book about which gossip is raving. Bud Fisher should stick to short stories. Zora should learn craftsmanship and surprise the world and outstrip her contemporaries as well. Bruce should be spanked, put in a monastery and made to concentrate on writing. Gwennie should stick to what she is doing. Aaron needs a change of scenery and a psychic shock. Eric ought to finish The Big Ditch or destroy it. I should commit suicide.

Don't mind such raving. I am distraught today, emotionally, and for no reason. When I get calm I'll write a long letter about adventures of a niggeratti in Southern Cal.

—

A QUESTIONNAIRE

THERE HAS LONG BEEN CONTROVERSY within and without the Negro race as to just how the Negro should be treated in art—how he should be pictured by writers and portrayed by artists. Most writers have said naturally that any portrayal of any kind of Negro was permissible so long as the work was pleasing and the artist sincere. But the Negro has objected vehemently—first in general to the conventional Negro in American literature; then in specific cases: to the Negro portrayed in the "Birth of a Nation"; in MacFall's "Wooings of Jezebel Pettyfer" and in Stribling's "Birthright"; in Octavius Roy Cohen's monstrosities. In general they have contended that while the individual portrait may be true and artistic, the net result to American literature to date is to picture twelve million Americans as prostitutes, thieves and fools and that such "freedom" in art is miserably unfair.

This attitude is natural but as Carl Van Vechten writes us: "It is the kind of thing, indeed, which might be effective in preventing many excellent Negro writers from speaking any truth which might be considered unpleasant. There are plenty of unpleasant truths to be spoken about any race. The true artist speaks out fearlessly. The critic judges the artistic result; nor should he be concerned with anything else".

In order to place this matter clearly before the thinking element of Negro Americans and especially before young authors, THE CRISIS is asking several authors to write their opinions on the following matters:

1. When the artist, black or white, portrays Negro characters is he under any obligations or limitations as to the sort of character he will portray?

2. Can any author be criticized for painting the worst or the best characters of a group?

3. Can publishers be criticized for refusing to handle novels that portray Negroes of education and accomplishment, on the ground that these characters are no different from white folk and therefore not interesting?

4. What are Negroes to do when they are continually painted at their worst and judged by the public as they are painted?

5. Does the situation of the educated Negro in America with its pathos, humiliation and tragedy call for artistic treatment at least as sincere and sympathetic as "Porgy" received?

6. Is not the continual portrayal of the sordid, foolish and criminal among Negroes convincing the world that this and this alone is really and essentially Negroid, and preventing white artists from knowing any other types and preventing black artists from daring to paint them?

7. Is there not a real danger that young colored writers will be tempted to follow the popular trend in portraying Negro character in the underworld rather than seeking to paint the truth about themselves and their own social class?

We have already received comments on these questions from Sinclair Lewis, Carl Van Vechten, Major Haldane MacFall and others. We shall publish these and other letters in a series of articles. *Meantime let our readers remember our contest for $600 in prizes and send in their manuscripts no matter what attitude they take in regard to this controversy. Manuscripts, etc., will be received until May 1, 1926.*

The Negro in Art

How Shall He Be Portrayed

A Symposium

WE have asked the artists of the world these questions:

1. When the artist, black or white, portrays Negro characters is he under any obligations or limitations as to the sort of character he will portray?

2. Can any author be criticized for painting the worst or the best characters of a group?

3. Can publishers be criticized for refusing to handle novels that portray Negroes of education and accomplishment, on the ground that these characters are no different from white folk and therefore not interesting?

4. What are Negroes to do when they are continually painted at their worst and judged by the public as they are painted?

5. Does the situation of the educated Negro in America with its pathos, humiliation and tragedy call for artistic treatment at least as sincere and sympathetic as "Porgy" received?

6. Is not the continual portrayal of the sordid, foolish and criminal among Negroes convincing the world that this and this alone is really and essentially Negroid, and preventing white artists from knowing any other types and preventing black artists from daring to paint them?

7. Is there not a real danger that young colored writers will be tempted to follow the popular trend in portraying Negro character in the underworld rather than seeking to paint the truth about themselves and their own social class?

Here are some answers. More will follow:

I am fully aware of the reasons why Negroes are sensitive in regard to fiction which attempts to picture the lower strata of the race. The point is that this is an attitude completely inimical to art. It has caused, sometimes quite unconsciously, more than one Negro of my acquaintance to refrain from using valuable material. Thank God, it has not yet harmed Rudolph Fisher! But the other point I raise is just as important. Plenty of colored folk deplore the fact that Fisher has written stories like "Ringtail" and "High Yaller". If a white man had written them he would be called a Negro hater. Now these stories would be just as good if a white man had written them, but the sensitive Negro—and heaven knows he has reason enough to feel sensitive—would see propaganda therein.

You speak of "this side of the Negro's life having been overdone". That is quite true and will doubtless continue to be true for some time, for a very excellent reason. The squalor of Negro life, the vice of Negro life, offer a wealth of novel, exotic, picturesque material to the artist. On the other hand, there is very little difference if any between the life of a wealthy or cultured Negro and that of a white man of the same class. The question is: Are Negro writers going to write about this exotic material while it is still fresh or will they continue to make a free gift of it to white authors who will exploit it until not a drop of vitality remains?

CARL VAN VECHTEN.

(See also Mr. Van Vechten's article in *Vanity Fair, Feb.*, 1926.)

---

1. The artist is under no obligations or limitations whatsoever. He should be free to depict things exactly as he sees them.

2. No, so long as his portrait is reasonably accurate.

3. I know of no publisher who sets up any such doctrine. The objection is to Negro characters who are really only white men, *i.e.*, Negro characters who are false.

4. The remedy of a Negro novelist is to depict the white man at his worst. Walter White has already done it, and very effectively.

5. This question is simply rhetorical. Who denies the fact?

6. The sound artist pays no attention to bad art. Why should he?

7. If they are bad artists, yes. If they are good, no.

It seems to me that in objecting to such things as the stories of Mr. Cohen the Negro shows a dreadful lack of humor. They are really very amusing. Are they exaggerations? Of course they are. Nevertheless they always keep some sort of contact with the truth. Is it argued that a white man, looking at Negroes, must always see them as Negroes see themselves? Then what is argued is nonsense. If he departs too far from plausibility and probability his own people will cease to read him. They dislike palpable falsifications. Everyone does. But they enjoy caricatures, recognizing them as such.

The remedy of the Negro is not to bellow for justice—that is, not to try to apply scientific criteria to works of art. His remedy is to make works of art that pay off the white man in his own coin. The white man, it seems to me, is extremely ridiculous. He looks ridiculous even to me, a white man myself. To a Negro he must be an hilarious spectacle, indeed. Why isn't that spectacle better described? Let the Negro sculptors spit on their hands! What a chance!

H. L. MENCKEN.

No. 1. If the author's object is the creation of a piece of art I feel that he should not be limited as to the sort of character he portrays. He should attempt that which moves him most deeply.

No. 2. If he is a sincere artist, no.

No. 3. Yes. On the grounds of bad business judgment, if nothing else. I feel that there is a growing public everywhere in America for literature dealing sincerely with any aspect of Negro life. The educated and artistic Negro, if presented with skill and insight, will find his public waiting for him when the publishers are willing to take the chance.

No. 4. Educated Negroes are rapidly arriving at a point where they are their own best refutation of this type of portrayal. They should, and doubtless will, soon be producing their own authentic literature.

No. 5. Emphatically yes. The point is that it must be treated *artistically*. It destroys itself as soon as it is made a vehicle for propaganda. If it carries a moral or a lesson they should be subordinated to the *artistic* aim.

6, 7. I cannot say. I think the young colored writer in America need not be afraid to portray any aspect of his racial life. And I may say further that I feel convinced that he alone will produce the ultimate and authentic record of his own people. What I have done in "Porgy" owes what social value it has to its revelation of *my* feeling *toward* my subject. A real subjective literature must spring from the race itself.

DUBOSE HEYWARD.

In a recent number of Harper's, J. B. Priestley discusses the American novel and describes a snag that has caught many an American writer. Our country contains so much variety in its background that our writers forget that this background is of comparatively little importance and think over-much of local color. They thus create fixed types. But the important thing, Priestley emphasizes, is to note "the immense difference between your neighbors".

With this in mind I can quickly answer a number of your questions. A novel isn't made up of all good or all bad, of all buffoons or all wise men. When a book overemphasizes one type, whether it be the buffoon, the villain or the heroically good young man, it isn't a true book and will soon be forgotten. What publishers, at least the best, want today is art, not propaganda. They don't want to know what the writer thinks on the Negro question, they want to know about Negroes.

Publishers will take books dealing with the educated Negro if he can be written of without our continually seeing his diploma sticking out of his pocket. Just as soon as the writer can believe that his reader knows there are educated Negroes, and doesn't have to be told that they live in pleasant homes and don't eat with their knives, he can begin seriously to write about them. Surely it is unimportant whether a book deals with the rich or the poor. Porgy and Crown and Bess are great figures in a powerful love story. John is a strong figure in Waldo Frank's "Holiday". So is Bob in Walter White's "Fire in the Flint".

Question six speaks of the "continual portrayal of the sordid, foolish and criminal among Negroes". This has not been true within the past few years. White artists are beginning to see the true Negro and colored writers are beginning to drop their propaganda and are painting reality.

Question seven, the danger of the Negro writer's following the popular trend, is a question every writer has to face. It has nothing to do with color. Are you so poor that you yield to the temptation to copy the trivial success? If you do you'll have plenty of company in this world of cheap popular magazines.

MARY W. OVINGTON.

(To be continued)

The Negro in Art

How Shall He Be Portrayed

A Symposium

WE have asked the artists of the world these questions:

1. When the artist, black or white, portrays Negro characters is he under any obligations or limitations as to the sort of character he will portray?

2. Can any author be criticized for painting the worst or the best characters of a group?

3. Can publishers be criticized for refusing to handle novels that portray Negroes of education and accomplishment, on the ground that these characters are no different from white folk and therefore not interesting?

4. What are Negroes to do when they are continually painted at their worst and judged by the public as they are painted?

5. Does the situation of the educated Negro in America with its pathos, humiliation and tragedy call for artistic treatment at least as sincere and sympathetic as "Porgy" received?

6. Is not the continual portrayal of the sordid, foolish and criminal among Negroes convincing the world that this and this alone is really and essentially Negroid, and preventing white artists from knowing any other types and preventing black artists from daring to paint them?

7. Is there not a real danger that young colored writers will be tempted to follow the popular trend in portraying Negro character in the underworld rather than seeking to paint the truth about themselves and their own social class?

Here are some answers. More will follow:

I think like this: What's the use of saying anything—the true literary artist is going to write about what he chooses anyway regardless of outside opinions. You write about the intelligent Negroes; Fisher about the unintelligent. Both of you are right. Walpool pictures the better class Englishman; Thomas Burke the sailors in Limehouse. And both are worth reading. It's the way people look at things, not what they look at, that needs to be changed.

LANGSTON HUGHES.

Are white publishers justified in rejecting novels dealing with the lives of cultivated colored people? If they publish mediocre white novels and reject mediocre colored novels, it is hard on a few colored writers, but should not the rest of us thank our stars that we are spared at least some of the poor books of the world? For surely, whatever the subject of the novel, it should be rejected if it is a mediocre book, and will not be rejected if it is really a powerful one; we may be sure that in the end a work of genius will find some form of publication.

This is the obvious answer to the crucial question in the questionnaire of THE CRISIS—indeed, an answer too obvious to be satisfactory. Complex problems cannot be solved in this airy way. For a novel, and in fact every other kind of book, is two things: It may be considered a contribution to the *literature* of the world or as a contribution to the *culture* of a race. The problems are so different that THE CRISIS questionnaire would demand a totally different set of answers in each case. From the standpoint of the critic, there is only one answer to the question as to what should be done with a mediocre book; but from the standpoint of Negro culture it may be important that some writers should get a hearing, even if their books are comparatively poor. The culture of a race must have a beginning, however simple; and imperfect books are infinitely better than a long era of silence. If the white publisher hesitates, on the ground that it is his business to be a publisher and not a champion of Negro culture, colored brains should create colored periodicals. The world will not close its ears to the voice of a great writer merely because of the imprint on the title-page.

The tendency today is to overestimate rather than underestimate colored books because of their subject, their delightfully exotic material. Their writers are valued by some people, as Dr. Johnson said of the first women preachers, not because they preached well but because of the surprise that they could preach at all. This will soon pass away; nothing disappears so quickly as a fashion in the subject of books. Great books may be made out of any subject under the sun; and colored writers will more and more have to depend not on their subjects but on their own excellence. In the meanwhile they should realize that all of the complex problems of literature cannot be magically solved by a childish formula like that of "art versus propaganda". They must understand that a book may be of high value to a race's culture without being of high rank in the world's literature, just as a man may be a very useful citizen yet a rather mediocre dentist. The Negro race should not sniff at the *Uncle Tom's Cabins* and the *Jungles* of its own writers, which are instruments of progress as real as the ballot-box, the school-house or a stick of dynamite.

J. E. SPINGARN.

It is unfortunate, it seems to me, that at the very time when Negro writers are beginning to be heard there should arise a division of opinion as to what or what not he should write about. Such a conflict, however, is, I suppose, to be expected. There are those who say that the only interesting material in Negro lives is in the lives of the lower or lowest classes—that upper class Negro life is in no wise different from white life and is therefore uninteresting.

I venture to question the truth of this statement. Like all other people who have struggled against odds, upper class Negroes have through that very struggle sharpened their sensitiveness to the intense drama of race life in the United States. They never come into contact with the outside world but there is potential drama, whether of comedy or tragedy, in each of those contacts. By this I do not mean simply unpleasant aspects of the lives of these people. This sensitiveness to pain and insult and tragedy has its compensation in a keener awareness and appreciation of the rhythmic beauty and color and joyousness which is so valuable a part of Negro life.

The lives of so-called upper class Negroes have advantages as literary material, judged even by the most arbitrary standards. "Babbitt" or "Jean Christophe" or any other novel is interesting in direct proportion to the ability of the writer to depict impingement of events and experiences, trivial or great, on the more or less sensitive photographic plates which are the minds of the characters. Life for any Negro in America has so many different aspects that there is unlimited material for the novelist or short story writer. For the reasons I have already given, there is no lack of this material among upper class Negroes if one only has the eye to see it.

Suppose we carry this objection to the utilization of experiences of educated Negroes to its logical conclusion. Would not the result be this: Negro writers should not write, the young Negro is told, of educated Negroes because their lives paralleling white lives are uninteresting. If this be true, then it seems just as reasonable to say that all writers, white or colored, should abandon all sources of material save that of lower class Negro life. Manifestly this is absurd. It makes no difference, it seems to me, what field a writer chooses if he has the gift of perception, of dramatic and human material and the ability to write about it.

Those who would limit Negro writers to depiction of lower class Negro life justify their contention by saying, "The artist must have the right to choose his material where he will; and the critic can judge him only by the artistic result." These same persons often nullify or negative their contention for freedom by following this assertion immediately with insistence that the Negro writer confine himself to one field. The Negro writer, just like any other writer, should be allowed to write of whatever interests him whether it be of lower, or middle, or upper class Negro life in America; or of white—or Malay—or Chinese—or Hottentot characters and should be judged not by the color of the writer's skin but solely by the story he produces.

I, myself, have not as yet written extensively of prostitutes or gamblers or cabaret habitues. Fortunately, or unfortunately, my life thus far has not given me as intimate a knowledge of these classes as I feel would be necessary for me to write about them. I am not boasting of this innocence, if one chooses to call it that. I am merely stating it as a fact. An honest craftsman, in my opinion, can only pour his knowledge and experience, real or imagined, through the alembic of his own mind and let the creations of his subjective or objective self stand or fall by whatever literary standards are current at the time. I do not mean that Zola or Flaubert had to live as "Nana" or "Emma Bovary" did to achieve subjective treatment of these characters—such obviously being a physical impossibility. But Zola *did* find himself drawn to write of the experiences of his character "Nana", as did Flaubert to the luckless "Emma". Certainly we could not have condemned either Zola or Flaubert if they had chosen instead to depict women less carnal minded.

To summarize specifically, it seems to me that:

1. The artist should be allowed full freedom in the choice of his characters and material.

2. An artist can rightly be criticized if he portrays only the worst or only the best characters of any group. (I, myself, was lambasted most enthusiastically by the South because Kenneth Harper in "The Fire in the Flint" seemed to me much more intelligent and decent than any of his white fellow townsmen.)

3. Publishers can and should be criticized for refusing to handle manuscripts, *provided they have merit*, that portray Negroes of superior talent because the lives of these Negroes do not vary from white people's.

4. When Negroes are painted only at their worst and judged accordingly by the public, Negroes must write stories revealing the other side and make these stories of such excellence that they command attention. (This is not an advertisement but in this same connection more Negroes must buy books by Negro writers for then sales will cause publishers actively to seek Negro writers of ability.)

5. The situation of the Negro in America *is* pregnant enough in drama and color and beauty to make of him a subject for artistic treatment.

6. Continual portrayal of any type to the exclusion of all others is not only harmful but bad art.

7. If young Negro writers can be saved or, better, save themselves from too hostile or too friendly critics, editors, publishers or public, from spending all their time and energy in restricted areas, they can have the freedom to explore whatever fields to which their fancy or inclination draws them.

In brief, sycophants and weaklings will follow whatever trend is mapped out for them; genuine artists will write or paint or sing or sculpt whatever they please.

WALTER WHITE.

I have yours of January 22 and will try to answer your questions promptly and briefly.

1. No.
2. No.
3. This question seems to me to be senseless.
4. To write books—fiction and non-fiction —to supply the deficiency.
5. Yes.
6. I doubt it.
7. I doubt it.

ALFRED A. KNOPF.

I feel that the Negro should be treated by himself and by others who write about him with just as little self-consciousness as possible. Realizing how untrue Octavius Roy Cohen's stories may be, they have amused me immensely, nor do they mean to me any very great libel on the Negro—any more than an amusing story about the Yankee would seem to me a libel on myself.

On the other hand, I have always thought that Walter White's novel was a trifle one sided, although I realize that I speak as one who does not truly know conditions in the South.

It therefore seems to me that although I realize it is inevitable under the circumstances that this discussion should arise, you will have Negroes writing about the Negro as the Jews have written about the Jews in "Potash and Perlmutter" and other such things, and that racial characteristics are bound to be presented in burlesque as well as real drama; and that, as Mr. Van Vechten has pointed out, the creative spirit, even though it may not be classed as art, will always disregard moral issues such as these.

JOHN FARRAR.

---

1. The only obligation or limitation that an artist should recognize is the truth.

2. He cannot be criticized unless he takes the worst as typical.

3. If a publisher takes the ground mentioned in this question, it would be absurd.

4. The Negroes must protest in print and must hope that by setting a good example in their lives they can correct the false impression.

5. Of course it calls for artistic treatment, sincere and sympathetic, but I have not read "Porgy".

6. There is a certain danger of this.

7. I think there might be a danger also here.

WILLIAM LYON PHELPS.

The Negro in Art

How Shall He Be Portrayed

A Symposium

WE have asked the artists of the world these questions:

1. When the artist, black or white, portrays Negro characters is he under any obligations or limitations as to the sort of character he will portray?

2. Can any author be criticized for painting the worst or the best characters of a group?

3. Can publishers be criticized for refusing to handle novels that portray Negroes of education and accomplishment, on the ground that these characters are no different from white folk and therefore not interesting?

4. What are Negroes to do when they are continually painted at their worst and judged by the public as they are painted?

5. Does the situation of the educated Negro in America with its pathos, humiliation and tragedy call for artistic treatment at least as sincere and sympathetic as "Porgy" received?

6. Is not the continual portrayal of the sordid, foolish and criminal among Negroes convincing the world that this and this alone is really and essentially Negroid, and preventing white artists from knowing any other types and preventing black artists from daring to paint them?

7. Is there not a real danger that young colored writers will be tempted to follow the popular trend in portraying Negro character in the underworld rather than seeking to paint the truth about themselves and their own social class?

Here are some answers. More will follow:

---

1. Neither the black nor the white artist should be under obligations or limitations as to the sort of character he will portray. His own experience and his inmost perception of truth and beauty, in its severest interpretation, should be his only criteria.

2. An author can be criticized for painting the worst or best characters of a group if his portrayal thereby becomes artistically false; he should be free to choose his characters according to his desire and purpose.

3. Publishers assuredly may be criticized for refusing to handle novels portraying Negroes of education and accomplishment, on the ground that these characters are no different from white folk and therefore not interesting. The Negro of this type has an artistic as well as a social right to speak for himself; and what he has to say is all too interesting, as a rule.

4. The work of such magazines as THE CRISIS and *Opportunity* suggests a possible way out. Through his songs, through drama, poetry and fiction, the Negro should make every effort to put before the public a true picture of the race, in totality; and white folk of sufficient intelligence and courage to recognize the issue as it stands should be enlisted as an auxiliary force to the same end.

5. The situation of the educated Negro in America surely merits all possible sincere and artistic treatment. If such enterprises seem doomed to failure in this country, they should be taken to Canada or England, or to the continental countries, and so finally reach the United States public with their prestige already established.

6. The portrayal of sordid, foolish and criminal types among Negroes is not convincing the world that such groups alone comprise the essentially Negroid, but it surely is doing a great deal to foster that opinion in the United States, where there are many anxious to believe it. The portrayal of such types by no means damns a race; look at the long line of English, French, Spanish and Russian novels and plays dealing with such characters; nor does one need to confine the list to those countries exclusively. Such portrayals have their place and deep significance artistically; but they at once become false and evil if used for propagandist purposes, or with ulterior racial motives.

7. Such a danger can scarcely be stated as a general phenomenon. The average young colored writer, if he be honest as an artist, will write the thing that is in his heart to write regardless of so-called "popular trends". Any artist who speaks the truth as he sees it and refuses to compromise with Mammon has none too easy a time; it is not a question of color, it is a question of courage. One has no reason to believe that the sincere black artist will be more easily daunted than a sincere white or brown or yellow artist. The one diffi-

culty that does seem to exist, in the light of a thoughtful reading of recent Negro novels and poems, is that many times an ingrained bitterness tinges work otherwise clearly and beautifully carried out. For that the Negro is not to blame, nor can one state the solution of the problem back of it. The only way out is up; and that seems to be the way which the younger Negro artists, singers and writers have chosen for themselves and for their people. More power to them.

VACHEL LINDSAY.

—

The Negro in Art

How Shall He Be Portrayed

A Symposium

WE have asked the artists of the world these questions:

1. When the artist, black or white, portrays Negro characters is he under any obligations or limitations as to the sort of character he will portray?

2. Can any author be criticized for painting the worst or the best characters of a group?

3. Can publishers be criticized for refusing to handle novels that portray Negroes of education and accomplishment, on the ground that these characters are no different from white folk and therefore not interesting?

4. What are Negroes to do when they are continually painted at their worst and judged by the public as they are painted?

5. Does the situation of the educated Negro in America with its pathos, humiliation and tragedy call for artistic treatment at least as sincere and sympathetic as "Porgy" received?

6. Is not the continual portrayal of the sordid, foolish and criminal among Negroes convincing the world that this and this alone is really and essentially Negroid, and preventing white artists from knowing any other types and preventing black artists from daring to paint them?

7. Is there not a real danger that young colored writers will be tempted to follow the popular trend in portraying Negro character in the underworld rather than seeking to paint the truth about themselves and their own social class?

Here are some answers. More will follow:

---

1. No.

2. No. Unless in a long series of articles he invariably chooses the worst types and paints them, even though truthfully, with evident malice.

3. I should think so. And what is more, it seems to me that white people should be the first to voice this criticism. Aren't *they* supposed to be interesting?

4. They must protest strongly and get their protestations before the public. But more than that they must learn to write with a humor, a pathos, a sincerity so evident and a delineation so fine and distinctive that their portraits, even of the "best Negroes", those presumably most like "white folks", will be acceptable to publisher and reader alike.

But above all colored people must be the buyers of these books for which they clamor. When they buy 50,000 copies of a good novel about colored people by a colored author, publishers will produce books, even those that depict the Negro as an angel on earth,—and the public in general will buy 50,000 copies more to find out what it's all about. Most best sellers are not born,—they're made.

5. I should say so.

6. I think this is true. And here I blame the publisher for not being a "better sport". Most of them seem to have an *idee fixe.* They, even more than the public, I do believe, persist in considering only certain types of Negroes interesting and if an author presents a variant they fear that the public either won't believe in it or won't "stand for it". Whereas I have learned from an interesting and rather broad experience gleaned from speaking before white groups that many, many of these people are keenly interested in learning about the better class of colored people. They are quite willing to be shown.

7. Emphatically. This is a grave danger making for a literary insincerity both insidious and abominable.

JESSIE FAUSET.

---

1. An artist must be free; he can not be bound by any artificial restrictions. At the same time we heartily wish that so many artists would not prefer today to portray only what is vulgar. There is beauty in the world as well as ugliness, idealism as well as realism.

2. This is really covered by 1. It may be added, however, that anyone, even an artist, becomes liable to criticism when his work gives a distorted idea of truth.

3. This question seems to me involved. However, aside from their other reasons for accepting or rejecting books, publishers can hardly be criticised for refusing to bring out books that do not promise a reasonable return on the investment. They are engaged in a business and not in a missionary enterprise.

4. When Negroes feel that they are imperfectly or improperly portrayed, they should find the way to truthful portrayal through any possible channel. Any plant that is struggling in the darkness must find its way to the light as well as it can.

5. Certainly.

6. Yes.

7. Yes.

General answer: Several of the questions seem to me to suggest that the Negro wants patronage. On the whole I think American publishers will be found to be hospitable; they have certainly been hospitable to the Negro in recent years. What we need to do first of all is to produce the really finished work of art. Sooner or later recognition will come.

BENJAMIN BRAWLEY.

---

1. No. The artist, black or white, must be in sympathy with his creations, or creatures, be they what they may be ethically and ethnically. If he is in sympathy with them, he has nothing to fear regarding the effect of his work. His art will justify itself.

2. No, not if he observes the laws of proportion, relation and emphasis. It is the artist's business to portray not merely the typical, the average, but the ultimate.

3. Publishers can be censured only for commercial stupidity.

4. Produce first-rate artistic works with which to kill travesties, as they are beginning to do.

5. Why not? No theme, absolutely none, offers greater opportunities to the novelist and the poet, whatever their race. It is a human situation. If white artists do not discern the potencies of this material in Negro life, the supreme artists in the near future will be black.

6. Yes, to all three questions: (1) But avowed fiction has not done such dastardly damage here as the daily press; (2) the white "artist" who thus takes his material second hand must be flayed; (3) the duty of the black artist is to be a true artist and if he is such he will show the "sordid", the "foolish", and the "criminal" Negro in the environment and the conditions—of white creation, of course—which have made him what he is. Let the black artist not hesitate to show what white "civilization" is doing to both races.

7. No. The cultivated Negro is up against a world hostile to him, ignorant of him, perplexed, uncomfortable, nonplussed by the contradictions arising. No one knows this better than the cultured Negro. It affords him laughter and tears—and out of these, lit by flames of anger, love, pride, aspiration, comes art, in which both the individual and the race are somehow expressed. The Negro artist is going to continue to be mainly concerned with himself, not with any grotesque caricature of him-

self—though he will not despise the broken image. ROBERT T. KERLIN...

Your critic, Mr. Emmett J. Scott, Junior, has every right to pour contempt on my literary gifts; but he has none to attribute to me "sustained contempt, almost hatred, for Negroes". He is again within his rights to find my novel feeble in wit and humour—though his own writing reveals scant glint of either, which I must suppose he is holding in reserve in order to show up my "sustained contempt, almost hatred, for Negroes". At the same time he admits "flashes of ability". But then he attacks Kemble! Surely as kindly an artist as the Negro ever had to utter the exquisite humour of a greatly humorous race! . . . .

When I was a youngster, I was left in command of a company of Zouaves at Port Royal in Jamaica. I was a mere boy. There was brought before me as prisoner a magnificent bronze god of a man whom they called "Long" Burke—he flits through my novel. I stood six feet high; this big fellow stood head and shoulders taller. Well—it appeared that he had knocked the stuffing out of a little black corporal, which is bad for discipline, and, being no hanging judge, I was grieved and worried when, to my relief, the corporal said he wished to add that Burke had always been a good soldier and he, the corporal, may have been over-impatient with him. I took it as a case of attempted murder with a recommendation to mercy. I talked to Burke like a father, and then told him that after what the corporal had said I would only give him a nominal punishment—changed his charge on the crime-sheet to a paltry offence—and, God forgive me, only confined him to barracks for three days. . . . . When I got back to my quarters I found an orderly waiting for me to tell me that Long Burke had "gone fantee" into the cocoa-nut grove with a rifle and ten rounds of ball cartridge to shoot me, and begging me not to go near the grove until Burke had been caught. Anyway, if I hate Negroes, the Negroes did not hate *me*, since they were prepared to risk their lives to save mine from harm. To cut a long story short, they waited until sunset, when Burke fell asleep, and they got him—took him to the guard room—and reported to me. I buckled on the sword of authority and made across the square in the twilight to the guard room. There the Sergeant-major and the Sergeant of the Guard begged me not to go near Burke who was in the cells foaming at the mouth—he had torn his uniform to tatters, and was sitting on the plank bed bare as Venus, scowling and vowing vengeance. Now I knew that this great mad devil of a man could crack me like a nut if he put his mind to it; but I knew equally well that if I did not close with him there and then I should live a life of misery as long as that man lived. And a brain-wave came to me. I called to the Sergeant of the Guard that I wanted to see Burke—what was he a prisoner for?—told him to throw open the door of the "clink", which he did most reluctantly,—and taking off my sword with a melodramatic air I handed it—in a majestic bluff and a gorgeous funk—to the Sergeant—walked boldly up to Burke who sat as naked as when born, a huge bronze god of sullen wrath on the plank bed—sat down beside him, laying my hand on his shoulder, and said: "Burke, they tell me that you wanted to shoot me—It's a shabby lie." I noticed that the Sergeant of the guard was "taking a bead" through the small window in the twilight on poor Burke—and he was a deadly sure shot!

The fellow said never a word; and the thought of that giant taking me by the throat made me feel about as small as I have ever felt. I turned to the open door:

"Sergeant," I called,—"it's all too damsilly about Burke. Send for his kit and let him go back to his barrack-room, and tell the men it was only Burke's joke. Good Lord! if it gets to the ears of the General that I only gave him three days confined to barracks for hitting my corporal, I shall have to leave the army." . . .

"Burke," said I,—"you would not see me punished for letting you off penal servitude, would you? Come, old man, get into your trousers, and be a man and a soldier! Damme, I've got you down for lance-corporal! Don't make me look a fool!"

I strolled out of the place, hoping to God he would not jump on my back . . . .

Long Burke became the most devoted friend to me for the rest of my service—and he maintained a discipline in my company such as I have never seen bettered. And it was not because of my contempt and hatred for Negroes. . . .

HALDANE MACFALL.

The Negro in Art

How Shall He Be Portrayed

A Symposium

WE have asked the artists of the world these questions:

1. When the artist, black or white, portrays Negro characters is he under any obligations or limitations as to the sort of character he will portray?
2. Can any author be criticized for painting the worst or the best characters of a group?
3. Can publishers be criticized for refusing to handle novels that portray Negroes of education and accomplishment, on the ground that these characters are no different from white folk and therefore not interesting?
4. What are Negroes to do when they are continually painted at their worst and judged by the public as they are painted?
5. Does the situation of the educated Negro in America with its pathos, humiliation and tragedy call for artistic treatment at least as sincere and sympathetic as "Porgy" received?
6. Is not the continual portrayal of the sordid, foolish and criminal among Negroes convincing the world that this and this alone is really and essentially Negroid, and preventing white artists from knowing any other types and preventing black artists from daring to paint them?
7. Is there not a real danger that young colored writers will be tempted to follow the popular trend in portraying Negro character in the underworld rather than seeking to paint the truth about themselves and their own social class?

Here are some answers. More will follow:

When it is fully realized that "a man's a man",—the problems of this sort will cease. Peoples long subjected to travail, depressing and repressing environment, and the long list of handicaps common to men of color, naturally find it difficult to reach the high levels *en masse.* It would be strange, miraculous if they did. The few who do break thru the hell-crust of prevalent conditions to high ground should be crowned, extolled and emulated.

This is the work of the artist. Paint, write, let the submerged man and the world see those who have proven stronger than the iron grip of circumstance.

Let the artist cease to capitalize the frailties of the struggling or apathetic mass—and portray the best that offers. This is naturally unpopular, and why? The thinker knows! To the ignorant it does not matter—yet. Depict the best, with or without approbation and renown.

GEORGIA DOUGLAS JOHNSON.

This question of what material the Negro writer should draw upon, and how he should use it, is no simon pure problem with a sure, mathematical conclusion; it has innumerable ramifications, and almost all arguments can be met with a dissenting *but* equally as strong. Opinions will probably be as various as the writers' several constitutions; moreover, it is a question of whether the work is the *thing,* or its moral, social and educational effect.

I should be the last person to vote for any infringement of the author's right to tell a story, to delineate a character, or to transcribe an emotion in his own way, and in the light of truth as he sees it. That is the one inalienable right into which the Negro author ought to be admitted with all other authors, as a slight compensation for other rights so described in which he does not share. I do believe, however, that the Negro has not yet built up a large enough body of sound, healthy race literature to permit him to speculate in abortions and aberrations which other people are all too prone to accept as truly legitimate. There can be no doubt that there is a fictional type of Negro, an ignorant, burly, bestial person, changing somewhat today, though not for the better, to the sensual habitue of dives and loose living, who represents to the mass of white readers the be—all and end—all of what constitutes a Negro. What would be taken as a type in other literatures is, where it touches us, seized upon as representative so long as it adheres to this old pattern. For Negroes to raise a great hue and cry against such misrepresentations without a t t e m p t i n g, through their artists, to reconstruct the situation seems futile as well as foolish. Negro artists have a definite duty to perform in this matter, one which should supersede their individual prerogatives, without denying those rights. We must create types that are truly representative of us as a people, nor do I feel that such a move is necessarily a genuflexion away from true art.

As far as I am concerned the white writer is totally out of the scene. He will write as he pleases, though it offend; and when he does offend, he can always plead the extenuation of a particular incident and of particular characters that appeal to him because of their novelty. He is not under the same obligations to us that we are to ourselves. Nor can he, as a member of a group with a vast heritage of sound literature behind it, quite rise to an understanding of what seems to him an oversensitiveness on our part; he cannot quite understand our disinclination as a people toward our racial defamation, even for art's sake.

I do not feel that we can so severely criticize publishers who reject our work on the score that it will not appeal to their readers. Publishers, in general, are caterers, not martyrs and philanthropists. But if they reject a treatment of educated and accomplished Negroes for the avowed reason that these do not differ from white folk of the same sort, they should reject those about lower class Negroes for the reason that they do not differ essentially from white folk of the same sort; unless they feel that, difference or no difference, the only time a Negro is interesting is when he is at his worst. This does not mean that the Negro writer has either to capitulate or turn away from his calling. Even among publishers there are those rare eccentrics who will judge a work on its merits.

The danger to the young Negro writer is not that he will find his aspiration in the Negro slums; I dare say there are as fine characters and as bright dream material there as in the best strata of Negro society, and that is as it should be. Let the young Negro writer, like any artist, find his treasure where his heart lies. If the unfortunate and less favored find an affinity in him, let him surrender himself; only let him not pander to the popular trend of seeing no cleanliness in their squalor, no nobleness in their meanness and no commonsense in their ignorance. A white man and a southerner gave us *Porgy*, the merits of which few will deny, nor wish away because the story deals with illiterate Negroes. Mr. Heyward gave us a group of men and women; the Negro writer can in strict justice to himself attempt no less than this, whether he writes of Negroes or of a larger world.

COUNTÉE CULLEN.

I am a bit excited about your magazine. There is in it stimulation for the darker races as well as a prod, a fetching good dig in the ribs, for the pale of face. There is perhaps one thing that needs stress and that is the proposition to forget race. Lay that old bogey man. And now may I give to you just an ordinary, average man's opinion in answer to your questionnaire? I know that my opinion is unsolicited but I wish to let you know that even an ordinary man may think upon the things you ask and to good advantage.

1. The inarticulate artist in me cries out that no man can be judged an artist by his race or creed. Paul Robeson is an artist first and a Negro next. When I have heard him sing I never think "What a wonderful Negro voice". I forget the qualification of race. The obligation of the artist is not to his race but to his talent.

2. An author can be criticized only when he deliberately falsifies with malice aforethought.

3. Such a publisher is missing his main chance. An absorbing tale can surely be written about Negroes of good education and refinement. A publisher who cannot see that is not on to his onions.

4. Bring out the supreme spectacle of the Nordic's obverse side. That ought to be a good tonic for all races.

5. No one but a numskull could treat him otherwise.

6. No. Wiley and Cohen are hardly artists. They are authors. Perhaps the latter is becoming one. He will I think some day write a real story of the Negro and do it with understanding. There is a false notion among a great number of peoples that the sordid-foolish-criminal side is all there is to the Negro. The Negro will have to fight that down as the Jew has had to fight down the same impression by proving the contrary.

7. The young author may have a tendency to pick-up easy money by writing only of the underworld but the compelling urge of a real artist, be he Negro or some other tint, will not allow mere facetiousness to mar his canvas. Things as he sees them —he paints.

Luck to your mission.

J. HERBERT ENGBECK.

Salt Lake City, Utah.

The Negro in Art

How Shall He Be Portrayed

A Symposium

WE have asked the artists of the world these questions:

1. When the artist, black or white, portrays Negro characters is he under any obligations or limitations as to the sort of character he will portray?
2. Can any author be criticized for painting the worst or the best characters of a group?
3. Can publishers be criticized for refusing to handle novels that portray Negroes of education and accomplishment, on the ground that these characters are no different from white folk and therefore not interesting?
4. What are Negroes to do when they are continually painted at their worst and judged by the public as they are painted?
5. Does the situation of the educated Negro in America with its pathos, humiliation and tragedy call for artistic treatment at least as sincere and sympathetic as "Porgy" received?
6. Is not the continual portrayal of the sordid, foolish and criminal among Negroes convincing the world that this and this alone is really and essentially Negroid, and preventing white artists from knowing any other types and preventing black artists from daring to paint them?
7. Is there not a real danger that young colored writers will be tempted to follow the popular trend in portraying Negro character in the underworld rather than seeking to paint the truth about themselves and their own social class?

Here are some answers. More will follow:

Please excuse my delay in answering your letter of Feb. 24th and the Questionnaire which you submitted to me. Many incidental circumstances have intervened and these, along with the exigencies of my own work and the need for careful reflection regarding your inquiries, have prevented an earlier reply.

Let me say at the outset that I am not a propagandist for or against the Negro; that for the most part I have small sympathy with propagandists of any kind or color. In my opinion, the minute any one becomes an advocate he ceases to be an artist. Propagandists may be able and admirable persons and, on occasion, be actuated by most worthy purposes; but, broadly speaking, it seems to me that special pleading is not conducive to the development of a judicial view-point.

I believe that the crying need among Negroes is a development in them of racial pride; and a cessation on their own part as well as on the part of other races, who attempt to portray their character, to estimate their worth according to their success in imitating their white brethren.

The Negro is racially different in many essential particulars from his fellow mortals of another color. But this certainly does not prove that he has not racial qualifications of inestimable value without the free and full development of which a perfected humanity will never be achieved.

Racial antagonisms are not necessarily a matter of color. Religion has produced and still perpetuates them in a most accentuated form. But pride of race has enabled the Hebrew to maintain himself against an age-old proscription; and it establishes him today as a recognized leader among the peoples of the earth.

So far as your complaint at the variety of derogatory portrayals of Negro life, character and self-expression, does it occur to an Irishman or a Jew to imagine for a moment that the cultural standing or development of their races are or could be seriously affected by the grotesqueries of "Mr. Jiggs" or "Mr. Potash"? The illiterate may feel irritated, but the Irishman or Jew who knows that his people have racially so lived and wrought and achieved that the world would be impoverished by the loss of their contribution to its civilization, laughs and is not remotely disturbed by these portrayals of Mr. McManus and Mr. Glass.

If America has produced a type more worthy of admiration and honor than the "Black Negro Mammy" I fail to have heard of it. The race that produced them has to its credit an achievement which may well be envied by any people. Without imitating anybody, often sinned against and seldom sinning, they wrote a page in human history that is not only an honor to themselves but to the Creator of life. Yet when a proposal was made in Congress that the nation erect a monument to commemorate the splendid virtues of these devoted black women, a number of Negroes protested against it, saying that their race wished to forget the days of its bondage.

It seems to me that a man who is not proud that he belongs to a race that produced the Negro Mammy of the South is not and can never be either an educated man or a gentleman.

My answer to all your queries may be summed up in my belief that the Negro must develop in himself and in his race such things as that race distinctly possesses and without which humanity and the civilization which represents it cannot permanently do.

Of course it is better for Mr. DuBose Heyward to write of him with pitying, pathetic sympathy than for Mr. Cohen (who may himself have felt the sting of racial antipathy and ridicule) to picture him as a perpetual exponent of primitive buffoonery. And it would be better for Negro authors to demonstrate that their race has things the white race has not in equal degree and that cannot be duplicated; to magnify these things instead of minimizing them.

A true artist, black or white, will search for these tokens of racial worth and weave around them his contribution to literature.

Yet it seems futile to cavil because one man writes this way and another, that, as varying abilities and inclinations may dictate.

I write about Negroes because they represent human nature obscured by so little veneer; human nature groping among its instinctive impulses and in an environment which is tragically primitive and often unutterably pathetic. But I am no propagandist for or against any race. I devoutly hope I shall never be one. I am interested in humanity *per se* without regard to color or conditions.

JULIA PETERKIN.

I am neither an artist nor a writer, yet I have traveled much, am a graduate of the school of hard knocks and have thought a great deal. So I would like to say something.

1. No.

2. No.

3. Yes, because these editors show their ignorance in the race question. Every race has its own peculiar talents and abilities. The danger in the United States is not that you have too many original minds and people, but the opposite is the case. No nation or people in the world are being moulded into such a sameness as the people of the United States. And if the Negro writes about the cultured of his race I am sure that these writings will be different from those of white writers and therefore should be welcome. Although the American Negro is, I am sorry to say, being Americanized, I think there will always be a difference between the coloured and white race, even in America. Therefore I think the portrayal of educated coloured folks and their lives will be as interesting if not more so than of the whites.

4. Be true to themselves. The Negro is no worse than the white man, given equal chances. Just here is where the Negro artist and writer must try to counteract the bad influence and as I have said before show up the cultured and good people of his race. If he cannot find white publishers then he must go into the publishing business himself. If the books are well written and the painter is a real artist, painting true to nature, he need not fear for the result.

5. Yes, and more so. The world, especially the European world, should be made acquainted with the condition of the educated Negro in the United States and wherever the Anglo Saxons rule. He has got to learn to be a fighter and to fight so hard till the conscience of the world is awakened and justice is done the coloured people.

6. I do not think so. Thinking people are beginning to see that a great, almost unspeakable injustice has been and is still being done to the coloured races, and scientists are pointing out that there are no inferior races. That those which appear backward are only so not in kind but in degree.

7. There may be some danger in that the Negro artist must not be afraid and must show up the coloured races true to nature, the good and the bad sides. Here is where the Negro must show himself master of the situation and must be willing to make the sacrifice for the benefit of his race. Even if for a time his work may be unpopular the time will come, if he is a true artist, when he will win out.

OTTO F. MACK,
Stuttgart, Germany.

The Negro in Art

How Shall He Be Portrayed

A Symposium

WE have asked the artists of the world these questions:

1. When the artist, black or white, portrays Negro characters is he under any obligations or limitations as to the sort of character he will portray?

2. Can any author be criticized for painting the worst or the best characters of a group?

3. Can publishers be criticized for refusing to handle novels that portray Negroes of education and accomplishment, on the ground that these characters are no different from white folk and therefore not interesting?

4. What are Negroes to do when they are continually painted at their worst and judged by the public as they are painted?

5. Does the situation of the educated Negro in America with its pathos, humiliation and tragedy call for artistic treatment at least as sincere and sympathetic as "Porgy" received?

6. Is not the continual portrayal of the sordid, foolish and criminal among Negroes convincing the world that this and this alone is really and essentially Negroid, and preventing white artists from knowing any other types and preventing black artists from daring to paint them?

7. Is there not a real danger that young colored writers will be tempted to follow the popular trend in portraying Negro character in the underworld rather than seeking to paint the truth about themselves and their own social class?

Here are some answers. More will follow:

---

1. The realm of art is almost the only territory in which the mind is free, and of all the arts that of creative fiction is the freest. Painting, sculpture, music, poetry, the stage, are all more or less hampered by convention—even jazz has been tamed and harnessed, and there are rules for writing free verse. The man with the pen in the field of fiction is the only free lance, with the whole world to tilt at. Within the very wide limits of the present day conception of decency, he can write what he pleases. I see no possible reason why a colored writer should not have the same freedom. We want no color line in literature.

2. It depends on how and what he writes about them. A true picture of life would include the good, the bad and the indifferent. Most people, of whatever group, belong to the third class, and are therefore not interesting subjects of fiction. A writer who made all Negroes bad and all white people good, or *vice versa*, would not be a true artist, and could justly be criticised.

3. To the publisher, the one indispensable requisite for a novel is that it should sell, and to sell, it must be interesting. No publisher wants to bring out and no reader cares to read a dull book. To be interesting, a character in a novel must have personality. It is perhaps unfortunate that so few of the many Negro or Negroid characters in current novels are admirable types; but they are interesting, and it is the privilege and the opportunity of the colored writer to make characters of a different sort equally interesting. Education and accomplishment do not of themselves necessarily make people interesting—we all know dull people who are highly cultured. The difficulty of finding a publisher for books by Negro authors has largely disappeared—publishers are seeking such books. Whether the demand for them shall prove to be more than a mere passing fad will depend upon the quality of the product.

4. Well, what can they do except to protest, and to paint a better type of Negro?

5. The Negro race and its mixtures are scattered over most of the earth's surface, and come in contact with men of other races in countless ways. All these contacts, with their resultant reactions, are potential themes of fiction, and the writer of genius ought to be able, with this wealth of material, to find or to create interesting types. If there are no super-Negroes, make some, as Mr. Cable did in his *Bras Coupé*. Some of the men and women who have had the greatest influence on civilization have been purely creatures of the imagination. It might not be a bad idea to create a few white men who not only think they are, but who really are entirely unprejudiced in their dealings with colored folk—it is the highest privilege of art to depict the ideal. There are plenty of Negro and Negroid

types which a real artist could make interesting to the general reader without making all the men archangels, or scoundrels, or weaklings, or all the women unchaste. The writer, of whatever color, with the eye to see, the heart to feel and the pen to record the real romance, the worthy ambition, the broad humanity, which exist among colored people of every class, in spite of their handicaps, will find a hearing and reap his reward.

6. I do not think so. People who read books read the newspapers, and cannot possibly conceive that crime is peculiarly Negroid. In fact, in the matter of serious crime the Negro is a mere piker compared with the white man. In South Carolina, where the Negroes out number the whites, the penitentiary has more white than colored inmates. Of course the propagandist, of whatever integumentary pigment, will, of purpose or unconsciously, distort the facts. My most popular novel was distorted and mangled by a colored moving picture producer to make it appeal to Negro race prejudice.

7. I think there is little danger of young colored writers writing too much about Negro characters in the underworld, so long as they do it well. Some successful authors have specialized in crook stories, and some crooks are mighty interesting people. The colored writer of fiction should study life in all its aspects. He should not worry about his social class. Indeed, it is doubtful whether the general reading public can be interested today in a long serious novel based upon the social struggles of colored people. Good work has been done along this line with the short story, but colored society is still too inchoate to have developed the fine shades and nuances of the more sophisticated society with which the ordinary novel of manner deals. Pride of caste is hardly convincing in a people where the same family, in the same generation, may produce a bishop and a butler, a lawyer and a lackey, not as an accident or a rarity but almost as a matter of course. On the other hand it can be argued that at the hand of a master these sharp contrasts could be made highly dramatic. But there is no formula for these things, and the discerning writer will make his own rules.

The prevailing weakness of Negro writings, from the viewpoint of art, is that they are too subjective. The colored writer, generally speaking, has not yet passed the point of thinking of himself first as a Negro, burdened with the responsibility of defending and uplifting his race. Such a frame of mind, however praiseworthy from a moral standpoint, is bad for art. Tell your story, and if it is on a vital subject, well told, with an outcome that commends itself to right-thinking people, it will, if interesting, be an effective brief for whatever cause it incidentally may postulate.

Why let Octavus Roy Cohen or Hugh Wiley have a monopoly of the humorous side of Negro life? White artists caricatured the Negro on the stage until Ernest Hogan and Bert Williams discovered that colored men could bring out the Negro's more amusing characteristics in a better and more interesting way.

Why does not some colored writer build a story around a Negro oil millionaire, and the difficulty he or she has in keeping any of his or her money? A Pullman porter who performs wonderful feats in the detection of crime has great possibilities. The Negro visionary who would change the world over night and bridge the gap between races in a decade would make an effective character in fiction. But the really epical race novel, in which love and hatred, high endeavor, success and failure, sheer comedy and stark tragedy are mingled, is yet to be written, and let us hope that a man of Negro blood may write it.

CHARLES W. CHESNUTT.

Criteria of Negro Art

W. E. BURGHARDT DU BOIS

So many persons have asked for the complete text of the address delivered by Dr. Du Bois at the Chicago Conference of the National Association for the Advancement of Colored People that we are publishing the address here.

I DO not doubt but there are some in this audience who are a little disturbed at the subject of this meeting, and particularly at the subject I have chosen. Such people are thinking something like this: "How is it that an organization like this, a group of radicals trying to bring new things into the world, a fighting organization which has come up out of the blood and dust of battle, struggling for the right of black men to be ordinary human beings—how is it that an organization of this kind can turn aside to talk about Art? After all, what have we who are slaves and black to do with Art?"

Or perhaps there are others who feel a certain relief and are saying, "After all it is rather satisfactory after all this talk about rights and fighting to sit and dream of something which leaves a nice taste in the mouth".

Let me tell you that neither of these groups is right. The thing we are talking about tonight is part of the great fight we are carrying on and it represents a forward and an upward look—a pushing onward. You and I have been breasting hills; we have been climbing upward; there has been progress and we can see it day by day looking back along blood-filled paths. But as you go through the valleys and over the foothills, so long as you are climbing, the direction,—north, south, east or west,—is of less importance. But when gradually the vista widens and you begin to see the world at your feet and the far horizon, then it is time to know more precisely whither you are going and what you really want.

What do we want? What is the thing we are after? As it was phrased last night it had a certain truth: We want to be Americans, full-fledged Americans, with all the rights of other American citizens. But is that all? Do we want simply to be Americans? Once in a while through all of us there flashes some clairvoyance, some clear idea, of what America really is. We who are dark can see America in a way that white Americans can not. And seeing our country thus, are we satisfied with its present goals and ideals?

In the high school where I studied we learned most of Scott's "Lady of the Lake" by heart. In after life once it was my privilege to see the lake. It was Sunday. It was quiet. You could glimpse the deer wandering in unbroken forests; you could hear the soft ripple of romance on the waters. Around me fell the cadence of that poetry of my youth. I fell asleep full of the enchantment of the Scottish border. A new day broke and with it came a sudden rush of excursionists. They were mostly Americans and they were loud and strident. They poured upon the little pleasure boat,—men with their hats a little on one side and drooping cigars in the wet corners of their mouths; women who shared their conversation with the world. They all tried to get everywhere first. They pushed other people out of the way. They made all sorts of incoherent noises and gestures so that the quiet home folk and the visitors from other lands silently and half-wonderingly gave way before them. They struck a note not evil but wrong. They carried, perhaps, a sense of strength and accomplishment, but their hearts had no conception of the beauty which pervaded this holy place.

If you tonight suddenly should become full-fledged Americans; if your color faded, or the color line here in Chicago was miraculously forgotten; suppose, too, you became at the same time rich and powerful;—what is it that you would want? What would you immediately seek? Would you buy the most powerful of motor cars and outrace Cook County? Would you buy the most elaborate estate on the North Shore? Would you be a Rotarian or a Lion or a What-not of the very last degree? Would you wear the most striking clothes, give the richest dinners and buy the longest press notices?

Even as you visualize such ideals you know in your hearts that these are not the things you really want. You realize this sooner than the average white American

Top Row: Eleanor Muriel Milton, Atlanta; Constance Marcheta Whitfield, Americus, Ga.; Parthenia Turner, Marshall, Texas; Emerson Du Bois Evans, Fitzgerald, Ga. Second Row: Clayton R., Jr., and Clara L. Yates, Atlanta; Darius Henry Keene, Jr., Philadelphia; George J. Ware, Iowa City, Iowa; Gloria M. Johnson, Washington, D. C. Bottom Row: Percy Lawrence Fleming, Akron, Ohio; Wellington Allen, Mobile, Ala.; Richard H. Allen, Jr., Mobile, Ala.; Charles P. Allen, Mobile, Ala.

because, pushed aside as we have been in America, there has come to us not only a certain distaste for the tawdry and flamboyant but a vision of what the world could be if it were really a beautiful world; if we had the true spirit; if we had the Seeing Eye, the Cunning Hand, the Feeling Heart; if we had, to be sure, not perfect happiness, but plenty of good hard work, the inevitable suffering that always comes with life; sacrifice and waiting, all that—but, nevertheless, lived in a world where men know, where men create, where they realize themselves and where they enjoy life. It is that sort of a world we want to create for ourselves and for all America.

After all, who shall describe Beauty? What is it? I remember tonight four beautiful things: The Cathedral at Cologne, a forest in stone, set in light and changing shadow, echoing with sunlight and solemn song; a village of the Veys in West Africa, a little thing of mauve and purple, quiet, lying content and shining in the sun; a black and velvet room where on a throne rests, in old and yellowing marble, the broken curves of the Venus of Milo; a single phrase of music in the Southern South—utter melody, haunting and appealing, suddenly arising out of night and eternity, beneath the moon.

Such is Beauty. Its variety is infinite, its possibility is endless. In normal life all may have it and have it yet again. The world is full of it; and yet today the mass of human beings are choked away from it, and their lives distorted and made ugly. This is not only wrong, it is silly. Who shall right this well-nigh universal failing? Who shall let this world be beautiful? Who shall restore to men the glory of sunsets and the peace of quiet sleep?

We black folk may help for we have within us as a race new stirrings; stirrings of the beginning of a new appreciation of joy, of a new desire to create, of a new will to be; as though in this morning of group life we had awakened from some sleep that at once dimly mourns the past and dreams a splendid future; and there has come the conviction that the Youth that is here today, the Negro Youth, is a different kind of Youth, because in some new way it bears this mighty prophecy on its breast, with a new realization of itself, with new determination for all mankind.

What has this Beauty to do with the world? What has Beauty to do with Truth and Goodness—with the facts of the world and the right actions of men? "Nothing", the artists rush to answer. They may be right. I am but an humble disciple of art and cannot presume to say. I am one who tells the truth and exposes evil and seeks with Beauty and for Beauty to set the world right. That somehow, somewhere eternal and perfect Beauty sits above Truth and Right I can conceive, but here and now and in the world in which I work they are for me unseparated and inseparable.

This is brought to us peculiarly when as artists we face our own past as a people. There has come to us—and it has come especially through the man we are going to honor tonight*—a realization of that past, of which for long years we have been ashamed, for which we have apologized. We thought nothing could come out of that past which we wanted to remember; which we wanted to hand down to our children. Suddenly, this same past is taking on form, color and reality, and in a half shamefaced way we are beginning to be proud of it. We are remembering that the romance of the world did not die and lie forgotten in the Middle Age; that if you want romance to deal with you must have it here and now and in your own hands.

I once knew a man and woman. They had two children, a daughter who was white and a daughter who was brown; the daughter who was white married a white man; and when her wedding was preparing the daughter who was brown prepared to go and celebrate. But the mother said, "No!" and the brown daughter went into her room and turned on the gas and died. Do you want Greek tragedy swifter than that?

Or again, here is a little Southern town and you are in the public square. On one side of the square is the office of a colored lawyer and on all the other sides are men who do not like colored lawyers. A white woman goes into the black man's office and points to the white-filled square and says, "I want five hundred dollars now and if I do not get it I am going to scream."

Have you heard the story of the conquest of German East Africa? Listen to the untold tale: There were 40,000 black men and

* Carter Godwin Woodson, 12th Spingarn Medallist.

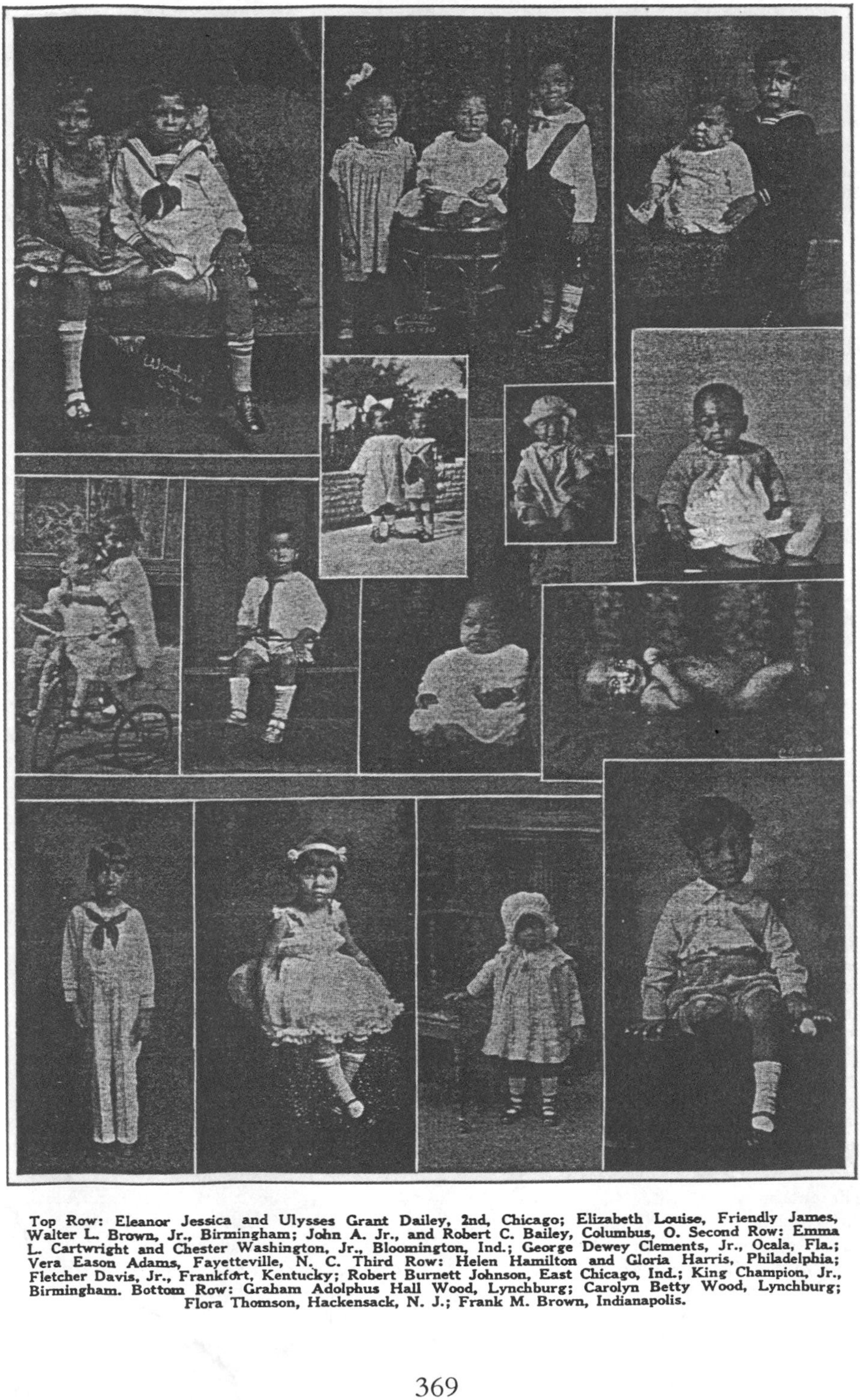

Top Row: Eleanor Jessica and Ulysses Grant Dailey, 2nd, Chicago; Elizabeth Louise, Friendly James, Walter L. Brown, Jr., Birmingham; John A. Jr., and Robert C. Bailey, Columbus, O. Second Row: Emma L. Cartwright and Chester Washington, Jr., Bloomington, Ind.; George Dewey Clements, Jr., Ocala, Fla.; Vera Eason Adams, Fayetteville, N. C. Third Row: Helen Hamilton and Gloria Harris, Philadelphia; Fletcher Davis, Jr., Frankfort, Kentucky; Robert Burnett Johnson, East Chicago, Ind.; King Champion, Jr., Birmingham. Bottom Row: Graham Adolphus Hall Wood, Lynchburg; Carolyn Betty Wood, Lynchburg; Flora Thomson, Hackensack, N. J.; Frank M. Brown, Indianapolis.

4,000 white men who talked German. There were 20,000 black men and 12,000 white men who talked English. There were 10,000 black men and 400 white men who talked French. In Africa then where the Mountains of the Moon raised their white and snow-capped heads into the mouth of the tropic sun, where Nile and Congo rise and the Great Lakes swim, these men fought; they struggled on mountain, hill and valley, in river, lake and swamp, until in masses they sickened, crawled and died; until the 4,000 white Germans had become mostly bleached bones; until nearly all the 12,000 white Englishmen had returned to South Africa, and the 400 Frenchmen to Belgium and Heaven; all except a mere handful of the white men died; but thousands of black men from East, West and South Africa, from Nigeria and the Valley of the Nile, and from the West Indies still struggled, fought and died. For four years they fought and won and lost German East Africa; and all you hear about it is that England and Belgium conquered German Africa for the allies!

Such is the true and stirring stuff of which Romance is born and from this stuff come the stirrings of men who are beginning to remember that this kind of material is theirs; and this vital life of their own kind is beckoning them on.

The question comes next as to the interpretation of these new stirrings, of this new spirit: Of what is the colored artist capable? We have had on the part of both colored and white people singular unanimity of judgment in the past. Colored people have said: "This work must be inferior because it comes from colored people." White people have said: "It is inferior because it is done by colored people." But today there is coming to both the realization that the work of the black man is not always inferior. Interesting stories come to us. A professor in the University of Chicago read to a class that had studied literature a passage of poetry and asked them to guess the author. They guessed a goodly company from Shelley and Robert Browning down to Tennyson and Masefield. The author was Countée Cullen. Or again the English critic John Drinkwater went down to a Southern seminary, one of the sort which "finishes" young white women of the South. The students sat with their wooden faces while he tried to get some response out of them. Finally he said, "Name me some of your Southern poets". They hesitated. He said finally, "I'll start out with your best: Paul Laurence Dunbar"!

With the growing recognition of Negro artists in spite of the severe handicaps, one comforting thing is occurring to both white and black. They are whispering, "Here is a way out. Here is the real solution of the color problem. The recognition accorded Cullen, Hughes, Fauset, White and others shows there is no real color line. Keep quiet! Don't complain! Work! All will be well!"

I will not say that already this chorus amounts to a conspiracy. Perhaps I am naturally too suspicious. But I will say that there are today a surprising number of white people who are getting great satisfaction out of these younger Negro writers because they think it is going to stop agitation of the Negro question. They say, "What is the use of your fighting and complaining; do the great thing and the reward is there". And many colored people are all too eager to follow this advice; especially those who are weary of the eternal struggle along the color line, who are afraid to fight and to whom the money of philanthropists and the alluring publicity are subtle and deadly bribes. They say, "What is the use of fighting? Why not show simply what we deserve and let the reward come to us?"

And it is right here that the National Association for the Advancement of Colored People comes upon the field, comes with its great call to a new battle, a new fight and new things to fight before the old things are wholly won; and to say that the Beauty of Truth and Freedom which shall some day be our heritage and the heritage of all civilized men is not in our hands yet and that we ourselves must not fail to realize.

There is in New York tonight a black woman molding clay by herself in a little bare room, because there is not a single school of sculpture in New York where she is welcome. Surely there are doors she might burst through, but when God makes a sculptor He does not always make the pushing sort of person who beats his way through doors thrust in his face. This girl is working her hands off to get out of this country so that she can get some sort of training.

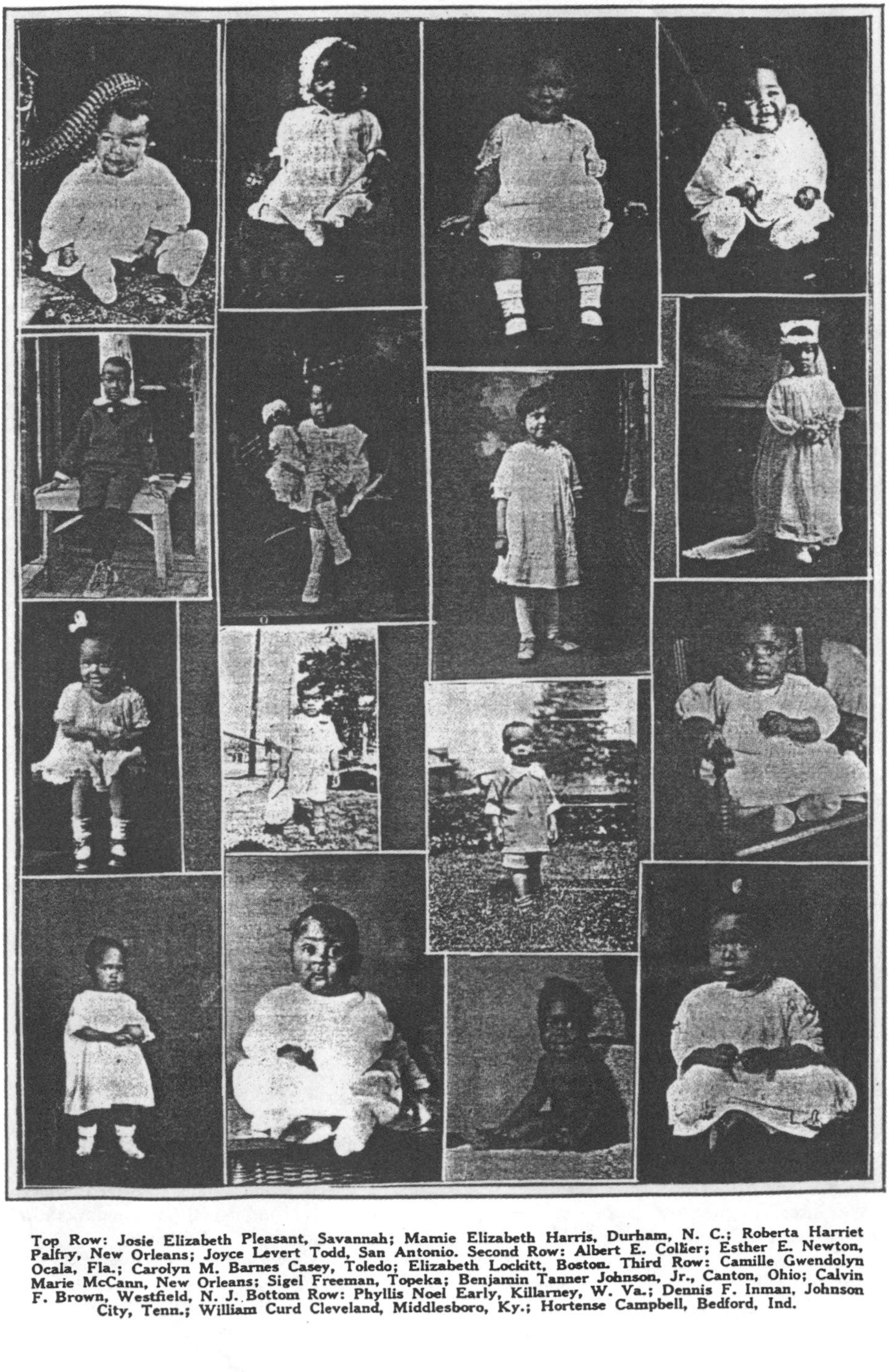

Top Row: Josie Elizabeth Pleasant, Savannah; Mamie Elizabeth Harris, Durham, N. C.; Roberta Harriet Palfry, New Orleans; Joyce Levert Todd, San Antonio. Second Row: Albert E. Collier; Esther E. Newton, Ocala, Fla.; Carolyn M. Barnes Casey, Toledo; Elizabeth Lockitt, Boston. Third Row: Camille Gwendolyn Marie McCann, New Orleans; Sigel Freeman, Topeka; Benjamin Tanner Johnson, Jr., Canton, Ohio; Calvin F. Brown, Westfield, N. J. Bottom Row: Phyllis Noel Early, Killarney, W. Va.; Dennis F. Inman, Johnson City, Tenn.; William Curd Cleveland, Middlesboro, Ky.; Hortense Campbell, Bedford, Ind.

There was Richard Brown. If he had been white he would have been alive today instead of dead of neglect. Many helped him when he asked but he was not the kind of boy that always asks. He was simply one who made colors sing.

There is a colored woman in Chicago who is a great musician. She thought she would like to study at Fontainebleau this summer where Walter Damrosch and a score of leaders of Art have an American school of music. But the application blank of this school says: "I am a white American and I apply for admission to the school."

We can go on the stage; we can be just as funny as white Americans wish us to be; we can play all the sordid parts that America likes to assign to Negroes; but for any thing else there is still small place for us.

And so I might go on. But let me sum up with this: Suppose the only Negro who survived some centuries hence was the Negro painted by white Americans in the novels and essays they have written. What would people in a hundred years say of black Americans? Now turn it around. Suppose you were to write a story and put in it the kind of people you know and like and imagine. You might get it published and you might not. And the "might not" is still far bigger than the "might". The white publishers catering to white folk would say, "It is not interesting"—to white folk, naturally not. They want Uncle Toms, Topsies, good "darkies" and clowns. I have in my office a story with all the earmarks of truth. A young man says that he started out to write and had his stories accepted. Then he began to write about the things he knew best about, that is, about his own people. He submitted a story to a magazine which said, "We are sorry, but we cannot take it". "I sat down and revised my story, changing the color of the characters and the locale and sent it under an assumed name with a change of address and it was accepted by the same magazine that had refused it, the editor promising to take anything else I might send in providing it was good enough."

We have, to be sure, a few recognized and successful Negro artists; but they are not all those fit to survive or even a good minority. They are but the remnants of that ability and genius among us whom the accidents of education and opportunity have raised on the tidal waves of chance. We black folk are not altogether peculiar in this. After all, in the world at large, it is only the accident, the remnant, that gets the chance to make the most of itself; but if this is true of the white world it is infinitely more true of the colored world. It is not simply the great clear tenor of Roland Hayes that opened the ears of America. We have had many voices of all kinds as fine as his and America was and is as deaf as she was for years to him. Then a foreign land heard Hayes and put its imprint on him and immediately America with all its imitative snobbery woke up. We approved Hayes because London, Paris and Berlin approved him and not simply because he was a great singer.

Thus it is the bounden duty of black America to begin this great work of the creation of Beauty, of the preservation of Beauty, of the realization of Beauty, and we must use in this work all the methods that men have used before. And what have been the tools of the artist in times gone by? First of all, he has used the Truth—not for the sake of truth, not as a scientist seeking truth, but as one upon whom Truth eternally thrusts itself as the highest handmaid of imagination, as the one great vehicle of universal understanding. Again artists have used Goodness—goodness in all its aspects of justice, honor and right—not for sake of an ethical sanction but as the one true method of gaining sympathy and human interest.

The apostle of Beauty thus becomes the apostle of Truth and Right not by choice but by inner and outer compulsion. Free he is but his freedom is ever bounded by Truth and Justice; and slavery only dogs him when he is denied the right to tell the Truth or recognize an ideal of Justice.

Thus all Art is propaganda and ever must be, despite the wailing of the purists. I stand in utter shamelessness and say that whatever art I have for writing has been used always for propaganda for gaining the right of black folk to love and enjoy. I do not care a damn for any art that is not used for propaganda. But I do care when propaganda is confined to one side while the other is stripped and silent.

In New York we have two plays: "White Cargo" and "Congo". In "White Cargo" there is a fallen woman. She is black. In "Congo" the fallen woman is white. In

"White Cargo" the black woman goes down further and further and in "Congo" the white woman begins with degradation but in the end is one of the angels of the Lord.

You know the current magazine story: A young white man goes down to Central America and the most beautiful colored woman there falls in love with him. She crawls across the whole isthmus to get to him. The white man says nobly, "No". He goes back to his white sweetheart in New York.

In such cases, it is not the positive propaganda of people who believe white blood divine, infallible and holy to which I object. It is the denial of a similar right of propaganda to those who believe black blood human, lovable and inspired with new ideals for the world. White artists themselves suffer from this narrowing of their field. They cry for freedom in dealing with Negroes because they have so little freedom in dealing with whites. DuBose Heywood writes "Porgy" and writes beautifully of the black Charleston underworld. But why does he do this? Because he cannot do a similar thing for the white people of Charleston, or they would drum him out of town. The only chance he had to tell the truth of pitiful human degradation was to tell it of colored people. I should not be surprised if Octavius Roy Cohen had approached the *Saturday Evening Post* and asked permission to write about a different kind of colored folk than the monstrosities he has created; but if he has, the *Post* has replied, "No. You are getting paid to write about the kind of colored people you are writing about."

In other words, the white public today demands from its artists, literary and pictorial, racial pre-judgment which deliberately distorts Truth and Justice, as far as colored races are concerned, and it will pay for no other.

On the other hand, the young and slowly growing black public still wants its prophets almost equally unfree. We are bound by all sorts of customs that have come down as second-hand soul clothes of white patrons. We are ashamed of sex and we lower our eyes when people will talk of it. Our religion holds us in superstition. Our worst side has been so shamelessly emphasized that we are denying we have or ever had a worst side. In all sorts of ways we are hemmed in and our new young artists have got to fight their way to freedom.

The ultimate judge has got to be you and you have got to build yourselves up into that wide judgment, that catholicity of temper which is going to enable the artist to have his widest chance for freedom. We can afford the Truth. White folk today cannot. As it is now we are handing everything over to a white jury. If a colored man wants to publish a book, he has got to get a white publisher and a white newspaper to say it is great; and then you and I say so. We must come to the place where the work of art when it appears is reviewed and acclaimed by our own free and unfettered judgment. And we are going to have a real and valuable and eternal judgment only as we make ourselves free of mind, proud of body and just of soul to all men.

And then do you know what will be said? It is already saying. Just as soon as true Art emerges; just as soon as the black artist appears, someone touches the race on the shoulder and says, "He did that because he was an American, not because he was a Negro; he was born here; he was trained here; he is not a Negro—what is a Negro anyhow? He is just human; it is the kind of thing you ought to expect".

I do not doubt that the ultimate art coming from black folk is going to be just as beautiful, and beautiful largely in the same ways, as the art that comes from white folk, or yellow, or red; but the point today is that until the art of the black folk compells recognition they will not be rated as human. And when through art they compell recognition then let the world discover if it will that their art is as new as it is old and as old as new.

I had a classmate once who did three beautiful things and died. One of them was a story of a folk who found fire and then went wandering in the gloom of night seeking again the stars they had once known and lost; suddenly out of blackness they looked up and there loomed the heavens; and what was it that they said? They raised a mighty cry: "It is the stars, it is the ancient stars, it is the young and everlasting stars!"

Acknowledgments

"A Note on the New Literary Movement." *Opportunity* 4 (March 1926): 80–81.
"Welcoming the New Negro." *Opportunity* 4 (April 1926): 113.
"For Negro Novelists." *Opportunity* 4 (April 1926): 113.
White, Walter. "The Negro Renaissance." *Palms* 4, No. 1 (October 1926): 3–7.
Braithwaite, William Stanley. "The Negro in American Literature." In Addison Gayle, Jr., ed., *Black Expression* (New York: Weybright and Talley, 1969): 169–81.
Brawley, Benjamin Griffin. "The Negro in American Fiction." In Addison Gayle, ed., *Black Expression* (New York: Weybright and Talley, 1969): 182–90.
Thurman, Wallace. "Negro Poets and Their Poetry." In Addison Gayle, ed., *Black Expression* (New York: Weybright and Talley, 1969): 70–82.
Robb, Izetta Winter. "From the Darker Side." *Opportunity* 4 (December 1926): 381–82.
"On the Need of Better Plays." *Opportunity* 5, No. 1 (January 1927): 5–6.
"Arthur Davison Ficke to Carl Van Vechten." nd [1927]. Transcribed letter. Original manuscript [Knopf/uncatalogued/permanent file folders/Hughes, Langston] is in the Harry Ransom Humanities Research Center, University of Texas at Austin. Reprinted with the permission of the Harry Ransom Humanities Research Center and the Estate of Carl Van Vechten.
Taussig, Charlotte E. "The New Negro as Revealed in His Poetry." *Opportunity* 5, No. 4 (April 1927): 108–11.
Brawley, Benjamin. "The Negro Literary Renaissance." *Southern Workman* 56, No. 4 (April 1927): 177–84. Reprinted with the permission of the Hampton University Archives.
Kerlin, Robert T. "Conquest by Poetry." *Southern Workman* 56, No. 6 (June 1927): 282–84. Reprinted with the permission of the Hampton University Archives.
Davis, Allison. "Our Negro 'Intellectuals.'" *Crisis* 35 (August 1928): 268–69, 284–86. Reprinted with the permission of the Crisis Publishing Company.
"Langston Hughes to the Editor of The *Crisis*, July 28, 1928." Letter in response to Davis essay [JWJ/Hughes/MSS 382] is located in the James Weldon Johnson Collection, Beinecke Rare Book Library, Yale University. Reprinted with the permission of the Yale University Beinecke Rare Book Library.
Carter, Elmer Anderson. "Harlem Goes to Work." *Opportunity* 6, No. 11 (November 1928): 326.

Edmonds, Randolph. "Some Reflections on the Negro in American Drama." *Opportunity* 8, No. 10 (October 1930): 303–5.

Chesnutt, Charles W. "Post-Bellum—Pre-Harlem." *Crisis* 38 (June 1931): 193–94. Reprinted with the permission of the Crisis Publishing Company.

"Introduction to a Speech by Langston Hughes Given at Fisk University, January 29, 1932." Typed transcript. Original manuscript [JWJ/76] is located in the James Weldon Johnson Collection, Beinecke Rare Book Library, Yale University. Reprinted with the permission of the Beinecke Rare Book Library and the Estate of Langston Hughes.

Gruening, Martha. "The Negro Renaissance." *Hound and Horn* 5, No. 3 (April–June 1932): 504–14.

Holmes, Eugene. "Jean Toomer—Apostle of Beauty." *Opportunity* 10, No. 8 (August 1932): 252–54, 260.

Starkey, Marion L. "Jessie Fauset." *Southern Workman* 61, No. 5 (May 1932): 217–20. Reprinted with the permission of the Hampton University Archives.

"Claude McKay to Nancy Cunard, September 18, 1932, from Tangier, Morocco." Typed transcription. Original manuscript [MS Cunard/recip/McKay, Claude] is located in the Harry Ransom Humanities Research Center, University of Texas at Austin. Reprinted with the permission of the Harry Ransom Humanities Research Center and the Estate of Claude McKay.

Braithwaite, William Stanley. "The Novels of Jessie Fauset." *Opportunity* 12, No. 1 (January 1934): 24–28. Reprinted with the permission of the National Urban League.

Calverton, V.F . "The Growth of Negro Literature." In Nancy Cunard, ed., *Negro: Anthology Made By Nancy Cunard 1931–1933* (London: Wishart & Co., 1934): 101–5.

Locke, Alain. "Sterling Brown: The New Negro Folk-Poet." In Nancy Cunard, ed., *Negro: Anthology Made By Nancy Cunard 1931–1933* (London: Wishart & Co., 1934): 111–15.

Matthews, Ralph. "The Negro Theater—A Dodo Bird." In Nancy Cunard, ed., *Negro: Anthology Made By Nancy Cunard 1931–1933* (London: Wishart & Co., 1934): 312–14.

Perry, Edward G . "Negro Creative Musicians." In Nancy Cunard, ed., *Negro: Anthology Made By Nancy Cunard 1931–1933* (London: Wishart & Co., 1934): 356–59.

Hughes, Langston. "Remarks Concerning Kay Boyle's Analysis of *On the Road*." Typed transcript. Original typed manuscript [MS Boyle, Kay/Misc/Hughes, Langston] is located in the Harry Ransom Humanities Research Center, University of Texas at Austin. Reprinted with the permission of the Harry Ransom Humanities Research Center and the Estate of Langston Hughes. Copyright 1995.

Du Bois, W.E.B. "Review of *The Book of American Negro Spirituals* by James Weldon Johnson." *Crisis* 31 (November 1925): 31. Reprinted with the permission of the Crisis Publishing Company.

Charlton, Melville. "Review of *Second Book of Negro Spirituals* by James Weldon Johnson." *Opportunity* 4 (December 1926): 393

Baldwin, William H. "Review of *Dark Laughter* by Sherwood Anderson." *Opportunity* 3 (November 1925): 342.

Cullen, Countee. "Review of *Porgy* by Du Bose Heyward." *Opportunity* 3 (December 1925): 379.

Du Bois, W.E.B. "Review of *Porgy* by Du Bose Heyward." *Crisis* 31 (March 1926): 240. Reprinted with the permission of the Crisis Publishing Company.

Locke, Alain. "Color—A Review." *Opportunity* 4 (January 1926): 14–15.

Du Bois, W.E.B. "Review of *The New Negro,* edited by Alain Locke." *Crisis* 31 (January 1926): 140–41. Reprinted with the permission of the Crisis Publishing Company.

Cullen, Countee. "A Review of *The Weary Blues* by Langston Hughes." *Opportunity* 4 (February 1926): 73–74.

Bagnall, Robert W . "Review of *The New Negro—An Interpretation,* edited by Alain Locke." *Opportunity* 4 (February 1926): 74.

Fauset, Jessie. "Review of *Color* by Countee Cullen." *Crisis* 31 (March 1926): 238–39. Reprinted with the permission of the Crisis Publishing Company.

Heyward, Du Bose. "The Jazz Band's Sob." [Review of *The Weary Blues*] *New York Herald Tribune* (August 12, 1926).

Fauset, Jessie. "Review of *The Weary Blues* by Langston Hughes." *Crisis* 31 (March 1926): 239. Reprinted with the permission of the Crisis Publishing Company.

Locke, Alain. "Review of *The Weary Blues* by Langston Hughes." *Palms* 4 (October 1926): 25–28.

Kerlin, Robert T. "Singers of New Songs." *Opportunity* 4 (May 1926): 162–64.

Kerlin, Robert T. "Review of *Poets of America* by Clement Wood." *Opportunity* 4 (June 1926): 196.

Horne, Frank. "Review of *Flight* by Walter White." *Opportunity* 4 (July 1926): 227.

Waring, Nora E. "Review of *Flight* by Walter White." *Crisis* 32 (July 1926): 142. Reprinted with the permission of the Crisis Publishing Company.

Imes [Larsen], Nella. "Correspondence." *Opportunity* 4 (September 1926): 295.

Horne, Frank. "Correspondence." *Opportunity* 4 (October 1926): 329.

White, Walter. "Correspondence." *Opportunity* 4 (December 1926): 397.

"Charles S. Johnson to Carl Van Vechten, August 10, 1926." Letter. Typed transcript. Original letter James Weldon Johnson Collection [JWJ/Van Vechten/ Corres.] is located in the Beinecke Rare Book Library, Yale University. Reprinted with the permission of the Yale University Beinecke Rare Book Library and the Estate of Carl Van Vechten.

Weatherwax, John M. "Review of *Color* by Countee Cullen." *Palms* 3 (January 1926): 121–23.

Johnson, James Weldon. "Romance and Tragedy in Harlem—A Review." *Opportunity* 4 (October 1926): 316–17, 330.

Du Bois, W.E.B. "Review of *Nigger Heaven* by Carl Van Vechten." *Crisis* 33 (December 1926): 81–82. Reprinted with the permission of the Crisis Publishing Company.

Frank, Waldo. "In Our American Language." *Opportunity* 4 (November 1926): 352.

Heyward, Du Bose. "Fine Clothes to the Jew." *New York Herald Tribune* (February 2, 1927).

White, Walter F. "The Growth of a Poet." *New York World* (February 2, 1927).

Larkin, Margaret. "A Poet for the People—A Review." *Opportunity* 5, No. 3 (March 1927): 84–85.

Root, E. Merrill. "Keats in Labrador: A Review." *Opportunity* 5, No. 9 (September 1927): 270–71.

Nelson, Alice Dunbar. "Review of *The Autobiography of an Ex-Colored Man* by James Weldon Johnson." *Opportunity* 5, No. 11 (November 1927): 337–38.

Purnell, Idella. "Review of *Caroling Dusk: An Anthology of Verse by Negro Poets*, edited by Countee Cullen." *Opportunity* 5, No. 11 (December 1927): 374–75.

Du Bois, W.E.B. "The Browsing Reader." *Crisis* 35 (January 1928): 20. Reprinted with the permission of the Crisis Publishing Company.

Du Bois, W.E.B. "The Browsing Reader." *Crisis* 35 (June 1928): 202. Reprinted with the permission of the Crisis Publishing Company.

Doggett, A.B., Jr. "Review of *Home to Harlem* by Claude McKay." *Southern Workman* 57, No. 5 (May 1928): 240. Reprinted with the permission of the Hampton University Archives.

Brickell, Herschel. "Review of *Home to Harlem* by Claude McKay." *Opportunity* 6, No. 5 (May 1928): 151–52.

Walton, Eda Lou. "Review of *Quicksand* by Nella Larsen." *Opportunity* 6, No. 7 (July 1928): 212–13.

Whipple, Leon. "Review of *Dark Princess* by W.E. Burghardt DuBois." *Opportunity* 6, No. 8 (1928): 244.

Aery, William A. "Review of *Dark Princess* by W.E. Burghardt DuBois." *Southern Workman* 57, No. 8 (August 1928): 334–36. Reprinted with the permission of the Hampton University Archives.

Du Bois, W.E.B. "The Lighter Touch in Harlem." [Review of *The Walls of Jericho* by Rudolph Fisher] *Crisis* 35 (November 1928): 374. Reprinted with the permission of the Crisis Publishing Company.

Botkin, B.A. "Review of *The Walls of Jericho* by Rudolph Fisher." *Opportunity* 6, No. 11 (November 1928): 346.

Du Bois, W.E.B. "The Browsing Reader." *Crisis* 36 (April 1929): 125, 138–39. Reprinted with the permission of the Crisis Publishing Company.

Du Bois, W.E.B. "The Browsing Reader." *Crisis* 36 (May 1929): 161. Reprinted with the permission of the Crisis Publishing Company.

Du Bois, W.E.B. "The Browsing Reader." *Crisis* 36 (July 1929): 234, 248–50. Reprinted with the permission of the Crisis Publishing Company.

Brown, Sterling A. "Review of *Mamba's Daughters* by DuBose Heyward." *Opportunity* 7, No. 5 (1929): 161–62.

Carter, Eunice Hunton. "Review of *The Blacker the Berry* by Wallace Thurman." *Opportunity* 7, No. 5 (May 1929): 162–63.

Bennett, Gwendolyn B. "Review of *Banjo* by Claude McKay." *Opportunity* 7, No. 8 (August 1929): 254–55.

Labaree, Mary Fleming. "Review of *Passing* by Nella Larsen." *Opportunity* 7, No. 8 (August 1929): 255.

Bennett, Gwendolyn. "Review of *Plum-Bun* by Jessie Fauset." *Opportunity* 7, No. 9

(September 1929): 287.

Shillito, Edward. "Review of *The Black Christ and Other Poems* by Countee Cullen." *Southern Workman* 59, No. 2 (February 1930): 92–93. Reprinted with the permission of the Hampton University Archives.

Wood, Clement. "The Black Pegasus." [Review of *The Black Christ and Other Poems* by Countee Cullen] *Opportunity* 8, No. 3 (March 1930): 93.

Bradstreet, Howard. "A Negro Miracle Play." [Review of *The Green Pastures* by Marc Connelly] *Opportunity* 8 (May 1930): 150–51.

Calverton, V.F. "This Negro."[Review of *Not Without Laughter* by Langston Hughes] *The Nation* (August 6, 1930): 157–58. Reprinted from "The Nation" magazine. Copyright the Nation Company, L.P.

Brown, Sterling A. "Review of *Not Without Laughter* by Langston Hughes." *Opportunity* 8, No. 9 (September 1930): 279–80.

Paxton, Alice M. "Review of *Not Without Laughter* by Langston Hughes." *Southern Workman* 59, No. 10 (October 1930): 476–77. Reprinted with the permission of the Hampton University Archives.

Carmon, Walt. "Away from Harlem." [Review of *Not Without Laughter* by Langston Hughes] Typed transcript. *The New Masses* (October 1930).

Thurman, Wallace. "Review of *Not Without Laughter* by Langston Hughes." nd [1930] Clipping [Knopf/uncatalogued/permanent titles folders/Hughes, Langston] is located in the Harry Ransom Humanities Research Center, University of Texas at Austin. Reprinted with the permission of the Harry Ranson Humanities Research Center.

Brown, Sterling A . "Review of *God Sends Sunday* by Arna Bontemps." *Opportunity* 9 (June 1931): 188.

Du Bois, W.E.B. "Review of *God Sends Sunday* by Arna Bontemps." *Crisis* 38 (September 1931): 304. Reprinted with the permission of the Crisis Publishing Company.

Kuyper, George A. "Two Book Reviews." *Southern Workman* 61, No. 3 (March 1932): 134–38. Reprinted with the permission of the Hampton University Archives.

Burgum, Edwin Berry. "Review of *The Chinaberry Tree* by Jessie Fauset." *Opportunity* 10, No. 3 (March 1932): 88–89.

Taylor, Lois. "Review of *Infants of the Spring* by Wallace Thurman." *Opportunity* 10, No. 3 (March 1932): 89.

Thurman, Wallace. "Infants of the Spring—Author Review." Typed transcript. Original manuscript is located in the Harry Ransom Humanities Research Center, University of Texas at Austin. Reprinted with the permission of the Harry Ransom Humanities Research Center.

Braithwaite, William Stanley. "*Along This Way*: A Review of the Autobiography of James Weldon Johnson." *Opportunity* 11 (December 1933): 376–78. Reprinted with the permission of the National Urban League.

Holmes, E.C. "Review of *The Ways of White Folks* by Langston Hughes." *Opportunity* 12, No. 9 (September 1934): 283–84. Reprinted with the permission of the National Urban League.

Zugsmith, Leane. "The Impact of Races." [Review of *The Ways of White Folks* by

Langston Hughes] *New York Times* (July 1, 1934). Reprinted with the permission of *The New York Times*.

Ellison, Ralph. "Stormy Weather." [Review of *The Big Sea* by Langston Hughes] *New Masses* (September 1940).

Wright, Richard. "Forerunner and Ambassador." [Review of *The Big Sea* by Langston Hughes] *The New Republic* (October 24, 1940): 600.

"Stories and Poetry of 1926." *Opportunity* 5, No. 1 (January 1927): 5.

Locke, Alain. "1928: A Retrospective Review." *Opportunity* 7, No. 1 (January 1929): 8–11.

Kerlin, Robert T. "A Decade of Negro Literature." *Southern Workman* 59 (May 1930): 226–29. Reprinted with the permission of the Hampton University Archives.

Locke, Alain. "This Year of Grace." *Opportunity* 9 (February 1931): 48–51.

Locke, Alain. "We Turn to Prose: A Retrospective Review of the Literature of the Negro for 1931." *Opportunity* 10, No. 2 (February 1932): 40–44.

Locke, Alain. "Black Truth and Black Beauty: A Retrospective Review of the Literature of the Negro for 1932." *Opportunity* 11, No. 1 (January 1933): 14–18. Reprinted with the permission of the National Urban League.

Locke, Alain. "The Saving Grace of Realism: Retrospective Review of the Negro Literature of 1933." *Opportunity* 12, No. 1 (January 1934): 8–11, 30. Reprinted with the permission of the National Urban League.

Locke, Alain. "The Eleventh Hour of Nordicism: A Retrospective Review of the Literature of the Negro for 1934." *Opportunity* 13, No. 1 (January 1935): 8–12; and *Opportunity* 13, No. 2 (February 1935): 46–48, 59. Reprinted with the permission of the National Urban League.

Locke, Alain. "Deep River: Deeper Sea: Retrospective Review of the Literature of the Negro for 1935." *Opportunity* 14, No. 1 (January 1936): 6–10; and *Opportunity* 14, No. 2 (February 1936): 42–43, 6. Reprinted with the permission of the National Urban League.

Locke, Alain. "God Save Reality!: Retrospective Review of the Literature of the Negro: 1936." *Opportunity* 15, No. 1 (January 1937): 8–13; and *Opportunity* 15, No. 2 (February 1937): 40–44. Reprinted with the permission of the National Urban League.

Locke, Alain. "Jingo, Counter-Jingo and Us: Retrospective Review of the Literature of the Negro: 1937." *Opportunity* 16, No. 1 (January 1938): 7–11, 27; and *Opportunity* 16, No. 2 (February 1938): 39–42. Reprinted with the permission of the National Urban League.

Locke, Alain. "The Negro: 'New' or Newer: A Retrospective Review of the Literature of the Negro for 1938." *Opportunity* 17, No. 1(January 1939): 4–10; and *Opportunity* 17, No. 2 (February 1939): 36–42. Reprinted with the permission of the National Urban League.

Shillito, Edward. "The Poet and the Race Problem." *Christian Century* 46, No. 29 (July 17, 1929): 915–16. Copyright (1929) Christian Century Foundation. Reprinted by permission of the Christian Century.

Berlack, Thelma E. "New Author Unearthed Right Here in Harlem." *New York Amsterdam News* (n.d.). Typed transcript. Original manuscript [Knopf/uncatalogued/permanent title folders/Larsen, Nella] is in the Harry Ransom Humanities Research Center, University of Texas at Austin. Reprinted with the permission of the Harry Ransom Humanities Research Center.

"*New York Telegram*, April 13, 1929." [Article on Nella Larsen] Typed transcript. Original article [Knopf/uncatalogued/permanent title folders/Larsen, Nella] is in the Harry Ransom Humanities Research Center, University of Texas at Austin. Reprinted with the permission of the Harry Ransom Humanities Research Center.

Starkey, Marion L. "Negro Writers Come into Their Own." Typed interview with Nella Larsen and Walter White. Original manuscript [Knopf/uncatalogued/permanent title folders/Larsen, Nella] is located in the Harry Ransom Humanities Research Center, University of Texas at Austin. Reprinted with the permission of the Harry Ransom Humanities Research Center.

Thompson, Louise. "Langston Hughes, Novelist." (nd [July 1930]). Typed transcript. Original manuscript [Knopf/uncatalogued/permanent title folders/Hughes, Langston] is located in the Harry Ransom Humanities Research Center, University of Texas at Austin. Reprinted with the permission of the Harry Ransom Humanities Research Center.

"Wallace Thurman to Langston Hughes." (nd [1928?]). Typed transcript. Original manuscript [JWJ/Hughes/Corres/Wallace Thurman] is located in the James Weldon Johnson Collection, Beinecke Rare Book Library, Yale University. Reprinted with the permission of the Beinecke Rare Book Library.

"Wallace Thurman to Langston Hughes from Mamaroneck." (nd [1928?]). Typed transcript. Original manuscript [JWJ/Hughes/Corres/Wallace Thurman] is located in the James Weldon Johnson Collection, Beinecke Rare Book Library, Yale University. Reprinted with the permission of the Beinecke Rare Book Library.

"Wallace Thurman to Langston Hughes from Santa Monica." (nd [1929?]). Typed transcript. Original manuscript [JWJ/Hughes/Corres/Wallace Thurman] is located in the James Weldon Johnson Collection, Beinecke Rare Book Library, Yale University. Reprinted with the permission of the Beinecke Rare Book Library.

"A Questionnaire." *Crisis* 31 (February 1926): 165. Reprinted with the permission of the Crisis Publishing Company.

"The Negro in Art, How Shall He Be Portrayed: A Symposium." *Crisis* 31 (March 1926): 219–20. Reprinted with the permission of the Crisis Publishing Company.

"The Negro in Art, How Shall He Be Portrayed: A Symposium." *Crisis* 31 (April 1926): 278–80. Reprinted with the permission of the Crisis Publishing Company.

"The Negro in Art, How Shall He Be Portrayed: A Symposium." *Crisis* 32 (May 1926): 35–36. Reprinted with the permission of the Crisis Publishing Company.

"The Negro in Art, How Shall He Be Portrayed: A Symposium." *Crisis* 32 (June 1926): 71–73. Reprinted with the permission of the Crisis Publishing Company.

"The Negro in Art, How Shall He Be Portrayed: A Symposium." *Crisis* 32 (August 1926): 193–94. Reprinted with the permission of the Crisis Publishing Company.

"The Negro in Art, How Shall He Be Portrayed: A Symposium." *Crisis* 32 (September

1926): 238–39. Reprinted with the permission of the Crisis Publishing Company.

"The Negro in Art, How Shall He Be Portrayed: A Symposium." *Crisis* 33 (November 1926): 28–29. Reprinted with the permission of the Crisis Publishing Company.

Du Bois, W.E. Burghardt. "Criteria of Negro Art." *Crisis* 32 (October 1926): 290–97. Reprinted with the permission of the Crisis Publishing Company.